Praise for
Jeremy Scahill and *Dirty Wars*

"[A] courageous and exhaustive examination of the way a number of clandestine campaigns—full of crimes, coverups, and assassinations—became the United States's main strategy for combating terrorism. It's about drones, but also, more profoundly, about what our government does on our behalf, without our consent, and arguably to our disadvantage."

—TEJU COLE, *The New Yorker*'s Best Books of 2013

"[A] fantastic piece of investigative reporting . . . "

—NOAM CHOMSKY

"*Dirty Wars* shows you why geography shouldn't join penmanship on the list of obsolete American school disciplines before you even read a single page—in the maps at the front of the book: the Middle East, Afghanistan and Pakistan, the Horn of Africa, Yemen, Mogadishu, Somalia—every one an American theater of war, no matter how few Americans realize it. For the next 500 pages, Scahill demonstrates how what we don't know can hurt us—and hurt lots of other people we don't know."

—*Los Angeles Review of Books*

"There is no journalist in America, in the world, who has reported on what the war on terror actually looks like under the Obama administration better than [Scahill]. This book is an unbelievable accomplishment. [W]hatever your politics, you should read this book. It is incredibly carefully reported. People who come to this book expecting a polemic, I think will be surprised to a find a book that really . . . lets the facts speak for themselves. What this book does is show a side of our unending wars that we haven't seen . . . I think every member of Congress should read this book."

—CHRIS HAYES, host of MSNBC's *All In with Chris Hayes*

"*Dirty Wars* will earn its place in history as one of the most important pieces of literature related to over a decade of failed American foreign policy strategy that continues to exist to this day. It's also one of the most grounded and thoroughly researched books I've read on the subject of covert US operations in the twenty-first century. A must-read for anyone that cares about this country and the direction we are heading."

—BRANDON WEBB, retired member of Navy SEAL
Team Three, former lead sniper instructor at the
US Naval Special Warfare Command and author of
the *New York Times* bestseller *The Red Circle*

"*Dirty Wars* is not politically correct. It is not a history of the last decade as seen from inside the White House, or from the pages of the *New York Times* and *Washington Post*. Scahill's book takes us inside Dick Cheney's famed 'dark side' and tells us, with convincing detail and much new information, what has been done in the name of America since 9/11."

—SEYMOUR HERSH, Pulitzer Prize–winning journalist

"[One] of the best intelligence reporters on the planet . . . Scahill has covered the worldwide wanderings of JSOC task forces and their intersection for years, and he takes a deeper look at their expanded post 9/11 mission set. He has incredible sources . . . "

—MARC AMBINDER, editor-at-large of *The Week*

"*Dirty Wars* is the most thorough and authoritative history I've read yet of the causes and consequences of America's post-9/11 conflation of war and national security. I know of no other journalist who could have written it: For over a decade, Scahill has visited the war zones, overt and covert; interviewed the soldiers, spooks, jihadists, and victims; and seen with his own eyes the fruits of America's bipartisan war fever. He risked his life many times over to write this book, and the result is a masterpiece of insight, journalism, and true patriotism."

—BARRY EISLER, novelist and former operative
in the CIA's Directorate of Operations

"There is no journalist in America who has exposed the truth about US government militarism more bravely, more relentlessly and more valuably than Jeremy Scahill. *Dirty Wars* is highly gripping and dramatic, and of unparalleled importance in understanding the destruction being sown in our name."

—GLENN GREENWALD, *New York Times*
bestselling author and former *Guardian* columnist

"A surefire hit for fans of *Blackwater* and studded with intriguing, occasionally damning material."

—*Kirkus Reviews*

"Scahill adds a thorough and unsentimental accounting of JSOC's brutal work in Iraq, including a review of the available evidence that prisoners interrogated at its facilities near Baghdad were tortured . . . Scahill weaves into his larger narrative the most detailed biography of Anwar Awlaki yet published. It is a riveting account."  —STEVE COLL, *The New Yorker*

"Jeremy Scahill's new book, *Dirty Wars: The World Is a Battlefield* is sort of like approaching a dark cavity in an old tree. How many of us would instinctively cry out, 'I don't want to look—there will be creepy crawly things in there and I'm better off not knowing!' . . . Luckily, reporter Scahill has cared to look, and poke at and examine . . . to shine a light inside the hole, and show us that whatever abomination lurks inside is, in reality, much worse than we had even imagined."

—KELLEY VLAHOS, antiwar.com

# DIRTY

## The
## World
## Is a
## Battlefield

# WARS

## JEREMY SCAHILL

**Nation Books**
*New York*

Copyright © 2013 by Jeremy Scahill

Published by Nation Books, a Member of the Perseus Books Group
116 East 16th Street, 8th Floor, New York, NY 10003
Nation Books is a co-publishing venture of the Nation Institute and
the Perseus Books Group.

First paperback edition published in 2014 by Nation Books.

Books published by Nation Books are available at special discounts
for bulk purchases in the United States by corporations, institutions,
and other organizations. For more information, please contact the
Special Markets Department at the Perseus Books Group, 2300
Chestnut Street, Suite 200, Philadelphia, PA 19103, or call (800)
810-4145, ext. 5000, or e-mail special.markets@perseusbooks.com.

Designed by Janet Tingey

Library of Congress Cataloging-in-Publication Data
Scahill, Jeremy.
Dirty wars : the world is a battlefield / Jeremy Scahill. — First edition.
pages cm
Includes bibliographical references and index.
ISBN 978-1-56858-671-7 (hbk.)
ISBN 978-1-56858-727-1 (eb)
ISBN 978-1-56858-968-8 (int. ed.)
1. United States—History, Military—21st century. 2. Special opera-
   tions (Military science)—United States—History—21st century.
   3. Terrorism—Prevention—United States—Government
   policy—History—21st century. 4. Targeted killing—United
   States—History—21st century. 5. Intelligence service—United
   States—History—21st century. 6. United States—Military poli-
   cy—History—21st century. 7. United States—Military policy—
   Moral and ethical aspects. I. Title.
E897.S33 2013
355.00973—dc23
                                                        2012051769

ISBN 978-1-56858-954-1 (paperback)

10 9 8 7 6 5 4 3 2 1

FOR JOURNALISTS—

*those imprisoned for doing their jobs and
those who have died in pursuit of the truth.*

"It is forbidden to kill; therefore all murderers are punished unless they kill in large numbers and to the sound of trumpets."

—VOLTAIRE

# CONTENTS

**MAPS**

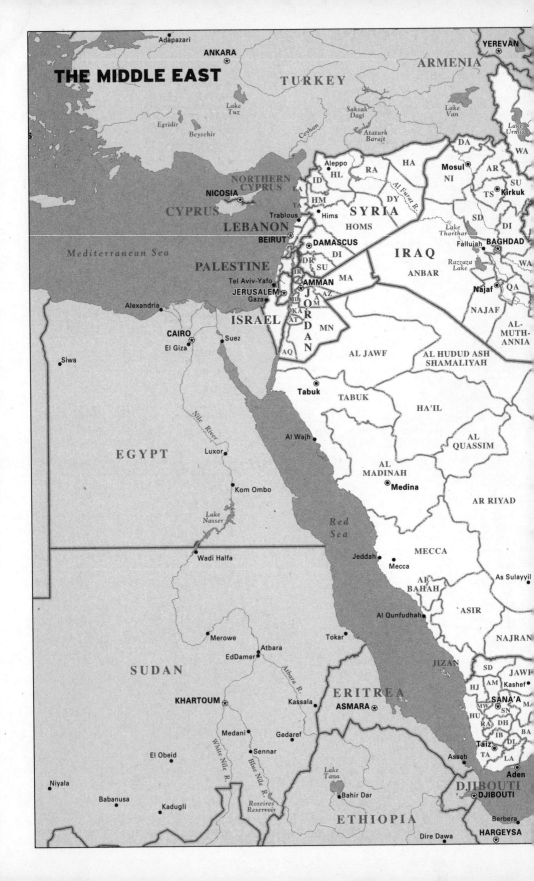

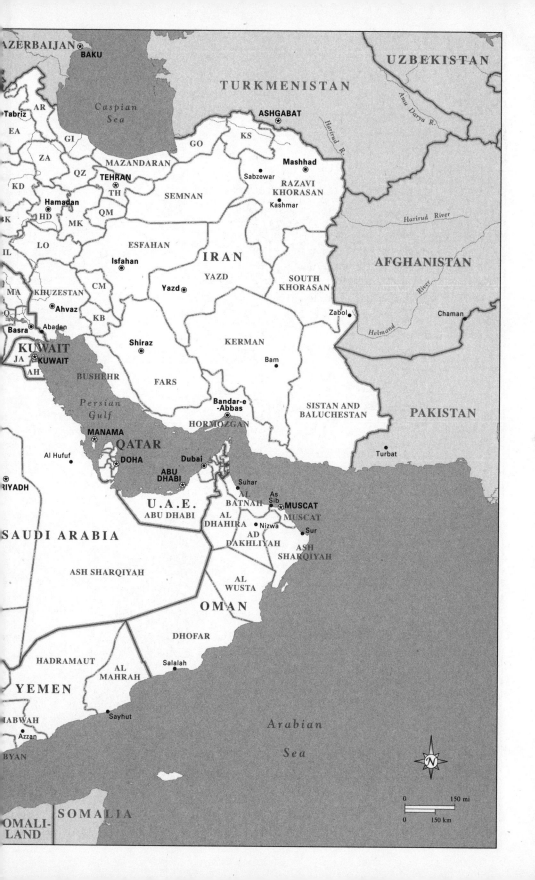

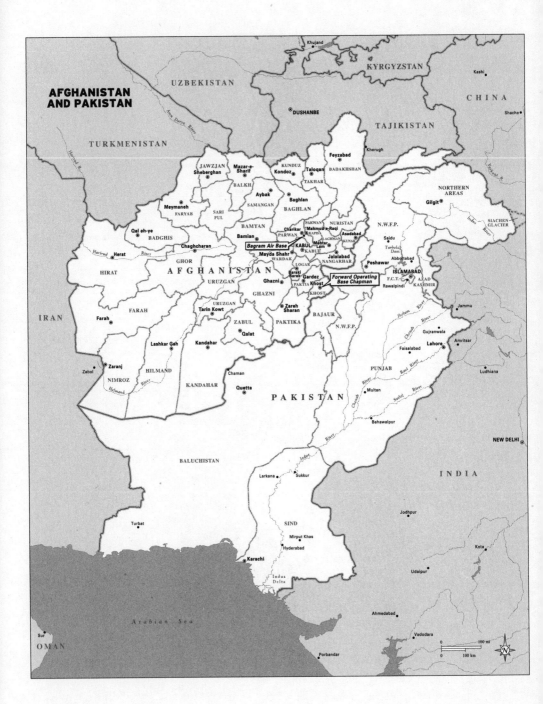

AFGHANISTAN
AND PAKISTAN

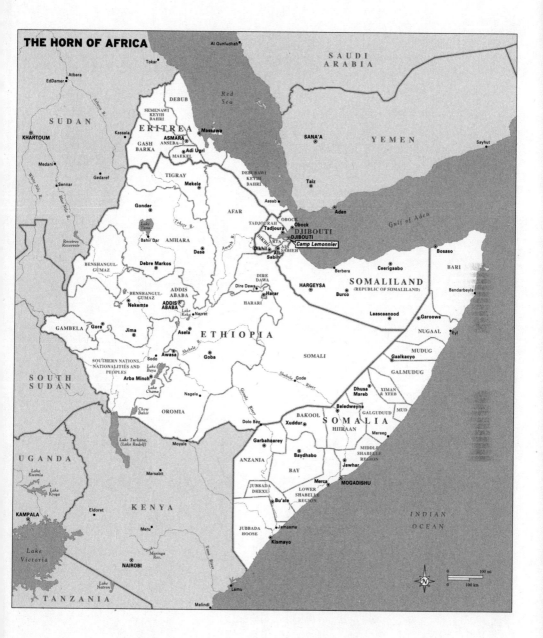

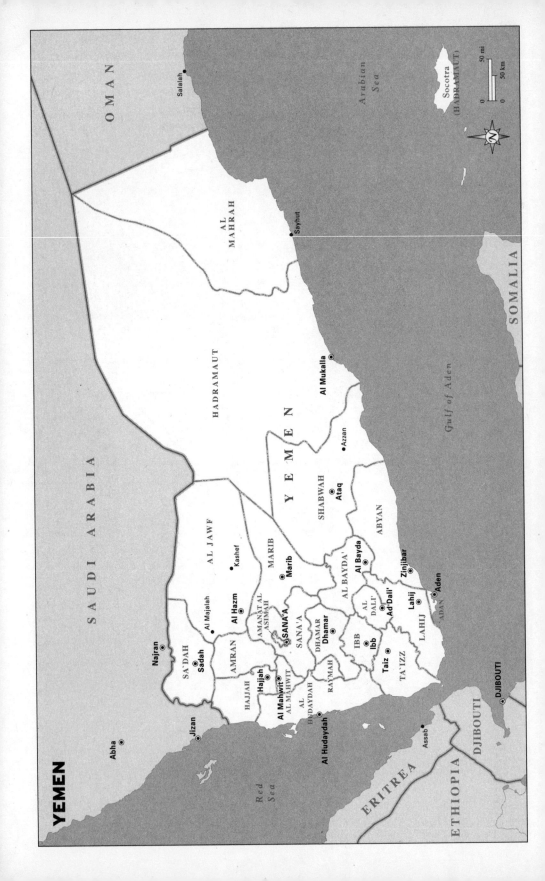

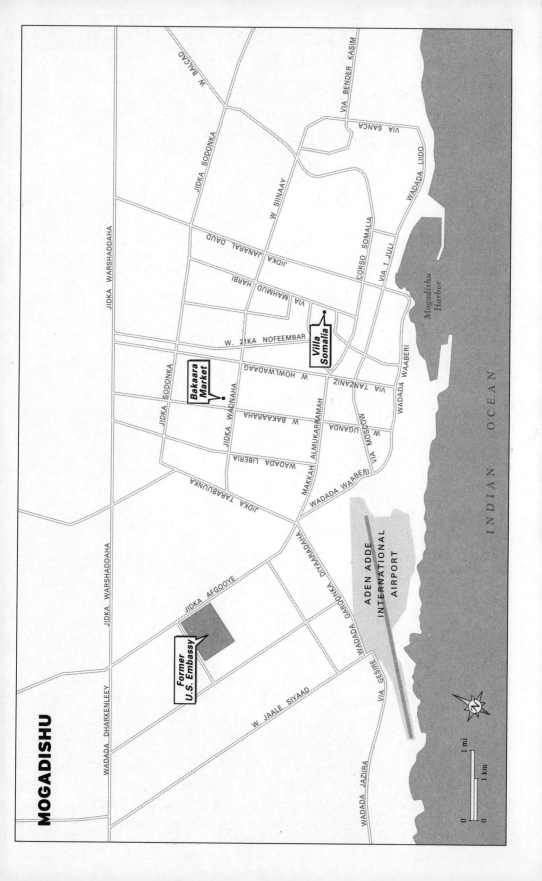

# MOGADISHU

Villa Somalia

Bakaara Market

Former U.S. Embassy

ADEN ADDE INTERNATIONAL AIRPORT

Mogadishu Harbor

INDIAN OCEAN

Wadada Liido

Corso Somalia

Via 1 Juli

Via Bender Kasim

Via Sanca

W. Balcad

Jidka Sodonka

W. Siinaay

Jidka Janaral Daud

Via Mahmud Harbi

W. 21ka Nofeembar

W. Howlwadaag

Via Tanzaniz

Wadada Waaberi

Jidka Warshaddaha

Jidka Sodonka

Jidka Wadnaha

W. Bakaaraha

Makkah Almukarramah

Jidka Liberia

Wadada Liberia

Via Moscow

Uganda

Jidka Tarabuunka

Wadada Waaberi

Via Gesire

Wadada Garoonka Diyaaradaha

Jidka Afgooye

Jidka Warshaddaha

Wadada Dharkenleey

W. Jaale Siyaad

Wadada Jazira

1 mi

1 km

0
0

N

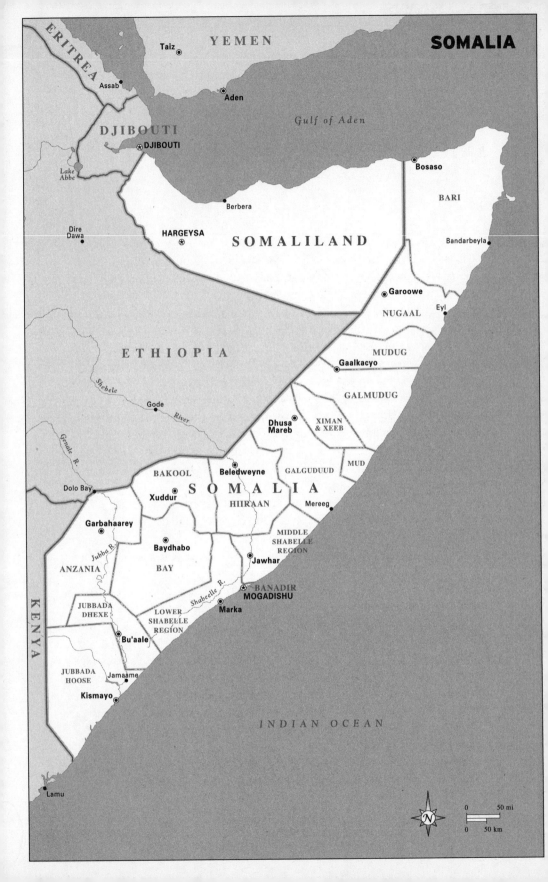

# A NOTE TO THE READER

THIS IS A STORY about how the United States came to embrace assassination as a central part of its national security policy. It is also a story about the consequences of that decision for people in scores of countries across the globe and for the future of American democracy. Although the 9/11 attacks dramatically altered the way the United States conducts its foreign policy, the roots of this story far predate the day the Twin Towers fell. In the post-9/11 world, there is also a tendency to see US foreign policy through a partisan lens that, on the one hand, suggests that President George W. Bush's invasion of Iraq was an utter disaster that led the nation into a mentality that it was in a global war and, on the other, that President Barack Obama was left to clean up the mess. In the eyes of many conservatives, President Obama has been weak in confronting terrorism. In the eyes of many liberals, he has waged a "smarter" war. The realities, however, are far more nuanced.

This book tells the story of the expansion of covert US wars, the abuse of executive privilege and state secrets, the embrace of unaccountable elite military units that answer only to the White House. *Dirty Wars* also reveals the continuity of a mindset that "the world is a battlefield" from Republican to Democratic administrations.

The story begins with a brief history of the US approach to terrorism and assassination prior to 9/11. From there, I weave in and out of several stories, spanning the course of Bush's early days in office and going into Obama's second term. We meet al Qaeda figures in Yemen, US-backed warlords in Somalia, CIA spies in Pakistan and Special Operations commandos tasked with hunting down those people deemed to be enemies of America. We meet the men who run the most secretive operations for the military and the CIA, and we hear the stories of insiders who have spent their lives in the shadows, some of whom spoke to me only on condition that their identity never be revealed.

The world now knows SEAL Team 6 and the Joint Special Operations Command as the units that killed Osama bin Laden. This book will reveal previously undisclosed or little-known missions conducted by these very forces that will never be discussed by those at the helm of power in the United States or immortalized in Hollywood films. I dig deep into the life of Anwar al Awlaki, the first US citizen known to be targeted for assassination by his own government—despite never having been charged with a crime. We also hear from those who are caught in the middle—the civilians who face drone bombings and acts of terrorism. We enter the home of Afghan civilians whose lives were destroyed by a Special Ops night raid gone wrong, transforming them from US allies to would-be suicide bombers.

Some of the stories in this book may, at first, seem to be disconnected, from people worlds apart. But taken together, they reveal a haunting vision of what our future holds in a world gripped by ever-expanding dirty wars.

—JEREMY SCAHILL

# DIRTY WARS

# PROLOGUE

*The young teenager sat outside with his cousins as they gathered for a barbecue. He wore his hair long and messy. His mother and grandparents had repeatedly urged him to cut it. But the boy believed it had become his trademark look and he liked it. A few weeks earlier, he had run away from home, but not in some act of teenage rebellion. He was on a mission. In the note he left for his mother before he snuck out the kitchen window as the sun was just rising and headed to the bus station, he admitted that he had taken money from her purse—$40—for bus fare, and for that he apologized. He explained his mission and begged for forgiveness. He said he would be home soon.*

*The boy was the eldest child in his family. Not just in his immediate family, which consisted of his parents and his three siblings, but in the large house they shared with his aunts and uncles and cousins and two of his grandparents. He was his grandmother's favorite. When guests visited, he would bring them tea and sweets. When they left, he would clean up after them. Once, his grandmother twisted her ankle and went to the hospital for treatment. When she limped out of the treatment room, the boy was there to greet her and make sure she got home safely. "You are a gentle boy," his grandmother always told him. "Don't ever change."*

*The boy's mission was simple: he wanted to find his father. He hadn't seen him in years and he was afraid that if he didn't find him, he would be left only with blurred memories: of his father teaching him to fish; to ride a horse; surprising him with an abundance of gifts on his birthday; taking him and his siblings to the beach or to the candy shop.*

*Finding his father would not be easy. He was a wanted man. There was a bounty on his head and he had narrowly escaped death more than a dozen times. That powerful forces in multiple countries wanted his father dead did not deter the boy. He was tired of seeing the videos of his father that painted him as a terrorist and an evil figure. He just knew him as his dad, and he wanted at least one last moment with him. But it didn't work out that way.*

*Three weeks after he climbed out the kitchen window, the boy was outdoors with his cousins—teenagers like him—laying a picnic for dinner beneath the stars. It was then he would have heard the drones approaching, followed by the whiz of the missiles. It was a direct hit. The boy and his cousins were blown to pieces. All that remained of the boy was the back of his head, his flowing hair still clinging to it. The boy had turned sixteen years old a few weeks earlier and now he had been killed by his own government. He was the third US citizen to be killed in operations authorized by the president in two weeks. The first was his father.*

**"There Was Concern...
That We Not Create an American Hit List"**

WASHINGTON, DC, 2001–2002—It was 10:10 a.m. on June 11, 2002, nine months to the day since the September 11 attacks. The senators and representatives filed into Room S-407 of the US Capitol. All of them were members of a small, elite group in Washington and were, by law, entrusted with the most guarded national security secrets of the US government. "I hereby move that this meeting of the committee be closed to the public," declared Republican Richard Shelby, the senior senator from Alabama, in a Southern drawl, "on the grounds that the national security of the United States might be compromised were a proceeding to become public." The motion was quickly seconded and the secret hearing was under way.

As the members of the Senate Select Committee on Intelligence and the House Permanent Select Committee on Intelligence gathered in Washington, DC, half a world away in Afghanistan, tribal and political leaders were convening a *loya jirga*, a "grand council," that was tasked with deciding who would run the country following the swift overthrow of the Taliban government by the US military. After 9/11, the US Congress had granted the Bush administration sweeping powers to pursue those responsible for the attacks. The Taliban government, which had ruled Afghanistan since 1996, was crushed, depriving al Qaeda of its sanctuary in Afghanistan. Osama bin Laden and other al Qaeda leaders were on the run. But for the Bush administration, the long war was just getting started.

At the White House, Vice President Dick Cheney and Defense Secretary Donald Rumsfeld were deep into planning the next invasion—Iraq. They had come to power with plans to topple Saddam Hussein in hand and, despite the fact that there was no Iraqi connection to the attacks, they used 9/11 as the pretext to push their agenda. But the decisions made in that first year of the Bush administration were much bigger than Iraq, Afghanistan or even al Qaeda. The men in power at that time were intent on changing the way the United States waged its wars and, in the process, creating unprecedented powers for the White House. The days of fighting uniformed enemies and national militaries according to the rules of the

3

Geneva Conventions were over. "The world is a battlefield" was the mantra repeated by the neoconservatives in the US national security apparatus and placed on PowerPoint slides laying out the plans for a sweeping, borderless global war. But terrorists would not be their only target. The two-hundred-year-old democratic system of checks and balances was firmly in their crosshairs.

Room S-407 was nestled in the attic of the Capitol building. It was windowless and accessible only by one elevator—or a narrow staircase. The room was classified as a secure facility and had been fitted with sophisticated counterespionage equipment to block any attempt at eavesdropping or monitoring from outside. For decades, the room had been used to house the most sensitive briefings of members of Congress by the CIA, the US military and scores of other figures and entities that inhabit the shadows of US policy. Covert actions were briefed and debriefed in the room. It was one of a handful of facilities in the United States where the nation's most closely guarded secrets were discussed.

As the senators and representatives sat in the closed-door session on Capitol Hill that morning in June 2002, they would hear a story of how the United States had crossed a threshold. The stated purpose of the hearing was to review the work and structure of US counterterrorism (CT) organizations before 9/11. At the time, there was a substantial amount of finger-pointing regarding US intelligence "failures" leading up to the attacks. In the aftermath of the most devastating terrorist strikes on US soil in history, Cheney and Rumsfeld charged that the Clinton administration had failed to adequately recognize the urgency of al Qaeda's threat, leaving the US homeland vulnerable by the time the Bush White House took power. Democrats pushed back and pointed to their own history of combating al Qaeda in the 1990s. The appearance of Richard Clarke before the US lawmakers on this particular day was, in part, intended to send a message to the congressional elite. Clarke had been President Bill Clinton's counterterrorism czar and chaired the Counterterrorism Security Group of the National Security Council (NSC) for the decade leading up to 9/11. He had also served on President George H. W. Bush's National Security Council and was an assistant secretary of state under President Ronald Reagan. He was one of the most experienced counterterrorism officials in the United States and, at the time of the hearing, was on his way out of government, though he still held a post as a special adviser to President George W. Bush on cyberspace security. Clarke was a hawkish figure who had risen to prominence under a Democratic administration and was known to have pushed hard when Clinton was in power for more covert action. So it made tactical sense that the Bush administration would put him forward to make the case for a regime of military and intelligence tactics that had previously been deemed illegal, undemocratic or, simply, dangerous.

Clarke described the dialogue within the national security community under Clinton as marked by great concern over the possibility of violating a long-standing presidential ban on assassination and a deep fear of repeating scandals of the past. Clarke said he believed that "a culture" had developed at the CIA "that said when you have large scale of covert operations, they get messy, and they get out of control, and they end up splattering mud back on the Agency."

"The history of covert operations in the 1950s and 1960s and 1970s was not a happy one," Clarke told the lawmakers. The CIA had orchestrated the overthrow of populist governments in Latin America and the Middle East, backed death squads throughout Central America, facilitated the killing of rebel leader Patrice Lumumba in the Congo and propped up military juntas and dictatorships. The spate of assassinations had become so out of control that a Republican president, Gerald Ford, felt the need to issue Executive Order 11905 in 1976, explicitly banning the United States from carrying out "political assassinations." The CIA officers who had come of age in the shadow of that era and rose to positions of authority at the Agency during the 1990s, Clarke said, "had institutionalized [the notion that] a sense of covert action is risky and is likely to blow up in your face. And the wise guys at the White House who are pushing you to do covert action will be nowhere to be found when [the Senate Select Committee on Intelligence] calls you up to explain the mess that the covert action became."

President Jimmy Carter amended Ford's assassination ban to make it more sweeping. He removed language that limited the ban to political assassinations and also extended the ban on participating in assassinations to US proxies or contractors. "No person employed by or acting on behalf of the United States Government shall engage in, or conspire to engage in, assassination," read President Carter's executive order. Although Presidents Reagan and George H. W. Bush maintained that language, no president's executive orders actually defined what constituted an assassination. Reagan, Bush and Clinton all developed work-arounds to the ban. Reagan, for example, authorized a strike on the home of Libyan dictator Muammar el Qaddafi in 1986 in retaliation for his alleged role in a bombing of a night club in Berlin. The first President Bush authorized strikes on Saddam Hussein's palaces during the 1991 Gulf War. Clinton did the same during Operation Desert Fox in 1998.

Clarke described for the lawmakers how, under the Clinton administration, plans were drawn up for killing and capturing al Qaeda and other terrorist leaders, including Osama bin Laden. President Clinton asserted that the ban did not apply to foreign terrorists engaged in plotting attacks against the United States. In the aftermath of the bombings of the US Embassies in Kenya and Tanzania in late 1998, Clinton authorized cruise missile attacks against alleged al Qaeda camps in Afghanistan and also a strike against a factory in Sudan that the administration alleged was a chemical weapons plant. It turned out that the plant was actually a pharmaceutical factory. Although this lethal authority was granted by Clinton, it was envisioned as an option that would be rarely used and only at the direction of the president on a case-by-case basis. Rather than granting a carte blanche authority to conduct these operations, the Clinton White House required each proposed action to be thoroughly vetted. Legal structures were put in place and "lethal findings" were signed by the president, authorizing the use of deadly force in pursuit of terrorists across the globe. Yet, Clarke said, the trigger was seldom pulled.

Clarke conceded that the Clinton-era authorizations for targeted killings "looks like a very Talmudic and somewhat bizarre series of documents," adding that they were crafted in a careful way to narrow the scope of such operations. "The administration, and particularly the Justice Department, did not want to throw out the ban on assassination in a way that threw the baby out with the bathwater. They wanted the expansion of authorities to be limited." He added that the Clinton-era authorizations for targeted killing look like "a very narrow casting. But that, I think, is because of this desire not to throw out altogether the ban on assassinations and create an American hit list."

Representative Nancy Pelosi, one of the most powerful Democrats in Congress at the time, admonished her colleagues in the closed chamber not to publicly discuss any of the highly classified memoranda that authorized the use of lethal force. The memoranda, she said, "were held to the most restricted form of notification at the highest level in the Congress. It is extraordinary...that this information is being shared here today." She warned against any leaks to the media and added: "There is no way that we can confirm, deny, stipulate to, acknowledge knowledge of the memoranda." Clarke was asked whether he thought the United States should lift its policy banning assassinations. "I think you have to be very careful about how broadly you authorize the use of lethal force," he responded. "I don't think the Israeli experience of having a broad hit list has been terribly successful. It doesn't—certainly hasn't stopped terrorism or stopped the organizations where they have assassinated people." Clarke said that when he and his colleagues in the Clinton administration issued authorizations for targeted killing operations, they were intended for very surgical and rare cases. "We didn't want to create a broad precedent that would allow intelligence officials in the future to have hit lists and routinely engage in something that approximated assassination....There was concern in both the Justice Department and in some elements of the White House and some elements of the CIA that we not create an American hit list that would become an ongoing institution that we could just keep adding names to and have hit teams go out and assassinate people."

Even so, Clarke was part of a small group of officials in the counterterrorism community under the Clinton administration who agitated for the CIA to be more aggressive in using that lethal authority and pushed the envelope of the assassination ban within the limits he outlined. "In the wake of 9/11," Clarke declared, "almost everything we proposed prior to 9/11 is being done."

It would soon be everything and more.

RUMSFELD AND CHENEY HAD PADDED the administration with leading neoconservatives who had spent the Clinton era effectively operating a shadow government—working in right-wing think tanks and for major defense and intelligence contractors, plotting their return to power. Among them were Paul Wolfowitz, Douglas Feith, David Addington, Stephen Cambone, Lewis "Scooter" Libby, John Bolton and Elliott Abrams. Many of them had cut their teeth in the Reagan and Bush White Houses. Some, like Cheney and Rumsfeld, went back to the Nixon era. Several were key players in building up a policy vision under the umbrella of the ultranationalist Project for the New American Century (PNAC). Despite Clinton's decisions to use force in Yugoslavia and Iraq and to conduct a series of air strikes in other nations, they viewed the Clinton administration as an almost pacifist force that had weakened the hand of US dominance and left the country vulnerable. They believed the 1990s had been a "decade of defense neglect." The neoconservatives had long advocated a posture that, in the wake of the Cold War, the United States was the lone superpower and should exert its weight aggressively around the globe, redrawing maps and expanding empire. At the center of their vision was a radical increase in US military spending, plans for which were drawn up by Cheney and his aides when he was defense secretary in 1992. The Cheney draft Defense Planning Guidance, the neocons asserted in PNAC's founding document, "provided a blueprint for maintaining U.S. preeminence, precluding the rise of a great power rival, and shaping the international security order in line with American principles and interests." Wolfowitz and Libby were the key authors of Cheney's defense manifesto, which argued that the United States must be the sole superpower and take all necessary actions to deter "potential competitors from even aspiring to a larger regional or global role."

Their plan, however, was scrapped by more powerful forces within the first Bush administration, namely, the chair of the Joint Chiefs of Staff, General Colin Powell, Secretary of State James Baker and National Security Adviser Brent Scowcroft. The final draft, much to Cheney's and the neocons' frustration, was greatly toned down in its imperialist language.

A decade later, even before 9/11, the neoconservatives—restored to power by the Bush administration—pulled those plans out of the dustbin of history and set about implementing them. Expanding US force projection would be central, as would building up streamlined, elite special ops units. "Our forces in the next century must be agile, lethal, readily deployable, and require a minimum of logistical support," George W. Bush had declared in a speech on the campaign trail in 1999 that was crafted by Wolfowitz and other neocons. "We must be able to project our power over long distances, in days or weeks, rather than months. On land, our heavy forces must be lighter. Our light forces must be more lethal. All must be easier to deploy."

The neocons also envisioned further asserting US dominance over natural resources globally and directly confronting nation-states that stood in the way. Regime change in multiple countries would be actively contemplated, particularly in oil-rich Iraq. "Ardent supporters of U.S. military intervention, few neo-cons have served in the armed forces; fewer still have ever been elected to public office," noted Jim Lobe, a journalist who tracked the rise of the neoconservative movement for a decade leading up to 9/11. They have a "ceaseless quest for global military dominance and contempt for the United Nations and multilateralism more generally." Lobe added: "In the neo-conservatives' view, the United States is a force for good in the world; it has a moral responsibility to exert that force; its military power should be dominant; it should be engaged globally but never be constrained by multilateral commitments from taking unilateral action in pursuit of its interests and values; and it should have a strategic alliance with Israel. Saddam must go, they argue, because he is a threat to Israel, and also Saudi Arabia, and because he has hoarded—and used—weapons of mass destruction." The PNAC crowd had concluded that the "United States has for decades sought to play a more permanent role in Gulf regional security. While the unresolved conflict with Iraq provides the immediate justification, the need for a substantial American force presence in the Gulf transcends the issue of the regime of Saddam Hussein." Within weeks of taking office, Rumsfeld and Cheney pressed to reverse President Clinton's signing, at the very end of his time in office, of the Rome Statute, which recognized the legitimacy of an international criminal court. They would not stand for US forces being subjected to potential prosecution for their actions around the world. Soon after becoming defense secretary, Rumsfeld wrote that he wanted his legal staff—and those of other US government agencies—to immediately determine "how we get out of it and undo the Clinton signature."

Even among the GOP foreign policy community of elders, these figures were viewed as extremists. "When we saw these people coming back in town, all of us who were around in those days said, 'Oh my God, the crazies are back'—'the crazies'—that's how we referred to these people," recalled Ray McGovern, who served for twenty-seven years at the CIA and was a national security briefer to George H. W. Bush when he was vice president and served under him when he was the director of the Agency in the late 1970s. McGovern said that once they were in power, the neoconservatives resurrected ideas that had been tossed in "the circular file" in previous GOP administrations by veteran Republican foreign policy leaders, adding that those extremist ideas would soon "arise out of the ashes and be implemented." These officials believed, "We've got a lot of weight to throw around, we should throw it around. We should assert ourselves in critical areas, like the Middle East," McGovern said.

For decades, Cheney and Rumsfeld had been key leaders of a militant movement outside of government and, during Republican administrations, from within the White House itself. Its mission was to give the executive branch of the US government unprecedented powers to wage secret wars, conduct covert operations with no oversight and to spy on US citizens. In their view, Congress had no business overseeing such operations but should only fund the agencies that would carry them out. To them, the presidency was to be a national security dictatorship, accountable only to its own concepts of what was best for the country. The two men first worked together in the Nixon White House in 1969 when Rumsfeld hired Cheney, then a graduate student, to be his aide at the Office of Economic Opportunity. It kicked off a career for Cheney in the power chambers of the Republican elite and a lifetime project to further empower the executive branch. As scandal rocked the Nixon White House in the 1970s— with the secret bombings of Laos and Cambodia, revelations of a domestic "enemies" list and the infamous break-in at the Democratic National Committee's headquarters at the Watergate Hotel—the US Congress began attacking the executive privileges and extreme secrecy that permeated the administration. Congress condemned the Laos and Cambodia bombings and overrode an attempt by Nixon to veto the War Powers Act of 1973, which limited the powers of the president to authorize military action. It mandated that the president "consult with Congress before introducing United States Armed Forces into hostilities or into situations where imminent involvement in hostilities is clearly indicated by the circumstances." In the absence of a formal declaration of war, the president would be required to inform Congress, in writing, within forty-eight hours, of any military action of "the circumstances necessitating the introduction of United States Armed Forces; the constitutional and legislative authority under which such introduction took place; and the estimated scope and duration of the hostilities or involvement." Cheney viewed the War Powers Act as unconstitutional and an encroachment on the rights of the president as commander in chief. He termed this era the "low point" in American presidential authority.

After the Watergate scandal forced Nixon's resignation, Cheney went on to serve as President Ford's chief of staff, while Rumsfeld served as the youngest defense secretary in US history. In 1975, Congress intensified its probes into the underworld of secret White House operations under the auspices of the Church Committee, named for its chair, Democratic senator Frank Church of Idaho. The committee investigated a wide range of abuses by the executive branch, including domestic spying operations against US citizens. The Church Committee's investigation painted a picture of lawless, secret activities conducted with no oversight whatsoever from the courts or Congress. The committee also investigated the involvement of the United States in the overthrow and eventual death of Chile's democratically elected socialist president Salvador Allende in 1973, though Ford invoked executive privilege and stymied the probe. At one point during the Church investigations, Cheney attempted to compel the FBI to investigate famed investigative journalist Seymour Hersh and to seek an indictment against him and the *New York Times* for espionage in retaliation for Hersh's exposé on illegal domestic spying by the CIA. The aim was to frighten other journalists from exposing secret controversial actions by the White House.

The FBI rebuffed Cheney's requests to go after Hersh. The end result of the Church investigation was a nightmare for Cheney and his executive power movement: the creation of congressional committees that would have legally mandated oversight of US intelligence operations, including covert actions. In 1980, Congress enacted a law that required the White House to report on all of its spy programs to the new intelligence committees. Cheney—and Rumsfeld—would spend much of the rest of their careers attempting to thwart those authorities.

By the end of the liberal Carter administration, Cheney concluded that the powers of the presidency had been "seriously weakened." Throughout the years of the Reagan administration, Cheney served as a Wyoming representative in Congress, where he was a fierce backer of Reagan's radical drive toward reempowering the White House. As Pulitzer Prize–winning author Charlie Savage noted in his book, *Takeover: The Return of the Imperial Presidency and the Subversion of American Democracy*, Reagan's Justice Department sought to end "the congressional resurgence of the 1970s," commissioning one report that called for the White House to disregard laws that "unconstitutionally encroach upon the executive branch." Instead, the Reagan White House could use presidential "signing statements" to reinterpret laws and issue presidential edicts that could be used to circumvent congressional oversight. In the early 1980s, the Reagan administration was deeply embroiled in fueling a right-wing insurgency against the leftist government of the Sandinistas in the Central American nation of Nicaragua. The centerpiece of this campaign was covert US support for the right-wing Contra death squads. Reagan also authorized the mining of the harbors around Nicaragua, bringing an unlawful use of force judgment against the United States at the World Court.

When the US Congress finally moved in 1984 to ban all US assistance to the Contras, passing the Boland Amendment, some officials within the Reagan White House, led by Colonel Oliver North, who worked on the National Security Council, began a covert plan to funnel funds to the right-wing rebels, in direct contravention of US law. The funds were generated by the illicit sale of weapons to the Iranian government, in violation of an arms embargo. Fourteen members of the Reagan administration, including his secretary of defense, were later indicted for their involvement. When the Iran-Contra scandal unfolded, and Congress aggressively investigated its origins, Cheney emerged as the White House's chief defender on Capitol Hill and issued a dissenting opinion defending the covert US program that most of his congressional colleagues had deemed to be illegal. Cheney's "minority report" defending the White House condemned the congressional investigation into Iran-Contra as "hysterical." The report charged that history "leaves little, if any doubt that the president was expected to have the primary role of conducting the foreign policy of the United States," concluding, "Congressional actions to limit the president in this area therefore should be reviewed with a considerable degree of skepticism. If they interfere with the core presidential foreign policy functions, they should be struck down."

President George H. W. Bush pardoned Cheney's allies convicted in connection with Iran-Contra, and Cheney went on to serve as his defense secretary during the 1991 Gulf War, where he continued building his vision of a supremely powerful executive branch. During his time as defense secretary, Cheney began planting the seeds for another program that would aid the consolidation of executive supremacy, commissioning a study from the oil services giant Halliburton that laid out a plan for privatizing as much of the military bureaucracy as possible. Cheney realized early on that using private companies to wage US wars would create another barrier to oversight and could afford greater secrecy for the planning and execution of those wars, both declared and undeclared. Cheney would then go on to head Halliburton for much of the 1990s, spearheading a drive to create a corporate shadow army that would ultimately become a linchpin of his covert and overt wars when he returned to the White House in 2001. During the Clinton era, Cheney also spent time at the neoconservative American Enterprise Institute, developing a political and military agenda that could be implemented once his party resumed power. When President George W. Bush was inaugurated, Cheney became the most powerful vice president in history. And he wasted no time in driving to expand that power.

ON SEPTEMBER 10, 2001, a day before American Airlines Flight 77—a Boeing 757—smashed into the western wall of the Pentagon, Donald Rumsfeld stood in that very building to deliver one of his first major speeches as defense secretary. Two portraits of Rumsfeld hung inside—one of him as the youngest defense secretary in US history, the other as its oldest. September 11 had not yet occurred, yet Rumsfeld was at the podium that day to issue a declaration of war.

"The topic today is an adversary that poses a threat, a serious threat, to the security of the United States of America," Rumsfeld bellowed. "This adversary is one of the world's last bastions of central planning. It governs by dictating five-year plans. From a single capital, it attempts to impose its demands across time zones, continents, oceans, and beyond. With brutal consistency, it stifles free thought and crushes new ideas. It disrupts the defense of the United States and places the lives of men and women in uniform at risk." Rumsfeld—a veteran Cold Warrior—told his new staff, "Perhaps this adversary sounds like the former Soviet Union, but that enemy is gone: our foes are more subtle and implacable today. You may think I'm describing one of the last decrepit dictators of the world. But their day, too, is almost past, and they cannot match the strength and size of this adversary. The adversary's closer to home. It's the Pentagon bureaucracy." The stakes, he declared, were severe—"a matter of life and death, ultimately, every American's." Rumsfeld told his audience, consisting of former defense industry executives turned Pentagon bureaucrats, that he intended to streamline the waging of America's wars. "Some might ask, How in the world could the Secretary of Defense attack the Pentagon in front of its people?" Rumsfeld told his audience. "To them I reply, I have no desire to attack the Pentagon; I want to liberate it. We need to save it from itself." It would be dubbed by Rumsfeld and his team his "revolution in military affairs."

Bush's all-star foreign policy team had come into power with an agenda to radically reorganize the US military, to end what they characterized as the Clinton-era weakening of national defenses and to reenergize the drive for massive missile defense systems favored by Reagan and other Cold Warriors. As Rumsfeld's deputy, Douglas Feith, recalled, "The threat of jihadist terrorism was on the list of U.S. government concerns at the start of the Bush administration in early 2001, but it got less attention than Russia did." The focus on "terrorism" in the early days of the administration centered on the threats posed by nation-states—Iran, Syria, North Korea and Iraq—and enacting regime change. Cheney and Rumsfeld had spent much of the 1990s plotting out a course to redraw the maps of the Middle East, but it was not focused on the asymmetric threat al Qaeda and other terrorist groups posed. Iraq, not al Qaeda, was their obsession. "From the start, we were building the case against Hussein and looking at how we could take him out and change Iraq into a new country," said former treasury secretary Paul O'Neill. "And, if we did that, it would solve everything. It was all about finding a way to do it. That was the tone of it. The President saying, 'Fine. Go find me a way to do this.'" At the new administration's second National Security Council meeting on February 1, 2001, Rumsfeld said bluntly, "What we really want to think about is going after Saddam."

Ironically—for all of Rumsfeld's bravado about the weakness of the Clinton era, and neocon charges that the Democrats had been asleep at the wheel watching al Qaeda—Rumsfeld himself was initially dismissive of the imminence of the threat posed by the group prior to 9/11. Journalist Bob Woodward detailed a meeting that reportedly took place on July 10, 2001, two months before the 9/11 attacks. CIA director George J. Tenet met with Cofer Black, the head of the CIA's Counterterrorism Center (CTC), at Langley, Virginia. The two men reviewed current US intelligence on bin Laden and al Qaeda. Black, Woodward reported, "laid out the case, consisting of communications intercepts and other top-secret intelligence showing the increasing likelihood that al-Qaeda would soon attack the United States. It was a mass of fragments and dots that nonetheless made a compelling case, so compelling to Tenet that he decided he and Black should go to the White House immediately." At the time, "Tenet had been having difficulty getting traction on an immediate bin Laden action plan, in part because Defense Secretary Donald H. Rumsfeld had questioned all the National Security Agency intercepts and other intelligence. Could all this be a grand deception? Rumsfeld had asked. Perhaps it was a plan to measure U.S. reactions and defenses." After reviewing the intelligence with Black, Tenet called National Security Adviser Condoleezza Rice from the car en route to the White House. When Black and Tenet met with Rice that day, according to Woodward, they "felt they were not getting through to Rice. She was polite, but they felt the brush-off." Black later said, "The only thing we didn't do was pull the trigger to the gun we were holding to her head."

Then the planes piloted by the 9/11 hijackers slammed into the Twin Towers and the Pentagon. It didn't take long for Rumsfeld and his team to envision how the fight against terrorism didn't undermine their Iraq plans but could actually provide the rationale to carry them out. Perhaps even more important, the post-9/11 moment allowed Rumsfeld, Cheney and their cohort to realize the ambitions they had long held for an all-powerful executive branch, with the virtually unlimited right to wage wars across all borders, justified in their minds by a global national security threat. The goals and plans that they had spoken of in hushed tones at unofficial gatherings would soon become the official policy of the United States.

As President Bush's war team began planning for a response to the 9/11 attacks, Rumsfeld led the charge to put Iraq on the target list immediately. In advance of the September 15–16, 2001, weekend meetings Bush convened at Camp David, Feith drew up a memo for Rumsfeld that listed "the immediate priority targets for initial action" as: al Qaeda, the Taliban and Iraq. "The agenda was very clear from the night of 9/11," General Hugh Shelton, at the time the chair of the Joint Chiefs of Staff and the most senior military adviser to President Bush, told me. He said that Rumsfeld and Wolfowitz immediately began pressing for an attack on Iraq. "We need to be going into Iraq. We need to go right now," he recalled them saying. "Although there wasn't one shred, not one iota of evidence that would say [9/11] was linked into Iraq," Shelton said. "But yet, that drumbeat started that night. They didn't like the fact that when I came up to the office that night with some plans that we had [to respond to 9/11] that none of them included the Iraq plans." Richard Clarke said that on September 12, President Bush told him three times to look for "any shred" of evidence linking Iraq to the attacks. Wolfowitz sent a strategy memo to Rumsfeld arguing that "even a 10 percent chance that Saddam Hussein was behind the 9/11 attack" meant that "maximum priority should be placed on eliminating that threat." Joining Shelton in the anti-Iraq invasion camp was one of his predecessors, General Colin Powell, the secretary of state. A decade earlier, during the Gulf War, Powell had clashed with Wolfowitz—at the time an undersecretary of defense—and the ideological civilian leaders at the Pentagon over their desire to send US troops all the way to Baghdad to overthrow Saddam. But Powell and traditional conservatives like former secretary of state James Baker and Brent Scowcroft won that debate. Now, with the 9/11 attacks fresh in everyone's minds, Wolfowitz and the ideologues were certain they could achieve their goals.

At Camp David, Shelton said, Wolfowitz continued to press for an Iraq attack even as Shelton, Powell and senior intelligence officials said there was no evidence to suggest Iraq had anything to do with the attacks. As discussion focused on Afghanistan and attacking al Qaeda's sanctuary, "True to form, Wolfowitz brought it up: 'We need to be using this as a reason to attack Iraq,'" Shelton recalled. Dr. Emile Nakhleh, a senior CIA analyst at the time, was also briefing the president during the immediate post-9/11 period. Nakhleh had been with the Agency for a decade and had spent much of it traveling under academic cover in Muslim countries across the globe. Having started the CIA's Political Islam Strategic Analysis Program and as its scholar-in-residence on militant Islamist movements and Middle Eastern governments, he was the Agency's equivalent of a three-star general. In response to Rumsfeld and Wolfowitz pushing for an invasion of Iraq in those first meetings, Nakhleh told me, he stood up at one point and said to them, "If you want to go after that son of a bitch [Saddam] to settle all scores, be my guest, but we have no information that Saddam was tied to al Qaeda or to terrorism and we have no clear information" about weapons of mass destruction (WMD). Nakhleh said, after the first several meetings post-9/11, "my conclusion and other analysts' conclusion was they were going to go to war. The train had left the station, regardless of the intelligence we presented." President Bush shelved the Iraq discussions for a time, having pledged as a candidate not to engage in "nation building." He said he wanted a "humble" foreign policy. But his views were rapidly evolving.

It would take some time—and more than a dozen visits to the CIA by Cheney and his chief of staff, "Scooter" Libby—to produce enough "evidence" of an active Iraqi WMD program to pull off their plans for an Iraq invasion. But, in the meantime, they had a war against government oversight and accountability to wage. The CIA and Special Forces campaign in Afghanistan was, in the beginning, a rout. While the Afghanistan war was producing spectacular headlines trumpeting the swiftness and decisiveness of the US military campaign against the weak Taliban government, Cheney and Rumsfeld and their neoconservative deputies were busy plotting a global war. This war would extend to the home front with warrantless wiretapping, mass arrests of Arabs, Pakistanis and other Muslim immigrants and a prodigious rollback of the civil liberties of American citizens. To wage it, they would have to dismantle and manipulate a bureaucracy of oversight and legal review that had been built up over successive administrations. All this would open the door for an array of tactics that had been used before but could now be deployed on an unprecedented scale: covert action, black ops, secret prisons, snatch operations and what amounted to a blanket rebranding of assassinations as "High Value Targeting."

COMING OUT OF THE REAGAN-BUSH ERA, in which the institution of covert action was marred by the Iran-Contra scandal, President Clinton put in place more oversight mechanisms and created a rigorous legal system for approving lethal covert action. When Clinton or his national security adviser proposed a covert action, it would be passed through an internal oversight system: first to the CIA, where the Agency's general counsel would review its legality before passing it on for further review (and possibly proposed changes as a result of the legal review) to two separate CIA committees—the Covert Action Planning Group and the Covert Action Review Group. After those committees reviewed the proposed action and suggested alterations, it would go back to the CIA's general counsel for a final legal review and then would be passed back to the White House. There, it would be put before the Interagency Working Group for Covert Action, comprising representatives from various agencies within the executive branch. The group would analyze the potential consequences of the proposed covert action and, again, review its legality. After a final review by the heads and deputies of the relevant agencies, the action would be presented to the president for authorization. These actions were rarely approved.

When President Bush was sworn in early in 2001, his administration indicated it intended to keep many of those same checks and balances in place. National Security Presidential Directive-1 (NSPD-1), signed by Bush on February 13, 2001, closely mirrored the Clinton-era system for approving covert actions. But in March, Bush asked National Security Adviser Condoleezza Rice to request that the CIA "prepare a new series of authorities for covert action in Afghanistan." Clarke and his CIA counterparts who ran the "bin Laden Unit" began laying out covert actions that could target al Qaeda, while the administration proposed beefing up the CIA's counterterrorism funding. Clarke pushed hard for a retaliatory strike against al Qaeda for the October 2000 bombing of the USS *Cole* off the coast of Yemen. As was the case under Clinton, many of the plans involved targeting al Qaeda leadership in Afghanistan. At the end of May, Rice and

Tenet met with Clarke, Cofer Black and the bin Laden Unit chief to discuss "taking the offensive" against al Qaeda. The CIA was running disruption activities against bin Laden at the time, but the consensus of these officials was that they needed a plan for "breaking the back" of al Qaeda. They also endorsed covert aid to Uzbekistan but stopped short of offering any significant support to the Northern Alliance and other anti-Taliban groups inside Afghanistan. In other words, they were continuing the Clinton-era approach to al Qaeda and Afghanistan, albeit with increased funding and focus.

A draft of a new Counterterrorism National Security Presidential Directive (NSPD) was circulated in June. Deputy National Security Adviser Stephen Hadley described the program to the 9/11 Commission as "admittedly ambitious," outlining a multiyear effort involving "all instruments of national power," including a far-reaching covert action program. But it would go through five more meetings at the deputy level before being presented to the principals. At one of these meetings, in August 2001, the NSC Deputies Committee had "concluded that it was legal for the CIA to kill bin Laden or one of his deputies" with a Predator drone strike.

Although the use of drones would eventually become one of the staples of the US targeted killing apparatus, before 9/11 there was great dissension on the topic in the ranks of Bush's counterterrorism team. In the last year of the Clinton administration, the United States began flying drones over Afghanistan out of a secret US base, called K2, in Uzbekistan. There was a program to create a weaponized drone under way, but it was not yet operational. Cofer Black argued that the drones should not even be used for reconnaissance, suggesting that the administration wait until they could be weaponized. He pointed out that a Predator had been spotted over Afghan territory in 2000, spurring the Taliban government to scramble MiG fighters. "I do not believe the possible recon value outweighs the risk of possible program termination when the stakes are raised by the Taliban parading a charred Predator in front of CNN," Black asserted. In the end, the administration decided to shelve the use of the drones for recon in Afghanistan until they could be loaded for strikes. But while Black, Clarke and others within the counterterrorism team pushed hard for the eventual use of the Predators to conduct targeted killing operations, the CIA's senior leadership expressed serious concerns about the Agency running such a program, echoing many of the concerns of the Clinton-era counterterrorism team about creating US hit lists. According to the 9/11 Commission, Tenet "in particular questioned whether he, as Director of Central Intelligence, should operate an armed Predator. 'This was new ground,' he told us. Tenet ticked off key questions: What is the chain of command? Who takes the shot? Are America's leaders comfortable with the CIA doing this, going outside of normal military command and control?" Charles Allen, who was the CIA's assistant director for collection from 1998 to 2005, said that he and the Agency's number-three man, A. B. "Buzzy" Krongard, "had said that either one of them would be happy to pull the trigger, but Tenet was appalled," adding that no CIA personnel had such authority to use drones to summarily assassinate people, even terrorists.

While these debates played out inside the Agency, it was not until a week before 9/11 that the Bush administration convened a meeting of "principals" to discuss the al Qaeda threat. At the September 4 meeting, a draft of the National Security Presidential Directive was officially presented and was approved "with little discussion" for presentation to Bush to sign. National Security Adviser Condoleezza Rice reportedly told President Bush that she thought it would take about three years to implement the ambitious program. On September 10, Hadley continued to press Director Tenet and the CIA to prepare draft legal authorities "for the 'broad covert action program' envisioned by the draft presidential directive." Hadley also instructed him to draw up findings "authorizing a broad range of other covert activities, including to capture or to use lethal force" against al Qaeda "command-and-control-elements." According to the 9/11 Commission report, this section would overwrite Clinton-era documents and ought to be broad enough "to cover any additional [Osama bin Laden]-related covert actions contemplated." Although the Bush administration was working to widen the scope of acceptable lethal force against bin Laden and his top deputies, the process was marked by the same concerns expressed during the Clinton era about granting sweeping lethal authority. The Bush White House was embarking on a path similar to the Clinton administration's, trying to circumvent the assassination ban while still requiring careful review of each proposed lethal operation.

On September 11, all of that would change.

As the World Trade Center towers crumbled to the ground, so too did the system of oversight and review of lethal covert ops that had been carefully constructed over the course of the previous decade.


"ONLY A CRISIS—actual or perceived—produces real change." So wrote the conservative icon Milton Friedman in his book *Capitalism and Freedom.* Friedman was a key adviser to successive Republican administrations and held tremendous influence over many officials in the Bush White House. He had mentored Rumsfeld early in his career, and Cheney and the leading neocons in the administration regularly sought his counsel. Friedman preached, "When that crisis occurs, the actions that are taken depend on the ideas that are lying around. That, I believe, is our basic function: to develop alternatives to existing policies, to keep them alive and available until the politically impossible becomes the politically inevitable."

For the senior officials in Bush's national security and defense teams who spent the eight Clinton years—and more—developing those alternatives, the 9/11 attacks, and almost unanimous support from the Democratic-controlled Congress, provided a tremendous opportunity to make their ideas inevitable. In an eerie prediction of things to come, the neocons of the Project for the New American Century had asserted a year to the month before 9/11 in their report, "Rebuilding America's Defenses," that "the process of transformation, even if it brings revolutionary change, is likely to be a long one, absent some catastrophic and catalyzing event—like a new Pearl Harbor." Cheney and Rumsfeld may not have been able to see 9/11 coming, but they proved masters at exploiting the attacks. "The 9/11 attack was one of those events in history potent enough to stimulate fresh thought and disturb the complacent," recalled Feith. "It created an opportunity to give many people—friends and enemies, in the United States and abroad—a new perspective. Rumsfeld, Wolfowitz, and I shared the view that the president had a duty to use his bully pulpit."

Under the Constitution, it is the Congress, not the president, that has the right to declare war. But seventy-two hours after 9/11, Congress took a radical step in a different direction. On September 14, 2001, the House and Senate gave President Bush unprecedented latitude to wage a global war, passing the Authorization for Use of Military Force (AUMF). It stated that "the President is authorized to use all necessary and appropriate force against those nations, organizations, or persons he determines planned, authorized, committed, or aided the terrorist attacks that occurred on September 11, 2001, or harbored such organizations or persons, in order to prevent any future acts of international terrorism against the United States by such nations, organizations or persons." The use of the term "persons" in the authorization was taken by the administration as a green light for assassinations. It passed the House with only one opposing vote and the Senate with no dissent. The lone "Nay" vote against the AUMF came from liberal California Democrat Barbara Lee. "However difficult this vote may be, some of us must urge the use of restraint," Lee declared, voice trembling, as she spoke on the floor of the House that day. "There must be some of us who say, let's step back for a moment and think through the implications of our actions today—let us more fully understand their consequences," she added in her submitted remarks. "We must be careful not to embark on an open-ended war with neither an exit strategy nor a focused target."

Lee's two-minute speech was the extent of any congressional push-back to the sweeping war powers and authority the White House was requesting.

Empowered by an overwhelming, bipartisan endorsement of a global, borderless war against a stateless enemy, the Bush administration declared the world a battlefield. We "have to work, though, sort of the dark side, if you will," Dick Cheney proclaimed on NBC's *Meet the Press* on September 16, 2001, hinting at what was to come. "We've got to spend time in the shadows in the intelligence world. A lot of what needs to be done here will have to be done quietly, without any discussion, using sources and methods that are available to our intelligence agencies, if we're going to be successful." The president publicly signed the AUMF into law on September 18, 2001, but it was the order he signed a day earlier in secret that was even more momentous. The secret presidential directive, which remains classified, granted the CIA authority to capture and hold suspected militants across the globe, which would lead to the creation of a network of what administration officials internally referred to as "black sites" that could be used to imprison and interrogate prisoners. The directive also wiped out the roadblocks of oversight and interagency review from the process of authorizing targeted killings. Perhaps most significantly, it ended the practice of the president signing off on each lethal, covert operation. The administration's lawyers concluded that the ban on assassinations did not apply to people it classified as "terrorists," and it gave great latitude to the CIA for authorizing kill operations on the go. In the beginning, President Bush wanted the CIA to take the lead. He had just the man for the job.

COFER BLACK spent much of his career in the shadows in Africa. He cut his CIA teeth in Zambia during the Rhodesian War and then in Somalia and South Africa during the apartheid regime's brutal war against the black majority. During his time in Zaire, Black worked on the Reagan administration's covert weapons program to arm anti-Communist forces in Angola. In the early 1990s, long before most in the counterterrorism community, Black became obsessed with bin Laden and declared him a major threat who needed to be neutralized. From 1993 to 1995, Black worked, under diplomatic cover, at the US Embassy in Khartoum, Sudan, where he served as CIA station chief. Bin Laden was also in Sudan, building up his international network into what the CIA would describe at the end of Black's tour as "the Ford Foundation of Sunni Islamic terrorism." Black's agents, who were tracking bin Laden, worked under a Clinton-era "operating directive" that restricted them to intelligence collection on bin Laden and his network. Black wanted the authority to kill the Saudi billionaire, but the Clinton White House had not yet signed the lethal findings it eventually did after the 1998 African embassy bombings. "Unfortunately, at that time permissions to kill—officially called Lethal Findings—were taboo in the outfit," said CIA operative Billy Waugh, who worked closely with Black in Sudan. "In the early 1990s we were forced to adhere to the sanctimonious legal counsel and the do-gooders." Among Waugh's rejected ideas was allegedly a plot to kill bin Laden in Khartoum and dump his body at the Iranian Embassy in an effort to pin the blame on Tehran, an idea Waugh said Cofer Black "loved."

In the early days of the Bush administration, Black began agitating once again for authorization to go after bin Laden. "He used to come in my office and regale me with all the times when he had tried to do something about Osama bin Laden, prior to 9/11," recalled Lawrence Wilkerson, who served as Secretary of State Colin Powell's chief of staff at the time. He told me Black said that "because of the lack of courage of Delta [Force], and lack of bureaucratic competence in the CIA, he'd never been able to do anything." According to Wilkerson, Black told him that "every time they presented a possibility to Delta, for example, they would come up with this list of questions they had to answer, like, 'What kind of nails are in the door?' 'What kind of lock is on the door?' 'Give us the serial number on the lock,' and all this kind of stuff, which is just standard SOF [Special Operations Forces] stuff for not wanting to do something." Much to Black's satisfaction, such meticulous practices would soon be dispensed with altogether.

On August 6, 2001, President Bush was at his Crawford, Texas, ranch, where he received a presidential daily brief titled "Bin Ladin Determined to Strike in US." It twice mentioned the possibility that al Qaeda operatives may try to hijack airplanes, saying FBI information "indicates patterns of suspicious activity in [the United States] consistent with preparations for hijackings or other types of attacks, including recent surveillance of federal buildings in New York." Nine days later, Black addressed a secret Pentagon counterterrorism conference. "We're going to be struck soon," Black said. "Many Americans are going to die, and it could be in the U.S."

After 9/11, Bush and Cheney rewrote the rules of the game. Black no longer needed to hold a gun to anyone's head to get permission for lethal operations. "My personal emotion was, It is now officially started," Black recalled. "The analogy would be the junkyard dog that had been chained to the ground was now going to be let go. And I just couldn't wait." In his initial meeting with President Bush after the 9/11 attacks, Black outlined how CIA paramilitaries would deploy to Afghanistan to hunt down bin Laden and his henchmen. "When we're through with them, they will have flies walking across their eyeballs," Black promised, in a performance that would earn him a designation in the inner circle of the administration as "the flies-on-the-eyeballs guy." The president reportedly loved Black's style. When he told Bush the operation would not be bloodless, the president said, "Let's go. That's war. That's what we're here to win." Philip Giraldi, a career CIA case officer who went through "The Farm," the CIA's training facility in rural Virginia, with Black, recalled running into him in Afghanistan shortly after the first US teams hit the ground post-9/11. "I hadn't seen him in many years," Giraldi told me. "I was astonished at how narrow-minded he had become. He would basically keep talking about bringing back bin Laden's head on a platter—and he meant his head on a platter." Giraldi said that Black "had a narrow view of things," and loathed America's closest European allies, including the British, saying, "He didn't trust them a bit." When it came to the emerging US global war, Giraldi said, Black was "a real enthusiast, which is unusual in the Agency. In the Agency, people tend to be kind of skeptical. If you're an intelligence officer in the field, you get skeptical of a lot of things real fast. But Cofer was one of these enthusiasts."

On September 19, the CIA team, code-named Jawbreaker, deployed. Black gave his men direct and macabre instructions. "Gentlemen, I want to give you your marching orders, and I want to make them very clear. I have discussed this with the President, and he is in full agreement," Black told covert CIA operative Gary Schroen and his team. "I don't want bin Laden and his thugs captured, I want them dead," Black demanded. "They must be killed. I want to see photos of their heads on pikes. I want bin Laden's head shipped back in a box filled with dry ice. I want to be able to show bin Laden's head to the President. I promised him I would do that." Schroen said it was the first time in his thirty-year career that he had been ordered to assassinate an adversary rather than attempting a capture. Black asked if he had made himself clear. "Perfectly clear, Cofer," Schroen told him. "I don't know where we'll find dry ice out there in Afghanistan, but I think we can certainly manufacture pikes in the field." Black later explained why this would be necessary. "You'd need some DNA," Black said. "There's a good way to do it. Take a machete, and whack off his head, and you'll get a bucketful of DNA, so you can see it and test it. It beats lugging the whole body back!" When Russian diplomats meeting with Black in Moscow ahead of the full US invasion of Afghanistan reminded Black of the Soviet defeat at the hands of the US-backed mujahedeen, Black shot back. "We're going to kill them," he said. "We're going to put their heads on sticks. We're going to rock their world." In a sign of things to come, the covert operations Black organized immediately after 9/11 relied heavily on private contractors. The initial CIA team consisted of about sixty former Delta Force, ex-SEALs and other Special Forces operators working for Black as independent contractors, making up the majority of the first Americans to go into Afghanistan after 9/11.

In the beginning, the list of people who had been pre-cleared for CIA targeted killing was small: estimates ranged from seven to two dozen people, including bin Laden and his deputy, Ayman al Zawahiri. And the operations were largely focused on Afghanistan. On October 7, President Bush officially launched "Operation Enduring Freedom," and the US military began a campaign of air strikes, followed by a ground invasion. In the early days of the Afghanistan campaign, CIA personnel and Special Forces worked in concert. "We are fighting for the CT [counterterrorism] objectives in the Afghan theater," the chief of counterterrorist special operations wrote in a memo to CIA personnel in October 2001. "And although this sets high goals in very uncertain, shifting terrain, we are also fighting for the future of CIA/DOD integrated counterterrorism warfare around the globe. While we will make mistakes as we chart new territory and new methodology, our objectives are clear, and our concept of partnership is sound." At the time, the CIA had a very small paramilitary capability, but as the lead agency responsible for hunting down those responsible for 9/11, the CIA could borrow Special Operations Forces for missions.

Rumsfeld had no interest in being the support team for the CIA, and the Agency's emerging centrality in the growing US war did not sit well with the defense secretary. Rumsfeld had nothing but contempt for the Clinton administration, and he, Cheney and their neoconservative allies thought that the CIA had become a watered-down liberal iteration of its former self. Covert action, they believed, had been handcuffed by lawyers and unnecessary and intrusive congressional oversight that would hinder what they perceived as life-and-death operations that needed to be conducted in secret. Although Cofer Black shared Rumsfeld's zeal for killing "terrorists," that was not enough. Rumsfeld wanted nothing to do with CIA oversight bureaucrats, and he didn't want his forces under CIA control. Cheney had made clear that under this administration, CIA lawyers and congressional committees would not be viewed as defenders of the law or as part of a necessary system of checks and balances. As Rumsfeld was fond of saying, these institutions were a hindrance to "taking the fight to the terrorists." Lawyers would be consulted to rubber-stamp secret policies and only certain, select members of Congress would be consulted. Briefings to Congress, including mandated full-access briefings to the elite "Gang of Eight" congressional members who were historically briefed on intelligence operations regarding covert actions, would be censored and redacted internally at the White House, meaning a sanitized version would be given to US lawmakers.

In the months after 9/11, Cheney, Rumsfeld and their teams launched several major initiatives aimed at ensuring that no bureaucracy would stand in the way of their plans for the unchecked use of the darkest US forces. Cheney wanted to disabuse the CIA of the idea that it had any kind of independence. Rather than having the Agency serve as the president's premier fact-checking and intelligence resource, the CIA's new job would be to reinforce predetermined policy. Cheney wanted to gut the interagency reviews of proposed lethal actions that were standard under Clinton. Soon after 9/11, the White House convened a group of senior administration lawyers whose job it would be to legally justify torture, kidnapping and assassination. The group secretly dubbed itself the "War Council" and was led by David Addington, Cheney's counsel and longtime adviser who had worked with him on the "minority report" defending Iran-Contra. It also included White House counsel Alberto Gonzales and his deputy, Tim Flanigan; the Pentagon's general counsel, William Haynes; and Deputy Assistant Attorney General John Yoo. The War Council explicitly excluded the State Department's general counsel and other military and Justice Department lawyers who had historically been included in reviewing legal structures for combating terrorism. This point was clear: this group was to develop legal justification for tactics in a covert dirty war, not to independently assess their legality.

To fight its global war, the White House made extensive use of the tactics Cheney had long advocated. Central to its "dark side" campaign would be the use of presidential findings that, by their nature, would greatly limit any effective congressional oversight. According to the National Security Act of 1947, the president is required to issue a finding before undertaking a covert action. The law states that the action must comply with US law and the Constitution. The presidential finding signed by Bush on September 17, 2001, was used to create a highly classified, secret program code-named Greystone. GST, as it was referred to in internal documents, would be an umbrella under which many of the most clandestine and legally questionable activities would be authorized and conducted in the early days of the Global War on Terror (GWOT). It relied on the administration's interpretation of the AUMF passed by Congress, which declared any al Qaeda suspect anywhere in the world a legitimate target. In effect, the presidential finding declared all covert actions to be preauthorized and legal, which critics said violated the spirit of the National Security Act. Under GST, a series of compartmentalized programs were created that, together, effectively formed a global assassination and kidnap operation.

Authority for targeted kills was radically streamlined. Such operations no longer needed direct presidential approval on a case-by-case basis. Black, the head of the Counterterrorism Center, could now directly order hits.

The day Bush signed the memorandum of notification, which among other initiatives, authorized a High Value Detainee program, CTC personnel and "selected foreign counterparts" were briefed on it in Washington, DC. "Cofer [Black] presented a new Presidential authorization that broadened our options for dealing with terrorist targets—one of the few times such a thing had happened since the CIA was officially banned from carrying out assassinations in 1976," recalled Tyler Drumheller, the former head of CIA clandestine ops in Europe. "It was clear that the Administration saw this as a war that would largely be fought by intelligence assets. This required a new way of operating." John Rizzo, a veteran CIA attorney who helped draft the authorization, later said, "I had never in my experience been part of or ever seen a presidential authorization as far-reaching and as aggressive in scope. It was simply extraordinary."

GST was also the vehicle for snatch operations, known as extraordinary renditions. Under GST, the CIA began coordinating with intelligence agencies in various countries to establish "Status of Forces" agreements to create secret prisons where detainees could be held, interrogated and kept away from the Red Cross, the US Congress and anything vaguely resembling a justice system. These agreements not only gave immunity to US government personnel, but to private contractors as well. The administration did not want to put terror suspects on trial, "because they would get lawyered up," said Jose Rodriguez, who at the time ran the CIA's Directorate of Operations, which was responsible for all of the "action" run by the Agency. "[O]ur job, first and foremost, is to obtain information." To obtain that information, authorization was given to interrogators to use ghoulish, at times medieval, techniques on detainees, many of which were developed by studying the torture tactics of America's enemies. The War Council lawyers issued a series of legal documents, later dubbed the "Torture Memos" by human rights and civil liberties organizations, that attempted to rationalize the tactics as necessary and something other than torture. "We needed to get everybody in government to put their big boy pants on and provide the authorities that we needed," recalled Rodriguez, who, with Black, would become one of the key architects of the torture policy. "I had had a lot of experience in the Agency where we had been left to hold the bag. And I was not about to let that happen for the people that work for me."

The CIA began secretly holding prisoners in Afghanistan on the edge of Bagram Airfield, which had been commandeered by US military forces.

In the beginning, it was an ad hoc operation with prisoners stuffed into shipping containers. Eventually, it expanded to a handful of other discrete sites, among them an underground prison near the Kabul airport and an old brick factory north of Kabul. Doubling as a CIA substation, the factory became known as the "Salt Pit" and would be used to house prisoners, including those who had been snatched in other countries and brought to Afghanistan. CIA officials who worked on counterterrorism in the early days after 9/11 said that the idea for a network of secret prisons around the world was not initially a big-picture plan, but rather evolved as the scope of operations grew. The CIA had first looked into using naval vessels and remote islands—such as uninhabited islands dotting Lake Kariba in Zambia—as possible detention sites at which to interrogate suspected al Qaeda operatives. Eventually, the CIA would build up its own network of secret "black sites" in at least eight countries, including Thailand, Poland, Romania, Mauritania, Lithuania and Diego Garcia in the Indian Ocean. But in the beginning, lacking its own secret prisons, the Agency began funneling suspects to Egypt, Morocco and Jordan for interrogation. By using foreign intelligence services, prisoners could be freely tortured without any messy congressional inquiries.

In the early stages of the GST program, the Bush administration faced little obstruction from Congress. Democrats and Republicans alike gave tremendous latitude to the administration to prosecute its secret war. For its part, the White House at times refused to provide details of its covert operations to the relevant congressional oversight committees but met little protest for its reticence. The administration also unilaterally decided to reduce the elite Gang of Eight members of Congress to just four: the chairs and ranking members of the House and Senate intelligence committees. Those members are prohibited from discussing these briefings with anyone. In effect, it meant that Congress had no oversight of the GST program. And that was exactly how Cheney wanted it.

THE BUSH ADMINISTRATION did not create the CIA's rendition program. It started under Clinton in the mid-1990s when he signed a presidential directive authorizing the CIA and US Special Operations Forces, in conjunction with the FBI, to snatch terror suspects from across the globe without the need to respect bilateral extradition agreements or international conventions. But the Clinton directive also allowed for these US officers to send terror suspects to Egypt, where, far removed from US law and due process, they could be interrogated by *mukhabarat* (secret police) agents not constrained by US prohibitions against torture. The program required direct authorization for each snatch operation. Under Clinton, more than seventy renditions were conducted. In some cases, US planes would land in countries and ferry their targets back to the United States for trial. Among these high-profile renditions conducted under Clinton were: Mir Aimal Kasi, a Pakistani national who had shot and killed two CIA employees outside the Agency's headquarters in 1993 and was rendered from Pakistan in 1997; Ramzi Yousef, the mastermind of the 1993 World Trade Center bombing; Wali Khan Amin Shah, who plotted to blow up multiple US airlines on a single day in 1995; and Japanese Red Army member Tsutomu Shirosaki, who bombed the US Embassy in Jakarta in 1986 and was eventually snatched in 1996. All of these renditions involved court orders from US judges and ended in civilian trials. However, in cases where the United States wanted intelligence rather than justice, it would render them to third countries where they would have no legal rights. In 1998, the US Congress passed legislation declaring that it is "the policy of the United States not to expel, extradite, or otherwise effect the involuntary return of any person to a country in which there are substantial grounds for believing the person would be in danger of being subjected to torture, regardless of whether the person is physically present in the United States." Bush's post-9/11 presidential directives threw those concerns out the door, and the CIA intensified its use of what human rights advocates came to call "torture taxis."

As the new kill/capture program began to kick into full gear in late 2001, the CIA's number-three man at the time, Buzzy Krongard, declared the "war on terror" would be "won in large measure by forces you do not know about, in actions you will not see and in ways you may not want to know about." A US official directly involved in rendering captives told the *Washington Post*, "We don't kick the (expletive) out of them. We send them to other countries so they can kick the (expletive) out of them." Another official who supervised the capture and transfer of prisoners told the paper, "If you don't violate someone's human rights some of the time, you probably aren't doing your job," adding, "I don't think we want to be promoting a view of zero tolerance on this. That was the whole problem for a long time with the CIA." Cofer Black put a fine point on it when he told Congress about the new "operational flexibility" employed in the war on terror. "This is a very highly classified area, but I have to say that all you need to know is that there was a before 9/11, and there was an after 9/11," Black said. "After 9/11 the gloves come off."

The early stages of the post-9/11 rendition program began what would be a multiyear battle between the FBI and the CIA over who would take the lead in investigating the terror attacks. It would also bring to the sur-

face how little regard the Bush White House had for anything vaguely resembling a law enforcement approach to the perpetrators of 9/11. As the
Taliban regime crumbled and US troops poured into Afghanistan, scores
of al Qaeda operatives began retreating across the border into Pakistan.
In November, Pakistani forces picked up al Qaeda trainer Ibn al Shaykh
Libi, who allegedly ran the Khalden training camp in Afghanistan where
the would-be "Shoe Bomber," Richard Reid, and Zacarias Moussaoui, the
so-called Twentieth Hijacker, were both trained. The Pakistanis handed
Libi over to FBI agents stationed at Bagram Air Base for questioning. The
FBI saw the prisoner as a potentially valuable source of intel on al Qaeda
and a possible witness against Moussaoui. New York–based FBI agent Jack
Cloonan told his agents in Afghanistan to "handle this like it was being
done right here, in my office in New York." He said, "I remember talking
on a secure line to them. I told them, 'Do yourself a favor, read the guy
his rights. It may be old-fashioned, but this will come out if we don't. It
may take ten years, but it will hurt you, and the bureau's reputation, if
you don't. Have it stand as a shining example of what we feel is right.'"
Libi's interrogators described him as cooperative and "genuinely friendly"
and said that he had agreed to give them information on Reid in return for
promises to protect his family.

However, just as the FBI believed it was making headway with Libi,
CIA operatives, on orders from Cofer Black, showed up at Bagram and demanded to take him into their custody. The FBI agents objected to the CIA
taking him, but the White House overruled them. "You know where you
are going," one of the CIA operatives told Libi as he took him from the FBI.
"Before you get there, I am going to find your mother and fuck her."

The CIA flew Libi to the USS *Bataan* in the Arabian Sea, which was also
housing the so-called American Taliban, John Walker Lindh, who had been
picked up in Afghanistan, and other foreign fighters. From there, Libi was
transferred to Egypt, where he was tortured by Egyptian agents. Libi's interrogation focused on a goal that would become a centerpiece of the rendition and torture program: proving an Iraq connection to 9/11. Once he was
in CIA custody, interrogators pummeled Libi with questions attempting to
link the attacks and al Qaeda to Iraq. Even after the interrogators working
Libi over had reported that they had broken him and that he was "compliant," Cheney's office directly intervened and ordered that he continue to
be subjected to enhanced interrogation techniques. "After real macho interrogation—this is enhanced interrogation techniques on steroids—he admitted that al Qaeda and Saddam were working together. He admitted that
al Qaeda and Saddam were working together on WMDs," former senior FBI
interrogator Ali Soufan told PBS's *Frontline*. But the Defense Intelligence

Agency (DIA) cast serious doubt on Libi's claims at the time, observing in a classified intelligence report that he "lacks specific details" on alleged Iraqi involvement, asserting that it was "likely this individual is intentionally misleading" his interrogators. Noting that he had been "undergoing debriefs for several weeks," the DIA analysis concluded Libi may have been "describing scenarios to the debriefers that he knows will retain their interest." Despite such doubts, Libi's "confession" would later be given to Secretary of State Powell when he made the administration's fraudulent case at the United Nations for the Iraq War. In that speech Powell would say, "I can trace the story of a senior terrorist operative telling how Iraq provided training in these weapons to al Qaeda." Later, after these claims were proven false, Libi, according to Soufan, admitted he had lied. "I gave you what you want[ed] to hear," he said. "I want[ed] the torture to stop. I gave you anything you want[ed] to hear."

The pattern that was emerging early on with the rendition and interrogation program centered on two primary objectives: dismantling al Qaeda's network and preventing any further attacks, and supporting the case for an invasion of Iraq. In pursuit of these goals, no options or tactics would be left off the table. While the State Department cautioned against declaring an ill-conceived global war and pushed for a narrow, law-enforcement response to 9/11, Cheney began drawing up plans for ambitious global kidnapping and assassination operations in which certain elements of the CIA would initially take a leading role. Cheney, according to former senior CIA and State Department officials, began effectively directing a global manhunt using a mesh of Special Operations Forces and operatives from the CIA's Special Activities Division, the paramilitary arm of the Agency. The former officials described a culture that permeated these operations in which ambassadors, the conventional US military commanders and even CIA station chiefs around the world were kept in the dark about clandestine or covert activities. To execute this program, Cheney relied on the gray area in US law and command authority between the jurisdiction of the CIA and the military.

In November 2001, Cheney convened a meeting at the White House to put the finishing touches on a presidential order, drawn up by Addington and other lawyers, that outlined how prisoners captured around the world would be tried. As had become custom, War Council lawyers were invited to the meeting, but senior State Department and National Security Council officials were shut out. Powell and the State Department's lawyers had told President Bush that they believed that, under the Geneva Convention, Taliban and al Qaeda detainees were entitled to legal protections and humane treatment while in enemy custody. They furthermore warned that in not offering America's enemies such protections, it would endanger the lives of US military personnel captured in the war. On February 7, 2002, President Bush made his decision. He signed another directive, based on a notion that the Geneva Convention was "quaint" and did not apply to al Qaeda or Taliban prisoners held by the United States. The order was issued just after the Bush administration began sending detainees snatched in Afghanistan and elsewhere to a US military prison at Guantánamo Bay, Cuba.

Although Congress was largely asleep at the wheel in its oversight responsibilities early on in the war on terror, the administration knew that would not last. By early 2002, some on Capitol Hill were already demanding that the CIA and administration brief them on the range of tactics being used by the Agency in pursuit of terror suspects. The full details of how those early post-9/11 "Cheney Program" operations were run and who exactly was operating them will likely never be fully revealed. "We deliberately kept the circle of people who knew where the black sites were to a very small number. We didn't tell the FBI," recalled Rodriguez, the CIA official who coordinated the construction and use of the black sites. "Many people, even those within the Agency with the highest security clearances, were not clued in. As far as I know, the location of the black sites was not even shared with the president." Rodriguez added that it was not that those senior officials kept outside the circle of knowledge were untrustworthy, "but rather that they simply did not have a 'need to know.'"

The strategies that fueled this force's ascent would become a model for a secret program that Rumsfeld would build at the Pentagon. Rumsfeld was watching as the CIA became the alpha dog in the GWOT under Cheney's direction. Rumsfeld became determined to break what he called the Pentagon's "near total dependence on CIA" and to build an iron curtain around the most sensitive activities of America's most elite warriors. This project was envisioned as a parallel intelligence operation to the CIA, but also as the most effective kill and capture machine the world had ever seen—one that, by its very nature, would answer to no one but the president and his inner circle.

## 2 Anwar Awlaki: An American Story

THE UNITED STATES AND YEMEN, 1971–2002—The world was a different place when George W. Bush was campaigning for president in 2000. The date 9/11 held no particular significance for Americans and Osama bin Laden was not the center of attention for the US military and intelligence machine. For many Arabs and Muslims, the Clinton era had resulted in crushed hopes that the Palestine issue would be negotiated in their favor. Many Muslim Americans saw Bush, not Clinton's vice president, Al Gore, as their best hope in the 2000 presidential election. But it wasn't just Palestine. Many Muslims also shared the conservative social values embraced by evangelical Christians like Bush, on issues of marriage, gay rights and abortion. One such American Muslim was a young imam from New Mexico named Anwar al Awlaki. "Yes, we disagree with a lot of issues when it comes to the foreign policy of the United States," Awlaki said in 2001. "We are very conservative when it comes to family values. We are against the moral decay that we see in the society. But we also cherish a lot of the values that are in America. Freedom is one of them; the opportunity is another."

In many ways, Awlaki's story was a classic tale of people from a faraway land seeking a better life in America. His father, Nasser Awlaki, was a brilliant young student from Yemen who came to the United States on a Fulbright scholarship in 1966 to study agricultural economics at New Mexico State University. "I read a lot about the United States when I was only fifteen years old," Nasser recalled. "My impression of the US, when I was young boy in elementary and junior high school, was that America is a land of democracy, and the land of opportunities. I yearned all the time to have my studies in the United States of America." When he arrived, Nasser went first to Lawrence, Kansas, to study English and then headed for New Mexico. "I wanted to know and meet people of the New World who built one of the most progressive nations the world has ever known," he declared in an essay introducing himself to fellow classmates in the United States. Nasser wrote that he wanted to get an education "in order to help my people become more progressive and advanced." He had married right after he completed high school but could not afford to bring his wife, Saleha, to live with him in the United States on his $167 monthly stipend. "Because I wanted to get my wife back, I finished my schooling for a bachelor's degree in agriculture in only two years and nine months," he told me when we met in his large, modern home in Sana'a, the Yemeni capital in December 2011. After graduating, Nasser headed back to Yemen, got his wife a visa and returned to Las Cruces, New Mexico, where he completed his master's degree. On April 22, 1971, their baby boy, Anwar, was born. "In those days, it was OK to distribute cigars to your fellow graduate students," he laughed. "It was written on it: 'It's a Boy.' And it was an unbelievable day for me, when Anwar was born. In Las Cruces Memorial Hospital."

Nasser wanted to raise Anwar as an American, not just in nationality but also in character. In 1971, when the family moved so Nasser could complete his PhD at the University of Nebraska, they signed young Anwar up for swimming lessons at the local YMCA. "He was actually swimming when he was only two and a half years old," Nasser recalled. "And he was very brilliant at it." As we sat in his living room at his home in Sana'a, Nasser pulled out the family photo album and showed me pictures of little Anwar, posed on a rug in a staged picture taken at a shopping mall. Eventually, the family settled down in St. Paul, where Nasser got a job at the University of Minnesota and enrolled Anwar at Chelsea Heights Elementary School. "He was an all-American boy," he said, showing me a picture of Anwar in his classroom. Anwar, with long, flowing hair, is smiling as he points out Yemen on a globe. Another family photo shows a lanky adolescent Anwar wearing sunglasses and a baseball hat at Disneyland. "Anwar was really raised like any other American boy, he used to like sports and he was very brilliant at school, you know. He was a good student, and he participated in all kinds of sports."

In 1977, Nasser decided to move the family back to Yemen—for how long he did not know. Nasser believed he had an obligation to use his US education to help his very poor home country. He knew that he wanted Anwar to return to the United States one day for university, but he also believed it would be good for the young boy to learn about his family's homeland. So, on the last day of 1977, the family returned to Sana'a. Six-year-old Anwar could barely speak Arabic, though he quickly picked it up. He had risen to number four in his class in Sana'a by the end of his first semester and within a year was speaking Arabic with ease. Nasser and his colleagues eventually started a private school that taught in both English and Arabic. Anwar was in the first class, along with Ahmed Ali Abdullah Saleh, the son of Yemen's president. The two boys would be classmates for eight years. Ahmed Ali would go on to become one of the most feared men in Yemen and the head of its Republican Guard. Anwar, meanwhile, set off on a course to follow in his father's academic footsteps.

Anwar would spend the next twelve years in Yemen, as his father became closer to his American friends in Sana'a. Nasser and several other US- and British-educated Yemenis worked with the US Agency for International Development (USAID) and started a college of agriculture with $15 million in funding from the United States. In 1988, Nasser was appointed Yemen's minister of agriculture. After Anwar finished high school in Yemen, a colleague of Nasser's from USAID offered to help find a good college for Anwar in the United States. Nasser wanted his son to study "civil engineering, particularly regarding hydraulics, and the problem of water resources in Yemen. Because Yemen is really suffering from the shortage of water." His USAID friend suggested Colorado State University (CSU) and helped Anwar get a US government scholarship. In order for Anwar to get the scholarship, he had to have a Yemeni passport. "At that time, I was just a regular university professor, I didn't have the finances to send my son to study in the United States at my own expense," recalled Nasser. "So the American USAID director told me it is easy, if Anwar can get a Yemeni passport, then he will be qualified for the scholarship from USAID. So, we got Anwar a Yemeni passport." The Yemeni authorities listed his birthplace as Aden, Yemen. This would later cause trouble for Anwar.

ANWAR LANDED AT O'HARE AIRPORT in Chicago on June 3, 1990, and then moved to Fort Collins, Colorado, to study civil engineering. "His dream, as a young man, was really to finish his studies [in the United States] and come and serve in Yemen," said Nasser. During Anwar's first year at the university, the United States launched the Gulf War against Iraq. Nasser recalled a phone call he received from Anwar when the US bombs started falling on Baghdad. He was watching Peter Arnett, the famed CNN correspondent, reporting from the Iraqi capital. "He saw pictures from CNN that it was a complete blackout over Baghdad. So Anwar was thinking that Baghdad was really, completely destroyed. Baghdad has a lot of cultural meaning to Muslims, because it was the site of the Abbasid dynasty. So he was really disappointed at what happened. And so at that time he started really to worry about general Muslim problems."

Anwar admitted that when he first went to the United States for college, he "was not [a] fully practicing" Muslim, but after the Gulf War began he started to become politicized and eventually headed up the Muslim Student Association on campus. Anwar had also become interested in the

war in Afghanistan and, during winter break in 1992, Anwar traveled to
the country. The US-backed mujahedeen had expelled the Soviet occupiers
in 1989, yet Afghanistan remained embroiled in civil war and the country was a popular destination for young Muslims, including a staggering
number of Yemenis, to explore a front of jihad. "The invasion of Kuwait
took place, followed by the Gulf War. That is when I started taking my religion more seriously," Anwar later recalled. "I took the step of traveling to
Afghanistan to fight. I spent a winter there and returned with the intention
of finishing up in the US and leaving to Afghanistan for good. My plan was
to travel back in summer; however, Kabul was opened by the mujahedeen
and I saw that the war was over and ended up staying in the US."

Anwar's grades started slipping at the university as he became more
invested in politics and religion. He later claimed that he lost his scholarship because of his activism. "Word came to me from a connection at
the US Embassy in Sana'a, that they have been receiving reports about my
Islamic activities on campus and the fact that I have traveled to Afghanistan and this was the single reason for the termination of my scholarship,"
he alleged. In retrospect, this appears to have been a defining moment in
Anwar's trajectory. A spark had been created that, when combined with
the events that followed it, altered his path. Years later, Anwar theorized
that the scholarship he was given was part of a US government plot to
recruit students from around the world as agents for America. "The US
government through its programs of scholarships for foreign students has
created for itself a pool of cadres around the world. From among these are
leaders in every field, heads of state, politicians, businessmen, scientists,
etc. They have one thing in common: They were all students in American
Universities," he wrote. "These programs have helped the US bolster its
strength worldwide and spread out its control. The way the US is managing an empire without calling it an empire is one of the great innovations
of our time." The story he told about himself was one of a rare individual
who had resisted this imperial design. "The plans to have me as one of the
many thousand men and women around the world who have their loyalty
to the US did not go through. I wasn't suitable for that role anymore. I was
a fundamentalist now!"

The members of the Awlaki family did not consider themselves particularly religious, just good Muslims who prayed five times a day and tried
to live their lives in accordance with the Koran. Religion was not unim-
portant by any means, but for the Awlakis, their tribal identity came first.
They were also modern people with relationships with international diplomats and businessmen. As he was becoming politicized, Anwar attended
a mosque near his university in Colorado and the local imam asked him

to deliver a sermon one Friday. Anwar agreed and realized he had a gift for public speaking. He began to think that maybe preaching, not engineering, was his true calling. "He was a very, very, very promising person. And we were hoping for a good future for him," recalled Anwar's uncle, Sheikh Saleh bin Fareed, a wealthy businessman and the head of the Aulaq tribe in Yemen. "I think Anwar was born to be a leader. It was in his blood, and his mentality."

Anwar graduated from CSU in 1994 and decided to stay in Colorado after graduation. He married a cousin from Yemen and took a job as an imam at the Denver Islamic Society. Nasser told me that Anwar never spoke of becoming an imam when he left for America but that he fell into it after being asked to preach a few times. "He thought this is an area where he can be [of help] and can do something. So I guess it started just by coincidence. But then I guess he liked it, so he decided to shift from professional engineering" to a vocation preaching Islam. Anwar became interested in the writings and speeches of Malcolm X and concerned about the plight of the African American community. In Denver, "He started to think about social issues in America, and he knew many black people and he went to see them in prisons, tried to help them," said Nasser. "So he became more involved in the social problems in the United States, regarding Muslims, and other minorities." A member of his mosque in Denver later said of Awlaki, "He could talk to people directly—looking them in the eye. He had this magic." An elder from Awlaki's Denver mosque later told the *New York Times* that he'd had a dispute with Awlaki after the young imam advised a young Saudi worshipper to join the Chechen jihad against Russia. "He had a beautiful tongue," the elder said. "But I told him: Don't talk to my people about jihad."

On September 13, 1995, Anwar's wife gave birth to their first child, a boy named Abdulrahman. A year later, in 1996, Anwar moved his young family to San Diego, California, where he became an imam at the Masjid al Ribat al Islami. He also began working on a master's degree in education leadership at San Diego State University. In the late 1990s, as the United States was gearing up for the 2000 presidential election, Nasser traveled to the United States to receive medical treatment and visited his son in San Diego. Nasser showed me a photo of a full-bearded Anwar on a boat, holding up a massive fish he caught. "He was already an imam with a big beard, you know," Nasser recalled, smiling at the picture of his son, who wore a yellow T-shirt emblazoned with the logo of a local Islamic organization and a baseball cap. A former San Diego neighbor of Awlaki's, Lincoln Higgie III, described Awlaki as "very outgoing and cheerful," with a "very retiring wife" and an "adorable" child. "He liked to go albacore fishing,"

Higgie recalled, "so every once in a while he would bring me some albacore fillets that his wife cooked up."

While visiting his son, Nasser attended Friday prayers and watched Anwar preach. "It was regular mosque. It had a capacity of about four hundred people, and most of the people who came to the mosque were regular Muslims: engineers, doctors, and people who had restaurants and things like that. From all over the Muslim world, from the Arab world," Nasser remembered. "I used to listen to his sermons. In fact, at that time, he was asking Muslims to participate in the democratic process in America, and he was encouraging—in fact, during the 2000 presidential campaign of George W. Bush, he thought the conservative Republicans would be better than the liberal Democrats, and he encouraged the Muslims there to elect George Bush. Because, he said, he was against abortions and things like that. These things conform to Muslim tradition," Nasser recalled. "So he was very active with the Muslim community, actually, and he never supported any violent things. He was very peaceful in America. All he did, really, was to represent Islam in its best."

In 1999, Anwar had his first run-in with the FBI, when he was flagged by the Bureau because of his alleged contact with Ziyad Khaleel, an al Qaeda associate who US intelligence believed had bought a battery for bin Laden's satellite phone. He had also been visited by a colleague of Omar Abdel Rahman, the "blind sheikh" accused of conspiring in the 1993 World Trade Center bombing. The 1999 investigation reportedly uncovered other ties the FBI found troubling, such as to the Holy Land Foundation, a Muslim charity vilified for raising funds for Palestinian charitable institutions linked to Hamas, a US State Department–designated terrorist organization. For two years while in San Diego, according to tax records procured by the FBI, Awlaki was the vice president of another organization, the Charitable Society for Social Welfare (CSSW). According to an FBI agent, this was merely another "front organization to funnel money to terrorists." Though no charges were ever brought against CSSW, federal prosecutors described it as a subsidiary of a larger organization founded by Abdul Majeed al Zindani, a well-known Yemeni with alleged al Qaeda ties. However, by this logic, the US Department of Labor would also be guilty by association, for providing CSSW projects with millions of dollars between 2004 and 2008. Anwar's family dismisses the suggestion that Anwar was raising money for terrorist groups and insists he was raising money for orphans in Yemen and elsewhere in the Arab world. The US investigation into Anwar was soon closed, for lack of evidence. In March 2000, the FBI concluded that Awlaki "does not meet the criterion for [further] investigation." But it wasn't the last time Anwar would hear from the FBI.

Two men who prayed at Anwar's mosque in San Diego, Khalid al Mihdhar and Nawaf al Hazmi, would soon be among the nineteen hijackers who conducted the 9/11 attacks. When Anwar moved the family to Falls Church, Virginia, in 2000, Hazmi also attended his mosque. After 9/11, US investigators would charge that Anwar was al Hazmi's "spiritual adviser." Nasser told me he asked his son about his connections to Hazmi and Mihdhar and told me that Anwar had only a sporadic, clerical relationship with the men. "I asked him myself. He said, 'They prayed in the mosque like anybody else, and I met them casually,'" Nasser asserted, asking, "How in the world do you think al Qaeda would have faith in Anwar to tell him about their biggest thing they were preparing for? It is unbelievable, because at that time he had no links whatsoever with any group like that. Definitely. And I'm 100 percent sure of that."

Listening to Anwar's sermons from this era, there is no hint that he had any affinity for al Qaeda. In 2000, Anwar began recording CDs of his sermons and selling them as box sets. The sermons were extremely popular among Muslims in the United States and elsewhere in the English-speaking world. He recorded more than a hundred CDs in all, most of them consisting of lectures on the lives of the Prophet Muhammad, and on Jesus and Moses, as well as theories about the "Hereafter." As the *New York Times* put it, "The recordings appear free of obvious radicalism." Invitations began streaming in, inviting Awlaki to speak to mosques and Islamic centers across the United States and around the globe. "I was very pleased with him," said Abu Muntasir, a founding member of a UK group called JIMAS, which hosted Awlaki several times. "He filled a gap for western Muslims who were seeking expressions of their religion which differed from the Islam of their parents' generation, to which they found it difficult to relate."

Despite the nonpolitical nature of his preaching, Anwar later alleged that US intelligence agents had sent "moles" into his San Diego mosque to gather information on its activities. "There was nothing happening at the mosque that would fall under the loose category of what we today refer to as terrorism but nevertheless, it is my firm belief that the government, for some reason, was actively trying to plant moles inside the mosque," he charged.

There is another strange mystery regarding Anwar's early run-ins with the FBI, one that will likely never be solved. While he was an imam in San Diego, Anwar was busted twice on charges of soliciting prostitutes. In the first case, he pleaded guilty to a lesser charge and paid a $400 fine and in the other, he was fined $240, given three years' probation and sentenced to two weeks of community service. The arrests would later be used to paint Anwar as a hypocrite, but the preacher offered up a different explanation:

the US government was trying to blackmail him into becoming an informant. In 1996, Anwar claimed, he was in his minivan at a stoplight waiting for it to turn green when his vehicle was approached by a middle-aged
woman who knocked on the passenger-seat window. "By the time I rolled
down the window and before even myself or the woman uttering a word
I was surrounded by police officers who had me come out of my vehicle
only to be handcuffed," he recalled. "I was accused of soliciting a prostitute
and then released. They made it a point to make me know in no uncertain terms that the woman was an undercover cop. I didn't know what to
make of the incident." Then, Anwar said, a few days later he was visited
by two men he said identified themselves as federal agents, who told him
they wanted his "cooperation." Anwar said they wanted him to "liaise
with them concerning the Muslim community of San Diego. I was greatly
irritated by such an offer and made it clear to them that they should never
expect such cooperation from myself. I never heard back from them again
until" a year later. That was his second bust for soliciting. "This time I was
told that this is a sting operation and you would not be able to get out of
it," Anwar recalled.

Perhaps he really was soliciting prostitutes, and his self-projection as a
pious man was an elaborate deception. But there would be other indications
later that Anwar Awlaki may not have been regarded by US intelligence
simply as a target of investigation, but also as a potential collaborator.

Anwar was unsettled by his run-ins with the law in California. "I believed that if the issue in San Diego was with local government I should
be safe from it if I move somewhere else," he recalled. Nasser arranged for
him to get a partial scholarship at George Washington University in Washington, DC, to pursue a PhD. By that point, Anwar's wife had given birth to
their second child and he needed to find employment. So, he lined up work
as a chaplain for the university's interreligious council and landed a job as
an imam at a popular mosque in Virginia, Dar al Hijrah. "Our community
needed an imam who could speak English...someone who could convey
[a modern narrative about Islam] with the full force of faith," said Johari
Abdul Malik, the outreach director at Dar al Hijrah. The mosque wanted
someone who could present the messages of the Koran to an audience of
American Muslims. Awlaki, Malik said, "was that person. And he delivered that message dutifully." The family settled into suburban Virginia in
January 2001. Although Anwar's reflections years later indicate that his
rage against the United States was building in the years preceding 9/11, if
that was true, he did a great job of masking it with his public profile as a
highly respected figure in the mainstream Muslim community.

ON THE MORNING OF SEPTEMBER 11, 2001, Anwar Awlaki was sitting in the backseat of a taxi. He had just arrived at Reagan National Airport in DC and was heading home after catching a red-eye back from a conference in Irvine, California. He heard the news of the attacks in the taxi and told the driver to head straight for his mosque. Awlaki and his colleagues were immediately concerned that the mosque could be targeted in the rage that was brewing. That night, police were called to Anwar's mosque after a man pulled his car up in front of the building and screamed threats at those inside for thirty minutes straight. The mosque closed for three days as a result and issued a press release condemning the attacks. "Most of the questions are, 'How should we react?'" Awlaki said to the *Washington Post*, explaining the leadership's reasons for shuttering the mosque. "Our answers are, especially for our sisters who are more visible because of the dress: Stay home until things calm down." When the mosque reopened, a Muslim-owned security firm was hired to search cars and handbags and pat down people entering the building. Local churches offered support to Dar al Hijrah, including escorts for Muslim women afraid to venture out to mosque. This was a fact that Anwar lauded publicly to his congregation and to reporters, but he also kept worshippers informed about anti-Muslim prejudice and hate crimes—such as one incident in which a Muslim woman stumbled into the mosque on September 12 after being attacked by a man with a baseball bat. In his first sermon after the reopening of the mosque, Anwar condemned the attacks as "heinous." "Our hearts bleed for the attacks that targeted the World Trade Center as well as other institutions in the United States, despite our strong opposition to the American biased policy towards Israel," he said, reading a condemnation of the attacks from Sheikh Yusuf al Qaradawi, the famous, controversial Egyptian theologian. "We came here to build, not to destroy....We are the bridge between America and 1 billion Muslims worldwide," Awlaki added.

When 9/11 happened, Awlaki didn't own a television. "I used to get my news through the Internet," he said days after the attacks. "But since this happened, I rushed to Best Buy and got a TV set. And we were glued to our TV sets. For Muslims, I think it was a very complicated issue because we suffer twice," he asserted. "We're suffering as Muslims and as human beings because of the tragic loss for everyone. And then in addition, we suffer the consequences of what will happen to us as an American Muslim community since the perpetrators are, so far, identified as Arabs or Muslims. I would also add that we have been pushed to the forefront because of these events. There has been huge media attention towards us, in addition to FBI scrutiny."

While Anwar huddled with other Muslim leaders to determine how they would respond to the 9/11 attacks, he once again popped onto the US government radar. "September 11 was a Tuesday," Anwar later recalled. "By Thursday the FBI were knocking on my door." US agents began questioning Awlaki about his dealings with two of the suspected hijackers. The agents showed him pictures of the hijackers—including the two who had attended his San Diego mosque as well as Hani Hanjour, who also had spent time in San Diego and, along with Hazmi, attended an Awlaki sermon in Falls Church, Virginia, in 2001. Awlaki "said he did not recognize Hazmi's name but did identify his picture. Although Awlaki admitted meeting with Hazmi several times, he claimed not to remember any specifics of what they discussed," according to the 9/11 Commission. Awlaki also said that he had not had any contact with Hazmi in Virginia, only in San Diego, and said he had never met Hanjour. Awlaki, according to the commission, "described Hazmi as a soft-spoken Saudi student who used to appear at the mosque with a companion but who did not have a large circle of friends." According to declassified FBI files on Awlaki's meetings with federal agents after 9/11, Awlaki described Hazmi as "a loner," adding that he was "a very calm and extremely nice person." Awlaki, according to the FBI, did not view Hazmi "as a very religious person, based on the fact that [Hazmi] never wore a beard and neglected to attend all five daily prayer sessions." Soon after that meeting, the FBI returned again and asked Awlaki to work with them in their investigation. The next time they visited, Awlaki got a lawyer. An FBI file after the meeting stated: "Investigation continues at WFO [the FBI's Washington Field Office] into the association between Anwar Aulaqi and persons connected to the September 11, 2001 terrorist attacks on the United States." [Awlaki's name is alternately spelled Aulaqi.]

According to subsequent FBI testimonies to the 9/11 Commission, Awlaki had a series of phone conversations in 2000 with Saudi Omar al Bayoumi, who helped Hazmi and Mihdhar find apartments in San Diego. An FBI investigator told the commission that he believed that the men were using Bayoumi's phone at the time, implying that Awlaki had had direct contact with the hijackers. Yet, based on those early interviews, the investigators concluded that Awlaki's interactions with the three hijackers were inconclusive. The 9/11 Commission asserted that the future hijackers "respected Awlaki as a religious figure and developed a close relationship with him" but added that "the evidence is thin as to specific motivations."

While the FBI dug into Awlaki's relationship with the hijackers, hundreds of people would pack Dar al Hijrah mosque to hear Awlaki preach on Fridays. He counseled families and helped new immigrants find apartments or employment. Among those who came to him for help was a Palestinian couple who attended all of his Friday sermons. They were having trouble with their son, who was a US military psychiatrist. The couple was concerned that their son was not taking interest in their religion. Nasser recalled Anwar telling him that they said, "Why don't you talk with [our son], so he will come with us to the mosque?" Awlaki agreed to help. Their son was named Nidal Malik Hasan, the man who, more than a decade later, would commit one of the worst massacres on a US military base in history. Just as his relationship with some of the 9/11 hijackers would result in government scrutiny of his life, Awlaki's interactions with Hasan would later be used to raise suspicions about Awlaki's role in other terror plots.

Undoubtedly, Awlaki's mosques seemed to attract an array of characters who would go on to become terrorists. But the extent of Awlaki's knowledge of who they were or what they were plotting is difficult to determine. In examining Awlaki's experiences and statements from this period, the mystery only deepens. What unfolded between Awlaki and the US government behind closed doors in the months after 9/11 and what played out publicly between Awlaki and the US media at the same time is a bizarre tale, filled with contradictions. It was as though Anwar Awlaki were living a double life.

In the weeks after 9/11, while Anwar dealt with the FBI agents in private, in public he became a media star, called upon by scores of media outlets to represent a "moderate" Muslim view of the 9/11 attacks. TV crews followed him around. National radio programs interviewed him. Newspapers quoted him frequently. Awlaki encouraged his followers to participate in blood drives for 9/11 victims, to donate money for the families. The leadership at the mosque described him as a man known for his "interfaith outreach, civic engagement, and tolerance," and the Associated Press reported that, among those who attended his sermons, "Most said they did not find him to be overtly political or radical." Although Awlaki at times delivered stinging indictments of US foreign policy, he also condemned the attacks in strong terms. Initially, he even indicated that the United States would be justified in waging an "armed struggle" against those responsible for the attacks. "Absolutely," Awlaki told PBS. "We have stated our position that...there must be a way for the people who did this, they have to pay the price for what they have done. And every nation on the face of the earth has a right to defend itself."

Awlaki was "a go-to Muslim cleric for reporters scrambling to explain Islam. He condemned the mass murder, invited television crews to follow him around and patiently explained the rituals of his religion," according to the *New York Times*. In a separate article, the paper reported that

Awlaki "is held up as a new generation of Muslim leader capable of merging East and West." Awlaki said in late September 2001, "I even feel that it's unfortunate that we have to state this position because no religion would condone this, so it should be common knowledge. But we were in a position where we had to say that Islam does not approve of this. There is no way that the people who did this could be Muslim, and if they claim to be Muslim, then they have perverted their religion." The *Washington Post* consulted Awlaki several times after 9/11, even commissioning him to star in a webcast about Ramadan. "Our position needs to be reiterated and needs to be very clear," Awlaki said during a sermon, televised nationally in the United States by PBS, a few weeks after the attacks. "The fact that the US has administered the death and homicide of...civilians in Iraq, the fact that the US is supporting the deaths and killing of thousands of Palestinians does not justify the killing of one US civilian in New York City or Washington, DC, and the deaths of [thousands of] civilians in New York and Washington, DC, does not justify the death of one civilian in Afghanistan. And that is the difference between right and wrong, evil and good, that everybody's claiming to talk about."

Even as he condemned the attacks, Awlaki pulled no punches in his analysis of the US posturing toward the Islamic world. In one sermon, a week after 9/11, Awlaki pushed back on the Bush administration's characterization of al Qaeda's motives. "We were told this was an attack on American civilization. We were told this was an attack on American freedom, on the American way of life," Awlaki declared. "This wasn't an attack on any of this. This was an attack on US foreign policy." As the United States began its push into Afghanistan in October 2001, Awlaki was interviewed by the Washington Times. "We're totally against what the terrorists [have] done. We want to bring those who [have] done this to justice," he said. "But we're also against the killing of civilians in Afghanistan." As the first Ramadan after 9/11 approached, Awlaki said, "There will be a higher level of anxiety in the community this year." The Muslim holiday will be overshadowed by "a gloomy mood because of the events that happened in September and the ongoing war overseas," he said, adding, "We always want Ramadan to come in quiet times, but unfortunately, this year that is not going to happen." He also made clear he was opposed to the launch of the US war against the Taliban. "In my personal opinion I feel that the US rushed into this war," he told an interviewer. "There could have been some other avenues to solve this problem, one of which was diplomatic pressure, taking advantage of all the Muslim countries who voiced their support for the US in this, and voiced their concern for what has happened on September 11. Very strong condemnations from all over the Muslim world. So that could have been used and capitalized on to put some pressure on Afghanistan or whoever did this, rather than rushing into the war that we've seen." More than a decade before the so-called Arab Spring, Anwar also criticized US support for autocratic leaders and their repressive regimes in Middle Eastern and predominantly Muslim countries. "There doesn't have to be a dramatic, sudden, overnight change in these regimes, but there needs to be at least some pressure on the part of the US for these regimes to open up a bit and provide more freedom to the people," he said.

Driving around suburban Virginia during Ramadan in late 2001, Awlaki spoke to a camera held by a journalist from the *Washington Post*. "Since the war started there have been a lot of casualties among civilians. A lot. And unfortunately that hasn't been reported, or hasn't been reported in a fair proportion in the media, so there's a lot of concern that the common people in Afghanistan are paying the price for this. They're pawns in this game of politics," he said.

After September 11th, the feelings of American Muslims were similar to the feeling of everybody else in America, feelings of sympathy for the families of the victims, and a sense that whoever did this needs to be brought to justice...that was the prevailing feeling amongst all American Muslims, in fact Muslims around the world. The war changed that a bit, because we have the memories of Iraq fresh in our minds. We were told in 1990 that this was going to be a war against Saddam Hussein. Well, after ten years he's still in power and the ones who are suffering are the Iraqi people. A million in Iraq died. So those memories are coming back to us now. They say it's to get the terrorists, but then here we go, casualties from the civilians.

The interviewer asked Awlaki what he thought of bin Laden and the Taliban. "They represent a very radical understanding, an extreme view, and a part of what feeds into [those] radical views are the conditions that exist in the Muslim world," he said. "It's definitely a fringe group. There have been teaching[s] that were twisted. It's a method of justifying views by using religious texts, and that could exist in any religion." Awlaki appears, in the video, to be struggling sincerely with how to respond to 9/11. He is also seen as a loving father, wiping his younger son's nose. At another point, he holds his trotting toddler's hand as they walk into the mosque. For a brief moment, Awlaki even sings part of the theme song from the children's show *Barney*: "I love you, you love me." It is difficult to watch the hours of footage and conclude that he was simply a good actor.

As incidents of anti-Muslim violence and bigotry spread, Awlaki watched as Muslim and Arab communities in the United States were targeted by the federal government. The people who came to his sermons told him of harassment they endured because of their race or their faith. People were rounded up, mosques were infiltrated, Muslim businesses were targeted by vigilantes and federal agents. Like many American Muslims, Awlaki believed that his people were being singled out, profiled because of their religion or race. "There is an element of feeling among the Muslims that they are targeted, or at least they are the ones who are paying the highest price for what's going on," Awlaki told National Public Radio in October 2001. "There has been a rise in negative reporting on Islam in the media since the events happened. There have been 1,100 Muslims detained in the US. There's a bombing going on over a Muslim country, Afghanistan. So there are some reasons that make the Muslims feel that, well, it is true that the statement was made that this is not a war against Islam, but for all practical reasons, it is the Muslims who are being hurt." When two members of his former San Diego mosque were detained on the basis of allegedly "strong connections" to the hijackers who had worshipped there, Awlaki rebuked the FBI. "There was no need to round them up in a crude fashion," he said. He and his colleagues had preached patience and cooperation with the authorities, Awlaki said, but argued that "our people won't listen to us when they see this is how the FBI is treating them. It strengthens our belief that we are a community under siege...whose civil rights are being violated." "It is not right," he went on, claiming that the two men had tried to voluntarily cooperate with authorities before being unfairly detained. "It gives the impression they have involvement in this. It just destroys their reputation. I am convinced they are innocent."

As the weeks went on after 9/11, Awlaki described in scores of media interviews the struggle that he and other Muslim leaders were facing in their communities, sparked by the perception that the United States was waging a war against Muslims and Islam. "It is the radical voices that are taking over, the ones who are willing to enter into an armed confrontation with their governments. So, basically, what we have now is that all of the moderate voices are silenced in the Muslim world," he said in one interview. In another, Awlaki said, "With American Muslims, there's this feeling of being torn between our nation and our solidarity with Muslims around the world." Awlaki began warning the United States that if it launched what Muslims perceived as a war against their religion, it would bring blowback. "My worry is that because of this conflict, the views of Osama bin Laden will become appealing to some of the population of the Muslim world," he said. "That's a very frightening thing, so the US needs to be very careful and not have itself perceived as an enemy of Islam."

IN ONE OF THE ODDER TWISTS in Awlaki's post-9/11 story, he was invited by officials at the US Department of Defense (DoD) to address a Pentagon luncheon on February 5, 2002. In a declassified e-mail, one of the organizers of the event, a Pentagon employee, wrote: "I had the privilege of hearing one of Mr. Awlaki's presentations in November and was impressed both by the extent of his knowledge and by how he communicated that information and handled a hostile element in the audience. I particularly liked how he addressed how the average Middle Eastern person perceives the United States and his views on the international media." The e-mail concluded that the event needed to be booked soon because Awlaki "will be leaving for an extensive period of time," adding, "I think you'll enjoy it if you come. [Awlaki] is very informative and this is certainly a hot topic that we all would like to learn a little more about." According to declassified Pentagon documents, "At that period in time, the secretary of the Army (redacted) was eager to have a presentation from a moderate Muslim," adding that Awlaki "was considered to be an 'up and coming' member of the Islamic community." After being vetted for security reasons, Awlaki "was invited to and attended a luncheon at the Pentagon in the secretary of the Army's Office of Government Counsel." (It is unlikely Awlaki dined on the "East Side West Side" sandwich offered at the event, which included beef, turkey and bacon on marbled rye.)

The Pentagon appearance may have just been a freak event that occurred thanks to poor vetting and Awlaki's public reputation at the time, shaped by his scores of media appearances, but it would also fuel speculation that Awlaki was cooperating with the US government in its 9/11 investigations. When I asked Nasser Awlaki, Anwar's father, about the Pentagon luncheon, he lit up. "Yes! You know, you cannot believe it," he told me. "At one time, he told me he will join the US Army in order to be Muslim chaplain." In one conversation he had with his son during this time, Nasser said Anwar "told me he was mad not to be invited to the White House. Like other Muslim dignitaries during Ramadan, when Bush started this event, asking people to come to Ramadan. He thought, how come they didn't ask him, because he was the imam of a big religious center in America." Awlaki may not have made it into the White House, but in early 2002, he was invited to lead a prayer service in the US Capitol. His sermon there was featured in the 2002 PBS documentary *Muhammad: Legacy of a Prophet.*

In March 2002, US federal agents conducted a series of sweeping raids against more than a dozen Muslim nonprofit organizations, businesses and private homes. The raids were conducted under the banner of an interagency task force and were part of a broad investigation into terror finances, code-named Operation Green Quest. Among the raided organizations were respected Islamic think tanks, such as the International Institute of Islamic Thought, as well as the Graduate School of Islamic and Social Sciences at Cordoba University in Virginia. The homes of various leaders and staffers of the organizations were also searched and their property seized. The raids were allegedly conducted as part of a targeted operation against terrorism financing. The agents seized computer hard drives, confidential files and books. The raids filled five hundred boxes with files seized in the actions. No charges were ever filed against any leaders of these institutions or the organizations themselves in connection with the raids. Mainstream Muslim organizations and civil liberties groups condemned the raids as a witch hunt. Awlaki delivered a stinging sermon saying Operation Green Quest "was an attack on every one of us" in "the Muslim community," warning, "If today this happened to these organizations, tomorrow you're going to be next." In another sermon, Awlaki declared, "Maybe the next day the Congress will pass a bill about Islam that it is illegal in America. Don't think that this is a strange thing to happen; anything is probable in the world of today because there are no rights unless there's a struggle for those rights."

Unbeknownst to Awlaki, he had been identified by the Green Quest task force as an active subject of its investigation, though it ultimately determined he had no connection to the targeted groups. At the same time, the FBI was actively trying to force him to cooperate in various investigations. Awlaki believed they were using the prostitution busts back in San Diego to try to flip him. Actually, his theory was not far-fetched. In fact, this was precisely what the feds were trying to do in the months after 9/11 when Awlaki was in Virginia. "FBI agents hoped al-Awlaki might cooperate with the 9/11 probe if they could nab him on similar charges in Virginia," *US News & World Report* later reported. "FBI sources say agents observed the imam allegedly taking Washington-area prostitutes into Virginia and contemplated using a federal statute usually reserved for nabbing pimps who transport prostitutes across state lines."

Awlaki was being feted in the media and presented as a voice of moderate Islam; a man who spoke eloquently of the Muslim community's struggle to navigate feelings of outrage at the 9/11 attacks and opposition to the wars the United States had launched in response. But privately, Awlaki was plotting his departure from America. Imam Johari Abdul Malik, who was the outreach director at Awlaki's Virginia mosque, said that he tried to persuade Anwar to stay in the United States in 2002. "Why are you leaving?" Malik asked him. He recalled Awlaki saying, "Because the climate here, you can't really do your work, because it's always antiterrorism, investigating this. The FBI wants to talk to you. That's not what I signed up for. I would rather go somewhere where I can preach, I can teach, I can have a discourse that's not about 9/11 every day." Awlaki also said he was considering running for parliament in Yemen and that he was interested in having his own TV show in the Gulf. Malik added that "Awlaki knew that he had been arrested for the solicitation of prostitutes, and that any revelation of this by US authorities would have ruined him."

Awlaki had also changed his tone about the United States. He was outraged over the crackdowns on Muslims and the wars abroad in Muslim countries. The raids, combined with the US war in Afghanistan and the threats of war against Iraq, spurred Awlaki to become sharper in his critique of the US government. "This is not now a war on terrorism. We need to all be clear about this. This is a war against Muslims. It is a war against Muslims and Islam. Not only is this happening worldwide but it is happening right here, in America, that is claiming to be fighting this war for the sake of freedom, while it is infringing on the freedom of its own citizens, just because they are Muslims," Awlaki said during a sermon. It was one of the last he would deliver in the United States. The US government surveillance of Muslims and mosques and imams enraged Awlaki, according to Nasser. "So Anwar suddenly was finding himself in a very difficult position. The country which he was born in, the country which he loved, the country where he wanted to preach his religion," in Anwar's eyes, "became really against Muslims. And he was mad. And he could not really practice his religion freely in America. So he thought maybe Britain will be a good country to go to," recalled Nasser. "And so he called me and said, 'Father, I cannot finish my PhD.'" Nasser was devastated. His dream was for his son to finish his PhD in America and return to Yemen to teach at the university, as he had done.

In leaving America for Britain in 2002, Anwar would also leave behind the "moderate" reputation he had built in the US media after 9/11. Was Anwar Awlaki a sleeper supporter of al Qaeda? A spiritual adviser to 9/11 hijackers, as the government would later allege? Or was he an American Muslim radicalized by his experiences in the United States after 9/11? Whether Awlaki was putting on a public show after 9/11 and hiding his true militant views on the United States or trying to escape the US government's investigations and interrogations, when he left Virginia he was on a collision course with history.

**Find, Fix, Finish: The Rise of JSOC**

WASHINGTON, DC, 1979–2001—On November 21, 2001, as the Global War on Terror was kicking into gear, Defense Secretary Donald Rumsfeld visited Fort Bragg, the headquarters of the Green Berets. "This is a world-wide war on terrorism, and every one of you, and each one of the organizations you represent are needed. And I know—I know of certain knowledge that when the call comes, you will be ready," Rumsfeld declared at the base. "At the start of the campaign, President George W. Bush said, 'We are at the beginning of our efforts in Afghanistan, but Afghanistan is only the beginning of our efforts in the world. This war will not end until terrorists with global reach have been found and stopped and defeated.' You are the men and women who will hand-carry that message to America's enemies, sealed with the muscle and might of the greatest warrior force on Earth." In his public appearance, Rumsfeld publicly thanked the "vanilla" Special Forces, the Green Berets, for their central role in Afghanistan, but when he spoke of those who would "hand-carry" America's message, he was referring to a particular group of warriors whom he viewed as his best and most secret weapon.

Although part of Rumsfeld's visit to Fort Bragg was public, he was also there for a secret meeting—with the forces whose units were seldom mentioned in the press and whose operations were entirely shrouded in secrecy: the Joint Special Operations Command, or JSOC. On paper, JSOC appeared to be an almost academic entity, and its official mission was described in bland, bureaucratic terms. Officially, JSOC was the "joint headquarters designed to study special operations requirements and techniques; ensure interoperability and equipment standardization; plan and conduct joint special operations exercises and training; and develop joint special operations tactics." In reality, JSOC was the most closely guarded secret force in the US national security apparatus. Its members were known within the covert ops community as ninjas, "snake eaters," or, simply, operators. Of all of the military forces available to the president of the United States, none was as elite as JSOC. When a president of the United States wanted to conduct an operation in total secrecy, away from the prying eyes of Congress, the best bet was not the CIA, but rather JSOC. "Who's getting ready to deploy?" Rumsfeld asked when he addressed the special operators. The generals pointed to the men on standby. "Good for you. Where you off to? Ahh, you'd have to shoot me if you told me, right?" Rumsfeld joked. "Just checking."

JSOC was formed out of the ashes of the failed mission to rescue fifty-three American hostages held in the US Embassy in Tehran, Iran, following the Islamic revolution of 1979. Code-named Operation Eagle Claw, the action involved an insertion of elite Delta Force operatives commanded by one of its famed founders, Colonel Charlie Beckwith, to secure an airstrip that could be used to launch an assault on the embassy. But when two of the helicopters went down in a sandstorm and a third was grounded, Beckwith and other commanders began fighting over whether to abort the mission. The loss of several crucial aircraft resulted in a standoff in the Iranian desert on whether to go forward with the mission. Beckwith fought with the air force commanders, naval officers and marine commanders. Eventually, President Carter issued an abort-mission order. Eight US service members died in the failed operation, when a helicopter crashed into a C-130 during the evacuation from Iran. It was a disaster. The Iranians scattered the American hostages around the country to prevent another rescue attempt. After 444 days in captivity, after a behind-the-scenes deal was brokered to swap the hostages for weapons, the Americans were eventually released—just minutes after President Reagan was sworn into office.

Behind the scenes, the White House and Pentagon reviewed what had gone wrong with the mission. It was determined that a unified, fully capable special operations all-star team was needed for such operations, one that would have its own aircraft, soldiers, SEALs and intelligence. Soon after Eagle Claw failed, the Pentagon established the Joint Test Directorate to begin preparing for another rescue operation, code-named Operation Honey Badger. The mission never launched, but a secret program would begin drawing up plans for a special ops team that would have full-spectrum capabilities to ensure that disasters like Eagle Claw would never happen again. Thus, in 1980, JSOC was officially formed, though the White House and the military would not publicly acknowledge its existence. JSOC was unique among all military and intelligence assets in that it reported directly to the president and was intended to be his small, private army. At least that was how the force was viewed in theory.

Colonel Walter Patrick Lang spent much of his military career in dark ops. Early in his army service, he helped coordinate the operation that led to the capture and killing of Che Guevara in Bolivia in 1967. He was a member of the Studies and Observation Group, SOG, which ran the targeted killing campaign for the United States during the Vietnam War, and eventually became the head of the secret Defense Intelligence Agency global human intelligence program. He was posted in Yemen, Saudi Arabia, Iraq and other hot spots around the globe. Lang also started the Arabic-language program at the West Point Military Academy. Throughout his career, he watched closely as the United States created this new special ops capability. The principal role of the "vanilla" Special Forces, like the Green Berets, was "training and leading indigenous forces, usually irregular forces against either regular forces or guerrilla forces. That's what they do, so they're attuned to foreigners. They seek to find people who are empathic, who work well with foreigners. Who like to sit around and eat with their right hand out of a common bowl bits of stringy old goat. And listen to somebody's gramma talk about the baloney, fictional ancestry of the tribe. They like to do that." Lang likened Green Berets to "armed anthropologists." JSOC, he said, was envisioned as "a counterterrorist commando outfit modeled on the British SAS [Special Air Service]. And the SAS does not do 'let's get happy with the natives' stuff. They don't do that. They're commandos, they kill the natives. These people are not very well educated about the larger picture of the effect that [their operations] have on the position of the United States in the world."

In the beginning, JSOC was a bit like an afterthought within the military bureaucracy. It did not have its own budget and was largely used as a force multiplier for hot conflicts under the command of the conventional military's Areas of Responsibility, the Pentagon's global system for organizing which forces oversee operations in specific regions. Delta Force had formed in the 1970s as a result of a series of terrorist attacks that spurred calls for the United States to expand the capacity of its unconventional warriors and special operations forces. "A lot of the military officers who had been brought up through this kind of, 'Charlie-Beckwith-counterterrorism-commando' thing, these are technicians of war, basically," Lang told me.

After the disaster of Eagle Claw in Iran, JSOC would be created as a highly compartmentalized organization with Special Mission Units (SMU) that would train and prepare for what were called "F³" operations: Find, Fix, Finish. In plain English, that meant tracking a target, fixing his location and finishing him off. The now world-famous Navy SEAL Team 6 that killed Osama bin Laden was created to support and conduct these missions. Its founding commander, Richard Marcinko, had served on the task force, known as the Terrorist Action Team, that planned Eagle Claw. Originally called Mobility 6, this elite unit of seventy-five Navy SEALs would develop into the leading counterterrorist unit available to the US government. Its name was itself propaganda. At the time of Team 6's founding, there were only two other SEAL teams, but Marcinko wanted the Soviets to think there were other teams of which they were unaware.

In the beginning, there were growing pains within JSOC, given that it was drawing its forces from a variety of elite units, including Delta Force, the SEALs and the 75th Army Rangers, that all believed in their own superiority. JSOC trained for operating in denied areas, conducting small-scale kinetic operations or direct actions, that is, lethal ops. A temporary military intelligence unit called the FOG, Field Operations Group, was formed. It would later become the in-house intelligence wing of JSOC and be known as "the Activity." Among its early highlights was providing signals intelligence for an operation to free Brigadier General James Dozier, who had been kidnapped by the Marxist Red Brigades in December 1981 from his home in Verona, Italy. Dozier was the only US flag officer to have ever been kidnapped. The Activity traced his location after several weeks of hunting, leading to a successful rescue operation by Italian antiterror forces.

Headquartered at Pope Air Force Base and Fort Bragg in North Carolina, JSOC would eventually command the army's Delta Force and 75th Ranger Regiment and SEAL Team 6, which was renamed the Naval Warfare Development Group, DEVGRU. Its air assets were drawn from the elite 160th Special Operations Aviation Regiment, known as the "Night Stalkers," as well as from the air force's 24th Special Tactics Squadron. JSOC's founders conceived of it as an antiterrorist force. But for much of its early history, it would be used for other types of missions. These teams would be deployed in secret and attach themselves to allied military forces or paramilitaries seeking to bring down governments perceived as hostile to US interests. At times the lines between training and combat were blurred, particularly in the dirty wars in Latin America in the 1980s. JSOC was used in Grenada in 1983 when President Reagan ordered a US invasion and throughout the 1980s in Honduras, where the United States was coordinating support for the Contras in Nicaragua and battling a guerrilla insurgency inside of Honduras. During his first term, President Reagan seemed eager to label terrorism a national security threat to be tackled by targeted kinetic force. Around the time of the 1983 Beirut bombing, Reagan publicly espoused "swift and effective retribution" against terrorists and signed a classified National Security Decision Directive (NSDD) and a subsequent secret finding authorizing "the use of sabotage, killing, [and] preemptive retaliatory strikes" against terrorist groups. The NSDD and the finding referred to a plan to form lethal CIA "action teams," but they reportedly authorized cooperation with JSOC forces.

JSOC operators liaised with foreign military forces throughout Latin America and the Middle East to combat hostage takers. They were also involved in the operation that led to the killing of Colombian drug lord Pablo Escobar in Medellín in 1993. Such operations led to the rise of a force of American fighters with a unique set of skills in counterinsurgency warfare. By the end stages of the Cold War, JSOC operators had become the most elite, seasoned combat veterans in the US military arsenal. In the 1990s, they went on to play central, but secret, roles in the wars in the Balkans, Somalia, Chechnya, Iran, Syria and throughout Africa and Asia. In the former Yugoslavia, JSOC helped lead the hunt for accused war criminals, though it failed to capture its two main targets, Bosnian Serb leaders Ratko Mladic and Radovan Karadzic. Under a secret presidential directive issued by President Clinton, JSOC was authorized to operate on US soil in counterterror operations and to confront any WMD threats, circumventing the Posse Comitatus Act, which prohibits the military from conducting law enforcement domestically.

In fact, some of JSOC's most sensitive missions were conducted at home. In 1993, Delta Force members participated in the disastrous raid against the Branch Davidian cult's compound in Waco, Texas. Some seventy-five people died in the raid, including more than twenty children and two pregnant women. JSOC also conducted security operations within America's borders when the 1994 World Cup and 1996 Summer Olympics were hosted by the United States.

By the end of the 1990s, the Department of Defense had officially acknowledged that teams such as JSOC existed, though its name was not made public. "We have designated Special Mission Units that are specifically manned, equipped and trained to deal with a wide variety of transnational threats," said Walter Slocombe, the undersecretary of defense for policy. An estimated 80 percent of JSOC's missions prior to 2000 remain classified.

"I would say they're the ace in the hole. If you were a card player, that's your ace that you've got tucked away." That's how General Hugh Shelton described JSOC to me. Shelton served as chairman of the Joint Chiefs of Staff under President Clinton and had spent most of his military career in Special Operations. Before Clinton named him chairman, Shelton had commanded the US Special Operations Command (SOCOM), which was technically the parent organization for JSOC's operations. "They are a surgical type of unit. They are not to be used to assault a fortress or anything—that's what the army and the marine corps does. But if you need someone that can sky dive from thirty miles away, and go down the chimney of the castle, and blow it up from the inside—those are the guys you want to call on." They're "the quiet professionals. They do it, and do it well, but they don't brag about it," he added. "You would not want to commit them to anything that required a mass force—and I guarded against that, when I was the chairman." On 9/11, Shelton was chairman. And Rumsfeld loathed him and his reservations.

Although JSOC's secret history was discussed, in hushed tones, in the halls of the Pentagon, many of its most decorated veterans believed it had been underutilized or, worse, misused. After an auspicious start and a far-reaching mandate, JSOC was viewed as a bastard child within the Pentagon and White House. The Iran-Contra scandal had placed a pox on the house of covert action. Despite some successes, such as the rescue of Kurt Muse, an American citizen, from a Panamanian prison during Operation Just Cause in 1989, Special Operations Forces (SOFs) were used with trepidation for the decade preceding 9/11.

During the 1991 Gulf War, United States Central Command (CENTCOM) Commander General Norman Schwarzkopf was reluctant to include JSOC in the war plan, though he ultimately lost that battle. JSOC deployed and—among other missions—hunted down SCUD missile systems to sabotage them. This distrust began to thaw slightly during the Clinton administration. According to SOCOM's official history, during this period, the operational tempo of Special Ops Forces increased more than 50 percent: "In 1996 alone, SOF were deployed in a total of 142 countries and engaged in 120 counterdrug missions, 12 demining training missions, and 204 Joint Combined Exchange Training exercises." But, rather than targeted kinetic ops, JSOC had mostly been used in large-scale operations, which increasingly became peacekeeping missions involving international coalitions, such as the wars in Bosnia-Herzegovina, Liberia, Sierra Leone, Haiti and Somalia. The kinetic, direct-action missions it was formed to conduct seldom seemed to go live. General Wayne Downing, who headed SOCOM from 1993 to 1996 and was a former JSOC commander, said that following the end of the Cold War, US Special Operations Forces' "unconventional warfare" role "had received reduced emphasis," adding that its "capabilities in this area had atrophied." JSOC, he said, "maintained superb counterterrorism and counterproliferation capabilities, but operated from a reactive rather than a proactive posture."

As the al Qaeda threat began to emerge in the 1990s, JSOC would propose missions aimed at targeting the network's leadership. Its commanders believed that this was its central role, and early drafts of planned operations against bin Laden and al Qaeda in the late 1990s reportedly included JSOC. But JSOC's commanders claimed that prior to 9/11 their forces "were never used once to hunt down terrorists who had taken American lives." According to Downing, during his tenure at SOCOM he participated in the preparation of approximately twenty operations targeting terrorist groups accused of killing American citizens, but the command "couldn't pull the trigger." Downing asserted that although JSOC "had superb, direct assault, 'finish' capabilities," it lacked "the 'find' and 'fix' and intelligence fusion capabilities essential to" fight a global war on terrorism.

"For many years, they were kind of a joke. They were the 'Big, Bad, Weightlifting Guys,' you know, down at Fort Bragg, inside their compound there," recalled Lang. "But they went on a lot of reconnaissance, and did things like that, but they never got to fight anybody, until the Clinton thing in Somalia [the infamous 1993 Black Hawk Down incident]. You gotta admit, they were brave as hell—there's no doubt about that—but in fact their real days of glory, as kind of worldwide scourers of the enemies of justice and truth, really only started after 9/11. They didn't really do a lot of fighting before that, really."

Rumsfeld came into office with an agenda to change that equation. He not only wanted the Pentagon to take over covert operations from the CIA but aimed to consolidate control over these operations himself, radically streamlining the established military chain of command. JSOC was created in secrecy to perform operations that were, by their very nature, meant to be kept hidden from virtually all other entities of military and government. After 9/11, Rumsfeld moved swiftly to create a structure to circumvent the Joint Chiefs and to begin directly coordinating with combatant commanders to conduct kinetic operations in their areas of responsibility. Under Title 10 of the US code, the chair of the Joint Chiefs of Staff was the senior military adviser to the president and was to serve as a conduit to the president. "[Rumsfeld] didn't like that at all," recalls Shelton. Rumsfeld "would try to diminish my authority or eliminate members of my staff," Shelton alleged. Rumsfeld, Shelton said, "wanted to be the policy and the operations guy." Shelton told me Rumsfeld sidelined "all that military expertise" and "he immediately wanted to figure out how he could start dealing directly with the combatant commanders and not dealing, as every other SECDEF [secretary of defense] had done, by presidential directive through the chairman of the Joint Chiefs." In his memoir, Shelton described Rumsfeld's model of the secretary of defense as being "based on deception, deceit, working political agendas, and trying to get the Joint Chiefs to support an action that might not be the right thing to do for the country, but would work well for the President from a political standpoint." He added, "It was the worst style of leadership I witnessed in 38 years of service or have witnessed at the highest levels of the corporate world since then."

Shelton said that during his time as chairman, under both Clinton and Bush, he personally intervened to stop operations he believed would have resulted in innocents being killed if they had gone ahead based on initial intel. But Rumsfeld wanted to streamline the process for green-lighting targeted killing operations and did not want to be bogged down by the military brass. "You've got to be careful when you start killing people, and make sure the ones you kill are the right people. And that requires using all the assets we got, to make sure we don't make a mistake. And it can be done fast, but it needs to be done as a cross-check," said Shelton. "Even though you don't want to miss an opportunity to grab a terrorist, you don't want to end up having an international incident that turns out to make us look like the terrorist." Far from Shelton's view of how these "surgical" forces should be deployed, Rumsfeld believed that JSOC had been underutilized, and he intended to transform it from the tip of the spear of a new global killing campaign to the spear itself. Rumsfeld—and many in the Special Ops community—believed that President Clinton and the military brass of the 1990s had lawyered forces like JSOC into a state of near irrelevance in the fight against terrorism. During the Clinton administration, "the possibility of hunting down the terrorists did receive ample attention at the top echelons of government," concluded a report commissioned by Rumsfeld three months after 9/11. "But somewhere between inception and execution, the SOF options were always scuttled as too problematic."

The author of the report was Richard Shultz, an academic who specialized in Special Operations warfare, and its purpose was to dissect Clinton's counterterrorism strategy. Rumsfeld wanted to ensure that any legal or bureaucratic barriers to unleashing JSOC would be smashed. Shultz was given a security clearance and free rein to conduct interviews with senior military officials and to review intelligence. The ultimate conclusion of the Shultz report was that the United States needed to take JSOC off the national security shelf and put it front and center in the war on terror.

The Shultz report, parts of which were later adapted into an unclassified article for the neoconservative *Weekly Standard*, also postulated that the Black Hawk Down incident in 1993 in Somalia had scared the White House into paralyzing Special Operations Forces. In late 1992, the United States was leading a UN peacekeeping mission aimed at delivering aid and, later, ridding Somalia of the warlords who had overthrown the country's government. But the warlords openly defied the US and UN forces and continued to pillage Somalia. In the summer of 1993, after a series of attacks on UN forces, Clinton gave the green light to JSOC to conduct a daring operation to take down the inner circle of the notorious warlord Mohamed Farrah Aidid, whose forces were rapidly consolidating their control of Mogadishu. But the mission descended into disaster when two of JSOC's Black Hawk helicopters were shot down over Mogadishu, sparking a massive battle between Special Ops Forces and Somali militia members. In all, eighteen US soldiers were killed. Images of some of the Americans being dragged through the streets were broadcast around the globe and ultimately spurred a US withdrawal. "The Mogadishu disaster spooked the Clinton administration as well as the brass, and confirmed the Joint Chiefs in the view that SOF should never be entrusted with independent operations," the Shultz report asserted. "After Mogadishu, one Pentagon officer explained, there was 'reluctance to even discuss pro-active measures associated with countering the terrorist threat through SOF operations. The Joint Staff was very happy for the administration to take a law enforcement view. They didn't want to put special ops troops on the ground.'" General Peter Schoomaker, who commanded JSOC from 1994 to 1996, said that the presidential directives under Clinton, "and the subsequent findings and authorities, in my view, were done to check off boxes. The president signed things that everybody involved knew full well were never going to happen," adding: "The military, by the way, didn't want to touch it. There was great reluctance in the Pentagon."

Shultz had interviewed several officials who served on the Joint Staff and in the special operations world under Clinton and who asserted that officials such as Richard Clarke, who advocated using Special Ops troops on the ground to engage in targeted kill or capture operations against bin Laden and other al Qaeda figures, were denounced by the brass as madmen who were "out of control, power hungry, wanted to be a hero, all that kind of stuff." One former official told Shultz, "when we would carry back from the counterterrorism group one of those SOF counterterrorism proposals, our job was" not to figure out "how to execute it, but how we were going to say no." Shultz denounced such "showstoppers," his label for the lawyering and bureaucratic restrictions imposed under Clinton that "formed an impenetrable phalanx ensuring that all high level policy discussions, tough new presidential directives, revised contingency plans, and actual dress rehearsals for missions would come to nothing." As Shultz saw it, these "mutually reinforcing, self-imposed constraints...kept the special mission units sidelined," under Clinton, "even as al Qaeda struck at...targets around the globe and trumpeted its intention to do more of the same."

The Shultz report painted a picture of Special Ops Forces being handcuffed by the military brass and civilian officials who preferred to launch cruise missiles and to approach bin Laden and his terrorist troops through a law-enforcement lens. The fear of failed missions or humiliation combined with concern over violating bans on assassination or killing innocents in the pursuit of the guilty paved the path to 9/11, in Rumsfeld's opinion. His strategy boiled down to this: he wanted America's best killers to kill America's enemies wherever they resided.

As the United States began its global war, Shultz began briefing senior Pentagon officials on his findings and recommendations. The report, which was classified as "SECRET," was scathing in its denunciation of Clinton's counterterrorism policies and advocated an aggressive promotion of JSOC within the US national security apparatus. Instead of being a force that could be called in to support the conventional US commanders in their areas of responsibility, those conventional commanders would be supporting JSOC. It was an unprecedented promotion of America's premier black ops force to a position of supreme authority. Rumsfeld, who only had to deal with General Shelton "for fifteen minutes," as Rumsfeld put it, forged ahead full speed after Shelton was replaced in October 2001 by a far more malleable chair of the Joint Chiefs, Richard Myers. If Rumsfeld was to "employ" JSOC to "conduct a global war on al Qaeda it must learn the right lessons of Mogadishu," the Shultz report concluded. "Those lessons reveal how good SOF units are, even when policymakers misuse them. Imagine if they were employed properly in the war on terrorism."

Whether it was proper or not, Rumsfeld was about to yank JSOC from obscurity and build its force to an unprecedented prominence and strength within the US war machine. To do it, he would need to invade the CIA's realm and create parallel structures that would answer to him—not to Congress or the State Department. They would also need a freestanding intelligence operation that would support their covert agenda.

FROM THE START of the Bush administration, Rumsfeld and Cheney frequently clashed with Secretary of State Colin Powell and were determined to make sure the highly decorated former chair of the Joint Chiefs didn't stand in the way of their wars. Powell was hardly a dove, but from the first moments after 9/11, he was advocating that the United States develop a tightly focused military response against al Qaeda. Powell and his deputies asserted that "our allies and friends abroad would be more comfortable with retributive U.S. strikes against the perpetrators of 9/11 than with a global war against Islamist terrorists and their state supporters," recalled Douglas Feith. Powell, he asserted, believed a "narrowly scoped campaign of punishment would keep U.S. policy more in line with the traditional law enforcement approach to fighting terrorism." But the neoconservatives were intent on waging preemptive wars against nation-states and sought to unleash the CIA from the legal and oversight bureaucracy. "Forget about 'exit strategies,'" Rumsfeld said two weeks after 9/11. "We're looking at a sustained engagement that carries no deadlines." As secretary of state, Powell was responsible for building up international relationships and alliances. His diplomatic agenda almost immediately came into direct conflict with that of the neocons. Powell and his ambassadors also had a hand in monitoring CIA activities around the globe. They were to be informed of all operations in countries around the world—a stricture Rumsfeld and Cheney bitterly resented.

Malcolm Nance, a career navy counterterrorist specialist who trained elite US Special Operations Forces, watched as experienced military figures within the administration were sidelined by Cheney, Rumsfeld and their militia of ideologues. "No one amongst those people had served in combat, but Colin Powell, Lawrence Wilkerson and his staff were all the combat personnel," Nance told me. "And it's funny, they were shuffled over at the State Department and the civilian ideologues were put over into the Pentagon and they were the people who came up with what we call TCCC, 'Tom Clancy Combat Concepts.' They came out and just started reading these books and magazines and start thinking, 'We're going to be hard, we're going to do these things, we're going to go out and start popping people on the streets and we're going to start renditioning people.' The decision makers were almost childlike in wanting to do high, Dungeons and Dragons, you know, dagger and intrigue all the time."

On 9/11, the CIA did not have a large in-house paramilitary capability—just six hundred to seven hundred covert operatives at most. So, many of its hits relied heavily on Special Forces and Special Operations Forces—which numbered more than 10,000—loaned to the Agency for specific missions. "All of the paramilitary expertise really came from the military, from Special Forces," recalled Vincent Cannistraro, a career CIA counterterrorism officer, who also did stints at the Pentagon and the National Security Agency (NSA). "It didn't really exist, except in a skeletal way, in the CIA," he told me. "The Special Forces had the expertise. The resources were Department of Defense resources, and the transfer of those under CIA direction was a policy decision made at the national level."

Initially, on orders from President Bush, the CIA was the lead agency in the global war. But Cheney and Rumsfeld realized early on that it certainly didn't need to be the only dark-side force and that there was another capability available to the White House that could provide far greater flexibility and almost no congressional or State Department meddling. Although some operations necessitated working through the CIA—particularly when it came to establishing "black sites" with the cooperation of foreign intelligence services—Cheney's crew did not trust the Agency's bureaucrats. "I think Rumsfeld, Cheney thought that the CIA was a bunch of pansies, much the way they thought about the State Department," recalled Wilkerson, Powell's former chief of staff. Wilkerson said that, during this period, he began to see a pattern of "what I consider assumption of presidential power, commander in chief powers, by the vice president of the United States." Cheney, in particular, he said, longed for the covert wars of the 1980s, "the Ronald Reagan period of helping the Contras to fight the Sandinistas" and the "almost symbiotic relationship between some of the Special Operations Forces and the clandestine operators in the CIA. That, I think comes to a real art form in the War on Terror, as one would suspect it would, because this is what Cheney wanted to do. Cheney wanted to operate on the clandestine side."

Rumsfeld saw the lending of US Special Ops Forces to the CIA as creating a problematic, obstructionist middle man whose operations could be lawyered to death. He wanted America's premier direct-action forces to be unrestrained and unaccountable to anyone except him, Cheney and the president. "The CIA can't do anything without the intelligence oversight committees knowing about it, or being informed almost immediately thereafter," said Cannistraro, who helped start the CIA's Counterterrorism Center. "When you had CIA carrying out a paramilitary operation, prior to 9/11, that meant that there were Special Forces elements that were attached to CIA, and therefore they were under civilian control [and] what they were doing for CIA was reported to the Intelligence Oversight Committee. But, if the military carries it out, it doesn't follow the same guidance, because it doesn't get reported to the intelligence oversight committees. They're military operations. And therefore they're part of a war, or 'military preparing.'" Cannistraro told me that some of the most controversial and secretive activities conducted globally would be done through "the military under the 'Cheney Program,' because it didn't have to be briefed to the Congress."

While Powell and the State Department were cautioning against widening the focus beyond Afghanistan, al Qaeda and the Taliban, Rumsfeld had been pushing to take the military campaign global. "You have no choice but to take the battle to the terrorists, wherever they may be," Rumsfeld declared in December 2001. "The only way to deal with a terrorist network that's global is to go after it where it is." Rumsfeld wanted Special Operations Forces front and center, and he asked General Charles Holland, the commander of Special Operations Command, to draw up a list of regional targets where the United States could conduct both retaliatory and preemptive strikes against al Qaeda. In late 2001, Feith directed Jeffrey Schloesser, then chief of the War on Terrorism Strategic Planning Cell,

J-5 of the Joint Staff, and his team to prepare a plan called "Next Steps." Afghanistan was just the beginning. Rumsfeld wanted plans drawn up to hit in Somalia, Yemen, Latin America, Mauritania, Indonesia and beyond. In a memo to President Bush two weeks after 9/11, Rumsfeld wrote that the Pentagon was "exploring targets and desired effects in countries where CIA's relationship with local intelligence services either cannot or will not tackle the projects for the U.S." This included countries that would invite the United States in "on a friendly basis," but also those that would not.

The world is a battlefield—that was the mantra.

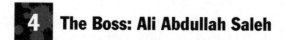

# 4 The Boss: Ali Abdullah Saleh

YEMEN, 1970–2001; WASHINGTON, DC, 2001—When the planes slammed into the World Trade Center, Ali Abdullah Saleh knew he needed to act fast. The Yemeni president was famous in intelligence circles as a wily survivor who had adeptly navigated his way through the Cold War, deep tribal divisions in his country and terrorism threats, largely unscathed. When 9/11 happened, Saleh was already in trouble with the United States following the bombing of the USS *Cole* off the port of Aden in southern Yemen, and he was determined that 9/11 would not mark the beginning of the end of his decades-long grip on power. As the Bush administration began to map out its plans for a borderless war in response to 9/11, Saleh hatched a plan of his own with one central goal: to hold on to power.

Saleh became Yemen's leader in 1990, following the unification of the north, which he had ruled since the 1970s, and the Marxist government based in Aden, in the south. In Yemen, he was known as "The Boss." Colonel Lang, who served for years as the US defense and army attaché to Yemen, first met Saleh in 1979. Fluent in Arabic, Lang was often brought into sensitive meetings as a translator for other US officials. Lang and his British MI-6 counterpart would often go hunting with Saleh. "We would drive around with a bunch of vehicles, and shoot gazelle, hyenas," Lang recalled, adding that Saleh was a "reasonably good shot." Of Saleh, Lang said, "He's really a very charming devil," describing Saleh's multidecade rule as "quite a run, in a country where it's 'dog-eat-dog.' It's like being the captain on a Klingon battle cruiser, you know? They're just waiting." Saleh, Lang said, proved a master of playing tribes against each other, co-opting them at crucial moments and outsourcing his problems. "There's a precarious balance all the time between the authority of the government and the authority of these massive tribal groups. The government normally only controls the land its forces sit on, or where it's providing some service that the tribal leaders and population wants, like medical service, or education. So you end up with a lot of defended towns, with a lot of checkpoints around them, and little punitive expeditions going on, all the time, by the government around the country, to punish people with whom they are quarreling over some issue."

During the mujahedeen war against the Soviets in Afghanistan in the 1980s, thousands of Yemenis joined the jihad—some of them coordinated and funded directly by Saleh's government. "They were all sent to Afghanistan to face the former Soviet invasion and occupation," Saleh asserted in an interview with the *New York Times* in 2008. "And the USA forced friendly countries at that time, including Yemen, the Gulf states, Sudan, and Syria, to support the mujahedeen—they called them freedom fighters—to go fight in Afghanistan. The USA used to strongly support the Islamist movement to fight the Soviets. Then, following collapse of Soviets in Afghanistan, the USA suddenly adopted a completely different and extreme attitude towards these Islamic movements and started to put pressure on the countries to have confrontation with these Islamic movements that were in the Arab and Islamic territories."

When the jihadists returned to their home country, Saleh gave them safe haven. "Because we have political pluralism in Yemen, we decided not to have a confrontation with these movements," said Saleh. Islamic Jihad, the movement of Ayman al Zawahiri, the Egyptian physician who rose to become bin Laden's number-two man, based one of its largest cells in Yemen in the 1990s. Saleh clearly did not see al Qaeda as a major threat. If anything, he saw the jihadists as convenient sometime allies who could be used for his own domestic agenda. In return for allowing them to move freely and train in Yemen, Saleh could use jihadists who fought in Afghanistan in his battle against southern secessionists and, later, against Shiite Houthi rebels in the north. "They were the thugs that Saleh used to control any problematic elements. We have so many instances where Saleh was using these guys from al Qaeda to eliminate opponents of the regime," Ali Soufan, the former senior FBI agent who worked extensively in Yemen, told me. Because of their value to Saleh's domestic agenda, "they were able to operate freely. They were able to obtain and travel on Yemeni documents. Saleh was their safest base. He tried to make himself a player by playing this card."

The consequence of this relationship was that as al Qaeda expanded during the 1990s, Yemen provided fertile ground for training camps and recruitment of jihadists. During the Clinton administration, this arrangement barely registered a blip on the US counterterrorism radar outside of a small group of officials, mostly from the FBI and CIA, who were tracking the rise of al Qaeda.

That would change on October 12, 2000, following a massive David versus Goliath attack on a billion-dollar US warship, the USS *Cole*, which had docked in the port of Aden to refuel. Shortly after 11:00 a.m., a small motorboat packed with five hundred pounds of explosives sped up to the ship and blasted a massive forty-by-forty-foot hole in the *Cole*'s side. The attack killed seventeen US sailors and wounded more than thirty others. "In Aden, they charged and destroyed a destroyer that fearsome people fear, one that evokes horror when it docks and when it sails," bin Laden later said in an al Qaeda recruitment video, reciting a poem one of his aides had written. The successful attack, according to al Qaeda experts, inspired droves of new recruits—particularly from Yemen—to sign up with al Qaeda and similar groups.

The FBI agents who traveled to Yemen in the aftermath of the attack were heavily monitored by Yemeni authorities and were greeted at the airport by Yemeni special forces pointing weapons at them. "Yemen is a country of 18 million citizens and 50 million machine guns," reported John O'Neill, the lead FBI investigator of the *Cole* bombing. He later said, "This might be the most hostile environment the FBI has ever operated in." In the summer of 2001, the FBI had to pull out completely after a series of threats against its agents and an alleged plot to blow up the US Embassy. "We regularly faced death threats, smokescreens and bureaucratic obstructions," recalled Soufan, who was one of the FBI's lead investigators. Saleh's government generally obstructed the US investigation into the bombing, but he was hardly the only source of frustration for the investigators. "No one in the Clinton White House seemed to care about the case," recalled Soufan. "We had hoped that the George W. Bush administration would be better, but except for Robert Mueller, the director of the F.B.I., its top officials soon sidelined the case; they considered it, according to Paul Wolfowitz, the deputy defense secretary, 'stale.'"

Soufan and a handful of US counterterrorism officials watched as the *Cole* bombing strengthened bin Laden's position. "The Strike on the Cole had been a great victory," observed Lawrence Wright in his definitive book on al Qaeda, *The Looming Tower*. "Al-Qaeda camps in Afghanistan filled with new recruits, and contributors from the Gulf states arrived carrying Samsonite suitcases filled with petrodollars, as in the glory days of the Afghan jihad." A week before 9/11, Saleh had boasted on Al Jazeera that his government had not allowed the FBI to interrogate or question any senior Yemeni officials about the attack. "We denied them access to Yemen with forces, planes and ships," declared Saleh. "We put them under direct monitoring by our security forces. They respected our position and surrendered to what we did."

The terrorist attacks on the World Trade Center on September 11, 2001, posed a new challenge to the relationship between Saleh's regime and the United States. Although he had been in power since the late 1970s, in the aftermath of 9/11, Saleh's world could have easily crumbled in an instant.

"Those who make war against the United States have chosen their own destruction," President Bush declared four days after 9/11. "Victory against terrorism will not take place in a single battle, but in a series of decisive actions against terrorist organizations and those who harbor and support them." The "harbor" part was taken as an ominous warning by Saleh—and rightly so.

The presidential findings and other directives issued by Bush after 9/11 had authorized the CIA and US Special Operations Forces to fight al Qaeda across the globe wherever its operatives were based. As US forces pushed into Afghanistan, Special Operations Forces and the CIA continued to track the movements of al Qaeda operatives with the aim of targeting them for kill or capture wherever they landed. After the United States swiftly overthrew the Taliban government in Kabul, many of the foreign fighters affiliated with bin Laden found themselves on the run and seeking refuge. One of the key safe havens they found was in the wilds of Yemen.

The Bush administration put Yemen on a list of potential early targets in the war on terror and could have swiftly dismantled Saleh's government, despite Saleh's cocky pre-9/11 declaration that "Yemen is a graveyard for the invaders." Saleh was determined not to go the way of the Taliban, and he wasted little time in making moves to ensure he wouldn't.

The first was to board a plane to the United States.

In November 2001, President Saleh arrived in Washington, DC, where he held talks with President Bush and Vice President Cheney, as well as FBI director Robert Mueller and CIA director George Tenet. He told anyone who would listen that Yemen was on the side of the United States. The media were brought into the White House for a photo session of the two leaders smiling and shaking hands. In his meetings with Bush, Saleh emphasized Yemen's "condemnation of the September 11 terrorist attacks on the U.S. and Yemen's denunciation of all forms of terrorism" and referred to his country as "a principal partner in the coalition against terrorism."

While the Saleh show played out in public, with the Bush administration portraying Saleh as an ally in the newly branded "Global War on Terror," behind closed doors senior US officials were brokering agreements with Saleh to expand the US footprint in Yemen. During his meetings in Washington, which included visits at his personal suite at the Ritz Carlton Hotel on Twenty-second Street by Mueller and Tenet, Saleh was presented with an aid package worth up to $400 million, in addition to funding from the World Bank and International Monetary Fund. Crucially for the United States, it would also include expanding the training of Yemen's special forces. It was this training that would permit US Special Forces to deploy inside Yemen while allowing Saleh to save face domestically. As part of Saleh's deal with the Bush administration, the United States set up a "counterterrorism camp" in Yemen run by the CIA, US Marines and American Special Forces that would be backed up by the US outpost in the nearby African nation of Djibouti, which also housed Predator drones. Tenet also arranged for the United States to provide Yemen with helicopters and eavesdropping equipment. Crucially, Saleh also gave Tenet permission for the CIA to fly drones over his territory.

"Saleh knew how to survive," said Dr. Emile Nakhleh, a former senior CIA intelligence officer. During his decades in power, Saleh had "learned how to speak the language of the Cold War, to endear himself to us and other Western countries by speaking the anti-communist language." After 9/11, Saleh "learned very quickly" that he had to speak the antiterrorism language, Nakhleh added.

"So he came here seeking support, seeking financing. But, Saleh, from day one, years back, never thought that terrorism posed a threat to him. He thought that Yemen was basically a platform for al Qaeda and other terrorist organizations and that the real target was al Saud, the House of Saud. So he found ways to deal with them," Nakhleh told me. "And yet, he would come here or speak to us in a language we would like and would understand, but then he would go home and do all kinds of alliances with all kinds of shady characters to help him survive. I don't think he really honestly believed that al Qaeda posed a serious threat to his regime."

Colonel Lang said Bush "was so taken with President Saleh as a personable, friendly, chummy kind of guy, that Bush was in fact quite willing to listen to whatever Saleh said about, 'We like you Americans, we want to help you, we want to cooperate with you,' that kind of business, and was quite willing to send them foreign aid, including military aid." During his meeting with President Bush in November 2001, Saleh "expressed his concern and hope that the military action in Afghanistan does not exceed its borders and spread to other parts of the Middle East, igniting further instability in the region," according to a statement issued by the Yemeni Embassy in Washington at the end of the visit. But to keep Yemen off Washington's target list, Saleh would have to take action. Or at least give the appearance of doing so.

Saleh's entourage was given a list of several al Qaeda suspects that the Yemeni regime could target as a show of good faith. The next month, Saleh ordered his forces to raid a village in Marib Province, where Abu Ali al Harithi, a lead suspect in the *Cole* bombing, and other militants were believed to be residing. The operation by Yemeni special forces was a categorical failure. Local tribesmen took several of the soldiers hostage and the targets of the raid allegedly escaped unharmed. The soldiers were later released through tribal mediators, but the action angered the tribes and served as a warning to Saleh to stay out of Marib. It was the beginning of what would be a complex and dangerous chess match for Saleh as he made his first moves to satisfy Washington's desire for targeted killing in Yemen while maintaining his own hold on power.

Soon after Saleh's Washington meetings, the United States established a task force for the Horn of Africa and Gulf of Aden. In late 2002, some nine hundred military and intelligence personnel would be deployed to a former French military outpost, Camp Lemonnier, in Djibouti, under the name Combined Joint Task Force–Horn of Africa (CJTF–HOA). Located just an hour from Yemen by boat, the secretive base would soon serve as a command center for covert US action in the Horn of Africa and the Arabian Peninsula and would serve as the launch pad for the CIA and JSOC to strike at will outside the declared battlefield of Afghanistan.

As construction began on Lemonnier, the United States beefed up the presence of military "trainers" inside Yemen. Although officially in Yemen to modernize Yemen's counterterrorism forces, the Americans quickly set out to establish operational capacity to track al Qaeda suspects to find and fix their location so that US forces could finish them off. "Over the years, there'd been a number of kinds of people that were dubious characters from the American point of view that had taken shelter in Yemen. And Saleh plays his own game, very much, so he variously offers people shelter and a place to refuge," recalled Colonel Lang. "So it was known that there were people in the country who were inimical to the United States, and they started tracking where these people were." A year after Saleh's meeting with Bush at the White House, the US "trainers" would set up their first "wet" operation.

## 5  The Enigma of Anwar Awlaki

THE UNITED KINGDOM, THE UNITED STATES AND YEMEN, 2002–2003—
When Anwar Awlaki arrived in the United Kingdom, he called his wealthy·
uncle, Sheikh Saleh bin Fareed, who had a home in the south of England.
"Uncle Saleh, I am here. May I come and see you?" Anwar asked. "You are
welcome," bin Fareed told him. When Anwar arrived at his uncle's home,
the two caught up on family affairs back in Yemen before the conversation turned to the events in the United States. "Do you have anything to
do with what happened?" bin Fareed recalled asking him, knowing that
Anwar had been interrogated multiple times by the FBI. He had also seen
news reports alleging that Anwar had met with some of the hijackers. "I
don't have anything [to do with 9/11], whatsoever," Anwar said, according to his uncle. "If I had anything to do with al Qaeda or those people,
I would not be sitting with you in England today. I travel freely. In the
UK they do not touch me." Anwar told his uncle that US agents had told
him, "We have nothing against you." Anwar stayed with his uncle while
he got situated in England and began preaching before Muslim audiences,
at community groups, religious centers and mosques, with an increasing
degree of passion, if not militancy, about the importance of defending and
promoting Islam at a moment when he believed it was under assault. "He
used to commute by train—he'd go to London, and he'd go to Birmingham,
to give speeches, and he'd come back," bin Fareed recalled.

In a speech he delivered during this period at the annual conference of
the charity JIMAS, an Arabic acronym for the Association to Revive the
Way of the Messenger, at the University of Leicester, Awlaki issued a challenge to Western Muslims to defend and preach their faith. "We should be
concerned about what is happening to our neighbors, to our friends, to our
coworkers, to the people whom we live with," he said. "We're not being
concerned if we know that our neighbors and friends, their fate is hellfire
and we're doing nothing about it. So our first role as a Muslim minority
of Muslims living among non-Muslims, is to proclaim the message publicly, and when we convey the message, we convey it in very plain and
clear terms, with no confusion." He cautioned them not to be aggressive

in promoting Islam, saying they should be like UPS, DHL or FedEx delivery people. "Rather than knocking on the door with a hammer, and then when the person opens the door you throw the package in their face—no," he said. "You knock on the door, very politely, and then when they open the door you have a big smile on your face."

In mid-2002, Awlaki returned to Yemen to study at the famed Iman University in Sana'a. "I was given permission from the administration of the University...to attend any class at any level and I took advantage of this and attended classes in Tafsir [exegesis of the Koran] and Fiqh [Islamic jurisprudence] for a period of a few months," Awlaki later wrote, adding that he "also benefited from the teachings of Shaykh Abdul Majid al Zindani the Rector of the University." But as Awlaki began to make his next moves, those investigating him in the United States had not forgotten about him.

While Awlaki traveled to Saudi Arabia and Yemen and studied Islam, back in the United States there were some within the US intelligence community who believed that his case should not have been closed, that the young imam was potentially connected to 9/11 and that all leads on him had not been pursued. Some believed he should not have been allowed to leave the United States. "When he left town, it was as if the air went out of the balloon," said one FBI source. Yet, according to the 9/11 Commission, the investigation into Awlaki's alleged involvement with the 9/11 hijackers did not produce evidence that "was considered strong enough to support a criminal prosecution."

In June 2002, the agents investigating him were able to get a warrant issued for his arrest, though they were skeptical he would return. The warrant was not issued for his alleged contacts with the 9/11 hijackers or for soliciting prostitutes, but rather for passport fraud, stemming from Awlaki's scholarship application back in the early 1990s, listing Yemen as his place of birth. When he arrived in the United States for college and applied for a Social Security number, he had also listed his birthplace as Yemen. When Awlaki was confronted about it at the time, he had resolved the issue with the US authorities, explaining that his Yemeni documents had been in error. Now, a decade later, the Feds wanted to reopen the case as a pretext to arrest him. "We were ecstatic that we were able to get a warrant on this guy," recalled a former Joint Task Force agent. The charges they wanted to pin on him for passport fraud carried up to ten years in prison and could potentially be used as a vise to pressure him to cooperate further in the 9/11 investigation.

Whether he would ever return to the United States, the investigators did not know. They got the Treasury Department to put Awlaki's name into the TECS II system, the Treasury Enforcement Communications System, which meant that any interaction he had with US Customs or Immigration officials would prompt a "look out" alert and result in his detention. If he tried to enter the United States, the FBI would be informed immediately.

It seemed like a long shot.

But Awlaki did return, much sooner than anyone expected, and when he did, a series of events unfolded that raise serious questions about the nature of Awlaki's relationship with the FBI.

IN SANA'A, Nasser Awlaki was arguing with his son. Anwar had told him he was done with living in the United States. The harassment from the FBI was too much, Muslims were being persecuted, jailed, investigated, he told Nasser. But the elder Awlaki would not give up his dream of having a truly American son and of him getting his PhD in the United States. "Give it another shot, Anwar," Nasser told his son in September 2002. Nasser and his wife offered to take care of Anwar's elder son, Abdulrahman, and daughter, Maryam, while Anwar and his wife and their younger son, Abdullah, returned to Virginia to see if they could salvage their life in the States. "It was like a trial," Nasser recalled. "If they found things will be good" in the United States, then Nasser would bring Abdulrahman and Maryam to join their parents. Anwar finally agreed. "It was really under encouragement from me. I told him, 'Go back, and see how things are, and if everything is OK, continue your PhD at George Washington University,'" said Nasser.

The FBI, it appears, had gotten wind of Anwar's plans. On October 8, 2002, Awlaki was the subject of a classified, limited-distribution FBI Electronic Communications (EC) intelligence memo. Its contents remain classified. The next day, on October 9, 2002, the US Attorney's Office in Colorado abruptly filed a motion to have the warrant for Awlaki's arrest vacated and dismissed. The US Attorney who withdrew the warrant said that the government had determined there was not enough evidence to win a conviction, adding that Awlaki could not be charged for "having a bad reputation." Two days after the FBI EC memo on Awlaki was sent and a day after the motion to quash the warrant for his arrest was filed, Awlaki and his family had arrived at JFK Airport in New York on a flight from Riyadh, Saudi Arabia, landing just after 6:00 a.m. When Awlaki went through passport control, his name popped up on the TECS II and terrorism watch lists. The reason provided on screen was: "ANTI-TERRORIST PASSENGER." When agents searched their databases, they also discovered the warrant that the US Attorney's Office in Colorado was trying to get vacated. It was still registering as active. Awlaki was pulled aside by Immigration and Nat-

uralization Service (INS) agents and, with his family, detained in a special
screening area of the airport for three hours. "Subject was escorted to INS
primary and secondary by U.S. Customs. He is a match," was the message
recorded by the agents in their incident log. Their luggage was searched
and the Customs officials informed their superiors that they had Awlaki
in custody. They tried to reach the FBI special agent listed as the point of
contact in the warnings that had popped up on their screens when Awlaki
came through. But initially they could not get through to that agent, Wade
Ammerman, because his cell phone number was invalid.

Ammerman was one of the lead agents in the Awlaki investigation. A
senior Customs official, David Kane, told the agents holding Awlaki that
he would track down Ammerman. By coincidence, Kane had years earlier
worked the Awlaki case when Awlaki was an imam in San Diego. Kane
was then relocated to Virginia and had also investigated Awlaki as part of
Operation Green Quest, targeting terror-financing networks. Although he
had tried to link Awlaki to those networks, Kane said, "We did not find a
link between that group and Awlaki." So, Kane knew exactly who it was
that Customs had at JFK Airport on October 10, 2002. But when Kane finally reached Agent Ammerman, he told Kane that Awlaki's "warrant had
been rescinded" and that he should be released. Kane said the FBI offered
"no explanation" for the order. In the incident log, the Customs officials
noted that they had "RECEIVED A CALL FROM S/A KANE NOTIFYING US THE
WARRANT ISSUED BY THE STATE DEPT. HAD BEEN PULLED BACK," adding that a
representative of the FBI's Washington Field Office had called them regarding the Colorado warrant, saying "THE WARRANT HAD BEEN REMOVED ON
10/9." Curiously, the warrant was not actually removed until October 11.

The US documents describing Awlaki's detention at JFK noted that the
Awlakis were released by the agents at 9:20 a.m. "with thanks for their"
patience and given a "comment card" to describe their experience with
the US authorities. An official from Saudi Arabian Airlines then escorted
the Awlakis to their connecting flight to Washington, DC. "The custom
officials were quite baffled at the situation and didn't know what to say,"
Awlaki later recalled. "I got an apology from one of them with a weird face
on him. Actually I myself was shocked and asked them: Is that it? They
said, yes sir, that's it. You are free to board!" The next day, the warrant for
Awlaki's arrest was officially vacated, though the FBI clearly knew about
it a day before it happened.

Now free to travel in the United States, Awlaki returned to Virginia. He
reconnected with old colleagues and began assessing what, if any, future
he could envision for his family in the United States. But then, a curious
meeting happened. In October 2002, Awlaki paid a visit to another charis-

matic preacher, an Iraqi American named Ali al Timimi. Timimi was the lead lecturer at Dar al Arqam, an Islamic center in Falls Church, Virginia. But Timimi was not just a religious figure; he was also a brilliant young scientist who had attended the elite Georgetown Day School in DC and had a degree in biology. At the time of Awlaki's visit, he was pursuing a PhD and working on cancer gene research. Timimi was identified by the FBI for potential involvement in the "anthrax plots" that were uncovered after 9/11, and the Bureau also believed he might be involved with a network that sought to train Western jihadists on US soil. No charges were ever brought against Timini in connection with the anthrax investigation.

The meeting between Timimi and Awlaki would help form the basis for an alternative theory on Awlaki's relationship with the FBI; one in which he was not simply the target or person of interest in an investigation.

Had the FBI actually flipped Anwar Awlaki and made him an informant?

The trail of clues supporting this theory is compelling. Special Agent Ammerman, who facilitated Awlaki's release at JFK Airport, had not only worked the Awlaki case; he was also one of the lead investigators into Timimi after 9/11. "I don't think anyone wants me talking 'bout what I was involved in," Ammerman told Catherine Herridge, a Fox News journalist who investigated the case and had close contacts with US law enforcement officials. Herridge believed that the FBI "was trying to cultivate al Awlaki as a human intelligence asset," as Awlaki himself had alleged years earlier. But had they succeeded?

When Awlaki came to his home, Timimi said, he started talking about recruiting Western jihadists. "Ali had never, in his whole life, even talked to the guy or met him," Timimi's lawyer, Edward MacMahon, told me. "Awlaki just showed up at the guy's house and asked him if he could assist him in finding young men to join the jihad." MacMahon said that Timimi was suspicious of Awlaki showing up "completely out of the blue." At the time, the Muslim community was under intense scrutiny from the government—Islamic groups had been raided, Muslims were being regularly detained for questioning and there were justifiable suspicions that moles and informants were infiltrating organizations. "You'd have to go back in time to understand," said MacMahon. "The community was sure there were all kinds of investigations and Ali was a pretty prominent Muslim. I mean, just look: Why was the guy [Awlaki] there? Why was he asking somebody he'd never met in his whole life to help him get young men for the jihad? It just stunk of entrapment. Ali threw him out of the house."

Timimi's friends said he suspected Awlaki may have been working with the FBI and trying to set him up. In 2003, Timimi's house was raided by federal agents. He was ultimately convicted on charges that he had incited

eleven young Muslims, mostly Americans, to join the Taliban in fighting the United States in Afghanistan. The prosecutors alleged his sermons
helped inspire the "Northern Virginia Paintball Jihad," which had trained
with paintball guns to join the fight in Afghanistan. In the legal proceedings, Timimi asserted that he believed Awlaki was wearing a wire when
he came to his house in late 2002 and that the FBI had recordings of the
meeting. When Timimi's lawyers filed for the alleged tapes in discovery,
government lawyers responded in writing, "Al-Timimi seeks the Court
to order the government to produce tapes he suggests that Aulaqi made
while visiting Al-Timimi. We are aware of no authority for this request."
MacMahon said that the government response suggested "it is a national
security issue and that it was classified." But it wasn't just the "out of the
blue" nature of Awlaki's visit with Timimi that MacMahon found suspicious. "We thought [Awlaki] was wearing a wire, and we wanted to know
how he got" to Timimi's house. MacMahon later learned that Awlaki was
driven to the meeting with Timimi by Nabil Gharbieh, an alleged member of the conspiracy who later cooperated with prosecutors. "How does
Anwar Awlaki end up at Ali's house?" asked MacMahon, before offering
his own theory: "Because [Special Agent] Ammerman made Gharbieh take
him there."

Ammerman met with Awlaki when he returned to the DC area in October 2002 and was in fact the agent who had Awlaki released from JFK
Airport so that Awlaki could make his flight to DC. Whether the two men
discussed Timimi, we do not know. But there are other lingering hints at
a connection. "In late 2002, the FBI's Washington field office received two
similar tips from local Muslims: Timimi was running 'an Islamic group
known as the Dar al-Arqam' that had 'conducted military-style training,'
FBI special agent John Wyman would later write in an affidavit," according
to the Washington Post, adding, "Wyman and another agent, Wade Ammerman, pounced on the tips."

Years later, this series of events spurred Republican congressman Frank
Wolf of Virginia to demand answers from the FBI. In a letter to FBI director
Mueller, Wolf asked: "Is there any connection between the timing of the
FBI's EC [Electronic Communication] on Aulaqi, the motion to vacate his
arrest warrant, and Aulaqi's sudden return to the U.S.?" Wolf also noted
that "following his detention at Kennedy [Airport] early on the morning
of October 10, 2002, an FBI agent—Special Agent Wade Ammerman in
the Washington Field Office—ordered that Aulaqi be released by U.S. customs agents after having been detained on an outstanding warrant," adding: "This is particularly questionable given the time of these events. The
Colorado U.S. Attorney's motion to dismiss the warrant was not approved

until October 11, 2002, a day after the FBI ordered Aulaqi released into the U.S. Why would the FBI order Aulaqi's release while the warrant for his arrest remained active?" When journalists filed a Freedom of Information Act request seeking the October 8, 2002, FBI intelligence memo and other documents on Awlaki, they were rebuffed. The Bureau sent back "twenty-seven pages of blankness," citing "national security and an executive order," according to Herridge, the Fox journalist.

Of course, there are other theories about Awlaki's visit to the United States and his meeting with Timimi—namely, that Awlaki was actually attempting to recruit young Westerners for jihad. It is also possible that the FBI intervened when Awlaki was detained at JFK to free him because the Bureau wanted to follow him once he was in the United States to investigate his movements and his contacts. It is not uncommon for law enforcement to allow suspects or persons of interest to walk around believing they are free so that they can be monitored.

As for Timimi, he was eventually sentenced to life in prison. Among those who testified against him as government witnesses was Gharbieh, the man who drove Awlaki to meet Timimi. Timimi's legal team alleged that Timimi was railroaded in a "faux terror" trial born of the post-9/11 panic that another attack was imminent. MacMahon maintained that Timimi was prosecuted based on fears—not evidence. "They weren't going to take any kind of a chance," he said. "But, we don't usually use our judicial system as kind of a holding pen like the British did with the Irish in Northern Ireland."

MacMahon alleged that the FBI deliberately concealed Awlaki's role in the Timimi case and believed that had they acknowledged it, Timimi would have been able to use it as evidence in the fight for his freedom. "If they had disclosed that Ammerman facilitated the trip, then I would have gotten into it in detail, but they withheld that information," he said. "The FBI just will not admit what they did. It would have been critical evidence in Ali's trial. The poor guy's serving life. You know, the charge in Ali's case was recruiting young men to go to the jihad. So, evidence that a government agent—somebody working for the government—came to him and asked him to do it—and he threw him out—would be admissible, would completely refute the charges."

Years later, Representative Wolf pressed the US government for answers. "How did Aulaqi end up at the home of Ali al Timimi with a government witness shortly after he was allowed back into the U.S.? Was the FBI aware of this meeting in advance" of Awlaki's return? Whether Awlaki had worked with the FBI in attempting to secure an indictment against Timimi will likely never be known. Awlaki spoke on numerous occasions of the FBI's attempts to turn him into an asset. Had they succeeded? "Wade Ammerman testified in [Timimi's] case. To me the evidence is overwhelming that Wade Ammerman tried to flip Anwar Awlaki. Or maybe even thought he had flipped him," said MacMahon. "I mean, Awlaki was one of the only people in the United States with contact in several states with the hijackers. He was not your garden variety FBI flip target. How could they not have arrested this guy [Awlaki] when they had him in the office? They're chasing people that are playing paintball when they've got this guy in their office."

Anwar "never told me he had the problem in New York," Nasser recalled. What about Anwar's interactions with the FBI and possible attempts to flip him? "He never told me about this," Nasser added. The FBI refused to shed light on what exactly happened with Awlaki in late 2002 and why. That leaves many unanswered questions, including ones that would weigh heavily on events to come. Did the Feds have Awlaki ensnared in their web because of threats of prosecution for soliciting prostitutes or his interactions with the hijackers? Did they blackmail him into cooperating? Was Awlaki cooperating with the FBI in an effort to pay his dues in return for being left alone by the government? If so, had he realized that the government would never leave him alone and he would forever be asked to work as an informant?

"My guess, and it is only a guess, is that there was a plan to attempt a recruitment," a former senior FBI counterterrorism agent told me. "If Awlaki was pitched and pretended to accept, that would explain the dismissal of the warrant after he was released. My guess is that he pretended to cooperate for a while and then just split. This would also explain the FBI's reluctance to reveal more about the active case that they had in San Diego. Too embarrassing." If this were the truth, it would be in neither party's interest to acknowledge it. In any case, said Nasser, Anwar "decided that it's not really good for him to stay around again in America." In late December, Awlaki left the United States, this time for good. A year later, an FBI official was asked why Awlaki had been allowed to leave. "We don't know how he got out," was the reply.

# 6 "We're in a New Kind of War"

DJIBOUTI, WASHINGTON, DC, AND YEMEN, 2002—In mid-2002, US intelligence operatives discovered that the man they had fingered as one of the masterminds of the 2000 USS *Cole* bombing, Abu Ali al Harithi, was in Yemen. US officials had dubbed him "the godfather of terror in Yemen." For months, JSOC teams and drones had been hunting him to no avail and US ambassador Edmund Hull had been meeting with tribal officials in Marib, paying them for information on Harithi's location and movements. Harithi used multiple mobile phones and regularly swapped out their SIM cards to avoid detection. On Sunday, November 3, the Special Ops signals intelligence team inside Yemen located Harithi in a compound in Marib after he used a mobile phone number that US intelligence had traced to him months earlier. "Our Special Ops had the compound under surveillance," recalled General Michael DeLong, at the time deputy commander of US Central Command. They were "preparing to storm in when Ali exited with five of his associates. They got into SUVs and took off."

As part of the operation, the CIA had launched an MQ-1 Predator drone from its outpost in Djibouti into Yemen's airspace. But this wasn't just a spy drone—it was armed with two antitank Hellfire missiles. The drone was under the operational control of the CIA's highly secretive Special Activities Division and a live video feed from the drone was piped into the Counterterrorism Center in Langley, Virginia, as well as to the command center in Djibouti. "Now we were involved in a high-speed Predator chase," according to DeLong.

The video feed from the drone showed Harithi and his cohorts driving off in a convoy at dawn in their dusty Toyota Land Cruiser, one hundred miles outside of Sana'a. The men were driving through Marib, where the US ambassador was scheduled to visit the following day. As the convoy circled the Yemeni desert, Harithi's driver shouted into a satellite phone, speaking to a man with whom the al Qaeda operatives were supposed to rendezvous. "We're right over here," he yelled. Intelligence analysts determined that Harithi's voice could be heard in the background giving instructions to the driver and that the drone had a solid lock on the jeep. "Our intel says that's him," DeLong said to CIA director George Tenet, as they both monitored the live feed from their respective locations. "One of them is an American—the fat guy. But he's al Qaeda."

Tenet called Saleh and informed him that he was going to give the go-ahead for the strike. Saleh consented but was emphatic that the mission be kept secret. Tenet agreed. "We didn't want publicity, either," DeLong recalled. "If questions did arise, the official Yemeni version would be that an SUV carrying civilians accidentally hit a land mine in the desert and exploded. There was to be no mention of terrorists, and no mention of missiles fired."

Once the formalities were taken care of, Tenet gave the green light for action. A five-foot-long Hellfire missile slammed into the jeep, blowing it up. One passenger survived the strike and managed to crawl about twenty-five yards before collapsing and dying. As the jeep's remnants continued to burn in the desert, a CIA operative went to examine the aftermath of the strike and to obtain DNA samples from the dead. A few days later, it was revealed that among those killed in the strike was Ahmed Hijazi, also known as Kamal Derwish, a US citizen born in Buffalo, New York. After the attack, US officials publicly tied Hijazi to what they described as a terror cell in Buffalo, known as the "Lackawanna Six." Hijazi had been named as an unindicted co-conspirator in the alleged plot of six Yemeni Americans to provide material support to al Qaeda. Civil liberties organizations alleged that the men had been encouraged and ultimately entrapped by the FBI. The men had been arrested two months before Hijazi's killing. FBI investigators in the case alleged that Hijazi was a "card carrying member of al Qaeda" who was helping to run a sleeper cell in Buffalo.

A day after the drone strike, President Bush was in Arkansas stumping for Republican candidates in the midterm congressional elections. Without specifically mentioning the strike, Bush sent a message about his strategy against al Qaeda operatives around the world. "The only way to treat them is [as] what they are—international killers," Bush declared. "And the only way to find them is to be patient, and steadfast, and hunt them down. And the United States of America is doing just that."

At the Pentagon, Defense Secretary Donald Rumsfeld deflected questions about the US role in the strike, saying only that if Harithi was killed, "it would be a very good thing if he were out of business." When pressed on the extent of US operations in Yemen, Rumsfeld would only say, "We have some folks in that country," adding, "I'm not going to get into the arrangements we have with the government of Yemen, other than to say what I said."

While the Bush administration characterized the attack that killed Hijazi and Harithi as a successful takedown of a dangerous high-value target, unnamed officials revealed in multiple media outlets that it was a US operation but said they were reluctant to discuss the US role because of the damage it could do to Saleh's government. "Most governments aren't keen on the idea of U.S. hit squads or unmanned Predators roaming their country, executing summary justice," reported *Newsweek*, adding that Saleh had given the United States "consent to go after Al Qaeda with its own high-tech resources." But then, on November 5, Paul Wolfowitz, the deputy defense secretary, openly confirmed it was a US strike, angering Saleh as well as the CIA. "It's a very successful tactical operation, and one hopes each time you get a success like that, not only to have gotten rid of somebody dangerous, but to have imposed changes in their tactics and operations and procedures," Wolfowitz declared on CNN. "And sometimes when people are changing, they expose themselves in new ways. So, we've just got to keep the pressure on everywhere we're able to, and we've got to deny the sanctuaries everywhere we're able to, and we've got to put pressure on every government that is giving these people support to get out of that business."

Saleh was described as being "highly pissed" at the disclosure. "This is going to cause major problems for me," Saleh complained to General Tommy Franks, the commander of CENTCOM. "This is why it is so difficult to make deals with the United States," said Yemeni brigadier general Yahya M. al Mutawakel. "They don't consider the internal circumstances in Yemen." To the American intel and special ops community, which had cooked up a cover story with Saleh's government to blame the hit on a truck bomb or a land mine, this was infuriating. But not everyone was displeased. When Senator Robert Graham, then chair of the Senate Intelligence Committee, was asked if the drone attack was "a precursor of more to come," he replied bluntly, "I hope so."

The targeted assassination of a US citizen away from the declared battlefield of Afghanistan sparked outrage from civil liberties and human rights groups. It was the first publicly confirmed targeted killing by the United States outside a battlefield since Gerald Ford implemented a ban on political assassinations in 1976. "If this was the deliberate killing of suspects in lieu of arrest in circumstances in which they did not pose an immediate threat, the killings would be extra-judicial executions in violation of international human rights law," declared Amnesty International in a letter to President Bush. "The United States should issue a clear and unequivocal statement that it will not sanction extra-judicial executions in any circumstances, and that any US officials found to be involved in such actions will be brought to justice."

Far from issuing such a statement, the Bush administration not only owned the operation but pushed back hard, asserting its right under US law to kill people it designated as terrorists in any country, even if they were US citizens. "I can assure you that no constitutional questions are raised here," National Security Adviser Condoleezza Rice said on Fox News a week after the attack. "The president has given broad authority to U.S. officials in a variety of circumstances to do what they need to do to protect the country. We're in a new kind of war, and we've made very clear that it is important that this new kind of war be fought on different battlefields." She added, "It's broad authority."

The targeted killing didn't just grab the attention of human rights groups. "To the extent you do more and more of this, it begins to look like it is policy," said the CIA's former general counsel, Jeffrey Smith. If used regularly, such attacks would "suggest that it's acceptable behavior to assassinate people....Assassination as a norm of international conduct exposes American leaders and Americans overseas."

In addition to launching a new kind of war in Yemen and the surrounding region, the drone strike that killed Hijazi would prove to be a precedent for Bush's successor, Barack Obama, who nearly a decade later asserted the right of the US government to kill another US citizen in Yemen.

In the bigger picture, the 2002 Predator drone strike in Yemen was a seminal moment in the war on terror. It was the first time the CIA's armed version of the Predator drone was used to attack al Qaeda outside Afghanistan. "It means the rules of engagement have changed," an ex-CIA official familiar with special operations told the *Los Angeles Times*. The attack was an early salvo in the US government's new borderless war. "The best way to keep America safe from terrorism is to go after terrorists where they plan and hide," President Bush said in his weekly radio address after the drone strike. "And that work goes on around the world." Bush reasserted that he had "deployed troops" in Yemen but emphasized they were only there in a training capacity.

As Bush spoke, plans were under way to put the new "world is a battlefield" doctrine into practice. In late 2002, US military and intelligence personnel worked around the clock upgrading and expanding Camp Lemonnier on the outskirts of Djibouti's airport, preparing it for its role as a clandestine base of operations for JSOC and other special operations teams to strike at will against targets in Yemen and Somalia deemed to be terrorists under President Bush's sweeping parameters of what constituted a combatant in the war on terror. On December 12, Donald Rumsfeld paid a surprise visit to the base as it was still under construction. "We need to be where the action is," Rumsfeld told several hundred soldiers dressed in military fatigues. "There's no question but that this part of the world is an area where there's action." He continued, "There are a number of terrorists, for example, just across the water in Yemen," declaring, "These are serious problems." That day, a US Army spokesman at Camp Lemonnier was asked if any missions had been launched from the new US base. "None that are conventional enough that we can speak about," he replied. On December 13, the base officially became fully operational.

The US force in Djibouti was bolstered by more than four hundred soldiers and sailors aboard the USS *Mount Whitney*, a command-and-control ship sailing the Horn of Africa and the Gulf of Aden. Its official mission: detect, disorganize, defeat and deny terrorist groups posing an imminent threat to coalition partners in the region. "We're coming, we're hunting, we're relentless," declared the *Whitney*'s senior officer, US marine major general John Sattler. His warship would help coordinate a covert US offensive encompassing Somalia, Yemen, Kenya, Ethiopia, Eritrea, Djibouti and Sudan. As Sattler spoke, in December 2002, his ship was decorated with paper Santas and other Christmas decorations, as well as a portrait of Osama bin Laden riddled with bullet holes. He described his mission as hunting terrorist leaders fleeing Afghanistan and heading to Yemen, Somalia and elsewhere in the region. "If they stumble, we'll bring them to justice. Even if they don't stumble, if they sleep a little too early one night or a little too late one morning, we'll be there."

Sattler refused to confirm his forces were involved in the November 2002 drone strike but said, "If I were a terrorist, and I thought I was happily driving down the road with my terrorist buddies, and all of a sudden—with no warning—I cease to exist, I would be looking left, right and, now, up, because we're out there." On December 22, Sattler met with President Saleh and other senior Yemeni officials in Sana'a. The US Embassy would not comment at the time about the meetings. The Yemeni government said only that the officials had discussed "coordination" in the "war against terrorism." At the time, the *New York Times* characterized the views of a senior Bush administration official on Yemen: "As long as Mr. Saleh allows the C.I.A. to fly pilotless Predator drones over Yemeni territory and cooperates with American Special Forces and C.I.A. teams hunting for Qaeda members," the administration would continue to back the Yemeni president.

The lethal US drone attack in Yemen and the construction of the base in Djibouti presaged an era of "direct action" by US counterterrorism forces in the region. "Needless to say a year ago, we weren't here," Rumsfeld said at Camp Lemonnier. "I suspect that if we looked out one or two or three or four years we would find that this facility would be here." In addition to the conventional US military forces building up around Yemen and the Horn of Africa, US Special Operations Forces, including troops from JSOC, discreetly based at the time in Qatar and Kenya, were put on standby for more clandestine incursions into Yemen and its neighbor across the Gulf of Aden, Somalia. Although the CIA would take the lead in many of the future US operations in the region, it was a key moment in the rise of US Special Operations Forces, particularly JSOC, to a position of unprecedented influence within the US national security apparatus.

# 7 Special Plans

WASHINGTON, DC, 2002—By 2002, the fight between the CIA and the Pentagon for supremacy over the global US fight against terrorism was itself beginning to resemble a small war. On April 17, the *Washington Post* ran a front-page story alleging that US military forces had allowed Osama bin Laden to escape after being injured at Tora Bora in Afghanistan in December 2001, asserting in its lead paragraph that it was the "gravest error in the war against al Qaeda." Rumsfeld was furious and believed that Cofer Black, then the counterterrorism chief at the CIA, had been the "deep background" source for the story. A month later, Black was "assigned to another position" at a CIA satellite office in Tysons Corner, Virginia. Some charged that it was Rumsfeld who had Black fired. Still, the CIA's Operations Directorate and the Counterterrorism Center were forging ahead with Cheney's black ops campaign globally. Black was replaced at the CTC by Jose Rodriguez, who, like his predecessor, was a zealous promoter of "enhanced interrogation techniques" and secret CIA "black sites." But the Agency's analytical division was a different animal.

CIA Iraq specialists and the State Department were causing problems for the administration's drive to war with Iraq. Cheney and his top aide, Scooter Libby, began visiting the Agency to pressure analysts to deliver intel linking Iraq to 9/11 or proving that Iraq had an active WMD program. At the time, the pro-Iraq-war clique was receiving significant push-back from Powell's State Department and CIA analysts. The intelligence community, on clear orders from President Bush and under tremendous pressure from the vice president's office, was poring over all intelligence going back to the early 1990s, looking for a connection between Saddam and al Qaeda, Iraq and 9/11. A consensus was building in the intelligence community that no significant links existed, that there was "no credible information" that Iraq was involved with 9/11 "or any other al-Qaida strike" and that rather than a cooperative partnership, according to a CIA brief presented to Congress, Iraq's relationship with al Qaeda "more closely resemble[d] that of two independent actors trying to exploit each other." Dissatisfied with this response, Rumsfeld and Cheney began establishing their own, private intelligence apparatus as they plotted out plans for an expansion of JSOC's direct action capabilities around the globe.

Within weeks of 9/11, Douglas Feith's office in the Pentagon became home to a secret "parallel, ad hoc intelligence operation" that would serve two purposes: collecting "intelligence" that would bolster the case for a "preemptive" war against Iraq and to provide Rumsfeld, Wolfowitz and Feith with "data they can use to disparage, undermine and contradict the CIA's own analyses." When it was revealed, Rumsfeld attempted to downplay the significance of the parallel intelligence operation. "It's [Feith's] shop. The people work for him," Rumsfeld said. "They have been looking at terrorist networks, al Qaeda relationships with terrorist states, and that type of thing." Wolfowitz told the *New York Times* that the parallel intelligence team was "helping us sift through enormous amounts of incredibly valuable data that our many intelligence resources have vacuumed up," describing "a phenomenon in intelligence work, that people who are pursuing a certain hypothesis will see certain facts that others won't, and not see other facts that others will." He added that "the lens through which you're looking for facts affects what you look for" but insisted that the team was "not making independent intelligence assessments."

By mid-2002, Feith's "shop" had grown into the Office of Special Plans, the primary plan being to create a justification for an invasion of Iraq, as would later become clear after the much-hyped WMDs failed to materialize and a somewhat embarrassed mainstream media began to reexamine the run-up to war. Wilkerson charged that Cheney and Rumsfeld, and their aides, insisted on viewing and analyzing raw, uninterpreted intelligence data from the field, believing that "they could do it a lot better than the Agency did," adding that their "read" of raw intelligence "would always produce a far more frightening threat scenario than would be produced by the Agency," because, in their view, "the Agency just couldn't do anything but equivocate." Wilkerson saw this as a dangerous development. "Any intelligence person of stature would tell you that you don't give raw intelligence to the laymen, because they don't know how to read it," he told me. "That's how Cheney, Feith and those people patched together a patchwork quilt—which is what it was—of Iraqi violations of the sanctions and Iraq [having a] WMD program and so forth and so on. They just picked out the [intelligence] that supported their own preexisting views and pieced them together."

In 2002 alone, Cheney personally made approximately ten visits to the CIA. His top aide, Libby, made repeated trips, as did former House speaker Newt Gingrich, at the time a Pentagon "consultant." William Luti, Feith's deputy for the Near East and South Asia, would also go to the Agency.

Some analysts said they felt pressured to conform their assessments with Cheney and company's political agenda and that Libby had inundated the CIA with requests for hundreds of documents that the analysts said would have taken a year to produce. Cheney would arrive at Langley and then commandeer a conference room on the seventh floor of CIA headquarters, to which he would summon various analysts and senior CIA officials. Cheney's staff, in particular, was "hell-bent on connecting Saddam and his regime to al Qaeda," recalled Jose Rodriguez, who was running the high-value interrogation program and the black sites at the time. The "connections between Iraq and AQ were remarkably thin," he conceded. "I could have given you a list of a half-dozen countries that had more substantial ties to bin Laden's organization than did Iraq."

It was not unheard of for a vice president to visit the CIA, but according to former senior CIA analyst Ray McGovern—who served as the national security briefer for Vice President George H. W. Bush in the 1980s—Cheney's "multiple visits" were "unprecedented," adding that Cheney was putting "unrelenting pressure" on analysts to produce the intelligence he wanted. "This is like inviting money changers into the temple. It's the inner sanctum," McGovern asserted. "You don't have policy makers sitting at the table, helping us come up with the correct conclusions, and that is the only explanation as to why Dick Cheney would be making multiple visits out there."

An investigative report prepared by Senator Carl Levin of the Senate Armed Services Committee concluded that Feith's office "developed and disseminated an 'alternative' assessment of the relationship between Iraq and al Qaeda that went beyond the judgments of intelligence professionals in the IC [Intelligence Community], and which resulted in providing unreliable intelligence information about the Iraq–al Qaeda relationship to policymakers through both direct and indirect means." Feith edited his reports depending on whom he was briefing. Cheney's office received all access briefings, but Feith's presentations to CIA director Tenet omitted PowerPoint slides critical of the Agency. The presentations to Cheney's staff, according to Levin's report, "conveyed a perception that the U.S. had firm evidence of a relationship between the Hussein regime and al Qaeda when it did not." Tenet was unaware that Feith's office was briefing the president and vice president behind his back and did not find out until a year after Iraq had already been invaded. "The nation's foremost intelligence experts, and the President's chief intelligence officer, were deprived of the opportunity…to correct inaccuracies" in Feith's briefings, Levin's report asserted. More important, the CIA was "deprived of the opportunity to inform the White House of significant concerns about the reliability of some of the reporting upon which Under Secretary Feith's White House briefing was based."

In August 2002, Feith's staff showed up at an Intelligence Community meeting at which a final draft of the US intelligence on Iraq was to be nailed down. Professional intelligence analysts who attended the meeting said that it was "unusual" because "members of an intelligence consumer organization" such as Feith's office "normally do not participate in the creation of intelligence products." At the meeting, Feith's staff complained that the report was not direct enough and contained too many caveats. They also pressured the analysts to include discredited intelligence that one of the 9/11 hijackers, Mohammed Atta, had met with an Iraqi intelligence official in Prague before the attacks. Feith's staff wrote a memo to Rumsfeld and Wolfowitz after the meeting. They alleged that the "CIA attempts to discredit, dismiss, or downgrade" the information Feith wanted included in the final report resulted in "inconsistent conclusions in many instances." They concluded: "Therefore, the CIA report should be read for content only—and CIA's interpretation ought to be ignored."

In the end, under great pressure from Cheney's team and Feith's office, the US Intelligence Community's final Iraq report included "questionable intelligence reports," according to a US Senate investigation, that fit the administration's predetermined policy of invading Iraq. Feith later presented a classified report to the Senate Select Committee on Intelligence. The *Weekly Standard* obtained the memo and held it up as evidence of a rock-solid connection between al Qaeda and the Iraqi regime. Feith's memo, author Stephen Hayes alleged, proved that "Osama bin Laden and Saddam Hussein had an operational relationship from the early 1990s to 2003," stating bluntly that "there can no longer be any serious argument about whether Saddam Hussein's Iraq worked with Osama bin Laden and al Qaeda to plot against Americans." Cheney's targeted pressure campaign at the CIA and other intelligence agencies, along with Feith's briefings, would form the basis for the dubious claims that would ultimately make the Iraq invasion a reality.

# 8 Survival, Evasion, Resistance, Escape

WASHINGTON, DC, 2002–2003—The November 2002 drone strike in Yemen was the opening salvo in the Bush administration's drive to expand US military action beyond the stated battlefield of Afghanistan. Although much of the media focus at the time was on the Bush administration's campaign to justify the invasion of Iraq, in secret the CIA was building up a black-site archipelago to deal with the rest of the world. Prisoners who had been snatched from various countries across the globe were being held in the gulags of foreign intelligence services, where they were interrogated and often tortured under the direction of US intelligence agents. CIA black sites were being constructed and "high value" detainees were being interrogated.

But infighting between the FBI and the CIA was becoming untenable. Some FBI personnel were disgusted with what they believed were extreme tactics being employed by the Agency's interrogators. Others, like Rumsfeld and Cheney, believed the CIA was not going far enough and was too restrained by its requirements to keep congressional committees abreast of its operations. By December 2002, CIA director George Tenet would boast that the United States and its allies had already detained more than 3,000 suspected al Qaeda operatives and associates, in more than one hundred countries. But despite such proclamations, the game was only just beginning. The post-9/11 fervor that had allowed Cheney's "dark side" operations to flow largely unabated and unchallenged by Congress and the media was fading. Journalists and lawyers were poking around. A few members of Congress were starting to ask questions. There were rumblings about "secret prisons."

Cheney and Rumsfeld were not content with the intelligence they were receiving from the CIA or the military's Defense Intelligence Agency (DIA) interrogators. "We have to start pushing on intel," Rumsfeld had noted in an internal memo in March 2002. "It is not going right." Rumsfeld asserted, "We are faced with the job of trying to find individual terrorists. That never used to be a DoD job. But terrorists today are well-organized and well-financed, they are trying to get weapons of mass destruction and can impose enormous damage on the United States. So finding them has become a Defense Department task." Rumsfeld and his deputies began seeking assistance from a secretive military program. The Joint Personnel Recovery Agency (JPRA) was responsible for coordinating the rescue of US military personnel trapped in enemy territory, including in "denied areas," where their very presence—if exposed—could cause a major international crisis or scandal. But of particular relevance to Rumsfeld was JPRA's other work: preparing US forces for resisting enemy attempts to extract information from captured US personnel. All US special operators went through JPRA's horrid torture mill, a program known as SERE, for Survival, Evasion, Resistance and Escape.

The SERE program was created to introduce US soldiers, sailors and airmen to the full spectrum of torture that "a totalitarian evil nation with a complete disregard for human rights and the Geneva Convention" could use on them if captured. At SERE training, soldiers would be subjected to a hellish regimen of torture tactics drawn from the techniques of vicious dictatorships and terrorists. During training, soldiers could be kidnapped from their quarters, beaten, hooded, shackled and stuffed into vans, flown in helicopters. They could be waterboarded, beaten with canes, have their heads slammed against walls. They would often be deprived of food and sleep and subjected to psychological torture. "At SERE school, 'enhanced interrogation techniques' are enemy torture methods," said Malcolm Nance, who worked on the SERE program from 1997 to 2001 and helped develop and modernize its curriculum. Nance and other SERE instructors studied the debriefings of US prisoners of war throughout history. They dissected the interrogation tactics of Communist China, North Korea, the Vietcong, Nazi Germany and scores of other regimes and terror groups. The institutional knowledge at SERE was "built in blood. They are written in blood. Everything we use at SERE, a US service member—or thousands of them in some instances—died from." SERE, Nance said, "was a repository of every known [torture tactic] out there. We had debriefs that went back—literally, the original debriefs—that went back to the Civil War." SERE's intended purpose was to prepare US military personnel to face the tactics of lawless foes. But Rumsfeld and his allies saw a different value for the program.

In the early stages of the High Value Detainee program, the CIA and the DIA were running the interrogation show, but personnel from JSOC were watching closely. Internally, JSOC had concluded that the methods being used by the US interrogators in Afghanistan were not producing results—not because they were too harsh but because they were not harsh enough. "From the beginning, there was incredible pressure on interrogators to elicit actionable intelligence from practically every individual we took into custody. Some of these detainees were complicit, others innocent; some were knowledgeable, some truly clueless," recalled Colonel Steven Kleinman, who spent twenty-seven years working in US intelligence and was one of the most experienced interrogators in modern US history. Among his positions was director of intelligence at JPRA's Personnel Recovery Academy. "In far too many cases, we simply erred in pressing interrogation and interrogators beyond the edge of the envelope. As a result, interrogation was no longer an intelligence collection method; rather, it had morphed into a form of punishment for those who wouldn't cooperate." Kleinman added that when the torture tactics "proved ineffective in producing the type of actionable intelligence required by senior leaders," veteran US interrogators, including some from the FBI and US military, suggested using alternative, noncoercive, nonviolent tactics. Top White House officials "ignored or rejected" those tactics as "irrelevant." "We instead opted for more of the same, except the pressure would be ratcheted up...in some cases to an alarming degree," Kleinman said. "When presented with the choice of getting smarter or getting tougher, we chose the latter."

To develop new tactics, Rumsfeld and his team looked inward at the very program used to train US forces in how to resist enemy torture. As JSOC reviewed the "failures" of the interrogation program the CIA and DIA were running at Bagram Airfield in Afghanistan, Rumsfeld and his team soon began reviewing the possibility of taking interrogation of enemy combatants captured on the battlefield to the next level. The SERE program, they believed, could be reverse-engineered. The medieval tactics they had studied from history's greatest torturers would be their new interrogation manual. "We are at war with an enemy that has flagrantly violated the laws of war," Rumsfeld had declared in late 2001. "They do not wear uniforms. They hide in caves abroad, and among us here at home." While denouncing the "enemy's" disregard for the laws of war, Rumsfeld and his team were preparing to follow suit. As early as December 2001, Rumsfeld's office began asking JPRA for assistance in detainee "exploitation."

Initially, the leadership at JPRA headquarters pushed back on Rumsfeld's requests to export their training tactics into the interrogation chambers of the war on terror. In a two-page memo to the Pentagon's general counsel, JPRA warned against using SERE's "torture" tactics on enemy prisoners. "The requirement to obtain information from an uncooperative source as quickly as possible—in time to prevent, for example, an impending terrorist attack that could result in loss of life—has been forwarded as a compelling argument for the use of torture.... In essence, physical and/or psychological duress are viewed as an alternative to the more time-consuming conventional interrogation process," JPRA's command asserted. "The error inherent in this line of thinking is the assumption that, through torture, the interrogator can extract reliable and accurate intelligence. History and a consideration of human behavior would appear to refute this assumption." JPRA noted that "upwards of 90 percent of interrogations have been successful" by developing a rapport with the detainee, and warned that after being subjected to harsh interrogation techniques, a prisoner's resolve to resist cooperation is strengthened. JPRA's memo noted that eventually, if tortured enough, prisoners "will provide answers that they feel the interrogator is seeking. In this instance, the information is neither reliable nor accurate."

But Rumsfeld and his team forged ahead. Feith and other Defense officials instructed JPRA to begin providing detailed information on the SERE program to US interrogators. By early 2002, JPRA began briefing DIA personnel on "detainee resistance, techniques, and information on detainee exploitation." Meanwhile, the senior SERE psychologist, Dr. Bruce Jessen, who was also a CIA contractor, began developing an "exploitation plan" for the Agency's interrogators to receive instructions on how to use SERE tactics on detainees. In early July 2002, CIA interrogators began receiving training from SERE instructors and psychologists on extreme interrogation tactics. Later that month, Rumsfeld's office requested documents from JPRA, "including excerpts from SERE instructor lesson plans, a list of physical and psychological pressures used in SERE resistance training, and a memo from a SERE psychologist assessing the long-term psychological effects of SERE resistance training on students and the effects of waterboarding," according to a Senate Armed Services Committee investigation. "The list of SERE techniques included such methods as sensory deprivation, sleep disruption, stress positions, waterboarding, and slapping. It also made reference to a section of the JPRA instructor manual that discusses 'coercive pressures,' such as keeping the lights on at all times, and treating a person like an animal." The Pentagon's deputy general counsel for intelligence, Richard Shiffrin, acknowledged that the Pentagon wanted the documents in order to "reverse-engineer" SERE's knowledge of enemy torture tactics for use against US detainees. He also described how JPRA provided interrogators with documents about "mind-control experiments" used on US prisoners by North Korean agents. "It was real 'Manchurian Candidate' stuff," Shiffrin said. JPRA's commander also sent the same information to the CIA.

The use of these new techniques was discussed at the National Security Council, including at meetings attended by Rumsfeld and Condoleezza Rice. By the summer of 2002, the War Council legal team, led by Cheney's consigliere, David Addington, had developed a legal rationale for redefining torture so narrowly that virtually any tactic that did not result in death was fair game. "For an act to constitute torture as defined in [the federal torture statute], it must inflict pain that is difficult to endure. Physical pain amounting to torture must be equivalent in intensity to the pain accompanying serious physical injury, such as organ failure, impairment of bodily function, or even death," Assistant Attorney General for the Office of Legal Counsel Jay Bybee asserted in what would become an infamous legal memo rationalizing the torture of US prisoners. "For purely mental pain or suffering to amount to torture under [the federal torture statute], it must result in significant psychological harm of significant duration, e.g., lasting for months or even years." A second memo signed by Bybee gave legal justification for using a specific series of "enhanced interrogation techniques," including waterboarding. "There was not gonna be any deniability," said the CIA's Rodriguez, who was coordinating the interrogation of prisoners at the black sites. "In August of 2002, I felt I had all the authorities that I needed, all the approvals that I needed. The atmosphere in the country was different. Everybody wanted us to save American lives." He added, "We went to the border of legality. We went to the border, but that was within legal bounds."

In September 2002, the congressional leadership was briefed on these specific interrogation techniques. Some Democrats, including Representative Nancy Pelosi, would later say that they were never briefed on the use of waterboarding. The CIA briefers and her Republican colleagues claimed otherwise, adding that none of the House and Senate leaders briefed on the method raised any objections to it. Pelosi later clarified that, at the time, she had been briefed on the tactic of waterboarding, but not its active use in interrogations. Whatever the truth, the torture program was now operating at full speed and, as far as the White House was concerned, with the legal backing of the US government. "Instead of co-opting these [al Qaeda] operatives and bringing them to our side, we used SERE methodologies, which are purely enemy methodologies," recalled Nance. "Taking those and inverting them and then taking them way past the safety margins... completely breaks the moral fiber of anyone who raises their hand in oath to support and defend the constitution of the United States."

Years after the black sites had been established and scores of prisoners were shuttled through them, the International Committee of the Red Cross compiled testimonials of fourteen prisoners who had survived. Some were snatched in Thailand, others in Dubai or Djibouti. Most were taken in Pakistan. The ICRC report described what would happen once US forces took a prisoner:

The detainee would be photographed, both clothed and naked prior to and again after transfer. A body cavity check (rectal examination) would be carried out and some detainees alleged that a suppository (the type and the effect of such suppositories was unknown by the detainees) was also administered at that moment.

The detainee would be made to wear a diaper and dressed in a track-suit. Earphones would be placed over his ears, through which music would sometimes be played. He would be blindfolded with at least a cloth tied around the head and black goggles. In addition, some detain-ees alleged that cotton wool was also taped over their eyes prior to the blindfold and goggles being applied....

The detainee would be shackled by [the] hands and feet and trans-ported to the airport by road and loaded onto a plane. He would usually be transported in a reclined sitting position with his hands shackled in front. The journey times...ranged from one hour to over twenty-four to thirty hours. The detainee was not allowed to go to the toilet and if necessary was obliged to urinate and defecate into the diaper.

According to the ICRC, some of the prisoners were bounced around to different black sites for more than three years, where they were kept in "continuous solitary confinement and incommunicado detention. They had no knowledge of where they were being held, no contact with persons other than their interrogators or guards." The US personnel guarding them wore masks. None of the prisoners was ever permitted a phone call or to write to inform their families they had been taken. They simply vanished.

During the course of their imprisonment, some of the prisoners were confined in boxes and subjected to prolonged nudity—sometimes lasting for several months. Some of them were kept for days at a time, naked, in "stress standing positions," with their "arms extended and chained above the head." During this torture, they were not allowed to use a toilet and "had to defecate and urinate over themselves." Beatings and kickings were common, as was a practice of placing a collar around a prisoner's neck and using it to slam him against walls or yank him down hallways. Loud music was used for sleep deprivation, as was temperature manipulation. If pris-oners were perceived to be cooperating, they were given clothes to wear. If they were deemed uncooperative, they'd be stripped naked. Dietary ma-nipulation was used—at times the prisoners were put on liquid-only diets for weeks at a time. Three of the prisoners told the ICRC they had been waterboarded. Some of them were moved to as many as ten different sites during their imprisonment. "I was told during this period that I was one of the first to receive these interrogation techniques, so no rules applied," one prisoner, taken early on in the war on terror, told the ICRC. "I felt like they were experimenting and trying out techniques to be used later on other people."

As the CIA began applying SERE tactics on more detainees at its black sites, Rumsfeld was not content with the Agency running interrogations. In late 2002, JSOC formed a task force to draw up plans for a potential role for its personnel in interrogating "designated unlawful combatants." The CIA was reporting to the White House—specifically Cheney's office—on its progress in using SERE tactics at its black sites, but JSOC could provide far greater flexibility and far less oversight. JSOC operators were tapped by the White House to participate in a parallel interrogation program known by its unclassified code name as Copper Green. Internally, the program was called Matchbox. Interrogation would be one of their key tactics, but Cheney and Rumsfeld had much broader plans for a new, unaccountable way of waging a global, secret war.

WITHIN THE US LAWS governing military and intelligence operations, there are gray areas. Title 50 of the US code, or federal law, sets out the rules and structures for intelligence operations, while Title 10 covers military actions. The code under which a particular operation is performed has serious implications for oversight and accountability. The terms "covert" action and "clandestine" operations are often thrown around as though they mean the same thing. They do not. "Covert action" is a doctrinal and legal term that, broadly speaking, refers to an activity whose sponsorship is meant to be a secret. It is meant to provide the United States with "plausible deniability." Such operations are extremely risky—not just in terms of the operational danger, but because they often involve secret US agents conducting operations inside the borders of a sovereign country without alerting its government. If the operation is exposed or disrupted, the potential for scandal is very real. The legal definition of covert action, according to Title 50, is "An activity or activities of the United States Government to influence political, economic, or military conditions abroad, where it is intended that the role of the United States Government will not be apparent or acknowledged publicly." A covert action requires a presidential finding and for the White House to brief the House and Senate Intelligence Committees on its contents. This briefing must occur before the covert action unless there are "extraordinary circumstances." The requirements for congressional involvement were established to prevent scandals such as the Bay of Pigs invasion of Cuba and Iran-Contra. Those operations were passionately supported by Cheney and Rumsfeld. Although they no doubt regretted the fact that Iran-Contra became public and stirred controversy, they did not regard the operation itself as a scandal but rather as a model for how the United States should conduct its dirty business.

Military doctrine defines another class of activities, "clandestine operations," in which the point of secrecy is to protect the integrity of the mission, not to conceal its sponsor, the US government. The military may conduct operations that are both covert and clandestine, but these are rare. Unlike covert actions, clandestine operations do not require a presidential finding if "future hostilities" are "anticipated" in the country where they are taking place. Nor is the administration required to report the operation to Congress. Such operations are defined as "Traditional Military Activities" and offer the intelligence committees no real-time oversight rights. Under US law, the military is not required to disclose the specific actions of an operation, but the US role in the "overall operation" should be "apparent" or eventually "acknowledged."

From where Rumsfeld and Cheney were sitting, the United States was at war, and the world was a battlefield. Therefore, hostilities were "anticipated" in every country on earth, necessitating dozens if not hundreds of potential "Traditional Military Activities" across the globe. Cheney and Rumsfeld realized that by using JSOC—a black-ops force whose activities arguably straddled both Title 10 and Title 50—they could operate in the crevice separating US military and intelligence law. Much of JSOC's operations could be classified under military doctrine as "Preparing the Battlespace," which is defined by the US Special Operations Command as "the umbrella term for all activities conducted prior to D-Day, H-Hour to plan and prepare for potential follow-on military operations...in likely or potential areas of employment, to train and prepare for follow-on military operations." Such activities could be conducted as Advance Force Operations (AFOs), which are "military operations conducted by forces which precede the main elements into the area of operations to prepare for follow-on operations." Unlike CIA operations, AFOs can be carried out with minimal external oversight—for a significant period of time—prior to an "overt" hostility, or for a "contingency" that may or may not occur.

The congressional intelligence committees viewed this logic as a workaround to oversight and reporting laws, charging that the Defense Department wanted to liberally deploy its increasingly formidable intelligence capabilities abroad under the pretense of operational planning for future military hostilities, without granting the intelligence committees their due oversight.

Adding another layer of bureaucratic complexity to this already murky area of US law was the fact that the armed services committees authorized the funding for operations, and the intelligence committees held the power to determine what constituted a covert action. Those committees often clashed on this very issue and fiercely guarded their turf, leaving a huge opening for potential abuses and the exploitation of gaps or gray areas.

Although the CIA was supposed to be the main agency conducting co-vert actions, the National Command Authority—which consisted of the president and Rumsfeld—could choose to use Title 50 authorities for orga-nizations other than the CIA, by delegating military assets to CIA opera-tions. JSOC, for example, had been used for covert actions in order to oper-ate in politically volatile areas without repercussions under international law or to supersede Congress's authority to declare war. Title 10 operations conducted in "Preparing the Battlespace" had even fewer congressional reporting requirements, and with the congressional resolution authoriz-ing a global war, the National Command Authority could use its power to direct military operations without having to classify them as covert actions. This had always been a gray area open for exploitation. And that was attractive to Cheney and Rumsfeld and their teams as they plotted their "Next Steps."

Rumsfeld had major plans for Special Ops—and they didn't include any CIA control or meddling. Cofer Black's departure opened a door for Rums-feld to assert more control over the dark wars. But it wasn't just the Agency or Congress that Rumsfeld wanted to cut out of the equation. It was also the conventional military bureaucracy and military brass, which he be-lieved had grown soft and gun-shy. "The worst way to organize for a man-hunt...is to have it planned in the Pentagon," Rumsfeld wrote in an inter-nal memo laying out a vision for SOF units to begin striking globally. "We must be willing to accept the risks associated with a smaller footprint." On July 22, 2002, Rumsfeld sent a secret directive to General Charles Hol-land, the SOCOM commander, envisioning a decentralized "manhunt" that would circumvent the traditional military command structure and operate more like a private hit team. He instructed Holland to "develop a plan" to deal with al Qaeda and associated groups. Rumsfeld explained that going forward, they would need to find a way to "cut through" the Pen-tagon bureaucracy and process deployment orders "in minutes and hours, not days and weeks." He added: "The objective is to capture terrorists for interrogation or, if necessary, to kill them, not simply to arrest them in a law-enforcement exercise." But Holland "did not respond as swiftly and dramatically as people in Washington thought he should," recalled Law-rence Wilkerson, a retired colonel who served thirty years in the army. "People in Washington, in this case, being Rumsfeld and Cheney." The general came back with a five-year plan when Rumsfeld wanted immediate action.

As Rumsfeld and Cheney pushed for Special Ops to start hitting globally, top military commanders expressed concern that those plans outpaced the military's abilities to collect and exploit intelligence. Some JSOC teams in Afghanistan had found themselves in turf battles with other JSOC teams and, though they did kill a tremendous number of Afghans and foreign fighters, whom exactly it was they were killing was not always clear. A big problem was a lack of solid intelligence. While the CIA was taking the lead in hunting down High Value Targets (HVTs), Rumsfeld was simultaneously pushing JSOC's men to yield results. But without good intel, they were chasing ghosts.

When Rumsfeld proposed beefing up JSOC and taking it global, General Holland pushed back. He told Rumsfeld he was concerned about the lack of "actionable intelligence" in the emerging proposed target regions. One senior military commander said bluntly that "the intelligence wasn't good enough to allow us to have a campaign like that." Rumsfeld and his deputies reportedly ridiculed the commanders, particularly General Holland, for what they saw as excessive caution. A Pentagon adviser who worked closely with Rumsfeld at the time told the investigative journalist Seymour Hersh that Rumsfeld and his team were convinced that "there [were] few four-stars leaning forward in the Special Operations Command," and that more "fighting generals" were needed, and further, the high-ranking military officers who came up during the Clinton years would need to be "reassessed."

More to Rumsfeld's liking was General Wayne Downing, who had been called out of retirement after 9/11 to serve as deputy national security adviser and coordinate the US campaign targeting terrorist networks and "those who support them." Although he technically reported to National Security Adviser Rice, he would be JSOC's advocate within the White House. Downing pushed for JSOC to return to its roots as a "blacker/lower visibility force," employing "a preemptive posture, with improved find and fix capabilities for sustained operations." He began pushing for Special Operations Forces to prepare for "the future indirect and clandestine GWOT fight in countries with which we are not at war" and to conduct operations "in multiple, sensitive, non-permissive and denied areas." He recommended that JSOC should report directly to the secretary of defense and not run its operations through the conventional chain of command.

In reality JSOC was already being freed. While Downing went through official channels, Wilkerson said Rumsfeld and Cheney had already "bypassed Special Operations Command and went straight into Fort Bragg and began giving directions for Special Operating Force activities, direct action in most cases, directly from the Vice President's office to the Joint Special Operations Command." Within months, Holland would be relieved of his SOCOM post.

It was the beginning of what would be a multiyear project by Rumsfeld and Cheney to separate this small, elite, surgical unit from the broader chain of command and transform it into a global killing machine. Before 9/11, they had big plans for JSOC, but the terrorist attacks gave them all the ammunition they would need to win their own war against oversight of these elite and highly lethal forces.

"What I was seeing was the development of what I would later see in Iraq and Afghanistan, where Special Operations Forces would operate in both theaters without the conventional commander even knowing what they were doing," said Wilkerson. "That's dangerous, that's very dangerous. You have all kinds of mess when you don't tell the theater commander what you're doing." Wilkerson told me that when he worked in the Bush administration, "You had JSOC operating as an extension of the [administration] doing things the executive branch—read: Cheney and Rumsfeld—wanted it to do. This would be more or less carte blanche. 'You need to do it, do it.' It was very alarming for me as a conventional soldier."

There was no love lost between the CIA and Rumsfeld and Cheney over the emerging Iraq War intelligence game. And, as they planned other wars, they didn't trust the CIA's analysts to provide them with intelligence required to hit, early and often, globally. Rumsfeld believed that Special Operations needed its own intelligence operation specifically aimed at fueling the global kill/capture campaign. JSOC already worked closely with the famed signals intelligence operation, the Intelligence Support Activity, or simply the Activity. Also known as Gray Fox, the unit specialized in operational electronic surveillance and intercepts. But Rumsfeld also wanted an entity that mirrored the capabilities of the CIA—one that was built on human intelligence, known in the community as HUMINT. In the spring of 2002, a commission chaired by former National Security Adviser Brent Scowcroft recommended that the NSA, the National Reconnaissance Office and the National Imagery and Mapping Agency be removed from Pentagon control and handed over to the CIA. Rumsfeld pushed back violently and moved US intelligence in the exact opposite direction.

In April 2002, Project Icon was launched. The funding for the program came from "reprogrammed" Pentagon funds and was not briefed to congressional intelligence committees. The "new clandestine teams" made up of "case officers, linguists, interrogators and technical specialists" were deployed alongside Special Ops Forces with renewed focus on gathering human intelligence—from the field interrogations, surveillance and the running of local sources and assets. After initially operating under classified code names, the secret program would later become known as the Strategic Support Branch, or SSB. In July 2002, President Bush transferred Gray Fox to the Special Operations Command by executive order, giving Rumsfeld control over a huge portion of US intelligence assets and systems. This new shop, consisting of Gray Fox working together with SSB, would provide real-time intelligence to Special Ops Forces to target suspected militants, prevent future attacks and "prepare the battlefield" for potential military operations. In short, it would fuel a global manhunt. If Doug Feith's intelligence shop was meant to threaten the supremacy of the CIA's analysts, the SSB was meant to supersede the authorities of the Agency's human intelligence structures.

Any country, friend or foe of the United States, would be fair game for operations. The CIA, the US ambassadors and the home government would not be looped in. Early planning memos by Rumsfeld indicated that he wanted the SSB to focus intelligence-gathering operations on "emerging target countries such as Somalia, Yemen, Indonesia, Philippines and Georgia." SSB was designed to "operate without detection and under the defense secretary's direct control." The *Washington Post* obtained internal Pentagon documents that called for a HUMINT branch that would be "directly responsive to tasking from SecDef." These SSB units would operate under "nonofficial cover," at times using false names and nationalities with the goal of covering the "full spectrum of humint operations." It was a direct challenge to the CIA, whose Directorate of Operations was the traditional agency tasked with covert missions, particularly when conducted in "friendly" nations or countries where "conventional war is a distant or unlikely prospect." There was pro forma language in the internal guidelines on the SSB defining "coordination" as giving the Agency seventy-two hours' notice before launching an intelligence-gathering mission, but the SSB was intended to radically streamline the pace and scope of lethal covert military operations against terrorist suspects, regardless of where they resided.

"Definitely Cheney, and also Rumsfeld to a lesser extent, viewed the CIA as a weak sister, and that basically they were not politically reliable," recalled Philip Giraldi, the career CIA case officer. "And, essentially, it was decided that we would go the JSOC route. But of course, the JSOC route has problems. When you use the military as your cutting edge on some of these activities where you're not at war with somebody, where you're getting involved with sending people into someone else's sovereign territory, then you're opening up all kinds of cans of worms that intelligence agencies were created to avoid." Covert actions permit US operatives to ignore international conventions and to violate other nations' domestic laws. US military operations, however, are required by US law to observe international laws, the laws of war and the Geneva Conventions, though the Bush administration clearly did not see it that way when it came to the status of certain military detainees. Using US Special Ops Forces for covert actions could mean they lose their Geneva Convention status, be accused of spying and ultimately be labeled "unlawful combatants." Critics worried that this would place US armed service members at risk should they be captured, with their captors enabled to ignore the Geneva Conventions' prohibitions on torture and inhumane treatment, citing the US precedent.

Although the SSB was officially run by Vice Admiral Lowell Jacoby, the head of the Defense Intelligence Agency, its real taskmaster was Stephen Cambone, a political ideologue recruited by Rumsfeld. A leading neocon, Cambone had first appeared on the Pentagon radar when he ran the Strategic Defense Initiative in 1990. Later, he worked on special projects for Rumsfeld on DoD commissions dealing with missile defense and space-based weapons. Bringing Cambone on board to help shape the hunter-killer Special Ops program that had been on Rumsfeld's mind since 9/11 opened the floodgates. Officially, Cambone was Rumsfeld's special assistant. In reality, he was Rumsfeld's point man on developing the DoD's version of the "dark side."

When, after 9/11, Rumsfeld sought to wrest control of the Global War on Terror from the CIA, he went to Cambone. In one of his famous "snowflake" memos, on September 23, 2001, Rumsfeld told his staff: "We want to think through designating Special Ops as the global terrorism CINC [commander in chief]. They've got a joint intelligence center. The effort has to be global." That day, Rumsfeld sent Cambone a note, subject: "Capabilities," asking him to look into "how we can develop additional unconventional capabilities in the Pentagon and troops, like Special Ops, only of a different type. We need greater flexibility and versatility." Three days later, on the morning of September 26, 2001, Rumsfeld sent Cambone another memo with the subject: "Opportunity." "Now is the time to fix intel," Rumsfeld wrote, saying that he wanted to remap the command structure of US forces across the globe, "to reorganize our forces in Europe and Asia, to accelerate Army transformation, to reduce headquarters and to get homeland defense humming. There may be other things we could do as well."

Cambone would become a powerful shadow player with access to Rumsfeld and his team. One of his primary jobs would be organizing Special Operations activities aimed at killing and capturing people designated as terrorists or enemies by Rumsfeld and the White House. "They are all cast in the same mode, which is 'let's get the most high-tech gadgets for communications and weapons, let's run these operations at the highest possible level of efficiency, let's get some really good intelligence, so we can pick out individuals, and we'll go kill them,'" said Colonel Lang. Rumsfeld had told Cambone, "We need to increase the total number of Special Forces."

In 2002, Cambone began reviewing ways to free up as many shooters as possible. This began with transferring some of the traditional tasks performed by SOFs to the conventional military, such as: training foreign forces, conducting airlift missions and serving as a Quick Reaction Force (QRF) for VIPs in Afghanistan. Rumsfeld and Cambone wanted all SOF hands on deck for kill/capture. Leave the rest to big army.

In mid-2002, Rumsfeld issued a classified planning order to General Richard Myers, the chair of the Joint Chiefs, advocating a sweeping change in the way JSOC and other Special Ops would operate. Rumsfeld wanted "preliminary pre-clearance" for operations and maximum authority for commanders on the ground to execute missions.

Rumsfeld's goal was to reorganize the structure of US Special Operations Forces, blowing up barriers to allow for fast, lethal, global operations with no bureaucratic meddling from anyone who did not have a need to know. The Special Mission Units (SMUs) of JSOC, Delta Force, which was officially known as CAG, or Combat Applications Group, and SEAL Team 6, were attractive to Rumsfeld because they were accustomed to operating autonomously, even in the old days of regional commands being responsible for all troops operating in their Area of Responsibility. These SMUs formed the National Missions Force and were permitted to operate discreetly and globally without coordinating with the conventional command authorities. Rumsfeld wanted to make this model apply to all Special Ops Forces.

"Today we're taking a number of steps to strengthen the U.S. Special Operations Command so it can make even greater contributions to the global war on terrorism," Rumsfeld declared. "Since 1987 the Special Operations Command has been organized as a supporting command, meaning it provides warriors and materiel to the various regional combatant commanders, who then plan and direct missions." No more. From now on, Rumsfeld asserted, SOCOM would be its own boss—with a headquarters in Tampa, Florida, and regional "Theater Special Operations Commands" that could organize hits and other direct actions on a rolling basis. Rumsfeld said this was necessary because of "the nature of the enemy and the need for fast, efficient operations in hunting down and rooting out terrorist networks around the world."

In 2003, Rumsfeld created a new portfolio for Cambone, one that had never existed in the Pentagon's civilian bureaucracy before, undersecretary of defense for intelligence. The new position was referred to internally as "defense intelligence czar"—and it came with unprecedented authority, as it forced all of the previously independent intelligence entities of the Pentagon to report directly to Cambone. This included the Defense Intelligence Agency and the National Security Agency. Steven Aftergood of the Federation of American Scientists charged that the position was part of a drive "to shift the intelligence community's center of gravity further into the Pentagon." What this meant in real terms was that 85 percent of the nation's total intelligence budget would be under Cambone's control, with the CIA director controlling just 12 percent. "Rumsfeld wasn't an evil man" a former aide to a Special Operations commander told me. "Rumsfeld had vision. He allowed people like Cambone to manipulate shit." Conventional uniformed military leaders reportedly despised Cambone, with one senior army officer quipping early in Cambone's tenure, "If I had one round left in my revolver, I'd take out Stephen Cambone."

Cambone's right-hand man was a legend in the dark world of covert military operations, Major General William "Jerry" Boykin, an original member of Delta Force who went on to serve in both JSOC and the CIA. He'd spent his entire career in the shadows of US foreign policy, engaged in unattributable operations across the globe. As Boykin saw it, "Through the 1980s and 90s, SOFs saw great opportunities to get boots on the ground, to prepare the battleground, to shape the environment, and to collect intelligence" but only received "approval for less than 10 percent of the opportunities that existed." These opportunities, he asserted, "were missed because of an unwillingness to take risks and a lack of vision and understanding of the benefits for preparing the battle space ahead of time. There was also a fear of consequences." Boykin believed that US counterterrorism operations had become subservient to intelligence standards that required nearly 100 percent certainty of the target and that civilians would not be killed. He said he rejected the term "actionable intelligence." "Give me action," Boykin declared. "I will give you intelligence."

Some, though, warned of the risks of this approach. Running US Special Operations Forces in CIA-type operations and "expanding their role in the way Rumsfeld intends could be very dangerous for U.S. foreign policy," argued Jennifer Kibbe of the Brookings Institution, adding that using Special Ops Forces was "much easier than using the CIA. And this facility seems to appeal to Rumsfeld." It meant that Special Operations "can conduct covert operations abroad without local governments' permission and with little or no congressional oversight or recourse. If Rumsfeld gets his way, administration hawks may soon start using special forces to attack or undermine other regimes on Washington's hit list."

Over at the State Department, Powell and Wilkerson began seeing the effects of this new, parallel operation being run out of the Pentagon. "Early in the so-called 'Global War on Terror,' we were encountering things like ambassadors calling or e-mailing, or messaging or cabling, that they had people walking around their capital cities, who were white people, six foot five, males, nineteen-inch biceps, and it didn't take too long for the ambassador to figure out who these people were, and why were they there," recalled Wilkerson. "We began to have to press Rumsfeld as to what he was doing, sending these Special Operating Forces around the world, without alerting the country team, without alerting our ambassador, the chief of mission in the country. It got to the point where we actually had a death down in South America where one of these people got a little bit inebriated one night and pulled his weapon and he killed a taxi driver in that country, and we had to whip him out of the country real quickly." Wilkerson added: "I am not even sure Rumsfeld knew some of the [operations] that the vice president's office was" running.

"It grew and went out of control under the vice president. It kinda went wild," Cannistraro, the former senior CIA officer, told me. "There were people at the Pentagon given the responsibility to run 'special Special Operations,' that didn't go through the regular chain of command, and that were kept separate from coordination with CIA, or the State Department, or other elements of the US government. And that was all justified on the basis that 9/11 meant that we were in a war, and this war would require special measures to deal with. And it got out of control. There were a couple of places where, because they weren't coordinated, they weren't informed, they killed people that were not real targets. They were wrong." He added, "It happened, frequently."

The House Permanent Select Committee on Intelligence would eventually conclude that the Pentagon had "shown a propensity to apply the [Preparing the Battlespace] label where the slightest nexus of a theoretical, distant military operation might one day exist." For some career army officers who had served in the conventional military, the developments they were witnessing inside the Pentagon felt ominous. "We know that the Geneva Convention was thrown under the bus, so to say, pretty early," Colonel Douglas Macgregor told me. Macgregor was a decorated army officer who led the most famous tank battle of the 1991 Gulf War. He was on the Pentagon team that was charting out the early stages of Iraq War planning in 2001 and 2002. He said he was disturbed by what he was witnessing inside the DoD as Cheney and Rumsfeld began building up the SSB and JSOC. "To be perfectly blunt with you, I stayed away from it. I didn't want to be involved in it, and I wasn't interested in participating in it, because I had this fear that we were ultimately breaking laws," he said. "Whether those laws were our own, or they turned out to be the Geneva Convention, or the 'Law of War' as we in uniform call it. One would have expected someone to stand up and say, 'I'm sorry, Mr. Secretary, Mr. Cambone, General

Boykin, you don't have the authority to suspend the Geneva Convention. That has been ratified by the United States Senate.' But, we have another problem. We have no interest in the Senate, in holding anyone account-able and enforcing the laws," he asserted. "So if you have no one in any branch—whether it's judicial, legislative or executive—who's interested in upholding the law, then you can do pretty much what you want. And I think that's ultimately what's happened."

Elsewhere in the military, there was great consternation at the possibil-ities for disaster presented by this newly forming power being asserted by Rumsfeld and Cheney and the global adventure they were plotting for US Special Operations Forces. "By entering the friendly country with military forces in execution of a military mission, the U.S. has committed an act of war even though our interest lies not with them but in the terrorist headquarters," noted Colonel Kathryn Stone in a July 2003 report for the US Army War College:

> Most of the world has come to look at CIA de facto wars as a way of life because most powers benefit from their own CIA-equivalents op-erating in foreign countries, with nothing to be gained politically by claiming an act of war when another's covert action is discovered. The world, however, is not likely to tolerate the U.S. throwing its regular military muscle around in a covert fashion. The world will rightly ask: Where does it stop? If the U.S. employs SOF to conduct deniable covert action, then is the next step a clandestine tomahawk missile strike, or maybe even a missile strike whose origin is manipulated to conceal U.S. fingerprints?

Colonel Stone's analysis would later prove prophetic, but such concerns were buried away. "I think a lot of 'back-dooring' went on and as a result they got a lot of running room. The President was kind of passive, in his first term he let them get away with a lot of stuff, and they had their own idea how to do things, which is much like the way the Israelis do things," recalled Colonel Lang. "You know, the famous 'Cheney one per-cent' thing—if there's any doubt, you kill 'em. That's basically it, either capture them, or kill them. And that's what they did for a long time."

Rumsfeld and Cheney were beginning to build up the infrastructure for waging an unaccountable, global war—and JSOC would be their prized weapon. They needed a forward-leaning general to run their secret war. They would find their man in the form of General Stanley McChrystal, US Army Ranger.

**The Troublemaker: Stanley McChrystal**

THE UNITED STATES, 1974–2003; IRAQ, 2003—Stanley McChrystal was the son of an army general. He enrolled at West Point Military Academy in 1972, where he said he earned a reputation for being a "troublemaker." He partied hard and seemed eager for action. One night, McChrystal and some friends staged a mock raid on one of the buildings on campus, using actual guns and balled-up socks as grenades. McChrystal was nearly shot by campus security and was later disciplined for his actions. A file full of disciplinary demerits, however, did not stand in the way of McChrystal making battalion commander. He graduated from West Point in 1976, finished Special Forces School at Fort Bragg in 1979 and commanded a Green Beret unit from 1979 to 1980, though he did not deploy during the most high-profile missions that were conducted during his early military career. "I missed Panama and Grenada and it bothered me," McChrystal recalled. "You always wonder how you'll do." In the years following West Point, McChrystal pursued a dual track that would earn him a reputation for being a "warrior-scholar." He picked up a master's degree in national security and strategic studies from the US Naval War College and another in international relations from the Salve Regina University. McChrystal rose through the ranks of the Rangers and served with Airborne units as well as Special Forces.

In 1986, McChrystal became the commander of the 3rd Battalion 75th Ranger Regiment and, by all accounts, revolutionized the training regime for Rangers, modernizing the technology available to its forces and increasing the tempo of physical training and for night operations. McChrystal's first known work with a JSOC team was in the lead-up to the 1991 Gulf War, when he served as the army special operations action officer for Operations Desert Shield and Desert Storm. While McChrystal was deployed to the Gulf to help coordinate special operations, he would spend the war in Saudi Arabia and at Fort Bragg. At the time McChrystal was entering the world of dark ops, he acknowledged, "I've never shot anyone." Instead, he would focus on the planning and execution of missions, developing leadership skills and moving up through the Special Ops ranks.

By the late 1990s, McChrystal had become the commander of the Rangers. Dalton Fury, who led a Delta Force team hunting bin Laden in Afghanistan, served as a staff officer under McChrystal in the Rangers before moving over to Delta. "My Ranger peers and I had a unique opportunity to see the good and the bad in [McChrystal]. I think if McChrystal were wounded on the battlefield, he would bleed red, black, and white—the official colors of the 75th Ranger Regiment. He is 110% US Army Ranger," Fury recalled. "Even with a bum back and likely deteriorating knees after a career of road marching and jumping out of planes he doesn't recognize the human pause button." Fury noted that as a Ranger, "McChrystal was considered a Tier II subordinate commander under the Joint Special Operations functioning command structure. The highest level, Tier I, was reserved exclusively for Delta Force and Seal Team 6. This always seemed to bother McChrystal. His nature isn't to be second fiddle to anyone, nor for his Rangers to be considered second-class citizens to the Tier 1 Special Mission Units."

Indeed, McChrystal fought for years to advance the position of the US Army Rangers in the Special Ops machinery, refusing to view them as a "farm team" for Delta Force. "The Rangers were, and still are, just as skilled in their Mission Essential Tasks as are the Tier I units in theirs," recalled a former Ranger who served under McChrystal. "He believed that losing quality officers and noncommissioned officers to what many considered the true tip of the spear outfits—those granted the most funding, most authority, and given the premier targets—hurt the Regiment." As Fury explained, in McChrystal's eyes, "the Rangers were just as skilled in their primary mission of Airfield Seizures and Raids as Delta was in land based Hostage Rescue or the SEALs were in assaulting a ship underway."

Fury recalled a conversation he had had with then-Colonel McChrystal in which they discussed the failed Eagle Claw operation in Iran, the Delta Force hostage rescue attempt in 1980 that remained a stain on the Special Ops community. "It was an interesting and enlightening conversation. The essence of the discussion centered on COL McChrystal's reasoning that Beckwith should have continued the mission with fewer operators and lift helicopters. Even though the risk would have increased significantly, COL McChrystal felt the embarrassment in the eyes of the world of failing to try was exponentially more devastating to our nation's reputation than executing a high risk mission that might have even an outside chance of success. McChrystal believed the American people would never accept such a decision like that again."

After establishing himself as an iconic figure in the Rangers, McChrystal burnished his credentials with stints at Harvard and the Council on Foreign Relations in New York. In 1998 Dick Cheney, who then chaired the Military Fellowship Selection Board at the CFR, recommended McChrystal for the fellowship to "broaden" his "understanding of foreign relations." At the CFR, McChrystal wrote an in-depth paper debating the merits of humanitarian intervention. In the paper, written before 9/11, McChrystal asserted, "It is military reality that the nation is incapable of unlimited action around the world. It is political reality that unconstrained or poorly justified US military intervention would be neither supported nor accepted, either by Congress or by other nations," adding, "Our actions, particularly interventions, can upset regions, nations, cultures, economies, and peoples, however virtuous our purpose. We must ensure that the cure we offer through intervention is not worse than the disease." McChrystal continued, "We must not put at risk our military capability to perform core missions crucial to national defense.... The cost of losing or significantly degrading the power of the United States," he argued, "is a price the world can ill afford." Ironically, McChrystal, who considered himself a political liberal, would ultimately owe his rise to fame to men who did everything he warned against in his CFR paper.

When the 9/11 attacks occurred, McChrystal was the chief of staff of the 18th Airborne. He was soon deployed to Afghanistan to help establish Combined Joint Task Force 180, which would become the forward headquarters for Operation Enduring Freedom. In the early days of CJTF 180, McChrystal ran a "hybrid organization" made up of Special Operations Forces, as well as conventional and Special Forces units. Based at Bagram Air Base, the task force had a mission to coordinate the full-spectrum war effort, directing operations targeting al Qaeda and Taliban leadership, in addition to other counterterrorism operations. The task force would take the lead in detention operations and interrogating prisoners for "actionable intelligence" in Afghanistan. CJTF 180 commanded many of the units that initiated the widespread use of night raids on suspected houses of al Qaeda or Taliban figures. These raids were considered a "blueprint for the war against terrorism" that would later be replicated elsewhere.

In July 2002, McChrystal was recalled to Washington, DC, for a promotion. Five months after he left Afghanistan, CJTF 180 became embroiled in a prisoner abuse scandal when it was revealed that in December 2002, two detainees in the task force's custody had died from blunt trauma, exposing the "enhanced interrogation techniques" being used there. Whether it was the task force that was responsible or the Special Mission Unit that was using the task force's facilities to conduct interrogations was never fully resolved. Two Military Police officers were tried in connection with the deaths. Although McChrystal's time in Afghanistan was brief, it was there that he strengthened his close working relationship with a legend of the military intelligence world, Major General Michael T. Flynn.

Flynn, who was McChrystal's deputy at the 18th Airborne, deployed with him to Kabul, where he served as director of intelligence for CJTF 180. Known in his early years as a hard-partying surfer, Flynn was commissioned in 1981 as an army second lieutenant and became an intelligence officer, doing multiple tours at Fort Bragg. He participated in the 1983 invasion of Grenada and the invasion of Haiti in the early 1990s. He spent his career working on sensitive military intelligence programs and building up systems for developing intelligence collection in "denied" areas. As McChrystal rose, Flynn rose with him. When McChrystal returned to Washington, Flynn returned to command the 111th Military Intelligence Brigade, whose members would, among other activities, deploy, "equipped with low density systems" such as unmanned aerial vehicles "to contingency operations throughout the world." This period marked a dramatic uptick in the use of a variety of drones that would later become central weapons in Washington's wars. Flynn would be on the knife's edge of the intelligence technology that would be at the center of the mounting, global kill/capture campaign.

McChrystal watched from the sidelines as the invasion of Iraq got under way. Before "Shock and Awe" began, an elite group of JSOC commandos, known as Task Force 20, deployed inside Iraq ahead of the larger invading force. Its mission was threefold: help invading forces develop targets for air strikes, uncover SCUD missiles and other weapons of mass destruction, and hunt down HVTs such as Saddam Hussein. The "super secret" Task Force 20 "had been operating in the Kurdish autonomous region of northern Iraq for more than a decade, and in 2002 its forces infiltrated Iraq proper," William Arkin reported in the *Los Angeles Times* in June 2003. "Commandos established 'hide sites' and listening posts, and they placed acoustic and seismic sensors on Iraqi roads to track activity. They penetrated Iraq's fiber-optic network to eavesdrop on communications." The task force, which numbered roughly one thousand personnel, included top-tier teams, each with a dozen commandos that would have free rein to travel throughout Iraq in pursuit of Saddam Hussein and the Baath Party leadership and military command structure.

Although TF-20 was given autonomy on the battlefield and coordinated its operations directly with Pentagon officials, at times its men attached themselves to conventional military units. "In 2003, JSOC soldiers were among the first troops in southern Iraq, riding in with the protection of an armored task force of the 3rd Infantry Division," Arkin and Dana Priest reported in their book, *Top Secret America*. "According to three JSOC commanders, these troops helped the division kill upward of five thousand Iraqis in perhaps the bloodiest portion of the war, the march to Baghdad.

'It sounded like World War II, there was so much noise,' said a JSOC commander who was there. The gunners on the armored vehicles faced human waves of Iraqi army forces, fedayeen, and their ragtag civilian supporters. They were ordered to kill anyone who got up on the vehicles. 'That's the dirty little secret, the dark underbelly of the war,' he said. 'There were bodies everywhere.'" Armored "vehicles also delivered the JSOC commandos on their own missions to capture or kill senior Iraqi Baathists loyal to Saddam Hussein and to find and secure weapons of mass destruction." They would never find any to secure.

McChrystal had returned from Afghanistan just as the Iraq War planning was kicking into full gear. His new position was as vice director of operations for the Joint Staff (J-2). Like many military and intelligence officials, he did not view Iraq as a terrorist threat and was not enthusiastic about the invasion. "There were a lot of us who didn't think Iraq was a good idea," McChrystal told journalist Michael Hastings. "We co-opted the media in the buildup to the Iraq War," he said. "You could see it coming."

The US efforts to fight against al Qaeda in Afghanistan, McChrystal asserted, were hindered by invading Iraq. He said:

> I think they were made more difficult in one sense from the military standpoint, but I really think they were made more difficult because they changed the Muslim world's view of America's effort. When we went after the Taliban in Afghanistan in 2001, there was a certain understanding that we had the ability and the right to defend ourselves. And the fact that al-Qaida had been harbored by the Taliban was legitimate. I think when we made the decision to go into Iraq, that was less legitimate with many of the observers. And so while there was certainly a certain resource strain and reduction in the ability of just our attention to be in multiple places, I think it was more important that much of the Muslim world now questioned what we were doing, and we lost some of the support that I think would have been helpful longer term.

Notwithstanding his misgivings, for the first month of the US invasion of Iraq, McChrystal would emerge from the shadows and become—at least for a month—one of the most public faces of the US military. At the Pentagon, he would address reporters and, behind closed doors, give classified briefings to Congress. In April 2003, Representative Jose Serrano, a Democrat from New York, dubbed the briefings "the daily lie." Serrano's sentiments were shared by other House Democrats. "I don't benefit a great deal from [the briefings]," said Representative John Conyers. "I get more from other sources that don't compromise my ability to speak" about the war, he said. "I thought it was not the best use of my time," Representative Bobby Rush told the press of the briefings.

Other lawmakers, however, viewed the McChrystal briefings as more candid and worthwhile than the blustery sessions given by Rumsfeld. "My staff goes to the ones in the morning," said then-Senator Joseph Biden, who supported the invasion of Iraq. "They are considerably more valuable than the celebrated ones when the secretary comes up." Senator John McCain said, "They simply give us the facts without embellishment.... I don't think [Rumsfeld] gives us the kind of pure military picture that these guys do."

During one press briefing, McChrystal opened a window into the prominence of Special Operations Forces in the Iraq War. "They are more extensive in this campaign than any I have seen. Probably, as a percentage of effort, they are unprecedented for a war that also has a conventional part to it," he declared. "It's probably the most effective and the widest use of Special Operations forces in recent history, clearly." The US military, McChrystal said, was using "a very precise and very focused targeting process against the regime." By April 14, McChrystal had practically declared the war a victory. "I would anticipate that the major combat engagements are over because the major Iraqi units on the ground cease to show coherence," he said. In reality the war was just beginning, and whether he thought invading Iraq was a "good idea" or not, McChrystal was about to taste the war firsthand, on the ground. Even as Bush declared "Mission Accomplished" in Iraq, McChrystal was being tapped by Cheney and Rumsfeld to run the most empowered kill/capture team in US history. In September 2003, he became the commander of JSOC.


THERE ARE DUELING MYTHOLOGIES that have developed around Stanley McChrystal. The dominant one, repeated breathlessly in various media profiles, is of the "warrior scholar" who is in better physical shape than any of the younger men under his command. He ate just one meal a day and ran twelve miles to and from the office every day in the 1990s when he was at the Council on Foreign Relations. He was well versed in the classics, yet enjoyed the Will Ferrell "dude" comedy *Talladega Nights*, and would quote it, and would cite Monty Python films frequently. His beer of choice was Bud Lite Lime. There is no doubt that men who served under McChrystal revered and adored him. "He's a unique warrior in American history. I obviously have an intense personal admiration for the guy," said Andrew Exum, a former Ranger who served under McChrystal in Iraq. "When you are a young Ranger platoon leader, and Stan McChrystal steps on the podium in front of you, then you are seeing everything you want to be in life: just a remarkable individual, a fantastic soldier, somebody who is just a tremendously capable individual and somebody who is widely admired. There's a reason why folks in the community call him 'the Pope.' He's the man above whom is no one else."

Actually, McChrystal was not the first JSOC commander to be called "the Pope." It was a reference dating back to the Clinton administration, when then-Attorney General Janet Reno complained that prying information from JSOC was like attempting to access the secret vaults of the Vatican. But, more than any commander before or after, to the JSOC community McChrystal was "the Pope." Although he thought the Iraq War was a bit of a fool's errand, McChrystal also saw it as an opportunity to revolutionize JSOC and push it to a more powerful position than ever before. "Stan was the epitome of a warrior. Stan is a man that, when he's given a directive from the commander in chief, he moves out smartly and executes an order," a former member of McChrystal's team told me. "What Stan came to realize is that with the proper political backing in the White House he would be able to accomplish things with his force that had never been done before."

Stanley "McChrystal is stubborn," observed Fury, who served as a staff officer under him, "and no one can argue that he isn't a man of extraordinary stamina, advanced intellect, and uncompromising dedication to his warriors, the American people, and our way of life. Personally, I don't know a man with more stamina and stomach for the fight than...McChrystal. He sets an incredible pace, expects excellence, demands results, but most importantly he listens to the men on the ground."

Once he took over at JSOC, McChrystal's Ranger roots provided the inspiration for him to Ranger-ize the command. When he had run the 75th Rangers, "Terms like 'kit', often used by Delta and Seal Team 6 operators to collectively describe the gear, weapons, and equipment an assaulter carries was banned from the Ranger lexicon," said Fury. "The term 'assaulter' or 'operator' was also verboten speak within the Regiment. The men wearing the red, black, and white scroll were Rangers, not assaulters and not operators. They also didn't carry kit. They carried standard military issue equipment." When he took command of JSOC, McChrystal believed that the various entities that made up the command should operate as a fluid team, with a "cross fertilization plan of skill sets and team building," rather than reserving the most sensitive operations to Delta and SEAL Team 6, the Special Mission Units. "From the very beginning" of his time as JSOC Commander, "McChrystal tried to shake up the status quo of the Tier I outfits. He now owned those assaulters and snipers from the Army and Navy, and even though he completely supported creative risk taking and out of the box thinking, he quickly moved to fit their actions into an easily managed color coded box. It didn't always work the way the General wanted though." McChrystal believed that the Delta and Team 6 guys should work in tandem, but Fury said McChrystal quickly understood that it might not be the best approach. "It took a little while, but the General eventually recognized that the two units were apples and oranges and squaring them in that color coded box resulted in a fruit salad of conflicting skill sets, SOPs [standard operating procedures], and even mindset." This ability to adapt became part of the McChrystal legend while he presided over the premier US counterterrorism units as the fight was increasingly going global.

But nearly invisible in the breathless media narrative of the warrior-leader's ascent is another McChrystal—a man who in reality had seen very little action before ascending to the post of JSOC commander after the Iraq invasion. This McChrystal was a climber who had cozied up to the right people politically, whether Democrats or Republicans, as well as key figures within the military bureaucracy. In essence, he was one of the chosen few. "A third generation soldier, [McChrystal] missed the end of Vietnam while attending West Point. Graduating in 1976, he entered an Army hollowed out after the unpopular conflict in Southeast Asia," asserted Carl Prine, the veteran military reporter. "With few wars to fight for nearly two decades, he advanced in a largely uncompetitive world, it all made perhaps even easier for him because his father—retired major general Herbert McChrystal—had been the Pentagon's director of planning before his son took a commission."

According to career military officers who knew McChrystal going back to West Point, he had been groomed for years to rise through the army ranks. "I like Stan very much, as a person," said Colonel Macgregor, who was McChrystal's roommate at West Point. But Macgregor charged that after 9/11, McChrystal had ingratiated himself with the neoconservatives, particularly Rumsfeld and Cheney. "He was someone that had made his reputation, in the Pentagon with Rumsfeld. He was someone who saw this 'global' Caliphate as a tremendous enemy, and kept beating the drum for that. And that endeared him to all of the key people." The military, Macgregor said, is run under a "system that rests ultimately on a foundation that is cronyism. In other words, are you one of the boys? If they judge you to be culturally reliable, amenable, then you're considered someone that should be advanced to the senior ranks. It's a kind of brotherhood selection: 'Is this man going to stay the course with us? Is he going to say whatever we tell him to say, do whatever we tell him to do?'" McChrystal, he told me, realized early on "that if he is going to advance, he's going to have to ingratiate himself. And he does this in the Pentagon."

Despite his stated concern about the way US military policy was alienating Muslims, McChrystal shared the political view that the United States was indeed in a war against Islam, according to a retired military officer who had known him from the beginning of his military career and went through Ranger training with him. "Boykin and Cambone and McChrystal were fellow travelers in the great crusade against Islam," the officer told me. "They ran what was for all practical purposes an assassination program." Macgregor said that when McChrystal was named JSOC commander, he was "given a mission under Mr. Cambone, who is Rumsfeld's intelligence director, and General Boykin, who was Cambone's right-hand man, to essentially go after the 'terrorists.' And of course we're defining terrorist very, very broadly." McChrystal, he said, "presided over this black world where any actions were justified against Muslims because you were fighting against the Caliphate."

While McChrystal was reorganizing JSOC, the White House and Pentagon were demanding results in Iraq. By late 2003, the war the United States had already declared won was just beginning. The neocons' vision for Iraq and their ill-conceived policies were fueling a nascent insurgency from both Sunnis and Shiites alike. The ground was laid during the year that L. Paul Bremer was running Iraq under the Coalition Provisional Authority.

BREMER WAS A CONSERVATIVE CATHOLIC CONVERT who had cut his teeth in government working for Republican administrations and was respected by right-wing evangelicals and neoconservatives alike. Forty-eight hours after 9/11, Bremer wrote in the *Wall Street Journal*, "Our retribution must move beyond the limp-wristed attacks of the past decade, actions that seemed designed to 'signal' our seriousness to the terrorists without inflicting real damage. Naturally, their feebleness demonstrated the opposite. This time the terrorists and their supporters must be crushed. This will mean war with one or more countries. And it will be a long war, not one of the 'Made for TV' variety." Bremer concluded, "We must avoid a mindless search for an international 'consensus' for our actions. Today, many nations are expressing support and understanding for America's wounds. Tomorrow, we will know who our true friends are."

In mid-April 2003, "Scooter" Libby and Paul Wolfowitz contacted Bremer about taking "the job of running the occupation of Iraq." By mid-May, Bremer was in Baghdad, leading the Coalition Provisional Authority.

During his year in Iraq, Bremer was a highly confrontational viceroy who traveled the country in a Brooks Brothers suit coat and Timberland boots. He described himself as "the only paramount authority figure—other than dictator Saddam Hussein—that most Iraqis had ever known." Bremer's first official initiative, reportedly the brainchild of Rumsfeld and his neoconservative deputy, Douglas Feith, was dissolving the Iraqi military and initiating a process of "de-Baathification," which in Iraq meant a banishment of some of the country's finest minds from the reconstruction and political process because party membership had been a requirement for many jobs in Saddam-era Iraq. Bremer's "Order 1" resulted in the firing of thousands of schoolteachers, doctors, nurses and other state workers, while sparking a major increase in rage and disillusionment. Iraqis saw Bremer picking up Saddam's governing style and political witch-hunt tactics. In practical terms, Bremer's moves sent a message to many Iraqis that they would have little say in their future, a future that increasingly looked bleak and familiar. Bremer's "Order 2"—disbanding the Iraqi military—meant that hundreds of thousands of Iraqi soldiers were forced out of work and left without a pension. "That was the week we made 450,000 enemies on the ground in Iraq," one US official told the *New York Times Magazine*.

Within a month of Bremer's arrival, talk of a national uprising had begun. As the bloody impact of his decision to dissolve the military spread, Bremer amped up his inflammatory rhetoric. "We are going to fight them and impose our will on them and we will capture or, if necessary, kill them until we have imposed law and order upon this country," he declared.

On May 1, President Bush, wearing a bomber jacket, stood on the USS *Abraham Lincoln* before a large "Mission Accomplished" banner. "My fellow Americans, major combat operations in Iraq have ended," he declared. "In the battle of Iraq, the United States and our allies have prevailed." It was a fairy tale. The Saddam regime may have been deposed and Saddam's days were numbered (not long after Bush's speech, on July 23, 2003, Saddam's sons, Uday and Qusay, were killed in a JSOC raid), but a guerrilla war—one with multiple warring forces—was just beginning.

Rumsfeld rejected claims that the United States was facing a "guerrilla" insurgency. "I guess the reason I don't use the phrase 'guerrilla war,'" he quipped, "is because there isn't one." But Rumsfeld's newly appointed CENTCOM chief, who was technically the on-the-ground commander of the Iraq War, disagreed. General John Abizaid said at a July 2003 press conference at the Pentagon that the United States was now facing a "classical guerrilla-type war" in Iraq. Abizaid knew another front of resistance was opening, and it was not being run by Saddam's "henchmen." By mid-August 2003, three months after Bremer arrived in Baghdad, resistance attacks against US forces and Iraqi "collaborators" were a daily occurrence. New militias were forming, with both Sunni and Shiite groups attacking American troops. Rumsfeld and Bush both downplayed the extent of the uprisings in Iraq, saying they were being driven by fallen regime "dead-enders," "criminals," "looters," "terrorists," "anti-Iraqi forces" and "those influenced by Iran." But there was one fact they couldn't deny: The number of Americans returning home in tin coffins was exploding as attacks against US forces increased by the day. "We believe we have a significant terrorist threat in the country, which is new," Bremer finally acknowledged on August 12. "We take this very seriously."

On August 19, a Kamaz flatbed truck pulled up to the United Nations headquarters at Baghdad's Canal Hotel and parked just below the office window of Sergio Vieira de Mello, the United Nations special representative in Iraq. Inside the building, a press conference was under way. Moments later, a massive explosion rocked the building. The truck had been driven by a suicide bomber and was filled with explosives, including a five-hundred-pound bomb from the former Iraqi military's reserves. In all, twenty-two people were killed, including de Mello. More than one hundred were injured. The United States and the United Nations alleged that the bomber had been sent by Abu Musab al Zarqawi, a Jordanian-born militant who headed up the group Jama'at al Tawhid wa'al Jihad. A few days after the bombing, Rumsfeld delivered a speech at a Veterans of Foreign Wars convention. "We still face determined adversaries, as we've seen in Iraq and Afghanistan, the dead-enders are still with us, those remnants of the defeated regimes who'll go on fighting long after their cause is lost," Rumsfeld declared. "There are some today who are surprised that there are still pockets of resistance in Iraq, and they suggest that this represents some sort of failure on the part of the Coalition. But this is not the case. Indeed I suspect that some of you in this hall today, especially those who served in Germany during World War II or in the period immediately after the war were not surprised that some Ba'athists have kept on fighting. You will recall that some dead-enders fought on during and after the defeat of the Nazi regime in Germany."

Rumsfeld tried to cling to the idea that the main resistance in Iraq was coming from such quarters, but the reality was, the most lethal forces rising in Iraq were responding to the invasion and occupation. While the United States was fighting multiple Sunni insurgent groups, Shiite leader Moqtada al Sadr was waging an uprising against the United States, along with a "hearts and minds" campaign to provide basic services to Iraqi neighborhoods. Because Sadr had brokered a tenuous alliance with some Sunni resistance groups, the United States was facing the possibility of a popular nationalist rebellion.

After the August bombing, the United Nations withdrew most of its six hundred international personnel from Iraq. In September 2003, the UN complex was bombed a second time, spurring the United Nations to withdraw all remaining non-Iraqi employees from the country. It was a powerful symbol of how far from accomplished the US mission in Iraq actually was.

That month, McChrystal became JSOC commander, tasked with crushing the insurgency that had been sparked by his bosses' own policies, about which he had harbored doubts. Next to Saddam and his henchmen, the Jordanian terrorist Zarqawi, who had come to Iraq to fight against the US occupation, would become target number one of McChrystal's task force.

Zarqawi had traveled to Afghanistan to fight with the US-backed mujahedeen against the Soviet occupation. In early 2000, he had been indicted in absentia in a Jordanian court for plotting to attack American and Israeli tourists. The Bush administration had tried to use Zarqawi to prove an al Qaeda tie to Iraq, after Zarqawi allegedly received medical treatment in Baghdad in 2002. When Bush made his case in a nationally televised address on October 7, 2002, that Saddam's regime posed a "grave threat," he cited "high-level contacts" between Saddam's government and al Qaeda, charging that "some al-Qaeda leaders who fled Afghanistan went to Iraq. These include one very senior al-Qaeda leader who received medical treatment in Baghdad this year, and who has been associated with planning for chemical and biological attacks." In his UN speech, Colin Powell called Zarqawi the leader of a "deadly terrorist network" that had been given safe haven by Saddam's government. But the charge that Zarqawi was in Baghdad with the consent of the Iraqi government was a dubious one. Saddam's regime and al Qaeda were rivals. Nonetheless, after the invasion, Zarqawi would eventually have a $25 million bounty on his head and JSOC hunting him in Iraq.

There is no doubt that Zarqawi was a savage character, but he was also a convenient villain for the United States. Washington was facing a mounting resistance in Iraq, and by inflating Zarqawi's importance, it could place the fight in Iraq within the context of the broader war on terror. Zarqawi played his role perfectly. A year after the UN bombing, Zarqawi and his group would pledge allegiance to Osama bin Laden and form al Qaeda in Mesopotamia, also known as al Qaeda in Iraq (AQI). Despite his declaration of loyalty, Zarqawi would ultimately prove problematic for al Qaeda. His ruthless attacks on Muslims—in both Iraq and Jordan—would eventually play into the hands of the US occupation and Washington's propaganda campaign against the Iraqi resistance.

IRAQ WOULD SERVE AS A laboratory for creating a new kill/capture machine, centered on JSOC, run by McChrystal and accountable to no one but a small group of White House and Pentagon insiders. Within months, the targeted kill/capture program would begin to resemble the CIA's Phoenix Program from the Vietnam War, in which the Agency, supported by US Special Operations Forces and indigenous militias, carried out a vicious campaign to "neutralize" the Vietcong and its support networks. In plain terms, the Phoenix Program was effectively a well-organized death squad. "They killed huge numbers, thousands and thousands, of suspected Vietcong operatives," said Gareth Porter, an independent historian who has written extensively about the Phoenix Program in Vietnam, as well as the history of JSOC. "Phoenix was in fact the grandfather of [the JSOC] approach to a war."

Dealing with the Iraq insurgency would become an almost totally consuming task for the bulk of America's most elite forces, though Rumsfeld and Cheney had global aspirations for JSOC's expanded use. Rumsfeld signed an executive order on September 16, 2003—the same month that Holland retired as SOCOM commander, and General Bryan "Doug" Brown took over—establishing JSOC as the principal counterterrorism (CT) force of the United States. It contained preauthorized lists of fifteen countries where CT action might be taken and specified which actions could be carried out. Brown, a SOF vet and founding member of the 160th Special Operations Aviation Regiment, told the Senate that "the nexus of the Department of Defense's global war on terrorism is at USSOCOM." SOCOM, a newly established, free-standing command, would be "the lead combatant commander for planning, synchronizing, and as directed, executing global operations against terrorist networks in coordination with other combatant commanders." A month later, Rumsfeld was demanding answers from his senior advisers. "Are we capturing, killing, or deterring and dissuading more terrorists every day than the madrassas and the radical clerics are recruiting, training, and deploying against them?" Rumsfeld wrote in a memo to Wolfowitz, Feith and Myers.

It was an interesting question and one many were debating in the counterterrorism community. But, as al Qaeda's leadership fled to countries throughout the Horn of Africa and Arabian Peninsula and into Pakistan, the premier US counterterrorism force would be given orders to focus entirely on a nation that had no al Qaeda presence before the US tanks rolled in a year earlier. The Pentagon had distributed decks of playing cards to troops in Iraq, assessing a value to various leaders of the former Baath regime. Saddam was the ace of spades. The tradition dated back to the US Civil War. But this time around, the cards were produced not just for the military but as a consumer product sold to the public. The Bush administration seemed to believe its own propaganda about how easy victory would be in Iraq, reasoning that by destroying the Baath Party and killing or capturing its leaders, the war could be won swiftly.

When McChrystal hit the ground in Iraq in October 2003, his Task Force 20, renamed Task Force 121, would lead the hunt. Its members included JSOC forces, British SAS commandos and some local Iraqi teams. Their job was to plow through the deck of cards. "The mission of the direct action, special operations task force was really to focus on the old regime leadership," recalled Andrew Exum, who led a platoon of Rangers in Iraq as part of McChrystal's task force. "The deck of cards—you know, the most wanted folks. I think that was based largely on the idea that the insurgency in Iraq, the fighting, kind of goes away if a lot of these guys go away." That theory would prove to be fatally flawed.

Whatever the strategic value of the effort, however, it had some success in its immediate goals—taking out selected individual targets. At McChrystal's right hand as the forward commander of JSOC's High Value Targeting task force was William McRaven, a Navy SEAL renowned for his scholarly ambition. Although McChrystal would receive much of the credit for building up JSOC's capabilities and overseeing its greatest hits, people in the Special Ops community knew that many of the key achievements of the HVT Task Force were largely McRaven's doing.

Raised in San Antonio, Texas, McRaven grew up with an appreciation for the military—his father flew Spitfire fighter planes in World War II. The young Bill McRaven was a big fan of James Bond films—he was particularly enthralled by Sean Connery's underwater exploits in *Thunderball*, according to his sister. "That was his favorite!" Nan McRaven told *Time* magazine. "I said to him, 'You can grow up to be 007.' I guess he did."

McRaven graduated from the University of Texas in 1977 with a degree in journalism. He enrolled in Navy ROTC on campus, and right after graduating with an ensign's commission, he entered SEAL training. After finishing his training he was deployed to the Philippines. When Richard Marcinko created the Naval Special Warfare Development Group, SEAL Team 6, in 1982, he asked McRaven to lead one of the constituent SEAL teams. Marcinko's freewheeling leadership soon put him at loggerheads with his young lieutenant. Marcinko bought his SEALS expensive cars and financed debauched parties on navy property that included prostitutes. "The SEALS were happy, I was happy, and nobody was getting in trouble except Bill McRaven," Marcinko told *Time* magazine, remembering McRaven as a killjoy. "He was a bright guy, but he didn't like my rude and crude way. If I was a loose cannon, he was too rigid. He took the special out of special warfare." McRaven saw it differently. "I was not some white knight on a horse going with my lance against the windmill," McRaven countered. Marcinko "was the boss, I was a very young lieutenant. There were some things I didn't think were exactly right...and he relieved me" of duty. According to a former Special Forces commander, Marcinko asked McRaven to carry out "some questionable activities," adding that McRaven refused and "would not back down." Other officers in SEAL Team 6 reportedly found McRaven's integrity heroic, but after his run-in with Marcinko, "thought it was the end of his career."

Actually, it was Marcinko whose career in black ops was coming to an abrupt end—while McRaven's was just getting started. In March 1990, Marcinko was sentenced to twenty-one months in prison on charges he defrauded the US government in a weapons sale. McRaven was soon given command of a platoon in SEAL Team 4, focusing on South and Central America. Very few details are publicly available about McRaven's combat history, though he was a "task unit" leader in the Persian Gulf War, according to his official biography. In 1991, he headed to the Naval Postgraduate School, and graduated in 1993. He helped to establish the Special Operations/Low Intensity Conflict program and was its first graduate. He received a dual degree, in SO/LIC and national security affairs. His graduate thesis, "The Theory of Special Operations," was published in book form and would become widely read and taught. The book analyzed several key Special Ops battles from World War II to Vietnam, presenting lessons that could be learned for future conflicts and wars. It is considered a seminal text in the study of Special Operations warfare. "Bill is reputed to be the smartest SEAL that ever lived," a former commander said in 2004. McRaven went on to serve as a "task group commander" in the Middle East, and he also commanded SEAL Team 3, which operates in Southwest Asia. By 2001, he was a naval captain, commodore of the SEALS Special Naval Warfare Group 1.

Shortly after 9/11, McRaven's SEAL team deployed to Afghanistan, but its commander could not join them. Two months before 9/11, McRaven had fractured his pelvis and part of his back during a parachute jump near his base in Coronado, California. Some predicted he might never fight again, let alone walk normally. McRaven resigned his command, but his career was not over. If anything, the parachute accident was fortuitous. Although McRaven was not on the battlefield initially, he would become a major player in the strategy that was to shape US counterterrorism operations for many years to come. Wayne Downing, newly appointed the deputy national security adviser for combating terrorism, asked McRaven to join his staff at the White House. McRaven ended up working for Downing for two years while he recovered from his injuries and is credited with having been the principal author of Bush's "National Strategy for Combating Terrorism." It was not a cushy job for a sidelined warrior. Captain McRaven would become the primary JSOC figure inside the National Security Council and coordinated the Office of Combating Terrorism. Among his jobs would be vetting and assembling lists of High Value Targets for JSOC to hunt down. He was one of the key players in militarizing US counterterror policy and building up the infrastructure for the creation of kill lists. McRaven's time at the NSC would put him on a path to becoming one of the most powerful figures in US military history and a transformative figure in the institutionalization of assassination as a central component of US national security policy.

After 9/11, no more than two dozen men were on the US kill list. Once McRaven got to work, the list grew every year. After helping build the structure for JSOC to engage in a global manhunt, McRaven would finally forward deploy to implement it. There are "three people who really improved Special Operations Forces and who can claim a great amount of credit for the way they have developed since 2001," Exum told me. "You can look at Bill McRaven, you look at Stan McChrystal and you look at Mike Flynn."

**"Their Intention and Our Intention Is the Same"**

SOMALIA, 1993–2004—In early January 2003, Mohamed Afrah Qanyare stood on the tarmac of the secluded airstrip he controlled just a few clicks north of Mogadishu. The tiny airport was a small fortress in a dangerous, lawless nation. Qanyare's private security force guarded its perimeter and land mines were strategically scattered "in the bush," making a sneak attack—or, for that matter, a casual visit—very risky. In the years following the fall of dictator Mohamed Siad Barre—who headed Somalia's last stable government—Qanyare had emerged as one of the most powerful warlords who ravaged Mogadishu and laid claim to their own plots of territory. The Daynile airstrip was Qayare's fiefdom. And it brought in money. A lot of money. For a decade, the airport's profits overwhelmingly came from smuggling *mira*, or khat, the addictive, narcotic-like leaf that is chewed by millions throughout the Horn of Africa and the Arabian Peninsula. It was the drug of choice among the thousands of militiamen who fought for Qanyare and his fellow warlords and a major factor in the insanity that had long gripped Somalia. But on this particular day—January 5, 2003—the aircraft that Qanyare awaited on the tarmac was not a Bluebird Aviation flight bringing in the foliage of chaos, but rather a small Gulfstream that carried a different kind of volatile cargo.

Qanyare said he couldn't recall which government agency the white men who stepped off the plane that day worked for, but they were definitely Americans. "I believe they were special military intelligence and CIA," Qanyare remembered. "But I really don't know. That's internal business for them. They were intelligence, American intelligence."

A few weeks earlier, Qanyare had been approached by a trusted friend who told him the CIA wanted to meet with him in Nairobi, Kenya. The day after Christmas, Qanyare sat in a hotel room with a handful of white men. "They requested to get together and I accepted, because America is a world power," he remembered. "We discussed intelligence business." The business they discussed was Washington's desire to track down and eliminate a small group of al Qaeda operatives on the CIA and JSOC radar. Among them, the Americans told Qanyare, were dangerous men who had planned and carried out the 1998 bombings of the US embassies in Kenya and Tanzania, killing more than two hundred people. Washington, they told Qanyare, was concerned that al Qaeda was planning to ratchet up its attacks in East Africa.

Indeed, on November 28, 2002, a month before Qanyare met the Americans in Nairobi, terrorists had carried out simultaneous attacks in Kenya. One was on a vacation resort in Kikambala, along the coast north of Mombasa; the other was on an Israeli jetliner at Mombasa's Moi International Airport. In the first strike, three men drove a vehicle laced with explosives into the Paradise Hotel, killing themselves and thirteen others, and wounding eighty more. Minutes later, two men fired surface-to-air missiles at Arkia Israel Airlines Flight 582. Both narrowly missed the plane. Washington suspected that the men who plotted these attacks were part of the same cell that had hit its embassies in 1998.

After the embassies in Kenya and Tanzania were bombed, several of the lead suspects ended up in Somalia—among them, Fazul Abdullah Mohammed, who was later indicted in the United States for his alleged role in the bombings. In late 2001, Fazul began assembling a team in Mogadishu that ultimately carried out the 2002 attacks in Kenya. Some of the weapons used in the Mombasa attacks were traced back to Somalia's thriving weapons black market, including the two Strela-2 surface-to-air missiles used against the Israeli plane. The finances for the operation were handled by a Sudanese national, Tariq Abdullah, also known as Abu Talha al Sudani, who moved between Somalia and the United Arab Emirates (UAE). A previously unknown operative, Saleh Ali Saleh Nabhan, came to the attention of US authorities when the car that blew up the Paradise Hotel was traced back to him. The Kenyan citizen of Yemeni descent was also accused of firing one of the rockets. Nabhan had supposedly been managing a Mombasa cell for years, perhaps serving as the principal intermediary between the Kenya cell and al Qaeda leadership in Afghanistan-Pakistan. After the November 2002 attacks, Nabhan, Fazul and their accomplices once again escaped to Somalia by boat.

These men were prominent on the list of High Value Targets that Washington wanted taken out, but there were larger, more systematic concerns, like the governmentless nation of Somalia being prime territory for al Qaeda to set down new roots, particularly as the US invasion of Afghanistan sent al Qaeda's leadership there into flight.

MOHAMED QANYARE IS A STRIKING PRESENCE, both physically and intellectually. He is tall and his eyes, ringed with many wrinkles, have a surreal intensity. As he tells it, he grew up "in the bush" in Somalia and conned his way into an education by Mennonite missionaries, who taught him the trade of accounting. As a young man, Qanyare parlayed his education into keeping the books for the Somali secret police, which kicked off his career in the dark corners of Somali war politics. He speaks fluent English and often laughs at his own jokes, many of which are actually funny. He often dresses in guayabera outfits, perfectly pressed, though his unkempt mane speaks to his rougher edge.

Over the three years that followed the first visit by the US operatives to Qanyare's airfield, the Americans would fly in once or twice a week. The US team often included a mixture of CIA operatives and "shooters" from JSOC. In the beginning, it was a CIA-led operation run out of the US Embassy in Nairobi. "The airport is inland, inside the bush. So the airport itself is very secretive," Qanyare boasted. "We designed it not to expose or to see easily who is landing. The Americans, they enjoy that." In one of the early visits, Qanyare drove the Americans to his villa. Over coffee, they placed a series of photos before the Somali warlord. He refused to say exactly what the Americans told him they wanted done with the men in the photos. "My agenda was to eliminate al Qaeda representatives in Somalia and whole East Africa," Qanyare told me. "My intention was to fight with these people with the help and the knowledge, and knowing of Americans. That was my intention. I can say that their intention and our intention is the same, and they wanted to eliminate the al Qaeda representatives in the Horn of Africa."

While CIA personnel worked with Qanyare and other warlords, members of JSOC's intelligence division—the Activity—would sometimes break away. Independently, they began building a network of surveillance and eavesdropping equipment across Mogadishu. They were "preparing the battlefield," not fighting on it. There was still no stomach in Washington for US boots on the ground in Somalia. But there was certainly an appetite for an old-fashioned proxy force, which Qanyare was happy to satisfy.

On average, Qanyare said, the Americans would pay him $100,000–$150,000 a month for his services and the use of his airport. Classified US diplomatic cables sent from the embassy in Nairobi detailed a plan to use "non-traditional liaison partners (e.g., militia leaders)" in Somalia. Its aim, according to the cables, was "locating and nullifying high value targets." Thus was born a US-funded coalition of warlords who would serve as Washington's men in Somalia. Its eventual name reeked of the Agency's involvement: the Alliance for the Restoration of Peace and Counterterrorism. Inside the US intelligence community at the time, however, it was known as "Operation Black Hawk," a clear reference to the disaster in

1993 that led to the withdrawal of US forces from Somalia. What started as a quiet intelligence-gathering operation against a handful of al Qaeda members would soon turn into a full-scale dirty war, reminiscent of the US support for the Contras in Nicaragua in the 1980s.

SOMALIA COULD HAVE TURNED OUT very differently from the country the United States and its warlords helped create after 9/11. Radical Islam was new to Somalia and was not widespread prior to the launch of the Global War on Terror. Many seasoned Somalia analysts believed that the handful of radicals in the country could have been contained and that the central aim of stabilizing the country should have been to disarm and disempower the warlords. Instead, Washington directly supported an expansion of their power and, in the process, caused a radical backlash in Somalia, opening the doors wide for al Qaeda to step in. While the CIA began cultivating its relationship with Qanyare and other warlords, the official government of Somalia watched from the sidelines. Made up of Western-educated technocrats, the "Transitional National Government" was little more than an idea that existed in hotel suites and coffee shops in Kenya and other neighboring countries. And Washington's counterterrorism agencies treated it as such.

After the 9/11 attacks and President Bush's "Either you are with us or you are with the terrorists" declaration, Somalia's foreign minister, Ismail Mahmoud "Buubaa" Hurre, swiftly penned a letter to the US secretary of state. "We are with you, and we are as much concerned with the possibility of Al Qaeda moving into [Somalia] as you are," Buubaa recalled writing. "But," he told me over coffee at a posh hotel in Nairobi, "the response was lukewarm." Instead of strengthening the Somali government, he said, "they started cooperating with the warlords, thinking that the best way to combat terrorism was to help the warlords become stronger, and chase away the fundamentalists from Somalia. That backfired."

On September 23, 2001, President Bush had signed Executive Order 13224, designating more than twenty-five groups and individuals as terrorists that could be targeted in the Global War on Terror. Ultimately the list would grow to more than 180. The order was officially a means "to disrupt the financial support network for terrorists and terrorist organizations," but it also revealed groups that could potentially be targeted militarily. Among the original targets was a Somali group, Al Itihaad al Islamiya (AIAI). Despite the fact that the group had largely disbanded prior to 9/11, it was often used as a generic umbrella under which to classify Islamist militants in Somalia. AIAI had participated in the insurrection against the

UN peacekeeping force in Somalia in the 1990s and took credit for a series of terrorist attacks and assassinations in Ethiopia. Allegations of an al Qaeda connection to the Black Hawk Down incident were largely linked to AIAI. Its inclusion in 13224 was an indication that the Bush administration was considering striking inside Somalia.

US war planners believed that when American forces invaded Afghanistan, al Qaeda operatives and other jihadists would seek refuge elsewhere. Yemen and Somalia were among the presumed destinations, so Washington and its allies set up a flotilla, known as Task Force 150, charged with intercepting the jihadists headed there. Speaking from NATO headquarters on December 18, 2001—following a briefing Rumsfeld gave to the defense ministers of member nations—German defense minister Rudolf Scharping told reporters that a US incursion into Somalia was "not a question of 'if,' but of 'how,' and 'when.'" Rumsfeld wasted little time denying what he called "a funny report about some German saying something," telling reporters at a DoD press briefing the following day that "the German was wrong." "He didn't mean to be, and he's probably sorry," Rumsfeld continued. "But he was flat wrong."

Although US forces did not immediately move into Somalia—with Afghanistan and Pakistan the top priorities—the expanded US base at Camp Lemonnier in Djibouti was rapidly becoming a hub in the Horn of Africa for JSOC and the CIA. The base would be tasked with keeping watch over Somalia, along with Yemen, its neighbor across a narrow sliver of water. Scharping may have been wrong in the short term, but "flat wrong" would prove to be an exaggeration. A few days after Rumsfeld denied US plans to move on Somalia, Secretary of State Colin Powell said Somalia's instability made it "ripe for misuse by those who would take that chaos and thrive on the chaos," adding, "That's why we're really looking at Somalia—not to go after Somalia as a nation or a government, but to be especially sensitive to the fact where Somalia could be a place where people suddenly find haven."

US officials in East Africa were also concerned that Kenya could potentially turn into a Pakistan of sorts, providing a hideout for an al Qaeda network they believed was "rebuilding its infrastructure in Kenya." Some within the US military began agitating for a robust, full-time US military presence in the Horn of Africa, and the news media were rife with speculation about Washington's agenda in Somalia. "The possibility of terror cells being in Somalia is real," declared Walter Kansteiner, who headed up the Africa division at the State Department at the time. "Identifying Somalia as a terrorist base for bin Laden's al Qaeda and other extremist organizations, U.S. reconnaissance planes...reportedly began surveying targets from the sky, while military and CIA agents contacted potential allies both inside Somalia and in neighboring Ethiopia," according to the *San Francisco Chronicle*. Deputy Defense Secretary Paul Wolfowitz said that in assessing terror threats in the Horn of Africa, "People mention Somalia for obvious reasons. It's a country virtually without a government, a country that has a certain al-Qaeda presence already."

Like the government of Ali Abdullah Saleh in Yemen, the ruling elites in Kenya and Ethiopia saw opportunity in the threat of terrorism after 9/11. Both governments welcomed increased US counterterrorism assistance, training of their forces and financial support in return for their assistance and allowing territorial access to US forces. Ethiopia, a longtime nemesis of Somalia, saw the country's indigenous Islamists as a threat and aggressively pushed the line that al Qaeda was a creeping menace to its neighbor to the east. While regional stakeholders invoked a burgeoning terrorist threat and rumors spread about possible US operations in Somalia, eminent analysts of the country's affairs were referring to the al Qaeda threat there as "small potatoes." "There's no need to be rushing into Somalia," former US ambassador to Ethiopia David Shinn said at the time. "If you think about military targets, I doubt they exist." Davidson University professor Ken Menkhaus, a Somalia scholar who had written several papers on political Islamic tradition in Somalia prior to 9/11, estimated that the number of Somali nationals with "significant links" to al Qaeda was between ten and twelve. A few foreign fighters might also be holed up there, but because of a dearth of intelligence—Shinn referred to it as "abysmal"—"snatch and grab" type tactics would be ill-advised, he warned.

Although some within the military, CIA and Bush administration wanted to hit in Somalia, those plans would have to wait. The Combined Joint Task Force for the Horn of Africa in Djibouti would largely take on a watch-and-wait posture, and many of the commandos, including JSOC and CIA assets, originally deployed to Camp Lemonnier post-9/11, would be refocused on the impending invasion and occupation of Iraq. As a former member of the Special Operations Command's Horn of Africa Task Force told me, there was initially a determination to "bring the full resources of the United States military, and specifically the Special Operations Command to bear. And we were going to ensure that [al Qaeda] would not be able to reconstitute themselves, or use any part of the Horn of Africa as a safe haven, for operations against the United States." However, he explained, "it did not turn out that way, to our detriment. At some point, the top policy makers made the decision that the preeminent national security threat to America was Iraq. And when the focus shifted to Iraq, the resources went with it. And that led to a lack of focus, and, more egregiously, a lack of resources within and around the Horn of Africa." JSOC's role in Somalia during the early years after 9/11 was relegated to in-country protection for the CIA, establishing surveillance equipment on the ground and having a team on standby in Djibouti, ready to swoop in if anything went wrong with the small CIA-led teams running the warlords.

As JSOC's resources were overwhelmingly dedicated to Iraq, the US approach in Somalia consisted of a covert CIA proxy war. And the United States made Mohamed Qanyare its man in Mogadishu. According to classified US diplomatic cables from the US Embassy in Nairobi, US intelligence fiercely dismissed internal critics of its use of the alliance of warlords to carry out targeted kill and capture operations. "Arguments from diplomatic and NGO [nongovernmental organization] colleagues that a subtler approach...will help us address our CT concerns fail to take into account the immediacy of the threat," read one cable. Certain individuals, the cables stated bluntly, "must be removed from the Somali equation."

It was the beginning of a multiyear relationship among a network of murderous warlords and the CIA that would set Somalia on a course toward even further chaos and bloodshed. It would also result in the very Islamist militant forces Washington wanted crushed emerging more powerful than they had ever been before.

FOR MOST AMERICANS, mention of the word *Somalia* evoked one of two images: a starving child or US soldiers being dragged through the streets of Mogadishu following the infamous Black Hawk Down incident of 1993. Al Qaeda's alleged role in the Mogadishu battle was included in a 1998 indictment against bin Laden in the United States, which charged that al Qaeda had trained Somali clans to oppose the UN mission, culminating in the killing of eighteen US soldiers and the wounding of seventy-three others in Mogadishu. Bin Laden certainly helped bolster that narrative. He had issued a declaration that year, calling the United States "the snake" and exhorting his followers to "cut the head off and stop [it]." Bin Laden later boasted in an interview that the militants who brought down the Black Hawks were among 250 jihadists sent by him to Somalia. He declared, "The youth were surprised at the low morale of the American soldiers and realized more than before that the American soldier was a paper tiger and after a few blows ran in defeat...dragging their corpses and their shameful defeat."

Nonetheless, many experts have cast doubt on al Qaeda's centrality to those events. Journalists interviewed Somalis who said they had "never heard of bin Laden until he began boasting about Somalia years later." Undoubtedly, during this period, bin Laden was seeking to make his mark, but Somali militias hardly needed his help to wreak havoc. The country had already descended into a perpetual state of civil war, with various warlords commanding militias that were terrorizing and destabilizing the country as they fought neighborhood to neighborhood for control. After the withdrawal of the UN force in 1994, Somalia plummeted deeper into chaos.

The "Battle of Mogadishu" was the bloody finale to a mission codenamed Operation Gothic Serpent. Run by Major General William Garrison, then commander of JSOC, it went down as one of the greatest disasters for the US Special Operations community since the botched rescue mission in 1980 to free American hostages in Tehran. Many within the JSOC community did not see it that way. Lieutenant General Boykin, one of the original members of Delta Force, served alongside Garrison on the Somalia mission as the Delta contingent's commander. "This ragged place had just chewed up and spit out elite fighters from the most powerful army in the history of the world," Boykin recalled thinking as he stood in Mogadishu after the battle. He blasted the Clinton White House for abandoning Somalia. In the aftermath of the disaster, Boykin and Garrison had pushed for more troops and called for ramping up the offensive, requests that were rejected. General Garrison retired from the military on August 3, 1996. It was exactly two days after Mohamed Farrah Aidid died in Somalia, having sustained injuries during a gun battle a few weeks earlier. Although Somalia would be largely ignored by the United States in the years to come, it was never far from the minds of the JSOC operators.

It was not until 1996, after bin Laden was expelled from Sudan, that al Qaeda began to make its presence felt in East Africa. In the summer of 1998, US agents in Albania facilitated the extraordinary rendition of five members of Islamic Jihad, Ayman al Zawahiri's organization. The men were transferred to Egypt, where some claimed they were tortured, including by electric shock to the genitals. On August 5, Zawahiri published a letter in a British paper vowing revenge against America in "a language they will understand." Two days later, on August 7, 1998, al Qaeda cells, organized out of Nairobi, carried out simultaneous truck bombings of the US embassies in Kenya and Tanzania, killing 224 people, including twelve Americans, and injuring 5,000 more. It was the first time much of the world had ever heard of bin Laden, and the FBI put him on its Ten Most Wanted List. The al Qaeda leader, in taking responsibility for the embassy attacks, initially said that they were payback for the US "invasion" of Somalia, but the chosen date of the attacks also coincided with the eighth anniversary of US troops deploying to Saudi Arabia.

"We will use all the means at our disposal to bring those responsible to

justice no matter what or how long it takes," President Clinton declared
in the Rose Garden after the bombings. Clinton signed a secret finding authorizing the covert use of lethal force in hunting down those responsible;
the White House had determined that a mission to kill bin Laden was "not
inconsistent with the ban on assassinations." While Clinton authorized
the CIA to use lethal force against bin Laden, subsequent instructions issued to CIA station chiefs globally emphasized that arresting bin Laden
was preferable. The option of using US Special Ops Forces was on the table,
but the administration concluded it "was much easier and much less risky
to fire off cruise missiles," according to the Pentagon report commissioned
by Rumsfeld that reviewed Clinton-era counterterrorism policy. General
Downing, the former commander of JSOC and SOCOM, described the attitude he encountered from Clinton administration officials as: "Don't let
these SOF guys through the door because they're dangerous.... They are
going to do something to embarrass" the country.

Although some US intelligence indicated that scouting missions for the
embassy bombings were coordinated in Somalia, the Clinton White House
would not permit any incursions into Somalia. Instead, the US response
was to strike suspected al Qaeda sites in Afghanistan and Sudan with long-
range cruise missiles in a mission code-named Operation Infinite Reach.
The target of the Sudan bombing, al Shifa factory, turned out to be a legitimate pharmaceutical plant, which produced half of Sudan's medications,
and not, as the United States alleged, a facility for manufacturing nerve
gas. Regardless, East Africa had been ripped wide open as a new front in
what was rapidly becoming a covert US war against al Qaeda. "We are
involved in a long-term struggle," Secretary of State Madeleine Albright
declared. "This is unfortunately the war of the future."

When the Bush administration came to power, Defense Secretary Rumsfeld agreed with Albright's assessment but viewed the Clinton administration's approach to fighting that "war of the future" with utter disdain. He
came into office determined to put the darkest of the US military forces
front and center in the US war machine, and 9/11 had accelerated his plans.
But, in the early years after 9/11, Somalia was, at best, a third-tier concern
for the Bush administration—behind the war in Afghanistan and, eventually, Iraq.

IN THE YEARS FOLLOWING the US and UN withdrawal from Mogadishu,
Somalia was further destroyed. The beautiful, Italian-influenced architec-
ture of the capital was transformed into a skyline of bullet-pocked skele-
tons of once gorgeous buildings. Jobless youth—many addicted to khat—

joined up with clan-based militias and devoted their existence to the cause of the warlords. "Everyone was thinking in terms of creating a small slice of Mogadishu as his turf," recalled Buubaa, the former foreign minister. "It was as if the Somali state was over and everybody wanted to create his little turf to collect money and to become powerful just for personal gains, not for national gains." This was the Somalia that the Americans flew into in 2003 when they first approached Qanyare, one of the very people who had helped destroy the country.

General Downing argued that "a low-to-invisible American profile in the region" was crucial to the US strategy in Somalia, warning that the United States should be careful not to "inflate the appeal of [al Qaeda's] rhetoric or the resonance of their extremist ideology." The Bush administration may have tried to follow the "low profile" part of Downing's advice, but its embrace of the warlords forcefully disregarded the second part.

Believing they had the support of Washington, Qanyare and his CIA-backed alliance soon morphed from thugs battling to control territory to paramilitary militias using the cover of the war on terrorism to justify their activities. CIA officers and Special Ops personnel would fly from Nairobi to Mogadishu, transporting cash and lists of suspects Washington wanted taken out. Initially, the focus was on rendition against foreign operatives. The CIA did not want the warlords to target Somalis for fear of further fueling the civil war. According to military journalist Sean Naylor, the head of the CIA's warlord program was John Bennett, at the time the Agency's Nairobi station chief. Bennett internally laid out ground rules for the program: "We will work with warlords. We don't play favorites. They don't play us. We don't go after Somali nationals, just [foreign] al-Qaida." The warlords, however, had their own plans. Qanyare told me his CIA handlers were reluctant to pull the trigger on kill operations, fearing that an American could be killed or captured. Instead, they left the dirty work to him and his fellow warlords.

After making their deal with the CIA, Qanyare and his comrades engaged in an all-out targeted kill and capture campaign against anyone—Somali or foreign—they suspected of being a supporter of any Islamic movement. In a handful of cases, the warlords caught someone the United States considered to be of value, such as suspected al Qaeda operative Suleiman Ahmed Hemed Salim, captured in the spring of 2003. One of Qanyare's fellow warlords, Mohamed Dheere, seized Salim and rendered him into US custody. Salim was reportedly later held in two secret prisons in Afghanistan. In 2004, directly contradicting Bennett's supposed "rules" for the warlord game, Qanyare's men carried out a raid on a home of a Somali militant, Aden Hashi Farah Ayro. Ostensibly aimed at capturing Abu Talha al Sudani, whom the United States was hunting in connection with the embassy attacks in Africa, they instead seized Ayro's brother-in-law, Mohamed Ali Isse, who was wanted in connection with a spate of assassinations in Somaliland in 2003–2004. According to Isse, he was taken aboard a US helicopter and transported to a US Navy vessel. *Chicago Tribune* journalist Paul Salopek tracked down Isse in a Berbera, Somaliland, prison years later. He told Salopek that once aboard the US ship, he was first treated for a gunshot wound and then detained and interrogated by US plainclothes agents for about a month. Then he was taken to Lemonnier, en route to a clandestine Ethiopian prison, where Isse contends he was tortured by US-trained Ethiopian military intelligence using electric shocks. He was then returned to the Somaliland gulag, where he would remain.

Scores of other "suspects" were abducted by the CIA-backed warlords and handed over to American agents. "The scramble by Mogadishu faction leaders to nab al Qaeda figures for American reward money has spawned a small industry in abductions. Like speculators on the stock market, faction leaders have taken to arresting foreigners—mainly, but not exclusively Arabs—in the hope they might be on a wanted list," according to a report by the International Crisis Group in 2005. "According to one militia leader who has worked closely with the Americans in counter-terrorism operations, as many as seventeen suspected terrorists have been apprehended in Mogadishu alone since 2003—all but three apparently innocent." In many cases, the United States would determine the prisoners had no intelligence value and repatriate them to Somalia. Sometimes, according to several former senior Somali government and military officials, the warlords would execute them to keep them from talking.

"These people were already heinous warlords, they were widely reviled in Mogadishu. And then they start assassinating imams and local prayer leaders," said Abdirahman "Aynte" Ali, a Somali analyst who has written extensively on the history of al Qaeda and warlord politics in Somalia. "They were either capturing them, and then renditioning them to Djibouti, where there is a major American base. Or in many cases, they were chopping their head off and taking the head to the Americans and telling them, 'We killed this guy.'" He added: "The vast majority of people they killed had nothing to do with the War on Terror."

In a diplomatic cable to the State Department from the Nairobi Embassy, US officials acknowledged that the use of the warlords and their militias to hunt down alleged terrorists "may seem unpalatable choices, particularly in light of civilian casualties in recent rounds of fighting in Mogadishu." But, they explained, "These partners are the only means currently available to remove" the terrorists "from their positions in Mogadishu."

When I met Qanyare, he denied that his forces were committing extrajudicial killings, or kidnapping and torturing prisoners, but when pressed on his operations, he acknowledged he was capturing people and interrogating them. Then he shot back. "When you are fighting an enemy, any option is open. If you want to fight al Qaeda, you have to fight them ruthlessly, because they are ruthless." He paused, before putting a fine point on his sentiment. "No mercy."

THE "US GOVERNMENT WAS NOT HELPING the [Somali] government, but was helping the warlords that were against the government," Buubaa, the former foreign minister, complained. Washington "thought that the warlords were strong enough to chase away the Islamists or get rid of them. But it did completely the opposite. Completely the opposite. It was folly, you know, a foolish idea."

As the CIA deepened its involvement with Somali warlords, most of the JSOC and US military assets in the Horn of Africa were refocused on the war Cheney and Rumsfeld had come into office dying to wage: Iraq. This was not going to be a CIA-led war like the early stages of Afghanistan. JSOC was going to be running the show. And it would have a new leader, a "rising star" and one of the "Jedi Knights who are fighting in what Cheney calls 'the shadows.'"

## 11  "A Defeated Enemy Is Not a Vanquished One"

YEMEN, 2003–2006—Shortly after 11:00 p.m. on May 12, 2003, multiple teams of al Qaeda militants carried out a well-coordinated attack in Riyadh, Saudi Arabia. Using a combination of car bombs and heavily armed commandos, the al Qaeda cells hit three separate compounds housing large numbers of Americans and other Westerners. Among the targets hit was a facility owned by a US defense contractor, the Vinnell Corporation, which was training the Saudi National Guard, and another owned by a pro-US Saudi billionaire. Thirty-five people were killed and more than 160 others wounded. A few months later, in November 2003, another bomb attack targeting the Al Mohaya housing compound in Laban Valley killed seventeen people and wounded more than 120. The two attacks sparked a campaign against al Qaeda networks in the kingdom—more than six hundred people were arrested, and others accused of complicity were hunted down and killed. Although the attacks were considered great successes by al Qaeda, the crackdown they spurred meant that the organization needed a safe base outside of Saudi Arabia. Many fled to Yemen.

During this time, the al Qaeda network in Yemen was in disarray. A year after the November 2002 drone strike, Harithi's successor, Muhammad Hamdi al Ahdal, was jailed, as were scores of other suspected militants. Under pressure from the United States, Saleh arrested more than one hundred people and locked them up, ostensibly on suspicion of involvement with the USS *Cole* attack.

The period that followed, from 2003 to 2006, was notable only insofar as the Bush administration seemed to take almost all focus off Yemen and potential al Qaeda threats emanating from the country. "There was an interlude of a little over two years in which it appeared as though al-Qaeda had largely been defeated in Yemen," recalled Princeton University professor Gregory Johnsen, widely considered a leading US expert on Yemen, in testimony before the Senate Foreign Relations Committee. "But instead of securing the win, both the US and Yemeni governments treated the victory as absolute, failing to realize that a defeated enemy is not a vanquished one. In effect, al-Qaeda was crossed off both countries' list of priorities and replaced by other, seemingly more pressing concerns. While the threat from al-Qaeda was not necessarily forgotten in 2004 and 2005 it was mostly ignored." Johnsen believed this "lapse of vigilance" was "largely responsible for the relative ease" that al Qaeda had when it rebuilt its infrastructure in Yemen in the period that followed. Another factor that ultimately worked in al Qaeda's favor was Saleh's imprisonment of hundreds of people on simple suspicion of being affiliated with al Qaeda—in some cases with little or no evidence—which effectively turned the prisons into radicalization factories. "These men were tossed in security prisons with other more experienced fighters who did much to radicalize their younger more impressionable fellow inmates in the shared cells," Johnsen told the Senate. "This problem was largely overlooked at the time" and "would come back to haunt both Yemen and the US throughout multiple phases of the war against al-Qaeda."

Policy makers in Washington seemed to lose interest in Yemen, but the US military, especially the Special Operations community, certainly did not. While Rumsfeld tapped most of the elite hunter-killer forces from JSOC for the high-value killing campaign in Iraq, Yemen remained on the radar of these very forces, whose stated mission was counterterrorism operations. Several Special Operations veterans from this period told me they were disillusioned by what they saw as a misdirection of their skills for operations in Iraq that could have been used to confront the more serious threat posed by al Qaeda elsewhere.

In mid-2003, in Yemen, the ground was being laid for a resurgence of al Qaeda, as President Saleh found himself fighting to put down a domestic insurrection. In 2004, the Houthi minority launched a military uprising in the north, spurring a military offensive by Saleh that resulted in the deaths of hundreds, including Hussein Badreddin al Houthi, the leader of the rebellion. His brother, Abdul-Malik al Houthi, eventually succeeded him and continued the fight against Saleh. In confronting the Houthis during the period known as "the six wars," which spanned from 2004 to 2010, Saleh used both al Qaeda and Saudi forces, as well as his own US-trained-and-equipped Special Operations Forces. An al Qaeda spokesman, Ahmad Mansur, claimed the Yemeni government had solicited al Qaeda's support in fighting the Houthis in return for "eas[ing] the persecution of our members." This account was backed up by several former senior US intelligence and military officials.

Saleh also relied heavily on the Saudis in this effort. At one point, the Saudis were reportedly giving Yemen $10 million a month to fight the Houthis. For the Saudis, the situation in Yemen presented an array of challenges beyond the Houthi rebellion. Overall, the kingdom was Yemen's biggest sponsor, giving Saleh's government an estimated $2 billion a year in aid. To justify their wars against the Houthis to the United States, Saleh and the Saudis consistently used allegations of Iranian support for the Houthis and deliberately conflated them with al Qaeda.

While he worked various angles to try to bolster his own military and political objectives, and the CIA and JSOC entrenched deeper in Yemen from the US base nearby in Djibouti, Saleh used the US desire to take custody of *Cole* bombing suspects to leverage additional support. Despite repeated requests from the FBI and other US agencies and officials, Saleh refused to hand over the top suspects in the bombing, including Jamal al Badawi, whom the United States explicitly asked be extradited after he was indicted in 2003 in federal court in the United States. "The Yemeni constitution prohibits handing over any Yemeni," Saleh told the *New York Times*.

Instead, Saleh brokered a scheme wherein most of the suspects would be prosecuted and sentenced in Yemen. In 2002, under pressure from Washington to do something, Saleh had created what he called a "dialogue council" to "confront" the jihadists on his soil through rehabilitation and reconciliation. "The Yemeni state felt an urgent need to act against radical Islamism," observed terrorism researcher Ane Skov Birk. "This need arose from a perceived danger to the state partly from the militants themselves, and partly from the possibility of an American led war on Yemen if the state failed to act against these militants." Hundreds of Yemenis were taken into custody as part of the program, and there were reports of torture and cruel treatment that amounted to "gross violations of the detainees' rights." Between 2002 and 2005, more than three hundred Yemenis were released. Several of the program's "graduates" would go on to return to the struggle, fighting in Iraq or joining al Qaeda or other militant groups in Yemen, and the program was eventually discontinued in 2005. For seasoned observers of Yemen, Saleh's game over the *Cole* suspects was akin to a hostage scheme aimed at wresting more money, training and military hardware from the United States. Handing them over to the United States would be a political disaster internally for Saleh and would take away his negotiating power with Washington.

"After the *Cole*, Saleh knew al Qaeda couldn't be trusted, but he wouldn't drop that card," said the former top US counterterrorism official who worked extensively in Yemen during this period. He told me that once al Qaeda suspects ended up in jail, Saleh would eventually "release them through a fictional 'rehabilitation' program where they would swear on the Koran to renounce terrorism or through pardons or by simply allowing them to escape." In 2003, ten of the leading *Cole* suspects escaped from prison, beginning a multiyear pattern of arrests, convictions, escapes and rearrests. "Al-Qaeda intends to cause just enough sporadic damage to persuade [Saleh's] regime that it is best to curtail its efforts to destroy al-Qaeda and to allow the group to operate relatively freely in and from Yemen as long as no major attacks are staged in the country," observed former senior CIA official Michael Scheuer. Saleh's approach to alleged al Qaeda operatives, Scheuer asserted, "almost certainly equates to a license for the militants to do what they want, where they want, as long as it is not in Yemen."

From 2003 to 2006, while Saleh's government remained largely off the Bush administration's radar, there was an occasional meeting to demand action on the *Cole* suspects. In 2004, James Pavitt, the CIA's deputy director of operations, told the 9/11 Commission, "Our operations, in concert with our partners, are gaining ground against the core of al Qaeda," adding: "Two and a half years ago we would have listed our top concerns: Yemen, Saudi Arabia, Southeast Asia," but today, "almost every senior target is gone in Yemen, killed or captured." In reality, a sleeping giant was just waking up.

# 12 "Never Trust a Nonbeliever"

THE UNITED KINGDOM, 2003—As the Iraq invasion was quickly transforming into an occupation, Anwar Awlaki returned to Yemen, but there, his father persuaded him to give Britain another shot. Anwar left his family in his parents' care and returned to the United Kingdom, where he would remain for almost two more years, often preaching at well-known mosques. Among Awlaki's sponsors were the Muslim Association of Britain and the Federation of Student Islamic Societies, both of which had strong ties to the global Muslim Brotherhood organization. His partnership with these organizations is likely to have been one of expediency, noted researcher Alexander Meleagrou-Hitchens, who conducted an extensive historical study of Awlaki's life, "whereby they sought to co-opt a charismatic young preacher in order to help them gain influence among Western Muslims, and in return, they opened up to him the benefits of their considerable organizational capacities, providing Awlaki with ready-made large audiences and venues." Awlaki went on a speaking tour across Britain in 2003, lecturing at prominent universities and colleges and community organizations on the "war against Islam" and the role of Muslims in the Western world. "His popularity in the West was now at its peak, and he drew in large crowds," according to Meleagrou-Hitchens. Dr. Usama Hasan, the former imam of the Tawheed Mosque in Leyton, North London, said that Awlaki had become "one of the icons of Western Salafism and would pack out every venue he spoke at. People were excited to see him."

Awlaki continued to spread his message and, though many of his speeches focused on religious teachings or making modern analogies to Muhammad and other prophets, his politics were clearly growing more militant. His sermons resonated with young people who were coming of age in an era where they perceived their religion as being demonized. "There is a global culture that is being forced down the throats of everyone on the face of the earth. This global culture is protected and promoted. Thomas Friedman, he is a famous writer in the US, he writes for the *New York Times*. He says the hidden hand of the market cannot survive without the hidden fist. McDonald's will never flourish without McDonnell Douglas—the designer of F-15s," Awlaki said in one sermon. "In other words, we are not really dealing with a global culture that is benign or compassionate. This is a culture that gives you no choice. Either accept McDonald's, otherwise McDonnell Douglas will send their F-15s above your head. It is very intolerant culture that cannot coexist with anything else. It uproots every other culture on the face of the earth. Just cuts the roots of it. And you have a quote here by [Russian historian and Soviet dissident] Alexander Solzhenitsyn...'To destroy a people, you must sever their roots.' And the only ideology that is standing up to this global culture is Islam." Awlaki decried the reality he perceived among young Western Muslims, that they

> have more in common with the rock star or a soccer player than they would have with the companions of Rasool Allah [the prophet Muhammad]. You would find that our youth know more about pop stars than they know about the Sahaba [companions] of Rasool. In fact even sometimes more than the Anbiya [Prophets]. How many of our youth know the names of all of the Anbiya of Allah? How many of our youth know the names of the Sahaba? But ask the same person to name the soccer players on their favorite team or their best basketball players and they would go down the list. So there is a serious identity crisis that is going on among Muslims.

Awlaki would weave in pop cultural references with stories from the Koran. He railed against the corporate media and international human rights organizations, which he denounced as propagandists for those who were "plotting to kill" Islam. In London, Awlaki delivered a speech in which he warned young Muslims not to be taken in by the perceived kindness of their non-Muslim neighbors or friends. "The important lesson to learn here is never, ever trust a *kuffar* [a nonbeliever]. Do not trust him. Now, you might argue and say, 'But my neighbor is such a nice person, my classmates are very nice. My coworkers, they are just fabulous people, they're so decent and honest. And, you know, the only problem is that we Muslims are giving Islam a bad name. If these terrorists would just stop what they're doing,'" Awlaki said. "Now, I'm not going to argue that your neighbor is not a nice person. Or your classmate. They truly might be decent and nice people. But, brothers," he added, "this person that you know is not the one calling the shots. And when the Quran talks about" the nonbelievers, "it talks about the leaders," those who "are pulling the strings. Don't make a judgment" based "on Jane Doe and John Doe. You don't make it based on Joe Six-Pack or Sally Soccer Mom." The nonbelievers, he said, were intent on destroying Islam. "We need to wisen up and not be duped," he told the rapt audience. "Malcolm X used to say, 'We've been bamboozled.'"

Awlaki spoke frequently of the harassment and detention of Muslims across the globe, from Guantánamo to London to Virginia and beyond. He

implored his followers to see their struggles in the West as the same as
those in Muslim countries. "We are watching one Muslim nation fall after
another, and we are watching, sitting back, doing nothing. When Palestine
was taken, we did nothing," he boomed at a sermon in London as part of an
event called "Stop Police Terror." "The Ummah [the global Muslim com-
munity] is watching while Iraq is being devoured. It's not going to end there,
because it will spill over to other countries like Syria and only Allah knows
who is next." He added, "When we allow a Muslim nation to fall down, we
have allowed the same thing to happen to every and each one of us."

The December 2003 lecture was organized as part of a series of events in
Britain opposing what the Muslim community saw as a racist crackdown.
Using antiterror laws similar to the PATRIOT Act in the United States,
British security forces began a campaign of mass arrests of Muslims—many
of them students—on suspicion of involvement with terror plots. "We are
arresting people continuously," Britain's top police official, John Stevens,
declared. "It is part of this massive effort we have been having since 11th
September. And it will continue." It was against this backdrop that Awlaki
told his audience, "Many Muslims have been arrested. You know when
you talk about Guantánamo Bay and all that stuff; there is a Guantánamo
Bay in this country. There were 524 Muslims who were arrested under
the new laws and only 2 of them have been charged. You have over 520
Muslims who are locked up in jail, and are left to rot in there, and there's
no crime—they have not committed anything and there are no charges
brought against them. They are left there for months at end, to just rot in
those prison cells. What have you done for them?" He called his followers
to action. "We just sit there watching and doing nothing. Thinking by
ducking down and by being quiet, we will be safe. If you don't stop it now,
it's gonna happen to you, it might happen to your wife, it might happen to
your own daughter. You need to stop it in its tracks before it grows.... So
you need to do whatever you are capable of doing. This is a responsibility—it's hanging on your neck. It is something that you owe to your Muslim
brothers, you owe it to the Ummah and you owe it to Allah."

In London, Awlaki's sermons became more political, condemning the
wars in Muslim countries and the detention of Muslims in the West.
Guantánamo and the US torture program clearly had a major impact on
him. "He became a social figure, you see," recalled his father. Although
many of his earlier sermons were apolitical and focused on the lives of
the prophets and Koranic interpretation, Anwar had become a political
activist. "Anwar, in all his lectures, tried to connect them with something
modern that was happening," Nasser said.

In his sermons, Awlaki would weave his theories about the United
States being at war with Islam with condemnations of torture, at times

taking his theories into the realm of conspiracy, particularly in his denunciations of human rights organizations. "The Jews and the Christians will not be pleased until you become like them. How can we have trust in the leaders of *kufr* [disbelief] when today, today, right now, right now, there are Muslim brothers in jail?" Awlaki declared in a lecture in Britain, his voice shaking with passion. "Every sinister method of interrogation is used against them. They would use against them homosexuals to rape them. They would bring their mothers and sisters and wives and they would rape them in front of these brothers. Now it's true that this is not happening in the West, but the West knows about it. The United Nations knows about it. Amnesty International knows about it and they're doing nothing. In fact, sometimes they are encouraging it."

Meleagrou-Hitchens has pointed out that in all of his time in Britain, Awlaki did not "make clear and public statements in support of violent jihad in a contemporary Western context," adding that "although Awlaki sought to spark an Islamist political awakening within his audience, he was not openly calling for violent jihad against Western countries." While Awlaki lectured on jihad and used historical Arab texts, such as *Book of Jihad*, authored by Ibn Nuhaas, a fourteenth-century scholar who died fighting against the Moguls and the Crusaders, he was careful in offering his rationale. "I want to state in the beginning and make it very clear that our study of this book is not an exhortation or an invitation to violence or a promotion of violence against an individual or society or a state," Awlaki said in one lecture on the book. "We are studying a book that is 600 years old…so that is the extent of what we are doing. It's a purely academic study of an old traditional book." It was clear that Awlaki was thinking of his next move, and Meleagrou-Hitchens believed that his "disclaimer" about not calling for violence "was likely made with the intention of avoiding the attention of British security authorities."

Awlaki's stock among young, English-speaking Muslims on the street was rising by the day, but his solitary life in Britain, away from his wife and children, was not sustainable.

Ultimately, Awlaki decided to return to Sana'a. Nasser Awlaki said it was because Anwar had been unable to afford to live in the West and wanted to pursue business and educational opportunities in Yemen. But some of Anwar's associates in the United Kingdom had a different view. Usama Hasan, who had fought against the Soviets in Afghanistan, suggested that Awlaki wanted to put his money where his mouth was. "I've got a feeling that he's always been yearning for it [to fight jihad], and our yearning was satiated in a way, but he never got that outlet," he said. "Add to that his strong links to Yemen, which has extensive connections to al-Qaeda, and the pull to jihad was too strong."

# 13 "You Don't Have to Prove to Anyone That You Did Right"

IRAQ, 2003–2005—Once the Iraq War was in full swing, Rumsfeld directed General John Abizaid, the CENTCOM commander, to disband the separate High Value Task Forces JSOC was running in Afghanistan and Iraq, TF-5 and TF-20. Instead, JSOC would run one unified task force, TF-121, that would have jurisdiction to operate and hit in both countries. The logic was that "tracking and then capturing or killing Qaeda and Taliban leaders or fleeing members of the former Iraqi government required planning and missions not restricted by the lines on the map of a region where borders are porous." It was a further blurring of the lines between "covert" and "clandestine" missions, but Rumsfeld had determined JSOC should forge ahead. In keeping with Rumsfeld's drive to make Special Operations Forces the lead agency in the "global manhunt," the task force would be run by McRaven and overseen by McChrystal, and they would have at their disposal the full range of US intelligence assets, including what was needed from the CIA. In addition to McRaven's Navy SEALs and McChrystal's Rangers, as well as members of Delta Force, the team would also have command over paramilitaries from the CIA's Special Activities Division and support from the Activity, JSOC's signals intelligence wing.

The days of JSOC operatives being regularly put on loan to the CIA were over. Cambone's Strategic Support Branch and the Activity were coordinating the feeding of all-access intel to the task force. "This is tightening the sensor-to-shooter loop," a senior defense official told the *Washington Times*. "You have your own intelligence right with the guys who do the shooting and grabbing. All the information under one roof."

While TF-121 was given a mission to kill or capture Osama bin Laden and Saddam Hussein by the spring of 2004, Washington was increasingly focused on Iraq. Veteran intelligence officials identify this period as a turning point in the hunt for bin Laden. At a time when JSOC was asking for more resources and permissions to pursue targets inside of Pakistan and other countries, there was a tectonic shift toward making Iraq the number-one priority.

The heavy costs of that strategic redirection to the larger counter-terrorism mission were of deep concern to Lieutenant Colonel Anthony

Shaffer, a senior military intelligence officer who was CIA trained and had worked for the DIA and JSOC. Shaffer ran a task force, Stratus Ivy, that was part of a program started in the late 1990s code-named Able Danger. Utilizing what was then cutting-edge "data mining" technology, the program was operated by military intelligence and the Special Operations Command and aimed at identifying al Qaeda cells globally. Shaffer and some of his Able Danger colleagues claimed that they had uncovered several of the 9/11 hijackers a year before the attacks but that no action was taken against them. He told the 9/11 Commission he felt frustrated when the program was shut down and believed it was one of the few effective tools the United States had in the fight against al Qaeda pre-9/11. After the attacks, Shaffer volunteered for active duty and became the commander of the DIA's Operating Base Alpha, which Shaffer said "conducted clandestine antiterrorist operations" in Africa. Shaffer was running the secret program, targeting al Qaeda figures who might flee Afghanistan and seek shelter in Somalia, Liberia and other African nations. It "was the first DIA covert action of the post–Cold War era, where my officers used an African national military proxy to hunt down and kill al Qaeda terrorists," Shaffer recalled.

Like many other experienced intelligence officers who had been tracking al Qaeda prior to 9/11, Shaffer believed that the focus was finally placed correctly on destroying the terror network and killing or capturing its leaders. But then all resources were repurposed for the Iraq invasion. "I saw the Bush administration lunacy up close and personal," Shaffer said. After a year and a half of running the African ops, "I was forced to shut down Operating Base Alpha so that its resources could be used for the Iraq invasion."

Shaffer was reassigned as an intelligence planner on the DIA team that helped feed information on possible Iraqi WMD sites to the advance JSOC teams that covertly entered Iraq ahead of the invasion. "It yielded nothing," he alleged. "As we now know, no WMD were ever found." He believed that shifting the focus and resources to Iraq was a grave error that allowed bin Laden to continue operating for nearly another decade. Shaffer was eventually sent to Afghanistan, where he would clash with US military leaders over his proposals to run operations into Pakistan to target the al Qaeda leaders who were hiding there.

Beginning in 2002 and into 2003, Special Ops and CIA units in Afghanistan began shifting their resources to Iraq. By the time it was disbanded in 2003, TF-5 in Afghanistan had already lost "more than two-thirds of its fighting strength," from about 150 commandos to as few as thirty. By the winter of 2003, it was reported that "nearly half the US intelligence and commando agents who had been in Afghanistan and neighboring Pakistan were reassigned to Iraq." Saddam was code-named Black List One, and

McRaven's force intensified the hunt, scouring Iraq for him. They yanked family members, former bodyguards and aides of Saddam from their homes or hiding places and pressed them for information on his whereabouts. By late 2003, the US military's conventional commanders were growing concerned about the techniques they heard were being used by TF-121 to interrogate prisoners. It sounded a lot like the descriptions they had heard in whispers about what the CIA was doing at its black sites. "Detainees captured by TF 121 have shown injuries that caused examining medical personnel to note that 'detainee shows signs of having been beaten,'" according to a classified military report prepared for top US generals in Iraq at the time. One officer was quoted in the report as saying, "Everyone knows about it." The report alleged that some of the treatment of detainees by TF-121 could "technically" be illegal and gravely warned that the mass detention of Iraqis could fan the flames of a brewing insurgency, adding that Iraqis could perceive the United States and its allies as "gratuitous enemies."

But, just as the military was uncovering a potentially illegal and counterproductive detention program being run by TF-121, the task force achieved a major victory that would grab international headlines and win much internal praise in the Pentagon. A former bodyguard captured and interrogated by the task force had given up the location of a farm outside of Saddam's hometown, Tikrit, which he claimed the deposed Iraqi leader used as a hiding place. McRaven's men, backed by scores of troops from the 4th Infantry Division and local Iraqi militiamen, descended on the farm after cutting off all of its electricity, causing it to go completely dark. After searching the buildings on the property, they were just about to give up when a soldier spotted a crack in the floor, partially covered by a rug. Underneath, they found a styrofoam plate concealing a hole.

ON DECEMBER 14, 2003, it seemed to the Bush administration that the Iraq War had an end—and victory—in sight. That morning, Paul Bremer, flanked by General Ricardo Sanchez, walked up to a podium at a press conference in Baghdad. "Ladies and gentlemen, we got him," Bremer said, barely able to contain his smile. The "him" in this case was none other than Saddam Hussein. The deposed Iraqi leader had been found hiding in a "spider hole" inside a mud brick hovel at the farm in Adwar, near Tikrit, with a pistol. They also recovered some AKs and $750,000 in hundred-dollar bills on the farm. When a member of Delta Force spotted Saddam hiding in the hole, the Iraqi leader told him: "I am Saddam Hussein. I am the president of Iraq. I want to negotiate." The soldier reportedly shot back, "President Bush sends his regards." Moments later, McRaven's men were whisking him to a JSOC filtration site, a temporary holding facility, near the Baghdad Airport. It was called Camp NAMA. Ironically, the facility that would become Saddam's temporary home had once served as one of his torture chambers. The media was shown images of Saddam being given a medical exam at the facility, but JSOC had already been putting it to much darker uses that would never make it onto TV.

"Now it is time to look to the future, to your future of hope, to a future of reconciliation. Iraq's future, your future, has never been more full of hope. The tyrant is a prisoner," Bremer confidently declared. "The economy is moving forward. You have before you the prospect of a sovereign government in a few months." General Sanchez said the operation was a team effort, involving "coalition special operations forces," but JSOC and its commanders were not given any direct credit. Neither McChrystal nor McRaven were at the podium that day, but people in the Special Ops community say that McRaven coordinated "Operation Red Dawn." McRaven and Assistant Secretary of Defense Thomas O'Connell, a veteran of the Activity, shared a cigar outside of Saddam's cell soon after the Iraqi leader's capture. Rumsfeld announced that he believed "the eight-month-long insurgency might begin to run out of gas." In reality, the war was just beginning, particularly for McChrystal and McRaven. And the CIA knew it.

"We are seeing the establishment of an insurgency in Iraq," Robert Richer, the head of the CIA Near East Division, had told Bush during an intelligence briefing in late 2003. "That's a strong word," Rumsfeld interjected. "What do you mean? How do you define insurgency?" When Richer explained what he meant, Rumsfeld quipped, "I might disagree with you." Finally, Bush weighed in. "I don't want to read in the *New York Times* that we are facing an insurgency," he declared. "I don't want anyone in the cabinet to say it is an insurgency. I don't think we are there yet." Despite the state of denial that Rumsfeld appeared to embrace, Richer was right. Iraq, which had no ties to al Qaeda or 9/11, was becoming a magnet for jihadist groups wanting to fight—and kill—Americans.

Although much lip service was paid during the ensuing period to the presence of al Qaeda in Iraq, it was seldom pointed out that the foreign fighters came because of the US invasion. If anything, Saddam's regime and al Qaeda were enemies. And though there was undoubtedly an al Qaeda presence after the March 2003 invasion, Zarqawi and AQI, or al Qaeda in Iraq, represented a tiny portion of those attacking US occupation forces. There were disparate militias, unemployed Iraqi Army units, Shiite guerrillas and various political factions vying for local power, all of which were rising against the United States. American attacks, such as the siege of Fallujah in April 2004 and a shootout in the Shiite holy city of Najaf, combined with the broader war against the popular cleric Moqtada al Sadr, were swelling the ranks of the insurgency. Despite all the talk of sharp sectarian divides in Iraq, the US occupation was actually uniting Iraqis, Shiite and Sunni, in a common cause against their occupiers. The United States should have realized early on that its own disastrous policies were driving the chaos in Iraq. But the US war planners were intent on planting the flag of victory in Iraq by force, and that meant the insurgency had to be crushed and its leaders killed or captured. "We had this assumption that, okay, you've got this group of dead-enders, so to speak, and that if you capture Saddam Hussein, if you are able to capture or kill his sons, then you can more or less deflate the insurgency," recalled Exum, the Army Ranger. "We were so focused on getting these high value targets, quite independent of any larger or any broader strategy for how we were going to pacify Iraq. I think we ended up exacerbating a lot of the drivers of conflict and exacerbating the insurgency."

There were two wars in Iraq. One being waged by the conventional army, which was largely an occupation; the other was a war of attrition being fought by JSOC. McChrystal's men did not believe in taking orders from conventional commanders. General Sanchez, who from 2003 to 2004 was the top commander in Iraq, told me that JSOC forces would barely give his command the courtesy of informing his office of when they were going to conduct operations, even in areas where the conventional US forces were holding territory. When they did, he said, it was just to alert the conventional forces that they'd be doing a hit and to have his men stand clear. Exum recalled of the JSOC relationship with the conventional military: "Lord knows we were depending on those guys for Medivac and for Quick Reaction Force if things got really bad, but we weren't really talking to them, at the command level." The task force's operations, Exum said, were "very compartmentalized, very stove-piped." JSOC was creating a system where its intelligence operations were feeding its action and often that intelligence would not be vetted by anyone outside of the JSOC structure. The priority was to keep hitting targets. "The most serious thing is the abuse of power that that allows you to do," said Wilkerson, the former chief of staff to Powell. He continued:

You go in and you get some intelligence, and usually your intelligence comes through this apparatus too, and so you say, 'Oh, this is really good actionable intelligence. Here's "Operation Blue Thunder." Go do it.' And they go do it, and they kill 27, 30, 40 people, whatever, and they capture seven or eight. Then you find out that the intelligence was bad and you killed a bunch of innocent people and you have a bunch of innocent people on your hands, so you stuff 'em in Guantánamo.

No one ever knows anything about that. You don't have to prove to anyone that you did right. You did it all in secret, so you just go to the next operation. You say, 'Chalk that one up to experience,' and you go to the next operation. And, believe me, that happened.

Exum recalled hunting Izzat Ibrahim al Douri, one of Saddam's senior military commanders, who had received the designation as the King of Clubs in the High Value Target deck of cards. They got a tip that Douri was in a particular house and conducted a night raid. As they began the raid, Exum's Ranger team came under fire from two men. His team returned fire and gunned the men down. "We found out later that we were on two weeks old intelligence," he remembered. "We killed them and, you know, we kind of realized later that these guys were just out guarding the neighborhood generator." The men, Exum speculated, likely thought the Rangers were thieves. "Now, I didn't lose any sleep over it, because these guys were shooting at me, but nonetheless, you start thinking about it from a strategic perspective, that's a loss."

McChrystal's forces realized quickly that the Iraqi resistance was growing, not shrinking, even as various key members of the fallen Baath regime were taken out. McChrystal and his deputy, Mike Flynn, began assessing the state of the insurgency. At the time, JSOC had been "tailored down to a relatively small size in the months following the initial invasion," McChrystal recalled. "We found a growing threat from multiple sources—but particularly from al Qaeda in Iraq. We began a review of our enemy, and of ourselves. Neither was easy to understand." From JSOC's small base outside of Baghdad, McChrystal and his team began mapping out the intel they had on AQI, using white dry-erase boards. "Like all too many military forces in history, we initially saw our enemy as we viewed ourselves," McChrystal later wrote in an article for *Foreign Policy:*

Composed largely of foreign mujahideen and with an overall allegiance to Osama bin Laden but controlled inside Iraq by the Jordanian Abu Musab al Zarqawi, AQI was responsible for an extremely violent campaign of attacks on coalition forces, the Iraqi government, and Iraqi Shiites. Its stated aim was to splinter the new Iraq and ultimately establish an Islamic caliphate. By habit, we started mapping the organization in a traditional military structure, with tiers and rows. At the top was Zarqawi, below him a cascade of lieutenants and foot soldiers. But the closer we looked, the more the model didn't hold. Al Qaeda in Iraq's lieutenants did not wait for memos from their superiors, much less orders from bin Laden. Decisions were not centralized, but were made quickly and communicated laterally across the organization. Zarqawi's fighters were adapted to the areas they haunted, like Fallujah and Qaim in Iraq's western Anbar province, and yet through modern technology were closely linked to the rest of the province and country. Money, propaganda, and information flowed at alarming rates, allowing for powerful, nimble coordination. We would watch their tactics change (from rocket attacks to suicide bombings, for example) nearly simultaneously in disparate cities. It was a deadly choreography achieved with a constantly changing, often unrecognizable structure.

The insurgency was far more complex than those in Washington or at the Pentagon were letting on. But the decision to move ahead with targeting any and all insurgents went unchanged. Instead of stepping back, they doubled down. "If you see a fledgling insurgency start to develop, then it doesn't take a genius to realize that by dragging people out of their homes in the middle of the night, by doing so in such a way that you are not communicating to the neighbors...why this person is being dragged out of their home in the middle of the night, it's not hard to see how this could inflame tensions, how this could actually exacerbate drivers of conflict," said Exum. "I think that that's probably what happened in 2003."

That's not how Rumsfeld saw it. He wanted the insurgency obliterated and its leadership decapitated. McChrystal was left to figure out a system for achieving those goals. He began building up a structure to obtain and share information that could be used to facilitate a major expansion of house raids and targeted killing operations. "It became increasingly clear— often from intercepted communications or the accounts of insurgents we had captured—that our enemy was a constellation of fighters organized not by rank but on the basis of relationships and acquaintances, reputation and fame," McChrystal remembered. "We realized we had to have the rapid ability to detect nuanced changes, whether the emergence of new personalities and alliances or sudden changes in tactics." JSOC "had to process that new information in real time—so we could act on it," he asserted. "A stream of hot cinders was falling everywhere around us, and we had to see them, catch those we could, and react instantly to those we had missed that were starting to set the ground on fire."

The HVT Task Force was broken down into four subunits: Task Force West, whose main unit was a SEAL Team 6 squadron, with support from Rangers; Task Force Central, made up of a Delta squadron with support from Rangers; Task Force North, a Ranger battalion with a group of Deltas; and Task Force Black, a British SAS saber squadron, with British paratroopers. Each of these subunits could be supplemented by a Special Forces company specializing in "direct action" missions. The pace of the raids increased with intelligence gained from one raid leading to two or three others. "General McChrystal and Mike Flynn, his intelligence deputy, really invigorated that Task Force and did some pretty innovative things," recalled Exum. "In the past, in large part because of the experience in Mogadishu in 1993, the iron rule was, you don't go anywhere unless you've got company of Army Rangers in reserve. Well, under McChrystal, nobody was in reserve. I mean, people were hitting targets every single night, in a very dispersed way. You had Ranger platoons [conducting operations] that previously only Tier One Special Mission Units would be doing."

McChrystal and Flynn's fusion approach to gathering intelligence relied on an infrastructure for targeting known by the acronym F3EA: Find, Fix, Finish, Exploit, and Analyze. "The idea was to combine analysts who found the enemy (through intelligence, surveillance, and reconnaissance); drone operators who fixed the target; combat teams who finished the target by capturing or killing him; specialists who exploited the intelligence the raid yielded, such as cell phones, maps, and detainees; and the intelligence analysts who turned this raw information into usable knowledge," wrote McChrystal. "By doing this, we speeded up the cycle for a counterterrorism operation, gleaning valuable insights in hours, not days."

Part of McChrystal and Flynn's strategy for targeting the insurgency revolved around technology, while the other depended on taking prisoners and extracting information from them as quickly as possible.

Strategically, Flynn and McChrystal were hailed as geniuses. But the whole system was ultimately dependent on human intelligence, not technology. And with an incredibly diverse spectrum of insurgents attacking the occupation forces, that was a major challenge. It was this urgent need for HUMINT and the pressure from the White House and Pentagon to produce results to crush the insurgency (which they had declared did not exist) that would lead to a brutal regime of abuse and torture of detainees held by JSOC. Unsatisfied with the pace of interrogations being conducted by the CIA and other US agencies in the early stages of the Global War on Terror, Rumsfeld and Cambone developed a parallel rendition and detention program to the CIA black sites authorized under Greystone. The new Special Access Program went by various code names, including Copper Green, Matchbox and Footprint. With only some two hundred people read into the Special Access Program (SAP), the highly classified program put Stephen Cambone's private intel shop in the Pentagon on steroids. "They weren't getting anything substantive from the detainees in Iraq" early on in the invasion, a former senior intelligence official told Seymour Hersh.

"No names. Nothing that they could hang their hat on. Cambone says, 'I've got to crack this thing and I'm tired of working through the normal chain of command. I've got this apparatus set up—the black special-access program—and I'm going in hot.' So he pulls the switch, and the electricity begins flowing."

Although it got its major kick-start in Iraq, Copper Green predated the 2003 invasion and the intent was for it to go global. The program was "Rumsfeld's answer to the CIA death squads envisioned by Cofer Black," reported investigative journalist Jane Mayer. "Members of the squads were given aliases, dead mail drops, and unmarked clothing. They worked in a loose structure outside the Pentagon's usually rigid chain of command." Hersh, who first reported the existence of Copper Green in the *New Yorker*, interviewed several former high-ranking intelligence and military officials about the program. "We're not going to read more people than necessary into our heart of darkness," a former high-level intelligence official told Hersh. "The rules are 'Grab whom you must. Do what you want.'"

When Lieutenant Colonel Shaffer was in Afghanistan, he saw the early stages of Copper Green. It was "authorized," he said, "but a lot of us felt it wasn't appropriate and just wasn't right." When he visited the task force's facility in Afghanistan, Shaffer said he was "blown away—and not in a good way—by what I saw." He described how the building had been "completely gutted. Rooms had been converted into holding cells or open areas, framed in wood and steel." It was "nothing like the interrogation areas I was familiar with." The task force's Copper Green interrogation rooms in Afghanistan, he said, "had holding points for a prisoner's arms and legs. They were designed for prisoners to be shackled and held in stress positions to maximize discomfort and pain." "I'd been led into a top-secret interrogation 'system' authorized by my boss at the time, Secretary of Defense Donald Rumsfeld, as well as Stephen Cambone, undersecretary of defense for intelligence, permitting highly coercive interrogation techniques on detained personnel in Afghanistan." As he stood in "the giant facility," Shaffer recalled, "I could feel a sense of tension in the air—palpable and raw—like walking on a beach before a hurricane is about to hit." The world knew about Guantánamo and would soon come to know the name Abu Ghraib. Shocking photos would leak into the media that portrayed barking dogs menacing cowering prisoners, pyramids of naked detainees positioned behind smiling guards, the eerie image of a hooded man, standing arms outstretched in a crucifix pose, on a box. The wires attached to his fingers, he was told, would electrocute him if he lost balance and fell. Abu Ghraib would be infamous the world over, but almost no one ever talked about Camp NAMA.

# 14  "No Blood, No Foul"

IRAQ, 2003–2004—In the first year of the Iraq War, a lot of JSOC's dirty business went down in a small cluster of buildings nestled in the corner of a Saddam-era military base near the Baghdad International Airport. US Special Operations Forces had taken over the base soon after the March 2003 invasion of Iraq and erected a fence around the cluster of buildings that made up Camp NAMA. At the center of the small compound, surrounded by barbed wire, was the Battlefield Interrogation Facility (BIF).

Members of the JSOC Task Force resided at NAMA, but it was hardly just a dormitory. This task force went by various code names, and the names were frequently changed for operational security and to make investigating it difficult. At various times, it was known as Task Force 20, Task Force 121, Task Force 6-26, Task Force 714 and Task Force 145. Suspected insurgents snatched in house raids or taken off the streets of Iraq cities were brought to NAMA and placed in one of two structures: "Motel 6" was a plywood barracks; "Hotel California" was an actual cellblock that a few months earlier had been used by Saddam's regime as a prison. The acronym NAMA stood for "Nasty-Ass Military Area." Its motto, as advertised in posters throughout the camp, was "No Blood, No Foul." A Defense Department official said it was a play on a task force adage: "If you don't make them bleed, they can't prosecute for it."

To develop their approach to interrogating prisoners they would snatch in Iraq, the Special Mission Units that made up the HVT Task Force worked from a copy of the interrogation standard operating procedure (SOP) that was developed while McChrystal was running the detention and interrogation operations in Afghanistan as part of CJTF 180. According to a Senate Armed Services Committee investigation conducted years later, the Iraq Task Force simply "changed the letterhead, and adopted the SOP verbatim." The SOP "included stress positions, sleep deprivation, and the use of dogs." The regime of torture techniques, built up on the demands from Rumsfeld, Cheney and their posses for more results in interrogations, was spreading.

The people taken to NAMA were not given rights as prisoners of war

(POWs). They were classified as unlawful combatants. They would not see lawyers, be visited by the Red Cross or be charged with any crimes. Rumsfeld had issued guidelines to JSOC for its own "black" detainee program, which was off-limits to the conventional military. The task force could hold prisoners for ninety days without giving them anything resembling rights or transferring them to above-board military prisons. In effect, this meant that the task force had free rein over the prisoners for three months to squeeze out any information they might have held. Prisoners were often subjected to "beatings, exposure to extreme cold, threats of death, humiliation, and various forms of psychological abuse or torture," according to Human Rights Watch. Access to NAMA was denied to the Red Cross, lawyers and family members. According to a former interrogator at NAMA, a colonel told him that "he had this directly from General McChrystal and the Pentagon that there's no way that the Red Cross could get in." Similarly, army investigators would not be allowed to set foot in Camp NAMA. The task force members were told that such moves were "very necessary for the efficacy of the operation, and we don't want people to know even our name, of the unit."

When Colonel Stuart Herrington was deployed by Major General Barbara Fast to investigate conditions at detention facilities and intelligence operations in Iraq in December 2003, he was rebuffed by the task force at NAMA.

So secretive was NAMA that when General Geoffrey Miller, the former commander of the Guantánamo Bay prison, tried to visit, he was not permitted to enter the camp until he took his request all the way up the chain of command. There was a special ID to get into Camp NAMA, and the only people permitted to enter without it were prisoners, shackled and hooded. Ironically, even though NAMA personnel didn't want General Miller in their camp, the general seemed to be on their side. During that trip to Iraq, while touring other facilities including Abu Ghraib, Miller reportedly chastised US military prison administrators for "running a country club," charging they were being too lenient on detainees. Miller suggested they "GTMO-ize" their detention facilities and, according to military officials who met with the "GTMO team," they discussed how using dogs was "effective in doing interrogations with Arabs" because of "Arabs being fearful of dogs."

The task force at NAMA was run by JSOC, but it was built by pulling personnel from a variety of agencies and units. There were CIA and DIA interrogators, air force interrogators, and a variety of analysts and guards. "They told us we can't tell our chain of command about who works here or what [the task force] does. You're completely shut off. You can only discuss it amongst yourselves. That's what they told us from the very first day," recalled an interrogator who worked at Camp NAMA in 2003–2004. "It was pretty loose as far as chain of command goes. There was no rank within the task force....We called the colonel by his first name, called the sergeant major by his first name....I couldn't tell you the sergeant major's last name if I tried. Same with the colonel. When you asked somebody their name they don't offer up the last name....The consensus was, more often than not, when they gave you their name it probably wasn't their real name anyway."

Many of the members of the task force would grow long beards and seemed eager to make themselves look as frightening or intimidating as possible. "This is the dark side of the forces. This is the realm where you have essentially a cadre of folks who have a great deal of freedom. The folks that get to this level are treated with a certain amount of deference," Lieutenant Colonel Anthony Shaffer told me. "The culture is that where everybody essentially goes by their first name, no matter what rank you are, and the basic bottom line is, when you get to that level you just know what you need to do, and there's no second guessing, there is no room for being babied."

Back at the State Department, Wilkerson watched as this parallel detention system was being built up by Rumsfeld and Cheney and believed they used the task force specifically to avoid any scrutiny. "There is no oversight and when there's no oversight you're all-powerful. And when you know there's no oversight, then you know that you can pretty much do whatever you want to do," he told me. "We forget that when we create these special operating units, we create at least within a percentage of them—and this percentage is heightened incredibly in the special operations forces—you've got people who are killing instruments. That's what they are. That's what they're honed and trained to be, is killing instruments. When you allow no oversight of them, and you allow them to repeat operations, over and over and over again, with no oversight, then you allow them to instinctually gain the knowledge that almost anything goes. Then, almost anything is going to go."

"Rather than going through the local command, the Baghdad command, up to CENTCOM and then back to the Pentagon, there seemed to have been some sort of an express elevator, from JSOC operations on the ground, straight back to the Undersecretary of Defense for Intelligence [Cambone], and then to the Secretary of Defense. So it was going straight back to Washington—very, very high levels," charged Scott Horton, a human rights attorney who, as president of the New York City Bar Association's Committee on International Human Rights, investigated the US torture program and JSOC's role in it. "We know that a number of the normal rules that had applied, concerning the way that detention operations went forward, and the way interrogation operations went forward, were not being applied to JSOC. They had their own rules. So there were Special Access Programs and we know that these operations were associated with a lot of brutality, people being beaten up, being severely mistreated. So often as not, the torture cases and the serious abuse cases were far more frequently linked to JSOC operations than anything else."

When JSOC first deployed to Iraq to lead the hunt for WMDs and Saddam's top leadership, the prisoners they took early on were prioritized in terms of what, if any, intelligence or information they may have possessed that would produce results to support either of those missions. The harsh interrogation methods that were being refined in black sites and in Afghanistan were to be unleashed in Iraq. "There were two reasons why these interrogations were so persistent, and why extreme methods were used," said a former senior intelligence official. "The main one is that everyone was worried about some kind of follow-up attack [after 9/11]. But for most of 2002 and into 2003, Cheney and Rumsfeld, especially, were also demanding proof of the links between al Qaida and Iraq that [former Iraqi exile leader Ahmed] Chalabi and others had told them were there."

The Bush administration also wanted to find WMDs and to retroactively prove that its claims of Iraq possessing them were true. Rowan Scarborough, a conservative military journalist who wrote two books for which he received extensive access to Rumsfeld and his team, recounted how furious Rumsfeld would become each day when he was briefed on the lack of WMDs in Iraq. "Each morning, the crisis action team had to report that another location was a bust. Rumsfeld grew angrier and angrier. One officer quoted him as saying, 'They must be there!' At one briefing, he picked up the briefing slides and tossed them back at the briefers," according to Scarborough. Horton added: "A lot of this intelligence gathering operation, at the outset...was driven by a need to produce information that would justify [the war]. And I think that the use of torture was authorized largely because of an expectation that that would produce results. I don't think there was ever any expectation that it was going to produce the truth, but it would produce people saying what they wanted them to say, that would somehow back this up."

But as the months went on in Iraq and the WMD and al Qaeda claims fell apart, the focus of the interrogations began shifting to crushing the insurgency. The list of targets and suspects quickly grew from the original deck of cards representing the Saddam regime to a potentially infinite catalog of names. "You saw the French do this in Algeria and you saw the Americans do this in 2003 in Iraq," recalled Exum, who was deployed to Iraq at the time. "You start out with a target list, and maybe you've got 50 guys on it, maybe you've got 200 guys on it, but you can work your way through those 50 or 200 guys, and then suddenly at the end of that target list you've got a new target list of 3,000 people on it."

McChrystal expanded JSOC's role in detainee operations, but NAMA was up and running before he set foot in Iraq. The CIA, which inflicted more than its share of dirty deeds on prisoners, had become so shocked at the torture at NAMA that it withdrew its interrogators from the base in August 2003, though it continued to provide intelligence to the task force. In fact, the month before McChrystal assumed command at JSOC, an army investigator, as well as intelligence and law enforcement officials, were already voicing their warnings about detainee abuse, suggesting that the harsh techniques were being employed by JSOC. In September 2003, after a request from the "commander of the Special Mission Unit Task Force," US military SERE (Survival, Evasion, Resistance and Escape) instructors, whose official job was to prepare US service members to endure torture and captivity, arrived at Camp NAMA.

The JSOC Task Force did not categorize Camp NAMA as a prison but rather as a "filtration site" where intelligence was being obtained. This gave cover for all the dirty activity and the secrecy that shrouded it. The Special Access Program that the task force operated under "would be given a mission and might be authorized to use all sorts of special practices, that not only deviate from normal military practices, but might actually violate military law, and military policy, and this would be done by means of a Special Access Program, that would usually come from the Undersecretary of Defense for Intelligence [Stephen Cambone]. There's very clearly some criminal conduct," said Horton, the human rights lawyer. "And yet, here in this special JSOC regime, this was being authorized—being incited—by officers who were running the camp, who were supposed to be prohibiting this kind of conduct."

The Battlefield Interrogation Facility at NAMA had four interrogation rooms and a medical screening room, where Saddam was first processed after his capture. Furnished with rugs, prayer mats, couches, tables and chairs, the "Soft Room" was where cooperative and high-ranking detainees were brought for questioning—and tea. The Blue and Red (or Wood) rooms were larger (about six by ten feet), rectangular and plain; the Blue Room had a coat of blue paint over the plywood walls. These rooms were used for medium-intensity interrogations, reportedly employing techniques approved by the US Army Field Manual. The Black Room was preserved from its days as a torture chamber under Saddam and, for good measure, the task

force kept the meat hooks that hung from the ceiling during the Iraqi dictator's reign of terror in place for their use. The Black Room was the largest
room—approximately twelve by twelve feet. It was here that JSOC would
perform its harshest interrogations.

Detainees were moved between rooms, depending on their cooperation
with the interrogators. "We would do that to show him if you tell us what
we want to hear, then this is the treatment that you'll get," recalled "Jeff
Perry," the pseudonym of a former interrogator at NAMA who provided
eyewitness testimony on his experiences at NAMA to Human Rights
Watch. "If you don't, then this is the treatment that you'll get. So there
was a lot of that, going back and forth between the rooms." If a prisoner
was believed to have info on Zarqawi, he would be sent to the Black Room.
It would also be used if "the interrogator thinks he's being lied to or he's not
going to get anywhere with just talking to him," Perry recalled. "We would
march with him into the black room." It would also be used if interrogators
were "angry at [a detainee] and want[ed] to punish him for some reason."

Inside the Black Room, the full-spectrum of SERE tactics were unleashed
on detainees, along with a slew of medieval freestyle techniques. "It was
painted black floor to ceiling. The door was black, everything was black,"
recalled Perry. "It had speakers in the corners, all four corners, up at the
ceiling. It had a small table in one of the corners, and maybe some chairs.
But usually in the black room nobody was sitting down. It was standing,
stress positions." The interrogations there often incorporated extremely
loud music, strobe lights, beatings, environmental and temperature manipulation, sleep deprivation, twenty-hour interrogation sessions, water
and stress positions, and personal, often sexual, humiliation. The forced
nudity of prisoners was not uncommon. Almost any act was permissible
against the detainees as long as it complied with the "No Blood, No Foul"
motto. But, eventually, even blood was okay.

One former prisoner—the son of one of Saddam's bodyguards—said he
was made to strip, was punched repeatedly in the spine until he fainted, was
doused with cold water and forced to stand in front of the air-conditioner
and kicked in the stomach until he vomited. Prisoners held at other
facilities also described heinous acts committed against them by interrogators and guards, including sodomizing detainees with foreign objects,
beating them, forcing water up their rectums and using extreme dietary
manipulation—nothing but bread and water for more than two weeks in
one case.

Members of the task force would beat prisoners with rifle butts and spit
in their faces. One member of the task force reported that he had heard
interrogators "beating the shit out of the detainee." According to a former

interrogator with the task force, one of his colleagues was "reprimanded and assigned to desk duty because he pissed in a bottle and gave it to a detainee to drink." Members of the task force would also interrupt non-harsh interrogations and begin slapping or beating detainees. On at least one occasion, they abducted the wife of a suspected insurgent being hunted by the task force "to leverage the primary target's surrender." The woman was a twenty-eight-year-old mother of three who was still nursing her six-month-old baby. After interviewing numerous members of the task force at NAMA, Human Rights Watch concluded, "the abuses appear to have been part of a regularized process of detainee abuse—'standard operating procedure.'"

Steven Kleinman, at the time a lieutenant colonel in the air force, arrived at Camp NAMA in early September 2003, just as McChrystal was taking over as commander of JSOC. Kleinman was a veteran interrogator and an air force SERE instructor. When he was first dispatched to Iraq, he believed his job was to observe the interrogations at the camp and analyze how they could be done more effectively. A year earlier, Kleinman had investigated the program at Guantánamo and found "fundamental systemic problems" that he believed had undermined the stated goals of the interrogations. But the task force at NAMA had different plans. They told Kleinman they were having trouble getting actionable or reliable intelligence from their prisoners, and they wanted Kleinman and his SERE colleagues to help them apply SERE tactics to the interrogations. In essence, they wanted Kleinman and his colleagues to use the very torture tactics against detainees that they had taught US military personnel to resist.

Kleinman agreed that the intel was a mess, but he did not believe it was because the interrogations were not harsh enough. He described a chaotic situation lacking any effective screening of new detainees, with some prisoners appearing to have no intelligence value. But the task force wanted Kleinman and his colleagues to participate in interrogations, and eventually, they were ordered to do so. Kleinman soon found himself in the Black Room at NAMA. "I walked into the interrogation room, all painted in black with [a] spotlight on the detainee. Behind the detainee was a military guard...with a[n] iron bar...slapping it in his hand," Kleinman recalled. "The interrogator was sitting in a chair. The interpreter was to his left... and the detainee was on his knees.... A question was asked by the interrogator, interpreted, the response came back and, upon interpretation, the detainee would be slapped across the face.... And that continued with every question and every response. I asked my colleagues how long this had been going on, specifically the slapping, they said approximately 30 minutes."

Kleinman said he considered the tactics used on the prisoner to be "di-

rect violations of the Geneva Conventions and [actions that] could constitute a war crime." Kleinman says he told the commander of the Special
Mission Unit at NAMA that his force was engaged in "unlawful" conduct
and systematic violations of the Geneva Convention. It had no impact on
the commander or Kleinman's other JPRA/SERE colleagues. Kleinman said
his superior told him that they had been "cleared hot to use SERE methods" in interrogations. Kleinman said he believed that was an "unlawful
order," adding that he "wasn't going to have any involvement with it, and
I didn't think that they should either." He was told that the prisoners were
not entitled to Geneva Convention protection because they were "unlawful combatants." The torture continued.

Kleinman also recalled a detainee whom the task force was trying to
break. His colleagues decided to make the man believe he was being released and actually drove him to a bus stop. Moments later, they snatched
him again and returned him to NAMA. The man "was literally carried by
two of the guards into the bunker struggling against them. He was taken
down there," Kleinman said. His two SERE colleagues "took over from
that point.... They ripped his [clothing] off—not cut—they ripped it off...
ripped off his underwear, took his shoes, they'd hooded him already, then
they—they had shackled him by the wrist and ankles—being screamed at
the entire time in his ear in English about essentially...what a poor speci-
men of human that he was.... And then the orders were given that he was
to stand in that position for 12 hours no matter how much he asked for
help, no matter how much he pleaded, unless he passed out, the guards
were not to respond to any requests for help."

Despite Kleinman's objection to SERE tactics being expanded at NAMA,
the task force and Kleinman's bosses forged ahead. In September 2003,
they began developing a CONOP, or "Concept of Operations," for HVT
"exploitation" for the camp. Similar to the "Exploitation Draft Plan" that
SERE's chief psychologist, Dr. Bruce Jessen, had developed a year earlier for
use in Afghanistan, it called for taking enemy torture tactics used to train
US forces and reverse-engineering them. The CONOP called for "tailoring
detainee punishment consequences to maximize cultural undesirability."
Less than a month after he arrived, Kleinman was pulled out of NAMA, in
the words of the Pentagon inspector general, because it "became apparent
that friction was developing" between the task force and Kleinman. Kleinman later told the US Senate that "friction" was an understatement and
that he believed his life was being threatened by members of the task force
in retaliation for his dissent. One task force member, he said, sharpened a
knife while telling Kleinman to "sleep lightly" because the task force does
not "coddl[e] terrorists."

Another source of torture at NAMA was that members of the HVT Task

Force responsible for hunting people would continue to have access to the prisoners they seized. According to Major General Miller, at times the task force at NAMA would use special operators as interrogators. That created scenarios where the rage from the battlefield would spill over into interrogations, even after the prisoner was disarmed and in custody. Malcolm Nance, the former SERE instructor, told me, "Captives captured on the battlefield, first thing you're going to learn is the guy that is capturing you is going to be very upset that you just lost the fire fight to him, and you killed some of his buddies so be prepared for having an ass whipping. It's just that simple." It becomes even worse when the soldiers who did the assault then have access to those prisoners for days on end. "It's army doctrine that when you take a prisoner, one of the things you do is secure that prisoner and then you speed him to the rear. You get him out of the hands of the unit that took him," recalled an army officer of his experience at a different filtration site. "Well, we didn't do that. We'd keep them at our holding facility for I think it was up to seventy-two hours. Then we would place him under the guard of soldiers he had just been trying to kill." The officer described one such incident where a detainee who was suspected of having killed a US soldier had his leg whacked by one of the soldier's comrades with a baseball bat.

Perry recalled an incident soon after he arrived at NAMA involving an alleged financier of Zarqawi who was taken to the camp. The man was allegedly refusing to give any information to his interrogators. "I had no part in this interrogation, I was just observing....There was kind of a garden-like area with dirt and mud and a hose out there," Perry recalled, adding:

> He was stripped naked, put in the mud and sprayed with the hose, with very cold hoses, in February. At night it was very cold. They sprayed the cold hose and he was completely naked in the mud, you know, and everything. [Then] he was taken out of the mud and put next to an air conditioner. It was extremely cold, freezing, and he was put back in the mud and sprayed. This happened all night. Everybody knew about it. People walked in, the sergeant major and so forth, everybody knew what was going on, and I was just one of them, kind of walking back and forth seeing [that] this is how they do things.

Perry also recalled watching a British SAS officer—not authorized to conduct any kind of interrogation—mercilessly beat a detainee until he and another soldier intervened. As early as the summer of 2003, the CIA's Baghdad Station was complaining to Langley that Special Operations troops were being too aggressive with detainees. The CIA's general counsel, Scott Muller, said that the techniques being used at NAMA were "more aggressive" than those the CIA was using.

The task force would fly new detainees to NAMA using unmarked helicopters. The prisoners were clad in blue jumpsuits, and during their journey, they would have blacked-out goggles placed over their eyes. Interrogators at NAMA used an "authorization template" on their computers to check off which harsh interrogation techniques they intended to use on detainees. The request to use harsh interrogation would, in theory, need approval from higher-ups. "I never saw a sheet that wasn't signed. It would be signed off by the commander, whoever that was," recalled Perry. "He would sign off on that every time it was done." Another interrogator added that "every harsh interrogation [was] approved by the J2 [the unit's chief intelligence officer] of the TF and the Medical prior to its execution." Perry continued: "Some interrogators would go and use these techniques without typing up one of those things just because it was a hassle, or he didn't want to do it and knew it was going to be approved anyway, and you're not gonna get in that much trouble if you get caught doing one of these things without a signature."

When Perry and a handful of colleagues began expressing their discomfort with the events at NAMA to their commanders, those commanders would call in military Judge Advocate General's Corps (JAG) lawyers, who lectured the dissenters on the distinction between unlawful enemy combatants and POWs, and the legal loopholes therein. "Within a couple hours a team of two JAG officers, JAG lawyers, came and gave us a couple hours slide show on why this is necessary, why this is legal, they're enemy combatants, they're not POWs, and so we can do all this stuff to them and so forth," Perry recalled. "I mean they had this two hour slide show all prepared, and they came in and gave it to us and they stopped interrogations for it. It was a PowerPoint." The lawyers, Perry alleged, said that "we didn't have to abide by the Geneva Conventions, because these people weren't POWs." Perry said he thought the lawyers "just came in and said whatever they had to say to patch it up and continue with the war."

All task force personnel were required to sign nondisclosure agreements. Interrogators were often told that the White House and Rumsfeld were watching their operations closely. Perry stated that he saw McChrystal at NAMA on more than one occasion. The personnel at NAMA, he alleged, were given the impression that the techniques had been approved from on high because they "were only like a few steps away in the chain of command from the Pentagon." The task force commanders, he said, would tell the interrogators that the White House or Pentagon had been directly briefed on their progress, particularly when it came to intel on Zarqawi. The commanders would tell them: "Rumsfeld was informed, such and such a report is on Rumsfeld's desk this morning, read by Secdef." He added, "It's a big morale booster for people working 14 hour days. Hey, we got to the White House!" Malcolm Nance told me, "When you have the President of the United States setting the pace, well you're gonna get Abu Ghraib, you are going to get abuse. You've got the intelligence community throwing the book out to the point where, in their world, no one was ever subjected to 'abuse' by the US Armed Forces."

Major General Keith Dayton, the commander of the Iraq Survey Group, which was established in June 2003 to coordinate the hunt for WMDs, described the situation at NAMA as "a disaster waiting to happen," warning the Pentagon's inspector general that he needed to "slam some rules on this place right away to basically keep ourselves from getting in trouble and make sure these people are treated properly." Dayton described cases of prisoners transferred to conventional military custody from the task force with signs of being "badly burned," having two black eyes, "back almost broken," "multiple contusions on his face." Soldiers and personnel from Camp Cropper (near Camp NAMA) stated under oath that detainees arrested and interrogated by the task force and SEAL Team 5 had been delivered to Camp Cropper showing obvious signs of abuse.

There are at least two known cases of Iraqis dying immediately after being transferred from the custody of task force Navy SEAL commandos. After what a SEAL team described as a "struggle," on April 5, 2004, the SEALs delivered prisoner Fashad Mohammad to a conventional base, where he was interrogated and then allowed to sleep, at which point he became unresponsive and later died. The medical examiner's report on his death, which was released under the Freedom of Information Act, said that Mohammad "died in U.S. custody approximately 72 hours after being apprehended. By report, physical force was required during his initial apprehension during a raid. During his confinement, he was hooded, sleep deprived, and subjected to hot and cold environmental conditions, including the use of cold water on his body and hood." Although the report described "multiple minor injuries, abrasions and contusions" and "blunt force trauma and positional asphyxia," it concluded that the cause of death was "undetermined." On November 4, 2003, Manadel al Jamadi died at Abu Ghraib prison, amid allegations that he had been beaten to death by members of SEAL Team 7. One team member was court-martialed but was ultimately acquitted—and nobody was charged with homicide.

By December 2003, a confidential Pentagon memo warned, "It seems clear that" the task force "needs to be reined in with respect to its treatment of detainees." But the torture and abuse at NAMA continued, particularly if a detainee was believed to have any information about Zarqawi or his network. All of the interrogations were aimed at extracting intel that would lead to the next raid, the next strike and the next capture or kill. In an "operations center" near NAMA, "task force analysts pored over intelligence collected from spies, detainees and remotely piloted Predator surveillance aircraft, to piece together clues to aid soldiers on their raids," the *New York Times* reported. "Twice daily at noon and midnight military interrogators and their supervisors met with officials from the C.I.A., F.B.I. and allied military units to review operations and new intelligence."

In early 2004, the International Committee of the Red Cross issued a scathing report on the mass arrests of Iraqis. It asserted that "over a hundred 'high value detainees' have been held for nearly 23 hours a day in strict solitary confinement in small concrete cells devoid of daylight" at a "High Value Detainees" section at the Baghdad Airport. Without specifically singling out the task force, the report described the raids that led to arrests of scores of Iraqis. Soldiers would burst into homes

> usually after dark, breaking down doors, waking up residents roughly, yelling orders, forcing family members into one room under military guard while searching the rest of the house and further breaking doors, cabinets and other property. They arrested suspects, tying their hands in the back with flexi-cuffs, hooding them, and taking them away. Sometimes they arrested all adult males present in a house, including elderly, handicapped and sick people. Treatment often included pushing people around, insulting, taking aim with rifles, punching and kicking and striking with rifles. Individuals were often led away in whatever they happened to be wearing at the time of arrest—sometimes in pyjamas or underwear—and were denied the opportunity to gather a few essential belongings, such as clothing, hygiene items, medicine or eyeglasses.

The report cited "military intelligence officers" who told the Red Cross "that in their estimate between 70% and 90% of the persons deprived of their liberty in Iraq had been arrested by mistake." The Red Cross findings echoed those of the classified military report in late 2003, which warned that the task force's abuse of detainees combined with the mass arrests of Iraqis gave the impression that the United States and its allies were acting like "gratuitous enemies" of the Iraqi people.

When the military finally was permitted to investigate NAMA, its agents received threats from personnel at the camp, while DIA interrogators had their vehicle keys confiscated and were "ordered" not to discuss what they had seen with anyone. On June 25, 2004, Vice Admiral Lowell Jacoby, then director of the DIA, sent a two-page memo to Stephen Cambone with a list of complaints from DIA personnel at Camp NAMA. One interrogator had his photos confiscated after taking pictures of injured detainees, and others complained that task force commandos forbade them from leaving the camp without permission, even for a haircut, and from talking to outsiders; they threatened them and screened their e-mails. Despite these efforts at suppression, news of detainee abuse at NAMA made its way up the ranks, and eventually to lawmakers.

In 2004, under pressure from a handful of lawmakers, Stephen Cambone, whose SSB was actually enabling the harsh interrogation ops at NAMA, scribbled a handwritten letter to his deputy, Lieutenant General Boykin. Dated June 26, 2004, it read, "Get to the bottom of this immediately. This is not acceptable. In particular, I want to know if this is part of a pattern of behavior by TF 6-26." An aide to Boykin said, "At the time [Boykin] told Mr. Cambone he had found no pattern of misconduct with the task force."

Despite all the whistleblowers' reports, an official US military report on alleged abuses at NAMA and other facilities concluded that the prisoners' descriptions of torture were lies. Accusations of wrongdoing and misconduct by members of the task force were handled in-house rather than through traditional military disciplinary procedures. In one case, when an Army Criminal Investigations Division (CID) agent attempted to investigate a member of the task force for abusing a detainee, it was quashed because, in the words of the CID, "the subject of this investigation is a member of TF 6-26" and the task force's own security officer "has accepted investigative jurisdiction in this matter."

In all, some thirty-four task force members would be "disciplined" for misconduct, and at least eleven members were removed from the unit. In 2006, Human Rights Watch reported that "a small number of task force members have been administratively disciplined, but not court-martialed. Five Army Rangers associated with the task force were reportedly court-martialed for abuses they carried out against detainees," but "the sentences were all six months or less. There are no indications that officers up the chain of command [were] held accountable, despite serious questions about officers' criminal culpability."

An air force interrogator who worked with the JSOC task force hunting Zarqawi told me that he "did not see any form of oversight for the kill or capture campaign." He said he witnessed and stopped several cases of abuse, which he communicated up the chain of command. "With the cases in which I reported abuses, there was no accountability. In one case, an interrogator was merely recalled from a remote location and then put right back to work at the main prison. The atmosphere was such that secrecy was the priority." He added, "My general impression is that occasional law-breaking would be tolerated as long as it never got out to the press."

The abuse and torture at Camp NAMA was not an anomaly, but rather a model. When the US government began probing how the shocking horrors meted out against prisoners at Abu Ghraib happened, how it all began, the investigation revealed that those running the prison had looked to the example set at Camp NAMA, Guantánamo and at Bagram in Afghanistan. When Abu Ghraib prison was taken over by US forces and converted from a Saddam-era prison and torture chamber into a US-run gulag, the Americans who set it up simply took the task force's standard operating procedures and, once again, changed the letterhead and implemented them.

The Abu Ghraib torture scandal broke wide open in April 2004, when major news organizations released photos showing systematic abuse, humiliation and torture of prisoners being held at the prison by the US military. As more photos became public, they showed naked prisoners stacked in pyramids, angry dogs growling over shuddering prisoners, mock executions. When Major General Antonio Taguba eventually investigated, he found documentary evidence of acts even worse than those depicted in the published photos, but the White House chalked up the torture and abuse to a few "bad apples," and the public would never see the full extent of the atrocities committed at Abu Ghraib.

The horrors of the US-run prisons of Iraq may never come fully into light, but one thing was abundantly clear: Tactics that, in the immediate aftermath of 9/11, had been considered the sovereign realm of America's most unsavory "dark side" forces, and that had required approval from the highest levels of power in the United States for each escalation, now had become the widely accepted standard operating procedure for handling detainees in a huge battlefield with massive numbers of prisoners being held by the US military.


CAPTAIN IAN FISHBACK graduated from West Point in 2001 and deployed with the 82nd Airborne to Afghanistan for a combat tour from August 2002 to February 2003. In late 2003, he deployed to Iraq, where he was based at Forward Operating Base Mercury. In both Afghanistan and Iraq, Fishback witnessed the migration of the tactics from the black sites to the military's own prisons and filtration sites. On May 7, 2004, Fishback heard Rumsfeld's congressional testimony. The defense secretary had said that the United States was following the Geneva Conventions in Iraq and the "spirit" of the conventions in Afghanistan. Rumsfeld's statement did not jibe with what Fishback had seen, so he began seeking answers through his chain of command. "For 17 months, I tried to determine what specific standards governed the treatment of detainees by consulting my chain of command through battalion commander, multiple JAG lawyers, multiple Democrat and Republican Congressmen and their aides, the Ft. Bragg Inspector General's office, multiple government reports, the Secretary of the Army and multiple general officers, a professional interrogator at Guantánamo Bay, the deputy head of the department at West Point responsible for teaching Just War Theory and Law of Land Warfare, and numerous peers who I regard as honorable and intelligent men," Fishback recalled, adding that he was "unable to get clear, consistent answers from my leadership about what constitutes lawful and humane treatment of detainees. I am certain that this confusion contributed to a wide range of abuses including death threats, beatings, broken bones, murder, exposure to elements, extreme forced physical exertion, hostage-taking, stripping, sleep deprivation and degrading treatment. I and troops under my command witnessed some of these abuses in both Afghanistan and Iraq."

When Fishback began asking questions about the torture and abuse he had witnessed, he was blackballed by the military. He was confined to Fort Bragg and was denied permission to leave the base to attend a scheduled briefing on Capitol Hill. In a letter to Republican senators Lindsey Graham and John McCain, Fishback wrote: "Some do not see the need for [investigations]. Some argue that since our actions are not as horrifying as Al Qaeda's, we should not be concerned. When did Al Qaeda become any type of standard by which we measure the morality of the United States?" Fishback's protest barely registered a blip on the radar.

In the summer of 2004, McChrystal officially moved the task force forty miles north of Baghdad to the Balad Air Base and brought the HVT interrogation and "filtration" site that had been housed at NAMA with him. But a change of venue would not end the abuses.

McChrystal flatly denied that commanders at NAMA "ordered the mistreatment of detainees," asserting that any abuse was the result of "lapses of discipline" among individual members of the task force. Allegations of systematized torture at NAMA, he said, were false. "That wasn't the case before I assumed command and wasn't true under my command nor under my successors," McChrystal wrote in his memoir.

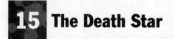

## 15 The Death Star

IRAQ, 2004—Balad was a massive air base that Saddam had built up with modern facilities and infrastructure. The kill/capture center JSOC established there was a microcosm of how Rumsfeld and Cheney wanted the whole national security apparatus in the United States to function: all US intelligence agencies and assets should be subordinate to the kill teams staffed by the Special Ops warrior class and directed by the White House and defense secretary. It would later be hailed by McChrystal and others as an unprecedented joint operation, but in reality it was a JSOC-run show where everyone else played their supporting parts. Journalist Mark Urban, who embedded with British commandos working with McChrystal's task force, said that some JSOC operatives referred to the Joint Operations Center at Balad as "the Death Star because of the sense that 'you could just reach out with a finger, as it were, and eliminate somebody.' Others who watched live the white splash of five-hundred-pound bombs on image-intensifier cameras referred to the screens above them as 'Kill TV.'" The JSOC command center was known as "the factory" or "the shop floor." McChrystal was fond of calling the kill/capture apparatus "the machine."

By mid-2004, the pace of the JSOC operations had accelerated dramatically. The CIA had liaisons assigned to the fusion center, along with satellite technicians from the National Geospatial-Intelligence Agency, surveillance experts from the NSA and, for good measure, Iraq "experts" from the State Department. "An NSA-created linkup called the Real Time Regional Gateway allowed operatives who seized scraps of intelligence from raids—a terrorist's cell phone contacts, receipts for bomb ingredients, even geolocated terrorist cell phones—to send their crucial data to different nodes across the network," reported Spencer Ackerman of *Wired* magazine. "One analyst might not appreciate the significance of a given piece of intel. But once JSOC effectively became an experiment in intel crowdsourcing, it soon got a bigger, deeper picture of the enemy it was fighting—and essentially emulating." In effect, JSOC was running the covert war buried within the larger war and controlling the intelligence.

In April 2004, Rumsfeld continued to hammer away on the theme that the Iraqi insurgency was being driven by remnants of the regime. After four private security contractors working for the mercenary firm Blackwater were killed in an ambush in Fallujah on March 31, 2004, Bush had ordered a massive revenge assault on the city, directing US commanders to "Kick ass!" and "Kill them!" With no apparent understanding that the uprising in Fallujah had been sparked by the US siege of the city, which disproportionately killed civilians, Rumsfeld thundered, "Thugs and assassins and former Saddam henchmen will not be allowed...to oppose peace and freedom." The US occupation was creating a situation in which new militant cells were popping up weekly, and the task force was struggling to keep them all straight, much less track them. The emerging US strategy was to loosen the definition of who was an insurgent and to engage in a sweeping war against anyone suspected of being a "militant." "The Americans were in total denial about the state of the insurgency," said a British intelligence officer. "The arrogance and hubris...were breathtaking."

In early April 2004, a young US businessman named Nicholas Berg went missing in Baghdad. Berg, like tens of thousands of other Americans, had come to Iraq to cash in on the post-invasion contracting boom. Under Saddam, Iraq had no real mobile phone networks and Berg saw dollar signs in the prospect of erecting mobile towers. He would never fulfill his dreams. On May 8, Berg's decapitated body was discovered on a Baghdad bridge by a US military patrol unit. Three days later, a video appeared online with the title "Abu Musab al-Zarqawi Slaughters an American." In the video, Berg was dressed in an orange jumpsuit—similar to those worn by US prisoners at Guantánamo. The young Jewish American made a brief statement identifying himself before being grabbed by masked men wielding weapons. Two of the men held him down, while another severed his head with a knife. One of the men screamed "Allah u Akbar," while another held the head in front of the camera. The narrator of the video declared, "We tell you that the dignity of the Muslim men and women in Abu Ghraib and others is not redeemed except by blood and souls. You will not receive anything from us but coffins after coffins," warning that more Americans would be "slaughtered in this way. How can a free Muslim sleep well as he sees Islam slaughtered and its dignity bleeding, and the pictures of shame and the news of the devilish scorn of the people of Islam—men and women—in the prison of Abu Ghraib?" The voice of the narrator was later determined by US intelligence to be that of Zarqawi.

Although Zarqawi's reference to the torture at Abu Ghraib was self-serving, it resonated with Iraqis who had lived to tell the tale of their ordeals there and other prisons or "filtration sites." There was no doubt that such acts were fueling the insurgency. In fact, Malcolm Nance, the former SERE instructor who worked in Iraq during this period, told me he saw direct evidence that the way the United States treated prisoners and housed them helped extremist groups recruit new operatives. The prisons, he said, became "the Jihadi Advanced University for Suicide Bomber Studies," explaining that "you put all the worst of the worst together with guys who would never consider being a jihadi, and suddenly you have guys who were released and now they're suicide bomber fodder."

Berg's killing by Zarqawi provided the Bush administration with a convenient opportunity to pivot from its claims that "regime dead-enders" were driving the violence in Iraq and shift the emphasis to al Qaeda terrorists. The US focus on Zarqawi, in turn, brought him notoriety and recognition, and he began raising new funds for his previously obscure network. Much of his money poured in from wealthy Saudis, Syrians and Jordanians. Although the Jordanian terrorist had already been on JSOC's radar for some time, Zarqawi became a propaganda bonanza for the Bush administration because it could now characterize the resistance in Iraq as being led by al Qaeda. "The execution of Nicholas Berg instantly catapulted Zarqawi into the media spotlight," recalled Richard Rowley, an independent journalist who spent extensive time in Iraq during that period, including in Zarqawi strongholds. He said:

> The United States was eager to publicly portray the insurgency as led by foreign extremists, and made Zarqawi Iraq's most wanted insurgent. They put a $20 million bounty on his head and retroactively identified him as the mastermind behind virtually every major terrorist attack in Iraq. The hunt for Zarqawi replaced the hunt for Saddam Hussein as a central public goal of the US campaign. The American attention was useful to Zarqawi, who quickly rose to prominence within the insurgency, and Zarqawi's prominence was useful to the Americans, who would use it to justify their bloodiest military operation of the war.

That operation would come in November 2004 with the second US siege of Fallujah, which had become a potent symbol of resistance to the US occupation. After that, a bloody civil war would break out in Iraq. Zarqawi would announce a war against Shiites, while the United States, in turn, would build up its own Shiite death squads.

At the center of the US contribution to Iraq's civil war were two Americans. One was General David Petraeus, who had close ties to the White House, particularly to Dick Cheney, and had been tapped by Rumsfeld in June 2004 to head the Multi-National Security Transition Command–Iraq. The other was retired US colonel James Steele, a former Enron executive who had been selected for a senior Iraq job by Wolfowitz.

Although Enron had been a major backer of the Bush campaign, Steele wasn't in Iraq because of his Enron days. He had a deep history with US "dirty wars" in Central America. As a colonel in the marines in the mid-1980s, Steele had been a key "counterinsurgency" official in the bloody US-fueled war in El Salvador, where he coordinated the US Military Advisory Group, supervising Washington's military assistance and training of Salvadoran Army units battling the leftist Farabundo Martí National Liberation Front guerrillas. In the late 1980s, Steele was called to testify during the Iran-Contra investigation about his role in Oliver North's covert weapons pipeline, which ran through the Salvadoran air force base at Ilopango, to the Nicaraguan Contra death squads.

Steele and Petraeus were central to a program known as the "Salvadorization of Iraq," or simply the "Salvador Option." The two men built up local Iraqi Special Ops units to be used in a counterinsurgency campaign, but they would soon turn into unaccountable death squads. "We will hit these people and teach them a good lesson they won't forget," Iraqi defense minister Hazim Shaalan said the day the first six-hundred-man battalion of Iraqi Special Operations forces was to put into action in June 2004. "Americans and allied forces have certain restrictions we won't have. It's our country, it's our culture, and we have different laws than you do." Enraged by another suicide bombing days later, Hazim declared, "We will cut off their hands and behead them."

On his own, Steele helped hatch a Special Police Commando Unit (also known as the Wolf Brigade), made up of former Republican Guard and Saddam-era SOFs recruited by the Ministry of Interior. According to a *New York Times Magazine* piece by Peter Maass from 2005, Petraeus didn't know about the unit right away; he found out about it, visited its base in the Green Zone, challenged the commandos to one of his famous push-up contests, and that was that. "He was not just embracing a new military formation; he was embracing a new strategy," Maass reported. "The hard men of the past would help shape the country's future. Petraeus decided that the commandos would receive whatever arms, ammunition and supplies they required," and he gave Steele his full support. After Ayad Allawi, the Sunni interim prime minister, lost the election in January 2005, the Wolf Brigade was taken over by Shiite militia members who then became the beneficiaries of Petraeus's support. It was the moment Iraq descended into unspeakable violence.

MCCHRYSTAL'S COMMAND CENTER at Balad was now up and running at a decent speed. "Vital months had been lost while the Pentagon leadership was in denial about the insurgency. By early 2004, it was mutating and

McChrystal was one of the few who both understood this and the need to get on top of it," reported Mark Urban, the journalist who embedded with British commandos working with McChrystal. "Teams from each of the different intelligence agencies were established at Balad. Once he had started to milk them for information, McChrystal put it all into a JSOC intranet similar to the one he'd created in Afghanistan. It would allow those at the cutting edge of the US counterterrorism effort to share information worldwide." Urban added: "McChrystal's counterterrorist Rome could not be built in a day. It would take much of 2004 to take shape."

With Saddam Hussein in prison and the High Value Task Force killing its way through Iraq, McChrystal and McRaven began refocusing the HVT efforts on Afghanistan and the hunt for Osama bin Laden. "If anyone is smart and cunning enough to get [bin Laden], McRaven and the Delta and SEAL Team Six guys he now commands will do it," General Downing said in 2004. Downing's remark about McRaven and Team 6 hitting bin Laden was prophetic, but he would not live to see it fulfilled—Downing passed away in 2007. Iraq was becoming engulfed in the flames of multiple insurgencies that were largely fueled by the US invasion and occupation, the abuse and torture of prisoners and the widely held perception among large swaths of the Iraqi population that the United States was a "gratuitous enemy." Zarqawi and his network grew stronger and made what was once a lie about an al Qaeda presence in Iraq a bloody reality. McChrystal would spend a great deal of time trying to find, fix and ultimately finish Zarqawi. But Afghanistan and Pakistan were also calling.

**"The Best Technology, the Best Weapons, the Best People—and Plenty of Money to Burn"**

AFGHANISTAN, IRAQ AND PAKISTAN, 2003–2006—AS in Iraq, JSOC ran its own detainee operations in Afghanistan and would maintain a list of people it wanted to kill or capture. Known as the Joint Prioritized Effects List (JPEL), it began with the leaders of the Taliban and al Qaeda, but would, in the ensuing years, grow to more than 2,000 people as the insurgency in Afghanistan widened. Just as JSOC found itself being ordered to kill its way through a constantly regenerating and growing list of "insurgents" in Iraq, it would eventually face a guerrilla war in which America's mightiest warriors would be fighting Afghans who previously had no serious connection to al Qaeda or the Taliban.

Anthony Shaffer, the career Defense Intelligence operative, had hit the ground in Afghanistan in July 2003, working with the leadership targeting cell that was tasked with hunting down al Qaeda and Taliban leaders, as well as those from Hezb-e-Islami Gulbuddin (HIG), a militant movement linked to al Qaeda. Shaffer had been given an alias and carried fake documents—Social Security number, driver's license, credit cards and a new passport. His cover name was Chris Stryker, inspired by John Wayne's character in the 1949 film *The Sands of Iwo Jima*. Shaffer found close allies among the JSOC ninjas who returned to Afghanistan to renew the hunt for bin Laden, Mullah Mohammed Omar and other al Qaeda and Taliban leaders, an operation coordinated from the Bagram Air Base. As the task force members "started to roll into Bagram, the very fabric of the base changed. It brought almost a surreal energy," Shaffer recalled. "At one point, fully loaded C-17 transport aircraft were landing at Bagram every thirty to forty-five minutes, spending about an hour off-loading and screaming rapidly back into the sky again. I could see pallet after pallet of material coming off the C-17s, neatly lined up and filled with enough high-tech gear to run a country." Shaffer said that the number of commandos and support staff for the High Value Target mission "swelled," adding that while the original task force "had been a tight unit of some 200," this one "was going to have more than 2,000." As Shaffer recalled, JSOC's force "had the best technology, the best weapons, the best people—and plenty of money to burn."

Once JSOC took over, the task force quickly assembled a large operations center, made up of a series of plywood "B-Huts" and tents that func-
tioned as everything from barracks to intelligence facilities. The heart of
the base was the Tactical Operations Center, housed in a gigantic tent. As
with the Joint Operations Center in Iraq, it was referred to as the "Death
Star." From this base, JSOC would attempt to hunt down and kill or capture the most wanted men in Afghanistan. Bearded Navy SEALs would
walk around the base in civilian gear, and almost no one wore any patches
to identify them to outsiders. The new JSOC presence didn't sit well with
the Green Berets and other "white" Special Ops guys who had been working for the past several years attempting to build up local connections by
spending considerable time traveling throughout Afghanistan's inhospi-
table terrain. Unlike the Green Berets, JSOC was not in the country to
win any hearts and minds. Once JSOC took charge, the mission would no
longer resemble anthropology. It was to be a manhunt, at times an assassination machine.

Early on in McChrystal's tenure at JSOC, Shaffer briefed him several
times in Afghanistan. Shaffer had been pushing for authority to conduct
operations inside Pakistan and had pushed his supervisor to clear ops
across the border against al Qaeda havens, saying that "the intel indicates
that most of the leadership is probably now in Pakistan." Shaffer's superior
officer told him that "for now, it's not an option. Frankly, and this cannot
leave the room, McChrystal is trying to get permission," but "CENTCOM
and the Pentagon have told us we have to stay on this side." McChrystal
was determined to change that.

PAKISTAN AND THE CIA have a long and complicated history, but particularly in the years after 9/11, the Inter-Services Intelligence (ISI) had
come to accept that it would have to live with the Agency's operatives
running around its territory. At times, the two entities would cooperate,
but more often the CIA found itself scrambling to thwart ISI attempts to
stymie its operations, while the ISI tried to keep track of all the operatives
the United States had working in Pakistan. It was a mutually agreed-upon
relationship based on mistrust, dishonesty, backstabbing and, in the end,
necessity. When the United States invaded Afghanistan in October 2001,
forcing al Qaeda and the Taliban leadership to flee, Pakistan's tribal areas
became the epicenter of Washington's counterterrorism operations. For
certain missions, such as the capture of people suspected of a connection
to the 9/11 attacks, Pakistan and the CIA would conduct joint operations.
But JSOC believed the CIA was getting played and that the United States

would have to operate unilaterally inside Pakistan if it was to break al Qaeda's safe haven.

To the consternation of the ISI, President Pervez Musharraf made a secret deal with JSOC in 2002 that allowed US forces to accompany Pakistani forces on raids against suspected al Qaeda cells in the country's tribal regions. Shaffer was elated. "The question became, of how deep, how severe, we would violate the sovereignty of Pakistan," he told me. Rules of Engagement for US Army Rangers and other elite "terrorist-hunting units" along the Afghanistan-Pakistan border stated that "entries into PAK [were] authorized" in the following cases: hot pursuit, troops in contact with the enemy, personnel recovery—and action against "the big three"—bin Laden, Zawahiri, and Taliban leader Mullah Mohammed Omar—approved by either the CENTCOM commander or the defense secretary. As a "general rule," these terrorist-hunting forces were to forge no deeper than ten kilometers into Pakistan. US and Pakistani authorities would technically need to be notified soon after any such actions. But the reality was different: central to the operations was Pakistan's ability to deny foreknowledge and to denounce violations of sovereignty after the fact. The United States would strike and then Musharraf would characterize any US incursions into Pakistan as an "invasion." But just as the JSOC campaign in Pakistan was getting started, it quickly lost steam after many of the JSOC assets originally focused on Pakistan were, once again, redirected to Iraq to confront the mounting insurgency. As a result, in 2003–2004, Pakistan remained largely a CIA-controlled operation.

IN 2004, the officials running the White House and Pentagon global manhunt issued a series of classified orders that would, when combined, prove to be an enduring blueprint for US assassinations and disregard for the sovereignty of nations the world over. The post-9/11 infighting between the CIA and Rumsfeld over who would be the prime entity responsible for running the manhunt and global wars had hit a defining moment. To fund the dramatically expanding scope of JSOC's operations, Rumsfeld asked for a 34 percent increase in the Special Ops budget, from $5 billion to $6.7 billion. It was 2004 that secured JSOC's place at the head of the counterterrorism table, a position it would keep through Republican and Democratic administrations. Seeking free rein for Special Operations Forces, President Bush developed an assertion that he and his successor, Barack Obama, would provide verbatim to Congress annually to justify the borderless war strategy that made the world a battlefield. "I will direct additional measures as necessary in the exercise of the right of the United

States to self-defense and to protect U.S. citizens and interests," Bush declared. "Such measures may include short-notice deployments of special operations and other forces for sensitive operations in various locations throughout the world. It is not possible to know at this time either the precise scope or duration of the deployment of U.S. Armed Forces necessary to counter the terrorist threat to the United States."

In early 2004, Rumsfeld signed a secret order that would streamline JSOC's ability to conduct operations and hit targets outside of the stated battlefields of Iraq and Afghanistan. Known as the Al Qaeda Network Execute Order, or AQN ExOrd, it allowed for JSOC operations "anywhere in the world" where al Qaeda operatives were known or suspected to be operating or receiving sanctuary. The order, which remains classified despite attempts by journalists to obtain it, reportedly named fifteen to twenty such countries, including Pakistan, Syria, Somalia, Yemen and Saudi Arabia, as well as several other Gulf nations. The AQN ExOrd was drafted in 2003, primarily by the Special Operations Command and the Office of the Assistant Secretary of Defense for Special Operations/Low-Intensity Conflict and was promoted by Wolfowitz and Cambone as a justification for special forces operating covertly—and lethally—across the globe. Part of the order provides for what a Special Operations source called "hot pursuit," similar to how some state police are permitted to cross borders into another state to pursue a suspect. "That's essentially what they have where they're chasing someone in Somalia and he moves over into Ethiopia or Eritrea, you can go after him," the source told me. The order was signed in the spring of 2004, but it took fifteen months for Rumsfeld to get "presidential approval" from the White House. Part of the delay was a result of "bureaucratic drag," but the CIA also offered up resistance, seeing it as another encroachment on its mandate as the lead agency tracking al Qaeda after 9/11.

The insertion of Special Ops personnel into US embassies under the cover of Military Liaison Elements (MLE) was extremely controversial with the CIA and State Department. But JSOC personnel were not limited to those operating with official cover. It also had operatives deploying in various countries under "non-official cover," at times using fake identities backed up by falsified passports, sometimes from other nations. Their job was to help prepare the battlefield for JSOC operations, and they often did not coordinate with the CIA or the ambassadors. If the SOCOM "presence in U.S. embassies abroad is an effort to pave the way for unilateral U.S. military operations or to enable defense elements to engage in covert action activities separate from the CIA, U.S. problems abroad will be certain to increase significantly," said John Brennan, a career CIA officer who spent a quarter of a century at the Agency and at the time ran the National

Counterterrorism Center. The use of MLE posts as cover for JSOC, combined with Cambone's intelligence operation, was seen by some on the civilian side of the war effort as a dangerous precedent. But Lieutenant General Boykin, the undersecretary of defense for intelligence, shot back at the program's critics, blasting what he called "an assumption that what the secretary is trying to say is, 'Get the CIA out of this business, and we'll take it.' I don't interpret it that way at all." Instead, he asserted, "The secretary actually has more responsibility to collect intelligence for the national foreign intelligence program" than "the CIA director."

It was during this period that Rumsfeld, Cambone and JSOC ran roughshod over the "covert" versus "clandestine" divide and did so with the backing of the White House. The Pentagon began defining "coordination" with the CIA as giving the Agency a seventy-two-hour heads-up that JSOC would be conducting an operation, and Cambone altered the definition of military "deployment orders," which are required to be provided to Congress. Cambone issued new guidelines that asserted the right of Special Ops Forces to "conduct clandestine HUMINT operations" before alerting Congress. Not only was the CIA being boxed out of operations it historically held sovereignty over, but the use of JSOC to conduct intelligence operations kept Congress even further at bay. Combined with the Copper Green program, this effectively meant that JSOC was free to act as a spy agency and a kill/capture force rolled into one. Even some well-connected Republican allies of the White House were disturbed by what they were witnessing. "Operations the CIA runs have one set of restrictions and oversight, and the military has another," a Republican member of Congress "with a substantial role in national security oversight" told the *Washington Post*. "It sounds like there's an angle here of, 'Let's get around having any oversight by having the military do something that normally the [CIA] does, and not tell anybody.' That immediately raises all kinds of red flags for me. Why aren't they telling us?"

Rumsfeld and his aides knew the CIA's paramilitary arm was far too small to conduct a global war, and once the case was made to Bush that the Special Operations Command should have a global mandate as its own command, it was a done deal. In addition to Rumsfeld's AQN-ExOrd, he persuaded President Bush to insert language into National Security Presidential Directive-38 (NSPD-38) that would codify SOCOM's global role in finding, fixing and finishing off terror suspects. NSPD-38's declassified description is as the "National Strategy to Secure Cyberspace." Yet the directive, which remains classified, gave unprecedented latitude for JSOC to hit across the globe, effectively pre-authorizing lethal operations outside of any stated battlefield. "There are a lot of things in NSPD-38 that are not cyber related," a Special Operations source told me, adding that authorization for Special Ops activities "were slipped in before signature." Among these was a "broad authorization to launch Find, Fix, Finish operations with SOCOM in the lead." He added that the classified directive was a "close hold" and estimated that "there are maybe five copies [that are] all in the physical NSC office space. Everyone jokes about the man-sized safe."

The global manhunt that JSOC was now fully empowered to engage in had multiple tracks. JSOC developed target lists of various al Qaeda figures they had authority to pursue globally, lists of "irreconcilables" who could be assassinated, others they would allow to move freely in an effort to gather intel on their contacts or cells. Although some may have seen what was happening in Iraq and Afghanistan with TF-121 as scandalous, it was in many ways the definitive vision of the type of wars Rumsfeld and Cheney had longed for: no accountability, maximum secrecy and total flexibility.

Scott Horton, the human rights lawyer, said the program "parallels something that the OSS [Office of Strategic Services] did during the Second World War, and that CIA did subsequently. Now, to a certain extent, the function is not unusual. It's not unusual for the military to have commandos who, in a theater of war, will seek out enemy command and control, with the purpose of identifying them and then killing them. And yes, that could be walking into a café and shooting somebody. And that would be traditional, authorized warfare." But, he added, "What's different here, is that suddenly the theater of war has become the entire globe—it's become everywhere. And they're looking at the possibility of assassinating people in Hamburg, Germany, in Norway, in Italy, as well as in Morocco, Jordan, Senegal, Turkey, Yemen, the Philippines and places in the African Horn. And, I'd say, in terms of law—it's pretty plainly illegal once you're outside of the normal theater of war."

At the end of 2004, Rumsfeld wrote a memo to his top advisers, including Cambone and Douglas Feith. It was classified FOUO, For Official Use Only, with the subject "Preparation of the Battlespace." In the memo, Rumsfeld wrote that he was concerned that "the old phrase 'preparation of the battlespace' may no longer be appropriate terminology." Today, Rumsfeld declared, "the entire world is the 'battlespace.'"


THE USE OF WEAPONIZED DRONES was still in its nascent stage in the global US wars, but surveillance drones had been in operation for years. The JSOC task force began using a system McChrystal's intelligence deputy Mike Flynn referred to as "The Unblinking Eye," in which drones and other aircraft would hover in a "long dwell airborne stakeout" to "apply multisensor observation 24/7 to achieve a greater understanding of how the enemy's network operates by building a pattern of life analysis" that could be used to conduct raids. Using what Flynn called "nodal analysis," patterns of movement were developed by tracking people suspected of being affiliated with an insurgent group or cell. Nodal analysis, Flynn believed, would have "the effect of taking a shadowy foe and revealing his physical infrastructure for things such as funding, meetings, headquarters, media outlets, and weapons supply points. As a result, the network becomes more visible and vulnerable, thus negating the enemy's asymmetric advantage of denying a target." He added, "The payoff of this analysis is huge but requires patience to allow the network's picture to develop over a long term and accept the accompanying risk of potentially losing the prey." Finally, the task force would conduct "vehicle follows," where they would monitor the movement of vehicles believed to be used by insurgents. At times, the task force would use three combat air patrols to surveil a target or a group of people. "It is not enough to have several eyes on a target—several eyes are needed on a target for a long period," Flynn asserted. This approach would allow for "persistent surveillance of a target while simultaneously developing the network's pattern of life through nodal analysis and vehicle follows. It gives the finishing force commander more options than merely killing or letting an observed enemy go; with sufficient ISR [Intelligence, Surveillance, Reconnaissance], a ground force commander can demonstrate much greater operational patience, thus allowing a larger insurgent network to emerge." What differentiated the JSOC forces from the conventional military, Flynn said, was that big army "forces tend to cover disparate targets for a shorter period than SOF, which tend to focus collection on a smaller number of targets for much longer." JSOC needed to understand "pattern[s] of life of an enemy network."

The Special Operations Command also began working on a program for monitoring suspected or known insurgents. It was straight out of a sci-fi film. Known as "Continuous Clandestine Tagging Tracking and Locating," or CTTL, it involved using advanced biometrics and chemistry to develop a long-range facial recognition program as well as a "Human Thermal Fingerprint" that could be isolated for any individual. They also used a chemical "bioreactive taggant" to mark people by discreetly swabbing a part of their body. The taggant would emit a signal that JSOC could remotely monitor, enabling it to track people 24/7/365. It was like a modern version of the old spook's tracking devices made famous in films, where spies would weave them into an enemy's clothes or place them on the bottom of a vehicle. The taggant allowed JSOC to mark prisoners and then release them to see if they would lead the task force to a potential terror or insurgent cell. Putting them on nonprisoners was a greater challenge, but it happened. The use of such technology, along with the accelerated pace of the killings and captures, would inspire President Bush's declaration that "JSOC is awesome."

While Iraq was vacuuming up most of the US counterterrorist resources, the White House and Pentagon continued on with their twilight wars elsewhere across the globe, and the war in Afghanistan festered, all but forgotten. Bin Laden was still at large, as were many of his top deputies, with Bush's "Wanted Dead or Alive" pronouncement relegated to a source of scorn and a symbol of a failing yet spreading war. Taliban leader Mullah Omar was underground, while Pakistan was heating up and Somalia and Yemen were increasingly showing up on the counterterror radar.

As the US body count in Iraq increased as a result of the widening insurgency, President Bush would press commanders on how many people they had killed on any given day. The conventional generals would often balk at the question, but the answer from the JSOC crew was unequivocal. When asked how many Iraqis the task force killed in Iraq, McChrystal's intelligence chief, Mike Flynn, replied, "Thousands, I don't even know how many." In Iraq, the task force had started to fulfill Rumsfeld and Cheney's wildest dreams of what a streamlined, well-funded, secret force could do—and accomplish away from the prying eyes of Congress and the media, or even the CIA.

Although Rumsfeld and Cheney had already been circumventing the conventional military chain of command and coordinating directly with JSOC, they now had all the pieces of their puzzle in place. The task force that had been built up and refined in Afghanistan and Iraq was going to take its actions global and away from declared battlefields. McChrystal began establishing a network of JSOC liaison offices in a variety of Middle Eastern and other countries to avoid relying on—or working with—US embassies or CIA station chiefs. "The Department of Defense is very eager to step up its involvement in counterterrorism activities, and it has set its sights on traditional CIA operational responsibilities and authorities," asserted Brennan, who at the time ran the National Counterterrorism Center. "Quite unfortunately, the CIA's important lead role in many of these areas is being steadily eroded, and the current militarization of many of the nation's intelligence functions and responsibilities will be viewed as a major mistake in the very near future." In the wake of the WMD scandal in the lead-up to the Iraq War, veteran intelligence professionals were already concerned that the independence of the CIA's analysis was being compromised to adhere to political agendas. With JSOC being used as a parallel intelligence operation to the CIA—and one with its own force to act free of independent review—the potential for abuse of substantial and secretive military power was significant.

Colonel Patrick Lang, who once ran the Defense Intelligence Agency's global human intelligence operations, concurred with Brennan about the risks of Rumsfeld and Cheney's innovations in the command structure. "When you made SOCOM a supported command rather than a support-ing command, then you've freed [JSOC] up to do all kinds of things," he said. "To do that kind of thing without coordinating with the US ambas-sador of that country, or with the host country's government is just kind of banditry, really. I mean, you're asking for retribution of some kind by somebody on your own turf, against your own people. It's not a good idea, at all."

Critics be damned, though, the JSOC Iraq model was about to go on tour. "You look at our Special Operations Forces, you have the ability to wage war, in a very low key way, and in a way that's not going to command a lot of congressional oversight," said Exum. The mindset, he said, was: "You have an empowered executive branch that more or less has license to wage war wherever it needs to, wherever it determines it needs to, worldwide. You've got this great hammer, and, you know, why not go hammer some nails?"

IN EARLY 2005, a behind-the-scenes scuffle broke out between the CIA, CENTCOM and the Pentagon over who should take the lead in targeting al Qaeda in Pakistan after some US intelligence reports suggested that al Qae-da's number-two man, Ayman al Zawahiri, was believed to be attending a meeting in the tribal area of Bajaur in Waziristan. General McChrystal pushed hard for a JSOC raid to capture Zawahiri, and some CIA officials wanted him to do so without informing the US ambassador in Islamabad, Ryan Crocker. Anthony Shaffer said that he and US Special Operations planners had wanted to conduct such missions without informing the CIA, either. "We felt that there was a likelihood at some point that CIA would—either inadvertently or with knowledge—give the ISI information relating to what we were doing," he told me. "The idea was, to be blunt about it, to go it alone. We felt that we could not trust the CIA or the Pakistanis, to any great degree." He added: "There are just some targets the Pakistanis would never cooperate with us to get."

The CIA, however, was well aware of this operation. Teams of Navy SEALs and Army Rangers in Afghanistan were actually preparing to board aircraft for the operation, which included as many as one hundred com-mandos, when the fighting among the CIA, CENTCOM and the Penta-gon leadership became so contentious that the operation was grounded. A former CIA officer told the *New York Times* that as the raid was being debated, he had "told the military guys that this thing was going to be the biggest folly since the Bay of Pigs."

Shaffer said that the rules for striking inside Pakistan had "changed dramatically" and "became much more restrictive to the point of where I think it was nearly impossible," adding, "The format of the war changed under our feet." General McChrystal, Shaffer said, "continued to push for authority to do things in Pakistan," adding, "I know for a fact that there was a policy decision made at some level that restricted our ability to do cross-border operations to deal with the things that we all believed from my level was the real issue. Pakistan was the real issue, not Afghanistan."

But then, in October 2005, Pakistan suffered a massive 7.6 magnitude earthquake. Some 75,000 Pakistanis died. Millions more were displaced. JSOC and the CIA took advantage of the disorder to fill the country with operatives, contractors and commandos, escaping requisite ISI background checks. According to journalists Marc Ambinder and D. B. Grady, the JSOC intelligence teams that entered Pakistan with the CIA had multiple goals, including the cultivation of informant rings to collect information on al Qaeda, as well as intelligence gathering related to how Pakistan transported its nuclear weapons. The elite US force also aimed to penetrate the ISI.

"Under a secret program code-named SCREEN HUNTER, JSOC, augmented by the Defense Intelligence Agency (DIA) and contract personnel, was authorized to shadow and identify members of the ISI suspected of being sympathetic to al-Qaeda," Ambinder and Grady wrote. "It is not clear whether JSOC units used lethal force against these ISI officers: one official said that the goal of the program was to track terrorists through the ISI by using disinformation and psychological warfare."

Despite this incredible opportunity, neither Afghanistan nor Pakistan would be given top billing in the Bush administration's war plan. Instead, the top-tier operators from JSOC and the CIA were again redirected to Iraq to confront the rapidly spreading insurgency, which had made a farce of the administration's claims that US forces would be welcomed as liberators. The CIA's unit responsible for hunting down bin Laden, Alec Station, was shut down. "This will clearly denigrate our operations against Al Qaeda," declared former senior CIA official Michael Scheuer, the unit's first director. "These days at the agency, bin Laden and Al Qaeda appear to be treated merely as first among equals."

The head of the CIA's clandestine operations branch, Jose Rodriguez, reorganized the CIA's secret US war in Pakistan under the code name "Operation Cannonball." In theory, it was an attempt to ratchet up the targeting of al Qaeda. But with most of the veteran CIA and Special Ops assets bogged down in Iraq, the operation was largely staffed by inexperienced operatives. "You had a very finite number" of agents with operational experience in the Islamic world, a former senior intelligence official told the *New York Times*. "Those people all went to Iraq. We were all hurting because of Iraq." The secret war in Pakistan became largely a drone bombing campaign, described by CIA officers at the US Embassy in Islamabad as "boys with toys." The drone campaign successfully took out several suspected al Qaeda figures and reportedly narrowly missed Zawahiri, but it also resulted in scores of civilians being killed, sparking protests and outrage among Pakistanis.

Although CIA drone strikes became the lead US weapon in Pakistan during this period, JSOC forces did, at times, manage to conduct sporadic ground operations, albeit "with a great deal of protest" from the Pakistanis, according to Shaffer. In a raid in 2006 in Damadola in Bajaur, Navy SEALs from DEVGRU targeted a suspected al Qaeda house and detained several people. "They choppered in, rappelled down and went into the compound," a former US official familiar with the operation told the *Los Angeles Times*. "It was tactically very well executed." Pakistani media sources characterized the operation a bit differently. "American soldiers had violated Pakistani airspace, flown to the village in helicopters, killed eight persons in the home of a cleric Maulana Noor Mohammad, and taken away five others to Afghanistan," reported journalist Rahimullah Yusufzai.

With resources spread thin in Pakistan as a result of the intensifying insurgency in Iraq, the Bush administration began outsourcing its war in Pakistan. Enter Blackwater, Erik Prince's secretive mercenary company already infamous for its work in Iraq. Like the CIA, Blackwater had its own cover: diplomatic security. From the early stages of the launch of the Global War on Terror, its operatives were able to deploy in large numbers to war zones as bodyguards for US officials. Blackwater was the elite Praetorian Guard for the senior officials running the US occupation of Iraq and simultaneously worked for the State Department, the Pentagon and the CIA providing security for their operations in hostile zones across the globe.

The company additionally won contracts for training foreign military forces, including Pakistan's Frontier Corps, the federal paramilitary force officially responsible for on-the-ground strikes against suspected terrorists or militants in the tribal areas.

Meanwhile, across the border in Afghanistan, Blackwater controlled four Forward Operating Bases, including the closest US base to the Pakistan border. All of this was very appealing to both JSOC and the CIA.

According to Shaffer, among Blackwater's roles for the CIA was training Afghan militias to do cross-border raids into Pakistan, which offered deniability to the United States. "I handled two of their—the CIA/Black-

water—KIAs [killed in action], killed while they were out on a mission...
essentially performing a Special Operations mission, training Afghan cadre
militia to do cross border stuff," Shaffer recalled. He added: "This is clearly
something they were doing that they didn't like having talked about." One
of the reasons Blackwater was used, he said, "was to avoid oversight."

Many of Blackwater's elite operatives, particularly those who worked for
its most sensitive division, Blackwater SELECT, were veterans of US Special Operations. It wasn't hard for them, therefore, to serve two masters:
the CIA and JSOC. While the CIA was, by mandate, concerned with an
array of intelligence functions, JSOC had one central mission worldwide:
the killing or capture of High Value Targets, HVTs. In 2006, twelve "tactical action operatives" from Blackwater were recruited for a secret JSOC
raid inside Pakistan, targeting an al Qaeda facility. The operation was code-
named "Vibrant Fury." The involvement of Blackwater demonstrated how
central the company had become to covert US actions.


IN 2005, Abu Musab al Zarqawi escalated his merciless campaign targeting Iraqi Shiites as well as Sunni Muslims he perceived as being weak
or ineffectual. Al Qaeda's central leadership, believing that the killing of
Muslims by Zarqawi would backfire, reached out to the Jordanian militant.
Ayman al Zawahiri wrote to Zarqawi in July 2005. Bin Laden's deputy
heaped praise on Zarqawi for his role in the jihad, while emphasizing that
the first goal in Iraq should be to expel the US invaders. The sectarian war
against Shiites, Zawahiri declared, was "secondary in importance to outside aggression" and al Qaeda in Iraq should focus on supporting a popular
revolt against the Americans. Zawahiri warned Zarqawi:

> In the absence of this popular support, the Islamic mujahed move-
> ment would be crushed in the shadows, far from the masses who are
> distracted or fearful, and the struggle between the Jihadist elite and
> the arrogant authorities would be confined to prison dungeons far
> from the public and the light of day. This is precisely what the secu-
> lar, apostate forces that are controlling our countries are striving for.
> These forces don't desire to wipe out the mujahed Islamic movement,
> rather they are stealthily striving to separate it from the misguided
> or frightened Muslim masses. Therefore, our planning must strive to
> involve the Muslim masses in the battle, and to bring the mujahed
> movement to the masses.

Zarqawi, however, seemed to pay Zawahiri no mind. In early 2006, Zarqawi's group formed a Shura Council of the Mujahedeen, which promptly

threatened Sunni leaders in Anbar Province—one of the front lines against the United States—that if they did not join al Qaeda, the group would "make you an example to each and every one." In February 2006, Zarqawi's group bombed one of the holiest sites in Shiite Islam, the Askariyya Mosque in Samarra, destroying its famed golden dome. The brief period of a unified national uprising against the Americans in Iraq was over. Zarqawi had made a tremendous tactical mistake by waging a war against the Sunni tribes in Anbar. It pushed the once anti-US tribes into an alliance with the occupation. America gave them arms, money and support in return for fighting Zarqawi's group. Combined with the US support for Shiite death squads, the United States had succeeded in an Iraqicization of its war on terrorism.

Although General Petraeus would be credited years later with "winning" the Iraq War through a troop "surge," he had also, along with Zarqawi, helped to destroy Iraq and create a sectarian bloodbath that would live on well past the US occupation. Petraeus would continue his rise to prominence and power within the US national security apparatus, but Zarqawi's days were numbered. In June 2006 JSOC found, fixed and finished the Jordanian terrorist. On June 7, members of the task force deployed in a palm grove in Hibhib, to which US and Jordanian intel had traced Zarqawi. Some of the commandos descended on the village after scaling down ropes dangling from helicopters. Within moments, the task force had the village surrounded. According to Iraqis on the scene, the US forces came under fire from a home situated in a date grove, sparking a brief firefight. The American forces decided not to take any risks to their personnel and called in an F-16, which fired a laser-guided five-hundred-pound bomb on the house. An identical strike hit the home a short time later. Zarqawi was dead.

## 17 "A Lot of It Was of Questionable Legality"

SOURCE: "HUNTER"—Despite the fact that I began covering US wars in the 1990s, spending extensive time in Yugoslavia and Iraq and elsewhere in the Middle East, JSOC was not on my radar until well after the US occupation of Iraq was under way. I had no sense of the scope of JSOC's operations or how it interacted (or didn't) with conventional military units or the CIA. My personal gateway into JSOC was through sources I had developed while working on my investigation into the private military contractor Blackwater, which employed an abundance of former Special Ops men, including many who had worked with JSOC and the CIA. In several of the Blackwater stories I was chasing, JSOC's name was popping up regularly. As I began investigating what was becoming an increasingly global covert war, I received an electronic communication from a man who could help make sense of this highly secretive world. When we first began communicating, I was a bit paranoid about him. My computer had just been hacked and I had received a series of threatening phone calls and e-mails pertaining to my work on Blackwater and on JSOC. So when he reached out to me, the timing seemed suspicious.

He presented himself to me as a patriotic American who believed in the Global War on Terror but said he was deeply concerned about the role that Blackwater was playing in it. He had read my book on the company, seen me on TV, and decided to get in touch. Initially, he didn't say anything about JSOC. We just talked about Blackwater. When I would press him on his own role in various US wars, he would change the subject or be so vague in his descriptions that he could have been almost anyone in any unit. Eventually, after we communicated through encrypted electronic methods for a few months, I came to believe that he was genuinely interested in helping me understand what the JSOC world was about. After we built up trust, he told me he would talk to me about what he does on one condition: we do it in person.

I decided to call him "Hunter" because when I finally met him, it was at a dingy motel a stone's throw from Fort Belvoir in Virginia, the home of JSOC's intelligence wing. The motel was called "The Hunter." It turned out to be an appropriate venue for the first of what would be many meetings over the years. Hunter had served under General McChrystal, Admiral McRaven and various Special Ops task force commanders, and he had a front-row seat for the secretive organization's operations at the most transformative moment in its history.

There is not much I can publicly reveal about what Hunter did or does because of the tight-knit nature of the Special Ops community and because I gave him my word that I would never compromise his identity. The members of that community almost never speak to reporters, and certainly not about some of the most sensitive operations they have conducted. What I can say is that after I began meeting with Hunter, I eventually pressed him to give me evidence that he was who he said he was and had participated in or witnessed the events he gave me information about. Over the years, he would show me his various DoD badges and evidence of his clearances, as well as photos of himself in countries around the world. I vetted his documents with knowledgeable sources, while concealing his identity, and verified that he was the real deal. Beyond saying that he worked with JSOC and on several classified task forces involving operations on acknowledged and unacknowledged battlefields, there is little more that I can, in good faith, share about him.

Over the course of several years and scores of meetings and conversations, Hunter shared with me his analysis of JSOC's rise. He was clear that he would not divulge classified information to me and would not compromise the integrity of any operations. He told me he has great reverence for General McChrystal and Admiral McRaven and described the people who make up JSOC as the best warriors available to the United States, calling them "people that have a true belief in the nation and our ideals." He described the training required to produce SEALs, Delta Force and other operators as the most rigorous on the planet. These Special Mission Units "are given a large degree of autonomy to execute direct action, special reconnaissance counterterrorism missions on behalf of the United States Government, almost exclusively in secrecy." Because of the nature of their work and the secrecy surrounding it, he said, "there is a potential for abuse there."

Hunter attributed JSOC's rise to prominence as the lead antiterrorism force after 9/11 to a belief within the Bush administration and the Special Ops community that the CIA was not up to the task of waging a global war. "There was a deep dissatisfaction with the level of human intelligence, and paramilitary operations that were being conducted on behalf of the Agency, and over time the Joint Special Operations Command, in effect, became a paramilitary arm of the administration, in that it would do the bidding of top policy makers in pursuit of political goals," he told me in one of our early meetings. After 9/11, JSOC's "mandate was expanded, significantly, and the funnel, if you will, was turned on. And there was billions upon billions of dollars poured into the Special Operations Command, which was then, in turn, directed to JSOC. And that coincided with a much greater latitude and freedom of movement—autonomy."

Hunter pointed to Cheney, in particular, as the administration figure most obsessed with transforming JSOC's role. "I was always under that impression that [Cheney] understood the ins and outs of the Department of Defense and all of its various components and agencies," Hunter recalled. Cheney "understood that in order to radically reshape the US military and put it on a different footing for a 'War on Terror' or a 'Long War'—what's now popularly referred to as 'countering extremism'—he would have to assert more and more authority and responsibility to darker elements of the military than before, which ultimately resulted in the Special Operations Command being given the lead when it came to prosecuting counterterrorism operations around the world."

The Bush administration, Hunter alleged, abused the authorities for "Operational Preparation of the Battlespace," which, as he described it, permits US military forces to "lay the groundwork for any potential or future military operations, by sending intelligence collectors, or linguists, into a theater, into a place where you have not necessarily declared war upon, to 'prepare the battlefield.'" Under the Bush administration, he charged, "this was somehow perverted into paramilitary operations, usually of a covert nature, with no semblance of accountability. They would tell Congress one thing, and do another." He described JSOC's parallel rendition program, which was used to snatch and interrogate prisoners. Among the people taken, he said, were individuals whom the administration "had made a calculation not to turn over to the Department of Justice and not to have the State Department or the Ambassador at Large for War Crimes or the Central Intelligence Agency get involved. They set up their own detainee operations."

Hunter told me that some of his colleagues began to question how they were being used. "There was a lot of trepidation on the part of people in that community about what we were being asked to do, and where, and for what purpose. A lot of it was of questionable legality, and most of it was outside of any stated battlefield," he recalled. He also made clear there was a sizable community of JSOC operators and support staff who "truly believed" in Rumsfeld and Cheney's vision "and were completely aware of the extralegal nature of the operations themselves, and were content with that and believed that they had been provided top cover from the office of the Secretary of Defense, and ultimately the White House." JSOC "guys are like wolf packs at the tip of the spear doing what some believe is God's work and some believe is America's work," he said. Rumsfeld and Cheney, he said, "would intentionally sidestep the Agency and go to Joint Special Operations Command with a set of mission parameters and goals and policy objectives that they wanted to meet for their own political purposes."

When I asked him what operations he found most objectionable, Hunter was quick in his response: "Utilizing Special Operations Forces to spy without the knowledge of the State Department or the Central Intelligence Agency; using Special Operations Forces to go in and capture or kill people who were supposedly linked to extremist organizations around the world, in some cases allied countries." He described operations conducted by JSOC in scores of countries, beyond Iraq and Afghanistan. Among them: Somalia, Algeria, the Philippines, Indonesia, Pakistan, Thailand, Mali, Yemen, Colombia, Peru, as well as various European and Central Asian countries. Across the globe, he said, JSOC was being used to conduct "kinetic operations—whether it's capture or kill, in some cases to detain people—as directed."

"Who were the people that would be targeted for killing?" I asked.

"People that were either linked to an extremist organization, or they were suspected of being affiliated with an extremist organization. Or they were people that were providing safe harbor or funding," he told me.

"What type of intelligence would be necessary to say, 'We've got a green light'" to conduct a targeted kill operation outside of a declared battlefield?

"Most of it was purely circumstantial," he replied. "The majority of the operations were predicated on actionable intelligence, but not necessarily definitive intelligence. I think that's the most worrisome aspect of the operations that transpired."

The mindset, he said, was, "The world is a battlefield and we are at war. Therefore the military can go wherever they please and do whatever it is that they want to do, in order to achieve the national security objectives of whichever administration happens to be in power."

**The Imprisonment of Anwar Awlaki**

YEMEN, 2004–2007—When Anwar Awlaki returned to Yemen in 2004, history was laying a path for him that would lead him toward international infamy and a showdown against JSOC, the CIA and the US assassination program. It seems unlikely he knew that at the time. How could he? His father, Nasser, said that Anwar's decision to return to Sana'a was a practical one, not an indicator of his growing radicalism. "He could not get a scholarship to study in Britain," Nasser asserted, so "he decided to come back to Yemen." But what happened to Awlaki when he did return would harden his views toward US policies and propel him to renounce any allegiance he had once professed to hold to the country of his birth.

Awlaki arrived in Sana'a and was contemplating his next steps. He had plans to study at Iman University and was invited to preach at some mosques. In a lecture at Sana'a University, he delivered a speech on the role of Islam in the world and condemned the US war in Iraq. He and his wife and their children settled into Nasser's home in Sana'a, just near the university. By that time, Awlaki's eldest son, Abdulrahman, was nine years old. Like his father, he had spent the first years of his life growing up as an American. He was a lanky, bespectacled boy and the spitting image of his father at that age. Anwar "thought about creating a center of learning Islam and also language—teaching non-Muslims Arabic, and things like that," recalled Nasser. "He thought about starting his own school, like an elementary school. He wanted to just do regular preaching, until he found some job which was appropriate for him."

But the United States had not forgotten about Awlaki, and Yemeni intelligence agents were on him from the day he arrived. Awlaki had grown accustomed to life under surveillance, and he did his best to make a living. But religion—his faith—was his real passion. He spent a lot of time in front of the computer, recording sermons and carrying on extensive correspondence with his followers across the globe. "He was mostly doing lecturing, through the Internet," said Nasser. "And also he got into trying to start some businesses, you know, real estate, some ventures. He was trying to work as a private person, buying and selling real estate." Nasser laughed, shaking his head, before adding, "You know, but this didn't work out." Awlaki's children were enjoying the time they spent with their grandparents, aunts and uncles, and the Awlakis began building a separate apartment for Anwar and his family inside their gated lot in Sana'a.

Awlaki's family members describe this period in Sana'a as a time of exploration for Anwar. It seems clear that by 2006, Anwar had come to terms with the fact that his life as an American was over. The FBI was not going to leave him alone. The wars in Iraq and Afghanistan enraged him. He spent endless days and nights toiling over questions of how Muslims should respond to the wars, from Iraq, to Gaza, to Afghanistan and beyond. His sermons were becoming sharper. He often debated the nature of jihad with those he corresponded with. He truly seemed to be struggling to discover his own truths about the post-9/11 world. But Anwar did not mention al Qaeda, at least not in any positive way. "Everything was normal, and we thought that he put everything back [in America] behind him," recalled Nasser. "And we were building our house, and we built him an apartment, and all that. So really, everything to me was very normal. And he himself was just only working on his preaching and things like that. And nothing else."

Nothing else, until Anwar was put in prison.

"That was a turning point," said Nasser.


ANWAR AWLAKI was a political prisoner. When he was arrested in mid-2006 by US-backed Yemeni forces, there was a cover story. Something about Anwar intervening in a tribal dispute. But, as with most political prisoners, it was just a thinly veiled excuse to take him off the streets. Anwar was taken at night and put in solitary confinement at the feared prison in Sana'a run by the PSO, the Political Security Organization. The PSO worked closely with US intelligence. After he was arrested, Yemeni intelligence agents confiscated his computer and tapes of lectures he had given at Iman University. There were never any real charges brought against him. Anwar swore that it was the US government that was keeping him locked up, so Nasser reached out to the US Embassy for help. He was their citizen, after all. Surely they knew Anwar, Nasser thought. He was the one on TV after 9/11. The "go-to imam." A counselor at the embassy said he could offer little more than an assurance they would "look after" Anwar.

"For the first nine months, I was in solitary confinement in an underground cell. I would say that the cell was about 8 feet by 4," Awlaki later recalled. "I was not allowed pen and paper, and no exercise whatsoever. I hadn't seen the sun for the entire period." He said he was allowed "no interaction at all with any person except with the prison guards."

There is no doubt the United States was involved in Anwar's imprisonment. "I believe that I was held at the request of the United States government," Anwar said. "I was taken into custody without any explanation."
When he was first arrested, he said Yemeni intelligence agents "began
asking me questions about my local Islamic activities here, and later on
it was becoming clear that I was being held due to the request of the US
government. That was what they were telling me here." They also told
Awlaki that the United States wanted its own agents to question him. A
report by the United Nations special rapporteur on extrajudicial summary
or arbitrary executions alleged that Awlaki was arrested "at the request of
the United States Government."

The *New York Times* reported that John Negroponte, who at the time of
Anwar's arrest was the US director of national intelligence, "told Yemeni
officials that the United States did not object to his detention." But it was
more than simply not objecting. A Yemeni source with close ties to Awlaki
and the Yemeni government told me about a meeting between Negroponte,
Yemen's ambassador to the United States and Prince Bandar bin Sultan, the
former Saudi ambassador to the United States. Bandar was extremely close
to the Bush administration and President Bush in particular—so close, in
fact, that his nickname was "Bandar Bush." The source told me he spoke
to the Yemeni ambassador, who told him that Negroponte had said something to this effect: "Oh, it is very nice that you locked Anwar in prison.
It is good. Because what bothers us is [his] preaching, and his sermons,
and we are afraid that he will influence young people in the West." The
Yemeni ambassador, according to the source, told Negroponte, "Look, if
there is nothing, no case against Anwar, we cannot keep him indefinitely
in prison. The tribal people in Yemen, [Anwar's] friends, civil rights groups
in America and in Britain, they write letters to Condoleezza Rice and to us,
regarding the imprisonment of Anwar. And so we cannot keep him indefinitely." Negroponte's reply, my source said, was, "Well, but you have to."

In November 2006, Nasser Awlaki ran into Yemeni President Ali Abdullah Saleh at a development conference in London. "I asked him to release
my son from prison," Nasser recalled. "And he said, 'there are some issues
with the Americans, I will try to solve them and I will release your son.'"
Saleh bin Fareed, Anwar's uncle, with whom he stayed briefly in Britain, is
one of the most powerful tribal sheikhs in Yemen. He is the head of the Aulaq tribe, Anwar's tribe, which numbers some 750,000 people. In Yemen,
it is the tribes, not the government, that hold the power and influence,
and the Aulaqs were not going to stand for Anwar being in prison without
charges. Bin Fareed told me he called President Saleh and asked him why
he was holding Anwar in prison. "The Americans asked us to keep him

in jail," bin Fareed said the president told him. The Americans told Saleh, according to bin Fareed, "We want you to keep him for three, four years." Saleh told him, "[Anwar is] well spoken—the reason they gave us is that he's very well-spoken, many people listen to him in United States, especially young people. And all over the world. And we want him to be kept [locked up] for a few years, until people forget about him."

When President Saleh visited Washington, DC, early on in Anwar's imprisonment, he met with FBI director Robert Mueller, CIA director George Tenet and other US intelligence officials. Saleh told Nasser that he raised Anwar's case with them. In fact, he said he asked President Bush directly about Anwar. "If you have anything against Anwar al-Awlaki, tell us," he said Saleh told Bush. "If you don't, we will release him from prison." President Bush, he said, responded, "Give me two months, and then I will answer you."

Two months passed and then Nasser received a call from the chief of Yemen's Political Security Organization, General Galib al Qamish. "Dr. Nasser," he said, "please ask your son to cooperate with the interrogators, who are coming from Washington to meet Anwar." So Nasser went to the prison to appeal to Anwar. "I told my son 'Please, you know, we want to settle this thing forever. Why don't you be helpful, and meet these people?' And [Anwar] said, 'I am willing to meet them. I met them in America, and I am going to meet them in Yemen.'"

When the FBI agents arrived to interview Anwar, they stayed for two days. Awlaki "was summoned to an office and as he entered upon the Americans, he didn't put himself into [an] accused position, rather he entered the office [and] acted like a boss," recalled Shaykh Harith al Nadari, who was imprisoned with Awlaki. "He chose to sit on the most appropriate seat, ate from the fruits prepared by the Yemenis to host the Americans and poured a cup of tea for himself. I had asked him about the nature of the investigation. He told me that the whole thing was to find any tiny violation that would permit them to prosecute him back in an American court. It was an interrogation, he said. Nevertheless, they didn't find what they were searching after." Yemeni intelligence insisted on having its own people in the room. Awlaki said that when the US agents interrogated him for two days, "There was some pressure, which I refused to accept and that led to a conflict that occurred between me and them, because I felt that it was improper behavior from their behalf....That was solved however, later on, and they apologized." Anwar, according to Nasser, cooperated with the interrogators. Still, days and weeks passed, and Anwar remained behind bars.

When the Awlaki family pressed the regime for answers, the Yemeni president made clear to them the stakes. Yemen's vice president, Abd Rab-buh Mansur Hadi, told Nasser that the Yemeni president had a grim choice for him: Do you want to keep Anwar locked up or do you want me to re-lease him "to be killed by an American drone?" "So, this is the president of Yemen telling me, 'Keep your son in prison rather than getting him out, because if he gets out he will be killed by an American drone,'" Nasser said, adding that at the time, he believed that "the only reason which made the United States targeting Anwar was because of his popularity among Muslims, English-speaking Muslims in the world." He concluded, "I think Ali Abdullah Saleh must have known something."

AS HIS FAMILY on the outside fought for his freedom, inside the prison, Anwar pored over books. Any books he could get. For the first two months, the only book he was permitted was the Koran. Awlaki later said he saw his "detention as a blessing," saying it offered him "a chance to review Qur'an and to study and read in a way that was impossible out of jail. My time in detention was a vacation from this world." He later said that "because they took everything away and gave the Qur'an, that is why the Qur'an had this different meaning," adding, "It is because of the distractions that are going around us, that we don't get the most benefit from Qur'an. But when a person is in that solitary environment, all of the distractions are taken away and his heart is fixed on the word of Allah," and the words take on "a completely different meaning."

Eventually, Awlaki got his hands on *In the Shade of the Quran* by Sayyid Qutb. There were some striking similarities between Awlaki's life experi-ence and those of Qutb. Qutb was an Egyptian scholar and thinker whose writings and teachings later were credited with forming the intellectual basis for militant Islamist movements. He was a dissident in Egypt who advocated for an Islamic government. Like Awlaki, he spent time studying in Colorado, where he enrolled at Colorado State College of Education in 1949. After his time in the United States, Qutb railed against what he perceived as the excesses of American culture—scantily clad women, jazz music, wrestling and football, alcohol. He labeled America a "primitive" society, writing that its people were "numb to faith in religion, faith in art, and faith in spiritual values altogether." When he returned to Egypt, Qutb developed close ties to the Muslim Brotherhood. In 1954, he was arrested and put in jail, where he would remain for most of the rest of his life. While Qutb was tortured in prison, he also wrote his most influential texts, including the book Awlaki would read in his own prison cell a half century later. In 1966, Qutb was hanged after being convicted of plotting to overthrow the Egyptian government.

Awlaki said he was "so immersed with the author I would feel that Sayyid was with me in my cell speaking to me directly. There was something about my reading in prison: I could feel the personality of the author through his words. So even though I was in solitary confinement I was never alone." Awlaki said that he tried to limit his reading to thirty pages a day, "But because of the flowing style of Sayyid I would read between 100–150 pages a day. In fact I would read until my eyes got tired. My left eye would get exhausted before the right eye so I would close it with my hand and carry on reading with my right eye until it can handle it no more and would just shut down. My vision started deteriorating especially in my left eye. Was it because of too much reading, or was it because of poor lighting, Allah knows best. I found that deteriorating eyesight along with kidney problems were the two most common complaints of the prisoners."

He also read the works of Charles Dickens (*Hard Times*), Shakespeare (*King Lear*) and Herman Melville (*Moby Dick*). "There was a particularly mean Prison Head who decided to ban me from having any Islamic books," Awlaki later wrote. "Shakespeare was the worst thing I read during my entire stay in prison. I never liked him to start with. Probably the only reason he became so famous is because he was English and had the backing and promotion of the speakers of a global language." Awlaki, however, praised Dickens's works. "What fascinated me with these novels were the amazing characters Dickens created and the similarity of some of them to some people today. That made them very interesting," he wrote. "For example: the thick and boastful Mr. Josiah Bounderby of Coketown was similar to George W. Bush; Lucy's father, Mr. Gradgrind, was similar to some Muslim parents who are programmed to think that only Medicine and Engineering are worthy professions for their children; the amazing cruelness of Stephen Blackpool was similar to some people who appear on the surface to be decent and kind human beings; and Uriah Heep was similar to some pitiful Muslims today."

Awlaki later reflected on the food in prison. Describing *kudam*, the "staple breads of prisoners and soldiers in Yemen," Awlaki wrote: "[They] are supposed to be multigrain. That is how it was in the old days. Now they are most likely whole-wheat. They are fermented so their taste resembles San Francisco's sourdough bread (those who live in America would know what I am talking about). They consist of a solid crust (and I mean really solid); they could be used for fights." He recalled, "Before my imprisonment, I had discussions with former prisoners about how it was in jail, so there was some mental preparation for what was to come. I remember the words of one of the shuyukh [religious figures] who had been to this same prison. He said the food was so horrible, so I was expecting the worst." His first morning in the prison, Awlaki recalled, "I began hearing the opening of the doors and soldiers screaming at prisoners to pick up their meals. It was my turn and I was already awake. They opened my door and there were two soldiers, one holding a bucket and the other dragging a sack full of kudam. The one with the bucket took my plate and poured in it a cupful of steaming pinto beans while the other handed me six" pieces of *kudam*. After a few weeks, he said, he had concluded: "This food stinks."

Eventually, the prison authorities permitted Awlaki to receive home-cooked meals from his family twice a week. "However the prison administration would use this as a method to pressure prisoners. Under the pretext of searching our food for contraband items I would sometimes receive my food in an inedible state. They once mashed together my rice, chocolate cake and salad and then poured over it a package of cranberry juice. Even the guard who delivered the meal to me was saddened by the state of my food," Awlaki recalled. Prison, he said, reaffirmed his commitment to his religion. "Islam is not something that we use to fill in the spiritual compartment of our life while we leave everything else to our whims and desires. Islam should rule over every aspect of our life."

After Anwar Awlaki had been locked up for seventeen months, the tremendous pressure from tribal groups that Saleh's regime had to keep on his side to maintain power, and from Anwar's influential family, finally forced his release. Sheikh Saleh bin Fareed had gone to see the Yemeni president to offer his personal guarantees that Anwar would not cause trouble if he was set free. "OK, if you have anything against Anwar, please take him to court," bin Fareed told the Yemeni president. "And if you prove anything, you kill him. We don't mind. If you have anything, any proof against him, we don't mind if you take him to court and you kill him. If you don't, then give us our son." The president, he said, told him, "To be honest, I have nothing against Anwar, whatsoever." That day, the order was given to release Awlaki. "The Americans were not happy about it," said bin Fareed.

A US diplomatic cable about Awlaki's release elevated Anwar to a "sheikh" and referred to him as "the alleged spiritual advisor to two of the 9/11 hijackers." The cable added that Yemeni government "contacts" told US officials that "they do not have sufficient evidence to charge [Awlaki] and can no longer hold him illegally." A few years later, the US government would characterize Awlaki's imprisonment as evidence he had long been involved with terror plots against the United States. Without providing any evidence to support the claim, the US Treasury Department statement alleged Awlaki "was imprisoned in Yemen in 2006 on charges of kidnapping for ransom and being involved in an al-Qa'ida plot to kidnap a U.S. official, but was released from jail in December 2007 and subsequently went into hiding in Yemen."

**"America Knows War. They Are War Masters."**

SOMALIA, 2004–2006—While JSOC came to dominate the expanding killing fields in Iraq, Afghanistan and elsewhere, Somalia continued its descent into chaos. The murderous warlords who were running the CIA's targeted kill/capture operations were widely feared and reviled. By 2004, the Agency's outsourced Somalia campaign was laying the groundwork for a spectacular series of events that would lead to an almost unthinkable rise in the influence of al Qaeda in the Horn of Africa. But it wasn't the CIA's warlord program alone that would spur a major uprising in Somalia. The civilian tolls the wars were taking in Iraq and Afghanistan, and the abuses at Abu Ghraib and Guantánamo, gave credence to the perception that the United States was waging a war against Islam. While the United States backed its own warlords in Mogadishu, Washington's post-9/11 actions led to the formation of a coalition of former warlords and religious movements that would challenge the rule of the US proxies in Somalia. It was blow-back sparked by US policies in Somalia and abroad.

Yusuf Mohammed Siad told me he was first approached by the CIA in Dubai in 2004. The notorious Somali warlord, who goes by the nom de guerre Indha Adde, or White Eyes, was—like Mohamed Qanyare—among the thugs who divided and destroyed Somalia during the civil war that raged through the 1990s. Indha Adde violently took control of the Lower Shabelle region, appointing himself governor of a reportedly brutal paramilitary occupation, earning him the moniker "The Butcher." He ran drug and weapons trafficking operations from the Merca port and cashed in on the lawlessness. Like Qanyare, he controlled a sizable militia and an array of technicals—weaponized pickup trucks. But unlike Qanyare, Indha Adde maintained a friendly relationship with the small group of Islamic radicals who dotted the chaotic Somali landscape of the 1990s. He openly admitted to providing shelter and protection to some of the very men Washington was hunting. That made him an attractive potential asset for the CIA. In Dubai, he said, he met the CIA's chief of East Africa operations. "They offered me money, they offered funding for the region I was controlling, they offered me influence and power in Somalia through US cooperation," he recalled when I met him at one of his homes in Mogadishu in June 2011.

"The CIA was always telling me that the men I was protecting were criminals who bombed the US embassies, who were also a threat to the world. They told me they wanted me to hand these guys over to them."

But Indha Adde had watched the CIA-backed warlord alliance in action and wanted nothing to do with it. As he saw it, they were killing Somalis in the service of a foreign power. "They were contracted to hunt down anyone who was wanted by the Americans. Their prisoners were all mistreated— they were stripped naked and had their mouths taped," he remembered. "The warlords would kill the prisoners who the Americans released, to keep them from talking about their imprisonment."

Moreover, Indha Adde was in the midst of a personal conversion from a heavy-drinking gangster to what he saw as a real Muslim. When the United States invaded Iraq in 2003, Indha Adde—like many Muslims around the globe—viewed the United States as "arrogant" and on a crusade against Islam. "The US president's words against Islam, the Iraq invasion and the Afghanistan war inspired me personally not to coöperate with the CIA," he recalled. "I refused all of their offers." Instead, Indha Adde made a decision to commit his forces to defeating the CIA's warlords. "The Bush administration overstated the strength of Al Qaeda and Osama [Bin Laden]. But when he invaded Iraq, we all thought that Islam was under attack. That was al Qaeda's biggest victory, and that is why we supported them."

When al Qaeda figures would seek his support or sanctuary in the areas he controlled, Indha Adde obliged. To him, the men were on the right side of history, fighting crusaders and their proxy warlords and defending Islam. "Personally, I thought of even Osama himself as a good man who only wanted the implementation of Islamic law," he remembered. "If there was accountability, Bush would have been executed like Saddam Hussein. But no one is powerful enough to hold the US to account."

While Qanyare worked with the Americans, Indha Adde soon became one of al Qaeda's key paramilitary allies and a commander of one of the most powerful Islamic factions to rise up in Somalia after 9/11. American activities that had started with a discreet meeting with Qanyare in a Nairobi hotel room in 2002 with the aim of killing or capturing five specific terrorists had transformed into death squads roaming Somalia, killing with impunity and widely viewed as being directly supported and encouraged by the United States. In a meeting with US officials in early 2006, according to a diplomatic cable, the internationally recognized Somali president "wondered aloud why the U.S. would want to start an open war in Mogadishu."

It was this horrific era that gave birth to the Islamic Courts Union (ICU), which would rise up against the US-backed proxies. The ICU was not a plot organized by al Qaeda, but rather an indigenous response to the lawlessness and brutality of the warlords, particularly those backed by the CIA. As Somalia disintegrated, small, regional Islamic courts began rising up. They created local justice systems based on Sharia law and sought to bring some level of stability. For several years, the courts were largely autonomous, clan-based entities. In 2004, the twelve courts united to become the Supreme Council of Islamic Courts of Somalia, known as "the Courts." Sheikh Sharif Sheikh Ahmed (known simply as Sheikh Sharif), a former schoolteacher and cleric from the Middle Shabelle region, was elected its leader. Indha Adde would eventually serve as its defense minister. "When the Islamic Courts Union formed, there was a civil war in Somalia. There was murder, robbery and rape. The powerless were victimized. Everyone suffered, but the weakest clans were the hardest hit," recalled Indha Adde. "Warlords ruled, and we searched for a way to unite and save our people. It is Islam that unites us, so we formed the Islamic Courts Union."

In 2005, foreign weapons and money poured into Somalia. Indha Adde and other Courts figures began receiving shipments of heavy weapons and ammunition, flown into private airstrips from Eritrea. Ethiopia, meanwhile, joined with the United States in supporting the CIA's warlords with finances, weapons and ammunition. Somalia's prime minister, Ali Mohamed Gedi, an Italian-educated veterinarian, watched as the CIA bankrolled and armed Qanyare and the other warlords, some of whom were actually ministers in his own government. "I was following very closely those warlords and particularly Qanyare, who was misleading the US intelligence organizations by saying, 'I can defeat this terrorist, this Islamist. Yes, I will catch them tomorrow, the next day.' And they were paying him," Gedi told me. The CIA, he charged, undermined his government and "encouraged the mushrooming of the Islamic Courts and their strength. [The United States] stimulated the Islamic Courts people by supporting the warlords and the 'antiterrorism group' at that time. So the whole mess started from that point."

In February 2006, as the Islamic Courts Union grew in strength, Qanyare and the CIA's warlord network went public, officially announcing the Alliance for the Restoration of Peace and Counterterrorism and calling on Somalis to join them in defeating the "jihadists." In March, at the White House, the National Security Council officially endorsed the US campaign to fund and support the warlords. State Department spokesman Sean McCormack said the US strategy was to "work with responsible individuals... in fighting terror. It's a real concern of ours—terror taking root in the Horn of Africa. We don't want to see another safe haven for terrorists created. Our interest is purely in seeing Somalia achieve a better day." Washington "chose to view the situation only through the prism of its 'war on terror,'" observed Salim Lone, a former UN official. "The Bush Administration supported the warlords—in violation of a UN arms embargo it helped impose on Somalia many years ago—indirectly funneling them arms and suitcases filled with dollars." Qanyare and his allies suddenly appeared far better armed than before. "To war with [al Qaeda], you need very well-trained forces. And enough numbers, and enough weapons, and enough logistics. And enough reinforcements," Qanyare told me. With no sense of the irony that his alliance had given rise to the ICU, Qanyare told his American handlers, "This war is easy, it will not take time." It would not even take six months, he predicted. He was right about the timeline, but not its outcome.

After the warlords openly declared war on the Islamic Courts, Mogadishu was rocked by its worst fighting in more than a decade. By May, the *Washington Post* was reporting battles that "were some of the most violent in Mogadishu since the end of the American intervention in 1994, and left 150 dead and hundreds more wounded." The UN Monitoring Group, in its report to the Security Council, cited "clandestine third-country" support for the warlords. It did not specify which country, but everyone knew. US diplomats in the region soon found themselves besieged by their colleagues from other nations, including European Union officials. According to one US cable from the Nairobi Embassy, some European governments, "having concluded that the U.S. is supporting individual warlords as a means to prosecute the GWOT, tell us they are concerned that such actions now may set back both CT and democratization objectives in Somalia." The EU, the cable noted, was preparing to release a report that would state bluntly: "There are worrying signs that the general population—riled by overt support of the United States for the warlords—is increasingly rallying to the cause of the jihadis." Some US officials were clearly irked by the CIA's warlord program. They privately told the *New York Times* that "the campaign has thwarted counterterrorism efforts inside Somalia and empowered the same Islamic groups it was intended to marginalize."

The once disparate Islamic Courts Union, at the urging of and with strong backing from local businessmen in Mogadishu and other cities, began a concerted mobilization to defeat the CIA's warlords. Indha Adde would lead its military campaign. The ICU called on Somalis to "join the jihad against the enemies of Somalia."

But it wasn't simply a religious cause. The warlords had been a disaster for business in Mogadishu. The "killing [of] prayer leaders and imams in local neighborhoods, and school teachers, really sparked a much-needed anger," said Abdirahman "Aynte" Ali, the Somali terrorism scholar. But, from a financial perspective, he said, the warlords "had been holding Mogadishu hostage for sixteen years. They failed to open the airport, the seaport; they all had small airstrips beside their houses—literally, their houses. And so they were holding people hostage." In late 2005, businessmen had begun funneling money to the ICU to buy heavy weapons to take on the CIA warlords. Somalis from all walks of life began signing up to fight alongside the ICU. "People would leave their jobs at 5 pm at the Bakaara Market, take their weapon and join the fight against the warlords," recalled Aynte. "And the next morning they would report back to their shop, or whatever. I mean, it was stunning."

THE ISLAMIC COURTS UNION was not a homogenous bunch. Many of the Courts' leaders and rank and file had no connection to al Qaeda, knew little of bin Laden and had an agenda that was squarely focused internally. Their meteoric rise in popularity had everything to do with hatred for the warlords, combined with a fierce desire for stability and some degree of law and order. "We deployed our fighters to Mogadishu with the intent of ceasing the civil war and bringing an end to the warlords' ruthlessness," said Sheikh Ahmed "Madobe" Mohammed Islam, whose Ras Kamboni militia, based in Jubba in southern Somalia, joined the ICU in 2006. He told me, "Those of us within the ICU were people with different views—liberals, moderates and extremists." Other than expelling the warlords and stabilizing the country through Sharia law, he said, there was "no commonly shared political agenda."

There were certainly elements of the ICU that had a Taliban-like vision for Somalia. But the regionally based courts were largely used to govern their specific clans or subclans, rather than as a national justice system. Although Somalia is an almost exclusively Muslim nation, it also has a strong secular tradition that would have come into direct conflict with a Taliban-style agenda imposed nationally. "The courts' promise of order and security appeals to Somalis across the religious spectrum. Their heterogeneous membership and the diversity of their supporters mean that attempts to label the *Shari'a* system 'extremist', 'moderate' or any other single orientation are futile. In reality, the courts are an unwieldy coalition of convenience, united by a convergence of interests," the International Crisis Group noted in its 2005 report "Somalia's Islamists." The ICG asserted that only two of the courts had been "consistently associated with militancy" and that they were counterbalanced by other courts. It concluded, "[M]ost courts appear to exist for chiefly pragmatic purposes. Rather than imposing an Islamist agenda on a new Somali government, most are likely to be absorbed willingly into any future judicial system."

That did not mean that extremists did not view the Courts as a vehicle to implement their radical agenda. "We share no objectives, goals or methods with groups that sponsor or support terrorism," declared Sheikh Sharif, the head of the ICU, in an appeal to the international community. "We have no foreign elements in our courts, and we are simply here because of the need of the community we serve." Sharif's declaration may have been technically true, but that is only because the Harakat al Shabab al Mujahideen was not officially one of the Courts.

More commonly known by its abbreviated name, al Shabab, or The Youth, the group of young Islamist militants had joined forces with the ICU during the war against the warlords. There are varying accounts of when al Shabab officially formed, ranging from the late 1990s to 2006. Based on his interviews with insiders, Aynte concluded it was sometime in 2003. Al Shabab was initially organized by Aden Hashi Farah Ayro, who the United States alleged trained at al Qaeda camps in Afghanistan and was behind the killing of foreign aid workers in Somalia. Another influential leader was Ahmed Abdi Godane, a well-known jihadist from Somalia's relatively peaceful north. The men began training a cadre of young Somalis for a holy war. "They were extremely secretive, and many people who were part of that training were not widely accepted in the society. They were not Islamic scholars, they were not clan elders," said Aynte. "They were looking for legitimacy, so they joined the Islamic Courts Union, and they were not going to lose anything. If the ICU morphed into a central government for Somalia, it was a great deal. If it disbanded, they knew they would capture the essence of it. They had foresight." Eventually, al Shabab would win a powerful ally in Hassan Dahir Aweys, a former Somali army colonel turned military commander of Al Itihaad al Islamiya (AIAI), following the overthrow of Barre's regime.

IN AL SHABAB, al Qaeda saw opportunity: the chance to actually penetrate a Somali political landscape that it had long struggled—and largely failed—to exploit. Among al Shabab's closest allies in those early days was Indha Adde, at the time a key member of Aweys's faction of the ICU. "I was protecting all of these people," he recalled of the foreigners who had begun appearing amid al Shabab. "I thought of them as good people." Among those he harbored was Abu Talha al Sudani, an alleged explosives expert and a key figure in the world of financing al Qaeda's East Africa operations. Indha Adde also sheltered the Comoro Islands–born Fazul Abdullah Mohammed, the alleged mastermind of the 1998 embassy bombings. "At the time, Fazul appeared to me as a stable man," Indha Adde recalled. "Actually he told us that he had nothing to do with the bombings." When the war against the CIA-backed warlords began, Indha Adde realized that Fazul "had great military experience. He and other [foreign fighters] were trained by Osama personally." To Indha Adde, the CIA and the US government were the aggressors, and the foreign fighters increasingly popping up in Somalia were part of a growing struggle to reclaim the country from the warlords. Backed by al Qaeda, al Shabab forces began using Qanyare and the other warlords' own tactics against them, assassinating figures associated with the CIA's warlord alliance.

Fazul may have convinced Indha Adde that he had nothing to do with terrorism. But in the chambers of the US counterterrorism community, Fazul had become Washington's number-one HVT in East Africa. Fazul was not just a terrorist; he was a believer. And, by all accounts, he was brilliant. Born in 1972 or 1974, depending on which of his many passports or ID cards you look at, Fazul grew up in a stable, economically viable family in the extremely unstable cluster of islands that make up the Comoros. The political backdrop of his childhood was filled with coups or attempted coups—at least nineteen in all—after the Comoros declared independence from France in 1975. As a kid, Fazul liked to pretend he was James Bond as he played spy games with his friends. He enjoyed mimicking Michael Jackson's dance steps and was, according to his teachers, an extremely bright child. By the age of nine, he had memorized much of the Koran and could be heard reciting its verses on national radio. As he grew older, Fazul began studying under preachers who subscribed to a Saudi Wahabist worldview.

By the time he arrived in Karachi, Pakistan, in 1990, Fazul was already fully radicalized. Originally enrolled as a medical student, he soon transferred to Islamic studies and was recruited to train with the mujahedeen, which had just expelled the Soviets from Afghanistan. It was in Peshawar, Pakistan, that he first heard Osama bin Laden preach. Soon thereafter he arrived in Afghanistan to receive training in guerrilla warfare, surveillance evasion, the use of various small and heavy weapons and bomb-making. In 1991, he wrote to his brother Omar that he "got confirmed" in al Qaeda. His first mission, in 1993, would be to travel to Somalia to help train the small groups of Islamic militants who had joined in the insurrection against the US and UN forces. He worked under Abu Ubaidah al Banshiri, whom bin Laden had placed in charge of al Qaeda's Somalia operations. For Fazul, it was the beginning of a long terrorist career in East Africa. It was there that he first hooked up with Aweys and members of Al Itihaad, the people who would later bring him into the fold of the Islamic Courts Union.

Fazul claimed that his team participated in the downing of the Black

Hawks in 1993, but al Qaeda failed to entrench itself in Somalia as the warlords divided up the country. Most of them had no use for bin Laden or foreigners. "The primacy of tribalism in Somalia ultimately frustrated al-Qa'ida's efforts to recruit long term and develop a unified coalition against foreign occupiers. Al-Qa'ida mistook its call for jihad in Afghanistan as a universal motivator for which Muslims in Somalia would join at an equal rate," noted a study conducted at West Point Military Academy's Combating Terrorism Center. "In 1993 Somalia, this call fell on somewhat deaf ears as survival against local competitors trumped jihad."

So Fazul turned his attention to Kenya.

The embassy bombings in Kenya and Tanzania took five years of careful planning and preparation. Working with al Qaeda operative Saleh Ali Nabhan, Fazul directly coordinated the Nairobi bombing, renting the house that would serve as a laboratory to manufacture the explosives for the job. During this time, Fazul became a rising star within al Qaeda. He became one of its prized couriers, funding cells throughout East Africa and, for a period, relocated his family to Khartoum, Sudan, where bin Laden was building up al Qaeda and preparing to declare war on the United States. By 1997, when bin Laden officially announced al Qaeda would attack US interests, Fazul had already left Sudan and was outraged that he learned it from CNN. The announcement resulted in raids, including on the home of one of Fazul's closest associates who was preparing the embassy bombing in Nairobi. In the end, despite several close calls with the Kenyan authorities, the embassy hits were a categorical triumph, catapulting bin Laden and al Qaeda to international infamy. It also put Fazul on a path to becoming the chief of al Qaeda's East Africa operations.

After the Nairobi bombings, the United States aggressively tried to freeze the assets of bin Laden and al Qaeda. In response, bin Laden sought new revenue streams and put Fazul in charge of an ambitious operation to penetrate the blood diamond market. From 1999 to 2001, Fazul would largely operate out of Liberia under the protection of its dictator, Charles Taylor. In all, al Qaeda took in an estimated $20 million in untraceable blood diamond money, much of it from the killing fields of Sierra Leone. By that point, Fazul was a wanted man, actively hunted by the US authorities, and al Qaeda spent huge sums of money to keep him safe. He had become a player.

In 2002, Fazul was dispatched to Lamu, Kenya—ironically just a stone's throw from the eventual JSOC base at Manda Bay. From there, he organized the Mombasa attacks on the Paradise Hotel and the Israeli aircraft. Some of the operatives for that mission began training in Mogadishu, and Fazul would regularly travel to Somalia to check in on their progress. During this period, he worked extensively with Nabhan. Following the Mombasa attacks, Fazul traveled discreetly between Kenya and Somalia. The CIA always seemed to be a step behind him. In 2003, they contracted Mohamed Dheere, who was part of the CIA's warlord alliance, to hunt him down. Qanyare also told me that Fazul's photo was shown to him as early as January 2003 by US intelligence agents. Qanyare claims that he showed US counterterrorism agents houses used by Fazul and Nabhan and gave them GPS coordinates, but that the US agents were reluctant to pull the trigger on any targeted killing operations in Mogadishu, saying they preferred for the warlords to capture them. "They were worried that innocent people would die because of their action," Qanyare told me. "But, to arrest them is not easy because they got protection from other local al Qaeda people." The warlords failed to catch Fazul or Nabhan.

In August 2003, while the CIA was deep in its hunt for Fazul and other suspected terrorists in East Africa, an e-mail address the Agency had linked to al Qaeda was traced to an Internet café in Mombasa. Working with a CIA case officer, Kenyan security forces raided the café and began to arrest two men who were at a computer and were logged in to the suspect e-mail account. As they led the men to a police wagon, the larger of the two suspects shoved the smaller one away, pulled out a grenade and blew himself up. Special Operations sources later told military journalist Sean Naylor that the larger man was a "suicide bodyguard" and that the smaller man, whom he was protecting, was in fact Fazul. "Security forces converged on the scene, but Fazul was too smart for them," Naylor reported. "He ran into a mosque and emerged disguised as a woman, wearing a *hijab* or some other form of Islamic facial covering." US intelligence later searched the apartment Fazul and his bodyguard were using in Mombasa and discovered an apparatus for forging passports and visas.

In 2004, US intelligence claimed to have intercepted communications from Nabhan indicating that al Qaeda was, once again, planning to attack the US Embassy in Nairobi using a truck bomb and a chartered plane. By then, US counterterrorism officials had declared Fazul and other members of al Qaeda's Somalia cell "among the most wanted fugitives on the planet," saying Fazul was "a master of disguise, an expert forger and an accomplished bomb builder" who was "maddeningly elusive" and "the most dangerous and...most sought after" al Qaeda figure in Somalia.

In Mogadishu, Fazul hooked up with Aweys and Aden Hashi Farah Ayro, a Somali militant who had trained in Afghanistan with al Qaeda, and other former comrades from Al Itihaad, as they began building up al Shabab. He and Nabhan served as al Qaeda's chief emissaries to the group. At that point US intelligence was not even aware of the group's name and referred

to it simply as "the special group." Al Shabab's training base, the Salahud-
din Center, was situated on the grounds of a former Italian cemetery that
had been rather gruesomely desecrated. It was heavily fortified and offered
recruits the opportunity to watch jihadist videos from Afghanistan, Iraq
and Chechnya, as well as videos featuring bin Laden. "Once the Salahud-
din Center was established by al Shabab, they provided the training and the
know-how, they brought in the experience that was needed," said Aynte.

When the Islamic Courts Union began to emerge as a force that could
expel the warlords, Fazul ensured that al Qaeda would be a part of it. "Fazul and Nabhan, all of the foreigners were with us," recalled Madobe. "At
the time they were engaged in making connections and coordination which
we believed to be part of the jihad, and we knew that they were members
of al Qaeda." Madobe said he was not concerned about Fazul and the other
al Qaeda figures when they began appearing around the ICU. Al Shabab,
he asserted, had very little backing from Somalia's biggest clans and were
minor players compared to the more powerful Courts. "They were out
numbered by those within the Courts who had positive agendas," he said.
"But I can say the US actions helped boost them."

AL SHABAB began making a name for itself in 2005 by carrying out a spate
of "headline-grabbing assassinations and cemetery desecrations in Mogadishu and other regions," according to Aynte. In his paper, "The Anatomy of al Shabab," Aynte alleged that after al Shabab formed "more than
[one] hundred people, mostly former military generals, professors, businessmen, journalists and activists were quietly assassinated over the next
few years." He noted that a former al Shabab field commander "said the
objectives of the assassinations were twofold: First, it was a deliberate,
preemptive attempt to eliminate dissent and potential roadblocks. Second,
it was designed to inject fear and terror in the hearts of the elite class in
Mogadishu, who at the time wielded significant influence by their sheer
domination of the business, media and academia."

While the CIA obsessed over the relatively small number of foreign
fighters among the ICU in Somalia, many within the Courts did not see
them as a problem. If they did become trouble for the ICU, most of its
leaders were confident they could be kept in check by the clans that were
supremely important in Somalia's power structure. But it was Washington's own actions that would soon make al Shabab and its al Qaeda allies
more powerful in Somalia than it—or the CIA—could ever have imagined.

Backed by overwhelming public support, it took the Courts just four
months to drive out the CIA's warlords, sending Qanyare and his strong-

men fleeing. "We have been defeated because of a lack of logistics, the kind a militia needs to live: ammunition, superior weapons, coordination. This is what was needed," Qanyare recalled. He claimed that the United States only gave him "pocket money." Despite this, Qanyare's faith in his CIA partners was unshaken. "America knows war. They are war masters. They know better than me. So when they fight a war, they know how to fund it. They know very well. They are teachers, great teachers." As the Courts pummeled Qanyare's forces, he claimed, the CIA refused to increase its support for him and the other warlords. "I don't blame them, because they were working under the instruction of their bosses," he said, adding that if the United States had provided more funding and weapons at that crucial moment when the ICU was besieging Mogadishu, "We should win. We should defeat them." As he prepared to flee Mogadishu, he said he warned Washington. "I told them it would be too expensive to defeat [al Qaeda and al Shabab], for you, in the future, in the Horn of Africa. Al Qaeda is growing rapidly and they are recruiting, and they have a foothold, a safe haven—vast land."

JSOC had a limited presence in Somalia up to this point, with the CIA largely controlling counterterrorism operations there. But as the Agency's favored warlords were being driven out of power, JSOC began agitating to take a more active role. General McChrystal, JSOC's commander, had already started coordinating video teleconferences focused on the Horn of Africa and began pushing for a broadening of JSOC's role within counterterrorism operations there.

ON JUNE 5, 2006, the ICU's forces officially took control of Mogadishu. Some Somalia experts within the US government hailed the expulsion of the warlords as "a wonderful piece of news," in the words of Herman Cohen, the former assistant secretary of state for African affairs. "The warlords have caused tremendous hardship....People were permanently insecure under the warlords," Cohen declared the day after the ICU took the capital. "It's very important to keep those warlords from coming back into Mogadishu." In backing the warlords, like Qanyare, Cohen said, "I think the U.S. government panicked. They saw an Islamic group; they said, 'Taliban is coming.'" As for the risk that Somalia would become an al Qaeda safe haven, Cohen said, "I think it's minor, because the people in the Islamic movement saw what happened to the Taliban and they don't want the same thing to happen to them."

The ICU's chair, Sheikh Sharif, immediately penned a letter to the United Nations, the US State Department, the Arab League, the African and European Unions and other international institutions denying that the ICU had any connection to terrorists and declaring that the Courts wanted to "establish a friendly relationship with the international community that is based on mutual respect and interest."

"The present conflict has been fueled by the wrong information given to the U.S. Government by these warlords," he wrote. "Their expertise is to terrorize people and they were able to use it and terrorize the American government by misinforming them about the presence of terrorists in Somalia." In a subsequent letter to the US Embassy in Nairobi, Sharif pledged his support in fighting terrorism and said the ICU wanted to "invite an investigative team from the United Nations to make sure that international terrorists do not use the region as a transit route or hiding ground."

The United States was not impressed with the letter. "While we are prepared to find positive elements within the ICU," one diplomatic cable from Nairobi declared, "acknowledgement of the foreign al Qaida presence will serve as a litmus test for our engagement with any of its leaders."

In general, the US view of the Islamic Courts taking power was not a unified one. Scores of US diplomatic cables from that period portray a confused and contradictory assessment from US officials. Sharif was consistently characterized as a "moderate" within the cables sent from the US Embassy in Nairobi. Yet, according to the *New Yorker*'s Jon Lee Anderson, "The Bush administration had gone so far as to contemplate killing Sharif." For its part, al Shabab viewed Sharif as a sellout whose attempts to curry favor with the West was apostasy.

US diplomats worked with the recognized government of Somalia to determine how to approach the ICU, but the US military and the CIA saw the Courts' taking of Mogadishu as a serious crisis. "Suddenly, this is becoming a major issue that people throughout government are concentrating on: Military analysts, intelligence analysts, all over. Somalia is suddenly catapulted onto everybody's radar screen," said Daveed Gartenstein-Ross, a frequent consultant to the US military, including CENTCOM, who has advised US military forces deploying to the Horn of Africa. "The immediate concern is twofold: One, is the Islamic Court's connection to al Qaeda. And the second concern is possible emergence of a terrorist safe-haven inside of Somalia." President Bush was in Laredo, Texas when word came that the ICU had chased the warlords from Mogadishu. "Obviously, when there's instability anywhere in the world, we're concerned. There is instability in Somalia," he said. "We're watching very carefully the developments there. And we will strategize more when I get back to Washington as to how to best respond to the latest incident there in Somalia."

While the White House strategized, the ICU did indeed implement a radical agenda in Mogadishu—but one that virtually all Somalis viewed as being for the better. The Courts began dismantling the insane maze of roadblocks that separated one warlord's kingdom from another's, leading to a significant drop in food prices. They reopened the ports and the airport, facilitating a dramatic increase in the amount of humanitarian aid that was able to reach Mogadishu. Robbery and other crime dropped substantially, and many residents told journalists that they felt safer than they had at any point in sixteen years. The ICU "brought a modicum of stability that's unprecedented in Mogadishu," recalled Aynte. "You could drive in Mogadishu at midnight, no problem, [with] no guards." US officials acknowledged the improvement in aid shipments and credited the ICU with reducing piracy around Somalia. Even officials within the US-backed Somali government in exile acknowledged that the ICU had achieved something important. "The Islamic Courts brought about some semblance of order and stability to Mogadishu," conceded Buubaa, the former foreign minister, who had opposed the ICU. "A lot of people in Mogadishu appreciated that."

That was not the case within the US Special Operations community.

After 9/11, JSOC had been tasked with hunting down the most wanted terrorists in the world as identified by the White House. The Islamic Courts' social program would not change that fact. The CIA's warlord adventure had been a categorical failure and had actually resulted in even greater protection for the al Qaeda figures on JSOC's radar. The invasion of Iraq was, in many ways, an enormous distraction from JSOC's core mission. "There's no question about that. Iraq fucked everything up," said Gartenstein-Ross. Somalia is a "country, which, relative to Iraq, would have been easier to stabilize. But resources were never devoted to that. The major problem is that no steps were taken to avert an insurgency—and indeed, very early on, you had an insurgency arise." More to the point, Washington's own policies had directly sparked the insurgency. Following the CIA's failure in Somalia, the US military began preparing for a campaign to crush the Courts. But with Black Hawk Down still dominating the US view of boots on the ground in Somalia, the White House began considering using Somalia's reviled neighbor, Ethiopia, as a proxy force that could provide cover for US hit teams, primarily from JSOC, to covertly enter Somalia and begin hunting "High Value Targets."

A UN cable from June 2006, containing notes of a meeting with senior State Department and US military officials from the Horn of Africa task force, indicated that the United States was aware of the ICU's diversity but would "not allow" it to rule Somalia. The United States, according to the notes, intended to "rally with Ethiopia if the 'Jihadist[s]' took over."

The cable concluded, "Any Ethiopian action in Somalia would have Washington's blessing." Some within the US government called for dialogue or reconciliation, but their voices were drowned out by hawks determined to overthrow the ICU.

US Special Operations teams had long been in Ethiopia, training its notorious Agazi commando units. The country also had US air assets and small pop-up military facilities where the United States had access. But, although Ethiopia would play a huge role in the events to come, another of Somalia's neighbors would provide the launching pad for JSOC's forces. The US military began building up Camp Simba in Manda Bay, Kenya, which was created shortly after the Black Hawk Down disaster. Although its original intent was to train and assist Kenyan maritime forces along the Somali coast, as the ICU rose to power and the United States began drawing up contingency plans, the base at Manda Bay took on a different role. JSOC teams, particularly members of DEVGRU/SEAL Team 6, began setting up shop. Their presence was thinly masked by the US military's civil affairs units that mingled with the locals—rebuilding schools and creating water purification projects—and trained conventional Kenyan forces. It was from Manda Bay that elite US hit teams would stage any potential operations inside of Somalia. The men who would be tasked with this mission were classified as Task Force 88.

Almost from the moment the ICU took power, the Ethiopians were salivating over the possibility of intervening. Since the two countries had fought a nasty war in the 1970s, the Ethiopian military regularly crossed the border into Somalia, angering locals. Somali militants, who viewed the Ogaden region of Ethiopia as their own, conducted raids and attacks inside Ethiopia. After the ICU took power, Addis Ababa took the opportunity to ratchet up its rhetoric about the threat of Somali jihadists across the region. As Qanyare fled Mogadishu, he went on national radio to warn that the ICU's victory would result in an Ethiopian invasion, saying that Somalis were making a huge mistake by supporting the Courts. "I never, ever supported Ethiopia to land in Somalia," Qanyare recalled. "Over my dead body, I never accepted that. Because I know who they are, what they want, what they are looking for." A month after the ICU took power, US diplomats began noting reports of "clandestine" Ethiopian "reconnaissance missions in Somalia in preparation for possible future operations."

The United States "had already misread the events by aiding heinous warlords. And they misread it again," Aynte told me. "They should have taken this as an opportunity to engage the ICU. Because out of the thirteen organizations that formed the Courts, twelve were Islamic courts, clan courts who had no global jihad [agenda] or anything. Most of them never left Somalia. These were local guys. Al Shabab was the only threat—that was it. And they could have been controlled. But again the situation was misread and Ethiopia was essentially being urged by the US to invade Somalia." For al Qaeda, he said, "it was the break that they were looking for."

Malcolm Nance, a twenty-five-year veteran of the US intelligence community's Combating Terrorism Program, spent the bulk of his professional career working covert ops in the Middle East and Africa. He studied the rise of al Qaeda and al Shabab and was familiar with the leadership of both organizations. Nance told me he believed that the United States dramatically mishandled its counterterrorism approach in Somalia. Prior to the rumors of an Ethiopian intervention, he said, al "Shabab was a sideline organization, they were fringe." Nance believed the United States should have tried to work with the ICU and work toward isolating the foreign al Qaeda operatives. "As an intelligence guy, here is what I would have done [with an al Qaeda figure]: Leave him there. Get as many assets as close to him as possible. Put resources on him and all of his lieutenants there. Find out as much as possible. Find out what the real depth of al Qaeda is there. Then he will have an unfortunate accident on the road—you know, a lorry hits him from the front."

Nance believed that, given the clan-based power structure that ruled Somalia—and its repeated marginalization of foreign agents and widespread rejection of foreign occupation—the United States could have waged a propaganda war against the relatively small number of al Qaeda operatives around the Courts to "break their mindset, break their reason for being." "Wouldn't it be a lot more fun to brand al Qaeda as a non-Islamic cult? And to the point where people won't sell them bread, to where when they go out in a battlefield, people will fight against them." US intelligence, he asserted, should have run disinformation ops to portray them as "Satanists or people who are anti-Islam." He added: "We should have gone after them that way, and that would have helped every dimension of breaking the organization." The potential for any success from Nance's proposed strategy is debatable, given the clan system in Somalia and the fierce opposition to outside influence. But it was never put to the test. He called the actual US strategy that followed, "absolutely mind-boggling."

Like JSOC and the CIA, al Qaeda was closely monitoring events in Somalia. As rumors of outside intervention spread, Osama bin Laden released a statement that made clear al Qaeda had no illusions that Ethiopia was making its own military decisions. "We warn all the nations of the world not to agree to America's request to send international forces to Somalia. We swear to Allah that we will fight its soldiers on Somali soil, and we reserve the right to punish on their own soil, or anywhere else, at the appropriate time and in the appropriate manner," he declared. "Take care not to wait and tarry, as some of the Muslims did when they tarried in saving the Islamic government in Afghanistan. This is a golden opportunity and a personal obligation upon everyone who is capable, and you must not miss this opportunity to establish the nucleus of the Caliphate."

THE ISLAMIC COURTS UNION—and the first period of relative peace to come to Mogadishu—lasted just six months. While US diplomats in the region privately warned their superiors of potentially dire consequences of an Ethiopian invasion and sought to identify paths to reconciliation between the ICU and the internationally recognized transitional government, the Bush administration's national security team was gearing up for a war to take down the ICU. By late 2006, Ethiopian forces were massing along various points of the Somali border. Although US diplomats expressed concern over the buildup, they seemed unaware that the US military was deeply involved in it.

The ICU saw the writing on the wall. Both Sheikh Sharif, who just months earlier pledged to cooperate with the United States and the United Nations, and Aweys called on Somalis to wage a "jihad" against any invading Ethiopian forces. Dressed in combat fatigues, Sharif would sometimes hold an AK-47 as he made his public pronouncements. "I want to tell the Somali people that they have to protect their country, and their religion," Sharif declared. "Somalia's ancient enemy has returned, and therefore I give my order to Islamic Courts soldiers: We are calling you for Jihad in Allah's way." In November, as Ethiopia began pushing US officials to back an invasion to unseat the ICU, US officials obtained an "executive order" written in Arabic and purportedly issued by Aweys, who had recently taken on the role of chairman of the ICU. It called for the assassination of sixteen officials of the Somali government in exile, including the president, Mohammed Yusuf, and Prime Minister Mohamed Gedi. Specifically, it called for "martyrs" from al Shabab to "execute the operations using the most deadly suicide methods carried out by mujahidin fighters in Iraq, Afghanistan, Palestine and other countries of the world."

By December, the United States had developed a strategy to partner with the Ethiopian military and Somalia's government in exile to drive the Courts from Mogadishu. The plan was to install the weak, but official, Somali government, which would be secured by Ethiopian-trained Somali forces and the Ethiopian military. As for the ICU leaders and foreign fighters, Task Force 88, based out of Manda Bay, would develop a plan to hunt them down and kill them.

On December 4, 2006, CENTCOM commander general John Abizaid touched down in Addis Ababa for a meeting with Prime Minister Meles Zenawi. Officially, it was a routine visit with a US ally. Behind the scenes, it was clear that war was imminent. "We saw what was happening as the chance of a lifetime," a Pentagon officer told *Time* magazine, "a very rare opportunity for the U.S. to move directly against al-Qaeda and get these terrorists."

Days after Abizaid's meeting in Ethiopia, the US State Department significantly escalated its rhetoric and began publicly characterizing the ICU as an al Qaeda front. "The Council of Islamic Courts is now controlled by Al-Qaeda cell individuals, East Africa Al-Qaeda cell individuals," declared Jendayi Frazer, US assistant secretary of state for African affairs and the top US official on Africa. "The top layer of the courts are extremist to the core. They are terrorists and they are in control." Much like the buildup to the 2003 Iraq invasion, major US media outlets began hyping the al Qaeda connection, printing the views of anonymous US officials as verified facts. Sensational headlines began appearing, warning of a "Growing Al-Qaeda Menace in Africa." Corporate TV reporters breathlessly offered up revisionist history of the Somalia conflict, conveniently omitting the US role in creating the crisis. On CBS, veteran correspondent David Martin declared, "Somalia has been a safe haven for Al-Qaeda ever since the U.S. military pulled out of the country following the infamous Black Hawk Down firefight." CNN's Pentagon correspondent Barbara Starr practically sounded like a Bush administration spokesperson: "Today, here in East Africa, the concern remains that unless Somalia is shut down as a terrorist safe haven, the threat of another attack remains very real."

While the Bush administration and some prominent media outlets hyped the Somali threat, not everyone was playing along. Even as the US military prepared for direct action, the director of national intelligence, John Negroponte, expressed skepticism about claims the Courts were run by al Qaeda. "I don't think there are hard and fast views," Negroponte said. Somalia "has come back on the radar screen only fairly recently," he observed, adding that the key question was whether the ICU "is the next Taliban." He concluded, "I don't think I've seen a good answer." John Prendergast, who served as an Africa specialist in the Clinton administration's NSC and State Department, labeled the Bush administration's Somalia policy "idiotic," charging that backing an Ethiopian invasion would make "our counterterrorism agenda nearly impossible to implement."

Then-Senator Joe Biden, who at the time was preparing to take over the chairmanship of the Foreign Relations Committee, spoke out forcefully and displayed a keen historical knowledge of the timeline of events leading up to the ICU coming to power. "By making a bad bet on the warlords to do our bidding," Biden charged, "the administration has managed to strengthen the Courts, weaken our position and leave no good options. This is one of the least-known but most dangerous developments in the world, and the administration lacks a credible strategy to deal with it."

Credible strategy or not, the administration had committed itself to taking down the Courts.

On December 24, 2006, Ethiopian warplanes began bombing runs, as tanks rolled across the Somali border. It was a classic proxy war run by Washington and staffed by 40,000–50,000 troops from Somalia's widely despised neighbor. The ICU's defense minister, Indha Adde, held a press conference and publicly invited foreign Islamists to come fight. "Let them fight in Somalia and wage jihad, and, God willing, attack Addis Ababa," he said.

As fighter jets bombarded Somalia and Ethiopian forces made their way toward Mogadishu, Frazer and other US officials denied Washington was behind the invasion. The claims were demonstrably false. "The US sponsored the Ethiopian invasion, paying for everything, including the gas that it had to expend, to undertake this. And you also had US forces on the ground, US Special Operations forces. You had CIA on the ground. US airpower was a part of the story as well. All of which gave massive military superiority to the Ethiopians," said Gartenstein-Ross. "The Ethiopians were not able to come in without the support of the US Government," recalled Gedi, who was then the prime minister in exile and worked with US intelligence and the Ethiopian government in planning the invasion. "American air forces were supporting us."

Qanyare watched while the Ethiopians replaced his CIA-backed alliance as Washington's newest proxy. To him, it was an incalculable disaster. The "international community brought [the Ethiopians], in the pretext of that they are fighting with al Qaeda," Qanyare alleged. "They kill the people, because of a grudge of the 1977 war. They finish the people, and they kill the women and children. Elimination. Under the pretext that they are fighting al Qaeda. I should believe if America knew their character, they'd never call them."

By New Year's Day, exiled prime minister Gedi was installed in Mogadishu. "The warlord era in Somalia is now over," he declared. In a sign of what was to come, demonstrations broke out against the forces that had installed him as people swiftly and angrily began to denounce the Ethiopian "occupation." The events of 2007 would send Somalia on a trajectory toward more horror and chaos, leading to a stunning rise in strength and size of the very forces Washington sought to combat. "Ethiopia and Somalia were archenemies, historical enemies, and people felt that this was adding insult to the injury," said Aynte. "An insurgency was born out of there."

"If there's one lesson in terms of military operations of the past ten years, it's that the US is a very effective insurgent force," said Gartenstein-Ross. "In areas where it's seeking to overthrow a government, it's good at doing that. What it's not shown any luck in doing is establishing a viable government structure." The US and Ethiopian actions, Buubaa, the former foreign minister, said, would end up "driving Somalia into the al Qaeda fold."

Nance, the veteran intelligence operative, agreed that the US-backed Ethiopian invasion was a boon for al Shabab: "The Shabab existed in a very small warlord-like infrastructure, prior to that, but once Ethiopia went in there—it's pretty obvious that they were acting as a [US] surrogate—al Qaeda said, 'Great! New full-on Jihadi battlefront. We've got 'em here. We've got the Christian Ethiopians, we've got American advisers. Now we just create a new battlefront and we will reinvigorate East Africa's al Qaeda organization.' And that is exactly what happened."

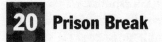

## 20 Prison Break

YEMEN, 2006—While the CIA's warlords were battling the Islamic Courts Union in Somalia and the Bush administration was almost singularly focused on the mounting insurgency in Iraq, a mass prison break in Sana'a occurred that would prove to be a seminal event in the reconstruction of al Qaeda in the region. Among those who escaped were several key figures who would go on to form the nexus of the leadership of a new organization, al Qaeda in the Arabian Peninsula (AQAP), including Nasir al Wuhayshi, bin Laden's former personal secretary. On February 3, 2006, Wuhayshi and twenty-two others escaped from their maximum security prison by tunneling out of a cell into a nearby mosque, though Wuhayshi later boasted that they performed morning prayers before literally walking out the front door. Wuhayshi would unite the Saudi and Yemeni branches of al Qaeda under the regional banner of AQAP. Qasim al Rimi, who escaped in the same breakout, would go on to become AQAP's military commander. "It is a serious problem," Rumsfeld said a few days after the prison break. "They were individuals who were deeply involved in al Qaeda activities and directly connected to the attack on the USS *Cole* and the death of the sailors that were on board that ship." But while Rumsfeld and other US officials focused almost exclusively on pressing Yemeni president Ali Abdullah Saleh to recapture Jamal al Badawi, whom the United States wanted to be extradited, and other *Cole* bombing suspects, it would be Wuhayshi and Rimi who would become the most notorious and problematic of the escapees.

Several former senior US intelligence, law enforcement and military officials who worked on Yemen operations and policy told me these prison releases were not accidental, and neither was AQAP's choice of Yemen totally beyond Saleh's control. While generally dismissing notions of direct collusion between Saleh and al Qaeda in planning attacks, the former officials described a multiyear pattern of Saleh's tacitly allowing acts of terrorism to be conducted on Yemeni soil, or exploiting such attacks after they occurred, as a way of reminding Washington of the threat posed by al Qaeda in Yemen. "Saleh knows how to play the game in order for everyone to know he is needed—from al Qaeda to the Saudis to the US," said the former top US counterterrorism official with extensive experience in Yemen. "And he plays it very well."

The game was about getting the money and weapons and specialized training for Saleh's most elite forces to battle the domestic rebellions he viewed as the real threat to his survival. "For years we have seen some of these regimes play these types of games," said Dr. Emile Nakhleh, the former senior CIA intelligence officer, in 2010. "They play it for survival, they play it to stay on our good side, they play it to get all kinds of military aid—and, in fact, the military aid is two or three times more than the economic aid that Yemen gets....Therefore, if that's true, then they are not necessarily serving [US] strategic, long-term counterterrorism policy."

Some seasoned Yemeni political analysts, however, believed that there was actually direct cooperation between the Saleh regime and al Qaeda. There were allegations that some members of the elite Republican Guard, the Political Security Organization and the Central Security Forces—all of which received support from Washington—were working with al Qaeda cells or had helped them with supplies, safe houses and intelligence on foreign diplomatic installations. The 2006 prison break struck some well-connected Yemeni security experts as "an inside job," asserted journalist Sam Kimball in a report for *Foreign Policy*. "The prison is an imposing fortress in the heart of Sana'a, with plainclothes soldiers patrolling its perimeter. Inmates' spare cells—only plastic silverware is allowed in—are inspected several times a day. Prisoners are only allowed a half-hour a day outdoors." Retired Yemeni colonel Muhsin Khosroof said, "We don't know how they got the tools to dig a 300-meter tunnel, and we don't know where the soil they dug out went." Short of direct support from prison officials, he asserted, "this operation would seem impossible."

The prison break would directly contribute to the growth of al Qaeda in Yemen. If what Colonel Khosroof and his colleagues alleged was true, it meant that the United States was backing the very government whose forces were facilitating al Qaeda's resurrection in Yemen.

Following the prison break, the Bush administration continued to increase military assistance to Yemen. According to the former top US counterterrorism official, Saleh had calculated that the political costs of cracking down on al Qaeda in a meaningful way—by handing over its leaders—would have been too great. "The moment he surrenders key figures, [Saleh's] gone off the cliff with al Qaeda. They won't support him any more. It means the relationship would be severely shaken." He added that Saleh "has given the US nothing of substance for the money he has received."

In July 2006, five months after the prison break, the United States launched a major expansion of Camp Lemonnier in Djibouti, from eighty-eight acres to almost five hundred. Its force had grown to 1,500 personnel, and it served as a major hub for the CIA and a stopover point for Special Operations Forces conducting covert or clandestine actions in the region. "Some teams use the base when not working 'downrange' in countries such as Kenya, Ethiopia and Yemen," reported *Stars and Stripes*, citing the camp's executive officer, Colonel Joseph Moore.

While Saleh played his game with the United States over the escaped prisoners, the United States was gradually building up its presence in the region, although Bush administration officials continued to treat al Qaeda's regrouping in Yemen as a secondary priority. In October 2007, Saleh received President Bush's top aide on homeland security and counter-terrorism, Frances Townsend, in Aden. During the meeting, Townsend asked Saleh for an update on Jamal al Badawi, the alleged mastermind of the *Cole* bombing. Saleh confirmed that he had been released and was "working on his farm" not far from where he and Townsend were meeting. Saleh added that he had just met with Badawi two weeks earlier. "Al-Badawi promised to give up terrorism and I told him that his actions damaged Yemen and its image; he began to understand," Saleh said. When Townsend "expressed dismay" over Badawi's release, Saleh told her not to worry because "he is under my microscope." It was Saleh who, according to a US diplomatic cable sent after that meeting, brought up Wuhayshi and told Townsend point blank that he had taken over as the head of al Qaeda in Yemen. Townsend, according to the cable, responded by changing the subject to Yemen's failed house-arrest system. Later in the meeting, Saleh discussed his fight against the southern secessionists, again portraying his survival as central to Washington's policies. "It is important that Yemen not reach a state of instability," he told Townsend. "We need your support." Townsend replied, "You do not even have to think about it. Of course we support Yemen."

Perhaps the most unusual moment during the Townsend-Saleh meeting came when Saleh brought in Faris Mana'a, a top Yemeni arms trafficker, and seated him next to Townsend. According to the United Nations, "Despite the Somalia UN arms embargo since 1992, Mana'a's interest in trafficking arms into Somalia can be traced back at least to 2003," and Mana'a "has directly or indirectly supplied, sold or transferred to Somalia arms or related material in violation of the arms embargo." As Mana'a entered the room, he was given a chair at Townsend's table. "Hey FBI," Saleh said to one of the US officials, "if he does not behave properly, you can take him... back to Washington in Townsend's plane or to Guantánamo." Saleh told Townsend his forces had recently intercepted a shipment of weapons from

Mana'a and given them to the Yemeni military. "He has donated weapons to the nation's military—he can be considered a patriot now," joked Townsend. Saleh laughed. "No, he is a double agent—he also gave weapons to the al-Houthi rebels." A US diplomatic cable Townsend authorized following the meeting proclaimed: "You Can't Make This Stuff Up." Putting an exclamation point on the whole episode, two years later, Mana'a would go on to serve as coordinator of President Saleh's "peace" efforts with the Houthi rebels.

Townsend's interaction with Saleh—and those of other US officials—showcased Saleh's prowess in playing multiple sides in his war to maintain power. "His use of the dual threats of terrorism and instability when referring to internal conflict is also not new," asserted the US diplomatic cable cleared by Townsend after her visit. "Saleh consistently uses this tactic when attempting to garner USG [US government] support." Saleh clearly used this approach because it was effective. When it came to al Qaeda, the less stable Saleh's government appeared, the more money and training he could squeeze out of the United States. "All these US officials were in way over their heads in dealing with Saleh," a former senior US military official who worked in Yemen told me. "When it comes to Yemen, he is so much smarter than them."

After the US drone strike in Yemen in 2002 and the subsequent arrest of scores of suspected militants, al Qaeda in Yemen had been severely disrupted and was largely a theoretical entity. But after the 2006 prison break, the escaped prisoners rebuilt the dormant organization. Saleh did little to stop them. The United States was obsessed with Saleh's recapturing Jamal al Badawi and another *Cole* suspect, a US citizen named Jabir al Banna, and paid scant attention to the others. "The US put a great deal of pressure on Yemen to track both men down," according to Gregory Johnsen, the Princeton Yemen scholar. "But, as is often the case, it was not the people the US was worried most about that caused the biggest problems, rather it was those it knew too little about that proved to be the most dangerous."

As Saleh told Townsend during her meeting with him in 2007, al Qaeda was indeed regrouping after the 2006 prison break. And, as he said, they were led by Wuhayshi, bin Laden's former secretary. Wuhayshi was a hardened jihadist who first went to Afghanistan in the late 1990s, where he hooked up with bin Laden. In 2001, when the United States invaded Afghanistan, Wuhayshi fought in the famed battle at Tora Bora and then fled to Iran, where he was arrested and held for two years before being handed over to Yemen in 2003. He was never charged with a crime. Upon his escape from the Yemeni prison, he rebranded al Qaeda in Yemen as a regional rather than a national group, called "The al Qaeda Organization of Jihad in the South of the Arabian Peninsula," which eventually became AQAP. Under Wuhayshi's leadership, al Qaeda in Yemen would "become more strident, better organized and more ambitious than it has ever been before," asserted Johnsen at the time. Wuhayshi "completely rebuilt the organization." That al Qaeda was back in business played well for Saleh because it required the Americans and Saudis to deal with him—and more important, to fund and arm his regime. But JSOC was growing impatient with Saleh and would soon begin to expand its own operations inside Yemen, with or without Saleh's permission.

## 21 Hot Pursuit

PAKISTAN, 2006–2008—Donald Rumsfeld's run as defense secretary met an inglorious end in late 2006. A half-dozen retired generals, some of whom were important commanders in the Iraq War, joined several Republican and Democratic lawmakers to spearhead a campaign demanding his resignation. Many sought to blame him for the deteriorating situation in Iraq, others for the abuses at Abu Ghraib prison. The Republicans suffered major losses in the 2006 midterm elections and handed the Democrats a majority in both the Senate and House, which many political analysts attributed to growing opposition to the Iraq War. Among those in the White House who had pushed hard for Bush to keep Rumsfeld on board was Dick Cheney. Although President Bush initially stood by Rumsfeld, he eventually accepted the resignation. Rumsfeld was undoubtedly a major figure in the secretive assassination and torture bureaucracy launched post-9/11, but his departure would not radically shift the course of the actions and programs he had helped to shape.

In December 2006, Robert Gates succeeded Rumsfeld. Gates had a close working relationship with the CIA, where he had spent much of his professional career. He first worked for the Agency in the late 1960s and ultimately went on to serve as its director in the early 1990s—the first basement-level recruit to rise through the ranks to become director. Gates had done several stints with the NSC and also had close ties to US Special Operations Forces. He was investigated over his alleged role in the Iran-Contra scandal, and though the independent counsel concluded Gates "was close to many figures who played significant roles in the Iran/contra affair and was in a position to have known of their activities," it was determined that his role "did not warrant indictment." Gates was also a key player in the US-fueled war in Afghanistan against the Soviets in the 1980s. Among his first acts at the Pentagon was to put Pakistan firmly back on the US targeted kill campaign's radar.

In testimony before the Senate Armed Services Committee three months into Gates's tenure, Lieutenant General Douglas Lute, director of operations for the Joint Staff, asserted that US military commanders had "kill-capture" or "direct action authorities in Afghanistan," making them "free to strike against those demonstrating a hostile act." Lute, however, added that those authorities also permitted operations inside Pakistan. If "the enemy" attempts "to flee across the border, [t]hen we have all the authorities we need to pursue." When asked about authority to engage in more invasive operations, such as directly targeting Osama bin Laden in Pakistan, Lute said he would only discuss it in closed session.

The "hot pursuit" arrangement had infuriated the ISI since it was first brokered by Musharraf and JSOC in 2002. Everyone in Pakistan knew the CIA was operating extensively in the country—every drone strike was a stark reminder—but the US military could not be perceived to be in the country for any purpose other than training Pakistani forces. While the Pakistani military and ISI were agitating for less US action on their soil, JSOC had been "pushing hard" for years to have greater latitude from the White House to strike inside Pakistan. JSOC wanted permission to hit, even in cases where the operation was more involved than the simple pursuit of suspected al Qaeda operatives across the border. "Give us greater latitude, we've got to hit where their sanctuaries are," was how a US official described JSOC's pitch at the time.

Although Pakistan was a fierce negotiator—at times outmaneuvering the United States—at the end of the day, it needed Washington's money, weapons and support. The bottom line, therefore, was that if Pakistan didn't want to deal with certain terrorist elements, JSOC and the CIA would. And the White House would sign off on it. In JSOC's case, that meant targeted raids into Pakistan. "I think this is one of those things that the Pakistanis looked the other way at times, much like the drone program," Anthony Shaffer, the DIA operative who worked on Pakistan extensively, told me. "I don't believe for a minute that President [Asif Ali] Zardari and [ISI chief] General [Ashfaq Parvez] Kayani, and even Musharraf before, didn't know we would be doing some of that."

By 2007, the budget for US special operations had grown by 60 percent from 2003 to more than $8 billion annually. In January, President Bush announced the "surge" in Iraq. The number of conventional US forces was expanded by 20,000, but Bush also authorized a dramatic increase in targeted killing operations, spearheaded by JSOC's forces. The operation was General McChrystal's swan song at JSOC. By the end of 2007, the president began declaring the Iraq surge a success. This freed up JSOC to refocus on Pakistan.

Late in 2007, the Bush administration began drafting plans for a substantial escalation of the use of US Special Operations Forces inside Pakistan. The plan, however, was stalled as a result of the ongoing fight for control of Pakistan operations between the CIA and the Pentagon, described by the *New York Times* as "bitter disagreements within the Bush administration and within the C.I.A." over "whether American commandos should launch ground raids inside the tribal areas."

An incident in June 2008 underscored the risks associated with a potential expansion of US special operations activity in Pakistan. A battle between US and Taliban forces in Afghanistan's Kunar Province spilled over into Pakistan. US forces called in air support and American choppers descended, launching missiles at the Taliban forces. The strikes also killed eleven Pakistani soldiers positioned on their side of the border. The action was denounced by Pakistan as an "unprovoked and cowardly" attack by the United States. "We will take a stand for sovereignty, integrity and self-respect," Pakistan's prime minister, Yousaf Raza Gillani told parliament. "We will not allow our soil [to be attacked]." The fact was, Pakistan could not back up such declarations.

Two days after the incident, on June 13, 2008, Vice Admiral William McRaven assumed command of JSOC from General McChrystal, inheriting the role of running the hunt for bin Laden and other HVTs. The botched raid that killed the Pakistani soldiers clearly didn't faze him. McRaven, a former Navy SEAL team leader and McChrystal's deputy commander at JSOC, began advocating for wider latitude to strike in Pakistan. In July 2008, President Bush approved a secret order—which had been the subject of much debate among the CIA, State Department and Pentagon—authorizing US Special Ops Forces to carry out targeted kill or capture operations. Unlike the early arrangement with President Musharraf, the US Special Operations Forces would not be working alongside Pakistani forces and they would not seek permission from Pakistan's government before conducting strikes on Pakistani soil. "To soothe the worries of U.S. Ambassador Anne Patterson about the mounting civilian deaths from JSOC raids in other countries, commandos brought her a Predator console so she could witness a raid in real time," according to reporters Dana Priest and William Arkin. In August 2008, Musharraf, long a malleable US ally, resigned from office under threat of impeachment. JSOC's forces almost immediately began testing his successor. As a Special Operations source who worked with McRaven at the time told me, "Bill rapidly expanded operations" in Pakistan.

On September 3, 2008, two helicopters carried a team of JSOC Navy SEALs across the Afghanistan-Pakistan border. Backed by a high-powered AC-130 Spectre gunship, with the capacity to do serious damage, they descended on a village near Angoor Adda, a small Pakistani mountain town in South Waziristan, near the Afghan border. The helicopters landed quietly, and more than two dozen SEALs, equipped with night-vision goggles, took up positions around the home of a fifty-year-old woodcutter and cattle herder. Some reports suggest that the Special Ops team had intel that an al Qaeda leader was inside. The *Washington Post* reported that it was "the first US ground attack against a Taliban target inside the country." In any case, once in position, the SEALs executed their raid.

What happened after the first shots were fired remains in dispute. According to US officials, "about two dozen suspected Qaeda fighters" were killed in "a planned attack against militants who had been conducting attacks against an American forward operating base across the border in Afghanistan." But according to local villagers, the SEALs opened fire, killing Payo Jan Wazir, the home's owner, along with six children, including a three-year-old girl, a two-year-old boy and two women. When Payo Jan's neighbors heard the gunfire and ran out to see what was happening, villagers said, the SEALs opened fire on them, killing ten more people. The Pakistani government said that all of the dead were civilians. The United States maintained they were al Qaeda militants. Pakistan's Foreign Ministry summoned Ambassador Patterson. In a statement it denounced the operation, calling it a "gross violation of Pakistan's territory" and a "grave provocation," alleging the raid had caused "immense loss of civilian life." The Foreign Ministry said it was "unfortunate" that US forces had "resorted to cross-border use of force against civilians," asserting that "such actions are counter-productive and certainly do not help our joint efforts to fight terrorism. On the contrary, they undermine the very basis of cooperation and may fuel the fire of hatred and violence that we are trying to extinguish."

After years of being directed to focus most of its resources on Iraq, JSOC was finally getting its chance to hit in a more concerted way in Pakistan. As it turned out, Rumsfeld's vision of the world as a battlefield was more fully realized after he left than when he was in power. His departure ushered in an era in which America's most potent dark side forces pivoted from Iraq to the US twilight wars in South Asia, Africa and beyond.

# 22 "Every Step Taken by the US Benefited al Shabab"

SOMALIA, 2007–2009—While much of the media focus on Somalia in early 2007 was on the Ethiopian invasion and occupation, JSOC was focused on hunting. It had quickly set up its makeshift "lily pad" at the discreet US base in Manda Bay, Kenya, in early January and was waiting to pounce. US war planners wanted the Ethiopian invasion to force the Islamic Courts Union leadership to flee the capital and head for strongholds, especially along the Kenyan border, where Task Force 88 could take them out. JSOC had AC-130 gunships positioned covertly at an airbase near Dire Dawa, Ethiopia, that could pummel retreating ICU leaders and foreign fighters, enabling follow-up JSOC teams based at Manda Bay to enter Somalia and finish the job, if necessary. US policy had boiled down to one mentality in Somalia: find, fix and finish. "It's kinetic, hard kill," asserted Malcolm Nance. "If it's not hard kill, it doesn't get played, you know?"

On January 7, an unarmed US Predator drone launched from Camp Lemonnier flew into southern Somalia, tracked down a convoy of vehicles and broadcast a live feed of them back to task force commanders. A short time later, an AC-130 flew into Somalia and strafed the convoy just before it disappeared into a forest along the Kenya-Somalia border. Reports suggested that the target was Aden Hashi Farah Ayro, al Shabab's military commander; or Fazul or Nabhan, the East Africa al Qaeda leaders. US officials claimed the strike killed between eight and twelve fighters, and rumors spread of an "al Qaeda leader" being among the dead. US and Ethiopian intelligence sources believed it might have been Ayro or Abu Talha al Sudani, the al Qaeda financier. A JSOC team from Manda Bay landed at the site of the strike in Somalia to take DNA samples from the dead. There, among the corpses and wreckage, they found Ayro's bloodied passport. They believed they had a major kill.

As it turned out, Ayro had indeed been in the convoy and was believed to have been injured, but he ultimately escaped.

On January 9, JSOC launched another strike "against members of the East Africa Al Qaeda cell believed to be on the run in a remote area of

Somalia near the Kenyan border," according to a US diplomatic cable from the Nairobi Embassy. Over the next few days there were several more air strikes that killed scores of civilians, according to witnesses and human rights groups. Whether these strikes were carried out by the United States or Ethiopia, or jointly, has never been confirmed. Undoubtedly, Ethiopia had its own helicopters and other aircraft pounding Somalia unilaterally. The Pentagon took credit for the January 7 strike but would not comment on the others, though anonymous US officials privately acknowledged they were American strikes. Initial US media reports portrayed the strikes as successful hits that were deftly picking off the "al Qaeda" leadership one by one in Somalia. Several reports, based on information provided by anonymous US officials, had Ayro and Fazul killed by US Special Ops troops. One particularly clownish report in the *New York Post*, claiming Fazul had been killed, bore the headline: "Qaeda Clobbered: U.S. Somalia Raid Kills Embassy Fiend." In reality, all but one of the major figures sought by the United States went unscathed in these operations. At some point, as US AC-130s, helicopters and Ethiopian aircraft strafed suspected al Shabab or al Qaeda strongholds, Sudani was randomly killed, though the United States did not learn of his death until months later.

This was the beginning of a concentrated campaign of targeted assassinations and snatch operations by JSOC in Somalia, but it initially produced few significant counterterrorism results. In fact, the men they were hunting would ironically become the beneficiaries of the very strikes that were aimed at killing them. "We were coming in and we were doing AC-130 strikes," Nance told me. "I mean it's a fine, fine instrument, when used against mass known troops, which is what the AC-130 is very good for." Rather than troops, he said, "We were wiping out groups of civilians."

Indeed, the AC-130 attacks resulted in a shocking number of Somali civilians being killed. In one particularly horrible incident, a large group of nomadic Somali herders and their families was attacked. The human rights group Oxfam alleged that seventy innocent Somalis were killed. "There were no combatants amongst them," said an Oxfam official. "It could possibly be related to a bonfire that the herdsmen had lit at night, but that's something they normally do to keep animals and mosquitoes away from their herd." Oxfam joined Amnesty International in questioning the legality of the air strikes. "Under international law, there is a duty to distinguish between military and civilian targets," Oxfam warned. "We are deeply concerned that this principle is not being adhered to, and that innocent people in Somalia are paying the price."

The US strikes focused intently on the areas around the Kenya-Somalia border, the stronghold of Ahmed Madobe and his Ras Kamboni militia.

Madobe was a protégé—and brother-in-law—of Hassan Turki, a career jihadist commander who founded the militia and led militant forces for each of Somalia's successive Islamist movements: AIAI, ICU and, eventually, al Shabab. When the strikes began, Madobe and his men were making their way back toward their home base near the Kenyan border, unwittingly putting them directly in the scope of JSOC's Task Force 88. Members of JSOC's intelligence division, the Activity, were tracking Madobe's movements and those of other ICU leaders. Like Indha Adde, Madobe had come to know and respect the international fighters who had come to Somalia and had helped in the battle against the CIA-backed warlords. His mentor, Turki, was now a US-designated terrorist. These facts, along with his leadership position within the Courts, put Madobe on a JSOC target list.

Madobe knew that the United States and Ethiopia were striking at fleeing ICU leaders and, after a few near misses, suspected he might be a target, so he and a small group made their way through the Somali countryside, trying to stay away from the growing number of aircraft overhead. "At night, we were afraid of lighting a fire to cook and in the daylight we did not want to create smoke," he told me when I met him at an outpost near the Kenyan border. "We had no precooked food, so it was really very tough." In retrospect, he said, it was likely technology that did him in. "We had Thuraya satellite phones, which clearly helped the Americans easily trace us."

On the night of January 23, 2007, Madobe and his group set up camp under a large tree. "At around 4:00 a.m., we woke up to perform the dawn prayers, and that's when the planes started to hit us," he remembered. "The entire air space was full of planes. There were AC-130s, helicopters and fighter jets. The sky was full of strikes. They were hitting us, pounding us with heavy weaponry." The eight people, whom Madobe said included both men and women who were with him in the camp, were all killed. Madobe himself was wounded. He believed that a ground force would come for him. "I picked a gun and a lot of magazines. I believed that death was in front of me and I wanted to kill the first enemy I saw," he remembered. "But it did not happen." Madobe lay wounded and losing blood and energy. Then, at around 10:00 a.m., he said US and Ethiopian forces landed by helicopter near his position. He recalled a US soldier approaching him as he lay shirtless on the ground. "Are you Ahmed Madobe?" the soldier asked. "Who are you?" he replied. "We are the people that are capturing you," he remembered the soldier telling him. The American held a photo of Madobe. As the American handcuffed Madobe, the guerrilla leader asked him why it was necessary. "You see I am half dead," he said.

They loaded Madobe onto a helicopter and took him to a makeshift base in Kismayo that the US and Ethiopian forces were using. The US forces, he said, immediately began interrogating him and only after Ethiopian agents intervened did they give him water and medical treatment. In Kismayo, as Madobe recovered from his injuries, he was regularly interrogated by the Americans. "They had names of different rebels and fighters on a list and they were asking me if I knew them or had information about them," he said. A month later, he was rendered to Ethiopia, where he was held for more than two years.

Unlike Madobe , the former chair of the ICU, Sheikh Sharif, was looking to make a deal. Even though senior US officials had suggested that the ICU was tantamount to the Taliban or was being run by al Qaeda, the United States actually viewed Sheikh Sharif as a "moderate." On December 31, 2006, as the ICU disintegrated, Sharif had made it to Kismayo, where he spoke by phone to the US ambassador in Nairobi. "The Ambassador told Sharif that it was the U.S. view that he could play an important role in helping to promote peace and stability in Somalia," according to a US diplomatic cable sent from Nairobi back to the State Department. The ambassador, who consulted with Washington before offering Sharif a deal, "indicated that the U.S. was prepared to recommend that Kenya help bring [Sharif] to Nairobi if he were prepared to give his commitment that he was willing to work to support peace and stability in Somalia...and to reject terrorism."

It was the beginning of a behind-the-scenes US campaign to rebrand Sharif. As Assistant Secretary of State Jendayi Frazer put it: It would be "preferable to co-opt a weak Sheikh Sharif Sheikh Ahmed, to prevent hard-liners from rallying around him." Sharif eventually escaped from Somalia to Kenya with the help of US intelligence. Ali Mohamed Gedi, the former Somali prime minister, told me, "I believe that [Sharif] was working with the CIA. They protected him." Gedi told me that when Sharif fled to Kenya in early 2007, the US government asked him to issue Sharif travel documents allowing him to travel to Yemen. Gedi says he also wrote letters on Sharif's behalf to both the Kenyan and Yemeni governments asking that Sharif be permitted to relocate to Yemen. "I did that, upon the request of the government of the US," he recalled. In Yemen, Sharif began organizing his eventual return to power in Mogadishu, this time with US support.

Unlike Sharif, many of those fleeing Somalia were at odds with the CIA and US intelligence. Kenyan security forces—sometimes acting at the behest of Washington—began arresting scores of people. Human Rights Watch reported that Kenya took into custody "at least 150 men, women, and children from more than 18 countries—including the United States, the United Kingdom, and Canada—in operations carried out near the Somali border. Suspecting the detainees of having links to terrorism, the Kenyans held them for weeks without charge in Nairobi. Over the course of three weeks from January 20 to February 10, 2007, the Kenyan government rendered dozens of these individuals—with no notice to families, lawyers or the detainees themselves—on flights to Somalia, where they were handed over to the Ethiopian military." In its investigation, Human Rights Watch concluded that when prisoners were rendered to Ethiopia, "they effectively disappeared" and were "denied access to their embassies, their families, and international humanitarian organizations such as the International Committee of the Red Cross." It added: "From February to May 2007, Ethiopian security officers daily transported detainees—including several pregnant women—to a villa where US officials interrogated them about suspected terrorist links." In all, Kenyan security and intelligence forces facilitated scores of renditions for the US and other governments, including eighty-five people rendered to Somalia in 2007 alone. At least one was sent to Guantánamo. Somalia was becoming a microcosm of the larger war on terror for both al Qaeda and the United States.

AS JSOC AND ETHIOPIAN FORCES intensified their hunt for the leaders of the Islamic Courts Union in Somalia in January 2007, Fazul Abdullah Mohammed left his family near the Kenyan border and disappeared. Eventually, he made his way back to Mogadishu to reunite with the al Shabab fighters he had helped to train and finance. Fazul had already become al Qaeda's most seasoned operative in the Horn of Africa, with several spectacular attacks under his belt, including the 1998 embassy bombings. He was about to take on a major role in a play al Qaeda had been producing since the early 1990s. The group had finally drawn the United States back into an asymmetric war in the heart of East Africa.

With the Somali ICU leaders on the run, al Qaeda saw Somalia as an ideal front line for jihad and began increasing its support for al Shabab. In early January 2007, bin Laden's deputy, Ayman al Zawahiri, addressed the situation in Somalia in a recording released online. "I speak to you today as the crusader invader forces of Ethiopia violate the soil of the beloved Muslim Somalia," he began. "I call upon the Muslim nation in Somalia to remain in the new battlefield that is one of the crusader battlefields that are being launched by America and its allies and the United Nations against Islam and Muslims." He implored the mujahedeen, "Launch ambushes, land mines, raids and suicidal combats until you consume them as the lions eat their prey."

In the disintegration of the ICU, al Qaeda had found its way into Somalia. "With the help of all these foreign fighters, the Shabab took over the fighting, with al Qaeda leadership," recalled Indha Adde, who had been the ICU defense minister. "The Shabab started ordering executions and innocent Muslims were killed. They even targeted members of [the ICU]. I was commander for all [ICU] military operations, and I turned against the Shabab, after seeing these violations against Islam." Indha Adde eventually went underground, along with Hassan Dahir Aweys, and began receiving support from Ethiopia's grand enemy, Eritrea. Both men would hover around the militant Islamist movement as they waited to see which way the chips would fall. Eventually, the two would go in very different directions.

By early February 2007, the Ethiopian invasion had become an occupation, which was giving rise to widening unrest. In a nation that had already suffered one of the worst fates in recent history, Somali civilians were paying yet another horrifying price. The occupation was marked by indiscriminate brutality against Somali civilians. Ethiopian and US-backed Somali government soldiers secured Mogadishu's neighborhoods by force, raiding houses in search of ICU loyalists, looting civilian property, and beating or shooting anyone suspected of collaboration with antigovernment forces. They positioned snipers on the roofs of buildings and would reportedly respond to any attack with disproportionate fire, shelling densely populated areas and several hospitals, according to Human Rights Watch. Extrajudicial killings by Ethiopian soldiers were widely reported, particularly during the final months of 2007. Accounts of Ethiopian soldiers "slaughtering" men, women and children "like goats"—slitting their throats—were widespread, Amnesty International noted. Both Somali Transitional Government forces, led by exiles and backed by the United States, and Ethiopian forces were accused of horrific sexual violence. Although forces linked to al Shabab were also accused of war crimes, a large proportion of those reported to Amnesty International, which included looting, rape and extrajudicial killings, were committed by Somali government and Ethiopian forces.

Some 6,000 civilians were reportedly killed in fighting in Mogadishu and across southern and central Somalia in 2007, and more than 600,000 Somali civilians were internally displaced from and around Mogadishu. An estimated 335,000 Somali refugees fled Somalia in 2007. The stability of the Islamic Courts had been replaced by a return of roadblocks, warlordism and, worse, troops from Somalia's archenemy, Ethiopia, patrolling the streets and regularly killing Somalis.

"The major problem is that no steps were taken to avert an insurgency—and indeed, very early on, you had an insurgency arise because of lack of stability in the country," recalled Daveed Gartenstein-Ross, who had advised CENTCOM on its Somalia policy. "What we ended up doing was basically depending upon the Ethiopians to stabilize Somalia. And that in itself was a terrible assumption."

With the ICU dismantled and the brutal Ethiopian occupation continuing for nearly three more years, al Shabab emerged as the vanguard in the fight against foreign occupation. "For them, it was the break that they were looking for," said Aynte. "It was the anger that they had been looking for, to harness the anger of the people and present themselves as the new nationalist movement that would kick Ethiopia out. So throughout the three years that Ethiopia was in Somalia, al Shabab never uttered a word of global jihad at all. They always said that their main goal was just to kick the Ethiopians out." For al Qaeda, this was just the beginning of a whole new world, made possible in no small part by Washington's actions. "What brought about the Islamic Courts?" Madobe asked. "The US-backed warlords. And if Ethiopia did not invade, and the US did not carry out airstrikes, which were viewed as a continuation of the warlords' and Ethiopia's ruthlessness, al Shabab would not have survived. Every step taken by the US benefited al Shabab."

By April, a full-blown insurgency had risen up against the Ethiopian occupation. In a four-day battle in April 2007, an estimated four hundred Ethiopian troops and Somali rebels died. Later that year, Somali mobs dragged Ethiopian soldiers through the streets, and al Shabab began targeting the leadership of the government that had been installed on the backs of Ethiopian tanks.

On June 3, 2007, a Toyota Land Cruiser packed with explosives burst through the security gates in front of Prime Minister Gedi's house in Mogadishu and detonated just outside his residence. The suicide attack killed six of his guards and wounded scores of others. After the attack, witnesses found severed limbs almost a mile from the scene. "They targeted me, and they sent a suicide bomb packed with more than two hundred kilos of explosives. They blew up my house," Gedi told me. "It was the start of the suicide bombing in Mogadishu, targeting the leaders and the government." It was the fifth assassination attempt against Gedi. Later that year, he resigned.

Although Ethiopia's prime minister, Meles Zenawi, proclaimed the invasion a "tremendous success," that was simply not true. If Somalia was already a playground for Islamic militants, the US-backed invasion blew open the gates of Mogadishu for al Qaeda. Washington was giving Osama bin Laden and al Qaeda an opportunity to achieve a status in Somalia that it had repeatedly failed to attain on its own. "I think when they [started to have] real power was when Ethiopia invaded," said Aynte. Fazul and Nabhan "had become the bridge between al Shabab and al Qaeda, tapping into the resources of al Qaeda, bringing in more foreign fighters, as well as financial resources—more importantly military know-how: How to make explosives, how to train people, and so on. So that's when they have gained the biggest influence that they needed."

While Aweys and his allies, including Indha Adde, vowed to continue the struggle against the Ethiopians and the Somali government, Sheikh Sharif intensified his cooperation with the Transitional Federal Government (TFG) and the US government. Al Shabab watched and waited, and in the power struggle saw opportunity.

On February 26, 2008, Secretary of State Condoleezza Rice officially designated al Shabab a terrorist organization and JSOC intensified its hunt. On March 2, 2008, the United States carried out missile strikes against a suspected al Shabab house believed to be housing Saleh Ali Saleh Nabhan, the senior al Qaeda leader in East Africa. Some reports indicated that he had been killed, but when the rubble cleared, the death toll was several civilians, some cows and a donkey, but no Nabhan.

On May 1, after three months of strikes that seemed to be killing more innocent people than intended targets, JSOC hit its mark. At 3:00 a.m., five Tomahawk cruise missiles rained down on the town of Dhusa Mareb in central Somalia, blowing up a house that CENTCOM alleged was used by "a known al-Qaeda operative and militia leader." The mission, military officials said, was the result of weeks of surveillance and tracking. Witnesses in the area described seeing the dead bodies of sixteen people. One of them was that of al Shabab's military commander, Aden Hashi Ayro. Although the US intelligence had been wrong several times about killing al Shabab leaders, this time there was little room for doubt. After the strike, al Shabab released a statement confirming Ayro's death, praising him as a hero. Attached to the release was the first publicly available photo of Ayro and a bio of their slain leader. Just before Ayro's death, according to a US diplomatic cable, the al Shabab leader had met with Indha Adde, a member of his Ayr clan, perhaps to broker a deal. US officials hoped his killing would isolate al Shabab from its former ICU allies and would lead to a "short-term disruption of terrorist operations." The strike may have deterred Indha Adde from deepening his alliance with al Shabab, but the assassination also emboldened al Shabab and made a martyr of Ayro.

THE ETHIOPIAN OCCUPATION began to wind down, following an agreement signed in Djibouti in August 2008 between Sheikh Sharif's faction and officials from the TFG. In reality, the al Shabab insurgency had bled the Ethiopians out, but the diplomatic charade served as a face-saving cover. The "Djibouti Agreement" paved the way for Sheikh Sharif to assume the presidency in Mogadishu. To veteran observers of Somali politics, Sharif's reemergence was an incredible story. The United States and Ethiopia overthrew his government, only to later back him as the country's president. When I met Sheikh Sharif at the presidential offices in Mogadishu, he refused to discuss this period of his career, saying only that it was not the right time. Ironically, Sheikh Sharif, who once declared himself a warrior against foreign occupation, would rely entirely on the US-backed African Union force that replaced the Ethiopians to keep his nominal grip on power.

When some members of the ICU and the Somali government merged following the Djibouti Agreement, Aweys and al Shabab predictably rejected it, believing that the ICU "had submitted themselves to the infidels," according to Aynte. Fazul and Nabhan were "fundamental in convincing the Shabab not to join the Djibouti Agreement. Because, if the Shabab had joined the Djibouti Agreement that brought about the current government under the leadership of Sheikh Sharif, Fazul and other al Qaeda players would not have been [able to remain] in Somalia. So I think it was a personal interest of al Qaeda figures, to make sure that that doesn't happen." Al Shabab's Somali leader, Ahmed Abdi Godane, declared Sharif an apostate and a "favorite puppet" for the "infidels." As the new government formed, al Shabab prepared to widen its insurrection, vowing to take down the new coalition government and to expel the US-backed African Union Mission in Somalia (AMISOM) forces that had replaced the Ethiopians.

With much of the ICU leadership dead, exiled or bickering over who would control what cabinet positions within the newly installed US-backed government, al Shabab capitalized on the disarray. The group welcomed the disillusioned fighters who felt that they had been sold out by the leadership of the Courts. Aside from its commitment to carry on the jihad, what separated al Shabab from the Somali government was its indigenous diversity. Its leadership consisted of figures from Somalia's four major clans, but it also put members of minority clans in influential positions. Also, true to its name, al Shabab began recruiting young Somalis whom it could easily indoctrinate. It gave them a sense of empowerment in a landscape once again dominated by brutal warlords and clan politics.

In 2008, al Shabab evolved into a broad-based movement and significant social force. While keeping up its military offensive, it began establishing itself in the south, by projecting soft power and cultivating popular support. Al Shabab members would make diplomatic "visits," as they called them, to towns, bringing with them food, money, and "mobile Sharia courts" to settle local disputes. Reminiscent of the ICU's approach, the Is-lamist militants would spend time moderating speedy court proceedings in each town, settling local disputes and sentencing criminals. Many of these takeovers of Somali towns were bloodless, involving lengthy negotiations with clan elders to convince them of al Shabab's noble intentions.

Al Shabab followed up on this diplomacy with popular social programs. One very important move was the further dismantling of roadblocks and checkpoints, a process the ICU had begun during its time in power. These checkpoints were historically used by warlords as tools of extortion rath-er than security. "The perception that [al Shabab] and other Islamist in-surgent groups are a rag-tag army of crude fanatics whose first instinct is to use force and terror to impose their radical vision is a caricature," noted a report by the International Crisis Group. "Their tactics have been well-adapted and more effective than those of their adversaries. They have largely succeeded in casting themselves as true Somali patriots opposed to the Ethiopian-allied TFG. As a result, they have been gaining popularity in central and southern Somalia, just as they did before the Ethiopian inva-sion in December 2006."

At the same time that it engaged in its version of a hearts-and-minds campaign, however, al Shabab also implemented policies reminiscent of the Taliban: banning popular Bollywood films, forcibly shaving the heads of men with "inappropriate" hairstyles and imposing harsh sentences for infractions against the al Shabab interpretation of Sharia law. By early 2009, al Shabab would control of most of southern Somalia. "In many areas al-Shabab is the only organization that can provide basic social services, such as rudimentary medical facilities, food distribution centers, and a basic justice system rooted in Islamic law," concluded a report for the Sen-ate Foreign Relations Committee. "Western diplomats fear that al-Shabab will continue to win converts by providing services similar to the way Hamas found success in the Gaza Strip. Experts strongly caution that there is little the United States can do to weaken al-Shabab." Further bombing by the United States or increased foreign military intervention, the report warned, could make al Shabab stronger.

While al Shabab consolidated local support, on the global scene, al Qaeda could now use the jihad in Somalia to recruit. In this narrative, a Christian nation, Ethiopia, backed by the United States—the root of all evil—had invaded Somalia and slaughtered Muslims. Jihadists had risen up and re-pelled the invasion, making Somalia a front-line battleground against the crusade bin Laden had long alleged the United States was waging. When the Ethiopians withdrew, according to Aynte, al Shabab "emerged far more popular and powerful than ever," transforming "its domestic, irredentist struggle into a global Jihadist dictum." Foreign fighters began pouring into Somalia in far greater numbers. Bin Laden released an audio address titled "Fight on, Champions of Somalia," amplifying calls for the overthrow of Sharif's "apostate" government. Al Shabab began easily taking territory throughout southern Somalia and soon found itself in control of a far greater swath of territory than the Somali government, despite the latter being backed by thousands of African Union forces funded and trained by the United States and other Western nations. Al Shabab would emerge as the premier jihadi force in Somalia—and would soon control more land than any other al Qaeda–affiliated group in history. US policy had backfired spectacularly, transforming a ragtag group of relative nobodies in Somalia, in just a few short years, into the new heroes of al Qaeda's global struggle.

## 23 "If Your Son Does Not Come to Us, He Will Be Killed by the Americans"

YEMEN, 2007–2009—During Anwar Awlaki's time in solitary confinement in a Yemeni prison, al Qaeda in Yemen had made a comeback. While the Bush administration's civilian leadership largely ignored the resurgence, JSOC was tracking al Qaeda's new organization in Yemen closely. On March 27, 2007, a Yemeni military unit in the province of Hadramaut discovered a US spy drone that had washed up on the shore of the Arabian Sea. The "Scan Eagle" was an unarmed aerial reconnaissance vehicle that had been launched off the USS *Ashland*, which deployed to the area in early 2007 to support Combined Task Force 150's counterterrorism operations in the Horn of Africa. Human rights groups also alleged that the *Ashland* was being used by US forces as a floating prison to hold al Qaeda suspects picked up in the region. The day after the Yemeni military recovered the aircraft, President Saleh spoke to the US chargé d'affaires in Yemen, who tried to assure Saleh that the Scan Eagle had crashed in the sea and had not entered Yemeni territory. Saleh told the US official he didn't buy that story but promised that Yemen would not "turn this into an international incident," according to a US diplomatic cable sent after the phone call, and "would instruct [Yemeni] government officials not to comment." Instead, Saleh's government put out a cover story that helped bolster Saleh's propaganda campaign against Iran. On March 29, official Yemeni media outlets reported that the Yemeni military had shot down an Iranian "spy plane" after consulting with "multinational forces" in the region. Saleh "could have taken the opportunity to score political points by appearing tough in public against the United States, but chose instead to blame Iran," according to the US cable. The crashed drone was an omen of things to come.

As al Qaeda regrouped in Yemen, it began to carry out a series of small-scale actions, primarily in Marib Province, the site of the 2002 US drone strike that killed Harithi, including suicide attacks against oil and gas facilities. In March 2007, they assassinated the chief criminal investigator in Marib, Ali Mahmud al Qasaylah, for his alleged role in the drone strike. In an audiotaped message, Wuhayshi's deputy, Qasim al Rimi, announced that Wuhayshi was officially the new head of al Qaeda in Yemen. In the message, Rimi vowed the group would continue to take revenge on those responsible for the US drone strike. Two weeks after Rimi's tape was released, suicide bombers attacked a convoy of Spanish tourists in Marib, killing eight of them, along with two Yemeni drivers.

After eighteen months in prison, Awlaki reentered a world in which the US wars he had grown to militantly oppose had spread. Now, it seemed, war was coming to Yemen. As JSOC and the CIA intensified their operations, Awlaki's story became like a mirror image. When Awlaki was freed in late 2007, he did not go into hiding, as the US government alleged. He went home to his family in Sana'a and tried to figure out a way to support them and to continue his preaching.

In an interview days after his release, Awlaki was asked if he would return to the United States or Britain to preach. "Well, I would like to travel. However, not until the US drops whatever unknown charges it has against me," he replied. "The truth of the matter is I am not banned from return to the US. I left the US on my own accord and refuse to return by my own choice," Awlaki said later. "In fact the opposite is true. The US consul encouraged me to return to the US during his visit to me while I was incarcerated. Alhamdulillah [thanks be to God], Allah has blessed me with living in a blessed land by the witness of Rasulullah [the prophet]. Why should I replace that with life in the US? But I refuse to even visit the US because the US government is not to be trusted as they are liars just like their media." As to what he would do next, Awlaki said, "I have a few opportunities open at the moment and I haven't chosen yet among them. I'm still sort of studying the situation at the time being."

In early 2008, the Internet became Awlaki's digital mosque, where he could reach Muslims across the globe. In February, he established his own website, www.Anwar-AlAwlaki.com, titled "Imam Anwar's Blog." He set up a Facebook page, which drew thousands of subscribers. "In the old times it used to take a few days to travel, for example, from Makkah to Madina which are only 450 km apart. Now we can communicate all over the globe within seconds; text, audio and video, all within seconds. So I would like to tell all of the brothers out there whom I personally know and whom I spent memorable time with: Assalamu alaykum and insha Allah I will never forget you," Awlaki wrote in his first blog post. "And to those whom I grew to know through these modern means of communication but the circumstances have separated me from meeting them, nevertheless, I still feel a bond with them and I love them for the sake of Allah because they have chosen to follow Islam: Assalamu alaykum, and if we don't meet in this world then we ask Allah to make us of those who would meet while reclining on the thrones of Paradise."

Awlaki's website had a vibrant comment section, and he built up a large online community to whom he was very responsive. The humanity—and an attention to mundane discussion—Awlaki showed in these discussions complicated the cartoonish descriptions of him in Western media and helped to explain his appeal, particularly to some Western Muslims. In one post headlined "Do You Like Cheese?" Awlaki posed a question: "Cheese is great. So if you are a fan of cheese you might be asking yourself the question, is cheese made by non-Muslims allowed or not?" In another blog post, Awlaki addressed Koran-compliant financial practices for Muslims living in the United States and warned against taking out home mortgages. "If you are a person whom Allah has bestowed wealth upon then you should avoid owning property in the US and you should diversify out of the dollar into gold and silver," he wrote. "In addition to this being the prudent thing to do from a financial point of view, it is also the recommended thing to do Islamicly. Muslims should not be supporting the economy of a nation that is fighting them. Finally, for those who are contemplating purchasing a home in the US based on mortgage which is a clear form of Riba (usury) they should fear Allah."

But Awlaki's posts also bristled with hostility to the United States and showed a clear radicalization of his own politics. Completely gone was any moderate tone about the United States or democracy. "Muslims do not try to infiltrate the system and work from within. It is just not our way. It is the way of the Jews and the munafiqeen (hypocrites) but not the way of the Muslims," he wrote in an August 2008 blog post. "As Muslims we should not subject Islam to the whims of the people, if they chose it we implement it, if they don't we accept the choice of the masses. Our position is that we will implement the rule of Allah on earth by the tip of the sword whether the masses like it or not. We will not subject sharia rule to popularity contests. Rasulullah (the prophet) says: I was sent with the sword until Allah alone is worshiped. That path, the path of Rasulullah, is the path we should follow." He added: "Today the Muslim world is under occupation and the statements of our scholars are clear that it becomes fardh ayn (a binding duty) on every able Muslim to fight to free the Muslim land. When something is fardh ayn it is fardh ayn. You cannot theorize or hypothesize otherwise. The ruling is clear and the implications of it are clear." Awlaki praised the Taliban in Afghanistan and the Islamic Courts Union in Somalia as two "successful examples, even though far from perfect," of a system of Islamic governance. Jihad, he wrote, "is what [military theorist Carl von] Clausewitz would refer to as 'total war' but with the Islamic rules of engagement. It is a battle in the battlefield and a battle for the hearts and minds of the people."

Awlaki began urging followers in the United States to break with its

government and society and to withdraw from any participation in the
political process:

> Today America is the home of an interesting assortment of sins that
> are handpicked from all over the nations that existed before us: the
> obstinacy of the people of Nuh; the arrogance of the people of Aad;
> the rejection of Allah's signs by the people of Thamud; the sodomy
> of the people of Lut; the financial deviance of the people of Shuayb
> as America is the biggest dealer and promoter of the interest based
> economy; the oppression of Abu Jahl et al; the greed, deception, love
> of the temporal life, and the bogusness of the children of Israel; along
> with the arrogance of the Pharaoh who had the misled notion that just
> because he is the leader of the most powerful nation on earth and is
> at the top of the greatest army of his time he can somehow defeat the
> servants of Allah.
>
> Brothers and Sisters this leads to the belief that the punishment of
> Allah is hovering over America. When? And how? Allah knows best.
>
> So if you are one of those unfortunate folks who turned out to be
> living in the wrong place at the wrong time then it is advisable for you
> to leave. That is obviously if you take heed. Many don't and are still
> living the utopia of the American dream. I am not talking about Mo
> and Mike who are still shaking to the tunes of MTV with their coke
> and big mac and are only Muslim by name, but I am talking about the
> practicing Muslims who sadly enough still think that the America of
> George W is the Abyssinia of the Negus.

The US intelligence community saw Awlaki's web sermons as a threat.
Some officials began a whisper campaign against him in the US press.
"There is good reason to believe Anwar Aulaqi has been involved in very
serious terrorist activities since leaving the United States, including plotting attacks against America and our allies," an anonymous US counterterrorism official told the *Washington Post* in February 2008, though no
evidence was presented.

On his blog and through e-mails, Awlaki fielded questions on whether
Western Muslims should participate in jihad and began debating the merits
of traveling to the front lines to fight. A new generation of young disenfran-
chised Muslims was eagerly seeking out Awlaki's videos and audio recordings. One of the most popular was "Constants on the Path of Jihad," an audio lecture believed to have been recorded in 2005. The lecture was based
on the teachings of Yusuf al Ayyiri, the first operational leader of al Qaeda
in the Arabian Peninsula and an articulate guerrilla warfare strategist who
was killed by Saudi security forces in 2003. In the lecture, Awlaki advanced

Ayyiri's teachings on jihad, weaving the stories of epic battles fought by Islamic warriors defending their faith into a current context. "Whenever you see the word terrorist, replace it with the word mujahid," Awlaki declared. "Whenever you see the word terrorism, replace it with the word jihad." Every "government in the world is united to fight against Islam," Awlaki added. "People try to find a way of bailing out of Jihad because they do not like it. The reality of war is horrible and that's why people try to avoid it, but fighting is proscribed upon you, it is an instruction from Allah." True Muslims, Awlaki said, citing Ayyiri's writings, define victory not as simple military triumph but as the act of sacrifice. "The Mujahid sacrificing 'his self' and his wealth is victory. Victory of your idea, your religion. If you die for your religion, your death will spread the da'wa [proselytizing on behalf of Islam].... Allah chooses Shuhada [martyrs] from amongst the believers. This is a victory."

CIA and FBI counterterrorism analysts began poring over Awlaki's sermons, looking for clues the preacher may have dropped about his potential connections to al Qaeda. They discovered no specifics, but they saw a threat in his influence and the inspiration others found in him. Intercepts from multiple terror investigations kept producing references to Awlaki's sermons, particularly the "Constants" lecture. "In a sense, al Awlaki crosses this bridge, speaking in Arabic but he also speaks in English and he's an American citizen and so he knows, therefore, how to address the youth," Dr. Emile Nakhleh, the former senior CIA officer who ran the Agency's Political Islam Division, told me. "And so the danger is not that he is another bin Laden—the fear of Awlaki among some people in the government is that he represents this new phenomenon of recruitment, recruiting ordinary people who fall under the radar."

As Awlaki's online popularity grew—many of his posts had hundreds of commenters asking him for advice—the United States was putting tremendous pressure on the Yemeni intelligence services to rearrest him. "The Americans were very, very angry with the [Yemeni] government," recalled Saleh bin Fareed, the leader of the Aulaq tribe, who would meet regularly with both US and Yemeni officials to resolve disputes between the government and Yemeni tribes. "They were really annoyed. And I think they put a lot of pressure on the [Yemeni] president to take him back" into custody. Awlaki was followed everywhere he went. "He was harassed, and he was under surveillance all the time he was in Sana'a. And he could not do anything," recalled Awlaki's father, Nasser, who lived with his son at the time. "They were watching him very closely," added bin Fareed. "And he did not like that. Wherever he goes, intelligence would be on his left and right. He goes to the mosque, they are with him; he goes by car, they are behind him; he goes to eat, they also eat. I think he did not feel free."

Awlaki's friend Shaykh Harith al Nadari recalled, "We were under intensified surveillance and harassment," and Awlaki determined that "Sana'a was no longer a suitable place for us to stay." Anwar ultimately decided to leave Sana'a to go to Ataq, the provincial capital of Shabwah, his family's tribal land in southern Yemen, near the Arabian Sea. He thought he would be left alone by the Yemeni intelligence services and the US government. He was wrong.

Washington was relentless in its pressure on the Yemeni regime. When Anwar left Sana'a, US intelligence demanded that Yemen's security services return him there. The head of Yemen's elite US-trained and -funded Counter Terrorism Unit, Yahya Saleh, told Nasser, "If your son does not come to us, he will be killed by the Americans." Nasser and bin Fareed both traveled to Shabwah to try to compel Anwar to return to Sana'a. "I went to Shabwah. I met Anwar. I tried to convince him," bin Fareed told me. "He told me, 'Uncle, I will not. I was born a free man. I don't want anybody to tell me where to sleep, where to put my head, which direction I will put it. I assure you I have nothing to do with terrorism, I have nothing to do with al Qaeda—I go from my house to the mosque, and those who attend are all from the village. I post on the Internet [and] people ask me questions, I answer. I preach Islam, and that's my job." Anwar told his powerful uncle, If you find any evidence I am involved with terrorism, "you come and take me and you put me in jail."

Awlaki had originally brought his wife and children with him to Ataq, but they eventually moved back to Sana'a to live with his parents. In Ataq, family sources told me, Anwar was subjected to continued surveillance by Yemeni intelligence agents. Awlaki decided to move further away to elude their grasp—leaving Ataq and moving to the family's small village, al Saeed, in rural Shabwah. "It's a small village. I mean, there are a few thousand people who live in the valley there. All of them are from the same tribe," bin Fareed told me. "If somebody comes from another village, it's known that he's a stranger. So, they know each other. I think the Americans did not like this." In his family's village, Awlaki continued his blogging, growing ever more radical. He began telling friends and family that he believed the United States was tracking him.

THE US HUNT FOR AWLAKI coincided with al Qaeda's own escalation of attacks in Yemen. On September 17, 2008, the group launched a massive kamikaze attack on the US Embassy in Sana'a. The fortresslike compound was hit in a coordinated assault with vehicle bombs, rocket-propelled grenades (RPGs) and automatic weapons, resulting in the deaths of thirteen guards and civilians, one of whom was an American. The six attackers all died as well. Al Qaeda declared it a successful strike. "This attack is a reminder that we are at war with extremists who will murder innocent people to achieve their ideological objectives," President Bush said as he sat next to General David Petraeus at the White House. "One objective of these extremists as they kill is to try to cause the United States to lose our nerve and to withdraw from regions of the world."

Petraeus would soon assume command of CENTCOM, where he would oversee the US wars—declared and undeclared—in the Middle East. One of his jobs would be to coordinate an expansion of covert US military strikes in Yemen. In May, shortly after he received word that he would become CENTCOM commander, Petraeus met in Qatar with the CIA director, Michael Hayden, as well as with JSOC's commander, Admiral McRaven, and others, to discuss plans for increasing the strikes against al Qaeda suspects wherever they operated.

As news of the embassy bombing broke in the United States, Petraeus's future boss, Senator Barack Obama, was on the campaign trail. "It just reminds us that we have to redouble our efforts to root out and destroy international terrorist organizations," Obama commented during a stop in Grand Junction, Colorado. Yemen was beginning to rise above its status as a back-burner issue.

Michael Scheuer, the twenty-two-year CIA veteran and the former head of the Agency's bin Laden unit, observed that "Al-Qaeda's organization in Yemen seems to have stabilized after the period of turmoil and governmental suppression that followed the November 2002 death of its leader Abu Ali Harithi." Scheuer added: "For al-Qaeda, Yemen provides a pivotal, central base that links its theaters of operation in Afghanistan, Iraq, East Africa and the Far East; it also provides a base for training Yemeni fighters and for the rest and refit of fighters from multiple Islamist groups after their tours in Afghanistan, Iraq and Somalia." In all, there were dozens of documented al Qaeda attacks on Yemeni soil from 2000 through the end of the Bush administration. Over the years, US military aid and CIA financing was increased. "When [al Qaeda] starts creating problems in Yemen, the US money starts flowing," asserted the former senior counterterrorism official. "For Saleh, al Qaeda is the gift that keeps on giving. They are his number one fund-raiser to get Saudi and US money."

In October 2008, the US base at Djibouti was officially placed under the control of AFRICOM, the Pentagon's sixth unified geographic command. Yemen remained under CENTCOM's area of responsibility and would become a major focus for Special Operations Forces under the banner of SOC(FWD)-Yemen (Special Operations Command-Forward Yemen). While Saleh managed his complex relations with the United States through official channels, on occasion, according to US Special Operations Forces veterans, JSOC teams carried out "unilateral, direct actions" against al Qaeda suspects in Yemen. These operations were never mentioned in public, and some may have been conducted without Saleh's knowledge or direct authorization. "During that period we were training and building the indigenous security forces in Yemen," a former aide to a senior JSOC leader told me. "Simultaneously we were targeting and then killing people who were suspected or had been confirmed to be al Qaeda extremists in and around the Peninsula, and within Yemen itself." Although Yemen was increasingly surfacing on the radar of JSOC and the CIA, the country would remain largely out of the headlines. During the three presidential debates between Barack Obama and John McCain in the 2008 election, Yemen was not mentioned once.

Barack Obama campaigned on the idea that Bush had drained resources in Iraq that should have been used to fight al Qaeda. "There was no such thing as Al Qaeda in Iraq until George Bush and John McCain decided to invade," Obama had declared in February 2008. "They took their eye off the people who were responsible for 9/11, and that would be Al Qaeda." The new president pledged to rearrange US priorities to Afghanistan, where he would place JSOC's former commander, General McChrystal, in charge of the war, but Obama would soon realize that his pledge to take the fight to al Qaeda would not be limited to Afghanistan. The tiny Arab nation of Yemen would become a major piece on Obama's counterterrorism chessboard.

AS THE EIGHT-YEAR-LONG BUSH ERA drew to a close, and the US election campaign entered its final weeks, Awlaki railed against the hopes that Muslims in the United States and globally were voicing about the candidacy of Barack Obama. "The promoters of participation in American elections argue that we are choosing the least of the two evils. This principle is correct but what they are missing is that in the process of choosing the lesser of the two evils they are committing an even greater evil," Awlaki wrote in October 2008. "The types of candidates that American politics has been spitting out is absolutely disgusting. I wonder how any Muslim with a grain of iman [faith] in his heart could walk up to a ballot box and cast his vote in endorsement of creatures such as McCain or Obama?!" He added: "No matter how irrelevant your vote is, on the Day of Judgment you will be called to answer for it. You, under no coercion or duress, consciously chose to vote for the leader of a nation that is leading the war against Islam." In a subsequent post, Awlaki wrote that "on most of the issues that concern Muslims there is very little difference" between McCain and Obama. "For example they have similar views on the war on terror and the issue of Palestine. Anyone with a simple understanding of the history of American politics would realize that on the major issues both parties share the same agenda."

As Awlaki escalated his rhetoric, the US intelligence community was elevating his perceived threat level. A month before Barack Obama's election, a tiny window was opened into how Awlaki was viewed when Charles Allen, the undersecretary of homeland security for intelligence and analysis, described Awlaki as "an al-Qaeda supporter, and former spiritual leader to three of the September 11 hijackers." This was the first time a US official had publicly linked Awlaki to terrorism. Allen charged that Awlaki "targets US Muslims with radical online lectures encouraging terrorist attacks from his new home in Yemen." When Allen's remarks were published, Awlaki shot back on his blog. Regarding the characterization of him as a "spiritual adviser" to some of the hijackers, Awlaki wrote: "This is a baseless claim that I have refuted again and again during the FBI's interrogations and with the media. The US government and the media still insist on spreading this lie around." As for encouraging terrorist attacks, Awlaki responded, "I would challenge him to come up with one such lecture where I encourage 'terrorist attacks.'" But, in the eyes of the US government, Awlaki's calls for jihad amounted to encouraging such attacks.

As president-elect Obama began to build his foreign policy and counterterrorism teams, Yemen would emerge as a major priority. Although most of the United States and the world had never heard of Anwar Awlaki, the new administration was monitoring his movements in Yemen. US authorities presented no concrete evidence that Awlaki was actively involved in any terror plots, but they asserted that he was an inspirational figure whose sermons kept popping up in investigations into various terror plots: in 2006, a group of Canadian Muslims charged with plotting to storm parliament and behead the prime minister were found to have listened to Awlaki speeches. In addition, some of the men convicted in the 2007 plot to attack Fort Dix in New Jersey were heard praising Awlaki, according to a recording made by a government informant. Other references to Awlaki were registering on the radar in investigations in the United Kingdom, as well as in Chicago and Atlanta. Awlaki was openly praising al Shabab in Somalia, where the United States was becoming increasingly concerned about Western Muslims joining the jihad. A group of young Somali Americans from Minneapolis who had traveled to Somalia to join al Shabab were allegedly inspired by Awlaki's "Constants on the Path of Jihad."

In a December 21, 2008, blog post titled "Salutations to al-Shabab of

Somalia," Awlaki wrote that the group's seizing of territory in Mogadishu and elsewhere in Somalia "fills our hearts with immense joy. We would like to congratulate you for your victories and achievements.... Al-Shabab not only have succeeded in expanding the areas that fall under their rule but they have succeeded in implementing the sharia and giving us a living example of how we as Muslims should proceed to change our situation. The ballot has failed us but the bullet has not." He contrasted al Shabab's armed insurrection against US proxies with the teachings of "Islamic universities run by Green Zone Scholars under governments headed by pimps," whose teachings advocated "weakness and humiliation." Awlaki asserted that the "university of Somalia" would "graduate an alumni" of "fighters who are hardened by the field and ready to carry on with no fear and hesitation. It will provide its graduates with the hands-on experience that the ummah [the global Muslim community] greatly needs for its next stage. But their success depends on your support. It is the responsibility of the ummah to help them with men and money."

Al Shabab replied to Awlaki's message and Awlaki posted the answer on his site. Addressing him as "beloved Sheikh Anwar," al Shabab's statement said, "We look to you as one of the very few scholars who stand firm upon the truth and defend the honor of the Mujahideen and the Muslims by continuously uncovering the feeble plots of the enemies of Allah. Allah knows how many of the brothers and sisters have been affected by your work so we ask you to continue the important effort you are doing wherever you are and never to fear the blame of the blamers." It concluded, "O Sheikh, we would not only look at you as only a soldier, but as the likes of Ibn Taymiya [an Islamic scholar known for resisting the Mongols in the thirteenth century]."

During the Israeli siege of Gaza, known as Operation Cast Lead, which began in late 2008, Awlaki's tone grew markedly more radical and warlike. "The illegal state of Israel needs to be eradicated. Just like Rasulullah drove them out of the Arabian peninsula the Jews of Palestine need to be driven out to the sea," Awlaki wrote. "There are no Israeli civilians unless they are Muslim. When the enemy targets our women and children we should target theirs."

Awlaki was influential among jihadist circles and with young, conservative Western Muslims, including those contemplating participating in the armed struggles against the United States and Israel and their proxies. His sermons had gone viral on jihadist web forums, which were heavily monitored by US intelligence. But there was no hard evidence presented that Awlaki had done anything that was not protected speech under the First Amendment to the US Constitution, or that would not require a major court battle to prove it was unconstitutional. There was, however, enough smoke around Awlaki for US intelligence to want him silenced, as he was during his eighteen months in a Yemeni prison. Now that Awlaki was out of jail and becoming more popular with every blog post, the digital surveillance on him intensified.

Unbeknownst to Awlaki, his e-mails were being intercepted and read, and his blog was being combed over for clues about his contacts. On December 17, 2008, the FBI intercepted an e-mail Awlaki received from Nidal Hasan, the army major whose parents had been members of Awlaki's mosque in Virginia in 2001. The last contact Awlaki had with Hasan was before he left the United States for Yemen—and then it was only to speak with him at the request of his parents. In retrospect, the e-mail is ominous. "There are many soldiers in the us armed forces that have converted to Islam while in the service. There are also many Muslims who join the armed forces for a myriad of different reasons," Hasan wrote Awlaki. "Some appear to have internal conflicts and have even killed or tried to kill other [US] soldiers in the name of Islam i.e. Hasan Akbar [a US soldier who was convicted of murdering two fellow soldiers in Kuwait], etc. Others feel that there is no conflict. Previous Fatwas seem vague and not very definitive." He then asked Awlaki, "Can you make some general comments about Muslims in the [US] military. Would you consider someone like Hasan Akbar or other soldiers that have committed such acts with the goal of helping Muslims/Islam (Lets just assume this for now) fighting Jihad and if they did die would you consider them shaheeds [martyrs]. I realize that these are difficult questions but you seem to be one of the only ones that has lived in the [US who] has a good understanding of the Qur'an and Sunna and is not afraid of being direct." Awlaki did not reply to that e-mail, but for months Hasan kept writing him.

Although federal investigators took no action against Hasan after that e-mail, a year later, after Hasan gunned down thirteen of his fellow soldiers at Fort Hood in Texas, Hasan's e-mails would help form part of the narrative that Awlaki was a terrorist. "Al-Awlaki condenses the Al Qaeda philosophy into digestible, well-written treatises," Evan Kohlmann, a self-proclaimed al Qaeda scholar and popular "expert witness" at terror trials, told the New York Times. "They may not tell people how to build a bomb or shoot a gun. But he tells them who to kill, and why, and stresses the urgency of the mission." Kohlmann was frequently brought in to brief the US government on al Qaeda—even though he did not speak Arabic and had done little traveling in any countries with a strong al Qaeda presence. Kohlmann briefed the US Justice Department and said he warned them of what he described as Awlaki's increasing ability to incite young Westerners to join foreign jihads or to conduct terror attacks in their own countries. Kohlmann alleged that there should be "little surprise that Anwar al-Awlaki's name and his sermon on 'Constants on the Path of Jihad' seem to surface in every single homegrown terrorism investigation, whether in the U.S., the U.K., Canada, or beyond." He labeled "Constants" a "lecture that over time has become the 'virtual bible' for lone wolf Muslim extremists."

Although Awlaki was undoubtedly grabbing the attention of an increasing number of counterterrorism officers and analysts in the United States, some within the intelligence community believed his importance was being inflated. Awlaki's sermons were indeed popping up in a variety of terror investigations, but he was a virtual nobody in the world of actual al Qaeda cells. Outside of English-speaking Western Muslims, he was not influential in most parts of the Muslim world. "I think the reason we tend to focus on him so much, is because he preaches in English. And because of that, we have more exposure to what he says and because we have more exposure to what he says, we assume that he has more influence than he really does," said Joshua Foust, who at the time was a Yemen analyst at the Defense Intelligence Agency. Foust said he was concerned about Awlaki's sermons influencing young Western Muslims, but he believed that some within the intelligence community were elevating the role his sermons played in terror plots. "I don't see any evidence whatsoever that [Awlaki] poses some kind of ideological threat against the United States. I would say that 99.99 percent of the all the people who either listen to, or believe in Awlaki's ideology, never act on it," Foust told me. "So if you're going to argue that ideology is what caused someone to do something, you need to actually—to me at least—to be intellectually honest and analytically rigorous. You need to explain why that ideology compelled that person to act, but it didn't compel everyone who didn't act to not act. And to me, I don't think its possible to really explain that. I haven't ever seen an argument that actually does that. So from the start, I think a lot of the focus on Awlaki doesn't make any sense, because we assign him a kind of importance and influence that he doesn't really have."

From Awlaki's perspective, he had been preaching a similar message for years before 9/11 and doing so in the United States. US Muslim "organizations used to support the Jihad in Afghanistan, in Bosnia, in Chechnya, and in Palestine. I was there, in America, at that time," Awlaki recalled. "We used to call from the pulpits...for Jihad for the sake of Allah, the establishment of the Caliphate. Allegiance and Disavowal. We could speak freely. The freedom in America allowed us to say these things, and we had much more freedom than in many of the countries of the Islamic world." Awlaki believed his message had not fundamentally changed, but the target of the jihad he advocated had. Lectures Awlaki had given advocating jihad in Chechnya or Afghanistan or Bosnia in the 1990s were on-message with US policy goals. A decade later, the same teachings—applied against the United States—took on a new meaning and cast Awlaki as a traitor to the country of his birth.

As 2008 drew to a close, Awlaki posted, "A New Year: Reality and Aspirations," a blog in which he provided an analysis of various wars around the Islamic world and cited countries where Muslim mujahedeen were progressing against Western powers. In Iraq, Awlaki wrote, "The US has come to the conclusion that they cannot do the job alone and they must seek the assistance of the munafiqeen [hypocrites]. With all of the outside and inside forces combining efforts to fight the carriers of the truth in Iraq our brothers do not need to win in order to be victorious. All they need to do is hang on. If they succeed in that they are [winning]. The invader cannot stay there forever." In Afghanistan, Awlaki asserted, "The mujahideen are winning, NATO are losing.... Obama is all hyped up about bringing an end to terrorism by focusing on Afghanistan. I pray the brothers teach him and his forces some good lessons this year." Awlaki also celebrated al Shabab's ascent in Somalia as "the best news of the year," writing, "Al-Shabab are winning on all fronts. Insha Allah we should witness the announcement of the establishment of an Islamic emirate. Ethiopia is tired of fighting a proxy war on behalf of America." Awlaki predicted that the United States would, once again, target Somalia, observing (presciently it would turn out), "The sea around Somalia is already occupied under the pretext of protection from piracy. This year could witness aerial bombardment with a renewed ground force invasion as a possibility."

Globally, Awlaki asserted, "The separation of believers from hypocrites which precedes any Muslim victory is underway." The "Jihad will carry on. And all of these are building stones for the ummah in its next stage. If Allah wants an end he prepares the means to it. Allah wants victory for this ummah and Allah is preparing the means for that. Let us not sit on the sidelines. Lets be part of that victory." In some ways, Awlaki's fixation on the Islamic players in an escalating global war of civilizations paralleled a different set of lists being secretly compiled by the Obama administration's counterterrorist teams. On these lists were scores of al Qaeda leaders, as well as militants much further down the food chain: "facilitators," "suspected militants," "propagandists." The administration was gearing up for a series of smaller wars in the Middle East, the Horn of Africa and the Arabian Peninsula, as well as a shift in strategy in Afghanistan that would seek to decapitate the Taliban leadership. At the center of Obama's new strategy would be a targeted assassination program that fulfilled Rumsfeld's vision of the world as a battlefield.

Awlaki predicted that the new US president would be a hawk against Islamic resistance movements. He was right. Obama would soon give carte blanche to JSOC and the CIA to wage a global manhunt. Capture was option two. Killing those whom the president deemed a threat to the United States was the primary mission, despite public assertions otherwise by military and government spokespeople. JSOC would not just be tasked with killing al Qaeda's top leadership, but with decimating its support infrastructure, killing its way down the chain. It was through this program that Awlaki would find himself in the new president's cross-hairs. He would soon become an American citizen sentenced to death with no trial.

**24** **"Obama Is Set to Continue the Course Set by Bush"**

THE UNITED STATES, 2002–2008—Barack Obama is an Ivy League–educated constitutional law professor whose political career was carefully plotted. In October 2002, when he was a state senator in Illinois, Obama had staked out a position on the Iraq War that foreshadowed the foreign policy vision he would later articulate as a presidential candidate. "I don't oppose all wars," Obama declared. "What I am opposed to is a dumb war. What I am opposed to is a rash war. What I am opposed to is the cynical attempt by…armchair, weekend warriors in this administration to shove their own ideological agendas down our throats, irrespective of the costs in lives lost and in hardships borne." Obama would often refer to that speech, but very few Americans heard it at the time. Obama burst onto the scene in 2004 when he delivered a widely praised, fiery keynote address at the Democratic National Convention, won a seat in the US Senate that year and then, three years later, announced his candidacy for president. "Let's be the generation that never forgets what happened on that September day and confront the terrorists with everything we've got," Obama said in his speech announcing his presidential run. "We can work together to track terrorists down with a stronger military, we can tighten the net around their finances, and we can improve our intelligence capabilities."

In crafting his campaign strategy on foreign policy, Obama and his advisers needed to straddle a fence between criticizing the national security policies of the Bush era while also appearing tough on terrorism. Obama conducted a dual-track approach in attacking his Republican opponent, John McCain: linking McCain to the war in Iraq and the unaccountability and secrecy of the Bush era, and simultaneously pledging to wage a "smarter," more focused war against al Qaeda.

On the morning of October 4, 2007, the *New York Times* ran a lengthy front-page story detailing a 2005 Justice Department opinion granting "an expansive endorsement of the harshest interrogation techniques ever used by the Central Intelligence Agency." Under newly arrived attorney general Alberto Gonzales, the CIA was "for the first time provided explicit authorization to barrage terror suspects with a combination of painful physical and psychological tactics, including head-slapping, simulated drowning and frigid temperatures." That morning Obama appeared on national television. "This is an example of what we've lost over the last six years and what we have to recapture," Obama told MSNBC anchor Mika Brzezinski. "You know, all of us believe we've got to track down and capture or kill terrorists who threaten America, but we have to understand that torture is not going to either provide us with information, and it's also going to create more enemies. And so as a strategy for creating a safer and secure America, I think it is wrongheaded, as well as immoral." Obama added: "I think this administration basically viewed any tactic as acceptable, as long as it could spin it and keep it out of the public eye."

As the presidential campaign rolled on, promises to reverse Bush-era policies became central to Obama's agenda. Torture, the prison at Guantánamo Bay, wars without justification or accountability and the evisceration of US civil liberties would come to an end, Obama vowed. "We have been governed by fear for the last six years, and this president has used the fear of terrorism to launch a war that should have never been authorized," Obama said in late October 2007. He argued that the political climate fostered by the Bush administration undermined the United States at home and abroad. "We haven't even talked about civil liberties and the impact of that politics of fear, what that has done to us in terms of undermining basic civil liberties in this country, what it has done in terms of our reputation around the world," Obama said.

But even as Obama won great praise and support from liberals and antiwar organizations in the United States, he articulated a foreign policy vision that, when it came to counterterrorism, made clear he intended to authorize covert and clandestine operations. "It was a terrible mistake to fail to act when we had a chance to take out an al Qaeda leadership meeting in 2005," Obama said. "If we have actionable intelligence about high-value terrorist targets and President Musharraf will not act, we will." McCain criticized Obama for his position that he would attack inside of Pakistan, calling it irresponsible. "You don't broadcast and say that you're going to bomb a country without their permission," McCain said. Obama shot back that the Bush administration had done "exactly that," declaring, "That is the position we should have taken in the first place...the fact is, it was the right strategy."

In accepting the Democratic nomination for president in 2008 in a massive football stadium in Denver, Colorado, Obama telegraphed a policy he intended to implement: escalating the war in Afghanistan and increasing US covert kill/capture operations globally. "John McCain likes to say that he'll follow bin Laden to the gates of Hell, but he won't even follow him to the cave where he lives," Obama said, reiterating that if he were elected, the United States would act unilaterally in Pakistan or elsewhere to kill terrorists. "We must take out Osama bin Laden and his lieutenants if we have them in our sights."

Obama's stump speeches on the campaign trail often focused on ending the war in Iraq, but he also articulated a hawkish position on unilateral US attacks that would necessitate a significant role for JSOC and the CIA. After his inauguration, as Obama built his foreign policy team, he stacked the administration with hawkish Democrats, including his vice president, Joe Biden, and secretary of state, Hillary Clinton, both of whom supported the 2003 invasion of Iraq. Susan Rice would serve as UN ambassador, and Richard Holbrooke would head up the civilian side of Obama's plan to expand the US war in Afghanistan. All of these figures had a track record of support for military interventions, neoliberal economic policies and a worldview consistent with the foreign policy arc that stretched from George H. W. Bush's time in office to the present. Obama also retained Bush's defense secretary, Robert Gates; tapped CIA veteran John Brennan as his senior adviser on counterterrorism and homeland security; and named General James Jones as his national security adviser.

Conservative Republicans heaped praise on Obama's picks. President Bush's senior adviser, Karl Rove, called Obama's cabinet selections "reassuring," and neoconservative leader and former McCain campaign staffer Max Boot beamed: "I am gobsmacked by these appointments, most of which could just as easily have come from a President McCain." Boot added that Hillary Clinton would be a "powerful" voice "for 'neoliberalism' which is not so different in many respects from 'neoconservativism.'" Boot's colleague Michael Goldfarb wrote in the *Weekly Standard*, the official organ of the neoconservative movement, that he saw "certainly nothing that represents a drastic change in how Washington does business. The expectation is that Obama is set to continue the course set by Bush in his second term."

Within weeks of assuming office in early 2009, Obama would send a clear message that he intended to keep intact many of the most aggressive counterterrorism policies of the Bush era. Among these were targeted killings, warrantless wiretapping, the use of secret prisons, a crackdown on habeas corpus rights for prisoners, indefinite detention, CIA rendition flights, drone bombings, the deployment of mercenaries in US wars and reliance on the "State Secrets Privilege." In some cases, Obama would expand Bush-era programs he had once blasted as hallmarks of an unaccountable executive branch.

Obama paid lip service on the campaign trail to holding Bush-era torturers accountable, but he later backed off such rhetoric, saying after his
election that "we need to look forward as opposed to looking backwards."
He said his job as president "is to make sure that, for example, at the C.I.A.,
you've got extraordinarily talented people who are working very hard to
keep Americans safe. I don't want them to suddenly feel like they've got to
spend all their time looking over their shoulders."

Early on in Obama's time in office, Dick Cheney charged that Obama
was moving "to take down a lot of those policies we put in place that kept
the nation safe for nearly eight years from a follow-on terrorist attack like
9/11." Cheney was wrong. If anything, Obama would guarantee that many
of those policies would become entrenched, bipartisan institutions in US
national security policy for many years to come. Whether these policies
have kept Americans safe—or have made them less safe—is another question.

## 25 Obama's Signature Strikes

PAKISTAN AND WASHINGTON, DC, 2009—As he settled into the Oval Office and his new role as commander in chief, President Obama tweaked Bush's expansive Global War on Terror rhetoric, rebranding it as a "war against al-Qaeda and its allies." On his third day in office, Obama signed a series of executive orders that were portrayed as "dismantling" the Bush-era torture and detention programs. "The message we are sending around the world is that the United States intends to prosecute the ongoing struggle against violence and terrorism, and we are going to do so vigilantly; we are going to do so effectively; and we are going to do so in a manner that is consistent with our values and our ideals," Obama declared as he stood with sixteen retired military officers. "We intend to win this fight. We're going to win it on our terms." But, while dispensing with the Bush-era labels and cowboy rhetoric that marked the previous eight years of US foreign policy, Obama simultaneously moved swiftly to expand the covert US wars that had marked his predecessor's time in office.

The day after Obama signed his executive orders, CIA director Michael Hayden briefed him on an operation the Agency was about to conduct inside Pakistan: a drone strike near the Afghan border. The targets, Hayden told the president, were upper-tier al Qaeda and Taliban members. Later that day, two Hellfire missiles hit compounds in North and South Waziristan. The first strike hit in a small village near Mir Ali, in North Waziristan, around 5:00 p.m. local time. The second struck a compound in the village of Karez Kot in South Waziristan at around 8:30 p.m. Hayden, weeks away from leaving the Agency, admitted to the president that the main HVTs had not been hit but told him that "at least five al Qaeda militants" had died. "Good," said Obama, who made clear that he favored escalating drone strikes in Pakistan.

As the US intelligence officers monitored the footage from the January 23 drone strikes, it became clear that civilians had been killed. John Brennan went straight to the president and told him what had happened. Five "militants" may have died in the strikes, but they were not the only ones killed. According to the Bureau of Investigative Journalism, the first strike in North Waziristan killed between seven and fifteen people, nearly all of them civilians. Many of the slain were from one family. One boy was reported to have survived, albeit with a skull fracture, a perforated stomach and the loss of an eye. The second strike in South Waziristan struck the "wrong house" and killed five to eight civilians, according to subsequent reports. Many of the dead, including at least two children, were the family members of a tribal elder, who was also killed. The elder was reportedly a member of a "pro-government peace committee."

Obama summoned Hayden for a face-to-face meeting and demanded a full briefing on the drone program's protocols. Despite the scores of national security briefings Obama had received from the time he became the Democratic nominee for president, it was the first the new president had heard of what the CIA called "signature strikes." Beginning in the closing months of the Bush administration, the Agency had begun targeting people based on patterns of life rather than specific intelligence. The CIA said that "military aged males" who were part of a large gathering of people in a particular region or had contacts with other suspected militants or terrorists could be considered fair targets for drone strikes. A positive ID was not necessary to strike, only some of the "signatures" the Agency had developed to identify suspected terrorists.

After some convincing from Hayden, Obama decided not to reject the signature strike policy, although he added a constraint: the CIA director was to have the final say on all strikes, an authority that had been occasionally delegated to the deputy director or the head of the Agency's counterterrorism center. Obama warned that he might withdraw the signature strike authority at a later time. But he didn't. In the ensuing months, the new CIA director, Leon Panetta, enlisted the help of "undercover officers" from the CIA's Counterterrorism Center and put the president through a "crash course" on targeted strikes. Panetta reviewed the drone program and other kinetic protocols, including the authorities needed in order to launch a strike. Obama and Panetta would hold one-on-one sessions after HVTs had been hit in Pakistan.

During that first year in office, Obama began to hold regular hourlong meetings with top officials to discuss all matters of national security and counterterrorism. According to participants, these early meetings had a "tutorial" character. Intelligence and security threats were discussed, but Obama was still being introduced to new capabilities. For much of the first year, discussions about capturing or killing people outside of Afghanistan and Pakistan were for the most part theoretical. The vice chair of the Joint Chiefs, General "Hoss" Cartwright, and Obama's top counterterrorism adviser, John Brennan, were increasingly central to the deliberations, as was Admiral McRaven, the commander of JSOC. One of the first tasks on Obama's national security agenda was a thorough review of Bush's military executive orders. When it came to counterterrorism, Obama would preserve much of his predecessor's policies, and he ended up sustaining most of the ExOrds without revision. In some cases, he sought to expand the authorities. Obama began striking Pakistan almost weekly.

OBAMA INHERITED an already escalating drone program from Bush. The strikes in Pakistan had become more frequent in the waning months of 2008. Just before Obama won the election, Bush had "reached a tacit agreement to allow [drone strikes] to continue without Pakistani involvement." The US policy was to inform Pakistan of attacks while they were under way, or minutes after they had been carried out. President Obama approved of the shift, which brought with it an uptick in drone activity, and he "fully endorsed the covert action program." Obama also kept in place "virtually all the key personnel" from the CIA who had run the covert campaign under Bush. Part of this program, which Obama was read into by outgoing director of national intelligence Mike McConnell right after the election, was a HUMINT network within Pakistan. The spies provided on-the-ground intel that was a necessary counterpart to the drone surveillance and targeting. The spy program, five years in the making and reportedly expensive, was "the real [secret] that Obama would carry with him from that moment forward."

Soon after he assumed office, Obama began pressing Panetta about the hunt for bin Laden. By May 2009, Obama told the CIA director that he needed to make the manhunt his "number one goal" and instructed Panetta to deliver a "detailed operation plan" for locating bin Laden. Panetta had thirty days to put the plan together and then began providing the president with weekly updates on progress made on the effort, even when there was little to report.

As the hunt for bin Laden intensified, the drone strikes continued. So too did the civilian deaths. On June 23, the CIA killed several alleged militants with a Hellfire missile in South Waziristan, then followed up hours later with an attack on the funeral mourning their deaths. Scores of civilians— estimates ranged between eighteen and forty-five—were killed. "After the prayers ended people were asking each other to leave the area as drones were hovering," said a man who lost his leg in the attack. "First two drones fired two missiles, it created a havoc, there was smoke and dust everywhere. Injured people were crying and asking for help...they fired the third missile after a minute, and I fell on the ground." US intelligence reportedly believed that Baitullah Mehsud, the leader of the Pakistani Taliban would be "among the mourners." He was not, at least when the drones struck.

The elusive Mehsud had already survived over a dozen reported attempts to kill him, between Bush and Obama, which had resulted in hundreds of collateral deaths. But then, in early August, US intelligence tracked Mehsud down to his father-in-law's house in a village called Zanghara in South Waziristan. On August 5, CIA drones fired at him as he reclined on the house's rooftop with family members and other guests. Two Hellfire missiles ripped Mehsud in half, killing eleven other people at the house.

In October 2009, Obama reportedly expanded the "target boxes" in Pakistan, broadening the area in which the CIA could go after targets, gave the agency authorization to acquire more drones, and "increased resources for the agency's secret paramilitary forces." Obama had already authorized as many drone strikes in ten months as Bush had in his entire eight years in office.

ALTHOUGH THE CIA WOULD TAKE MUCH of the credit and criticism for the US drone program in Pakistan, it was not the only player. JSOC had its own intelligence operations inside Pakistan and, at times, conducted its own drone strikes. At the center of both the JSOC and CIA targeted-killing programs were members of an elite division of Blackwater, who assisted in planning the assassinations of suspected Taliban and al Qaeda operatives, "snatch and grabs" of high-value targets and other sensitive actions inside Pakistan. Some elite Blackwater SELECT personnel worked for the CIA at "hidden bases in Pakistan and Afghanistan, where the company's contractors assemble and load Hellfire missiles and 500-pound laser-guided bombs on remotely piloted Predator aircraft."

Blackwater operatives also worked for JSOC on a parallel program that was run out of Bagram Air Base in neighboring Afghanistan. US military intelligence and company sources told me that some Blackwater personnel were given rolling security clearances above their approved level. Using Alternative Compartmentalized Control Measures (ACCMs), the Blackwater personnel were granted entry to a Special Access Program. "With an ACCM, the security manager can grant access to you to be exposed to and operate within compartmentalized programs far above 'secret'—even though you have no business doing so," a US military intelligence source told me. It allowed Blackwater personnel who "do not have the requisite security clearance or do not hold a security clearance whatsoever to participate in classified operations by virtue of trust," he added. "Think of it as an ultra-exclusive level above top secret. That's exactly what it is: a circle of love." As a result, Blackwater had access to "all source" reports that were culled in part from JSOC units in the field. "That's how a lot of things over the years have been conducted with contractors," said the source. "We have contractors that regularly see things that top policymakers don't unless they ask."

The military intelligence source said that the Blackwater-JSOC operation in Pakistan was referred to as "Qatar cubed," in reference to the US forward operating base in Qatar that served as the hub for the planning and implementation of the US invasion of Iraq. "This is supposed to be the brave new world," he told me. "This is the Jamestown of the new millennium and it's meant to be a lily pad. You can jump off to Uzbekistan, you can jump back over the border, you can jump sideways, you can jump northwest. It's strategically located so that they can get their people wherever they have to without having to wrangle with the military chain of command in Afghanistan, which is convoluted. They don't have to deal with that because they're operating under a classified mandate."

In addition to planning drone strikes and operations against suspected al Qaeda and Taliban forces in Pakistan for both JSOC and the CIA, the Blackwater teams also helped plan missions for JSOC inside Uzbekistan against the Islamic Movement of Uzbekistan. Blackwater did not actually carry out the operations, the military intelligence source told me, which were executed on the ground by JSOC forces. "That piqued my curiosity and really worries me because I don't know if you noticed but I was never told we are at war with Uzbekistan," he said. "So, did I miss something? Did Rumsfeld come back into power?" When civilians are killed, "People go, 'Oh, it's the CIA doing crazy shit again unchecked.' Well, at least 50 percent of the time, that's JSOC [hitting] somebody they've identified through HUMINT or they've culled the intelligence themselves or it's been shared with them and they take that person out and that's how it works."

CIA operations were subject to congressional oversight, unlike the parallel JSOC ops. "Targeted killings are not the most popular thing in town right now and the CIA knows that," my source told me in 2009. "Contractors and especially JSOC personnel working under a classified mandate are not [overseen by Congress], so they just don't care. If there's one person they're going after and there's thirty-four [other] people in the building, thirty-five people are going to die. That's the mentality." He added, "They're not accountable to anybody and they know that. It's an open secret, but what are you going to do, shut down JSOC?"

As President Obama and his new cabinet began reviewing the covert actions and programs built up under Bush, they were faced with a series of tough choices on which to end and which to continue. The labyrinth of the CIA-JSOC-Blackwater covert action program in Pakistan was a legacy of the infighting and secrecy that had played out within the US counter-terrorism community since the early days after 9/11. As a senator, Obama was critical of Blackwater and introduced legislation to try to hold it and other private security companies accountable. Now, as commander in chief, he was confronted by briefings from the CIA and US military about their necessity to covert US operations. Laying out policy visions on the campaign trail was one thing, but confronting the most secretive, elite forces in the US national security apparatus would be no easy task. And, for the most part, Obama elected to embrace—not restrain—those very forces. The more the president became involved with the day-to-day running of the targeted killing program, the more it expanded. By the end of his first year in office, Obama and his new counterterrorism team would begin building the infrastructure for a formalized US assassination program.

# 26 Special Ops Want to "Own This Shit Like They Did in Central America in the '80s"

WASHINGTON, DC, AND YEMEN, 2009—The day Obama signed an executive order mandating that the Guantánamo prison be shut down, opponents of his order received a substantial boost to their cause when it was revealed that a former Gitmo prisoner who was released as part of a US-supported rehabilitation program run by Saudi Arabia had resurfaced in Yemen and declared himself an al Qaeda leader. Logged at Guantánamo as prisoner number 372, Said Ali al Shihri was one of the first detainees taken to the prison, on January 21, 2002, after being captured on the Afghan-Pakistan border. According to the Pentagon's version of events, Shihri had trained in urban warfare tactics in Afghanistan and was an "al Qaeda travel facilitator," funding fighters. According to documents from his administrative review at Guantánamo, Shihri said he had gone to Afghanistan after 9/11 to participate in humanitarian relief operations. Ultimately, in November 2007, the Defense Department decided to repatriate Shihri to Saudi Arabia. After he completed the rehabilitation program, which was supported by the Bush administration, he went missing. Whether he was a member of al Qaeda before going to Guantánamo is the subject of debate. What happened after he was released is not.

In January 2009, Shihri appeared on a video with another Saudi who had been imprisoned at Guantánamo, Abu Hareth Muhammad al Awfi, and two infamous Yemeni members of al Qaeda: Nasir al Wuhayshi and Qasim al Rimi. In the video, posted on YouTube in late January, the four men, dressed in a mishmash of tribal garb and military gear, announced the formation of a new, regional organization, al Qaeda in the Arabian Peninsula (AQAP). "By Allah, imprisonment only increased our persistence in our principles for which we went out, did jihad for, and were imprisoned for," declared Shihri, wearing a keffiyeh on his head and sporting a belt of bullets slung over his shoulder. Although the name AQAP was known in some intelligence circles, particularly in Saudi Arabia, prior to the posting of the video, for much of the world it was the debut of a rebranded al Qaeda. It was no coincidence that the quartet of men in the video was evenly split between Saudis and Yemenis. It was a statement about the perceived illegitimacy and collusion of the Saudi and Yemeni governments. The new AQAP "transformed al Qaeda in Yemen from a subsidiary of the franchise into its primary regional office by swallowing its once-larger sibling in Saudi Arabia," according to Middle East scholar Barak Barfi, a research fellow at the New America Foundation. Wuhayshi "and his cadres have effectively rebuilt a dead organization and even made it stronger." That month, Saudi Arabia released a list of its "85 Most Wanted" individuals. Twenty of them, according to Saudi intel, had joined AQAP in Yemen.

Al Qaeda was back with a vengeance in Yemen. A National Counter-terrorism Center report released in early 2009 concluded: "The security situation in Yemen deteriorated significantly over the past year as al-Qa-ida in Yemen increased its attacks against Western and Yemeni govern-ment institutions." For much of the first year of the Obama presidency, Yemen was seldom mentioned publicly outside of a small circle of national security officials and journalists. Instead, the administration focused on its escalation of the war in Afghanistan and a drawdown of the US troop presence in Iraq.

The covert counterterrorism approach for much of the first year of the Obama presidency was dominated by ratcheting up the CIA's drone bombing campaign in Pakistan, coupled with occasional covert action from JSOC. The president repeatedly said the focus of the US war against al Qaeda was centered in the tribal areas straddling the Afghan-Pakistan border. "I don't think there's any doubt any longer that there has been a developing syndicate of terror, and those tentacles reach far and wide," Obama's new secretary of state, Hillary Clinton, said in one of her first major appearances in front of the Senate. "Yes, they do reach to Somalia, to Yemen, to the Maghreb, et cetera. But they are focused and grounded in the border area between Pakistan and Afghanistan." Obama's senior national security officials, though, knew early on that the harder they hit in Pakistan, the more likely it was for al Qaeda to find havens elsewhere.

When Admiral Dennis Blair, Obama's newly appointed director of national intelligence, testified before the House Permanent Select Com-mittee on Intelligence on February 25, 2009, he asserted that al Qaeda's headquarters were in the tribal areas of Pakistan but added, "We are con-cerned about their ability to move around. It's kind of like toothpaste in a tube." Blair said, "Of particular concern are the expanding al Qaeda networks" in "North Africa and the emerging and intensifying al Qaeda presence in Yemen." Yemen, he said, "is re-emerging as a jihadist battle-ground," adding bluntly: "We are concerned about the potential for home-grown American extremists, inspired by al Qaeda's militant ideology, to plan attacks inside the United States."

Obama's newly appointed CIA director echoed Blair's concerns. "This is a very persistent enemy that we're dealing with," Panetta told a group of journalists he invited to Langley for a roundtable discussion. "When they are attacked, they go and they find ways to regroup; they find ways to make their way to other areas. And, that's why I'm concerned about Somalia, that's why I'm concerned about Yemen...because of that kind of possibility. So I don't think we can stop just at the effort to try to disrupt them; I think it has to be a continuing effort because they aren't going to stop." He warned that Yemen and Somalia could "become safe havens" for al Qaeda.

During the presidential campaign, John McCain and other Republicans had attempted to portray Obama as ill equipped to deal with the threat of international terrorism. But from the first days of his administration the new president was, in fact, extremely focused on escalating the covert US war against al Qaeda and expanding it far beyond Bush-era levels, particularly in Yemen.

Two days after the election, when president-elect Obama received a global security briefing from director of national intelligence McConnell, he told Obama that, second to the al Qaeda presence in the tribal areas of Pakistan, an "immediate threat was al Qaeda in Yemen." Two weeks later, when Obama met with Admiral Mike Mullen, chair of the Joint Chiefs, Obama was told that despite substantial US intelligence on the resurrection of al Qaeda in Yemen, "adequate plans" did not exist for confronting it. Less than a year into Obama's presidency, a senior White House official publicly blamed the Bush administration for allowing al Qaeda to "regenerate" in Yemen and Somalia, "establishing new safe-havens that have grown over a period of years."

In the beginning of 2009, the Obama administration found itself in a challenging predicament with President Saleh. Obama had campaigned on a pledge to close Guantánamo and had signed an executive order mandating its closure. Almost half of the more than two hundred prisoners at the camp when Obama took office were from Yemen. Given President Saleh's track record of prison breaks and false rehabilitation programs, the administration did not trust Saleh to handle the prisoners if they were repatriated. Although the Saudis had "rehabilitated" Shihri only to have him appear as a leader of AQAP, the White House favored transferring the Yemeni prisoners to Saudi custody.

President Obama made John Brennan, his chief counterterrorism adviser, his point man on dealing with Yemen. Fluent in Arabic, Brennan had spent twenty-five years in the CIA, where he went from being an analyst and a spy to running the Agency's operations in Saudi Arabia. In 1996, Brennan was station chief in Riyadh when the Khobar Towers were bombed and nineteen US military personnel were killed. Throughout most of the Bush years, he was at the epicenter of US intelligence operations and eventually headed up the National Counterterrorism Center, tracking intel on terrorists worldwide. Brennan joined the Obama transition team after the election, helping coordinate the new administration's intelligence strategy. Obama had initially picked Brennan to be director of the CIA, but Brennan withdrew his name when it became clear that his past statements in support of "enhanced interrogation" techniques and extraordinary rendition of prisoners would make confirmation difficult. Instead, Brennan would serve as the deputy national security adviser for homeland security and counterterrorism, a position that did not require Senate confirmation. The position was made more powerful when Obama combined the portfolios of homeland security and national security and authorized Brennan to have "direct and immediate" access to the president.

In his role as Obama's Yemen point man, Brennan would find himself playing a dual role: negotiating access to Yemen's territory for Special Operations and CIA operations, along with training for Yemeni units; and dealing with the issue of the Guantánamo detainees. Predictably, Saleh would link the two at times, using the prisoners as bargaining chips.

In February 2009, after reaching agreements with tribal leaders, Saleh released 176 of the men taken into custody over the years on suspicion of being linked to al Qaeda. On March 15, in the southern historic fortified city of Shibam, four South Korean tourists were blown up as they posed for photographs near the UN World Heritage site. The next day, Brennan and the National Security Council director for counterterrorism, John Duncan, met with Saleh in Sana'a to try to persuade the Yemeni president to allow the United States to send Yemeni prisoners to Saudi Arabia. Brennan, according to a subsequent US diplomatic cable, was "repeatedly rebuffed." Saleh demanded the prisoners be returned to Yemen and placed in a rehabilitation center that, Saleh suggested, should be funded by the United States and the Saudis. "We will offer the land in Aden, and you and the Saudis will provide the funding," Saleh told them, adding that he thought $11 million in aid money should be enough to construct the facility. Brennan suggested that Saleh had "his hands full" dealing with al Qaeda and was too busy to run such a center. Saleh, according to the diplomatic cable, "appeared alternately dismissive, bored, and impatient during the 40-minute meeting."

At the meeting, Brennan delivered a letter from President Obama to Saleh. Yemen's official Saba News Agency reported that the letter "deal[t] with cooperation between the two countries in security field and fighting terror" and "praised Yemen's efforts in fighting terror and affirmed the United States' support to Yemen." A US diplomatic cable said the letter only addressed the Guantánamo situation. Before leaving Sana'a, Brennan told Saleh's nephew, a senior counterterrorism official in Yemen, that he "would report to President Obama his disappointment that [Yemen] was being inflexible in dealing" with the Guantánamo issue. A few weeks after the meeting, Saleh told *Newsweek*, "We are not obedient soldiers of the United States. We don't say just OK to everything that they ask us."

Colonel Patrick Lang first met Brennan when Brennan was assigned as a CIA analyst to Saudi Arabia. "I don't think [Brennan]'s up to dealing with Saleh in terms of sheer craftiness and wiles," Lang told me at the time, adding, the Yemenis "know how to deal with us."

WHILE BRENNAN AND OTHER CIVILIAN OFFICIALS haggled with Saleh over Guantánamo prisoners, the topic was far from the center of Washington's counterterrorism policy. The Obama administration became consumed with the Afghanistan war strategy and would spend the next several months frequently debating how many additional troops to send to Afghanistan and how to deal with al Qaeda sanctuaries in Pakistan.

The CENTCOM commander, General Petraeus, pushed hard for Obama to appoint General Stanley McChrystal to run the Afghan War, knowing that McChrystal shared his passion for kinetic action and clandestine operations. Petraeus, meanwhile, focused on plans for the United States to intensify its direct action inside Yemen and elsewhere in his area of control. In April, in front of the Senate Armed Services Committee, Petraeus outlined the posture of CENTCOM, speaking in sweeping terms that were very much in line with the Bush-era view of the world as a battlefield. "Success against the extremist networks in the CENTCOM AOR [Area of Responsibility]—whether in Iraq, Afghanistan, Pakistan, Yemen, Lebanon, or elsewhere—requires all forces and means at our disposal employed in a strategic approach grounded in the principles of counterinsurgency," Petraeus declared. "Our counter-terror efforts, which seek to dismantle the extremist networks and their leadership, often through the use of military force, are critical."

That month, Petraeus approved a plan developed with the US Embassy in Sana'a and the CIA and other intelligence agencies to expand US military action inside Yemen. Part of the plan involved special ops training for Yemeni forces, but it would also involve unilateral strikes against AQAP. Petraeus complained about what he saw as the "inability of the Yemeni government to secure and exercise control over all of its territory," which he said "offers terrorist and insurgent groups in the region, particularly Al Qaeda, a safe haven in which to plan, organize, and support terrorist operations." Petraeus said bluntly, "It is important that this problem be addressed, and CENTCOM is working to do that." Although Petraeus paid lip service to the cooperation between the United States and Yemen, he was clear that the United States would strike in Yemen whenever it pleased. "When he was CENTCOM commander, then he was in a position to start to apply this 'sacred doctrine' to other places in the theater for which he was commander, and Yemen was one of those that was available," recalled Colonel Lang. "And it's very easy when you're sitting in your headquarters to entertain thoughts like that." Lang paused, then added: "Let it be done, you know, and it is done."

At the time, in the summer of 2009, General McChrystal had left JSOC and was serving as the director of operations for the Joint Chiefs of Staff. Although McChrystal would soon take over as commander of the Afghan War, he advised President Obama to transform the way JSOC was being used under the Bush administration and to utilize the unit more intimately in task forces run by combatant commanders rather than as a stand-alone force. Along with Petraeus, McChrystal pushed Obama to authorize the expansion of covert ops against al Qaeda to a dozen countries throughout the Middle East, the Horn of Africa and Central Asia. The president gave the plan the green light. In the case of Yemen, that meant "direct actions" would fall under Petraeus's command and be carried out by JSOC's ninjas.

On May 28, the CIA's deputy director, Stephen Kappes, boarded a Yemeni Air Force helicopter in Sana'a and flew 120 miles south to the city of Taiz, where he was taken to one of President Saleh's private residences. Saleh greeted him in a white dress shirt and black pants. Saleh had a small cut over his left eye from an accident he'd had in his pool about a week earlier at his palace in Sana'a. The focus of the forty-minute meeting was operations against AQAP and intelligence sharing between Yemen and the United States, but first Saleh confirmed for Kappes that he had decided to support the transfer of some of the Yemeni Guantánamo prisoners to Saudi Arabia—a move he had told Brennan he would not make. Kappes thanked Saleh on behalf of President Obama, and then Saleh repeated his request for an $11 million rehab center of his own, adding that the Bush administration had assured him he would get it. The two then moved on to the central issue for Kappes: AQAP. Kappes told Saleh that the United States was concerned that al Qaeda might try to assassinate Saleh. The Yemeni leader replied that he was also concerned about this possibility, adding that he had already broken up a plot to down one of his presidential planes on his recent trip to Aden. When Kappes told Saleh that the Obama administration was intent on destroying al Qaeda worldwide, Saleh replied, "I hope this campaign continues and succeeds. We're doing the same here. Our position is unshakable."

What stood out most to Kappes from the meeting was Saleh's "decision to reverse himself and characterize AQAP as the most serious threat facing Yemen." Kappes and his entourage observed that Saleh's prime focus on AQAP versus the Houthis or the southern secessionists "was almost certainly taken with his [US government] interlocutors in mind" and "meant to elicit the necessary level of political, economic and military assistance to forestall Yemen's collapse, and the negative effects it would have on regional stability and security." During his meeting with Kappes, Saleh also pushed his line that the Houthis in the north were being backed by Iran and Hezbollah. Unbeknownst to Kappes, Saleh was laying the groundwork for another offensive in the north. The two men agreed that their intelligence cooperation was moving ahead smoothly and would only grow stronger.

ON JUNE 1, 2009, Abdulhakim Mujahid Muhammad, a US citizen, carried out a drive-by shooting outside a US military recruiting center in Little Rock, Arkansas. He killed Private William Long and wounded Private Quinton Ezeagwula as they stood in front of the center. Born Carlos Bledsoe, Muhammad, a convert to Islam, had traveled in 2007 to Yemen, where he would marry and remain for a year and a half. While in Yemen, he was arrested by local authorities after he was stopped at a checkpoint carrying a fake Somali passport and weapons manuals as well as literature by Anwar Awlaki. Muhammad subsequently spent four months in prison, where his lawyer says he was tortured by Yemeni authorities and radicalized by other prisoners. "If you ever get out of this godforsaken place, we'll hound you 'til the day you die," a visiting FBI agent told Muhammad during a visit with him in the Yemeni prison, according to his lawyer.

Eventually, the US government persuaded the Yemeni government to deport Muhammad to the United States. Once on US soil, he was investigated by the FBI's Joint Terrorism Task Force but was not taken into custody. Muhammad told police officials who interrogated him that he was motivated by the US wars in Iraq and Afghanistan.

After the drive-by shooting in Arkansas, as Muhammad's lawyer prepared his defense, Muhammad sent a handwritten letter to the judge in the case, announcing his intent to plead guilty. Muhammad said the shooting was "a jihadi attack on infidel forces," declared his allegiance to Wuhayshi and AQAP and proclaimed, "I wasn't insane or post traumatic nor was I forced to do this act. Which I believe and it is justified according to Islamic laws and the Islamic religion jihad—to fight those who wage war on Islam and Muslims." Whether Muhammad had actual ties to AQAP may never be known. His father suggested his son was brainwashed and "might be trying to link himself to Al Qaeda because he believes it will lead to his execution and make him a martyr." Whether it was an AQAP attack or not would soon become irrelevant, though, as other deadly incidents contributed to a perception that the group was intent on striking in the United States.

Shortly before the recruiting center shooting, former vice president Dick Cheney launched a scathing public assault on President Obama's counterterrorism policies. In a speech before the neoconservative American Enterprise Institute, Cheney blasted Obama's formal halting of "enhanced interrogation" techniques and celebrated congressional defunding of Obama's attempt to transfer Guantánamo detainees to US soil, a move that effectively blocked the closing of the prison. Cheney called Obama's counterterrorism policies, particularly the banning of torture, "recklessness cloaked in righteousness," charging they "would make the American people less safe."

While Cheney attacked in public, behind the scenes the Obama administration was preparing to launch a far more expansive and sophisticated counterterrorism campaign than that waged by Cheney and his former boss, particularly when it came to Yemen, drawing on the controversial Bush doctrine that declared the world a battlefield. Obama "doubled down on Bush policy," said Joshua Foust, who worked as a Yemen analyst for the Defense Intelligence Agency in the first half of the Obama administration. Shortly after he left the DIA, in early 2011, Foust told me that Obama's approach to Yemen was "heavily militarized, heavily focused on directly neutralizing the threat, instead of kind of draining the swamp."

From the start, the men who would be in charge of "neutralizing the threat" were, in fact, two of the major players in the Bush administration's war team. While General McChrystal coordinated the escalation in Afghanistan and Pakistan, General Petraeus would oversee the "small wars" in other areas of CENTCOM, particularly in Yemen, in coordination with McChrystal's successor at JSOC, Admiral McRaven. Under the task force structure, JSOC was designated as the lead force for covert action inside Yemen. For many JSOC operators, Yemen seemed more relevant to their skill set than Afghanistan, where al Qaeda had been largely wiped out or forced on the run. "These guys are scalpels. They don't like being used as sledgehammers," the former aide to the special operations commander told me. "In Afghanistan they were used as sledgehammers, chasing down Taliban goatherders. In Yemen, they could be scalpels again, knocking off actual al Qaeda." He added that: Special Operations "wants to own this shit like they did in Central America in the '80s. They don't want Jamba Juice, COIN [counterinsurgency] and 'nation building.'"

Following Kappes's visit with Saleh in May, as part of the coordinated CIA-military-JSOC-State Department plan on Yemen, Hillary Clinton authorized the US ambassador in Yemen, Stephen Seche, to negotiate with Saleh for the United States to be able to fly drones and US helicopters over Yemen's territorial waters at will. Seche was directly told not to put anything on paper and to discuss the proposal only in person. The official reason Seche was to give Saleh for the flyover rights was that CENTCOM needed access for its drones to "interdict the smuggling of weapons into Gaza." Among Seche's talking points with Saleh was US intelligence purportedly showing that a "significant volume of arms shipments to Hamas make the short 24-hour transit across the Red Sea from Yemen to Sudan." Another was that the United States had discovered that "a weapons smuggling network originating in Yemen is supplying weapons to individuals in Africa who are delivering them to various entities there, potentially including al-Qa'ida associated terrorist groups." Yemen's cooperation with the drones and helicopters "would greatly enhance CENTCOM's ability to gain the intelligence required to identify and track" the shipments. Although part of the US intent in brokering this agreement may well have been to track weapons smuggling, its timing suggests it was a cover story.

General Petraeus flew to Yemen on July 26, 2009, to continue laying the groundwork for the joint CIA-military plan to escalate targeting of AQAP. The general brought a gift for Saleh—official confirmation that Obama was increasing military aid to Yemen. In return, Petraeus pressed Saleh to go directly after al Qaeda. For both Saleh and the United States, it was important that Yemen appear to be fighting AQAP on its own and to conceal the extent of US involvement, which was expanding by the day.

A week after the meeting with Petraeus, Saleh deployed his nephew, Ammar Muhammad Abdullah Saleh—a senior commander of the National Security Bureau—to Marib, a hotbed of al Qaeda activity. Ammar's mission was to take down a suspected al Qaeda cell in an operation intended to show Washington that Saleh was serious. It was a disaster. Despite Ammar's negotiations with local tribal leaders on the terms of the assault, the Yemeni counterterrorism units botched it. Instead of shelling the al Qaeda safe house, they hit a tribal compound, sparking a gun battle in which tribal fighters actually joined with AQAP in attacking the government forces. A military supply truck got lost and was captured by al Qaeda operatives. In the end, Saleh's forces lost five tanks and several troops, and seven of their soldiers were taken prisoner. AQAP quickly capitalized on the debacle, naming it the "Battle of Marib" and posting a video online that featured the captured soldiers. Although the operation was a colossal failure, it was also useful for the United States and Saleh because it was a very public show that the Yemeni government was fighting AQAP, thus helping to cloak US actions in Yemen.

On August 10, in a town hall meeting with US troops, Admiral Mullen was asked "what regions we as the military can expect to focus on in the coming not year, two years, but five years and 10 years." Mullen responded that what he had "watched al-Qaeda do in the last five or six years is federate," adding, "I worry about safe havens being created in Yemen and Somalia, for example. Not unlike what they had in Afghanistan when this started in 2001." He also mentioned North Africa, the Philippines and Indonesia. "It is a growing network over time," Mullen said.

The Obama administration expanded the number of US Special Operations Forces trainers in Yemen. "They [the Yemenis] got free training from the elite of the elite of the US military—the best of the best," the former aide to a special operations commander told me. "The 'Advise and Assist' guys, mostly led by DEVGRU. Their job is to teach you how to blow shit up and fly choppers and do night raids and they are very good at it." While the training expanded, so too did unilateral, covert, lethal operations by JSOC.

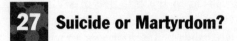

## 27 Suicide or Martyrdom?

YEMEN, 2009—As President Obama was settling into the Oval Office, Anwar Awlaki was busy building up his website and spreading his message. He posted an essay on his blog titled "Suicide or Martyrdom?" Although cloaked in the language of a debate about whether suicide is a mortal sin in Islam, it ultimately was a defense of suicide bombing. "Today the world turns upside down when one Muslim performs a martyrdom operation. Can you imagine what would happen if that is done by seven hundred Muslims on the same day?!" Awlaki wrote. "Brothers and sisters whether you agree or not with martyrdom operations let's leave our differences behind us, and let us support our Muslim brothers who are in the frontlines. Just like we disagree on many other issues, we should not let our disagreements stand in the way of our solidarity in the face of our adversaries." The post received more than three hundred comments, many of them praising Awlaki. A few weeks before he published that essay, Awlaki had posted links to one of his most popular treatises, "44 Ways to Support Jihad." In February, Awlaki posted links for free downloads of many of his most popular lectures. With each new blog entry, Awlaki was thumbing his nose at the US authorities who had tried to silence him and bury him away in a Yemeni dungeon. Now, here was Awlaki, operating online in full view, encouraging Muslims to fight against the disbelievers and labeling the United States and its allies a "scourge" and "the greatest terrorists of all."

In March 2009, Awlaki addressed a religious conference in Pakistan via Internet stream. "I'm speaking to you from Yemen at the moment, and there are some similarities between Yemen and Pakistan, so when speaking about one, it is like speaking about the other," Awlaki, his voice tinged with the effects of digitization, told the gathering. "Both countries are important US partners in the war on terror. Both countries have lost their sovereignty to the US by having drones strike within their territory." Both have "been used as supply stations for America's war against Muslims. And both countries are ruled by crooks." Awlaki said he wanted to talk straight to his audience because "sugar coating is not going to do anyone any benefit. So, if we want to change our situation, we really need to sit down and think about it and decide what the illness is, what the symptoms are, and how to cure it."

During his speech, he called on all able-bodied Muslims to join the jihad against the United States in Afghanistan, Iraq and elsewhere, and he encouraged those who could not fight to donate money to the causes. "We're following the tails of cows, and we have left jihad in the path of Allah. And that's why we are being humiliated now. And this humiliation will not be lifted," he said. The United States and its allies depend on "might—their powerful aircrafts, their carriers in the ocean, their soldiers with their hi-tech weaponry and their advanced missiles. This is might. So how can we restrain their might? Is it through negotiations? Is it through giving up? Is it through surrendering? Is it through bending backwards for them?" Awlaki asked rhetorically. "Brothers and sisters, if we are not going to fight today, then when will we fight? Muslim land is occupied, oppression is wide spread, the laws of Quran are neglected, what other time is better for jihad than today?"

Nasser Awlaki was growing concerned about his son. Everything the elder Awlaki was hearing from his friends and colleagues in the Yemeni government was ominous. Senior intelligence officials were warning him that the Americans intended to kill Anwar. They spoke of drones taking him out in the hinterlands of Shabwah, where Anwar was living. The Yemeni president personally called Nasser and begged him to persuade Anwar to return to Sana'a. "At that time, when the president was calling me, and telling me to bring my son, there was a directive from the minister of interior and the security people to capture him," Nasser told me. "And the governor of Shabwah called me and said, 'Look, we have an order from the Ministry of Interior, and the security people to capture your son.'"

This was no surprise to Anwar. In his family's village in Shabwah, Anwar was living in his grandfather's four-story mud house, recording sermons and writing his blog. Soon after he arrived, Yemeni security forces began regularly positioning their vehicles and weapons at the *wadi* (valley) that ran along the front of the house. Anwar told his father that they would point their automatic weapons at the house, trying to intimidate him. "Look, my son, I don't want you to be harassed because you either will kill somebody, or somebody will kill you," Nasser told Anwar in a phone call. "So please keep calm. No matter what they do, please be calm." Nasser feared that if the Yemeni forces tried to seize Anwar, a firefight could break out between the Aulaq tribe and Yemeni security forces.

In May 2009, at the behest of the Yemeni president, Nasser and his wife traveled to Shabwah to meet with Anwar and ask him to return to Sana'a with them. "This is what the president wants," Nasser told his son. "He's under pressure from the Americans." They discussed the order for Anwar's arrest. "You are my father," Anwar told Nasser. "How can you bring me to Sana'a when these people want to put me in prison? How can you be assured, father, that the Americans will not do something against me?" Nasser told his son that he could not provide him with any guarantees, but he believed it was Anwar's safest move. Anwar would not budge. "I will not allow the Americans to tell me which direction to position my bed," Anwar said. "It was a heated discussion," Nasser later told me. "And that was unfortunate, for me, because it was last time I talked to him, and we were not on very good terms at that time."

Saleh bin Fareed also spoke to Anwar and concluded that his nephew wasn't doing any harm in rural Shabwah. If anything, he thought Anwar would get into less trouble there. Bin Fareed called Yemen's intelligence chief, General Galib al Qamish. "You and the Americans, I think, are wrong," he told the general. Anwar "sits there, in a village of 1,000 or 2,000 people. If you think he is dangerous, and he comes to Sana'a, he will be meeting 2 million people. It's better to leave him there." Qamish sighed. "It's not what the Americans want." Why the Americans were so obsessed with Anwar was not clear to bin Fareed. How could a preacher in rural Yemen pose a threat to the most powerful nation on earth? he wondered.

Anwar didn't care what the Americans wanted. When his parents returned to Sana'a, Anwar began plotting his next move. As he saw it, his family had acted as intermediaries for the Yemeni government, which wanted Anwar arrested. The Americans were calling the shots. They knew where he was and their drones could find him. He had no choice: surrender or go underground. His wife and children would be left in Sana'a under the care of his parents. Anwar was being pushed, and eventually he sought the comradeship and protection of other outlaws being hunted in Yemen. "What am I accused of? That I call to the truth? That I call to Jihad for the sake of Allah, and in defense of the Islamic nation's causes?" Awlaki asserted. "The same goes for the Americans. I have no intention of turning myself in to them. If they want me, let them search for me."

NIDAL HASAN, the US army psychiatrist, kept writing to Anwar Awlaki, even though his e-mails were receiving no responses. He posed questions to Awlaki about theology and about Hamas's fight against the Israeli government, asking, among other things, "Is it Permissible to Fire Unguided Rockets into Israel?" After a few lengthy e-mails, Hasan shifted gears and started asking Awlaki how he could donate money to his causes. He suggested that Awlaki give an address where money orders or checks could be sent, rather than using online services. "This can assure privacy for some who are concerned," Hasan wrote. That same day, Hasan wrote Awlaki again. "InshAllah, A $5,000.00 scholarship prize is being awarded for the best essay/piece entitled 'Why is Anwar Al Awlaki a great activist and leader'. We would be honored if you would award the prize." Hasan added a P.S.: "We met briefly a very long time ago when you were the Imam at Dar al-Hijra. I doubt if you remember me. In any case I have since graduated medical school and finished residency training." Awlaki finally replied. "I pray this message reaches you at the best state of emaan [health]," he wrote Hasan. "Jazakum Allahu khairan [May Allah reward you in goodness] for thinking good of me. I don't travel so I wont be able to physically award the prize and I am too 'embarrassed' for a lack of the better word to award it anyway. May Allah assist you in your efforts."

Awlaki gave no indication that he remembered Hasan at all. Hasan wrote back, once again offering money to Awlaki and adding a postscript saying he was "looking for a wife that is willing to strive with me to please Allah.... I will strongly consider a recommendation coming from you." Awlaki replied, "Thanks for the offer for help. Well it is needed but I just don't know how to do it. There are poor people, orphans, widows, dawa [proselytizing on behalf of Islam] projects, and the list goes on. So if you have any ideas on how to get help across and in accordance to law in a climate that is strict to start with please let me know. Tell more about yourself. I will keep an eye for a sister." Sent on February 22, 2009, that was the last e-mail Awlaki is known to have sent to Hasan.

Over the next several months Hasan continued to e-mail Awlaki. "I know your busy. Please keep me in your rolodex in case you find me useful and feel free to call me collect," Hasan wrote. From there on out, the communications were a one-way road. The tone of Hasan's e-mails became like that of a patient in therapy attempting to work through difficult life decisions. In one e-mail, sent in May 2009, Hasan pontificated on the morality of suicide bombings and raised "the issue of 'collateral damage' where a decision is made to allow the killing of innocents for a valuable target. [In] the Qur'an it states to fight your enemies as they fight you but don't transgress. So, I would assume that suicide bomber whose aim is to kill enemy soldiers or their helpers but also kill innocents in the process is acceptable. Furthermore, if enemy soldiers are using other tactics that are unethical/unconscionable than those same tactics may be used." Hasan ended his note by telling Awlaki, "We miss hearing from you!"

AWLAKI'S BLOG had become far less active than it had been throughout 2008. With the US and Yemeni governments breathing down his neck, he had more pressing issues to deal with. Awlaki began moving throughout his family's tribal areas, while keeping a low profile. When he could get access to an Internet connection, he would post an essay or two.

As Awlaki began preparing for a life underground, the Obama administration was ratcheting up the pressure on the Yemeni government to hunt down al Qaeda–linked militants in the country. On August 1, 2009, Awlaki posted an analysis of battles between the Yemeni government and "the Mujahideen" in Marib, writing, "The first face to face fight between the army and the mujahideen ended in a resounding victory for the mujahideen. May Allah bless them with further victories. The army pulled out after asking for a truce from the mujahideen." Awlaki concluded: "May this be the beginning of the greatest Jihad, the Jihad of the Arabian Peninsula that would free the heart of the Islamic world from the tyrants who are deceiving the ummah and standing between us and victory." For Awlaki, the jihad he had advocated in speeches over the years was becoming a reality. As he saw it, a war was now beginning in Yemen, and he would need to decide if the blog was mightier than the sword.

On October 7, Awlaki popped up again with an essay titled "Could Yemen be the Next Surprise of the Season?" He wrote:

> The American people gave G.W. Bush unanimous backing to fight against the mujahedeen and gave him a blank check to spend as much as needed to fulfill that objective. The result? He failed, and he failed miserably. So if America failed to defeat the mujahedeen when it gave its president unlimited support, how can it win with Obama who is on a short leash? If America failed to win when it was at its pinnacle of economic strength, how can it win today with a recession—if not a depression—at hand?
>
> The simple answer is: America cannot and will not win. The tables have turned and there is no rolling back of the worldwide Jihad movement. The ideas of Jihad are proliferating around the world, the mujahedeen movements are gaining strength and the battlefields are expanding with the mujahedeen introducing new fronts....
>
> The Jihad of this era started in Palestine, followed by Afghanistan, then Chechnya, then Iraq, then Somalia, then the Maghreb, and the new front might very well turn out to be Yemen.
>
> And when this new front of Jihad starts in Yemen it might become the single most important front of Jihad in the world.... The Arabian Peninsula has always been a land of mujahedeen even though there has been no fighting occurring on its soil. In Afghanistan, Bosnia, Chechnya, and Iraq the participation of mujahedeen from the Arabian Peninsula represented the largest block of foreign mujahedeen. When Jihad starts in the Arabian Peninsula, Jihad would be coming back to

its home....The Arabian Peninsula is home to Makkah and Madinah [Mecca and Medina, the Islamic holy cities]. To free the Holy places from the rule of apostasy and tyranny is to free the heart of Islam....

America and its allies in the area are plotting against the mujahedeen, nevertheless their growth increases by the day. May Allah grant the true believers victory and grant them steadfastness on His path.

By accident or design, Anwar Awlaki found himself on the run just as al Qaeda in Yemen was growing into a real force with its core in Shabwah and Abyan, the Aulaq tribal areas. Fahd al Quso, who was still being hunted by the United States for his role in the 2000 USS *Cole* bombing, was a member of Awlaki's tribe, as were several other key figures in al Qaeda in the Arabian Peninsula.

Many Yemenis had fought the jihad elsewhere in the world, as Awlaki pointed out, but now Yemen would see the rise of an al Qaeda affiliate within its own borders. "If we go back to 2001 or 2002, Al Qaeda was not more than ten or twenty individuals in Yemen, and it was not an organization," journalist Abdul Rezzaq al Jamal, an independent Yemeni reporter who interviewed many of the founding members of AQAP, told me. "It had no structure until 2009." As AQAP formed, Awlaki believed it was his obligation to support his brother jihadists in their struggle against the Yemeni regime and what he believed would be a coming American war against them. "I lived in the US for twenty-one years. America was my home," Awlaki later recalled. "I was a preacher of Islam, involved in non-violent Islamic activism. However, with the American invasion of Iraq, and continued US aggression against Muslims, I could not reconcile between living in the US and being a Muslim... and I came to the conclusion that Jihad against America is binding upon myself just as it is binding on every other able Muslim."

Awlaki had long been viewed as a nuisance by the US government, and the US counterterrorism community wanted him silenced. But as AQAP rose in Yemen, the perception was that Awlaki was becoming an increasingly active threat. The events of the last two months of 2009 would seal Awlaki's fate. Awlaki's own words also crossed a line during this time, as he lent his powerful endorsement to specific acts of terrorism on US targets.

Less than a year into President Obama's term, Yemen would be catapulted to the top of the list of trouble spots on the US counterterrorism radar and Awlaki would become an epic figure, with senior US officials eventually comparing him to Osama bin Laden and labeling him one of the greatest terrorist threats facing the country.

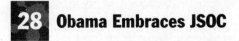

## 28 Obama Embraces JSOC

SOMALIA, EARLY 2009—For the first year of the Obama presidency, much of the administration's foreign policy attention was directed at Afghanistan and the president's pledge to escalate the war there. Despite estimates that there were fewer than one hundred al Qaeda operatives remaining in the country, Obama was weighing a dramatic increase in the number of US troops he would deploy to Afghanistan, to continue an intervention Obama had characterized as the "right war" during his presidential campaign. But while Afghanistan was the administration's top international concern, the Horn of Africa and the Arabian Peninsula were experiencing a dramatic uptick in al Qaeda mobilizations.

With the Islamic Courts Union in Somalia decimated, al Shabab had become the dominant armed group in Somalia and was in control of substantial territory in Mogadishu and elsewhere. The United States and its African Union proxies were supporting a weak transitional government headed by Sheikh Sharif, the former chair of the ICU. In May 2009, fighting in the capital between Sharif's government and al Shabab–linked groups became so intense that the United Nations accused al Shabab of trying "to seize power by force" in "a coup attempt."

Around that time, al Shabab released two highly produced videos featuring a young bearded American named Omar Hammami. The former University of South Alabama student declared himself a member of al Shabab and called on other Western Muslims to join him on the battlefield of Somalia. Hammami—whose name comes from his father, a Syrian immigrant—grew up as an average American in the South, playing soccer and chasing girls. In high school, he converted from Christianity to Islam. He eventually dropped out of college, married a Somali woman and had a child. Hammami had begun a process of radicalization and was speaking of wanting to fight jihad and frequenting Islamic web forums. In 2006, he visited Egypt, where he met Daniel Maldonado, another US citizen, whom he knew from online chat rooms. Maldonado persuaded Hammami to travel to Somalia to witness the Islamic revolution firsthand. So he headed there, initially staying with his Somali wife's grandmother in Mogadishu. By December, the two men had hooked up with al Shabab on the eve of the Ethiopian invasion. "I made it my goal to find those guys should I make it to Somalia," Hammami asserted, saying that he "signed up for training."

Maldonado was eventually captured by "a multinational counter-terrorism team" along the Kenya-Somalia border. He was extradited to the United States and indicted on federal terror-related charges in early 2007. But Hammami evaded capture and remained among the ranks of al Shabab. According to US counterterrorism officials, he caught the eye of al Qaeda leaders Fazul and Nabhan, who viewed him as a potential asset because of his American citizenship. In late 2007, a year after he first arrived in Somalia, Hammami appeared on Al Jazeera—with a keffiyeh covering much of his face, explaining why he had joined al Shabab. "Oh, Muslims of America, take into consideration the situation in Somalia," he declared, using the nom de guerre Abu Mansoor al Amriki, or the American. "After fifteen years of chaos and oppressive rule by the American-backed warlords, your brothers stood up and established peace and justice in this land."

Hammami would become al Shabab's most prominent online recruiter for young, Western Muslims. He grew closer to Nabhan and Fazul and eventually became one of al Shabab's key foreign operatives. By that point, Somali officials estimated that more than 450 foreign fighters had come into Somalia to join al Shabab in its struggle. "The only reason we are staying here, away from our families, away from the cities, away from—you know—ice, candy bars, all these other things, is because we're waiting to meet with the enemy," Hammami said, in the first video al Shabab released about him, as he sat dressed in camouflage and wearing a keffiyeh on his head in a tree-lined area. "If you can encourage more of your children, and more of your neighbors, and anyone around you to send people...to this Jihad, it would be a great asset for us."

In Hammami's video, another English speaker—this one masked and wielding an AK-47—calls on other Western youth to join al Shabab, saying, "We're calling all the brothers overseas, all the Shabab, wherever they are, to come and live the life of the mujahid. They will see with their own eyes, and they will love it." In other videos, Hammami is seen with key al Shabab leaders reviewing maps and helping to plan operations. In 2008, another US citizen, Shirwa Ahmed, blew himself up in a suicide attack in Northern Somalia, making him the first known American suicide bomber to hit in Somalia. He wouldn't be the last.

The increasing number of cases in which American Muslims traveled to the Horn of Africa to join al Shabab ranked high among the Somalia threat assessments awaiting Barack Obama after he won election in November

2008. Obama had said little about Somalia on the campaign trail, though he did refer obliquely to the growing national security imperative in Africa. There would, he said, be "situations that require the United States to work with its partners in Africa to fight terrorism with lethal force."

BY THE TIME PRESIDENT OBAMA TOOK OFFICE, Somalia was becoming a mounting concern in the US counterterrorism community. When the Islamic Courts took power in 2006, al Shabab was a little-known militia on the outskirts of the movement with little clan power. Its foreign fighters, particularly Fazul and Nabhan, were dangerous people with a proven ability to plan and implement large-scale attacks. But they were not in a position to conquer Somalia or hold substantial territory. Now, though, thanks in large part to a backlash against US policy, al Shabab's ranks were growing and its territory expanding. Sheikh Sharif officially assumed the presidency in Somalia the same month Obama was sworn in, but Sharif could barely lay claim to being the mayor of Mogadishu. He loosely governed a small slice of territory in the capital—with the authority of a city council member surrounded by far more powerful enemies who wanted to kill him.

"The idea that Somalia is just a failed state somewhere over there, where people are fighting with one another over heaven knows what, is a construct that we adopt at our peril," declared Hillary Clinton during her Senate confirmation hearing to become secretary of state. "The internal conflict within the groups in Somalia is just as intense as it's ever been, only now we have the added ingredient of al-Qaida and terrorists who are looking to take advantage of the chaos."

The Obama administration increased funding and arms shipments to the African Union Mission in Somalia, the peacekeeping force known as AMISOM. The Ugandan military, supported by Burundi, effectively took over where the Ethiopians had left off and began expanding its military base adjacent to Mogadishu's international airport. By this point, al Shabab had the Somali government and the African Union forces surrounded at the airport and in the Green Zone–like Somali government complex known as Villa Somalia. Al Shabab forces were better paid than the Somali army and were far more willing to die than the AMISOM peacekeeping troops, who had no personal stake in the conflict. In February 2009, al Shabab operatives carried out double-suicide attacks, killing eleven Burundian troops. AMISOM commanders found their base under constant mortar attack and acknowledged the bombardment was reaching an "unprecedented level." A retaliatory attack aimed at al Shabab sparked an exchange of fire that resulted in fifteen deaths in Mogadishu, and more than sixty others wounded, many of them from a stray mortar that slammed into a civilian area. The *New York Times* called the fighting "the heaviest of its kind since Ethiopian troops withdrew from Somalia."

A few months into Obama's presidency, top officials had begun to debate military strikes against al Shabab camps, despite the absence of a concrete threat outside of Somalia. The *Washington Post* reported a divide between DoD officials critical of a perceived "failure to act" and reticent civilian officials heavily influenced by the disastrous Bush policies of the previous few years. The Obama administration was "walking slowly, and for the players with continuity, the frustration continues to grow," one official said. "There is increasing concern about what terrorists operating in Somalia might do," a US counterterrorism official told the *Post*. By that point, the FBI had already been investigating at least twenty cases of young Somali Americans leaving the United States to join the Somali insurgency.

While al Shabab continued to broaden its authority, the first major crisis Obama directly confronted in Somalia did not come from the Islamist group, but rather from a totally different threat increasingly making its presence felt around the Horn of Africa and the Arabian Peninsula: pirates. It was this confrontation—with pirates, rather than al Qaeda—that would cement the growing affinity President Obama had for JSOC.

THE PIRACY INDUSTRY HAD DEVELOPED in Somalia following the fall of Siad Barre's regime in 1991. During the six months that the ICU ruled Somalia, it cracked down substantially on hijackings. Following the Ethiopian invasion, the pirates reclaimed the high seas around Somalia. Although the pirates were often condemned as terrorists and criminals, there was a seldom-mentioned context to their actions. International corporations and nation-states had taken advantage of the permanent state of instability in Somalia, treating the Somali coast as their private, for-profit fishery, while others polluted it with illegal waste dumping. Initially, piracy was at times a response to these actions and some pirates viewed themselves as a sort of Somali coast guard, taxing ships that sought to profit from what was once the realm of Somali fishermen. Those aims were eventually sidelined as the pirates realized they could make huge sums of money by hijacking ships, taking hostages and negotiating large ransoms. Piracy was big business in Somalia. In some cases, the hostages went unharmed, ransoms were paid and everyone moved on. On rare occasions, hostages were killed or, more frequently, died of disease or neglect.

The hijacking on April 8, 2009, was a day Somali pirates hit the wrong ship. On that day, the *Maersk Alabama*, a US-flagged cargo ship, was making its way through the Indian Ocean to Mombasa, passing along the Somali coast, when it was approached by a small vessel carrying four armed pirates. The crew on board the *Alabama* had received counterpiracy training and it did everything it was supposed to do: crew members shot off flares and began moving people on board the ship into a secured safe room. The crew maneuvered the *Alabama*'s rudders in an attempt to throw the much smaller ship off course, then shut down the ship's power and incapacitated its engines. But the young Somalis in the small boat were experienced pirates. In fact, the ship they were using in the attack on the *Alabama* was launched from the FV *Win Far 161*, a Taiwanese vessel they had just seized. After some struggle with the *Alabama* crew's counterpiracy maneuvers, the four Somali pirates managed to board the *Alabama*. They had no idea that the ship they were hijacking belonged to a major US Defense Department contractor or that this operation would be any different from others they had carried out.

When the White House learned that a US-flagged vessel had been seized and that the ship's captain and other members of the twenty-man crew were Americans, the hijacking became a major priority. President Obama was swiftly briefed on the crisis. It was the first registered, US-flagged vessel to be hijacked since the early 1800s. Hours after the hijacking, Obama authorized the deployment of a destroyer, the USS *Bainbridge*, to respond.

By the time the *Bainbridge* reached the scene, on April 9, the *Alabama*'s captain, Richard Phillips, had been taken hostage by the pirates and was in a smaller, encapsulated lifeboat en route to the Somali mainland. One of the pirates had sustained an injury during the hijacking and was ultimately captured by US Navy forces. The other three pirates had abandoned the *Alabama* and were attempting to flee with the only negotiating chip they had left, Captain Phillips. As the standoff continued, President Obama and his national security team worked around the clock with US military commanders to run through various scenarios of how to resolve the crisis and free Phillips unharmed. Two other ships, the guided missile frigate USS *Halyburton* and the amphibious assault ship, USS *Boxer*, were deployed to the scene.

Two days after Phillips was captured, President Obama received two national security briefings on the situation. Defense Secretary Gates said that US commanders twice requested the authority to use lethal force, which Obama granted "virtually immediately." The first authorization was issued at 8:00 p.m. on April 10, after US Navy personnel watched a day earlier from the *Bainbridge* as Captain Phillips tried to escape his captors before being quickly retaken. In response, the pirates threw into the ocean the only communications devices they had on the lifeboat, fearing they were being used to conduct surveillance or to communicate secretly with Phillips. That left the US naval forces with only eyes on the ship and the White House fearing that a US citizen would die very publicly at the hands of pirates only three months into Obama's presidency. On April 11, at 9:20 a.m., President Obama granted a second authorization to use lethal force to an "additional set of US forces."

It was the seizing of the *Alabama* that would very directly introduce President Obama to JSOC and its capabilities. It was "the first time I know of that Obama, himself, had sort of a direct encounter or experience with these units, [and] in a sense, came to grips with the reality of his own power, as chief executive," recalled Marc Ambinder, a journalist with very close ties to the Obama administration's national security team. The president authorized JSOC personnel in the United States to deploy to the Horn of Africa immediately. Obama was also briefed on the presence of a SEAL Team 6 unit based at Manda Bay, Kenya, that could make it to the *Bainbridge* in forty-five minutes. Those men, the president was told, were the best snipers available in the US military.

"If it comes down to putting sharpshooters up on the deck of an aircraft, and making sure that first shot doesn't miss, who do you want to do it?" asked General Hugh Shelton, the former chair of the Joint Chiefs and an ex-commander of the Special Operations Command. Referring to Team 6, he told me, "They're deadly accurate." With the SEAL snipers in place, the commanders on board the ship asked for authorization to neutralize the pirates. Within the administration, "there was a little bit of debate," recalled Ambinder. "Obama, the National Security Council and lawyers, they wanted to do this, because it was the first instance, the first time really, where they were creating an op from top to bottom, so they wanted to do it very carefully. They wrote very clear, careful, rules of engagement."

On April 12, believing that the pirates intended to kill Phillips, the JSOC commander aboard the *Bainbridge* was patched into the White House Situation Room, directly to President Obama. "The President is essentially asking the commander a series of questions," said Ambinder. "'Are these conditions satisfied? Is there any way to do this, save this guy without causing undue harm to US troops? Do you have a clear shot? Is there any chance of other collateral casualties or damage?' 'No, sir.' And then the commander asked, 'Do I have your permission to execute?' And the President says, 'Yes, you do.' The commander gives his order."

Pop. Pop. Pop.

Three shots, fired almost at the exact same moment by three different snipers. Three dead Somali pirates.

Captain Richard Phillips was rescued and returned to the United States with much fanfare. President Obama won praise from across the political spectrum for his leadership in taking down the pirates and bringing an end to the hostage situation without losing a single US life and with just three bullets fired. Behind the scenes, it was a powerful lesson for President Obama about the clandestine force that President Bush once praised as "awesome"—JSOC. In thanking the teams that worked on the *Maersk Alabama* operation, President Obama for the first time publicly used the name of Admiral William McRaven, JSOC's commander, who oversaw the operation. "Great job," Obama told McRaven when he called him after the operation. "The Somali pirates are dead, the captain is rescued and Obama, I think, really tangibly, physically gets it that he has this power as the President," recalled Ambinder.

Deploying Special Ops Forces in Afghanistan or Pakistan was one thing, but to use them in a truly unconventional, unanticipated operation brought the capability of this force home. After the takedown of the pirates, Admiral McRaven became a much more frequent guest of the president and, just as under President Bush, the troops from JSOC became Obama's prized ninjas. After the *Alabama* operation, "The President personally invited the leaders of the Special Operations forces to the White House, and asked them to have an integral role in policy," recalled a Special Ops source who worked on Horn of Africa policy at the time. Obama "asked for their professional military advice in how best to carry out these operations. That was absolutely unheard of in the previous administration, in that they would dictate what the policy was and they would tell the Pentagon, and the Pentagon would ensure that the subordinate commands would carry that out." Obama, he said, embraced the Special Ops leaders, particularly Admiral McRaven. His time at the White House in the early stages of the Global War on Terror "taught him how to anticipate policymakers' needs and desires, so JSOC was always ahead of the curve, they always had the perfect policy prescription for the White House," he added. JSOC "knew what they were gonna be asked to do before they were asked. That's key. This is why McRaven is a pivotal figure—he bridges those worlds."

While Afghanistan and Pakistan would be the primary front lines of JSOC's wars, the situations in Yemen and Somalia were demanding significant attention from Obama's counterterrorism team. Much of the foreign policy energy would be publicly focused on Afghanistan, but in the dark, both al Shabab and JSOC were expanding their targeted killing operations, quietly transforming Somalia into one of the premier battlegrounds for asymmetric warfare.

IN JUNE 2009, an al Shabab suicide bomber carried out a bold attack on a hotel near the Ethiopian border, killing Somalia's security minister and more than a dozen others, including a former Somali ambassador. That same week, insurgents killed Mogadishu's police chief in a gun battle. By July 2009, al Shabab had advanced so far into Mogadishu that its forces came within a few hundred yards of Villa Somalia, threatening to over-run the Mogadishu Green Zone, which housed Sheikh Sharif's government. The attack was repelled only when the US-backed African Union intervened. Officials from Somalia's fragile government were besieged and scared. "The government is weakened by the rebel forces," Sheikh Aden Mohamed Nur, the speaker of the parliament declared after the police chief was killed. "We ask neighboring countries—including Kenya, Djibouti, Ethiopia and Yemen—to send troops to Somalia within 24 hours." That would not happen.

That summer, the United States announced a shipment of forty tons of weapons to Somalia's government forces. In August, Secretary Clinton held a press conference in Nairobi with Sheikh Sharif. Putting an exclamation point on the Somali president's extraordinary journey from the head of the Islamic Courts, deposed by the United States only to return as the US-backed leader of choice, Clinton called Sharif the "best hope we've had in quite some time." But the US priority was not Sharif's government. It was the hunt. "We have presented President Obama with a number of actions and initiatives against al Qaeda and other terrorist groups," said John Brennan, Obama's counterterrorism adviser. "Not only has he approved these operations, he has encouraged us to be even more aggressive, even more proactive, even more innovative, to seek out new ways and new opportunities for taking down these terrorists." Most prominent in Obama's scope, Brennan said, were "those who attacked our embassies in Africa eleven years ago...and our homeland eight years ago."

In the summer of 2009, Somalis began seeing clusters of large naval ships appear off the Mogadishu coast. They were part of a US battle group—and they were there with a purpose.

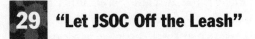

# 29 "Let JSOC Off the Leash"

SAUDI ARABIA, WASHINGTON, DC, AND YEMEN, LATE 2009—In late August 2009, Saudi prince Mohammed bin Nayef received a phone call from one of the kingdom's most wanted men, al Qaeda operative Abdullah Hasan Tali al Asiri. Prince bin Nayef was the son of the powerful Saudi interior minister, Prince Nayef bin Abdel-Aziz, third in line to the throne. In addition to serving as his father's deputy, bin Nayef was also Saudi Arabia's head of counterterrorism. As part of his official duties, bin Nayef encouraged al Qaeda fighters to turn themselves in through the kingdom's terrorist rehabilitation program. Asiri, who was placed on the Saudi's eighty-five most wanted persons list in February 2009, had fled the kingdom and was living in neighboring Yemen. If Asiri was calling the prince to turn himself in, it would be an unthinkable coup for the Saudis. Asiri was reportedly recruited to join al Qaeda by his brother, Ibrahim Hassan al Asiri, whom Saudi and US intelligence alleged was the chief bomb maker for AQAP.

"I need to meet you to tell you the whole story," Asiri told Prince bin Nayef.

"If you come, I will sit with you," the prince replied.

Asiri told the prince that he would meet with him in person if Prince bin Nayef sent a private jet to pick him up in a Saudi town just across the border with Yemen and bring him to bin Nayef's palace. The prince agreed. On August 27, the two men met in person.

According to Richard Barrett, the head of the United Nations' al Qaeda and Taliban monitoring team, as the meeting began, Asiri presented the prince with a mobile phone. "Asiri said, 'Oh, you need to speak to my friends because they also want to give themselves up, and if they hear from you, they'll certainly come.'"

While Prince bin Nayef was on the phone with Asiri's alleged cohorts in Yemen, Asiri's phone activated a bomb, Barrett explained. Incredibly, Asiri had managed to board a Saudi royal plane with a bomb made of pentaerythritol tetranitrate, known as PETN, pass multiple security checkpoints and make it onto the grounds of Prince bin Nayef's palace in Jeddah. The reason the Saudis hadn't detected it was because the one-pound bomb was lodged in Asiri's rectum. As Prince bin Nayef held the phone, Asiri exploded. "It was really very fortunate for the prince that all he did was hurt his finger, because the blast blew downwards and blew upwards, and not across towards the prince," said Barrett. The attack was caught on a video. "You see the guy's left arm embedded in the ceiling—so the blast must have been quite considerable—and bits of him scattered all over the room," recalled Barrett.

Although Prince bin Nayef survived the attack, it still represented a symbolic triumph for al Qaeda in the Arabian Peninsula. It was the first known assassination attempt against a Saudi royal in decades and the first significant al Qaeda attack since a twenty-month rash of bombings and killings across Saudi Arabia by al Qaeda in 2003–2004. Asiri's brother Ibrahim was believed to have manufactured the bomb. AQAP was on the map.

Within days of the attempted assassination of Prince bin Nayef, President Obama's chief counterterrorism adviser, John Brennan, was in Saudi Arabia delivering a personal letter from Obama to bin Nayef expressing his "outrage" at the attack. "I met with Prince Mohammed bin Nayef," Brennan later said. "I went to the room where the attack took place. We worked very closely with the Saudis." He added: "We're very concerned about it from an assassination standpoint, and we continue to look at all the evidence that is out there so we can take the steps necessary to prevent any types of attack from taking place."

To the UN's Barrett, the attack raised the prospect of bombs concealed inside the body, such as Asiri's, being used to attack airlines. "Here is a guy who got on a plane, he went through at least two security checks. He would have passed a metal detector. So he could get on any plane. That technique would work on any airline anywhere, regardless of what sort of security measures there are in the airport. And this is likely to have some severe consequences: What can you do? How much protection can you provide when this is possible?"

After meeting with the Saudis following the August 27, 2009, attack on Prince bin Nayef, Brennan said, "There was no indication...that al Qaeda was trying to use that type of attack and that modus operandi against aircraft." Brennan was wrong about that. The attempted bin Nayef assassination wouldn't be the last the Americans or Saudis heard from Asiri's bomb-making brother. But the attack sharpened the focus on al Qaeda's base in Yemen for both Riyadh and Washington.

ON SEPTEMBER 6, 2009, a week after Asiri carried out his assassination attempt on Prince bin Nayef, John Brennan once again sat face to face with President Saleh in Sana'a. Saleh boldly complained that the "current level" of US aid for counterterrorism was inadequate and claimed that his offensive against the Houthi rebels was in Washington's interest. "This war we're launching is a war on behalf of the US," he told Brennan. "The Houthis are your enemies too." In his meeting with Brennan, Saleh accused Iran of trying to undermine his relationship with Washington by backing the Houthis and tried to implicate Hezbollah as well. (In a subsequent classified cable, US officials acknowledged that the Houthis hadn't attacked US interests or personnel since the fighting began in 2004 and raised serious questions about the extent of Iranian involvement.) Brennan told Saleh it would be against the law to give him military support against the Houthis because the United States considered the Houthis a "domestic insurgency." Saleh countered that the lack of US support and Washington's refusal to declare the Houthis terrorists were undermining claims of friendship and cooperation. US officials described Saleh as being in "vintage form" as he met with Brennan, "at times disdainful and dismissive and at others, conciliatory and congenial."

According to the classified US diplomatic cable on the meeting, Saleh "repeatedly requested more funds and equipment to fight" AQAP. In return for increased aid, which Saleh undoubtedly wanted more for his domestic wars than to fight al Qaeda, he offered Brennan a valuable card. "President Saleh pledged unfettered access to Yemen's national territory for U.S. counterterrorism operations," the cable noted. "Saleh insisted that Yemen's national territory is available for unilateral CT [counterterrorism] operations by the U.S."

Brennan and other US officials saw Saleh's offer as an attempt to take out an insurance policy in the event of any future attacks on the US Embassy or other American targets. "I have given you an open door on terrorism," Saleh told Brennan, "so I am not responsible." In Brennan's view, Saleh's "interest in outsourcing the CT effort in Yemen" to the US government was linked to his desire to free up and better equip his own forces to battle the domestic insurgencies. "A concerted [US government] anti-terrorism campaign in Yemen will free Saleh to continue to devote his limited security assets to the ongoing war against Houthi rebels," the cable stated. "The net effect, and one we strongly suspect Saleh has calculated, of both the American and [Yemeni] 'iron fist' unleashed at the same time in Yemen will be a clear message...[to] any other party interested in generating political unrest in the country that a similar fate awaits them."

Regarding the Brennan-Saleh meetings, Colonel Lang, who dealt with Saleh for years, said, "What they tell you at a meeting like that doesn't mean a damn thing. You have to see what they're really willing to do when you talk to people at the operational level behind the scenes. And the more you understand them, the less easily you are bullshitted about this, to be honest about it, the more willing they are to come to some sort of reasonable arrangement."

Regardless of Saleh's motives, the meeting satisfied Brennan that the United States was getting the official green light to conduct special operations inside Yemen. In Yemen, Brennan delivered a letter to Saleh from President Obama, pledging increased support in the "fight against terrorism." Yemen's security, Obama wrote, "is vital to the security of the United States and the region, and America will adopt an initiative to help Yemen." During this period, according to US Special Operations sources, the Obama administration began authorizing plans for more lethal US operations in Yemen.

Some within the Pentagon feared the focus on Yemen was coming too late. "Not enough people in the intelligence community or the military paid the right attention to [the region], and al Qaeda has taken advantage of that to our disadvantage," a senior defense official told the *Washington Times* shortly after Brennan's visit to Yemen. "This is going to be a serious problem for us in the near future."

ON SEPTEMBER 30, 2009, Michael Leiter, the director of the National Counterterrorism Center, appeared before the US Senate. "Al Qaeda's under more pressure today and is facing more challenges and is more vulnerable than any time since 9/11," Leiter told the Homeland Security and Governmental Affairs Committee. "But that being said, they remain a robust enemy. And although I believe we have done much to deter attacks and defend against attacks, attacks in the United States remain quite possible." Even though "al Qaeda's safe haven in Pakistan is shrinking and becoming less secure," Leiter said, the group was growing in other countries.

Leiter warned the senators that al Qaeda offshoots were beginning to "pose an increasing threat to the homeland." Some "have proven capable of attacking Western targets in their regions," he said, but "they aspire to expand even further." In particular, he warned about the growing threat in Yemen posed by AQAP. "We have witnessed the reemergence of Al-Qaeda in the Arabian Peninsula, with Yemen as a key battleground and potential regional base of operations from which Al-Qaeda can plan attacks, train recruits, and facilitate the movement of operatives," Leiter asserted. "We are concerned that if AQAP strengthens, Al-Qaeda leaders could use the group and the growing presence of foreign fighters in the region to supplement its transnational operations capability."

That day, President Obama convened a meeting of his top military and political advisers in the Situation Room of the White House to discuss the US strategy in Afghanistan. At the meeting were Vice President Joe Biden; Secretary of State Hillary Clinton; Defense Secretary Robert Gates; CIA director Leon Panetta; the chairman of the Joint Chiefs of Staff, Admiral Mike Mullen; the director of national intelligence, Admiral Dennis Blair; and General Petraeus. The details of what was discussed at the meeting remain classified, but clearly Afghanistan wasn't the only issue on the table.

Shortly after that meeting, General Petraeus signed a seven-page secret order authorizing small teams of US Special Operations Forces to conduct clandestine operations off the stated battlefields of Iraq and Afghanistan. It was marked "LIMDIS," for limited distribution. Hard copies were given to about thirty people. Its original code name was "Avocado." The directive, known as a Joint Unconventional Warfare Task Force (JUWTF) Execute Order, served as a permission slip of sorts for US military Special Operations teams to conduct clandestine actions without the president's direct approval for each operation. "Unlike covert actions undertaken by the C.I.A., such clandestine activity does not require the president's approval or regular reports to Congress," reported Mark Mazzetti of the *New York Times*, who was allowed to read the execute order.

The order spoke volumes about the continuity of foreign policy from the previous administration to the Obama White House. Under the Bush administration, the Pentagon regularly justified clandestine special ops by insisting that the forces were not at war but rather "preparing the battlefield." Petraeus's 2009 "ExOrd" continued and solidified the Bush-era justification for expanding covert wars under President Obama. "While the Bush administration had approved some clandestine military activities far from designated war zones, the new order is intended to make such efforts more systematic and long term," the *New York Times* reported. "Its goals are to build networks that could 'penetrate, disrupt, defeat or destroy' Al Qaeda and other militant groups, as well as to 'prepare the environment' for future attacks by American or local military forces, the document said."

Moreover, the Petraeus order made clear that the United States was authorizing the US military, not just the CIA, to conduct such secret operations. "The Obama administration had been reluctant to allow such an expansion of nontraditional military activities in countries where the U.S. formally has no presence. That practice was unfavorably associated with the Bush-Cheney administration's disregard for international norms," observed journalist Marc Ambinder at the time. "But political imperatives, the threat of terrorism, and the knowledge of what the U.S. military can accomplish if its strings are cut away has slowly changed the minds of some of Obama's senior advisers. It is helpful that Congress has generally given the military a wide berth to conduct activities that intelligence agency paramilitaries would find objectionable."

In addition to authorizing direct actions by Special Operations Forces, the Petraeus order also focused on intelligence gathering, including by American troops, foreign businesspeople, academics and others, aimed at identifying insurgents or terrorists and their locations. The order, which Petraeus drafted in coordination with Admiral Eric Olson, head of the US Special Operations Command, laid out a plan for clandestine operations "that cannot or will not be accomplished" by regular US military forces or intelligence agencies. Among those who would oversee the activities of Special Operations Forces around the globe under Obama was Michael Vickers, a former CIA paramilitary with the Special Activities Division and a major player in the CIA's weapons- and money-smuggling operations to the mujahedeen in Afghanistan in the 1980s.

Colonel Lang said that at the time the order was issued, JSOC's forces in Afghanistan believed they had already killed or captured their way through the high-value targets in Afghanistan, at a minimum forcing them into other countries. "That's why it becomes very tempting to start going after people in other countries. Because you've got these highly skilled operators going after targets that are not really worthy of their skills," he told me. "The temptation for the leadership—the three-star [general] and above level—is to look for places to employ their lads in greener fields." Lang, who is a former Green Beret, described the men from JSOC who would fight Petraeus's small wars as "sort of like Murder, Incorporated," adding, "Their business is killing al Qaeda personnel. That's their business. They're not in the business of converting anybody to our goals or anything like that."

According to the former aide to a senior Special Operations Forces commander who served during both the Bush and Obama presidencies, the Obama administration's expansion of Special Ops activities globally was actually a continuation of the secret AQN Execute Order signed in early 2004 by Rumsfeld, known as the "AQN ExOrd," or Al Qaeda Network Execute Order. That AQN ExOrd was intended to cut through bureaucratic and legal processes, allowing US Special Operations Forces to move into denied areas or countries beyond the official battle zones of Iraq and Afghanistan. The mindset in the Obama White House, the Special Ops source told me, was that "the Pentagon is already empowered to do these things, so let JSOC off the leash. And that's what this White House has done." He added: "JSOC has been empowered more under [the Obama] administration than any other in recent history. No question."

Despite some initial hesitation, it became clear that Obama wanted to expand and codify the Bush-era order. "The Obama administration took the 2004 order and went above and beyond," he told me. "The world is the battlefield. We've returned to that," he added. "We were moving away from it for a little bit, but Cambone's 'preparing the battlefield' is still alive and well. It's embraced by this administration."

Under the Bush administration, JSOC and its then-commander Stanley McChrystal were coordinating much of their activity with Vice President Dick Cheney or Defense Secretary Rumsfeld. Under the Obama administration, JSOC's relationship became more formalized with the administration as a whole. As the former aide told me, "It used to be the strategy was to insulate the president. Now they directly interface with these people regularly."

On October 4, 2009, a few days after the execute order was signed and a month after Brennan's meeting with Saleh, Admiral McRaven made a discreet trip to Yemen to meet with President Saleh. McRaven was dressed in his naval uniform with yellow stripes on the sleeves. Saleh, in a perfectly tailored suit, sat in a gold-colored armchair. Saleh's government said the two men discussed "cooperation" in "combating terrorism." The US Embassy in Sana'a said it had discussed "cooperation between the U.S. and Yemen against al-Qaeda in the Arabian Peninsula," adding, "These discussions support the U.S. government's ongoing efforts to assist Yemen in eliminating the threat al-Qaeda poses to its security and stability." Well-informed Yemeni sources, however, said that McRaven pressed Saleh to let at least three of JSOC's drones operate regularly in Yemen and to allow "the implementation of some special operations similar to what is happening in Pakistan and Somalia." Saleh granted the requests, following through on the pledge he had made to Brennan to obtain the US military aid he needed.

On October 9, President Obama met with his national security team to discuss their primary foreign policy question, Afghanistan. During the meeting, Brennan suggested that there was a greater threat posed by al Qaeda in Yemen and Somalia than in Afghanistan. "We're developing geostrategic principles here," Brennan said, "and we're not going to have the resources to do what we're doing in Afghanistan in Somalia and Yemen."

# 30 Samir Khan: An Unlikely Foot Soldier

THE UNITED STATES AND YEMEN, 2001–2009—In retrospect, the path to Yemen's becoming a major counterterrorism concern for the Obama administration in late 2009 seems remarkably clear. By November, Yemen was all over the news and seemingly connected to every new alleged terror plot against the United States—with Anwar Awlaki's tentacles touching every incident. But for many Americans, it seemed to pop out of nowhere.

The Yemen media frenzy kicked off on November 5, 2009, when the young US Army psychiatrist Major Nidal Malik Hasan—who had written a series of e-mails to Awlaki—walked into the Soldier Readiness Processing Center in Fort Hood, Texas, shouted, "Allah u Akbar," and opened fire on his fellow soldiers, killing thirteen people and wounding forty-three others before being shot and paralyzed. By most accounts, Hasan was motivated by a combination of factors centering on his work in treating soldiers who had fought in Afghanistan and Iraq. He had reportedly sought to have some of the patients he saw prosecuted for war crimes after they disclosed their actions on the battlefield to him, but those requests were rejected. Hasan had complained to friends and relatives that fellow soldiers had harassed him because of his religion. They said he tried to get out of the military as he struggled increasingly to reconcile his faith with his work for an armed force waging war in Muslim lands.

In a 2007 PowerPoint presentation Hasan gave before a gathering of army doctors, he stated: "It's getting harder and harder for Muslims in the service to morally justify being in a military that seems constantly engaged against fellow Muslims." Hasan advocated for conscientious objector status for Muslims to ward off what he termed could be "adverse events." At the time of the shooting, Hasan was facing an imminent deployment to Afghanistan. Soon after the shooting, the media began reporting that he had been in contact with Awlaki, adding that Hasan had attended Awlaki's Virginia mosque in 2001, though the fact that Awlaki had only met him once was not reported. That the two men exchanged at least eighteen e-mails beginning in December 2008 became a major focus of attention and hype from journalists and politicians. But when US counterterror officials reviewed the e-mails, they determined them to be innocuous. According to the *New York Times*, "a counterterrorism analyst who examined the messages shortly after they were sent decided that they were consistent with authorized research Major Hasan was conducting and did not alert his military superiors." Awlaki later told a Yemeni journalist that Hasan had reached out to him and primarily asked him religious questions. Awlaki claimed he neither "ordered nor pressured" Hasan to carry out any attacks, a contention supported by the e-mails once they were made public. But Awlaki's reaction to the shooting made such details irrelevant in the eyes of the US public and government.

A few days after the Fort Hood shootings, Awlaki published a blog post with the not-so-subtle title: "Nidal Hasan Did the Right Thing." Hasan, Awlaki wrote, "is a hero. He is a man of conscience who could not bear living the contradiction of being a Muslim and serving in an army that is fighting against his own people. This is a contradiction that many Muslims brush aside and just pretend that it doesn't exist." Hasan "opened fire on soldiers who were on their way to be deployed to Iraq and Afghanistan. How can there be any dispute about the virtue of what he has done? In fact the only way a Muslim could Islamically justify serving as a soldier in the US army is if his intention is to follow the footsteps of men like Nidal." Awlaki called on other Muslims within the US Army to carry out similar operations. "Nidal Hassan was not recruited by Al-Qaida," Awlaki later said. "Nidal Hassan was recruited by American crimes, and this is what America refuses to admit." It was the last blog post Awlaki would publish.

The morning after the shooting, President Obama met with his top military and intelligence commanders "and ordered them to undertake a full review of the sequence of events that led up to the shootings." In his weekly address following the shooting, Obama said, "We must compile every piece of information that was known about the gunman, and we must learn what was done with that information. Once we have those facts, we must act upon them." He added: "Our government must be able to act swiftly and surely when it has threatening information. And our troops must have the security that they deserve."

Although there was no actual evidence presented to tie Awlaki to the planning of the Fort Hood shootings and investigators determined Hasan was not part of a broader terrorist conspiracy, the alleged connection to Awlaki became a major part of the story and became fodder for those agitating for more aggressive action by the Obama administration in Yemen. On November 18, Senator Joseph Lieberman called the shooting the "most destructive terrorist attack on America since 9/11." A month later Lieberman would call for preemptive strikes against Yemen.

Awlaki monitored the news from his hideout in Shabwah. He scoured news reports and his "Google Alerts" on his name started pinging every few minutes. He may have been famous before among English-speaking Muslims, but now his name was truly global. Whether Awlaki had played any role in Hasan's murderous rampage became irrelevant in the United States. The fact that he had openly and gleefully praised it became a media obsession. Awlaki was presented in the media as the "9/11 Imam," with new stories coming out every day examining his life history. The prostitution arrests, his alleged contacts with the 9/11 hijackers, his past speeches on jihad and his blog all were woven together to make it seem as though Awlaki had been plotting acts of terror against the United States his whole life. Terror "experts" on television opined on his ability to recruit Western jihadists for al Qaeda's cause.

Not long after the Fort Hood shootings, Awlaki's days as a blogger came to an abrupt end. The United States took down his website, whose URL was registered through Wild West Domains, a company based in Scottsdale, Arizona. "They shut down my website following Nidal Hasan's operation," Awlaki recalled. "Then I read in the *Washington Post* that they were monitoring my communications. So I was forced to stop these communications." Awlaki saw the media attention being focused on him as an ominous sign: he had to change locations and erase any digital trail that could lead the Americans to him. He knew they wanted him arrested—but now he feared that Obama wanted him dead.

IN OCTOBER 2009, a young Pakistani American named Samir Khan landed in Sana'a. Like hundreds of other Muslims from across the globe who come to Yemen each year, Khan was there to study Islam and Arabic at the country's famous ancient universities. At least that was what he told his family and friends back home. In the decade leading up to his flight into Yemen, Khan had grown increasingly militant in his politics and his interpretation of Islam. Like Awlaki, the events of 9/11 and the crackdown on Muslims in the United States had a profound impact on him. Khan was born in 1985 in Riyadh, Saudi Arabia, to Pakistani parents, one of whom was a US citizen. "He's a Christmas child," recalled his mother Sarah Khan, "born on Christmas day." When Samir was seven, they immigrated to the United States and settled into Samir's grandparents' house in Queens, New York. His relatives were conservative Muslims, but they also considered themselves patriotic Americans. "We actually wanted to have a better future for the children," Sarah told me. "We had great hopes for this country." Khan's high school classmates recalled a slightly awkward boy in baggy jeans, a junior varsity football player despite his shyness, with an enthusiasm for hip-hop and the school newspaper. "He was always interested in sports," Samir's mom recalled. "He would always tell me that he wants to be in the NFL."

Samir's interests began to change in August 2001, when at age fifteen, he attended a weeklong summer camp at a mosque in Queens, sponsored by IONA (Islamic Organization of North America), a prominent conservative Islamist organization tied to the Pakistani Tanzeem-e-Islami organization. In an interview years later, Khan said the camp was a formative experience for him and that he returned to school that year knowing "what I wanted to do with my life: be a firm Muslim, a strong Muslim, a practicing Muslim." He ditched the baggy pants and the rap music, making an exception only for the now disbanded hip-hop group called Soldiers of Allah. He became involved with the Islamic Thinkers Society, a Jackson Heights–based group that used nonviolent activism such as "street *dawahs* (invitations)" to call for an Islamic Caliphate. When 9/11 happened, Khan made no effort to hide his new attitudes toward religion and politics from his friends and family. He refused to recite the Pledge of Allegiance and got into debates with classmates over his contention that Americans had deserved the attack.

"Before 9/11, people still saw his change but didn't make much of it," said one classmate. "But afterwards, more people decided to question his ideology and be, like, 'Is he trying to be like them [the September 11 terrorists]? Does he think like them?'" Another classmate said Khan would sometimes be the target of ethnic slurs. In tenth grade, Khan was wearing a kufi hat to school every day.

Samir Khan's father noticed that his son had begun to frequent jihadist websites, and staged the first of several interventions. In his high school yearbook, Khan referred to himself as a "mujahid" and wrote that his future plans included going "overseas [to] study Islamic Law and other subjects that dealt with Islam." He also included a word of advice: "If you give Satan an inch, he'll be a ruler."

By 2003, the year Khan graduated from high school and the United States invaded Iraq, he had taken up a staunchly radical view on US foreign policy. The family relocated to North Carolina, where Khan's father, Zafar, took a job as an information technology executive. Samir enrolled in a community college and had a job on the side selling kitchen knives and other household items. He attended a mosque and would get into debates with fellow attendees about what he perceived as the spinelessness of religious leaders in the face of America's spreading wars.

He also began spending much of his time on the Internet, seeking out like-minded Muslims. He blogged and aggregated news of the jihad abroad, often writing under the tag "Inshallahshaheed," or "a martyr if God wills." Khan operated multiple blogs out of his parents' house, several times retiring blogs and switching servers when his vitriolic content came under attack or was taken down by server administrators.

Khan eventually found a home at Muslimpad, run by Islamic Network (one time employer of Daniel Maldonado, who was convicted for traveling to ICU training camps in Somalia). One of his blogs, also called Inshallahshaheed, was started in 2005 and had become wildly popular by 2007, ranking among the top 1 percent of 100 million websites in the world by the traffic counter Alexa.com. His other blogs went by names such as Human Liberation–An Islamic Renaissance and Revival. On his blogs, Khan would extol the victories and virtues of al Qaeda central and its affiliated militants, but his writings also helped to popularize a broader ideological movement that included radical sheikhs and scholars many Americans would not have known about. A later blog featured in its "About" section a list of men he described as "scholars of Islam...who we take knowledge from," and included Abu Musab al Zarqawi, Abu Layth Libi, and Anwar Awlaki.

One of the contributors to Khan's Inshallahshaheed blog was Zachary Chesser, an American who would be arrested in 2010 for attempting to travel to Somalia and join al Shabab. On his various websites, Khan would celebrate attacks against US soldiers in Iraq, promote the writings of bin Laden and call for victory of jihadists over US and Israeli forces across the globe.

During this period, Khan began to receive attention from the press, notably the *New York Times*, which first profiled him in 2007, describing the American as an "unlikely foot soldier in what Al Qaeda calls 'Islamic jihadi media.'" In the United States, Khan became a new face of the emergent and diversifying digital militant culture, which had started with grainy video uploads of Zarqawi severing heads in Iraq and had found full expression in what the *Times* called a "constellation of apparently independent media operators who are broadcasting the message of Al Qaeda and other groups," to people all over the world, including, increasingly, the West.

Khan told the *New York Times* that a video of a suicide bomber hitting a US outpost in Iraq "brought great happiness to me." Of the American families who had relatives serving in Iraq, he said, "Whatever happens to their sons and daughters is none of my concern," calling them "people of hellfire."

Although he denied links to terrorist groups and told a local news station that he was not actively recruiting American fighters, Khan hinted that he might go on to wage violent jihad himself one day, but he stopped just shy of directly inciting violence. He even hired a lawyer to counsel him on the parameters of protected speech before the launch of his first blog. Sure enough, the authorities barely touched him, though he had certainly gotten their attention: Homeland Security agents, as well as analysts at the Combating Terrorism Center, were following him closely. Sue Myrick, a Republican representative from North Carolina, later told the *Washington Post* that she had been involved in efforts to "shut [Khan] down through the FBI," which were ultimately unsuccessful, "because he was not inciting violence, he was simply putting out information, and because he kept changing his server."

Khan believed the authorities were doing more than reading his blogs. "Back in NC, the FBI dispatched a spy on me who pretended to convert to Islam," Khan later wrote. On several occasions, FBI agents visited the Khan home in an attempt to get Samir's parents to encourage him to stop blogging. According to Sarah Khan, the FBI agents told the family that Samir was not breaking any laws and was engaged in free speech, but that they were concerned about the direction he appeared to be heading. Samir's father, Zafar, had gone as far as to disconnect the home's Internet connection and attempted more rounds of interventions. He invited an imam, Mustapha Elturk, to try to persuade Samir to reconsider his radicalism. Elturk knew Samir's father as "a moderate Muslim devoted to his faith." He said Zafar "tried whatever he could within his means to talk to his son and also [to] have him meet with imams and Muslim scholars to persuade" Samir that "the ideology of violence is not the right course." Samir "became very much convinced that America is an imperialist country that supports dictators and supports Israel blindly....He had the opinion that the use of indiscriminate killing was justified," Elturk recalled. "I tried to bring arguments from the Koran and scholars, and said, 'Whatever you are thinking it is not true.'"

Samir was unmoved and continued with his work. The fruit of his final months in the United States was *Jihad Recollections*, an online PDF magazine, overrelying on graphics and featuring translations of al Qaeda speeches as well as original pieces by Khan and other contributors. By late 2009, Samir had made a decision to leave the United States. As he saw it, the FBI was watching him around the clock and he was sick of being around Muslims he considered to be co-opted by American culture.

Khan put out the fourth and final issue of *Jihad Recollections* in September 2009. "I knew the real truth wouldn't be able to reach the masses unless and until I was above the law," he later wrote. Khan left for Yemen the following month, under the pretense of studying Arabic and teaching English. Terror analysts in the United States speculated that he had already received an invitation from Awlaki to come to Yemen and help lead the "media jihad." But according to Sarah Khan, Yemen was not Samir's first choice. He had looked at schools in Pakistan and the United Kingdom, but the Yemen paperwork came through first. "We knew his desire to learn Arabic, and he was searching to find proper schools that would teach him the Arabic language as well as where he could learn more about Islam and understand the Koran better," she recalled. When Samir told his parents he was leaving for Yemen, Sarah was worried but thought "he will be fine, he's grown up. He needs to probably look around, see the world for himself."

But Khan was going through a very different thought process than his parents understood. He had decided he was finished with what he regarded as the banality and sins of suburban America. The Internet had been his best classroom, where he found the preaching of Muslim leaders who inspired him. He had watched the horrors of the post-9/11 wars and invasions and concluded that it was his obligation to join other Muslims in fighting against forces he perceived as Crusaders. "After my faith took a 180-degree turn, I knew I could no longer reside in America as a compliant citizen. My beliefs had turned me into a rebel of Washington's imperialism," he later wrote. "How could anyone claim sanity and remain sitting on their hands? For me, it wasn't possible. My guilty [conscience] became my mode of thinking; I could never imagine myself as one who left the opportunity of a lifetime, to save the Islamic nation from its plight."

Despite the surveillance, Khan had little trouble leaving the United States. "It took thirty minutes extra to get my boarding pass in North Carolina since, as the receptionist told me, I was being watched," Khan later wrote, admitting surprise that his exit went almost totally unremarked. Khan spent some time in Sana'a teaching English before he made plans to head south to seek out the mujahedeen. "I was about to officially become a traitor of the country I grew up in for most of my life," he recalled. "I thought about many of the possible effects it could have on my life; but whatever they were, I was ready for it."

MORTEN STORM says he first met Anwar Awlaki in Sana'a in 2006, shortly before Awlaki was tossed in a Yemeni prison for eighteen months at Washington's request. Storm was a former motorcycle gang member and a convicted criminal who converted to Islam. In the late 1990s, the Denmark native began running in radical Islamist circles under the name Murad Storm. He'd had a troubled childhood, committing his first armed robbery at the age of thirteen, and circulated in and out of jail as a teen. Storm eventually fell in with the Bandidos biker gang. In 1997, however, he renounced his life of drugs and crime, telling friends and family that he had converted to Islam. He moved to Yemen, where he married a Moroccan woman in 2000. Two years later they had a son. They named him Osama.

A video from 2005 shows Storm attending a speech given by radical Muslim cleric Omar Bakri Mohammed in London. Storm claimed he met Awlaki a year later in Sana'a. At the time Storm was a student at Iman University, where Awlaki was taking classes and delivering lectures. Storm claimed he and Awlaki "talked freely to each other" in the months that led up to Awlaki's arrest and developed a friendship. While Awlaki was imprisoned, Storm said he began to have a change of heart about the version of Islam he was practicing: "I found out that what I believed in was, unfortunately, not what I thought it was." Storm claimed he approached the Danish Intelligence Service, PET, and offered his assistance. He said he was introduced to British intelligence representatives and the CIA. The PET, he claimed, assigned him a handler.

When Awlaki was released from prison, Storm became a potentially important asset for the CIA. The CIA and the PET "knew that Anwar saw me as his friend and confidant. They knew that I could reach him, and find out where he stayed," Storm said in an interview with Denmark's second-largest newspaper, *Jyllands-Posten*. Storm claimed that Danish intelligence officials provided him with money "to bring materials and electronic equipment" to Awlaki. According to Storm, the CIA wanted to install a tracking device in the equipment he was providing to Awlaki, making it possible for the Americans to monitor and potentially kill the cleric with a drone strike.

In September 2009, Storm returned to Yemen and traveled to Shabwah Province, where Awlaki was in hiding. Storm said he stayed at the home of someone he described as an al Qaeda sympathizer in Shabwah. Storm alleged that when he met with Awlaki, he asked Storm to get hold of some solar panels or a transportable refrigerator, materials he could use to cool explosives parts. "We also discussed the terrorist attacks. He had some plans that would hit large shopping centers in the West or elsewhere with many people with poison attacks," Storm alleged. Storm's claims cannot be independently verified, but he definitely passed them on to the CIA at a time when the United States was building a case against Awlaki.

I asked Awlaki's father about Storm's allegations. "I don't believe many things he said about Anwar," Nasser said. "I think this man was part of a conspiracy to get Anwar—the man and the character—in order to reduce or eliminate his influence on Muslim men and women around the world. So, America and Denmark found a guy who was all his life an evil man and committed an armed robbery when he was only thirteen years old. Anwar, during his forty years in this life, never was involved in any act of violence against any person or group."

What is indisputable is that Awlaki asked Storm to find him an additional wife. Awlaki had married a second Yemeni wife while he was on the run and had a daughter with her. But this time, he specifically wanted a white Muslim convert to act as his "companion in hiding," Storm claimed. "He asked if I knew a woman from the West he could marry. I think that he lacked someone who could better understand his Western mindset," Storm told the Danish paper. Storm agreed to help. "There are two things that I would like to stress," Awlaki allegedly wrote Storm in a late 2009 e-mail, which he asked Storm to relay to a potential bride. "The first is that I don't live in a fixed location. Therefore my living conditions vary widely. Sometimes I even live in a tent. Second, because of my security situation I sometimes have to seclude myself, which means me and my family would not meet with any persons for extended periods. If you can live in difficult conditions, do not mind loneliness and can live with restrictions on your communications with others then alhamdulillah [thanks be to God] that is great."

When Storm returned to Copenhagen, he met with CIA and PET officials. He said he was shown satellite images of the area where he had been in Shabwah and he identified the home where he had stayed. Yemeni forces launched an assault on the house a short time later, but Awlaki had already moved on. The owner of the home was killed. Storm had also told them about Awlaki's desire to find a Western wife. In that request, the CIA saw opportunity. The American agents, he said, were "overjoyed." Along with agents from the PET, Storm claimed, the CIA came up with a plan. "The idea was to find someone who shared [Awlaki's] ideology and mentality so that both of them would be killed in an American drone attack," Storm said. "I helped the CIA and PET track Anwar so the Americans could send a drone after him. That was the plan."

## 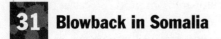 Blowback in Somalia

SOMALIA AND WASHINGTON, DC, 2009—As summer 2009 began, JSOC was well aware of the fact that the men they had identified as the most dangerous threats to US interests in East Africa, Saleh Ali Nabhan and Fazul Abdullah Mohammed, were still at large. The latter was believed to have undergone plastic surgery, and intelligence analysts could only guess his exact whereabouts. The trail on both men had gone largely cold as al Shabab spread its areas of control in Somalia, giving them more options to hide or operate discreetly.

US intelligence believed that Nabhan had become more deeply embedded within al Shabab's operations since the overthrow of the ICU and was running three training camps that produced several suicide bombers, including a US citizen. A secret diplomatic cable from the Nairobi Embassy noted, "Since Nabhan's selection as senior trainer for al-Shabab's training in summer 2008, the flow of foreigners to Somalia has broadened to encompass fighters from south Asia, Europe, and North America, Sudan, and East Africa, particularly trainees from Kenya." Those fighters would, according to the cable, travel to Mogadishu to fight against the US-backed African Union and Somali government forces. The "camps continue to generate increasing quantities of foreign graduates," it concluded.

Washington was desperate to take Nabhan out and in July 2009, US intelligence facilitated a potential breakthrough. That month, Kenyan security forces burst through the door of the home of a young Kenyan of Somali descent named Ahmed Abdullahi Hassan, who was living in Eastleigh, the congested Somali slum in Nairobi. The next night, Hassan's captors took him to Wilson Airport: "They put a bag on my head, Guantánamo style. They tied my hands behind my back and put me on a plane," Hassan recalled, according to a statement from Hassan provided to me by a human rights investigator. "In the early hours we landed in Mogadishu. The way I realized I was in Mogadishu was because of the smell of the sea—the runway is just next to the sea-shore." From there, Hassan was taken to a secret prison in the basement of Somalia's National Security Agency, where he was interrogated by US intelligence officials. An intelligence report leaked by the Kenyan Anti-Terrorism Police Unit alleged that "Ahmed Abdulahi Hassan aka Anas" was a "former personal assistant to Nabhan" and "was injured while fighting near the presidential palace in Mogadishu in 2009." He was viewed as a high-value prisoner. "I have been interrogated so many times," Hassan alleged in the statement, which was smuggled from the prison and provided to me. "Interrogated by Somali men and white men. Every day new faces show up."

On the campaign trail and after becoming president, Barack Obama pledged that the United States would no longer use certain Bush-era torture and detention tactics. CIA director Leon Panetta had stated in April 2009 that the "CIA no longer operates detention facilities or black sites" and announced a "plan to decommission the remaining sites." Yet three months later, Hassan found himself in a secret prison being interrogated by Americans.

According to a US official who spoke to me on condition of anonymity, Hassan was not directly rendered from Kenya to Somalia by the US government. But, the official said, "The United States provided information which helped get Hassan—a dangerous terrorist—off the street." That description supported the theory that Kenyan forces were rendering suspects on behalf of the United States and other governments. Another well-informed source said that Hassan had been targeted in Nairobi because of intelligence suggesting that he was the "right-hand man" of Nabhan, then the presumed head of al Qaeda in East Africa.

Two months after Hassan was rendered to the secret prison in Mogadishu, on September 14, 2009, a JSOC team took off in helicopters from an aircraft carrier positioned off the Somali coast and penetrated Somali airspace. The man they were stalking, they learned from recently obtained "actionable" intelligence, had been making regular trips between the port cities of Merca and Kismayo, near the Kenyan border. On this day, their target was traveling in a Land Cruiser, supported by several technicals. According to witnesses, the helicopters "buzzed" over a rural village en route to the convoy. In broad daylight, the JSOC team attacked the convoy from the helicopters, gunning down the people inside. The American commandos then landed and collected at least two of the bodies. One of them was later confirmed to be that of Saleh Ali Nabhan. Pentagon spokesman Bryan Whitman would not comment on "any alleged operation in Somalia," nor would the White House. That day, when al Shabab confirmed that Nabhan, five other foreigners and three Somali al Shabab fighters had been killed in the attack, there was little room for doubt. JSOC had taken down their most-wanted man in East Africa in the first known targeted killing operation inside of Somalia authorized by President Obama.

To veteran counterterrorism operators, like Malcolm Nance, the Nabhan hit was an example of what the United States should have done instead of backing the Ethiopian invasion. "I am a firm believer in targeted assassinations when they are people who are no longer of value to your collection processes. If they are too strong for your ability to negate their capacity in the battlefield, then you are just going to have to put a Hellfire in 'em," Nance told me. "We were much more successful using the surgical strikes, where we went in—to tell you the truth, very Israeli-like—and we did the drone strike, and/or Hellfire strike and we blasted the individual car of a known guy who was known to be in that vehicle. We flew in, we snatched his body, we confirmed it, we got the intelligence and went away. That's the way we should be doing it. We could have been doing that for the [preceding] ten years."

The Nabhan strike won Obama much praise from the counterterrorism and Special Ops community, but in other circles it raised serious questions about the emerging bipartisan consensus on assassinations, renditions and secret prisons. "These are like summary executions," said Evelyn Farkas, a former Senate Armed Services Committee staffer who worked on oversight for SOCOM from 2001 to 2008. "Who's giving authority? Who's making the [target] lists? Is it a kill or capture [mission], or is it a kill mission?" Candidate Obama laid out a vision of how he would radically depart from the policies of the Bush era, but in the Nabhan case he relied on some of the most controversial of them. "Has our policy shifted at all since the previous administration?" Farkas asked. "My sense is 'no.'"

Jack Goldsmith, who served as an assistant attorney general in the Bush administration, said that the belief that "the Obama administration has reversed Bush-era policies is largely wrong. The truth is closer to the opposite: The new administration has copied most of the Bush program, has expanded some of it, and has narrowed only a bit. Almost all of the Obama changes have been at the level of packaging, argumentation, symbol, and rhetoric."

While declaring an end to the secret prisons, Obama and his counterterrorism team found a backdoor way of continuing them. In Somalia, the CIA had begun using the secret underground prison where Hassan was held as a center to interrogate suspected al Shabab or al Qaeda prisoners there. Although not technically run by the United States, American agents would be free to interrogate the prisoners. Lawyers retained by the family of Hassan, the alleged right-hand man of Nabhan, saw his case as showcasing a slightly cleaned-up continuation of Bush's detention policies. "Hassan's case suggests that the US may be involved in a decentralized, out-sourced Guantánamo Bay in central Mogadishu," his family's Kenyan legal team asserted, noting that Hassan had not been provided access to lawyers, his family or the Red Cross. It would also soon be clear that Hassan was not the only prisoner being held in Somalia's underground secret prison—and that Washington's role in that prison was not limited to occasional interrogations of high-value detainees.

With Nabhan gone, Fazul became the most senior al Qaeda figure known to be operating in Somalia. Although al Shabab had suffered two major blows at the hands of JSOC, it was undeterred. Its asymmetric battle was just beginning. Nabhan's death, like so many of Washington's most passionately embraced "strategic" victories in Somalia, would result in blowback. Even when perfectly executed, targeted strikes had the potential to help bolster the ranks of insurgent groups and provide them with martyrs to be emulated. By the end of 2009, at least seven US citizens had died fighting on behalf of al Shabab and scores of others were believed to be among the group's ranks and in its training camps preparing for future action. Although al Shabab was unable to strike directly at the United States, it was showing that it could recruit American citizens and wreak havoc on its puppets and proxies in Mogadishu. In the process, al Shabab would draw the United States, the African Union and the Somali government into a potentially disastrous replay of the CIA warlord era, mixed with the worst excesses of the Ethiopian occupation period.

OF COURSE, the Obama administration saw developments in Somalia differently. Following the perfectly executed assassination of the Somali pirates, President Obama's relationship with JSOC and its commander, Admiral McRaven, deepened. The administration carefully reviewed the existing orders issued by President Bush that authorized US military forces to strike at terrorists wherever they resided, the "world is a battlefield" doctrine developed by Stephen Cambone and other architects of the war on terror. They decided that they wanted such authority expanded. Defense Secretary Gates and Obama's newly appointed CIA Director, Leon Panetta, worked diligently to bridge the CIA-JSOC divide, which, fueled by Rumsfeld and Cheney, had persisted during the Bush administration. Obama wanted a seamless counterterrorism machine. After the Nabhan strike, then–CENTCOM commander David Petraeus issued his update to the AQN-Execute Order, giving US military forces, particularly those from JSOC, far greater latitude to operate in Yemen, Somalia and elsewhere. Asymmetric attacks that had been relatively infrequent during the Bush administration—with Iraq as a draining focus of counterterrorism attention—would become the focal point of Obama's rebranded global war.

During his first year in office, President Obama and his advisers endeavored to reframe US counterterrorism policy as a more comprehensive, full-spectrum effort to reduce extremism, largely based on regional security. Defense Secretary Gates summed up the purported stance of top civilian and military officials in the Obama administration when he stated in April 2009 that there would not be a "purely military solution" to piracy or civil war in Somalia. The US approach to Somalia would have to shift away from containment. "The National Security Council has brought together the Department of State, the Department of Defense, USAID, the intelligence community, and a variety of other agencies to work to develop a strategy that is both comprehensive and sustainable," noted Assistant Secretary of State for African Affairs Johnnie Carson on May 20, 2009, during an appearance before the Senate Foreign Relations Committee. Increasing assistance to the Somali government and AMISOM would be priorities, but the major focus remained targeting the leadership of al Shabab and al Qaeda.

The priorities laid out in Obama's first annual budget request earlier in May were telling: the president continued the arc of a militarized Africa policy, while increasing security assistance to African states. The budget, noted Daniel Volman, director of the African Security Research Project, showed "the administration is following the course laid down for AFRICOM by the Bush administration, rather than putting these programs on hold until it can conduct a serious review of US security policy towards Africa." The US request for arms sales to Africa went up to $25.6 million, from $8.3 million in fiscal year 2009, including $2.5 million set aside for Djibouti, $3 million for Ethiopia, and $1 million for Kenya. Military training programs to those countries expanded as well. Further spending was proposed for Camp Lemonnier, as well as naval assets for security operations in the Indian Ocean. In addition to the drone capability at Camp Lemonnier, the Obama administration reached a deal with the government of the Seychelles to position a fleet of MQ-9 Reaper drones there beginning in September 2009. Although the stated purpose of the drones was for unarmed surveillance to support counterpiracy operations, US counterterrorism officials began pushing for the drones to be weaponized and used in the hunt for al Shabab. "It would be a mistake to assume that Obama will not take further military action if the situation in Somalia escalates," Volman concluded. He was right.

As Obama's national security team began mapping out a new, lethal strategy to deal with al Shabab in Somalia and AQAP in Yemen, al Shabab was also reorganizing. Fazul had taken over for Nabhan and was deeply embedded within the al Shabab leadership structure. By late 2009, al Shabab had benefited tremendously from the Ethiopian invasion. "Now we are dealing with a group that's in there and they are entrenched," Nance told me. By September 2009, the AMISOM force in Mogadishu had expanded to

5,200 troops from just over 1,700, thanks in large part to increased funding and support from Washington. In the aftermath of Nabhan's death, there were rumors that the AMISOM force was preparing for a post-Ramadan offensive against al Shabab later in the year.

After Nabhan was killed, al Shabab operatives stole two UN Land Cruisers from central Somalia and brought them to Mogadishu. On September 17, the al Shabab agents drove the vehicles up to the gates of Mogadishu's international airport, where the AMISOM forces were meeting at their base with Somali security officials. They positioned the Land Cruisers outside the offices of a US private security contractor and a fuel depot. The UN vehicles exploded in a spectacular, stealth suicide bombing. In the end, more than twenty people were killed in the attack, seventeen of them African Union troops. Among the dead was the deputy commander of the AMISOM force, Major General Juvenal Niyoyunguruza of Burundi. "This was very tactical," an AMISOM official told the *New York Times*. "It's like these guys had a map of the place." It was the single deadliest attack against AMISOM since it arrived in Somalia in 2007.

Al Shabab's spokesperson, Sheikh Ali Mohamud Rage, claimed credit for the strike and said it avenged the death of Nabhan. "We have got our revenge for our brother Nabhan," Rage declared. "Two suicide car bombs targeting the AU base, praise Allah." He added: "We knew the infidel government and AU troops planned to attack us after the holy month. This is a message to them." Rage said that, in all, five al Shabab agents participated in the suicide mission. Soon after the attack, witnesses who saw the Land Cruisers being prepared for the suicide mission said they heard two of the bombers speaking English. "They spoke English and identified themselves as being from the United Nations," said Dahir Mohamud Gelle, the Somali information minister. A Somali news site, known to be reliable, later reported that one of the attackers was a US citizen. While the US was celebrating the takedown of Nabhan, al Shabab had launched its own targeted killing campaign.

ON DECEMBER 3, 2009, dozens of proud young Somalis poured into the Shamo Hotel in Mogadishu wearing blue-and-yellow graduation caps and gowns. In a city that desperately needed doctors, they would literally become lifelines. All of them were to receive their medical degrees that day from Benadir University, which was established in 2002 by a group of Somali doctors and academics. In a video of the ceremony, which was given to me in Mogadishu, the young graduates-to-be smiled as they posed for pictures, their friends and families looking on with pride. As the ceremony began and people took their seats, dignitaries settled into the front row. Among them were five Somali government ministers, including those from the departments of education, sports and health. Three of the five were diaspora Somalis, who had returned to try to help rebuild the Somali government. The higher education minister, Ibrahim Hassan Addou, was a US citizen, and the health minister, Qamar Aden Ali, was a British Somali woman. Cameramen lined the perimeter of the stage, as they would for a high-profile press conference. The graduation was to be a message to Somalia and the world: this is our bright future.

Among those who filed into the meeting hall at the Shamo Hotel that day were several women wearing burkas or abayas—which cover much of the head and body. Former minister of health Osman Dufle welcomed the crowd and was beginning the proceedings when one of the burka-clad figures stood up, addressed the dignitaries in the front row and, in a distinctly male voice, said, "Peace." Before anyone could react, the man under the burka blew himself up. The camera filming the proceedings went blank for a moment. When the video resumed, the smoke-filled room had become a grisly panorama. Severed limbs laid next to the bodies they were once connected to, and three of the government ministers were dead.

"Suddenly, the hall shook and I heard a PAW! sound from the front of the ceremony, where most government officials and dignitaries were sitting. I got down on the ground and looked back. Dozens of people were on the ground under a huge cloud of smoke. Others were stampeding to the exit for safety," recalled Somali journalist Abdinasir Mohamed, who was stepping out for a drink of water when the bomber struck. "I looked to my right and saw one of my colleagues dead and bleeding. I couldn't help him. I saw the government officials' chairs empty and bloody, and many people badly wounded. The ceremony hall became very dark, and seemed like a slaughterhouse" with "blood flowing on the ground."

In all, twenty-five people were killed that day: among them would-be doctors and their family members as well as journalists. A fourth government minister later died from his injuries. Some fifty-five others were wounded. What had been planned as a message of hope had been transformed into a "national disaster," in the words of Somalia's information minister. President Sheikh Sharif blamed the attack on al Qaeda and desperately pleaded for outside aid. "We beg the world to help defend us from these foreign fighters," he implored. The bomber was later identified as a Danish citizen of Somali descent.

As word of the massacre spread across the world, al Shabab denied it had carried out the attack. "We declare that al-Shabab did not mastermind that explosion," said Sheikh Rage. "We believe it is a plot by the government itself. It is not in the nature of al-Shabab to target innocent people." Although attacks against the US-backed, foreign forces from AMISOM may not have sparked outrage among ordinary Somalis—and were quite possibly quietly supported by a significant portion of the population in Mogadishu—blowing up a medical school graduation was indefensible. Perhaps al Shabab wanted to distance itself from the bombing for that reason, or maybe it was a unilateral al Qaeda operation carried out by a foreign operative. No matter who planned the attack, though, it struck fear into Somalis of all walks of life.

IN EARLY DECEMBER, President Obama delivered a major address at West Point Military Academy in New York. Although the speech was focused on the coming surge of US troops in Afghanistan, the president hinted at the ongoing and broadening asymmetric wars his administration was waging behind the scenes. "The struggle against violent extremism will not be finished quickly, and it extends well beyond Afghanistan and Pakistan," Obama declared. "It will be an enduring test of our free society, and our leadership in the world. And unlike the great power conflicts and clear lines of division that defined the 20th century, our effort will involve disorderly regions, failed states, diffuse enemies." He added: "We'll have to be nimble and precise in our use of military power. Where al Qaeda and its allies attempt to establish a foothold—whether in Somalia or Yemen or elsewhere—they must be confronted by growing pressure and strong partnerships."

A week after his West Point speech, President Obama accepted the Nobel Peace Prize in Oslo, Norway. His remarks would win praise from hawkish Republicans for his forceful defense of the projection of US power across the globe and for his assertion that the wars America was waging were "just wars." "Perhaps the most profound issue surrounding my receipt of this prize is the fact that I am the Commander-in-Chief of the military of a nation in the midst of two wars," Obama said. Obama praised the legendary nonviolent activists Gandhi and Martin Luther King Jr.—a previous recipient of the prize—in his speech before laying out why he disagreed with their pacifism.

"As someone who stands here as a direct consequence of Dr. King's life work, I am living testimony to the moral force of non-violence. I know there's nothing weak—nothing passive—nothing naïve—in the creed and lives of Gandhi and King," Obama said. "But as a head of state, sworn to protect and defend my nation, I cannot be guided by their examples alone. I face the world as it is, and cannot stand idle in the face of threats to the American people. For make no mistake: Evil does exist in the world. A non-violent movement could not have halted Hitler's armies. Negotiations cannot convince al Qaeda's leaders to lay down their arms. To say that force may sometimes be necessary is not a call to cynicism—it is a recognition of history; the imperfections of man and the limits of reason."

Karl Rove, the former senior adviser to President Bush, called the speech "superb," "tough" and "effective," while a slew of neoconservatives also heaped praise on Obama. Newt Gingrich, the former Republican Speaker of the House, praised the fact that a "liberal president" went "to Oslo on behalf of a peace prize and reminds the committee that they would not be free, they wouldn't be able to have a peace prize, without having force." Noting the praise from hawkish Republicans for Obama's speech, columnist Glenn Greenwald dubbed it "the most explicitly pro-war speech ever delivered by anyone while accepting the Nobel Peace Prize." When Obama returned from Oslo with his Peace Prize, his administration was about to initiate a new, covert US war and herald an era in US foreign policy that would put at its center the expansion of the US global assassination program.

# 32 "If They Kill Innocent Children and Call Them al Qaeda, Then We Are All al Qaeda"

WASHINGTON, DC, AND YEMEN, 2009—On December 16, 2009, top US national security officials were given a file of "baseball cards" containing the bios of three alleged AQAP members whom Admiral McRaven wanted taken out by JSOC in a proposed "series of targeted killings" inside Yemen. Their code names were Objectives Akron, Toledo and Cleveland. JSOC wanted to move on the targets in less than twenty-four hours and needed an answer from the lawyers: yes or no. The officials who made up the killing committee had little time to review the intelligence. Both Harold Koh, the State Department's legal adviser, and his counterpart at the Pentagon, Jeh Johnson, reportedly had just forty-five minutes from the time they received the files until the JSOC-led teleconference that would decide if the missions were a go. This meeting was larger than most targeting meetings, involving some seventy-five officials. The Obama administration was about to start bombing Yemen, and the national security establishment was mobilized.

Admiral McRaven was beamed into the meeting via teleconference and, with the cold and direct tone he was famous for, laid out the military case for "kinetic action" against the "targets." The main target, "Akron," was Mohammed Saleh Mohammed Ali al Kazemi, whom the United States had identified as an AQAP deputy in Yemen's Abyan Province. JSOC had been hunting Kazemi and McRaven's men had "tracked him to a training camp near the village of al-Majalah." Kazemi had evaded JSOC for months. Now, McRaven said, the US intelligence had a dead lock on his position. After ruling out a capture operation and weighing other military options, the team decided on a JSOC-led cruise missile attack on the camp.

Johnson felt "heavy pressure exerted by the military to kill" and believed he had been "rushed and unprepared" to weigh all of the options. Still, he gave his thumbs up. A short time later, Johnson watched the satellite imagery of al Majalah from a command center in the Pentagon. Figures that appeared to be the size of ants moved around. And then with a massive flash they were vaporized. The feed Johnson watched was referred to internally at JSOC as "Kill TV." Now Johnson knew why.

On the morning of December 17, Sheikh Saleh bin Fareed's BlackBerry started ringing. Tribesmen from his Aulaq tribe told him there had been a horrible incident in a tiny Bedouin village in Abyan Province called al Majalah. Early that morning, missiles had rained down on the modest dwellings of a dozen families that lived in the remote, barren, mountainous village. Dozens of people had been killed, the callers told bin Fareed, many of them women and children. Bin Fareed turned on Al Jazeera just as the news was breaking. The announcer read a press release from the Yemeni government, which said that Yemeni warplanes had conducted an attack against an al Qaeda training camp, dealing a devastating blow to the militants. Bin Fareed called his chief bodyguard and his driver and ordered them to get his SUV prepared for the half-day's drive from Aden to al Majalah.

BIN FAREED is one of the most powerful men in southern Yemen. His family's lineage traces back to the sultans who once ruled the Arabian Peninsula. After British colonialists arrived in southern Yemen in 1839, the Aulaq tribe became one of their most prized tribal allies. From 1937 to 1963, the southern Yemeni city of Aden existed as a Crown colony, with remote areas governed through a series of treaties with tribes. Bin Fareed, whose father was a sultan, was educated in British schools and grew up as royalty. In 1960, he went to the United Kingdom for college and military schooling and then returned to Yemen, where he joined the army. In 1967, Marxists took control of southern Yemen and the British withdrew. Bin Fareed and his family fled Yemen, believing they would return in a few months. It would be nearly a quarter century.

Eventually, bin Fareed came to terms with the fact that he would live in exile. He worked much of his young adult life building up businesses elsewhere in the Gulf, and he spent extensive time at his family's estate in the south of England. As the years passed, he became a major transportation and construction contractor in the Gulf. By 1990, bin Fareed was an extremely wealthy man. That year President Saleh unified North and South Yemen and he called bin Fareed. Saleh needed the tribes to help him consolidate his control over the south of the country, so he cut a deal with the tribal sheikhs to return. In 1991, bin Fareed was back in Yemen.

By the time al Qaeda began to formally organize an affiliate in Yemen in 2009, bin Fareed had once again become a powerful figure in the country. He was a member of parliament, leader of a huge tribe and was building a massive private resort right on the Gulf of Aden. He knew there were a handful of people who had ties to al Qaeda, including members of his own tribe, but he primarily saw them as tribesmen and was not particularly troubled by the jihadis, as Yemen was full of veterans of the mujahedeen war in Afghanistan and elsewhere. What's more, those men were widely considered to be national heroes. Bin Fareed remembered when Fahd al Quso was arrested for his role in the *Cole* bombing. Quso's job was to film the bombing, but he had overslept. When the government took Quso into custody as a conspirator in the plot, bin Fareed was called in to mediate, as Quso was a member of the Aulaq tribe. "That's the first time I heard that any Awlaki belongs to al Qaeda," he said. "And it was just limited to him, and I think, one or two others."

Now, nine years later, bin Fareed watched as news reports alleged that an al Qaeda stronghold was right in the middle of his tribal areas. The reports said "that our government attacked al Qaeda in al Majalah where al Qaeda has a base, and a field for training. And they have huge stores for all kinds of weapons and ammunition, and rockets, all this. And it was a successful attack," bin Fareed recalled. "And they did not mention the Americans at all." Bin Fareed found it impossible to believe that there was an al Qaeda base in al Majalah. Even if there were al Qaeda members there, he thought, the government could easily have sent in a ground force to root them out. The reports he was getting about air strikes made no sense to him. It was a remote area, but it wasn't Tora Bora.

As soon as bin Fareed arrived in al Majalah, he was horrified. "When we went there, we could not believe our eyes. I mean, if somebody had a weak heart, I think he would collapse. You see goats and sheep all over, you see the heads of those who were killed here and there. You see their bodies, you see children. I mean some of them, they were not hit immediately, but by the fire, they were burned," he told me. Body parts were strewn around the village. "You could not tell if this meat belongs to animals or to human beings," he remembered. They tried to gather what body parts they could to bury the dead. "Some of the meat we could not reach, even. It was eaten by the birds." As bin Fareed surveyed the carnage, most of the victims he saw were women and children. "They were all children, old women, all kinds of sheep and goats and cows. Unbelievable." He examined the site and found no evidence that there was anything even vaguely resembling a training camp. "Why did they do this? Why in the hell are they doing this?" he asked. "There are no [weapons] stores, there is no field for training. There is nobody, except a very poor tribe, one of the poorest tribes in the south."

I later met with several survivors of the attack, in Abyan, including a local tribal leader named Muqbal, spared because he had gone out to run errands in a nearby village. "People saw the smoke and felt the earth shake—they had never seen anything like it. Most of the dead were women, children and the elderly. Five pregnant women were killed," he told me. After the missiles hit, "I ran to the area. I found scattered bodies and injured women and children." A woman who survived the strike sobbed as she recalled for me what happened. "At 6:00 a.m. [my family members] were sleeping and I was making bread. When the missiles exploded, I lost consciousness. I didn't know what had happened to my children, my daughter, my husband. Only I survived with this old man and my daughter. They died. They all died." In all, more than forty people were killed at al Majalah, including fourteen women and twenty-one children.

Muqbal, who adopted an orphaned child, was incredulous at the allegation that his village was an al Qaeda base. "If they kill innocent children and call them al Qaeda, then we are all al Qaeda," he told me. "If children are terrorists, then we are all terrorists."

As bin Fareed examined the wreckage, he saw missile parts that appeared to be from Tomahawk cruise missiles. "Of course, our government does not have this kind of rockets. I mean, any ordinary man could tell that this belongs to a big nation, a big government," he told me. Then he found a missile part labeled: "Made in the United States." Al Majalah was also littered with cluster bombs. A few days after the strike, three more people were killed when one exploded.

Bin Fareed believed the Yemeni government was lying and that the Americans had bombed al Majalah and massacred dozens of innocent people. And he set out to prove it. As did a young Yemeni reporter.

ABDULELAH HAIDER SHAYE was a rare kind of journalist in a country with a media dominated by regime sycophants. "We were only exposed to Western media and Arab media funded by the West, which depicts only one image of al Qaeda," recalled his best friend, Kamal Sharaf, a well-known dissident Yemeni political cartoonist. "But Abdulelah brought a different viewpoint." Shaye had no reverence for al Qaeda, but he did view the group's ascent in Yemen as an important story, according to Sharaf. Shaye was able to get access to al Qaeda figures in part because of his relationship, through marriage, to the radical Islamic cleric Abdul Majeed al Zindani, the founder of Iman University and a US Treasury Department–designated terrorist.

Although Sharaf acknowledged that Shaye used his connections to gain access to al Qaeda, he added that Shaye also "boldly" criticized Zindani and his supporters: "He said the truth with no fear." Shaye had done in-depth profiles on Wuhayshi and Shihri, the leaders of AQAP, and had documented their bomb-making capabilities. In one story, Shaye nervously tried on a suicide vest that AQAP had made. He was the leading chronicler of the rise of the movement. His journalism was famous inside Yemen and across the world.

Shaye had long been known as a brave, independent-minded journalist in Yemen, and his collision course with the US government appeared to have been set when al Majalah was bombed. As the story spread across the world, Shaye traveled to the village. There he discovered the remnants of the Tomahawk cruise missiles and cluster bombs, neither of which were in the Yemeni military's arsenal. He photographed the missile parts, some of them bearing the label "Made in the United States," and distributed the photos to international media outlets and human rights organizations. He reported that the majority of the victims were women, children and the elderly. After conducting his own investigation, Shaye determined that it was a US strike, and he was all over the media telling anyone who would listen. The young journalist was becoming a thorn in America's side. But when he started interviewing Anwar Awlaki, he would become a target.

BIN FAREED AND SHAYE WERE RIGHT. Al Majalah was the opening salvo in America's newest war. Unlike the CIA's "covert action" programs, which require formal notification to the House and Senate intelligence committees, this operation was done under a military "Special Access Program," which gives the armed forces wide latitude to conduct lethal, secret operations with little, if any, oversight. In Yemen, the operations were all being coordinated by US Special Operations Forces based at the US-Yemen joint operations center in Sana'a, with JSOC's intelligence division coordinating the intel, directing Yemeni forces in on-the-ground raids and providing coordinates for US missile strikes. Inside the facility, US and Yemeni military and intelligence officials had access to real-time electronic and video surveillance, as well as three-dimensional terrain maps. The US personnel inside Yemen fed intel and operational details back to the NSA in Fort Meade, the Special Operations Command in Tampa and to other intelligence and military agencies.

This is how al Majalah went down. It was December 17 in Yemen. Soon after Obama's committee met in Washington and approved the operation to assassinate Kazemi and the other al Qaeda members on Admiral McRaven's kill list, JSOC launched surveillance aircraft to monitor the intended targets. The operation kicked off in the early morning hours, as Tomahawk cruise missiles were fired from a submarine positioned in the waters off Yemen's coast. It was armed with cluster munitions. The missiles slammed into a collection of dwellings in al Majalah. Meanwhile, another strike was launched in Arhab, a suburb of the capital, Sana'a, followed up by raids on suspected al Qaeda houses by Yemeni special ops troops from the US-trained CTU, backed by JSOC. Authorization for the US strikes was rushed through President Saleh's office because of "actionable" intelligence that al Qaeda suicide bombers were preparing for strikes in the Yemeni capital. The target in Arhab, according to intel reports, was an al Qaeda house believed to be housing a big fish: AQAP leader Qasim al Rimi. In Abyan, an anonymous US official told ABC News, "an imminent attack against a U.S. asset was being planned."

A military source familiar with the operation told me al Majalah was a "JSOC operation with borrowed Navy subs, borrowed Marine Corps, Air Force and Navy surveillance aircraft and close coordination with CIA and DIA on the ground in Yemen. Counting the crew of the sub we're talking 350–400 [people] in the loop."

When word of the strikes first broke, Saleh's government publicly took responsibility. Yemen's defense ministry said its forces had mounted "successful pre-emptive operations" against al Qaeda, saying they had killed thirty-four terrorists and arrested seventeen others. The Pentagon refused to comment, directing all inquiries to Yemen's government, which released a statement taking credit for the coordinated strikes, saying in a press release that its forces "carried out simultaneous raids killing and detaining militants." President Obama called Saleh to "congratulate" him and to "thank him for his cooperation and pledge continuing American support." Egyptian dictator Hosni Mubarak also phoned to express his satisfaction to Saleh.

But as images of the al Majalah strike emerged, some military analysts who reviewed the footage of the aftermath questioned whether Yemen had the type of weapons used in the Abyan hit. Al Jazeera broadcast video of artillery shells with visible serial numbers and speculated that the attack was done with a US cruise missile. Abdulelah Haider Shaye was interviewed on the network describing the dead civilians he had seen in al Majalah. Among the munitions found at the scene were BLU 97 A/B cluster bomblets, which explode into some two hundred sharp steel fragments that can spray more than four hundred feet away. In essence, they are flying land mines capable of shredding human bodies. The bomblets were also equipped with an incendiary material, burning zirconium, that set fire to flammable objects in the target area. The missile used in the attack, a BGM-109D Tomahawk, can carry more than 160 cluster bombs. None of these munitions were in Yemen's arsenal.

As news of the strike spread, Admiral Mike Mullen, the chair of the Joint Chiefs, sat aboard his military aircraft returning from a trip to Iraq and Afghanistan and praised what he characterized as Yemeni operations supported by the United States. "We've actually done quite a bit there. I think we're on a pretty good track," he said. Referring to the attacks, Mullen said, "I really do applaud what they did, who they went after and specifically going after the Al Qaeda cell which has grown significantly over the last couple of years there."

But the vast majority of the victims killed in the strike were not, in fact, al Qaeda terrorists. Many of the victims, according to a classified US diplomatic cable, were "largely nomadic, Bedouin families who lived in tents near the AQAP training camp." A senior Yemeni defense official described them as "poor people selling food and supplies to the terrorists, but were nonetheless acting in collusion with the terrorists and benefiting financially from AQAP's presence in the area." For al Qaeda, the takeaway was clear: the strikes were a US operation. AQAP could use the images of the aftermath, including those of dead and disfigured children, to rally Yemenis to their cause.

SALEH BIN FAREED WAS LIVID as he watched the way the al Majalah bombing was covered in the international media. Virtually every Western news outlet that covered the story said that Yemen had targeted an al Qaeda training camp and that the strike had been a success. But bin Fareed had been there. He'd helped scrape the remains of poor Bedouin villagers off of trees. He had seen the bodies of dead children pulled from rubble. He had promised newly orphaned children that he would take care of them, and he had seen the markings on the missile parts that showed they came from the United States. He was determined to make sure that the world understood that the victims of the strike were not al Qaeda—and that America was responsible.

On December 20, bin Fareed organized a massive gathering of tribal leaders from across Yemen—nearly 150 of Yemen's most powerful sheikhs. It was no small feat. There were age-old disputes, current feuds and lethal hatred among some of the powerful tribesmen in attendance. But bin Fareed persuaded them all to pledge that they would put aside their differences for the task at hand. "We made an open invitation to many sheikhs from all tribes. They came from Marib, al Jawf. They came from the North, they came from the South," he recalled. "We drove all the way from everywhere to Majalah, just to prove, and show all media that what our government says is not true. The Majalah disaster was done by the Americans. And there was not al Qaeda whatsoever."

Bin Fareed's goal was to gather tens of thousands of Yemenis from across the country in al Majalah to show their solidarity with the victims of the missile strike. One of his estates was about one hundred miles from al Majalah, and he offered all of the visiting tribal leaders hospitality the night before, so that they could travel together as one unit to the demonstration the next day.

At about 9:30 at night, as the tribesmen finished up their dinner and discussion of the logistics for the following day, one of bin Fareed's guards approached him. He whispered to the sheikh that there were about a half dozen men who had pulled up to the compound. "They want to see you," the guard told bin Fareed, who waved for them to be allowed into the house. "But they are heavily loaded with machine guns, with hand grenades, with rocket launchers," the guard told him. "Does not matter," bin Fareed replied. "We are equipped the same. They are not enemies."

The men entered the house. They were young and well dressed, clean-cut. They made small talk. Bin Fareed asked them their names. He knew their tribes, but not the individuals. He asked them what they did for a living. The men laughed and looked at each other. "We are unemployed," one said. Then he added, "They say we are al Qaeda." "Are you?" bin Fareed asked. The men eventually admitted they were. "There is not one single American, or one single Israeli, or one single Brit, here in Shabwah," bin Fareed admonished them. "You are making a lot of trouble for your people. You are giving a bad reputation, to us and to our tribe. If you want to fight the Israelis, then I will buy you some tickets and I will send you to Palestine."

Bin Fareed was losing his patience. "What can I do for you?" he asked. The men told him that they had heard about the gathering in al Majalah and asked bin Fareed if they could address the crowd. "If you are coming tomorrow, as ordinary tribesmen, you are welcome," bin Fareed told them, but not as al Qaeda representatives. "No," one of them responded. "We want to come and give a speech and talk about al Qaeda." Bin Fareed lost his temper. "This means that you are really idiots. Really idiots," he told the young men. "Our gathering is to prove to the whole world that there is no al Qaeda" in al Majalah and that "those people who were killed were innocent." If they came, he told them, the "media will say that all of us, we are al Qaeda." He warned them not to show up. "If you do come," he told them, "you shave my beard, if you survive three days." It was a grave warning. In Yemen, under tribal customs, to have one's beard shaved in public by another man is to be humiliated for life. Bin Fareed was telling the young al Qaeda men that he would have them killed if they stepped foot in al Majalah.

The next morning at 4:30, bin Fareed and the scores of tribal leaders he had gathered at his home caravanned to al Majalah. When they arrived, tens of thousands of Yemenis had already assembled. Tents had been set up and there were cars as far as the eye could see. "We estimate that day, that the gathering was between 50,000 and 70,000, some estimate it was more," bin Fareed said. As bin Fareed settled into one of the massive tents and began going over the program for the day, his guards burst in. They told him that the men from last night—the members of al Qaeda—were standing on a car, giving a speech through a megaphone. Bin Fareed grabbed his automatic weapon and darted out of the tent. His men held him back. "Either they will kill me or I will kill them," bin Fareed said. "I warned them." It was too late. The al Qaeda men had already achieved their goal.

As bin Fareed was grabbing his machine gun, one of the al Qaeda men, Muhammad al Kilwi, was standing on a car speaking to a crowd on the periphery of the demonstration. With a henna-dyed beard and a military jacket, he declared, "Al Qaeda's war in Yemen is against the United States, not against the Yemeni military." Standing aside the other al Qaeda men, who were wielding rifles, Kilwi vowed to avenge the deaths at al Majalah. "Our issue is with the Americans and their lackeys." He finished his brief speech, and then he and his cohorts jumped back in the vehicles and disappeared into the mountains. That night, video of the speech was broadcast across the globe. Bin Fareed's gathering was portrayed as an al Qaeda rally, just as he had feared.

"They really spoiled our meeting," bin Fareed recalled. But he was vindicated in the end. The men who had hijacked his rally were killed a few days later when the United States launched another cruise missile attack. Maybe the Americans had tracked them after they showed up at the rally, bin Fareed speculated. "They were killed," he said. "All of them."

IN YEMEN, outrage about al Majalah was spreading, fueled largely by the assumption that it was a US bombing. The Yemeni parliament dispatched a delegation to do an on-the-ground investigation. When they arrived in the village, they "found that all the homes and their contents were burnt and all that was left were traces of furniture" along with "traces of blood of the victims and a number of holes in the ground left by the bombing...as well as a number of unexploded bombs." Their investigation determined that the strike had killed forty-one members of two families, including fourteen women and twenty-one children. Some of the dead were sleeping when the missiles hit. The Saleh government insisted that fourteen al Qaeda operatives were killed, but the Yemeni parliamentary investigators said the government could only provide them with one name of an al Qaeda operative killed in the bombing—Kazemi, the "leader" known as Akron on

JSOC's list. Various Yemeni journalists and security analysts I interviewed were puzzled as to why Kazemi was being portrayed as an al Qaeda leader, pointing out that he was an aging veteran of the earlier wars in Afghanistan and was not a major figure within AQAP.

After the strike, a senior Yemeni official told the *New York Times*, "The involvement of the United States creates sympathy for Al Qaeda. The co-operation is necessary—but there is no doubt that it has an effect for the common man. He sympathizes with Al Qaeda."

On December 21, ambassador Stephen Seche sent a cable from Sana'a back to Washington. Referencing the strikes, he said the Yemeni government "appears not overly concerned about unauthorized leaks regarding the U.S. role and negative media attention to civilian deaths." Seche said that Deputy Prime Minister Rashad al Alimi told him that "any evidence of greater U.S. involvement such as fragments of U.S. munitions found at the sites—could be explained away as equipment purchased from the U.S." But the United States and Yemen knew Saleh's forces did not have those bombs. In his cable, Ambassador Seche asserted that Yemen "must think seriously about its public posture and whether its strict adherence to assertions that the strikes were unilateral will undermine public support for legitimate and urgently needed CT operations, should evidence to the contrary surface."

Indeed, months after the strike, Amnesty International published photo-graphic evidence of the US bombs found at the scene. The Pentagon would not respond to the group's inquiries about the munitions. "A military strike of this kind against alleged militants without an attempt to detain them is at the very least unlawful," said Philip Luther, deputy director of Amnesty International's Middle East–North Africa division. "The fact that so many of the victims were actually women and children indicates that the attack was in fact grossly irresponsible." Amnesty noted that neither Yemen nor the United States had signed the Convention on Cluster Munitions, a treaty designed to ban the very weapons used in the strikes. Without publicly con-firming the strike was a US operation, unnamed American officials "cited strained resources" in the decision to use the cruise missile, alleging that with "the C.I.A.'s armed drones tied up with the bombing campaign in Pakistan...cruise missiles were all that was available at the time."

Yemeni officials told the US ambassador they had given the governor of Abyan $100,000 to pay off the victims and the families of the dead. Meanwhile, anonymous senior US counterterrorism officials defended the strikes. One told the *New York Times* they had been "conducted very methodically" and that reports of civilian deaths were "very much exag-gerated." But according to journalist Daniel Klaidman, Jeh Johnson, the

Pentagon lawyer who signed off on the strikes, reportedly said of his role in the al Majalah bombing, "If I were Catholic, I'd have to go to confession." For his part, Saleh told the United States he wanted such operations to continue "non-stop until we eradicate this disease," with Alimi adding that Yemen "'must maintain the status quo' with regard to the official denial of U.S. involvement in order to ensure additional 'positive operations' against AQAP," according to a US cable sent four days after the strike. Yemen's foreign minister, Abu Bakr al Qirbi, asked the United States to "stay quiet" on its role in the strikes, saying it "should continue to refer inquiries to the Yemeni Government, highlight the [Yemeni government's] indigenous CT capabilities, and stress that al-Qaeda represents a threat not only to the West, but also to Yemen's security." While US diplomats continued to develop the cover story with their Yemeni counterparts, more operations were being planned.

The role of the US government in the attacks in Yemen was only revealed through leaks. But it was clear who was calling the shots. Amid demands from the Yemeni parliament to explain the al Majalah massacre, Deputy Prime Minister Alimi started spinning an updated version of the story, saying, "Yemeni security forces carried out the operations using intelligence aid from Saudi Arabia and the United States of America in our fight against terrorism." Although closer to the truth, that version of events was also false. "It was cruise missile strikes in combination with military units on the ground," said Sebastian Gorka, an instructor at the US Special Operations Command's Joint Special Operations University, who had trained Yemeni forces. "It was a very distinct signal from the Obama administration that they are serious in assisting Yemen to remove these al Qaeda facilities from its soil. That was very much something executed by the United States, but with heavy support by the Yemeni government."

According to senior US military and intelligence officials, during the ground raid that followed the December 17 Arhab strike near Sana'a, Yemeni Special Operations Forces working with the JSOC team discovered someone they claimed was a surviving al Qaeda would-be suicide bomber, who still had his vest on. He was taken into custody and interrogated, producing what the United States believed was actionable intelligence. A week after the deadly Abyan air strike and the ground raids near Sana'a, President Obama signed off on another hit, based in part on information provided by the prisoner taken in the Arhab raid. This time the target was an American citizen.

**"The Americans Really Wanted to Kill Anwar"**

YEMEN, LATE 2009–EARLY 2010—Nasser Awlaki had not heard from his son since May. On December 20, 2009, he received a call from President Saleh that caused his stomach to plummet. "He called me at three o'clock in the afternoon. He said, 'Nasser, have you heard the news?' I said, 'What news?' He said, 'Four hours ago, your son was killed by an American airplane.' I said, 'What American airplane? Where?'" Saleh told him the location, a mountainous area of Shabwah. Nasser hung up and started calling tribal leaders in the area, desperate for any information. There had been no air strikes reported. "I don't know why the president told me that," Nasser later told me, adding that he believes the Americans had told Saleh they were going to hit Anwar on that day but that the operation had been called off for some reason. Regardless of the reason, it was now clear: "The Americans really wanted to kill Anwar."

Four days after President Saleh called Nasser, on December 24, US forces carried out an air strike four hundred miles southeast of Sana'a in the Rafd mountain valley in Shabwah. According to official accounts, US and Yemeni intelligence indicated Awlaki was meeting with the two most important figures in the growing AQAP organization, Nasir al Wuhayshi, bin Laden's former secretary, and AQAP leader Said Ali al Shihri. Yemeni officials charged they were "planning an attack on Yemeni and foreign oil targets."

The air strikes killed thirty people, and media outlets began reporting that Awlaki was dead, along with the two al Qaeda figures. Former intelligence officials and Yemen "experts" appeared on news programs characterizing the killings as "a huge victory for the struggle against al-Qaida in Yemen." An unnamed senior administration official told the *Washington Post* that the Obama administration had no problems with targeting a US citizen who it believed had joined al Qaeda, saying, "It doesn't really change anything from the standpoint of whether we can target them" because "they are then part of the enemy." The fact that the president had authorized an assassination strike against a US citizen went almost entirely unchallenged by Democrats and Republicans alike.

Although reports of the strikes being US operations made it onto major media outlets, primarily through leaks from US officials intent on showing they were hitting al Qaeda, there was no official ownership of the attacks by the White House or Pentagon. "While the U.S. has escaped the brunt of criticism to date, continued leaks from Washington and international media coverage of American involvement could stir up anti-American resentment in Yemen," declared a cable sent from the US Embassy in Sana'a back to Washington.

Nasser watched the news reports that his son had been killed. He managed to reach a tribal figure who was in contact with Anwar. "I got information that day that my son was not there, and he was not killed," he recalled. When a reporter for the *Washington Post* called Nasser to get a comment from him on Anwar's death, Nasser told him Anwar was alive. Meanwhile, CBS News interviewed a source in Yemen who said that not only was Awlaki still alive, but the attacks were "far from his house and he had nothing to do with those killed." Whether they were ever there or not, Wuhayshi and Shihri were not killed in the attack, either.

"They decided to kill [Anwar] at the end of 2009," Nasser told me. "Is it legal for the United States to kill an American citizen, without a legal process, without due process? I want any decent American lawyer to tell me that it is right for the United States government to kill an American citizen, on the basis that he said something against the United States, or against American soldiers. I don't understand 100 percent the American Constitution, but I don't believe that the American Constitution, American law, will allow the killing of an American citizen because he said something against the United States."

While the American government was hunting for Anwar Awlaki from the skies, Yemeni journalist Abdulelah Haider Shaye managed to track him down for an exclusive interview, which was broadcast around the globe and translated into multiple languages. In the United States, it was reported by major US television networks and printed in newspapers. Far from coming off as sympathetic, Shaye's interview was tough and seemed aimed at actually getting answers. Among the questions he asked Awlaki: How can you agree with what Nidal Hasan did as he betrayed his American nation? Why did you bless the acts of Nidal Hasan? Do you have any connection with the incident directly? Shaye also confronted Awlaki with inconsistencies from his previous interviews.

Under Shaye's questioning, Awlaki went into great depth articulating his defense of Nidal Hasan's massacre at Fort Hood, and he told Shaye he wanted to "clarify" his position on Hasan's shooting spree. "I did not recruit Nidal Hasan, but America did with its crimes and injustice, and this is what America does not want to admit. America does not want to admit that what Nidal carried out, and what thousands of Muslims besides Nidal are doing in fighting against America, is because of its oppressive policies against the Islamic world," Awlaki told the journalist. "Nidal Hasan, before he became an American, is a Muslim, and he is also from Palestine and he sees what the Jews are doing through oppressing his people under American cover and support. Yes, I may have a role in the intellectual direction of Nidal, but the matter does not exceed that, as I don't try to disconnect myself with what Nidal has done because of disagreement with it, but it would be an honor to me if I had a bigger role in it."

Awlaki provided his e-mail correspondence with Hasan to Shaye so the journalist could reach his own conclusions about its contents. "I gave it to you to publish it because the American administration has prohibited publishing it," Awlaki told him. "Why do they not want it out? What is the reason? Do they want to cover their security failure? Or, do they not want to confess that Nidal Hasan was a man of principle and that he did what he did as a service to Islam? Do they [want] to show it as a sudden, individual act with no relation to the actions of the criminal American Army?" Awlaki pointed out that the US government had been intercepting his e-mails with Hasan, including the first one, sent a year before the Fort Hood shootings, in which Hasan "asked whether killing American soldiers and officers is lawful or not." Awlaki said the e-mails revealed the failure of US intelligence agencies. "I wonder where were the American security forces that one day claimed they can read the numbers of any license plate, anywhere in the world, from space."

Shaye had caused trouble for the United States and the Yemeni government when he reported on the US role in the al Majalah bombing and other strikes. Now he was in contact with Anwar Awlaki, giving the preacher another opportunity to get his message out. Shaye was a serious journalist, chasing down important stories inside his own country. If anything, Shaye's interviews provided the US intelligence community, politicians and the pro-assassination pundits with ammunition to support their campaign to kill Awlaki. Nonetheless, the United States perceived Shaye as a threat—and one that had to be dealt with.

Awlaki, meanwhile, was quickly becoming a household name. In the aftermath of the December strikes and raids, the media and Congress began to awaken to the reality that the United States seemed to be heading toward an undeclared war in Yemen. The events of Christmas Day in 2009 would shake the entire country.

PRESIDENT BARACK OBAMA and his family were singing Christmas carols in Hawaii when one of the president's aides interrupted the festivities, pulling Obama aside for an urgent phone call with John Brennan, his top counterterrorism adviser.

A few hours earlier, a young Nigerian man, Umar Farouk Abdulmutallab, had boarded Northwest Airlines Flight 253 in Schiphol Airport in Amsterdam. Three days before, he had turned twenty-three years old. At around 8:00 a.m. local time, he made his way down the aisle of the plane and settled into seat 19A. At 8:45 a.m., the plane was wheels up, headed across the Atlantic en route to Detroit. Abdulmutallab's father, Alhaji Umaru Mutallab, was a retired businessman, former federal commissioner for economic development in Nigeria, and one of the wealthiest men on the African continent.

The path that led the wealthy young Nigerian to Flight 253 ran straight through Yemen. Abdulmutallab had attended elite private schools in Lomé, Togo, where he was known to be a devout Muslim and was described by one instructor as "every teacher's dream." In 2005, he spent part of the year studying Arabic in Sana'a and, like many figures being watched in Yemen by the US counterterrorism apparatus, attended lectures at Iman University. Later that year, Abdulmutallab moved to London, where he enrolled in college. There, he became president of the University College of London's Islamic society and participated in nonviolent protests against the US-UK wars in Muslim countries. He organized a conference to protest the "war on terror."

On at least two occasions, Abdulmutallab traveled to the United States for visits and, in 2008, was given a multiple-entry visa. In August 2008, he attended lectures at an Islamic institute in Texas before returning to Yemen to study Arabic. During that period, Abdulmutallab's father described his son as growing increasingly radical, becoming obsessed with Sharia law and what he called "the real Islam." Eventually, Abdulmutallab fell off the map. His father grew so concerned that on November 19, 2009, he went to the US Embassy in Nigeria and met with two US security officials, later identified as CIA, to tell them that his son had gone missing in Yemen. During the meeting, he described his son's "extreme religious views."

As Flight 253 began its descent into Detroit, Abdulmutallab complained that he had a stomachache and went into a bathroom, where he remained for about twenty minutes. When he returned to his seat, he covered himself with a blanket. Moments later, other passengers say they heard a noise that sounded like a firecracker. In a flash, Abdulmutallab's pants leg was on fire, as was part of the plane's inner wall. A nearby passenger jumped on him, and flight attendants scrambled to put out the fire. When a flight attendant asked Abdulmutallab what he had in his pants, he reportedly responded, "Explosive device."

It was Christmas morning and families across the United States were opening presents and preparing for celebrations when the news broke that there had been an attempted attack on a US airliner. Abdulmutallab quickly became known as the "Underwear Bomber" after it was revealed that he had smuggled explosives in his undergarments. It didn't take long before Abdulmutallab's Yemen connection was out in the open, with intense focus on the possible involvement of AQAP. The fact that PETN was among the explosives in Abdulmutallab's makeshift underwear bomb was cited as evidence of the involvement of Ibrahim Asiri, who made the pentaerythritol tetranitrate bomb his brother had used in the attempt to kill Prince bin Nayef of Saudi Arabia a few months earlier.

As the Obama administration scrambled to respond, the US intelligence community and congressional Republicans began to spring leaks. Before long, Abdulmutallab was presented as an AQAP operative who had been sent on a suicide mission by Anwar Awlaki. Yemeni intelligence officials told the United States that Abdulmutallab had traveled to Awlaki's tribal area of Shabwah in October 2009. There, they say, he hooked up with members of AQAP. A US government source said that the National Security Agency had intercepted "voice-to-voice communication" between Abdulmutallab and Awlaki in the fall of 2009 and had determined that Awlaki "was in some way involved in facilitating this guy's transportation or trip through Yemen. It could be training, a host of things. I don't think we know for sure," the anonymous source told the *Washington Post*.

A local tribal leader from Shabwah, Mullah Zabara, later told me he had seen the young Nigerian at the farm of Fahd al Quso, the alleged USS *Cole* bombing conspirator. "He was watering trees," Zabara told me. "When I saw [Abdulmutallab], I asked Fahd, 'Who is he?'" Quso told Zabara the young man was from a different part of Yemen, which Zabara knew was a lie. "When I saw him on TV, then Fahd told me the truth."

Awlaki's role in the "underwear plot" was unclear. Awlaki later claimed that Abdulmutallab was one of his "students." Tribal sources in Shabwah told me that al Qaeda operatives reached out to Awlaki to give religious counseling to Abdulmutallab, but that Awlaki was not involved in the plot. While praising the attack, Awlaki said he had not been involved with its conception or planning. "Yes, there was some contact between me and him, but I did not issue a fatwa allowing him to carry out this operation," Awlaki told Abdulelah Haider Shaye in an interview for Al Jazeera a few weeks after the attempted attack: "I support what Umar Farouk has done after I have been seeing my brothers being killed in Palestine for more than sixty years, and others being killed in Iraq and in Afghanistan. And in my tribe too, US missiles have killed" women and "children, so do not ask me if al-Qaeda has killed or blown up a US civil[ian] jet after all this. The 300 Americans are nothing comparing to the thousands of Muslims who have been killed."

Shaye pressed Awlaki on his defense of the attempted downing of the plane, pointing out to Awlaki that it was a civilian airliner. "You have supported Nidal Malik Hasan and justified his act by saying that his target was a military not a civilian one. Umar Farouk Abdulmutallab's plane was a civilian one, which means the target was the US public?" Shaye pressed him. "It would have been better if the plane was a military one or if it was a US military target," Awlaki replied. But, he added:

> The American people live [in] a democratic system and that is why they are held responsible for their policies. The American people are the ones who have voted twice for Bush the criminal and elected Obama, who is not different from Bush as his first remarks stated that he would not abandon Israel, despite the fact that there were other antiwar candidates in the US elections, but they won very few votes. The American people take part in all its government's crimes. If they oppose that, let them change their government. They pay the taxes which are spent on the army and they send their sons to the military, and that is why they bear responsibility.

Soon after the attempted bombing, AQAP posted a web statement praising Abdulmutallab as a hero who had "penetrated all modern and sophisticated technology and devices and security barriers in airports of the world" and "reached his target." The statement boasted that the "mujahedeen brothers in the manufacturing department" made the device and that it did not detonate due to a "technical error." Four months after the attempted attack, AQAP released a video showing Abdulmutallab, armed with a Kalashnikov and wearing a keffiyeh, at a desert training camp in Yemen. In the video, masked men conducted live-ammunition training. One scene showed AQAP operatives firing at a drone flying overhead. At the end of the video, Abdulmutallab read a martyrdom statement in Arabic. "You brotherhood of Muslims in the Arabian Peninsula have the right to wage jihad because the enemy is in your land," he said, sitting before a flag and a rifle and dressed in white. "God said if you do not fight back, he will punish you and replace you."

The incident gave ammunition to Republicans and former Bush administration officials who accused President Obama and his national security team of missing repeated warning signs leading up to the incident, saying that Abdulmutallab's father's warning at the embassy in Abuja, Nigeria, should have been taken more seriously. An intelligence official pushed back, telling *Newsweek*, "While this is the season for second-guessing and finger-pointing, I have not seen anything to come from the meeting in Abuja that suddenly would have rocketed Abdulmutallab to the no-fly list. You had a young man who was becoming increasingly pious and was turning his back on his family's wealthy lifestyle. That alone makes him neither Saint Francis nor a dead-eyed killer. Every piece of data, of course, looks different when you know the answer, as everyone does now."

At the same time, Republicans used the incident to portray Obama as a naïve peacenik. "The Obama administration came in and said, 'We're not going to use the word "terrorism" anymore. We're going to call it "man-made disasters,"' trying to, you know, I think, downplay the threat from terrorism," quipped Representative Pete Hoekstra, then the ranking member of the House Intelligence Committee, on Fox News two days after the failed attack. On December 30, former vice president Cheney launched another scathing public attack on Obama. "As I've watched the events of the last few days it is clear once again that President Obama is trying to pretend we are not at war," declared Cheney. "He seems to think if he has a low-key response to an attempt to blow up an airliner and kill hundreds of people, we won't be at war. He seems to think if he gives terrorists the rights of Americans, lets them lawyer up and reads them their Miranda rights, we won't be at war." Cheney's attack was bold, not least for its hypocrisy. When the so-called Shoe Bomber, Richard Reid, tried to blow up a flight in a similar way, the Bush administration prosecuted him in civilian courts and Rumsfeld declared that the case was "a matter that's in the hands of the law enforcement people." Unlike Obama, who responded to the incident swiftly, it took President Bush six days to address Reid's attempted attack.

Cheney further charged that Obama "seems to think if he gets rid of the words, 'war on terror,' we won't be at war. But we are at war and when President Obama pretends we aren't, it makes us less safe." Cheney's statement was a phenomenal misrepresentation. Obama had already bombed Yemen more times in his first year in office than Bush and Cheney had in the entire eight years of their term in the White House. "A lot of the knuckleheads I've been listening to out there on the network shows don't know what they're talking about," Brennan fumed to the *New York Times*. "When they say the administration's not at war with Al Qaeda, that is just complete hogwash. What they're doing is just playing into Al Qaeda's strategic effort, which is to get us to battle among ourselves instead of focusing on them." At his inauguration, Obama had declared, "Our nation is at war against a far-reaching network of violence and hatred." When it came to Yemen, Obama certainly viewed the country's al Qaeda presence as a priority target, despite Cheney's very public allegations.

While the Obama administration was facing intense scrutiny over its handling of the incident, it was also ratcheting up US military action against AQAP. "We have a growing presence there, and we have to, of Special Operations, Green Berets, intelligence," Senator Joe Lieberman asserted on Fox News. Lieberman, who had traveled to Yemen in August, said, "Somebody in our government said to me in Sana'a, the capital of Yemen: 'Iraq was yesterday's war. Afghanistan is today's war. If we don't act preemptively, Yemen will be tomorrow's war.' That's the danger we face." Like Cheney, Lieberman, it seemed, was late to the game. The war in Yemen was already well under way.

IN EARLY 2010, the Obama administration continued to downplay the US role in Yemen, with officials publicly repeating a version of the same line: the United States is only providing support to Yemen's counterterrorism operations. "People ask me—the question comes up—Are we sending troops into Yemen?" Admiral Mike Mullen, the chair of the Joint Chiefs, said in a lecture at the US Naval War College on January 8. "And the answer is we have no plans to do that and we shouldn't forget this is a sovereign country. And sovereign countries get to vote on who comes in their country and who doesn't." Those comments were echoed two days later by the president himself. "We've known throughout this year that al-Qaeda in Yemen has become a more serious problem," Obama said on January 10. "And as a consequence, we have partnered with the Yemeni government to go after those terrorist training camps and cells there in a much more deliberate and sustained fashion." Obama said bluntly: "I have no intention of sending U.S. boots on the ground" in Yemen. It was an incredible statement from a commander in chief who, for a full year, had troops on the ground who were entrenched, operational and growing in ranks. While the US footprint was small, JSOC was on the ground with the president's direct authorization.

In Sana'a, the State Department noted "steadily growing military elements based at the [US] embassy" as part of an expanding "U.S. military footprint." Under National Security Decision Directive-38 (NSDD-38), issued in 1982, the US ambassador had authority to approve all personnel entering Yemen. In June 2010, the embassy reported that it was managing a "daily flow of proposals for engagement by the U.S. military" and requests for intelligence and military personnel to be granted "country clearances" for "temporary duty." The Special Operations Command liaison to the embassy was Lieutenant Colonel Brad Treadway, who had served as a liaison for a team of SEALs from the Naval Special Warfare Group in Iraq in the early stages of the US invasion. He was undoubtedly a busy man, as Special Operations teams began a substantial expansion. By late January, JSOC had been involved with more than two dozen ground raids and air strikes in Yemen since the December 17 bombing of al Majalah. Scores of people were killed in the raids and strikes, and others were taken prisoner. At the same time, JSOC began operating its own drones in the country. What started as a day of coordinated strikes was turning into a sustained targeted killing campaign in Yemen coordinated by JSOC.

"After the December thing with Abdulmutallab, [President Saleh] had to kind of show more support for our actions," recalled Dr. Emile Nakhleh, the former senior CIA officer. "He would play the game, he would kind of look the other way when we would do certain kinds of military operations, kinetic operations against some radical groups there. When he was put under pressure, he would say it was his own operations. He played the game."

While US military and intelligence agencies began plotting more strikes in Yemen, General Petraeus traveled to Sana'a for another round of meetings with President Saleh and his top military and intelligence officers to ensure mission continuity after the December strikes and the failed Christmas Day bombing plot. On January 2, Petraeus kicked off the meeting by informing Saleh that the United States would be more than doubling "security assistance" to Yemen, including $45 million to train and equip Yemen's special operations forces for aerial warfare against AQAP. Saleh asked Petraeus for twelve attack helicopters, saying that if the US "bureaucracy" held up the transfer of the choppers, Petraeus could strike a backdoor deal with Saudi Arabia and the United Arab Emirates to handle the transfers for the United States. Petraeus told Saleh he had already discussed such an arrangement with the Saudis.

Saleh told Petraeus the United States could position fixed-wing aircraft around Yemen's territory "out of sight" and authorized them to strike AQAP when "actionable intelligence" was available. Officially, Saleh told Petraeus, Yemen did not want US forces conducting operations on the ground in Yemen. "You cannot enter the operations area and you must stay in the joint operations center," Saleh said. But everyone at the meeting must have understood that this "requirement" would not be enforced, as it had not been in the past.

While praising the December strikes, Saleh "lamented" the use of cruise missiles used to bomb al Majalah, according to a US diplomatic cable on the meeting, because they were "not very accurate." In the meeting, Petraeus claimed "the only civilians killed were the wife and two children of an AQAP operative at the site," which was blatantly false. Saleh told Petraeus he preferred "precision-guided bombs" fired from fixed-wing aircraft. Saleh even made Yemen's deception explicit: "We'll continue saying the bombs are ours, not yours," he told Petraeus. Yemen's deputy prime minister, Rashad al Alimi, then joked that he had just "lied" by telling the Yemeni parliament that the bombs in Arhab, Abyan and Shabwah were American-made but deployed by Yemen.

Shortly after that meeting, Alimi told reporters in Yemen, "The operations that have been taken...are 100 percent Yemeni forces. The Yemeni security apparatus has taken support, information and technology that are not available here, and that's mostly from the U.S. and Saudi Arabia and other friendly countries." But most Yemenis were not buying the story. Ahmed al Aswadi, a leader of the opposition Al Islah Party, said that "it is believed by most Yemenis" that the recent strikes had been "actually carried out by U.S. forces," adding, "U.S. policy in this region of the world is no secret. If the government doesn't comply with U.S. demands, then they bring in drones." During his meeting with Saleh, Petraeus had complained, "Only four out of fifty planned U.S. Special Operations Forces Command training missions with the Yemeni Air Force had actually been executed in the past year." In interviews, Special Forces operators with experience in Yemen characterized the special ops forces they were training there as not having the will to fight and told me they increasingly felt a need to take matters into their own hands.

In early 2010, the Obama administration canceled the scheduled repatriation of more than thirty Yemenis held at Guantánamo who had already been cleared for release. "Given the unsettled situation [in Yemen], I've spoken to the attorney general and we've agreed that we will not be transferring additional detainees back to Yemen at this time," President Obama said on January 5. Lawyers for some of the Yemeni prisoners called the decision "unconscionable," saying it would "effectively prevent any meaningful progress towards closing Guantánamo, which President Obama has repeatedly argued will make our nation safer." It was clear that for the Obama administration, the Guantánamo issue, a central pillar of the president's election campaign, was far less pressing than its counterterrorism agenda in Yemen, which had more citizens at the prison than any other nation.

At the State Department, Hillary Clinton declared, "The instability in Yemen is a threat to regional stability and even global stability." On January 15, more air strikes targeted suspected AQAP operatives, with missiles hitting two vehicles. Four days later, on January 19, the US government formally designated AQAP as a "Foreign Terrorist Organization." That day, the UN Security Council, at the urging of US ambassador Susan Rice, took similar action. State Department spokesman P. J. Crowley said the moves "support the U.S. effort to degrade the capabilities of this group. We are determined to eliminate AQAP's ability to execute violent attacks and to disrupt, dismantle, and defeat their networks."

On January 20, missile attacks once again targeted alleged AQAP operatives in Marib. As with the January 15 strikes, the Yemeni authorities claimed to have killed senior AQAP figures who would later prove to be alive, including Qasim al Rimi. The attacks, which included a strike on a convoy of vehicles, suggested that armed US drones were being used in Yemen. Both strikes seemed to be aimed at decapitating the AQAP leadership in Marib, centered on the suspected local leader Ayad al Shabwani. During the January 20 raids, the editor in chief of the *Yemen Post*, Hakim Almasmari, described sustained air strikes. "Today, there have been seventeen raids inside Marib, most of them trying to attack Shabwani and his friends," he said. "Until now, there is only one al-Qaida leader killed. [Yemeni security forces] have troops on the ground, but doing nothing. Most of the attacks are from the air." Eyewitnesses said that villagers were using antiaircraft guns to fire at menacing planes.

The author in Gardez, Afghanistan, walking with survivors of a deadly US night raid conducted in February 2010. Two pregnant women were killed, along with an Afghan police commander and several others.

Afghan police commander Mohammed Daoud Sharabuddin (fourth from the left) standing with American soldiers. Daoud was killed by US Special Operations Forces in a night raid based on faulty intelligence. He had long fought the Taliban and had been trained by the US.

⬤ Afghan forces who accompanied McRaven offered to sacrifice a sheep to ask for forgiveness for the deaths caused by the night raid.

◀ Admiral William McRaven, then–JSOC commander, visited Gardez, Afghanistan, in March 2010, a month after a botched US night raid.

◀ Hajji Sharabuddin, whose family members were killed in the night raid in Gardez, holds a picture of his two sons who died in the raid. "I don't accept their apology," he said. "Americans not only destroyed my house, they destroyed my family."

◆ Mohamed Afrah Qanyare was one of the first Somali warlords contracted by the CIA after 9/11 to hunt down people on the US kill list. "America knows war," he said. "They are war masters."

PHOTO © RICHARD ROWLEY, FROM THE FILM *Dirty Wars*

⬤ The Mogadishu Cathedral, built in 1928 when Somalia was under Italian colonial rule, now lies in ruins. Since 2002, US-backed warlords have battled Islamic militias for control of Somalia.

Somali warlord Yusuf Mohammed Siad, ⬤ known as "Indha Adde" (White Eyes), controls large sections of Mogadishu. Once an ally of al Qaeda, he now fights on the US side against al Shabab. "If we capture a foreigner, we execute them so that others will see we have no mercy," he said.

⬤ The author on the front lines near Mogadishu's Bakaara market in June 2011.

PHOTO © RICHARD ROWLEY, FROM THE FILM *Dirty Wars*

PHOTO © RICHARD ROWLEY

◗ Dr. Nasser Awlaki at his home in Sana'a, Yemen. After his son, US citizen Anwar Awlaki, was put on the kill list, he filed a lawsuit in an effort to save his son's life. He wrote a personal letter to President Obama asking him to "reconsider your order to kill...my son."

◖ Nasser Awlaki holding his first son, Anwar, who was born in New Mexico in 1971. Anwar "was an all-American boy," he said.

◖ In 2001, Anwar Awlaki was the imam at a large mosque in Virginia. After 9/11, Awlaki was interviewed frequently by US media outlets and offered commentary on the experience of American Muslims. He was frequently described as a moderate voice. Awlaki said the 9/11 attackers had "perverted their religion."

◗ In early 2010, Awlaki was identified as being on the US kill list. His sermons had become increasingly radical, and he embraced the very identity he once professed to oppose. "I eventually came to the conclusion that Jihad against America is binding upon myself just as it is binding on every other able Muslim," Awlaki declared. Awlaki became the first known US citizen to be targeted for assassination by his own government.

◖ CIA contractor Raymond Davis shot two Pakistanis in Lahore in 2011. He was arrested by Pakistani authorities but eventually freed after the victims' families were forced to accept a payment of "blood money." Many Pakistanis rallied, calling for him to be executed.

Admiral William McRaven, who led ◖ the operation that killed Osama bin Laden, with President Barack Obama at Fort Campbell in Kentucky days after the raid in Abbottabad, Pakistan. Since 2001, McRaven has been one of the key US officials running the targeted killing program.

◗ Part of the US missile that hit the Yemeni village of al Majalah on December 17, 2009. In all, more than forty people were killed, including fourteen women and twenty-one children. The Yemeni government took responsibility for the strike, alleging it was a successful attack on an al Qaeda training camp.

PHOTO © RICHARD ROWLEY

PHOTO © IONA CRAIG

PHOTO © RICHARD ROWLEY, FROM THE FILM *Dirty Wars*

⬆ Muqbal, a tribal leader from al Majalah, Yemen. "If they kill innocent children and call them al Qaeda, then we are all al Qaeda," he said. "If children are terrorists, then we are all terrorists."

◀ Yemeni journalist Abdulelah Haider Shaye was imprisoned soon after he exposed the US cruise missile attack on al Majalah and interviewed Anwar Awlaki. After the Yemeni president decided to pardon him, President Obama personally intervened and the pardon was rescinded.

◀ Posters demanding Shaye's release were hung throughout Sana'a. His trial was roundly condemned as a sham by human rights and media freedom groups.

⬇ Then–JSOC commander Admiral William McRaven with Yemeni president Ali Abdullah Saleh in Sana'a in October 2009.

⬤ Abdulrahman Awlaki's birth certificate, showing he was born in Denver, Colorado, in 1995. Anwar Awlaki's eldest son, he lived with his grandparents after his father went underground in 2009.

◗◗ Abdulrahman Awlaki, a sixteen-year-old US citizen, was killed in a US drone strike on October 14, 2011. His father had been assassinated two weeks earlier. Abdulrahman was eating dinner with his teenage cousin and some friends when he was killed. The US government has never explained his death.

◢ A young girl who survived the December 2009 US missile strike in al Majalah, Yemen.

A young girl at an ◗ anti-Saleh protest before Friday prayers in Sana'a.

**34** "Mr. Barack Obama...I Hope That You Reconsider Your Order to Kill...My Son"

WASHINGTON, DC, AND YEMEN, EARLY 2010—In January 2010, the news leaked in the US media that JSOC had officially elevated Anwar Awlaki to the capture or kill category on its list of High Value Targets. The decision to clear a US citizen for potential targeted assassination was made following a review by the National Security Council, which green-lit the proposal to kill Awlaki. "Both the CIA and the JSOC maintain lists of individuals, called 'High Value Targets' and 'High Value Individuals,' whom they seek to kill or capture," reported the *Washington Post*. "The JSOC list includes three Americans, including Aulaqi, whose name was added late last year. As of several months ago, the CIA list included three U.S. citizens, and an intelligence official said that Aulaqi's name has now been added."

When the *Post* story was published on January 26, the CIA was quick to say that it had not cleared Awlaki for assassination. The *Post* issued a correction stating that "the military's Joint Special Operations Command maintains a target list that includes several Americans." The quibble highlighted the benefit for the White House of using JSOC to conduct lethal operations. "I think it's a very dubious legality, because of the fact that we're not at war," Colonel Patrick Lang told me shortly after it was revealed that Awlaki was on a JSOC hit list. "And he's not a member of an enemy force that is legally at war with the United States. I like law, when it comes to war. Otherwise things get very messy, very fast." Constitutional law expert Glenn Greenwald observed at the time:

> Obviously, if U.S. forces are fighting on an actual battlefield, then they (like everyone else) have the right to kill combatants actively fighting against them, including American citizens. That's just the essence of war. That's why it's permissible to kill a combatant engaged on a real battlefield in a war zone but not, say, torture them once they're captured and helplessly detained. But combat is not what we're talking about here. The people on this 'hit list' are likely to be killed while at home, sleeping in their bed, driving in a car with friends or family, or engaged in a whole array of other activities. More critically still, the

Obama administration—like the Bush administration before it—defines the 'battlefield' as the entire world.

Representative Jane Harman, a Democrat who at the time chaired the House Homeland Security Subcommittee on Intelligence, described Awlaki as "probably the person, the terrorist, who would be terrorist No. 1 in terms of threat against us." She added that the Obama administration has "made very clear that people, including Americans who are trying to attack our country, are people we will definitely pursue...are targets of the United States." On February 3, Admiral Dennis Blair, then the director of national intelligence, testified before the House Permanent Select Committee on Intelligence. He confirmed that the Obama administration believed it had the right to kill US citizens, saying "a decision to use lethal force against a U.S. citizen must get special permission" and asserted that "being a U.S. citizen will not spare an American from getting assassinated by military or intelligence operatives overseas if the individual is working with terrorists and planning to attack fellow Americans."

"I don't know how comfortable people who follow these issues are when you begin to put a US citizen in the same category as a non-US citizen," Nakhleh, who had left the CIA before Awlaki was placed on JSOC's target list for assassination, told me. "There is some unease about this approach among people I talk to about targeting US citizens without due process." The Obama administration apparently had little unease, however. Speaking of the US relationship with Yemen that allowed the United States to strike at will in the country, an anonymous senior administration official told the *Washington Post*, "We are very pleased with the direction this is going." In Yemen, Nasser Awlaki read the story. And he decided to write directly to Obama. His letter, which was relayed to US officials by an American journalist, received no response:

TO: MR. BARACK OBAMA, President of the United States of America

I was very pleased when you were elected as President of the United States of America. In fact I spent the whole election night without sleep until it was declared by media that you were "President elect."

I read your book "Dreams Of My Father" and I was really moved by it. You know that I myself went to America in 1966 on a Fulbright scholarship to study Agricultural Economics when I was twenty years old. My son "Anwar" was my first born child and I distributed many cigars to my faculty and friends at the New Mexico State University when he was born in 1971.

Because of my love of America I sent Anwar also to Colorado State University to get American education.

My son continued his education to graduate school where he began PhD Program at George Washington University in 2001.

Because of the unfortunate events of September eleven it became difficult for him to continue his education because of the bad treatment he got at the University and decided to go to the United Kingdom to complete his education, but he could not afford the expensive cost of his education and returned to Yemen. Since that time, he spent his time learning and preaching his religion and nothing else.

However, he was put into prison for more than 18 months as a result of a request from the U.S. Government. The FBI interviewed Anwar for two days in 2007 and found no links between him and the events of September eleven. After he was released from prison, he continued to be harassed and decided to leave Sana'a, the Capital of Yemen and live in a small town in Southern Yemen. Again, US spy plane was flying over the town for many months and when it was known that he was being tracked to be put in prison again he went to the mountains in Shabwa Province the land of his ancestors.

The *Washington Post* published an article on Wednesday, January 27, 2010 by Dana Priest in which she reported that you ordered the December 24th strike where "Anwar was supposed to be meeting with Al-Qaeda leaders."

The Post reported that the CIA and the JSOC added Anwar to a list of so-called "High Value targets" whom they seek to kill or capture on the assumption that Anwar Al-Aulaqi is "an Al- Qaeda" figure. You know and I know that Anwar Al-Aulaqi has never been a member of this Organization and I hope that he will never be. He is simply a preacher who has the right to spread the word of Islam and wherever he likes and this is definitely lawful and protected by the American Constitution. So, I hope that you reconsider your order to kill or capture my son based on the wrong assumption that he is a member of Al-Qaeda. Again, I would like to inform you Mr. President Obama that my son is innocent, has nothing to do with violence and he is only a scholar of Islam and I believe that this has nothing to do with terrorism. So I plead again to you that you respect American law and if Anwar ever did anything wrong he should be prosecuted according to the principles of American law.

Sincerely yours,
Nasser A. Al-Aulaqi
Professor of Agricultural Economics
Sana'a University
The Republic of Yemen

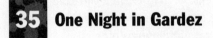

## 35 One Night in Gardez

WASHINGTON, DC, 2008–2010; AFGHANISTAN, 2009–2010—Stanley McChrystal had been off the battlefield since early 2008. After McRaven took the helm at JSOC, McChrystal returned to Washington to serve as the director of the Joint Staff, a powerful position within the Pentagon bureaucracy. His nomination had been held up by a handful of senators who wanted his possible role in the abuse and torture of prisoners in Iraq and elsewhere investigated, but he was ultimately confirmed. The move was not a demotion for McChrystal. If anything, it put him at the center of future decisions on troop deployments and the makeup of the forces that would be used in military operations. At the Joint Staff, McChrystal was instrumental in persuading Obama to spread out control of Special Operations Forces and shift some command authority over unconventional warfare to the combatant commanders. These moves, in turn, expanded the covert battlefield and facilitated the lethal operations Obama was increasingly authorizing in Yemen and other countries.

For the first several months of the Obama administration, his national security team engaged in a heated debate over how to proceed in Afghanistan. Some military commanders had pressed for a sizable increase to the US force and a replay of the counterinsurgency tactics mythologized in the narrative about the "success" of the troop surge in Iraq, but Vice President Joe Biden and National Security Adviser James Jones advocated for a shift in the focus of the campaign to Pakistan, using a combination of Special Ops Forces and drones. "I don't foresee the return of the Taliban and I want to be very clear that Afghanistan is not in imminent danger of falling," General Jones said in October 2009. "The al Qaeda presence is very diminished. The maximum estimate is less than 100 operating in the country, no bases, no ability to launch attacks on either us or our allies."

McChrystal and McRaven had pressed Obama to surge US forces in Afghanistan and, along with other powerful US military figures, including Petraeus, convinced the new commander in chief that it was the right course. Obama and McRaven "actually have a fairly good relationship, and

328

McRaven, when McChrystal was in Afghanistan, worked hand in glove with McChrystal, designing the counter al Qaeda strategies," a source close to the administration told me at the time. McRaven "played a significant, hidden role in developing the McChrystal plan that Obama eventually signed off on."

In December 2009, Obama announced a surge in Afghanistan. By the summer of 2010, Obama wanted to increase the number of US troops in the country from 68,000 to 100,000 US forces. Their goal, as President Obama explained in late 2009, was "to disrupt, dismantle, and defeat al Qaeda in Afghanistan and Pakistan, and to prevent its capacity to threaten America and our allies in the future" and to "reverse the Taliban's momentum." Obama asserted that he was "convinced that our security is at stake" and "that new attacks are being plotted as I speak. This is no idle danger; no hypothetical threat." To confront that "threat," Obama chose General McChrystal as his man in Afghanistan.

In appointing McChrystal as the commander of the International Security Assistance Force (ISAF) and commander of US forces in Afghanistan, Obama revealed the extent to which his counterterrorism policies centered on JSOC. Obama selected a man who was more closely aligned than almost any other figure with the most aggressive military policies of the Bush administration, except, perhaps, General Petraeus, to run the war Obama would soon claim as his own. "I was somewhat stunned when McChrystal was selected to be the commander in Afghanistan," recalled Colonel Lawrence Wilkerson, who had struggled with JSOC's secrecy during the Bush administration. "This guy has been kept away from the public. He's been a clandestine operator. He's a guy who's used to direct action. He's a guy who's used to getting his own way. He's a guy who's used to having it all happen without any transparency."

Other sources with whom I spoke put a different spin on McChrystal's appointment. They pointed to the problems the conventional command had long had with JSOC's forces conducting operations without informing them and observed that such actions were undermining the COIN, or counterinsurgency, strategy. "The Kabul Command just felt as if they were outside of the picture, JSOC was out doing its own show, JSOC wasn't toeing the line with respect to counterinsurgency doctrine" and "most of the tactics that were being used by JSOC in fact *did* undermine the legitimacy of the [Afghan] government," said Scott Horton, the human rights lawyer who has studied JSOC extensively. "So I think one way of reconciling these things, was in fact to put Stanley McChrystal in charge of the command in Kabul. And make him implement the counterinsurgency doctrine. Put in someone that JSOC would have to listen to."

Although many of these Special Ops Forces operated outside of the coalition chain of command, in his review of the war effort in Afghanistan,
McChrystal made it clear that closer coordination with JSOC was among
his key goals and that he sought to bring SOFs into the overall strategy of
defeating the insurgency. Vice Admirals McRaven and Robert Harward (a
JSOC veteran and the head of a new detention task force), were brought
into the White House Afghanistan strategy meetings in the fall of 2009.
Like McChrystal, McRaven and Harward pressed for a "heavy, heavy,
heavy COIN presence" in major population centers, while using CT teams
to stalk targets throughout the country. The region near the border with
Pakistan was to receive renewed attention, and McRaven also wanted to be
sure that operations inside of Pakistan would not be off the table. "They're
focusing on the main population centers that they think they can save
with manpower on the ground, and everything else will be cross border,"
a staffer on the NSC told journalist Spencer Ackerman in November 2009.
"JSOC is already ramping up for that."

As the man credited with systematizing the mass killing and detention
of suspected insurgents in Iraq, McChrystal may have seemed an unlikely
champion of counterinsurgency in Afghanistan. But he made a show of embracing its core tenets, such as a significant troop surge and a renewed focus
on securing population centers and promoting good governance. During
his confirmation hearing in June, McChrystal had stressed that bringing
down coalition-caused deaths and injuries was "essential to [the] credibility" of the mission, and that a tactical victory there would be "hollow and
unsustainable" if it resulted in popular outrage. The "complete elimination of al-Qaeda" from Pakistan and Afghanistan was still a primary goal.
However, he said, the metric of success in Afghanistan would "not be [the
number of] enemy killed" but "the number of Afghans shielded from violence." McChrystal issued directives that significantly reduced air strikes
in Afghanistan, which had been associated with a staggering number of civilian deaths. In May 2009—a month before McChrystal's confirmation—a
US air strike killed more than ninety-seven Afghan civilians in Farah Province, many of them women and children. McChrystal also developed new
rules for house raids that required that "any entry into an Afghan house
should always be accomplished by Afghan National Security Forces, with
the support of local authorities."

While McChrystal and the "COIN Doctrine" received much hype in
the media, the reality on the ground was that the United States was simultaneously escalating two wars in Afghanistan: the public COIN-centric
campaign of the conventional military forces and the covert war being
waged by Special Ops Forces. The week that McChrystal was confirmed as
the Afghan war commander, 1,000 Special Operations Forces and support-

ing personnel deployed to the country, bringing the total number of SOFs in Afghanistan to about 5,000. JSOC's High Value Target list was no longer limited to al Qaeda; McChrystal's counterinsurgency strategy needed teeth, and as conventional forces worked to secure the cities and towns, the SOF teams set to mowing down the midrank Taliban leadership as well as other militant groups such as the Haqqani network. "By any objective reckoning [McChrystal] was absolutely unqualified to do anything except carry out targeted killing. That's all he had done for five years, from 2003 to 2008," historian Gareth Porter told me. Porter, who spent extensive time in Afghanistan during McChrystal's tenure, said that putting McChrystal in charge of the war "really sent the signal that the United States was going to in fact be putting more and more emphasis on targeted killing in Afghanistan. It's as simple as that—and that's exactly, of course, what happened."

Upon assuming command in Afghanistan, McChrystal escalated JSOC-style night raids and expanded the list of names on the kill list in the country. By October 2009, there were more than 2,000 people on the Joint Prioritized Effects List. In May 2009, Special Ops Forces were conducting about twenty raids a month in Afghanistan. By November, under McChrystal, that had increased to ninety and was climbing steadily. Afghan forces would be used to gain entry, but according to the new rules, these raids were conducted by US Special Forces. By December 2009, the number of raids carried out by JSOC each month had increased fourfold. "This is Gen. McChrystal's play," a senior US official told the *Los Angeles Times*, "They have to show they can reverse momentum. He has to show he is making headway." The uptick in raids also resulted in a swelling of the ranks of prisoners taken into custody.

As in Iraq years earlier, JSOC ran its own detainee operations in Afghanistan. Prisoners they believed had intelligence that could lead to HVTs were taken to secretive US-run detention centers, known as Field Detention Sites, situated on US bases throughout Afghanistan. Although NATO had guidelines limiting the detention of militants by coalition forces to ninety-six hours, Special Ops Forces could find ways to hold detainees at interim detention facilities for up to nine weeks. There was also a secret prison within the larger Bagram prison, known as the Black Jail, for holding HVTs. As with Camp NAMA in Iraq, the Black Jail was off-limits to the Red Cross. Human rights workers who investigated the facility reported forced nudity, environmental manipulation and solitary confinement, and former prisoners described being beaten while in custody.

Although Obama had pledged to defeat al Qaeda in Afghanistan, McChrystal's time at the helm during the war would see a notable rise in support for the Taliban and a record number of US soldiers killed.

OBAMA'S EMERGING TWILIGHT WARS in Pakistan, Yemen and Somalia received very little media attention in the early stages of his presidency. The overwhelming focus was on Afghanistan and the debate over the troop surge, but there was a far more significant development in the works. The White House, working closely with General McChrystal, began to apply its emerging global kill list doctrine inside Afghanistan, buried within the larger, public war involving conventional US forces. When I visited Afghanistan in 2010, Afghan police commanders told me that US Special Ops teams would enter their areas of responsibility without coordinating with local authorities or informing the main US military bases in the area. They would conduct operations, sometimes killing people in night raids or snatching people and flying them to other provinces. The raids, the commanders explained, were causing a major backlash against the conventional US forces and the US-supported Afghan police units. They told me that the night raids were actually helping the Taliban.

The White House was well aware by that point of how serious the damage was in Afghanistan. In September 2009, a senior US diplomat in Afghanistan submitted a letter of resignation, in which he delivered a stinging indictment of the US war. Matthew Hoh, a decorated combat marine who had done multiple tours in Iraq and went on to serve as the top US civilian official in Zabul Province in Afghanistan, asserted that the "U.S. and NATO presence and operations in Pashtun valleys and villages" amounted to "an occupation force against which the insurgency is justified." In a letter to the State Department, Hoh stated bluntly, "The United States military presence in Afghanistan greatly contributes to the legitimacy and strategic message of the Pashtun insurgency." He wrote:

> I find specious the reasons we ask for bloodshed and sacrifice from our young men and women in Afghanistan. If honest, our stated strategy of securing Afghanistan to prevent al-Qaeda resurgence or regrouping would require us to additionally invade and occupy western Pakistan, Somalia, Sudan, Yemen, etc. Our presence in Afghanistan has only increased destabilization and insurgency in Pakistan where we rightly fear a toppled or weakened Pakistani government may lose control of its nuclear weapons.

The *Washington Post* reported that Hoh's letter "sent ripples all the way to the White House." Senior US officials, including the US ambassador and Obama's Af/Pak envoy, Richard Holbrooke, tried to offer Hoh other jobs to keep him from resigning. Holbrooke told the *Post* that he asked Hoh, "If he really wanted to affect policy and help reduce the cost of the war on lives and treasure," shouldn't he be "inside the building, rather than outside, where you can get a lot of attention but you won't have the same political impact?" Hoh ultimately declined the job offers and went public with his opposition to the war.

When I met Hoh soon after his resignation, we discussed the night raids and the role JSOC was playing in Afghanistan. Hoh made clear that he had tremendous respect for Special Ops teams and that he believed there are dangerous people who "need to be killed." But Hoh questioned the use of such an elite force to fight against what had effectively become a popular insurgency against a foreign occupation. JSOC, he said, is "the best strike force the world's ever known," yet "we've got them in Afghanistan chasing after mid-level Taliban leaders who are not threatening the United States, who are only fighting us really because we're in their valley." Hoh told me, "We found ourselves in this Special Operations form of attrition warfare." He estimated that there were "fifty to a hundred" al Qaeda operatives in Afghanistan at the time.

Under McChrystal, the pace of night raids accelerated as JSOC mowed its way down a kill list that seemed bottomless. McChrystal knew how to promote his agenda with the White House, and when he fought for his vision to be embraced, he did so "with the same fearlessness he used to track down terrorists in Iraq: Figure out how your enemy operates, be faster and more ruthless than everybody else, then take the fuckers out," noted journalist Michael Hastings, who traveled with McChrystal and spent time in Afghanistan. McChrystal and McRaven's Special Ops task forces began expanding the target list, going after Taliban "facilitators" and "suspected militants." The intelligence feeding the operations relied heavily on Afghan sources. Hoh told me it was common for Afghans to accuse their enemies of being Taliban operatives to settle grudges over land disputes or tribal conflicts. The feeding of such false intel to the American forces, in turn, created an environment in which a tremendous number of innocent Afghans found themselves facing US commandos bursting into their homes in the middle of the night, snatching or killing people. "A lot of times, yeah, the right guys would get targeted and the right guys would get killed," Hoh recalled. "And then, plenty of other times, the wrong people would get killed. Sometimes it'd be innocent families. Other times it would be people and their families who had been turned in because of grudges or because of rivalries that existed well before we showed up. It was very much, whoever got to the Americans first was the person who turned his rival, or his enemy, or his antagonist in."

Hoh said there were also times when a JSOC task force "would kill someone who was important to us. They would kill a tribal leader or some type of government administrator who was working with us or we were making inroads with. In the middle of the night, you end up shooting the guy." He added: "There's nothing like going into a village in the middle of the night, knocking a door down and killing a woman or child to just undo" any progress civilian or conventional military officials had made in areas around Afghanistan. In Afghanistan, I investigated several botched night raids, in which it was clear that innocent people had been targeted. None of them was more gruesome than what happened just outside of Gardez in Paktia Province, in February 2010.

ON FEBRUARY 12, 2010, Mohammed Daoud Sharabuddin had much to celebrate. He was a respected police officer who had recently received an important promotion, becoming head of intelligence in one of the districts of Paktia Province, in southeast Afghanistan. He was also the father of a newborn son. That night, Daoud and his family were celebrating the naming of the boy, a ritual that takes place on the sixth day of a child's life. The party was taking place at their compound, in the village of Khataba, a short distance from Gardez, the capital of Paktia. There were two dozen people at their home for the celebration, along with three musicians. "We invited many guests and had music," Daoud's brother-in-law Mohammed Tahir told me when I visited the family. "During the party, people were dancing our traditional dance, the Attan."

The Sharabuddin family was not ethnic Pashtun, the dominant—almost exclusive—ethnicity of the Taliban. Their main language was Dari. Many of the men in the family were clean-shaven, or wore only mustaches. They had long opposed the Taliban. Daoud, the police commander, had gone through dozens of US training programs, and his home was filled with photos of himself with American soldiers. Another family member was a prosecutor for the US-backed local government, and a third was the vice chancellor at the local university. The area where they lived was near a Taliban stronghold, and the Haqqani network—an insurgent group that the United States alleged had close ties to al Qaeda and Pakistan's ISI spy organization—had been staging attacks against government and NATO forces. So when they began to notice something was amiss outside their compound, the family feared it might be a Taliban attack on their home.

It was around 3:30 a.m., as the celebration was winding down, that the family and their guests noticed the main light to the compound had been shut off by someone outside the party. Around that time, one of the musicians went into the courtyard to use the outhouse and saw lasers scoping the grounds from the perimeter. The man ran back inside and told the others. "Daoud went to see what was happening," Tahir told me. "He thought the Taliban had come. They were already on the roof." As soon as Daoud and his fifteen-year-old son, Sediqullah, stepped out into the courtyard, they were both hit by sniper rounds and fell to the ground. The family began hearing the voices of their attackers. Some were shouting commands in English, others in Pashtun. The family suspected the attackers were Americans.

Panic broke out inside the house.

"All the children were shouting, 'Daoud is shot! Daoud is shot!'" Tahir recalled. Daoud's eldest son was behind his father and younger brother when they were hit. "When my father went down, I screamed," he told me. "Everybody—my uncles, the women, everybody came out of the home and ran to the corridors of the house. I sprinted to them and warned them not to come out as there were Americans attacking and they would kill them." Meanwhile, Daoud's brothers, Mohammed Saranwal Zahir and Mohammed Sabir, tried to come to his aid. "When I ran outside, Daoud was lying here," Mohammed Sabir told me as we stood in the dusty courtyard at the very spot where Daoud was shot. "We carried Daoud inside."

As Daoud lay bleeding out on the floor in a hallway inside the compound, his brother Zahir said he was going to try to stop the attack by speaking to the Americans. He was a local district attorney and knew some English. "We work for the government!" he shouted outside. "Look at our police vehicles. You have wounded a police commander!" Three women from the family, Bibi Saleha, aged thirty-seven, and Bibi Shirin, aged twenty-two, and Gulalai, aged eighteen, clutched at Zahir's clothes, pleading with him not to step outside. It didn't make a difference. Zahir was gunned down where he stood, with sniper rounds hitting him and the three women. Zahir, Bibi Saleha and Bibi Shirin died quickly. Gulalai and Daoud held on for hours, but their besieged family members could do nothing for them and they eventually died from their injuries.

Somehow, in a matter of minutes, a jubilant family event had become a massacre. Seven people had died in all, according to family members. Two of the women had been pregnant. The women had sixteen children among them.

IT WAS 7:00 A.M. A few hours earlier, Mohammed Sabir had just seen his brother, his wife, his niece and his sister-in-law gunned down. Now he stood, shell-shocked, above their corpses in a room filled with American soldiers. The masked commandos had burst into the home and proceeded to raid it, searching every room. Sabir told me that Daoud and Gulalai were still alive at that point. US soldiers kept saying they would get them medical attention. "They didn't let us take them to the hospital and kept saying that they have doctors and they would take care of the injured folks," he said. "I kept asking them to let me take my daughter to the hospital because she had lost a lot of blood and we had a car right there," Mohammed Tahir, Gulalai's father, recalled. "But they didn't let me take her to hospital. My daughter and Daoud were still alive. We kept asking, but we were told that a helicopter is coming and our injured will be taken to the hospital." Both of them died before any helicopter came to retrieve them.

Even as the American raid was under way, Mohammed Sabir and his nephew Izzat, along with the wives of Daoud and Sabir, prepared burial shrouds for those who had died. The Afghan custom involves binding the feet and head. A scarf secured around the bottom of the chin is meant to keep the mouth of the deceased from hanging open. They had managed to do this before the Americans began handcuffing them and dividing the surviving men and women into separate areas. Several of the male family members told me that it was around this time that they witnessed a horrifying scene: US soldiers digging the bullets out of the women's bodies. "They were putting knives into their injuries to take out the bullets," Sabir told me. I asked him bluntly, "You saw the Americans digging the bullets out of the women's bodies?" Without hesitation, he said, "Yes." Tahir told me he saw the Americans with knives standing over the bodies. "They were taking out the bullets from their bodies to remove the proof of their crime," he said.

Mohammed Sabir would not be able to attend his own wife's burial, nor those of any of his dead family members. Following the raid, the American forces made everyone kneel or stand in the courtyard, barefoot, on a brutal winter morning, with their hands tied behind their backs. Witnesses told me that those who tried to speak or plead with the soldiers were beaten. "They told me to raise my hands, but I thought it was my own house, why should I?" Daoud's eldest son, Abdul Ghafar, told me. "They hit me several times. They fired on me and around me. I put myself on the ground. I told the [American's Afghan] translator to tell them not to kill women, just do their search. We are pro-government people. We work with the government. They kicked me several times. I tried to stand, but they kicked me." A witness later told a UN investigator that at least ten people were assaulted by the US and Afghan team, including Hajji Sharabuddin, the sixty-five-year-old head of the household. "They told us that they were informed that forty to fifty Taliban are here," Sharabuddin told me. "But, in fact, all of them were from my family and work for the government." Sharabuddin demanded to know why they burst into his home in the middle of the night. "You could have searched my house in the morning," he recalled telling them. "And if you could find any Talib in my house, then you could do anything to me or destroy and spoil my house and I would not blame you."

A subsequent UN investigation conducted two days after the raid, which was never publicly released, determined that the survivors of the raid "suffered from cruel, inhuman and degrading treatment by being physically assaulted by US and Afghan forces, restrained and forced to stand bare feet for several hours outside in the cold," adding that witnesses alleged "that US and Afghan forces refused to provide adequate and timely medical support to two people who sustained serious bullet injuries, resulting in their death hours later."

Mohammed Sabir was one of the men singled out for further interrogation after the raid. With his clothes still caked with the blood of his loved ones, Sabir and seven other men were hooded and shackled. "They tied our hands and blindfolded us," he recalled. "Two people grabbed us. They pushed us, one by one, into the aircraft." They were flown to a different Afghan province, Paktika, where the Americans held them for days. "My senses weren't working at all," he recalled. "I couldn't cry. I was numb and I didn't eat for three days and nights. They didn't give us water to wash the blood away." The Americans ran biometric tests on the men, photographed their irises and took their fingerprints. Sabir described to me how teams of interrogators, including both Americans and Afghans, questioned him about his family's connections to the Taliban. Sabir told them that his family was against the Taliban, had fought the Taliban and that some of them had been kidnapped by the Taliban.

"The American interrogators had beards and didn't wear American uniforms. They had big muscles," Sabir recalled, adding that, at times, they would shake him violently. "We told them truthfully that there were not Taliban in our home." One of the Americans, he said, told him they "had intelligence that a suicide bomber had hidden in your house and that he was planning an operation." Sabir told them, "If we would have had a suicide bomber at home, then would we be playing music in our house? Almost all guests were government employees." After three days in captivity, he told me, the Americans released him and the others. "They told us that we were innocent, that they are very sorry, and it was a very bad thing that they did in our house." In public, however, the United States and its allies put forward a very different story about what happened that night in the compound in Gardez.

WHILE MOHAMMED SABIR and the others were in US custody, the headquarters of the International Security Assistance Force wasted little time in issuing a statement on the incident. Just hours after the raid, ISAF and the Afghan Ministry of Interior put out a joint press release. They asserted that a combined Afghan-international "security force" had made a "gruesome discovery" the night before. The force had been on a fairly routine operation near the village of Khataba. Intelligence had "confirmed" the compound to be the site of "militant activity." As the team approached, they were "engaged" in a "fire fight" by "several insurgents," the statement read. The force killed the insurgents and was securing the compound when they made their discovery: three women who had been "bound," "gagged" and then executed inside the compound. The force, the press release alleged, found them "hidden in an adjacent room."

"ISAF continually works with our Afghan partners to fight criminals and terrorists who do not care about the life of civilians," Canadian army brigadier general Eric Tremblay, ISAF's spokesman, told the press, referring to the raid. He portrayed the commandos who had raided the home as heroes. A number of men, women and children were detained by the force as they tried to leave the compound, the release stated, and eight men had been taken into custody for further questioning. During the incident, medical support had been called in, the statement said.

A few news agencies picked up the story that day and published more assertions from US, Afghan and ISAF officials. A "senior U.S. military official" told CNN that four victims had been found at the compound, two men and two women. The official confirmed the original statement's lurid details of the women's executions, adding that the killings seemed to have extreme cultural motives. "It has the earmarks of a traditional honor killing," the official said, the implication being that the four people could have been murdered by their own family members. The official speculated that adultery or collusion with NATO forces could have been the motivation.

The *New York Times* put out a brief the following day, largely summarizing NATO's account. The *Times* reporter, Rod Nordland, spoke to the Paktia Province police chief, Aziz Ahmad Wardak, who, he wrote, confirmed many details of the incident but said that three women and two men had been killed. He claimed the group had been killed by Taliban militants who attacked during a party celebrating a birth. US officials would later tell the press that the victims appeared to have deep cuts and puncture wounds, suggesting they had been stabbed.

While international news agencies largely put forward the US version of events, local reporters began speaking with Afghan officials and family members. The Pajhwok Afghan News Agency spoke with the deputy police chief in the province, Brigadier General Ghulam Dastagir Rustamyar, who said that "US Special Forces" had killed the five people during an operation, evidently in response to an inaccurate or falsified tip-off. "Last night, the Americans conducted an operation in a house and killed five innocent people, including three women," Shahyesta Jan Ahadi, a deputy provincial council member in Gardez, told a local reporter for the Associated Press. "The people are so angry." Ahadi denied the NATO claim that it was a joint Afghan–US force. "The [Afghan] government didn't know about this," he said. "We strongly condemn this."

Within days of the raid, UN human rights investigators in Gardez spoke to "local authorities," who said that US Special Forces had come from Bagram to Gardez days before the operation. They were also told that Afghan security officials had been notified about an impending operation but had not been given any details about the time or place. The United Nations concluded that neither the local Afghan National Security Forces (ANSF) nor ISAF troops were involved in the raid.

NATO had promised a "joint investigation," but it never happened. After the incident, Afghan officials from the provincial capital were barred from entering the compound. "By the time we got there, there was a foreign guy guarding the bodies, and they wouldn't let us come near," said Wardak, of the Paktia police. Ultimately, the Interior Ministry in Kabul dispatched a delegation, headed by Kabul's top criminal investigator, to investigate the raid. The group appeared to have worked largely independent of NATO.

By the time Mohammed Sabir returned home after being held in American custody, he had missed the burial of his wife and other family members. Racked with grief, he imagined avenging his loved ones. "I didn't want to live anymore," he told me. "I wanted to wear a suicide jacket and blow myself up among the Americans. But my brother and father wouldn't let me. I wanted jihad against the Americans."

THERE WAS CLEARLY A COVER-UP. The family knew it. The United Nations knew it. And the Afghan investigators knew it. The force that raided the home was US-led, but who were the Americans who had stormed into that home in the middle of the night?

It wasn't until a British reporter, Jerome Starkey, began a serious investigation of the Gardez killings a month after they took place that the full story would begin to unfold. When Starkey first read the ISAF press release, he said he "had no reason to believe it wasn't true." When I visited him at his home in Kabul, Starkey told me, "I thought it was worth investigating because if that press release was true—a mass honor killing, three women killed by Taliban who were then killed by Special Forces—that in itself would have made an extraordinary and intriguing story." But when he visited Gardez and began assembling witnesses to meet him in the area, he immediately realized ISAF's story was likely false.

The family had significant evidence that undercut the story circulated by ISAF and picked up by many news organizations. The family in Gardez showed Starkey and me a video from the night of the raid in which the musicians are seen playing and Daoud and his relatives are dancing in celebration of the naming ceremony for Daoud's son. "I suppose the closest approximation we'd have is like a christening party," Starkey recalled. "It's the sixth night after a child is born. It's named, usually by its grandparents, and you celebrate that by inviting all your friends and neighbors and cousins over to your house, effectively for a sort of feast or banquet and the dancing and music." Starkey realized that the nature of the celebration "didn't chime with the suggestion that they were Taliban. The Taliban are notorious for their very strict rules, and musical instruments were banned when they were in power. So here we've got video of guys, of a three-piece band, and we interviewed the musicians, who corroborated the story. It just, it really didn't stack up. They clearly weren't Talibs."

Starkey visited Gardez about a month after the raid and spoke to more than a dozen survivors, as well as local government and law enforcement officials and a religious leader. He also spoke to UN human rights investigators in the area who had conducted an investigation of their own. All of the people Starkey spoke to insisted that the mysterious US and Afghan shooters had killed the five people. In addition to learning new details about the killings on February 12, Starkey found that conventional coalition forces had likely not been behind the strike, suggesting that US "Special Forces" had been involved. US soldiers based in the area denied having been a part of any night raid in Khataba that day. And Afghan officials who, according to NATO protocol, should have been notified of an operation within their jurisdiction said they'd received no notice of a planned raid. "Nobody informed us," said the deputy governor of Gardez, Abdul Rahman Mangal. "This operation was a mistake."

Under NATO rules, the team conducting the operation should have left information about its unit with the local people, but the family said they had received nothing. The family further accused the soldiers of trying to cover up the raid, abetted by NATO's misinformation.

Starkey contacted Rear Admiral Greg Smith, General McChrystal's deputy chief of staff for communications, and confronted him with the discrepancies. NATO was guilty, Smith said—of poor word choice. The women, he conceded, had probably been prepped for a funeral, rather than "bound and gagged." But Smith denied that a "cover-up" had taken place and insisted that the women had been dead for hours. He confirmed that the men had been killed by the US and Afghan forces. "They were not the targets of this particular raid," Smith admitted. But they had been armed and showing "hostile intent," he claimed, justifying the escalation of force. "I don't know if they fired any rounds," he said. "If you have got an individual stepping out of a compound, and if your assault force is there, that is often the trigger to neutralize the individual. You don't have to be fired upon to fire back."

Despite the UN investigation and a smattering of mostly local news reports questioning ISAF's version of events, the US-led NATO command wasn't forced to publicly account for the wild discrepancies between what the family said happened and ISAF's assertions. That is, until Starkey published a story in the *Times* of London, headlined: "Nato 'Covered Up' Botched Night Raid in Afghanistan That Killed Five." Within hours of his story coming out, Starkey was receiving phone calls from his colleagues, warning him. "I was getting information from other journalists in Kabul, who were my friends, that NATO was briefing against me," Starkey told me. "NATO was trying to discredit me, trying to say that the story was inaccurate, and effectively trying to kill it dead."

Rear Admiral Smith had put out a statement that dispensed with the diplomacy and allusion typical of official press releases. McChrystal's press team was naming names. "The allegation made by Times UK reporter Jerome Starkey that NATO 'covered up' an incident that was conducted outside Gardez in Paktia province is categorically false," the statement read. It went on to accuse Starkey of misquoting Admiral Smith in the article and claimed that the ISAF Joint Command had sent an investigative team to the compound within twelve hours of the incident. Smith and Duncan Boothby, McChrystal's civilian press aide at the time, also "called up rival outlets and reporters to 'brief' against Starkey, saying he wasn't a credible journalist" because of a stint at a British tabloid. "I've been living in Afghanistan for four years," Starkey said. "I can't remember another case where that has happened. To my knowledge, that was the only time that they've named a journalist, and singled out a journalist so specifically in a denial."

NATO "claimed to have a recording of my conversation which contradicted my shorthand record," Starkey wrote in a Nieman Watchdog blog post the following week, referring to the alleged misquote. "When I asked to hear it, they ignored me. When I pressed them, they said there had been a misunderstanding. When they said recording, they meant someone had taken notes. The tapes, they said, do not exist."

Starkey pressed on, publishing another story describing the community's anger over the raid and subsequent responses of NATO and the Afghan authorities. "I don't want money. I want justice," the family's patriarch, Hajji Sharabuddin, told Starkey. He said that the government had offered them compensation for each slain family member after protests paralyzed the provincial capital. "All our family, we now don't care about our lives. We will all do suicide attacks and [the whole province] will support us."

"Nato officials continued to brief journalists in Kabul yesterday that the women were victims of an 'honour' killing," Starkey wrote. "However, they did not explain why the bodies would have been kept in the house overnight, against Islamic custom, nor why the family had invited 25 guests to celebrate the naming of a newborn child the same evening."

"My father was friends with the Americans and they killed him," Daoud's son, Abdul Ghafar, told Starkey, showing him a photograph of his father with three smiling American soldiers. "They killed my father. I want to kill them. I want the killers brought to justice."

ON MARCH 15, 2010, the *New York Times* reported that General Mc-Chrystal had decided to bring most of the US Special Operations Forces in Afghanistan under his command. The decision was motivated in part by concerns about civilian casualties, the article noted, which were often caused by elite forces operating outside of the NATO command structure. The *Times* report largely seconded Starkey's account of the Gardez raid, confirming that "Afghan police special forces paired with American Special Operations forces" had been behind the operation. Again, Admiral Smith avoided taking responsibility for the deaths of the women. "The regret is that two innocent males died," Admiral Smith said. "The women, I'm not sure anyone will ever know how they died." He added, however, "I don't know that there are any forensics that show bullet penetrations of the women or blood from the women." Smith added that the women appeared to have been stabbed and slashed by knives, rather than shot. The *Times* spoke to Sayid Mohammed Mal, the father of Gulalai's fiancé and the vice chancellor of Gardez University. "They were killed by the Americans," he said. "If the government doesn't listen to us, I have 50 family members, I'll bring them all to Gardez roundabout and we'll pour petrol on ourselves and burn ourselves to death."

Weeks later, in early April, Starkey received an unexpected phone call. "NATO phoned me up," Starkey told me, "and they said, 'Jerome, we just wanted to let you know that we're preparing to put out a press release. We're changing our version of events.'" A so-called joint investigation had "determined that international forces were responsible for the deaths of three women who were in the same compound where two men were killed by the joint Afghan-international patrol searching for a Taliban insurgent." The report added, "While investigators could not conclusively determine how or when the women died, due to lack of forensic evidence, they concluded that the women were accidentally killed as a result of the joint force firing at the men."

The statement maintained that the men had shown "hostile intent" but were "later determined not to be insurgents." "The [original] statement noted the women had been bound and gagged, but this information was taken from an initial report by the international members of the joint force who were not familiar with Islamic burial customs," the statement said. When Starkey received the phone call, he had just filed another story for the *Times* of London. This was his most explosive story to date, based on a conversation with a senior Afghan official involved in the government investigation, as well as members of the family.

The delegation had finished its report, and McChrystal was briefed on the findings as well. The press release, followed by news that McChrystal was ordering a second review of the incident, was meant to preempt a gruesome revelation. "US special forces soldiers dug bullets out of their victims' bodies in the bloody aftermath of the botched night raid, then washed the wounds with alcohol before lying to their superiors about what happened," Starkey asserted in his story, which came out the following day. Afghan investigators told Starkey that the US soldiers had also removed bullets from the scene. Their investigation had determined that eleven bullets were fired, but only seven had been found. The missing bullets, combined with photographic evidence and witness testimony, had brought them to their conclusion about what the US Special Forces had done. "In what culture in the world do you invite...people for a party and meanwhile kill three women?" the senior Afghan official told Starkey. "The dead bodies were just eight meters from where they were preparing the food. The Americans, they told us the women were dead for 14 hours." The Afghan government investigators had confirmed what the family had told Starkey—and later me—about the US forces digging bullets out of the women's bodies. "Because we were aware that what we were looking into was potentially so controversial, we wanted to make sure that we were on solid ground," Starkey told me, referring to the digging out of the bullets. "That allegation I left out of my original story. But when I heard it again, from this very senior, very credible Afghan source, we published that."


THAT SAME DAY, the *New York Times* reported some of the conclusions of the Afghan investigation. "We came to the conclusion that the NATO patrol was responsible for the killing of the two men and the three women, and that there was evidence of tampering in the corridor inside the compound by the members" of the assault team, said the lead investigator, Merza Mohammed Yarmad. "There was a mess at the scene." NATO said the allegations had prompted another investigation but nonetheless rejected them outright. "We strongly deny having dug any bullets out of bodies. There simply is no evidence," said a NATO military official. The officer appointed to conduct the second review was put under McChrystal's direct "operational control" while still conducting the investigation. The results remained classified, but NATO continued to insist that there was "no evidence of a cover-up."

AS RAGE IN AFGHANISTAN MOUNTED over civilian deaths in raids like that in Gardez, there was a fierce debate within NATO about how to respond. At one point there was a plan for General McChrystal to travel to the village to personally apologize to the family. Instead, the actual commander of the force responsible for the raid would travel to Gardez and in the process reveal exactly which unit was behind the gruesome killings and cover-up of the massacre. It would also publicly reveal the face of JSOC. On the morning of April 8, shortly after 11:00, Admiral William McRaven, JSOC's secretive commander, pulled up to the gates of the Sharabuddin compound.

The family had been told the night before that they would be receiving an important visitor. They thought it would be McChrystal himself. Mohammed Sabir and other family members told me that they had actually discussed killing McChrystal when he came the next day, but their local imam counseled them to instead show him hospitality and listen to him. Faced with this imminent meeting, the family decided to call an international witness: Jerome Starkey. NATO had tried to conceal the details and timing of the visit, but once Starkey got the call, he began the half-day drive to Gardez from Kabul. "We were obviously very keen to make sure that we were there when it happened and that was very, very difficult because nobody wanted to tell us. And I think, from the sort of PR spin side of things, that the image management within NATO probably didn't really want to draw attention," he told me. "They admitted they'd got it wrong. Again they were hoping it was going to go away but it wasn't."

Starkey arrived at the family compound early in the morning and was sitting with the family drinking tea and talking. "At about eleven o'clock, up rolls a huge convoy of massive American armored cars, armored land cruisers, countless, I mean literally countless Afghan officers and soldiers," Starkey recalled. "And among them is a man wearing a uniform that I recognized as sort of U.S. Marines, but it says U.S. Navy on his lapel." His name tag simply read "McRaven." "I didn't know who he was at that stage," said Starkey, one of the most experienced Western reporters in Afghanistan at the time. "And so, there unfolded perhaps one of the most extraordinary things I've ever seen in Afghanistan as they off-loaded a sheep from the back of an Afghan Army pickup truck. And three Afghan soldiers knelt on this sheep on the street outside the home where this operation had taken place, in the exact same place where these soldiers had been when they started the raid. And there with a knife, they sharpened the knife and there was an Afghan Army mullah who started praying and they were offering to sacrifice this sheep."

Hajji Sharabuddin, the family elder, intervened. "Don't do it," he told the soldiers. Starkey said that the Afghan forces and McRaven's men had put the family in a difficult position. "When people come to your gate and ask forgiveness, according to Afghan law, it's difficult to reject them," Sharabuddin told Starkey, who added that the practice was "an ancient Afghan ritual known as *nanawate* where you offer to sacrifice a sheep at somebody's door in order to ask for forgiveness." The family, Starkey said, "was left with no option, no honorable dignified option other than to let these men into [their] house."

The Afghan soldiers tried to prevent Starkey's photographer, Jeremy Kelly, from taking photos and to expel Starkey from the room once McRaven had entered. But the family insisted he remain. Otherwise, there would have been no evidence that this extraordinary event occurred, no proof of who the killers were. Inside the house, the commander of JSOC stood face-to-face with the survivors of the raid, including the fathers and husbands of the women his men had killed. "Admiral McRaven stood up and he gave an extraordinary speech. He drew similarities between himself and Hajji Sharabuddin, and he described them both as spiritual men, as men of God. He drew comparisons and found similarities between Christianity and Islam," Starkey recalled. "Sir, you and I are very different," McRaven told Sharabuddin. "You are a family man with many children and many friends. I am a soldier. I have spent most of my career overseas away from my family, but I have children as well and my heart grieves for you. But we have one thing in common. We have the same god. He is a god who shows great love and compassion. I pray for you today, sir, that in your grief he will show you love and compassion and ease your pain. I also pray today that he will show mercy on me and my men for this awful tragedy." Starkey said McRaven then told the family, "My soldiers were responsible for deaths of these members of your family," and then apologized. The Afghan generals handed the family a pile of money—almost $30,000, according to relatives. Major international news outlets reported that Hajji Sharabuddin had accepted McRaven's apology.

Months later, when I sat with Sharabuddin at his home, his anger seemed only to have hardened. "I don't accept their apology. I would not trade my sons for the whole kingdom of the United States," he told me, holding up a picture of his sons. "Initially, we were thinking that Americans were the friends of Afghans, but now we think that Americans themselves are terrorists. Americans are our enemy. They bring terror and destruction. Americans not only destroyed my house, they destroyed my family. The Americans unleashed the Special Forces on us. These Special Forces, with the long beards, did cruel, criminal things."

"We call them the American Taliban," added Mohammed Tahir, the father of Gulalai, one of the slain women. As I spoke to other family members, Mohammed Sabir, whose brothers and wife were killed, approached me with his six-year-old daughter, Tamana. He told me that we should leave soon and head back to Kabul because the Taliban control the roads at night. As we stood there, he asked his daughter, "Tamana, who did the Americans kill?" She bounced against her father's legs as she recited the list of dead. She then stared into the distance, blankly. "She remembers everything from that night," Sabir told me. "The Americans' arrival, their shootings, the destruction, everything." As we loaded up the car, he told me, "I have this message to people of America to help us: take these special forces of theirs back, and have them sentenced because they are killing innocent people."

FOR MORE THAN A YEAR, I tried to get access to any documents the US military had about the incident at Gardez. I asked for the "after action" reports and for any information on any disciplinary actions taken against the soldiers who killed the three women and two men and then dug the bullets from the women's bodies. I filed Freedom of Information Act requests that were bounced around the military before ending up in an unnamed "agency" awaiting review. As of this writing, in early 2013, I have received no documents. Starkey told me his attempts to get documents had met the same fate.

Not long after I returned from Afghanistan in late 2010, I met with General Hugh Shelton, the former chairman of the Joint Chiefs, and asked him about the Gardez incident. He told me he was not familiar with all of the details. And though he said that an internal review should be done on behalf of the commander to determine what happened and if any soldiers should face a court martial, he said he believed that it should not be investigated further. "If that police chief [Daoud], and those two pregnant women were killed, as a result of JSOC, based on all the intelligence that they had pointing to this is going to be a terrorist operation that's taking place here, and if they go flying in, and try to get to this place, and meet any kind of resistance at all—I mean, shots are fired—then I'm sorry that they got killed," he told me. "But in the wrong place, at the wrong time, our guys were doing what they thought they should do, and protecting themselves and their buddies in the process. I'm OK with that. I don't think it ought to be investigated; I think you write it off as one of those damn acts of war."

The fact that Daoud was a US-trained police commander meant little to Shelton. "Now, just because he's a police chief, he could have been a terrorist as well. He could have been working both sides," he told me. "The two pregnant women? The fact that they were pregnant is very, very unfortunate. But it's also unfortunate that they were women. But on the other hand, I've been shot at by women myself. So, that doesn't—and I mean shot at. So that doesn't excuse them. They die just like men do if they shoot at us."

As the pace of night raids increased in Afghanistan under McChrystal, the Special Ops Forces continued to enjoy the freedom to operate with no accountability for their actions, a fact that did not seem lost on McChrystal. "You better be out there hitting four or five targets tonight," McChrystal would tell a Navy SEAL in Afghanistan, before adding, "I'm going to have to scold you in the morning for it, though." But with each new raid, more protests began spreading across Afghanistan.

The conditions that drove Matt Hoh to resign his State Department post in protest in late 2009 persisted in 2010. If anything, things had gotten worse. Civilian deaths from NATO operations had killed upward of ninety civilians in the first few months of 2010, a 75 percent increase from the previous year. And it wasn't just in night raids. More than thirty Afghans were killed at checkpoint shootings from the time McChrystal took charge in Afghanistan to the spring of 2010. "In the nine-plus months I've been here, not a single case where we have engaged in an escalation of force incident and hurt someone has it turned out that the vehicle had a suicide bomb or weapons in it and, in many cases, had families in it," McChrystal conceded in March 2010, during a teleconference with US troops. "We've shot an amazing number of people and killed a number and, to my knowledge, none has proven to have been a real threat."

While McChrystal ostensibly put in place greater restrictions on night raids and almost entirely stopped air strikes, the ground truth was still the same: innocent people were dying and Afghans were growing ever more enraged. By May 2010, the United States was conducting as many as 1,000 night raids a month. US Special Ops Forces "were authorized to shoot any armed man on sight," reported Gareth Porter, "so the raids were resulting in many Afghan civilians being killed during the raids, all of whom were automatically categorized by SOF as insurgents."

When I met with Mullah Abdul Salam Zaeef, the former Taliban spokes-person, in late 2010, he told me bluntly that the US raids were aiding the Taliban, just as Hoh alleged. "They are encouraging the people to become extremist," he said as we sat in his home in Kabul, where he was under de facto house arrest, being watched day and night by Afghan police officers positioned outside his building. US political and military leaders, he said, "are thinking, 'When we scare the people, they should be quiet.' But this is a different nation. When you are killing one person, four or five others rise against you. If you are killing five people, twenty, at least, are rising against you. When you are disrespecting the people or the honor of the people in one village, the whole village becomes against you. This is creating hatred against Americans."

The US killing of civilians, combined with a widely held perception that the Afghan government existed only for facilitating the corruption of pow-erful warlords, drug dealers and war criminals, had produced a situation in which the Taliban and the Haqqani network gained support from commu-nities in the Pashtun heartland that would not otherwise be backing them. Zaeef told me that since 2005, when he was released from the US prison at Guantánamo, "the Taliban have become stronger." "Are the Taliban coming from the sky?" Zaeef asked. "No, it's new people."

When I asked Hoh what he thought of Zaeef's comments, he said they were accurate. "I think we're engendering more hostility. We're wasting a lot of very good assets going after midlevel guys who don't threaten the United States or have no capacity to threaten the United States," he told me. "If we say that al Qaeda recruits based on an ideology that they are defending the Muslim world against Western attack, this only feeds into that ideology."

By June 2010, Afghanistan had become the longest-running war in Amer-ican history. That summer, the number of US dead passed the 1,000 mark. From June 2009 to May 2010, the number of improvised explosive device attacks had swelled from 250 per month to more than 900. As the situation in Afghanistan deteriorated and the Taliban and other insurgent groups gained ground, a stunning scandal rocked the US military and the Special Ops community that would ultimately lead to the resignation and retire-ment of General McChrystal, one of the architects of the post-9/11 US killing machine. But his demise had nothing to do with any of his actions with JSOC in Iraq or his involvement in covering up the friendly-fire death of Pat Tillman, the former NFL player turned Army Ranger in Afghanistan in 2004 or his role in transforming JSOC into a global hit squad. Instead, McChrystal was brought down by an article in *Rolling Stone* magazine written by Michael Hastings that captured McChrystal and his inner circle making disparaging remarks about President Obama, Vice President Biden and other top US civilian officials. Before the issue of *Rolling Stone* even hit newsstands, excerpts of it boomeranged throughout the chambers of power and the media in Washington. McChrystal was finished, his run as the commander of the most elite units in the US military brought down by a story published in an issue of a magazine that featured on its cover an almost naked Lady Gaga sporting a brassiere with two rifles protruding from it.

On June 23, President Obama, flanked by Biden, Admiral Mullen, Defense Secretary Gates and General Petraeus, announced that "with considerable regret," he had accepted McChrystal's resignation. "It is the right thing for our mission in Afghanistan, for our military and for our country," Obama said outside the White House. "I believe that it is the right decision for our national security," he added. "The conduct represented in the recently published article does not meet the standard that should be set by a commanding general." Obama thanked McChrystal "for his remarkable career in uniform."

"This is a change in personnel," Obama declared. "But it is not a change in policy."

That point was driven home as the president announced that General Petraeus, one of the key architects of the expansion of the global US battlefield, would be taking over for McChrystal. Almost as soon as Petraeus took command of the war, the pace of night raids increased and air strikes resumed. As the civilian death toll mounted, the Afghan insurgency intensified. The US "targeted" killing program was fueling the very threat it claimed to be fighting.

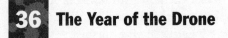

# 36 The Year of the Drone

YEMEN AND THE UNITED STATES, 2010—As thousands of US troops deployed and redeployed to Afghanistan, the covert campaign in undeclared battlefields elsewhere was widening. US drone strikes were hitting Pakistan weekly, while JSOC forces were on the ground in Somalia and Yemen and pounding the latter with air strikes. All the while, al Qaeda affiliates in those countries were gaining strength. When I met again with Hunter, who worked with JSOC under Bush and continued to work in counterterrorism under the Obama administration, I asked him what changes had taken place from one administration to the next. He quickly shot back, "There's no daylight. If anything, JSOC operations have intensified under this administration, there's been a greater intensity in what they're being asked to do, where they're being asked to do it and how they're being asked to do it," he told me. "There are things that are transpiring now, around the globe, that would be unthinkable to the Bush administration, not just because of vocal opposition within the cabinet, or within the Pentagon, but because they would not have the ultimate support of the president. In this administration, the president has made a political and military calculation—and this is his prerogative—that it is best to let the Joint Special Operations Command run wild, like a mustang, in pursuit of the objectives that [Obama] has set."

The Obama administration, Hunter told me, worked diligently to bring an end to the CIA-JSOC divide and to bring all forces together in a unified global antiterrorist campaign, though it would be an uphill task. What became clear in the first year of the Obama administration was that JSOC had won the decade-long war of ideas within the US counterterrorism community. Its paramilitary-focused direct actions would become the central strategy in the new administration's various small wars, not just Afghanistan. "The operations have been institutionalized to a point where it is an integral part of any campaign, in any theater, and at some point we crossed a threshold where Joint Special Operations Command *is* the campaign," Hunter told me. "In places like Yemen, it is Joint Special Operations Command, and that's it. And they make the rules. It's their house, and they do what it is that they need to do." As the JSOC-ization of US counterterrorism policy spread, the CIA was steadily increasing its paramilitary capabilities and expanding its drone strikes and target lists. In a way, it resembled a mini turf war between JSOC and the CIA over who would mow through the kill lists faster.

By early 2010, there were at least three entities within the US government that were maintaining kill lists: the National Security Council, which Obama dealt with directly during weekly meetings; the CIA; and the US military. The CIA had its own "parallel, more cloistered process" for selecting targets and executing strikes, which were for the most part in Pakistan. The NSC and the DoD had little oversight of that process. Obama exercised final authority over "more complex and risky strikes" in Pakistan. At least twice a month, the CIA's top lawyer would receive a file from the Counterterrorism Center (often no more than two to five pages long) containing targeting recommendations and intelligence. The lawyer would hold small meetings that included CTC lawyers and the head of the National Clandestine Service, formerly known as the Directorate of Operations, which coordinates the CIA's covert operations across the globe. Lawyers from the White House and the National Security Council would review the CIA's list, and the Gang of Eight on Capitol Hill would have to approve it, as well.

The military list, according to reporters Dana Priest and William Arkin, "was really more than one, since the clandestine special operations troops" from JSOC had their own internal list. These lists often overlapped, but as Priest and Arkin noted, "even these highly classified kill lists were not coordinated among the three primary agencies involved in creating them."

A YEAR INTO HIS PRESIDENCY, Obama and his counterterrorism team were fully committed to formalizing the process for conducting assassinations against terror suspects and other "militants." They had, in their own way, embraced the neoconservative vision of the world as the battlefield, and the kill lists they built would encompass the globe. Unlike President Bush, who often delegated decisions on assassinations to commanders and CIA officials, Obama insisted on personally signing off on most strikes. On Tuesday afternoons, the president would preside over meetings that senior officials dubbed "Terror Tuesdays," during which proposed targets would be "nominated" for spots on the kill list. Many of them were known operatives in Pakistan, Yemen or Somalia, but at times they were only loosely affiliated with other suspects or were simply residents of a particular region of a country.

"This secret 'nominations' process is an invention of the Obama administration, a grim debating society that vets the PowerPoint slides bearing the names, aliases and life stories of suspected members of Al Qaeda's branch in Yemen or its allies in Somalia's Shabab militia," reported the *New York Times*. "The nominations go to the White House, where by his own insistence and guided by Mr. Brennan, Mr. Obama must approve any name. He signs off on every strike in Yemen and Somalia and also on the more complex and risky strikes in Pakistan," the *Times* noted. The Terror Tuesday meetings would take place after a larger group—sometimes more than 100 of the administration's national security lawyers and officials— debated names to be added or subtracted from the list. JSOC, according to sources knowledgeable about the meetings, would dominate the process and "groomed" State Department, CIA and administration officials, in the words of one JSOC source, to accept a targeted killing campaign that would hit the "infrastructure" of the networks to move much further down "the food chain" in a variety of countries.

Although Obama had campaigned, in part, on a pledge to unilaterally use US force in pursuit of known terrorists, he had kept its scope narrowed to Osama bin Laden and his top deputies. Once in office, the system he was building would be far more sweeping. In essence, the kill list became a form of "pre-crime" justice in which individuals were considered fair game if they met certain life patterns of suspected terrorists. Utilizing signature strikes, it was no longer necessary for targets to have been involved with specific plots or actions against the United States. Their potential to commit future acts could be a justification for killing them. At times, simply being among a group of "military-aged males" in a particular region of Pakistan would be enough evidence of terrorist activity to trigger a drone strike. In Yemen, Obama authorized JSOC to hit targets even if the mission planners did not know the identities of those they were bombing. Such strikes were labeled Terrorist Attack Disruption Strikes, or TADS.

While Obama chaired the Terror Tuesday meetings, the administration's assassination policy was being coordinated by two key architects with vast experience in targeted killing: John Brennan and Admiral William McRaven. Brennan had worked extensively on the kill program under the Bush administration; McRaven had helped develop the post-9/11 version when he worked for Bush's National Security Council. Under Obama, both men were now in a position to formalize and streamline the kill programs they had worked on in the shadows for much of their careers.

In Pakistan, the CIA would take the lead on drone strikes and Obama granted the Agency a wider authority for strikes and supplied it with more drones to do so. By late 2009, Leon Panetta had declared that the CIA was "conducting the most aggressive operations in our history as an agency." Most of the rest of the world would belong to JSOC, which had been empowered under Obama with far greater latitude to strike across the globe. Although some of the behind-the-scenes conflicts that raged between JSOC and the CIA under the Bush administration would continue, both McRaven and Brennan saw an opportunity to move forward with more of a unified counterterrorism front than had been possible in the previous eight years. President Obama's credentials as a popular, liberal Democrat and a constitutional lawyer who pledged to end the excesses of the Bush war machine would be of tremendous value in selling their cause.

In interviews with the *New York Times* and other major media outlets, senior White House officials consistently hit on the themes of the "just war" theory that Obama had embraced in his Nobel Prize speech, noting that Obama was a fan of St. Augustine and Thomas Aquinas. "If John Brennan is the last guy in the room with the president, I'm comfortable, because Brennan is a person of genuine moral rectitude," State Department lawyer Harold Koh said. Koh, who had been a major critic of the Bush administration's counterterrorism policies, had changed his tune. "It's as though you had a priest with extremely strong moral values who was suddenly charged with leading a war."

On a counterterrorism front, Obama's first year in office was marked by an aggressive embrace of assassination as a centerpiece of US national security policy. In part, the preemptive strikes were motivated by fear of another attack against the United States. Politically, Obama's advisers knew that a successful terrorist attack could damage his presidency, and they expressed this quite bluntly to reporters. But expanded use of JSOC operatives and drones also bolstered the narrative that Obama was waging a "smarter" war than his predecessor. Obama could say that he was taking the fight to the terrorists while simultaneously claiming he was winding down the Iraq occupation he had opposed. Although Obama received praise from many Republicans for his aggressive counterterrorism policies, others saw it as a way of circumventing the controversial issue of how to lawfully detain terror suspects. "Their policy is to take out high-value targets, versus capturing high-value targets," declared Senator Saxby Chambliss, the most senior Republican on the Senate Intelligence Committee. "They are not going to advertise that, but that's what they are doing." Very few Democrats spoke in opposition to Obama's emerging global kill campaign. "It is the politically advantageous thing to do—low cost, no U.S. casualties, gives the appearance of toughness," said Admiral Dennis Blair, Obama's former director of national intelligence, explaining how the administration viewed its policy. "It plays well domestically, and it is unpopular only in other countries. Any damage it does to the national interest only shows up over the long term."

The administration heavily utilized the State Secrets Privilege and claims of protecting national security to keep the details of its kill program concealed from the public. When convenient, the administration would leak details of operations to journalists. In doing so, it continued many of the same practices that liberal Democrats had railed against when Bush and his team were steering the ship. Jack Goldsmith, the former Bush administration lawyer, asserted that "perhaps the most remarkable surprise of his presidency" was that "Obama continued almost all of his predecessor's counterterrorism policies." When Obama conducted a review of the proposed assassination of Anwar Awlaki, one of his senior advisers recalled the president declaring, "This is an easy one." Easy as it may have been, the Obama administration refused to release its findings on how such an operation would be legal. "This program rests on the personal legitimacy of the president, and that's not sustainable," former CIA director Michael Hayden told the *New York Times*. "I have lived the life of someone taking action on the basis of secret O.L.C. [Office of Legal Counsel] memos, and it ain't a good life. Democracies do not make war on the basis of legal memos locked in a D.O.J. [Department of Justice] safe."

Obama and his team created a system "where people are being killed, you don't know what the evidence is, and you have no way to redress the situation," former CIA case officer Phil Giraldi told me. "It's not that there aren't terrorists out there, and every once in a while one of them is going to have to be killed for one good reason or another, but I want to see the good reason. I don't want to see someone in the White House telling me, 'You'll have to trust me.' We've had too much of that."

BY MID-2010, the Obama administration had increased the presence of Special Operations Forces from sixty countries to seventy-five countries. SOCOM had about 4,000 people deployed around the world in countries besides Iraq and Afghanistan. "The Special Operations capabilities requested by the White House go beyond unilateral strikes and include the training of local counterterrorism forces and joint operations with them," the *Washington Post* reported at the time. "Plans exist for preemptive or retaliatory strikes in numerous places around the world, meant to be put into action when a plot has been identified, or after an attack linked to a specific group."

John Brennan laid out the new counterterrorism vision under the Obama administration: We "will not merely respond after the fact" to terrorist attacks. We will "take the fight to al-Qaeda and its extremist affiliates wherever they plot and train. In Afghanistan, Pakistan, Yemen, Somalia and beyond."

Well-placed special operations sources told me that among the countries where JSOC teams had been deployed under the Obama administration were: Iran, Georgia, Ukraine, Bolivia, Paraguay, Ecuador, Peru, Yemen, Pakistan (including in Baluchistan) and the Philippines. These teams also at times deployed in Turkey, Belgium, France and Spain. JSOC was also supporting US Drug Enforcement Agency operations in Colombia and Mexico. But the two greatest priorities outside of Afghanistan and Pakistan were Yemen and Somalia. "In both those places, there are ongoing unilateral actions," a Special Operations source told me in 2010.

One senior military official told the *Washington Post* that the Obama administration had given the green light for "things that the previous administration did not." Special Operations commanders, the paper reported, had more direct communication with the White House than they did under Bush. "We have a lot more access," a military official told the paper. "They are talking publicly much less but they are acting more. They are willing to get aggressive much more quickly." Under Obama, Hunter told me, JSOC was able to hit "harder, faster, quicker, with the full support of the White House."

While the Obama administration ratcheted up its drone strikes and targeted killing campaign, al Qaeda affiliates were growing stronger, emboldened in part by the US escalation. Although the Obama administration boasted that it had al Qaeda on the ropes, its global assassination program was becoming a recruitment device for the very forces the United States claimed to be destroying.

## 37 Driving Anwar Awlaki to Hell

YEMEN, 2010—In early February 2010, AQAP leader Said Ali al Shihri, whom the Yemenis had claimed to have killed multiple times, released an audiotape. "We advise you, our people in the Peninsula, to prepare and carry your weapons and to defend your religion and yourselves and to join your mujahideen brothers," he declared, adding that US "espionage planes," presumably drones, had been killing women and children.

On March 14, the United States struck again. Air strikes hit Abyan in southern Yemen, killing two alleged AQAP operatives, including its southern chief, Jamil al Anbari. As it did after the al Majalah bombing, Yemen took credit for a US attack while Washington remained silent. AQAP leader Qasim al Rimi confirmed the deaths in an audio recording released soon after the strikes. "A US strike targeted our brother," he declared. "The attack was carried out while our brother Jamil was making a phone call via the Internet." As for Yemen's claims to have carried out the strike, Rimi said, "This nonsense is similar to their allegations" in the December 2009 strikes. "May God disgrace lying and liars." A few months later, AQAP would avenge the deaths by launching a brazen attack against a government security compound in Aden, killing eleven people. The claim of responsibility was signed: "Brigade of the martyr Jamil al-Anbari."

A week after the March 14 strike, one of the key US officials running the Obama administration's covert war in Yemen, Michael Vickers, accompanied then-undersecretary of defense for intelligence James Clapper for talks with President Saleh and other Yemeni officials. The US Embassy released a brief statement on the meeting, saying only that they were there "to discuss the ongoing counterterrorism cooperation" between the two countries and "to express the appreciation of the United States for Yemen's continuing efforts to counter" AQAP. A month later, Vickers gave a closed-door briefing to the Senate Armed Services Committee on covert US action in Yemen and Somalia. An internal e-mail circulated within Vickers's office at the time, and provided to me in confidence, acknowledged that "a task force operating in Yemen has helped Yemeni forces kill terrorism suspects, but it has also carried out unilateral operations," adding: "The intelligence community, including the Defense Intelligence Agency and the Central Intelligence Agency vets the lists of targets and decides who needs to be captured for the purposes of intelligence collection, or who can be killed."

While JSOC forces continued to operate inside Yemen, at times training Yemeni forces and, at others, conducting kinetic actions, the air strikes continued. In late May, General James "Hoss" Cartwright, vice chairman of the Joint Chiefs, briefed President Obama on a High Value Target that JSOC had a lock on. The president green-lit a strike. On May 24, a US missile hit a convoy of vehicles in the Marib Desert that "actionable intelligence" had concluded was heading to a meeting of al Qaeda operatives. The intelligence was only partly correct. The men inside the vehicle were not al Qaeda members but prominent Yemeni local mediators in the government effort to demilitarize members of AQAP. Among those killed was Jabir al Shabwani, the deputy governor of Marib Province. Shabwani was in a key position to negotiate, given that his cousin Ayad was the local AQAP leader whom US and Yemeni forces had tried to take out in a pair of strikes in January. Shabwani's uncle and two of his escorts were also killed in the attack. A local official said the "deputy governor was on a mediation mission to persuade al-Qaeda elements to hand themselves over to the authorities."

As in the cases of the other US strikes, the Yemeni authorities took public responsibility, and Yemen's Supreme Security Council apologized for what it said was a government raid gone wrong. But this hit came with much higher stakes because the attack killed one of their own people. Within hours of the attack, Shabwani's tribe attacked the main oil pipeline running from Marib to the Ras Isa port on the Red Sea coast. The tribesmen also attempted to take over the presidential palace in the province but were repelled by Yemeni army forces and tanks. Yemeni lawmakers demanded that Saleh's government explain how the strike happened and who was really behind the widening aerial war in Yemen.

Months after the attack, some US officials began to believe that the Saleh regime had actually fed the United States bad intelligence to take out Shabwani, after a political feud had broken out between Jabir al Shabwani and "key members" of President Saleh's family. "We think we got played," a US source with access to "high-level" Obama administration discussions on Yemen said. The White House, the US military and the US ambassador to Yemen had all approved the strike. "It turned out you didn't really know who was at all those [Yemeni] meetings," a former US intelligence official told the *Wall Street Journal*. A former US official told the paper the strike showed that the United States was "too susceptible to the Yemenis saying, 'Oh, that's a bad guy, you go get him.' And it's a political bad guy—it's not a real bad, bad guy." Brennan was reportedly "pissed" about the strike. "How could this have happened?" Obama later demanded of General Cartwright. The general told him it was bad intel from the Yemenis. Cartwright said he "got a pretty good chest-thumping from the commander-in-chief."

After the Tomahawk cruise missile strikes that killed scores of civilians in al Majalah in December 2009 and the disastrous strike that killed Shabwani, the CIA began agitating for a shift from JSOC's Tomahawk strikes to the CIA's weapon of choice: drones. Surveillance satellites were repositioned, and more Predator drones were deployed in secret bases near Yemen. "The drones are flying over Marib every twenty-four hours and there is not a day that passes that we don't see them," said Sheikh Ibrahim al Shabwani, another brother of the government mediator who was killed in the May 25 strike. "Occasionally they fly at a lower altitude while at other times they fly at a higher altitude. The atmosphere has become weary because of the presence of US drones and fear that they could strike at any time." Stoking such insecurity seemed a central part of the emerging US strategy aimed at making it lethally dangerous for local tribes to support AQAP. But to some it seemed to be backfiring, particularly with local tribal leaders who often had family members on various sides of the war.

Some reports alleged that, far from having intended to get Shabwani killed, Saleh, who depended on tribes to support his regime, demanded a pause in US covert actions as a result of the strike. But US officials insisted that it did not shake the covert arrangement allowing the United States to strike inside Yemen. "At the end of the day, it's not like he said, 'No more,'" an unnamed Obama administration official told the *New York Times*. "He didn't kick us out of the country."

What cannot be disputed is that the strikes, especially those that killed civilians and important tribal figures, were giving valuable ammunition to al Qaeda for its recruitment campaign in Yemen and its propaganda battle against the US-Yemen counterterrorism alliance. Yemeni government officials said the series of US strikes from December 2009 to May 2010 had killed more than two hundred civilians and forty people affiliated with al Qaeda. "It is incredibly dangerous what the US is trying to do in Yemen at the moment because it really fits into AQAP's broader strategy, in which it says Yemen is not different from Iraq and Afghanistan," asserted Princeton professor Gregory Johnsen in June 2010, after Amnesty International released a report documenting the use of US munitions in the Yemen strikes. "They are able to make the argument that Yemen is a legitimate front for jihad," said Johnsen, who in 2009 served as a member of USAID's conflict assessment team for Yemen. "They've been making that argument since 2007, but incidents like this are all sort of fodder for their argument."

In the summer of 2010, after months of sustained US and Yemeni air strikes and raids, AQAP hit back. In June, a group of AQAP operatives dressed in military uniforms carried out a bold raid on the Aden division of Yemen's secret police, the Political Security Organization (PSO). During an early morning flag ceremony at the compound, the operatives launched rocket-propelled grenades and opened fire with automatic weapons as they stormed the gates. They gunned down at least ten security officers and three cleaning women. The purpose of the raid was to free suspected militants being held by the PSO, and it was successful. That raid was followed by a sustained assassination campaign during the summer aimed at high-level Yemeni military and intelligence officials. During the holy month of Ramadan, which began in August, AQAP launched a dozen attacks. By September as many as sixty officials had been killed, with a substantial number shot dead by assassins riding on motorcycles. The method of attack became so common that the government actually banned motorcycles in urban areas in Abyan. The use of "motorbikes in terrorist operations to assassinate intelligence officers and security personnel" has "massively mounted over the past nine months in the province," said a Yemeni Interior Ministry official.

As Yemen's government found itself under siege and US covert actions expanded, Anwar Awlaki released a "Message to the American People." In the speech, Awlaki said that Umar Farouk Abdulmutallab's attempt to bring down the airplane over Detroit was "in retaliation to American cruise missiles and cluster bombs that killed women and children," and he declared, "You have your B-52's, your Apaches, your Abrams and your cruise missiles, and we have small arms and simple improvised explosive devices. But we have men, who are dedicated and sincere, with hearts of lions." Awlaki also launched into a diatribe against the US and Saleh governments. If "Bush is remembered as being the President who got America stuck in Afghanistan and Iraq, it's looking like Obama wants to be remembered as the President who got America stuck in Yemen," Awlaki declared. He said:

Obama has already started his war on Yemen, by the aerial bombings of Abyan and Shabwah. By doing that he has waged a publicity campaign for the Mujahideen in Yemen, and within days accomplished for them the work of years....The corrupt Yemeni government officials and some of the tribal chiefs who claim to be your allies are having a ball these days. The word being passed around among them is that this is the time to extort the gullible American. Your politicians, military and intelligence officers are being milked for millions. The Yemeni government officials are giving you big promises and handing you big bills: welcome to the world of Yemeni politicians.

What was remarkable about Awlaki's statement on the US relationship with Saleh was how true it rang to many veteran Yemen analysts. During this time, Awlaki began to achieve almost mythical status in the US media and government narrative on terrorist threats. But the real question was how big a threat he *actually* posed. Although the dispute did not play out publicly, there was deep division in the intelligence community over how to approach Awlaki. There was abundant evidence that he had praised attacks against the United States after the fact and had been in touch with Hasan and Abdulmutallab. There was also evidence that he called for violent jihad against the United States and its allies. But there was no conclusive evidence presented, at least not publicly, that Awlaki had played an operational role in any attacks.

In October 2009, the CIA had reportedly concluded that "the agency lacked specific evidence that he threatened the lives of Americans—which is the threshold for any capture-or-kill operation" against an American citizen. President Obama now disagreed with that assessment. Awlaki would have to die.

IN FEBRUARY 2010, journalist Abdulelah Haider Shaye once again managed to find Awlaki and conducted the first interview with the American citizen since the news of his threatened assassination at the hands of the US government was made public. "Why do you think the Americans want to kill you?" Shaye asked Awlaki. "Because I am a Muslim and I promote Islam," Awlaki responded, adding that the allegations against him—in the media, not in a court of law—were based around the idea that he had "incited" Nidal Hasan and Abdulmutallab and that his taped teachings had been found in the possession of accused conspirators in more than a dozen alleged terror plots. "All this comes as part of the attempt to liquidate the voices that call for defending the rights of the Umma [the global Muslim community]." He added: "We call for the Islam that was sent by Allah to Prophet Muhammad, the Islam of jihad and Sharia ruling. Any voice that calls for this Islam, they either kill the person or the character; they kill the person by murdering or jailing them, or they kill the character by distorting their image in the media."

Shaye asked Awlaki, "Do you think Yemen's government would facilitate your assassination?"

"The Yemeni government sells its citizens to the United States, to earn the ill-gotten funds it begs the West for in return for their blood. The Yemeni officials tell the Americans to strike whatever they want and ask them not to announce responsibility for the attacks to avoid people's rage, and then the Yemeni government shamelessly adopts these attacks," Awlaki replied. "The people of Shabwah, Abyan and Arhab have seen the Cruise missiles, and some people saw cluster bombs that did not explode. The state lies when it claims responsibility, and it does so to deny collaboration. US drones continuously fly over Yemen. What state is that which allows its enemy to spy on its people and then considers it as 'accepted cooperation'?"

In Yemen, Awlaki was now completely underground and was having difficulty posting any sermons. His blog had been shut down by the US government, and drones hovered in the skies over Shabwah. While US media outlets, terror "experts" and prominent government officials were identifying Awlaki as a leader of AQAP, those allegations were dubious. Awlaki had entered dangerous territory in openly praising terrorist attacks on the United States and calling for Muslims in America to follow the example of Nidal Hasan. But the available evidence regarding al Qaeda's relationship with Awlaki in 2010 suggests that Awlaki was not an operational member of the group but was seeking out an alliance with like-minded individuals. Some, like his uncle, even argued that he was pushed into an alliance with AQAP after he was marked for death alongside its leaders.

Sheikh Saleh bin Fareed had been Anwar's protector in Yemen. It was bin Fareed's tribal leadership that allowed Awlaki safe passage through Shabwah and other tribal areas. But the sheikh was under great pressure from the Yemeni regime to bring in Anwar. Awlaki's father, Nasser, was convinced that Anwar would remain in hiding and that the US government would continue to try to kill him. Bin Fareed decided to give it one more try. He went to visit Anwar in Shabwah. When he arrived, he said he saw drones "circling our valley twenty-four hours—not one minute they were stopped. Of course we see them when the sun is out—but we can hear them very clearly. And they were after, I think, Anwar," he told me.

When bin Fareed met his nephew, Anwar told him that he had heard that Obama had marked him for death. "In Sana'a now, I think they are under pressure," bin Fareed told Anwar. "Now the president gave the order that they either capture you or kill you." Awlaki told bin Fareed that he had not been charged with any crime by the US government and would not turn himself in to face charges that didn't exist. "You tell them, I have nothing, until today, I have nothing to do with al Qaeda," Anwar told his uncle. "But if [Obama] will not withdraw his [order], and I am wanted, maybe they'll drive me to hell. I have no choice."

Bin Fareed told me he believed that the threats against Anwar inadvertently drove him closer to AQAP. "Of course, we realized that [Anwar] had no choice. And really, they did drive him to hell." The announcement by the US government that Anwar was marked for death, bin Fareed told me, "was a very, very big mistake."

On May 23, 2010, al Qaeda's media wing in Yemen, al Malaeim, released a video titled "The First and Exclusive Meeting with Sheikh Anwar al-Awlaki." In the video, Awlaki thanked his interviewer, a bearded man dressed in all white, for "taking all these pains in order to reach here." Awlaki was dressed in traditional Yemeni garb, sitting before a bookshelf filled with religious books. On his waist was a *jambiya* dagger, a tribal symbol worn by many men in Yemen. In the interview, Awlaki praised a recent speech given by al Qaeda's number-two man, Ayman al Zawahiri, but also referred to "you people in Al Qaeda" and did not claim to be a member of the group. The interviewer, who repeatedly thanked him for giving them an "exclusive" interview, did not address Awlaki as a fellow member of al Qaeda.

The interviewer for this al Qaeda propaganda video was remarkably direct, asking Awlaki many questions about the targeting of civilians, his relationship with Nidal Hasan and Abdulmutallab and his interpretation of various fatwas. He also asked Awlaki about the reports that he had been targeted. Speaking in Arabic, Awlaki told the interviewer, "It is not true that I am a fugitive. I move around among my tribesmen and in other parts of Yemen because the people of Yemen hate the Americans, and support the people of truth and the oppressed. I move around among the Aulaq tribe, and I get support from wide sectors of the people in Yemen." Awlaki praised various mujahedeen movements across the globe, from Iraq and Afghanistan to Somalia. "To the Muslims in general and to the inhabitants of the Peninsula especially, we should participate in this Jihad against America," he said.

Awlaki was undoubtedly developing an affinity for al Qaeda's principles—and his public remarks were becoming indistinguishable from the pronouncements of al Qaeda. Still, words are not actions. To former DIA analyst Joshua Foust, it appeared as though some within the US intelligence community were elevating Awlaki's status based on the fear he was able to inspire through his words. Although he found Awlaki's praise for al Qaeda and calls for terrorist attacks against the United States reprehensible, Foust did not believe these statements constituted evidence of a senior operational role in al Qaeda. "Within AQAP itself, he's literally middle management," he told me at the time. "Even the AQAP leadership treats him like he's just a subordinate, who needs to shut up and do what he's told." Foust added: "I think a lot of the focus on Awlaki doesn't make any sense, because we assign him a kind of importance and influence that he doesn't really have."

After the Christmas Day bomb plot, the White House changed its tune on Awlaki, claiming he had gone operational, with some officials comparing him to Osama bin Laden. "I think it's an exaggeration, frankly, to think he is necessarily a new bin Laden," Nakhleh, the former senior CIA officer, told me. "We would not have even thought much about him if it weren't for Abdulmutallab, the underwear bomber."

Although Awlaki was developing relationships with various al Qaeda figures in Shabwah and elsewhere, and his status was rising within its ranks, well-connected Yemenis who had interviewed AQAP leaders told me that he was not an operational member of the group. "Anwar al Awlaki was not a leader in al Qaeda, he did not hold any official post at all," said journalist Abdul Rezzaq al Jamal. He told me that AQAP viewed Awlaki as an ally and that "the thing that united him and al Qaeda is the hostility to the US." Awlaki "agrees with al Qaeda in vision, rationale and strategies. The efforts that were made by Awlaki in the framework of AQAP's work, especially in terms of recruiting in the West, were very big."

Nasser Awlaki acknowledged that his son was beginning to refer to members of al Qaeda as "my brothers" in interviews, but he did not believe his son was a member of AQAP. "He never said that he was member of al Qaeda," he told me, speculating that "maybe in ideology, maybe Anwar came to believe in some of the ideas of al Qaeda, that you cannot take back your land by peaceful means, you have to fight for it. Anybody who attacks you, you have to defend yourself." Nasser added, "Anwar is a very courageous man. I tell you, definitely, I know my son. If he was a member of that organization, he will have no problems to say it." After all, having already been marked for death by the United States, he had nothing to lose.

Even members of Yemen's government were concerned that the United States was inflating Awlaki's status as a terrorist leader. Yemen's foreign minister, Abu Bakr al Qirbi, told reporters in Sana'a, "Anwar al-Awlaki has always been looked at as a preacher rather than a terrorist and shouldn't be considered as a terrorist unless the Americans have evidence that he has been involved in terrorism."

Awlaki had not been charged with any crimes by the US government. Nor had the Americans publicly offered any evidence that Awlaki was the AQAP ringleader they made him out to be. Awlaki's case would cut to the heart of one of the key questions raised by the increasing role targeted assassinations were playing in US foreign policy: Could the American government assassinate it own citizens without due process?

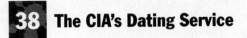

## 38 The CIA's Dating Service

DENMARK AND YEMEN, 2010—While the US manhunt for Anwar Awlaki in Yemen intensified, Morten Storm was busy trying to find Awlaki a European wife. Unbeknownst to Awlaki, the Danish intelligence asset was coordinating his bride search with the CIA. Storm had posted messages on websites frequented by Awlaki's fans and soon received a note from a Croatian woman who had recently converted to Islam. "Aminah" was the name she had adopted after her conversion, though she was raised as a Catholic. She had been a track star in high school and worked with troubled youth in Zagreb. "I was wondering will he search for second wife, I proposed him a marriage. I don't know how silly it is," Aminah wrote to Storm. "I deeply respect him and all the things he do.... I would go with him anywhere. I am 32 years old and I am ready for dangerous things. I am not afraid of death or to die in the sake of Allah."

Storm continued corresponding with Awlaki and told him about Aminah. He also informed the PET, the Danish intelligence agency, that he was in the process of arranging a marriage for Awlaki. The PET contacted the CIA. Storm claimed the intelligence officials were "overjoyed." Together, the intelligence agencies came up with a plan, should the marriage plans work out: Storm would provide Aminah with a suitcase outfitted with a tracking device that would ultimately reveal Awlaki's location.

Awlaki contacted Storm again on February 17, 2010, and said he wanted to meet Aminah. "If you visit her, I can upload a video recording of myself as [an] encrypted file, and you can get her to hear it, so she is sure that [it] is me," he wrote. Days later, Awlaki wrote again to describe his improved living conditions: "I currently do not live in a tent, but in a house [that] belongs to a friend. I'm not leaving the house, and am in a situation for my wife to be with me all the time. I prefer this residence [to] a tent in the mountains, because it gives me ability to read, write and research." Following the message, Storm said he met with CIA and PET officials in Helsingør, Denmark. Taking part in the meeting was a veteran Denmark-based CIA contact who went by the name Jed and, according to Storm, a CIA official who flew in from Washington and called himself Alex.

Storm met with Aminah in Vienna, Austria, on March 8, 2010, outside the international bus station. His trip was verified by multiple receipts reviewed by the Danish newspaper *Jyllands-Posten*. Storm claimed that when he met Aminah, he was shadowed by his PET and CIA handlers. Aminah, Storm alleged, convinced him she was willing to accept the potential consequences of her decision to travel to Yemen to marry Awlaki. Storm taught the young woman to send encrypted e-mails at Awlaki's request, and at a second meeting, he showed her a video the cleric had made for her. "This recording is done specifically for Sister Aminah at her request and the brother who's carrying this recording is a trustworthy brother," Awlaki said in the video. "So having said that, I pray Allah guides to that which is best for you in this life and in the hereafter. And guides you to choose what is better for you regarding this proposal. I would also suggest, if possible, if you could also do a recorded message and send it over. That would be great." According to Storm, the video moved Aminah to tears.

Aminah responded with two videos of her own. In the first she wore a hijab, leaving only her face visible. She described feeling "nervous" and said the experience was "awkward." In the second video, she removed her veil. "Brother, it's me without the scarf, so you can see my hair," she said in accented English. "I hope you are happy with me, inshallah." The two agreed to marry in Yemen.

Awlaki sent Storm an encrypted e-mail describing the things Aminah would need to bring to Yemen: "Warm weather clothing, her personal hygiene stuff, etc. Anything she would need during a month to two month period. She shouldn't have more than a medium sized suitcase and a carry-on bag. She should have with her at least $3,000." The CIA then contacted Storm. In a document obtained by *Jyllands-Posten*, Awlaki is referred to as "the Hook" and Aminah "the sister." The CIA suggested that Storm could "use the Hook's guidance as a reason to give the sister the suitcase and the cosmetic case."

Storm returned to Vienna on May 18, 2010, to purchase Aminah's ticket to Yemen and provide her with clothing and $3,000, all of which he said was paid for by the CIA. He also gave Aminah the bugged suitcase that, if things went according to plan, would set her and Awlaki up for execution by drone. Aminah flew to Yemen on June 2. Storm said he went to a safe house rented by the CIA and PET in Denmark. "We sat there, had a barbecue and had a great party," Storm told *Jyllands-Posten*. Aminah's journey, he recalled, was constantly monitored.

Two days later Storm received a text message from his Danish handler. "Congratulations brother, you just got rich, very rich," it read. The intelligence agent included smiley face emoticons in the text message. Storm claimed he collected his reward on June 9, 2010, at the Crowne Plaza Hotel near Copenhagen, adding that both a CIA and PET officer were present at the exchange and that the PET officer was handcuffed to the briefcase that contained his reward. The suitcase was filled with $250,000 in bundled $100 bills. Storm asked for the code to open the suitcase. "Try 007," the CIA agent told him. Storm snapped a photo of the cash in the briefcase and later provided it to *Jyllands-Posten* as evidence to support his story. Multiple sources confirmed that he received the payment.

The CIA and its allies celebrated what they believed would be a break in the hunt for Awlaki, but their plot soon ran into trouble. Aminah was scheduled to attend a language school in Sana'a for two weeks before meeting her groom-to-be. When Awlaki's aides arrived to pick her up to bring her to Awlaki, they told her she could not bring her suitcase but could only bring a plastic bag containing her belongings. The CIA's bugged suitcase would not make the trek. Soon after, Awlaki and Aminah were married. The CIA had inadvertently found a European wife for one of its most-wanted targets. Awlaki later sent Storm a message thanking him for the hookup.

**"The Auction of the Assassin"**

WASHINGTON, DC, 2010—In the halls of the US Congress, lawmakers fell into two basic camps on the issue of targeting Anwar Awlaki, a US citizen, for assassination: silence or support. It was not until three months after the plan was revealed that a US representative spoke out against it. "I don't support it—period," Democrat Dennis Kucinich told me at the time. "I think people in both parties that are concerned about the Constitution should be speaking out on this." Kucinich said he had sent several letters to the Obama administration raising questions about the potential unconstitutionality of the policy, as well as possible violations of international law, but said he had received no response.

"With all the smart people that are in that administration, they've got to know the risks that they're taking here with violations of law," Kucinich said. He called the policy "extra-constitutional, extra-judicial," saying it "vitiates the presumption of innocence and the government then becomes the investigator, policeman, prosecutor, judge, jury, executioner all in one. That raises the greatest questions with respect to our constitution and our democratic way of life." He added: "All this is being done in the name of national security. How do we know why certain people are being killed? I mean, who's making that decision? It's like a God-like power. You can put your finger on someone's image and say, 'This person is gone.'"

The fact that a US citizen was on the hit list was not Kucinich's only concern. A popular Democratic president and constitutional law scholar pushing the boundaries beyond the extreme policies of the Bush administration, Kucinich believed, would have far-reaching consequences. "We are acting out of fear. We've forgotten who we are," he told me. "We're knocking out pillars of our democratic traditions here. The right to a trial? Gone. The right to be able to confront those who are accusing you? Gone. The right to be free from cruel and unusual punishment? Gone. All of these anchors are being pulled away." He added, "Don't think for a moment that we can do these kinds of things without it having a direct effect here at home. You can't have one America abroad and another one at home. It's all the same. The erosion of integrity, the erosion of democratic values, the erosion of a benevolent intent all augurs a nation in which the basic rights of our own people can no longer be secured. They are up for the auction of the assassin."

In July 2010, Kucinich introduced a bill, HR 6010, "to prohibit the extrajudicial killing of United States citizens." In the bill, Kucinich referred to the various executive orders dating back to the Ford administration prohibiting assassination, including Executive Order 12333, which stated: "No person employed by or acting on behalf of the United States Government shall engage in, or conspire to engage in, assassination." In short, the bill called on Congress to affirm that American citizens had a right to due process before being executed. "The use of extrajudicial force against a citizen of the United States that is outside of the internationally recognized battlefields of Iraq and Afghanistan constitutes a violation of the law of armed conflict," the bill declared. "It is in the best interest of the United States to respect the rule of law and set the example for upholding the principles of international and domestic law."

Only six other members of the House of Representatives, and not a single senator, signed on to support Kucinich's bill. It died immediately.

By July, US intelligence officials acknowledged there had been "almost a dozen" strikes aimed at killing Awlaki. None of them had succeeded. The leading US organizations that had fought the Bush administration's war on terror policies—the Center for Constitutional Rights (CCR) and the American Civil Liberties Union (ACLU)—had been assessing the Obama administration's targeted killing program, primarily focused on the increased US drone strikes in Pakistan. But now that a US citizen had been identified as a target of the program, they believed it needed to be challenged in the US justice system. It was "a very important opportunity to challenge the [assassination] program because we actually have the name of someone—it is not an after-the-fact killing—it's a case we can bring to try to stop killing with respect to someone that we know, based on what has been reported, is on a kill list," said Pardiss Kebriaei, a CCR senior staff attorney.

Kebriaei and her colleagues reviewed the publicly available facts about Awlaki and came to the conclusion that Awlaki's sermons and comments in interviews, while offensive to many Americans, "look very much like protected First Amendment activity to us" and that, "if he does present a threat, and if what he is doing is not protected and criminal, then he should be charged and tried and given due process like anyone, particularly a US citizen." Kebriaei said that if the United States killed one of its own citizens in a foreign country where war had not been declared without charging the individual with a crime, it would amount to "a statement by the US that it is in fact claiming this authority and carrying out this authority to use lethal military force against suspects of terrorism, wherever they may be found. And the implications of that legally, morally, politically are terrifying to me."

After CCR and ACLU lawyers reached Nasser Awlaki through their legal partners in Yemen, he retained them to represent him on a pro bono basis in a lawsuit challenging the right of the Obama administration to kill his son without due process. "I will do my best to convince my son to [surrender], to come back, but they are not giving me time. They want to kill my son. How can the American government kill one of their own citizens? This is a legal issue that needs to be answered," Nasser said.

Days after Nasser first spoke with the lawyers in the United States, the Obama administration took swift action to try to ensure that the case would never be heard in US courts. On July 16, 2010, the Treasury Department officially labeled Anwar Awlaki a "Specially Designated Global Terrorist." Rather than the president or defense secretary or the CIA director, the White House put forward the Treasury Department's undersecretary for terrorism and financial intelligence, Stuart Levey, to make the case that Awlaki had become "operational," directly accusing him of "preparing" and instructing Abdulmutallab "for his operation," alleging that "after receiving this direction from Awlaki, Abdulmutallab obtained the explosive device he used in the attempted Christmas Day attack." Levey declared that Awlaki had "involved himself in every aspect of the supply chain of terrorism—fundraising for terrorist groups, recruiting and training operatives, and planning and ordering attacks on innocents" but provided no evidence for these charges.

The designation by the Treasury Department made it a crime for American lawyers to represent Awlaki without getting a license from the government. On July 23, the ACLU and CCR filed an urgent request for a license. When they were not granted one, they sued the Treasury Department. On August 4, in response to the lawsuit, the Treasury Department changed its position, allowing the lawyers to represent Awlaki. A month later, the CCR and ACLU filed a lawsuit against President Obama, CIA director Panetta, and Defense Secretary Gates, challenging their intention to target Awlaki for assassination, charging that it was unlawful. "Outside of armed conflict, both the Constitution and international law prohibit targeted killing except as a last resort to protect against concrete, specific, and imminent threats of death or serious physical injury," the suit alleged. "The summary use of force is lawful in these narrow circumstances only because the imminence of the threat makes judicial process infeasible. A targeted killing policy under which individuals are added to kill lists after a bureaucratic process and remain on these lists for months at a time plainly goes beyond the use of lethal force as a last resort to address imminent threats, and accordingly goes beyond what the Constitution and international law permit." They asked a federal judge to bar the president, the CIA and JSOC "from intentionally killing" Awlaki and to order them "to disclose the criteria that are used in determining whether the government will carry out the targeted killing of a U.S. citizen."

The Obama administration responded forcefully to the lawsuit, invoking an argument that was used throughout the Bush administration to quash lawsuits seeking to hold Donald Rumsfeld and other officials liable for their role in extrajudicial killings, torture and extraordinary rendition: the military and state secrets "privilege." Justice Department lawyers asked the judge to dismiss the case on other grounds, but said the court should use the "state and military secrets privilege" if all else failed, saying it would be "necessary to protect against the risk of significant harm to national security." Awlaki's lawsuit, Assistant Attorney General Tony West argued, "puts directly at issue the existence and operational details of alleged military and intelligence activities directed at combating the terrorist threat to the United States." He characterized the case as "a paradigmatic example of one in which no part of the case can be litigated on the merits without immediately and irreparably risking disclosure of highly sensitive and classified national security information." He referred to Awlaki as "an operational leader of AQAP."

The government submitted sworn declarations from Panetta, Gates and Clapper asserting the State Secrets Privilege and outlining the threat to national security they believed would be posed by litigating the case. Panetta wrote that he was invoking state secrets "to protect intelligence sources, methods and activities that may be implicated by the allegations in the Complaint" and argued that if he revealed the basis for invoking that privilege, it could harm "US national security." Gates asserted that "the disclosure of intelligence information related to AQAP and Anwar al-Aulaqi would cause exceptionally grave harm to national security" and that the US military "cannot reveal to a foreign terrorist organization or its leaders what it knows about their activities and how it obtained that information." In essence, the government was asserting that it had the right to kill a US citizen but that the justification for doing so was too dangerous to reveal to the American public.

Awlaki's lawyers responded, charging:

> The government's sweeping invocation of the state secrets privilege to shut down this litigation is as ironic as it is extreme: that Anwar Al-Aulaqi has been targeted for assassination is known to the world only because senior administration officials, in an apparently coordinated media strategy, advised the nation's leading newspapers that the National Security Council had authorized the use of lethal force against him.... Had the government itself adhered to the overriding

secrecy concerns so solemnly invoked in its pleadings, those senior officials would not have broadcast the government's intentions to the entire world, and intelligence officials, speaking on the record, would have refused all comment rather than providing tacit acknowledgement that Plaintiff's son is being targeted.

They asserted: "The government has clothed its bid for unchecked authority in the doctrinal language of standing, justiciability, equity, and secrecy, but the upshot of its arguments is that the executive, which must obtain judicial approval to monitor a U.S. citizen's communications or search his briefcase, may execute that citizen without any obligation to justify its actions to a court or to the public."

INSIDE THE WHITE HOUSE, the Obama administration had already been preparing its own legal framework for killing one of its own citizens. Although the government's threat to kill Awlaki was met with almost no outrage or questioning from the US Congress, those in the administration knew that once they killed Awlaki, the case would almost certainly end up back in court. Senior administration officials began leaking intelligence they claimed to have on Awlaki to journalists—intelligence that indicated that Awlaki had become operational and was actively engaged in plots to attack the United States, including with biological and chemical weapons.

The administration had already determined it intended to assassinate Awlaki, and President Obama wanted to be able to argue to the American people that it was the right decision. The State Department's senior legal adviser, Harold Koh, wanted to lay out the case publicly before Awlaki was killed. He was tired of hearing scathing criticisms of the targeted killing program from European diplomats and human rights groups. In an earlier life, Koh had been known as a liberal, pro–human rights, pro–civil liberties lawyer, and so his stamp of approval was useful to the administration as it sought to defend its assassination policy in general—and bolster its decision to target a US citizen without trial.

The White House also believed a public defense of the program from Koh would be a strong preemptive strike against the critics. "The military and the CIA, too, loved the idea," reported *Newsweek* correspondent Daniel Klaidman, author of the book *Kill or Capture*, about the targeted killing campaign. "They called the State Department lawyer 'Killer Koh' behind his back. Some of the operators even talked about printing up T-shirts that said: 'Drones: If they're good enough for Harold Koh, they're good enough for me.'"

In advance of his public speech, the CIA and military gave Koh access to their intel on Awlaki. Koh settled in for a long day of reading in a Secured

Classified Intelligence Facility. According to Klaidman, whose book was based almost entirely on leaks from administration officials, Koh

> had set his own legal standard to justify the targeted killing of a US citizen: evil, with iron-clad intelligence to prove it. It was not exactly a technical, legal standard but it was a threshold he was comfortable with. Now he was reading about multiple plots to kill Americans and Europeans, all of which Awlaki had been deeply involved in at an operational level. There were plans to poison Western water and food supplies with botulinum toxin, as well as attack Americans with ricin and cyanide. Awlaki's ingenuity at coming up with newer, deadlier plots was chilling. Koh was shaken when he left the room. Awlaki was not just evil, he was satanic.

When Koh delivered his speech, on May 25, 2010, he declared, "US targeting practices, including lethal operations conducted with the use of unmanned aerial vehicles, comply with all applicable law, including the laws of war." Koh's audience for the address was the annual convention of the American Society of International Law. He gave a full-throated defense of the administration's targeted killing police, saying:

> Some have argued that the use of lethal force against specific individuals fails to provide adequate process and thus constitutes *unlawful extrajudicial killing*. But a state that is engaged in an armed conflict or in legitimate self-defense is not required to provide targets with legal process before the state may use lethal force.... Some have argued that our targeting practices violate *domestic law*, in particular, the long-standing *domestic ban on assassinations*. But under domestic law, the use of lawful weapons systems—consistent with the applicable laws of war—for precision targeting of specific high-level belligerent leaders when acting in self-defense or during an armed conflict is not unlawful, and hence does not constitute "assassination."

Nasser Awlaki's lawyers did not take the position that Anwar Awlaki was an innocent man. Rather, they reasoned, if he was what the US government alleged he was—a terrorist and an operational member of al Qaeda—evidence should be presented that would hold up in a court of law. If what the administration was leaking to journalists about Awlaki's deep involvement in terror plots, including chemical attacks against the United States, was true, then why not indict Awlaki and demand his extradition from Yemen to face trial? "If someone poses a threat, if there's evidence against him, fine, charge him and give him due process," said Kebriaei, one of Awlaki's lawyers. "The president and the Defense Department or CIA, cannot just, on their own, determine in secret that these people are threats and we can not only detain them, but we can kill them."

The administration continued to leak intelligence it claimed proved Awlaki was an operational member of al Qaeda, and media coverage began referring to Awlaki as a leader or *the* leader of AQAP. When Awlaki's lawyers tried to challenge in court the government's claims that he was a leader of AQAP and was operational, the US government lawyers shut it down. The government's "attorney did walk into court and open with: 'The context of this case is that we're talking about a leader of AQAP and everything else is a state secret. We can't talk about the evidence, but you should know,'" Kebriaei recalled. "It can be maddening to hear the government make allegations that are completely unsupported by any real facts that we've seen and not have any access to that information, to be in this position of seeing that reporting [in the press] and not being able to respond. The Bush administration claimed a global detention authority in the context of this war on terror, and what the Obama administration is doing is actually extending that and claiming a global killing authority," including the right to kill American citizens.

ANWAR AWLAKI, meanwhile, was spending his days and nights on the run. He knew the Americans were actively trying to kill him. He would see drones and occasionally see missiles strike nearby. Awlaki had certainly become increasingly radical in his views of the United States, but from his perspective, it was America that had changed, not him. Not that long before, Awlaki had advocated voting for George W. Bush and praised America's freedoms. He spoke with passion when he condemned al Qaeda and the 9/11 attacks, and talked of Muslims peacefully coexisting with the United States. But between the global crackdown that followed 9/11 and the US government's campaign to hunt him down, something in Awlaki shifted, and he was no longer torn between allegiance to the country of his birth and his religion. "To the Muslims in America I have this to say: how can your conscience allow you to live in peaceful co-existence with the nation that is responsible for the tyranny and crimes committed against your own brothers and sisters? How can you have your loyalty to a government that is leading the war against Islam and Muslims?" Awlaki asked in one of his audio messages posted online. "Imperial hubris is leading America to its fate: a war of attrition, a continuous hemorrhage that would end with the fall and splintering of the United States of America."

Johari Abdul Malik, who succeeded Awlaki as imam of Dar al Hijrah mosque in Virginia, was dumbfounded. He remembered Awlaki as a moderate and as a Muslim leader who bridged two worlds deftly. "To go from that individual to the person that is projecting these words from Yemen is a shock," he said. "I don't think we read him wrong. I think something happened to him."

**"Martyrdom Is Why We Came Here, My Brother"**

YEMEN, 2009–2010—Early on in his stay in Yemen, Samir Khan lost his mobile phone. Such things happen to tourists and students the world over. But the stakes were higher for Khan. His phone was his only way of communicating with the people he had come to Yemen to find: the mujahedeen. Khan had the mobile number of a man he had been told could put him in touch with AQAP, and the two men had been texting and making plans to meet when Khan's phone went missing. The young Pakistani American panicked. "He was heartbroken, as this was the only means of communication between him and the mujahideen," recalled his friend Abu Yazeed, a self-professed jihadist. "Despite that, he never thought about turning back." Khan went to mosques hoping to find someone who could reconnect him. One night he was performing Ishaa, the evening prayer, when he felt a tap on his shoulder. "Are you Samir?" the man asked him. Khan nodded. "I am the brother to whom you have been texting," the man told him. Soon thereafter, Khan was packing his bags, leaving behind Sana'a and any pretense that he was there to teach English or study Arabic at one of its universities. He was on his way to study jihad with mujahedeen, who would embrace him as one of their muhajireen, or emigrants.

Khan felt he had been in the car "for what seemed like years," heading over the rough roads that one must cross to get from Sana'a to southern Yemen. The driver dispatched to take Khan to a mujahedeen camp had a nashid, a hymn, playing on repeat. It was called "Sir Ya Bin Laden." Khan had heard the homage to bin Laden before, but now that he was on his way to meet the warriors from AQAP, it had taken on a new significance. "Something had struck me at that moment. The nashid repeated lines pertaining to fighting the tyrants of the world for the purpose of giving victory to the Islamic nation. But it also reminded the listener that Shaykh Usama bin Ladin is the leader of this global fight," Khan recalled in an essay he wrote several months later. "I looked out the window at the tall mud houses below the beautiful sky and closed my eyes as the wind blew through my hair. I took a deep breath to let it all out." He thought, "I am an individual convinced that Islam's claim to power in the modern world is not going to be as easy as walking down a red carpet or driving through a green light. I am acutely aware that body parts have to be torn apart, skulls have to be crushed and blood has to be spilled in order for this to be a reality. Anyone who says otherwise is an individual who is not prepared to make sacrifices that heroes and champions make."

As they got closer to the camp, Khan gazed out the window at the rural landscape. "As my eyes passed over the mysterious twirls of the sand dunes, I was reminded of the enigma of jihad in the contemporary world. It's just absolutely enthralling to know that guerrillas can fight off global superpowers with the bare minimum resulting in great enemy losses, drainage of the enemy's economy and a rising popular support for the mujahidin."

Back in North Carolina, FBI agents showed up at Khan's house. "They came to know that Samir had left for Yemen," recalled his mother, Sarah Khan. "And they were asking how he went there and things like that, and if we have any contact with him. They were questioning us about [Samir] going to Yemen." The agents asked the Khans "whom he's been in contact with over there and stuff like that. We had been seeing different situations that had been appearing in the news, online and the papers about how the FBI has been keeping a tab on Muslims, so, we thought it was just one of those things." Sarah Khan had watched the news about the US cruise missile strikes in Yemen and the "underwear bomb" plot. As a parent with a son they believed was studying in Yemen, she told me, "of course it was very scary. It was a very scary moment for us." But, she reasoned, "Samir was at the university, so we didn't think that he was in any danger." But Samir was not at the university anymore. He was heading straight into the heart of an expanding US war against AQAP.

People don't just show up at an al Qaeda camp in Yemen and be greeted with open arms. There is a vetting process. But Khan was already a known quantity through his blogs and web magazine, and AQAP's leadership welcomed the prospect of an American jihadi among their ranks. Khan went through training in rural Yemen and was eager to see battle. "Samir's love for Martyrdom in Allah's sake was extraordinary," his friend recalled. Khan once sent him a text message that read: "Martyrdom is why we came here, my brother. We won't leave until we get what we came for." AQAP would eventually publish photos of Khan wielding weapons and practicing hand-to-hand combat, but the mujahedeen believed that Khan's greatest possible contribution to their cause lay in his role as a propagandist. When he eventually made it to an AQAP base, the Yemeni and Saudi jihadists he met listened to his stories of FBI surveillance and harassment by the US government. They reviewed his writings and previous work on his online magazines.

"I realized that he traveled [a] very long distance under very difficult circumstances, not to mention the fact that he was being wanted and hunted by the CIA," recalled Abu Yazeed. "His weapons to defend Islam were very simple; a laptop and a camera. However, he was loaded with ammunition. That ammunition was the creed of jihad in Allah's path." Khan's new friends found his broad, toothy smile infectious and would often ask him to laugh "in English." They "considered him a motivation and an inspiration for them since he crossed the ocean to support Islam's cause."

Although Khan was enthusiastic about getting weapons training, the leadership of AQAP assigned him to its media division. They wanted his help in creating an English-language publication that could spread their message to the Muslim diaspora. It was to be a glossy, well-produced magazine called *Inspire*. Khan had studied Internet technology during his stint in community college back in North Carolina and had already created several of his own websites, as well as an online magazine much like the one envisioned by AQAP. "After some time passed in the company of the mujahidin, I quickly acknowledged that success does not rely upon the job you undertake from nine to five, nor does it rely upon the wealth that you have accumulated, nor does it rely upon how far you have taken your studies in college. All of these things are respectable, but by being with the mujahidin, it helped open my eyes that our reason in life has nothing to do with any of these things," Khan remembered. "The only thing in the entire world that matters to me, more than ever before, is the condition of my heart when I die."

As Khan settled into life with AQAP, his main role would become "connecting and facilitating disparate groups of individuals online," said Aaron Zelin, a scholar who has studied and written about AQAP extensively. "He was [such] an important connective tissue and node that without him it is likely recruitment would have been more difficult, especially after Awlaki's site went down. He also understood how to connect with youth in the West without having pretension and as being a co-equal to show, 'Look, I'm an average guy, not even a religious scholar and I made it to the fields of jihad to fight the apostates and Zionist-Crusaders: so can you.'"

As the first issue of *Inspire* went into production, Khan did graphic design and editing, as well as some translation. He adopted more than one nom de guerre, among them al Qaqa al Amiriki and Abu Shidah, the Father of Harshness. "He—as I understood—wanted to choose the toughest of nicknames in order to terrorize the enemies of Islam," Abu Yazeed recalled. Khan poured himself into work on *Inspire* and studied the Arabic language with a passion. When colleagues tried to practice their English with him, Khan would respond in Arabic. "I cannot remember a time that we met except that he asked me something related to Arabic vocabulary," his friend remembered. "Every time I met him, I would realize an improvement in his Arabic. Over the time he stayed, he progressed a lot in the Arabic language to the point that you couldn't easily tell if he was an English speaking brother."

Khan became involved with AQAP at the very moment that it was ringing massive alarm bells in Washington. AQAP intended *Inspire* to promote its mission to an English-speaking audience and to encourage "lone wolf" jihadists in the West to conduct attacks, but it also played into the US propaganda campaign aimed at presenting AQAP as a grave threat. In English, AQAP's agenda was laid out for all to see. And, from the first issue, Anwar Awlaki would be a prominent commentator and religious analyst in the pages of *Inspire*.

There was very little published in *Inspire* that had not already been said much earlier in AQAP's Arabic-language publication, *Sada al-Malahim*. Now personnel at US intelligence agencies, which had a limited number of analysts fluent in Arabic, could read its statements in English. "By the time the first issue of *Inspire* came out, AQAP had already released thirteen issues of its Arabic-language magazine, which had far richer content on AQAP," said Zelin. *Inspire*'s publication, he told me, coincided "with AQAP pursuing its global ambitions more thoroughly in light of the Christmas Day plot. AQAP always wanted to hit the US. *Inspire* was a way to rally the Western sympathizers and to try and further bolster its roster so they can more easily plan attacks against the West."

The first issue of the magazine was released online, but it was hardly a smashing success. The sixty-seven-page issue only contained four actual pages of the magazine. The other sixty-three contained a computer code that, when deciphered, turned out to be cupcake recipes featured on the popular US daytime talk show *Ellen*, hosted by gay comedian Ellen DeGeneres. It is unclear how the file was corrupted, though some reports suggested it was a cyberattack by anti-AQAP hackers, MI-6 or the CIA itself.

Regardless, issue one of *Inspire* eventually hit the Web in uncorrupted format in June 2010. "Allah says: 'And inspire the believers to fight,'" read the opening line of the letter from *Inspire*'s unnamed editor. "It is from this verse that we derive the name of our new magazine." *Inspire*, the editor wrote, was "the first magazine to be issued by the al-Qaeda Organization in the English language. In the West; in East, West and South Africa; in South and Southeast Asia and elsewhere are millions of Muslims whose first or second language is English. It is our intent for this magazine to be a platform to present the important issues facing the ummah today to the wide and dispersed English speaking Muslim readership."

The issue of *Inspire* featured an "exclusive" interview with the head of AQAP, Nasir al Wuhayshi, also known as Abu Basir, as well as translated works from bin Laden and Zawahiri. It also included an essay praising Abdulmutallab, the failed underwear bomber. The magazine was well produced, with a layout that resembled a typical US teen magazine, though without fashionably dressed women and celebrities. Instead, it featured photos of children alleged to have been killed in US missile strikes and pictures of armed, masked jihadis. An article written under the byline AQ Chef and titled "Make a Bomb in the Kitchen of Your Mom," provided instructions on how to manufacture explosive devices from basic household goods. Another article gave detailed directions on how to download military-grade encryption software for sending e-mails and text messages.

Perhaps most disturbing, the magazine contained a "Hit List" of people who it alleged had created "blasphemous caricatures" of the Prophet Muhammad. In late 2005, *Jyllands-Posten*—the Danish newspaper that would later publish Morten Storm's story—commissioned a dozen cartoons of the Prophet, ostensibly to contribute to a debate about self-censorship within Islam. It had enraged Muslims across the world at the time, sparked massive protests and resulted in death threats and bomb threats against the newspaper. The hit list published by *Inspire* included magazine editors, anti-Muslim pundits who had defended the cartoons, as well as the novelist Salman Rushdie. But it also included Molly Norris, a Seattle-based cartoonist who initiated "Everybody Draw Mohammed Day." Norris said she did it in response to the US Comedy Central network's decision to edit out a scene in its popular animated program *South Park* that addressed the controversy, after receiving a threat.

*Inspire*'s hit list was accompanied by an essay penned by Awlaki encouraging Muslims to attack those who defame the image of Muhammad. "I would like to express my thanks to my brothers at Inspire for inviting me to write the main article for the first issue of their new magazine. I would also like to commend them for having this subject, the defense of the Messenger of Allah, as the main focus of this issue," Awlaki wrote. He then laid out a defense for assassinating those who engaged in blasphemy of Muhammad. "The large number of participants makes it easier for us because there are more targets to choose from in addition to the difficulty of the government offering all of them special protection." He continued:

But even then our campaign should not be limited to only those who are active participants. These perpetrators are not operating in a vacuum. Instead they are operating within a system that is offering them support and protection. The government, political parties, the police, the intelligence services, blogs, social networks, the media, and the list goes on, are part of a system within which the defamation of Islam is not only protected but promoted. The main elements in this system are the laws that make this blasphemy legal. Because they are practicing a "right" that is defended by the law, they have the backing of the entire Western political system. This would make the attacking of any Western target legal from an Islamic viewpoint....Assassinations, bombings, and acts of arson are all legitimate forms of revenge against a system that relishes the sacrilege of Islam in the name of freedom.

When *Inspire* was published, some within the US intelligence community panicked. The first concern was protecting the people who had been identified as targets for assassination. The FBI took immediate precautions to guard the Seattle cartoonist, whom they feared could be murdered. She eventually changed her name and moved. Law enforcement agencies in other countries took similar measures.

The "Hit List" embodied the fears that Awlaki would incite young Western Muslims to commit "lone wolf" acts of terror. *Inspire* magazine would become one of the primary US sources of intelligence on AQAP and Awlaki, with intelligence analysts scouring each new issue for clues about his whereabouts or potential new plots. "The more the US talked about *Inspire* and Anwar al-Awlaki, the more the media focused on the magazine and the man, which then resulted in AQAP promoting them more and more, essentially taking advantage of free advertising," recalled Gregory Johnsen, the Princeton University Yemen scholar. "It was a bit of a shock to see the US government's reaction to *Inspire*, as AQAP had been saying many of the same things for years—only they had been saying it in Arabic in the pages of *Sada al-Malahim*. When *Inspire* was first published, a lot of people in the US government who didn't have the tools to read *Sada al-Malahim* suddenly found out what AQAP had been saying, which, coming in the months after the attempted Christmas Day bombing in 2009, led to an overreaction and a sense of panic within certain agencies."

Awlaki and Khan seemed to take great pride in the reaction of the US government to *Inspire*. In subsequent issues, *Inspire* would highlight quotes from US officials condemning the magazine and reacting to the various threats published in its pages. Samir Khan was suddenly a star figure in the international jihadi scene. "Khan is widely believed by all serious scholars to be the editor of *Inspire* magazine. This is not only because of his articles being published in it, but because of the similarity between it and Khan's previous *Jihad Recollections* publication, which he edited and posted online prior to his trip to Yemen," said Zelin. In Yemen, Khan began to develop a close relationship with Awlaki, a man he had long admired from afar. "Khan is someone who clearly idolized Awlaki both for his preaching and for the stance he took with his life," said Johnsen. Eventually, he added, Khan would become a "sort of executive aide" to Awlaki. And Anwar Awlaki was putting himself out front in a clear alliance with AQAP. His connections to previous plots had been vague. Now he was openly encouraging assassinations of specific people around the world.

AQAP leader Nasir al Wuhayshi clearly saw value in the US obsession with Awlaki. So much so that he actually sent a message to Osama bin Laden proposing that he name Awlaki as the new head of AQAP. On August 27, 2010, bin Laden ordered his deputy Shaykh Mahmud, also known as Atiya Abdul Rahman, to relay a message to Wuhayshi. Bin Laden seemed to view Awlaki as an ally and a potentially valuable asset to al Qaeda's goals. The problem, bin Laden explained, was that Awlaki was an unknown quantity to al Qaeda central, a man who had yet to prove his mettle in actual jihad. "The presence of some of the characteristics by our brother Anwar...is a good thing, in order to serve Jihad," bin Laden wrote, adding that he wanted "a chance to be introduced to him more." Bin Laden explained, "Over here, we are generally assured after people go to the battlefield and are tested there." He asked Wuhayshi for "the resumé, in detail and lengthy, of the brother Anwar al-Awlaki," as well as a written statement from Awlaki himself explaining his "vision in detail." Wuhayshi, bin Laden asserted, should "remain in his position where he is qualified and capable of running the matter in Yemen."

Samir Khan relished his newfound fame and penned numerous essays holding up his own experience as an example for other young Westerners to join the jihad. "I am a traitor to America because my religion requires me to be one. A traitor can either be praiseworthy or despicable. The good and bad are defined by a certain political agenda in the eyes of someone," Khan wrote. "I am proud to be a traitor in America's eyes just as much as I am proud to be a Muslim; and I take this opportunity to accentuate my oath of allegiance *(bai'yah)* and the mujahidin of the Arabian Peninsula's bai'yah to the ferocious lion, the champion of jihad, the humble servant of God, my beloved Shaykh, Usama bin Ladin, may Allah protect him. Verily, he is the man that has shook the thrones of the tyrants of the world. We pledge to wage jihad for the rest of our lives until either we implant Islam all over the world or meet our Lord as bearers of Islam. And how reputable, adventurous and pleasurable is such a life compared to those who remain sitting, working from nine to five?"

## 41 The Persecution of Abdulelah Haider Shaye

YEMEN, SUMMER 2010—In the months after the al Majalah bombing, the young journalist Abdulelah Haider Shaye would not give up on the story. He regularly raised the issue on Al Jazeera and continued to report on other US strikes inside Yemen. He had interviewed Awlaki numerous times and had become famous inside and outside of Yemen as a major critic of the widening covert US war in Yemen. "He was focusing on how Saleh was using the al Qaeda card to gain more money and logistical support from the United States," recalled cartoonist Kamal Sharaf, Shaye's closest friend. "Abdulelah was the only person critical and speaking the truth about al Qaeda, so he had significance in the Arab world and in America." Shaye was working with the *Washington Post*, ABC News, Al Jazeera and many other major international media outlets, often producing stories that cast US policy in Yemen in a negative light.

In July 2010, seven months after the al Majalah attack, Shaye and Sharaf were out running errands. Sharaf stepped into a supermarket while Shaye waited outside. When Sharaf came out of the store, he told me, "I saw armed men grabbing him and taking him to a car." The men, it turned out, were Yemeni intelligence agents. They snatched Shaye, hooded him and took him to an undisclosed location. The agents, according to Sharaf, threatened Shaye and warned him against making further statements on TV. Shaye's reports on the bombing and his criticism of the US and Yemeni governments, Sharaf said, "pushed the regime to kidnap him. One of the interrogators told him, 'We will destroy your life if you keep on talking.'" Eventually, in the middle of the night, Shaye was dumped back onto a street and released. "Abdulelah was threatened many times over the phone by the Political Security agents and then he was kidnapped for the first time, beaten and investigated over his statements and analysis on the Majalah bombing and the US war against terrorism in Yemen," Shaye's Yemeni lawyer, Abdulrahman Barman, told me. "I believe he was arrested upon a request from the US."

Shaye responded to his abduction by going back on Al Jazeera and describing his own arrest. Mohamed Abdel Dayem, who headed the Committee to Protect Journalists's Middle East and North Africa program, happened to be in Yemen the night Shaye was arrested. Dayem was in the country to research a special tribunal that had been established by the Yemeni regime to prosecute journalists who were critical of the government. Two days before Shaye was arrested, Dayem had met the Yemeni journalist. "Immediately I could tell this was a very smart journalist and a journalist who really was willing to put a lot on the line to get the tough stories, because everybody can get the easy stories," he recalled. The night Shaye was arrested, Dayem was in the Sana'a studios of Al Jazeera preparing to do an interview when his phone rang. It was Shaye. "I'm on my way out of prison," Shaye told him. "I'm going to go home. I'm putting on a different jacket. This one has blood on it. I'll be there in twenty minutes." Dayem said that Shaye arrived at the studio and "spilled the beans on the air," describing his abduction and why he believed he was being targeted.

Around this time, the US government began privately telling major US media outlets that were working with Shaye that they should discontinue their relationships with him. One source inside a prominent US media organization told me that the government had warned the outlet that Shaye was using his paychecks to support al Qaeda. A US intelligence official told another journalist for a prominent US magazine that "classified evidence" indicated that Shaye was "cooperating" with al Qaeda. "I was persuaded that he was an agent," said the official. Just as it wanted Awlaki silenced, the US government wanted anyone who was putting out Awlaki's perspective or interviewing leaders of AQAP shut down.

When I met him at a café in Sana'a in 2011, Sharaf shook his head in disbelief at the notion that Shaye was pro–al Qaeda. "Abdulelah continued to report facts, not for the sake of the Americans or al Qaeda, but because he believed that what he was reporting was the truth and that it is a journalist's role to uncover the truth," Sharaf told me. "He is a very professional journalist," he added. "He is rare in the journalistic environment in Yemen where 90 percent of journalists write extempore and lack credibility." Shaye, he explained, is "very open-minded and rejects extremism. He was against violence and the killing of innocents in the name of Islam. He was also against killing innocent Muslims with the pretext of fighting terrorism. In his opinion, the war on terror should have been fought culturally, not militarily. He believes using violence will create more violence and encourage the spread of more extremist currents in the region."

In the meantime, Sharaf was encountering his own troubles with the Yemeni regime over his drawings of President Saleh and his criticism of the Yemeni government's war against the minority Houthi population in the north of Yemen. He had also criticized conservative Salafis. And his close friendship with Shaye put him at risk.

On August 16, 2010, Sharaf and his family had just broken the Ramadan fast when he heard shouting from outside his home: "Come out, the house is surrounded." Sharaf walked outside. "I saw soldiers I had never seen before. They were tall and heavy—they reminded me of American marines. Then, I knew that they were from the counterterrorism unit. They had modern laser guns. They were wearing American marine–type uniforms," he told me. They told Sharaf he was coming with them. "What is the accusation?" he asked. "They said, 'You'll find out.'"

As Sharaf was being arrested, Yemeni forces had surrounded Shaye's home as well. "Abdulelah refused to come out, so they raided his house, took him by force, beat him and broke his tooth," Sharaf said. "We were both taken blindfolded and handcuffed to the national security prison, which is supported by the Americans." They were separated and thrown in dark, underground cells, said Sharaf. "We were kept for about thirty days during Ramadan in the national security prison where we were continuously interrogated."

For that first month, Sharaf and Shaye did not see each other. Eventually, they were taken from the national security prison to Yemen's political security prison, where they were put in a cell together. Sharaf was eventually released, after he pledged to the authorities that he would not draw any more cartoons of President Saleh. Shaye would make no such deal.

Shaye was held in solitary confinement for thirty-four days with no access to a lawyer. His family did not even know where he had been taken or why. Eventually, his lawyers received a tip from a released prisoner that Shaye was in the political security prison, and they were able to see him. "When Abdulelah was arrested, he was put in a narrow dirty and foul-smelling bathroom for five days. I noticed that one of Abdulelah's teeth was extracted and another one was broken, in addition to the presence of some scars on his chest," recalled Barman. "There were a lot of scars on his chest. He was psychologically tortured. He had been told that all his friends and family members had left him and that no one had raised his case. He was tortured by false information."

On September 22, Shaye was eventually hauled into a court. Prosecutors asked for more time to prepare a case against him. A month later, he was locked in a cage in Yemen's state security court, which was established by presidential decree and had been roundly denounced by human and media rights groups as illegal and unfair. The Yemeni government called it a trial. "Yeah. The trial does not pass the laugh test, at all. And the court does not pass the laugh test," said Dayem, of the Committee to Protect Journalists. "I could not locate a single case that was tried in this specialized criminal tribunal...that met, even remotely, fair trial standards."

The judge read out a list of charges against Shaye. He was accused of being the "media man" for al Qaeda, recruiting new operatives for the group and providing al Qaeda with photos of Yemeni bases and foreign embassies for potential targeting. "The government filed many charges against him," said Barman. "Some of these charges were: joining an armed group aiming to target the stability and security of the country, inciting al Qaeda members to assassinate President Ali Abdullah Saleh and his son, recruiting new al Qaeda members, working as propagandist for al Qaeda and Anwar Awlaki in particular. Most of these charges carry the death sentence under Yemeni law." As the charges against him were read, according to journalist Iona Craig, a longtime foreign correspondent who reported regularly for the *Times* of London from Yemen, Shaye "paced slowly around the white cell, smiling and shaking his head in disbelief."

When the judge finished reading the charges against him, Shaye stood behind the bars of the holding cell and addressed his fellow journalists. "When they hid murderers of children and women in Abyan, when I revealed the locations and camps of nomads and civilians in Abyan, Shabwah and Arhab when they were going to be hit by cruise missiles, it was on that day they decided to arrest me," he declared. "You notice in the court how they have turned all of my journalistic contributions into accusations. All of my journalistic contributions and quotations to international reporters and news channels have been turned into accusations." As security guards dragged him away, Shaye yelled, "Yemen, this is a place where, when a young journalist becomes successful, he is viewed with suspicion."

## 42 The President Can Write His Own Rules

WASHINGTON, DC, AND YEMEN, LATE 2010—While US counterterrorism operations expanded in Yemen in the summer of 2010, Washington and other political and economic forces were drawing up plans for a neoliberal restructuring of Yemen's economy. Organized under the banner of "Friends of Yemen," the US and British governments joined with the European Union, the International Monetary Fund and some of Yemen's neighbors. "Progress against violent extremists and progress toward a better future for the Yemeni people will depend upon fortifying development efforts," US secretary of state Hillary Clinton said at an early meeting of the group in January 2010. This included what Aaron W. Jost, the National Security Council's director for Arabian Peninsula affairs, called "greatly expanded... economic and humanitarian assistance to the Yemeni people."

The Obama administration increased USAID funding, humanitarian assistance and "democracy promotion" funds for Yemen from $14 million two years earlier to $110 million in 2010. "There is no doubt AQAP is a serious threat to Yemen, the United States, and our allies," Jost asserted. "However, support for operations against AQAP is only one piece of the United States' strategy for Yemen." But as a condition of the increased aid Yemen was to receive, President Saleh was forced to accept IMF structural adjustments, among them "the gradual reduction in the level of Government subsidies on fuel." A declaration from the "Friends" openly acknowledged that "necessary economic reforms would have an adverse impact on the poor."

Washington and its allies made clear to Saleh that continued military aid was conditioned on his cooperation with the economic reforms. "The Yemeni people and the international community are both confronted by real threats from AQAP, and it may take years to decisively defeat it," Jost declared. "However, we believe that the future belongs to those who build, not to those who are focused on destruction. And the United States stands with the people of Yemen as they seek to build a more positive future and reject AQAP's efforts to kill innocent men, women and children."

Saleh's main priority was not fighting AQAP, but rather suppressing the

internal rebellions he faced from the Houthis and the southern secessionists. But in order to continue receiving the US military aid he needed for
these internal fights, he had to prove to Washington he was serious about
fighting AQAP. Colonel Lang, who spent years dealing with Saleh as US
defense attaché, said that Saleh was very weary of what he perceived as
an attempt by the Obama administration to apply the counterinsurgency
doctrine in Yemen but had to play the game to keep the military aid flowing. "Saleh doesn't really want us to get involved to the extent that the
full implications of that doctrine would imply, because then he would be
increasingly relegated to the position of a Karzai-like state—and, in fact,
whereas Afghan President [Hamid] Karzai has never been able to play the
game with sufficient skill, to manipulate all the factors to some end that
approximates something that he wants, Saleh has. With great skill," Lang
said at the time. He added that Saleh knew that the type of money allocated by the "Friends of Yemen" and USAID and for political reform would
be monitored by the United States "so that any graft that occurs does not
excessively benefit him and his cronies, and other things like that which
will tend to reduce his net power. So he's not gonna be really in favor of
that." But with the intense US focus on AQAP, Saleh's military aid lunch
ticket, he needed to play the game.

In August 2010, following the rash of killings of Yemeni military and
intelligence officials by the motorcycle assassins, Yemeni forces launched
a major offensive in the Lawdar District of Abyan, an alleged AQAP stronghold. In several days of gun battles, a dozen Yemeni soldiers were reportedly
killed, along with nineteen people the Yemeni government identified as al
Qaeda figures. At least three civilians were also killed, and scores of others
fled their homes. "Security forces have taught the terrorists of Al-Qaeda
a hard lesson and inflicted painful hits on them, forcing those terrorist
elements that tried to hide, to flee after dozens were killed and wounded,"
Yemen's deputy interior minister, General Saleh al Zaweri, declared.

That assessment was not shared in Washington. JSOC forces were scor-
ing occasional victories against AQAP, but Yemeni Special Operations
Forces were perceived as lazy and largely incompetent by their American
counterparts and Saleh's double-dealing often resulted in shoddy intelligence. In short, there was what senior US officials described as a "dearth
of solid intelligence" in Yemen. JSOC's forces were certainly more than
capable of finding, fixing and finishing targets, but those operations required solid intelligence. "All Land Rovers look pretty much alike," a
former high-ranking U.S. intelligence official familiar with operations in
Yemen told the *Washington Post*. "You have to have something that tells
you this is the one to follow." The CIA had historically culled personnel

from JSOC and other special operations units for lethal missions, but the ascent of JSOC within the Bush and Obama administrations had altered that process. JSOC, insiders told me, wanted to run point—and the CIA was not happy about it.

The day the Lawdar offensive was over, on August 25, the *Washington Post* and *Wall Street Journal* both ran front-page stories that were clearly based on leaks from the CIA and its allies in the administration. "For the first time since the Sept. 11, 2001, attacks, CIA analysts see one of al-Qaeda's offshoots—rather than the core group now based in Pakistan—as the most urgent threat to U.S. security," the *Post* story began. The *Wall Street Journal* added that the administration was considering plans to "mount a more intense targeted killing program in Yemen." The *Post* went on to quote an unnamed senior administration official as saying that AQAP was "on the upswing," adding that, between Pakistan and Yemen, "the relative concern ratios are changing. We're more concerned now about AQAP than we were before." The official said, "We are looking to draw on all of the capabilities at our disposal," describing plans for "a ramp-up over a period of months."

The leaks appeared to reflect a power play by the CIA to assert a greater role in Yemen operations, which had become dominated by JSOC. "You're not going to find bomb parts with USA markings on them," the senior official said, clearly referencing JSOC's December 2009 Tomahawk strike in al Majalah and the misinformed attack in Marib that killed the deputy governor on his negotiation mission. The official made it clear that the White House was considering a plan to deploy more CIA drones.

"The Agency has taken advantage of every criticism of the performance of JSOC as an argument to regain control over covert operations," said Colonel Lang, who spent his career working with both Special Operations Forces and the CIA, including operationally in Yemen. "The competition between the military clandestine services and the CIA is greater than ever before." Although the CIA was clearly seeking an advantage in its power struggle with JSOC over control of the Yemen ops, there was also a crucial strategic interest on the part of the administration in making a shift in the CIA's direction: placing JSOC forces under the sponsorship of the CIA would, under US law, allow "elite U.S. hunter-killer teams" to operate far more freely in Yemen without the consent of Yemen's government.

In September 2010, as Obama's senior counterterrorism adviser, John Brennan, visited Yemen, Saleh launched yet another offensive against AQAP, this time in the city of Hawta in Shabwah Province, sixty miles from the home of Anwar Awlaki. Led by CTU forces trained and armed by the United States, Yemeni commandos laid siege to the town, shelling it with artillery and launching helicopter attacks. Although the extent of the US role remains classified, military officials confirmed US forces were involved in a limited capacity. As thousands of people fled their homes, Brennan was in Sana'a on September 20 for meetings with Saleh. The timing of the offensive was classic Saleh, enabling him to point to a concrete, ongoing operation against AQAP in his meetings with Brennan. As the two men met, the Friends of Yemen group was preparing to hold ministerial-level talks in New York on aid to the country. According to a statement released by the National Security Council, Brennan and Saleh "discussed cooperation against the continuing threat of al-Qa'ida, and Mr. Brennan conveyed the United States' condolences to the Yemeni people for the loss of Yemeni security officers and citizens killed in recent al-Qa'ida attacks." Although Yemen's government publicly hailed its success in Hawta and Lawdar, the operations amounted to a failure, as the main al Qaeda targets of the raids in both places escaped and tribal rage increased against the government.

A MONTH AFTER MEETING WITH SALEH, Brennan received a late-night phone call on October 28, 2010, from his friend Prince Mohammed bin Nayef. Saudi intelligence, the prince said, had uncovered a plot by AQAP to bring down US cargo planes. The bombs, he said, were already in place. Shortly after 10:30 p.m., Brennan warned President Obama of a "potential terrorist threat" to the US homeland. Saudi intelligence provided US and British intelligence with tracking numbers for packages they believed contained explosives. By the time Brennan heard of the plot, one of the planes carrying the alleged bomb had already left Sana'a. The package was transferred to a UPS plane and flown to Germany, where it was transferred again before arriving at 2:13 a.m. local time at East Midlands Airport in Leicestershire, one hundred miles north of London. British security forces recovered the package, which was addressed to a synagogue in Chicago.

The package contained an office-sized printer cartridge equipped with a circuit board. Instead of toner, the cartridge contained white powder. Initial tests performed in Britain, including with bomb-sniffing dogs and explosive detection equipment, indicated it was not a bomb. The package was kept in Britain for further tests and the plane was cleared to continue its journey to Philadelphia. The suspicious package, meanwhile, was flown by helicopter to the Defense Science and Technology Laboratory at Fort Halstead for analysis. It was later revealed that the powder contained 400 grams of PETN, the same material used in Abdulmutallab's underwear device and in the attempt on Prince bin Nayef's life. The package was armed with an alarm clock on a Nokia mobile phone's circuit board. Scotland Yard subsequently said that had the bomb not been removed, "activation could have occurred over the eastern seaboard of the U.S.," with detonation set to occur at 5:30 a.m. Eastern time. A senior British counterterrorism official told the *Guardian* newspaper that the device was "one of the most sophisticated we've seen. The naked eye won't pick it up, experienced bomb officers did not see it, x-ray screening is highly unlikely to catch it." A second bomb was discovered in Dubai on board a FedEx plane. It contained 300 grams of PETN. Like the other package, it was addressed to a Jewish organization based in Chicago. Ironically, neither of the addresses was current. Investigators suspected that whoever sent the packages had obtained outdated information online.

The packages were sent to the Jewish organizations in Chicago but addressed to two infamous and long-dead historical figures. One was addressed care of Diego Deza, the brutal grand inquisitor who, for a period, led the Spanish Inquisition. The other was addressed to Reynald Krak, a French knight of the Second Crusade known for his mass murder of Muslims. Krak was eventually beheaded by Saladin, the Muslim warrior who defeated the Crusaders in the twelfth century.

On Friday, October 29, Americans watched as breaking news coverage showed US warplanes escorting a cargo plane to an emergency landing at JFK Airport. Images were broadcast of other planes being swept at Philadelphia and Newark Airports. And reports of more potentially dangerous packages spread. That night, President Obama said that the explosives had posed a "credible terrorist threat." In the end, none of the bombs detonated and the speculation of explosives aboard other planes proved to be just that. Once the Yemen connection was clear, there was no debate within the administration: all eyes focused on AQAP.

In November, AQAP published a "special issue" of *Inspire*. The cover featured a foggy image of a UPS cargo plane with the simple headline: "$4,200." That was the cost, according to AQAP, of the attempted bombings, which the group labeled "Operation Hemorrhage." The magazine featured photos purporting to show the printer cartridge bombs before they were shipped and articles outlining the objectives and technical details of the bombs. AQAP also claimed that it had succeeded in taking down a UPS plane a few months earlier, on September 3. "We have succeeded in bringing down the UPS plane but because the enemy's media did not attribute the operation to us we have remained silent so we may repeat the operation," the magazine stated. A UPS plane did indeed crash that day, killing two crew members. Investigators said the accident occurred after a fire broke out in the plane. US officials dismissed suggestions it was a terror attack. "We would like to ask: Why didn't the enemy reveal the truth about what happened with the downed UPS plane?" AQAP's statement read. "Is it because the enemy could not discover why the plane was brought down? Or was it because the Obama administration wanted to conceal the truth so it doesn't expose the failure of his administration especially...during an election season?" AQAP labeled September 3, "The day a tree fell into a forest that no one heard."

As for the attempted bombings in October, AQAP's "Head of Foreign Operations" wrote in *Inspire* that bringing down the planes would have been a bonus but that the "objective was not to cause maximum casualties but to cause maximum losses to the American economy. That is also the reason why we singled out the two U.S. air freight companies: FedEx and UPS for our dual operation." Noting that the US and other governments would likely spend substantial amounts of money reviewing and changing airport screening procedures, he wrote, "You either spend billions of dollars to inspect each and every package in the world or you do nothing and we keep trying again." He said they had selected addresses in Chicago because it was "Obama's city." The magazine also featured a picture of a beat-up copy of a Dickens book. It was a title that Awlaki had read in prison. "We were very optimistic about the outcome of this operation," the alleged head of foreign ops wrote. "That is why we dropped into one of the boxes a novel titled, *Great Expectations.*"

Four days after the cargo bombs were discovered, Yemen indicted Awlaki in absentia on charges unrelated to the bomb plot. The official charge was "incitement to kill foreigners and members of security services." The judge ordered prosecutors to hunt down Awlaki and bring him to justice dead or alive. Regardless of the specific charges against Awlaki, it was clear that the indictment was coordinated with Washington and intended to give legitimacy to the continued targeting and potential assassination of Awlaki while placing responsibility once again on the Yemenis.

JUDGE JOHN BATES, a 2001 appointee of President George W. Bush, heard oral arguments in *Al-Aulaqi v. Obama*, challenging the administration's placement of a US citizen on an assassination list. "How is it that judicial approval is required when the United States decides to target a U.S. citizen overseas for electronic surveillance, but that, according to defendants, judicial scrutiny is prohibited when the United States decides to target a U.S. citizen overseas for death?" the judge asked. The government's lawyers maintained that the matter of Anwar Awlaki was a state secret, was a national security policy determined by the president and did not belong in the courts. Judge Bates called the lawsuit "a unique and extraordinary case" in which "vital considerations of national security and of military and foreign affairs (and hence potentially of state secrets) are at play." Bates asked: Can a US citizen "use the U.S. judicial system to vindicate his constitutional rights while simultaneously evading U.S. law enforcement authorities, calling for 'jihad against the West,' and engaging in operational planning for an organization that has already carried out numerous terrorist attacks against the United States? Can the Executive order the assassination of a U.S. citizen without first affording him any form of judicial process whatsoever, based on the mere assertion that he is a dangerous member of a terrorist organization?" Judge Bates concluded, "These and other legal and policy questions posed by this case are controversial and of great public interest."

But Judge Bates dismissed the case on December 7, 2010, on procedural grounds, ruling that Anwar's father, Nasser, did not have standing to file suit on behalf of his son and that the case would not have survived a review of the "political questions" it raised regarding the president's authority to wage war. Judge Bates concluded that "the serious issues regarding the merits of the alleged authorization of the targeted killing of a U.S. citizen overseas must await another day."

Awlaki's lawyers were disappointed but not surprised by the ruling. The CCR and ACLU had spent eight years fighting the Bush administration on the very same issues, though they asserted that this case was more far-reaching in its implications. "If the court's ruling is correct, the government has unreviewable authority to carry out the targeted killing of any American, anywhere, whom the president deems to be a threat to the nation," said the ACLU's Jameel Jaffer after the ruling was announced. "It would be difficult to conceive of a proposition more inconsistent with the Constitution or more dangerous to American liberty." In a way, the Awlaki case was a microcosm of President Obama's evolving approach to counterterrorism, which was remarkably similar to that of his predecessor: the president can write his own rules.

# Al Qaeda's "Foothold in Somalia Has Probably Been Facilitated"

SOMALIA, 2010—While the legal battle played out over whether the United States could assassinate one of its own citizens, the White House's counterterrorism team was not just concerned with Awlaki or AQAP in Yemen. It was also confronting an increasingly broad-based threat in Somalia, thanks to a newly emboldened and unified Islamist movement there. The militant group al Shabab had signed an "agreement for unification" with Hassan Turki's Ras Kamboni militia, with the explicit aim of "establishing an Islamic state that will implement Shariah law." But it was the last point of their agreement that mattered most in US counterterrorism circles. "In order to restore the damaged dignity of Muslims, their political power, economic strength and military might, all Muslims in the region should be united and end the hostility among them created by colonial powers," the statement declared. "To prevent invasion by the international crusaders and the attacks they have carried out against our Muslim people, the Jihad in the Horn of Africa must be combined with the international Jihad led by the Al-Qaeda network and its Amir Sheikh Osama bin-Laden."

Al Shabab, in justifying its alliance with al Qaeda, conflated its embrace of the terror group with resistance against foreign aggression. The opportunity to paint itself that way was a gift that Osama bin Laden could only have dreamed of in the 1990s. And Washington's missteps and miscalculations had helped to deliver it. "The United States has launched air strikes to target high-level members of al-Shabab it believes have links to Al Qaeda. But experts say these air strikes have only increased popular support for al-Shabab. In fact, they argue that two of the only actions that could galvanize al-Shabab and increase its support within Somalia are additional air strikes by the United States, or a return of Ethiopian troops," a report by the Senate Foreign Relations Committee concluded in early 2010. "Al Qaeda is now a more sophisticated and dangerous organization in Africa," the report asserted, noting that al Qaeda's "foothold in Somalia has probably been facilitated by the involvement of Western powers and their allies."

Although al Shabab's jihad had, to that point, been confined to the borders of Somalia, the group would soon mark its formal declaration of unity with al Qaeda by hitting its enemies on their own territory.

SOMETHING HAPPENED to the Somali militia leader Ahmed Madobe during his two years in Ethiopian custody after JSOC nearly killed him in 2007. After reaching an agreement in 2009 with the Ethiopian and Somali governments that he would renounce al Shabab and actively fight them, Madobe was back in his region of Somalia. As he tells it, he had planned to go back to Jubba and try to figure out the best deal he could make. If it was with the Somali government, so be it. If it wasn't, well, once a guerrilla, always a guerrilla.

But when he returned to his region, Madobe discovered that it was no longer his. Madobe's mentor, Hassan Turki, had merged Ras Kamboni with al Shabab and pledged allegiance to al Qaeda. Madobe was given a choice by his former comrades: with us or against us. Madobe says he tried to negotiate a power-sharing agreement for the region, but al Shabab rejected it. So Madobe chose the only real option available to him. At least that is how he prefers to tell it. "The view I had about Ethiopia greatly changed, as did the one I had about international policy on Somalia," he told me. In early 2010, Madobe announced his forces were at war with al Shabab and supporting Somalia's government; and it was clear that he had forged a new relationship with the Ethiopians, who had long funded various Somali warlords and political figures. "We were fighting against the Ethiopians and the Americans and considered them enemies," he asserted. "But these guys from al Shabab are worse than them because they spoiled the image of Islam and our peoples' values. So now, the differences between me, the Ethiopians and the US are small in contrast with the differences I have with al Shabab."

Turki's alliance with al Shabab was of particular concern to the United States, as it gave the alliance ownership of the key port town of Kismayo. Control of that port, along with "the secondary ports of Marka and Baraawe...emerged as the most important source of income for [al Shabab]," according to a UN report. Al Shabab "generates between $35 million and $50 million per year from port revenues, of which at least $15 million is based on trade in charcoal and sugar." The United States wanted that cash flow cut off. So, the Americans began backing Ahmed Madobe, a former member of the Islamic Courts Union whom JSOC had tried to kill in 2007. Madobe had once been an ally of both al Shabab and Hasan Turki's Ras Kamboni militia. Madobe and his men began receiving "training and support" from US-backed Kenyan military forces. They rode around in new technicals and, during battles with al Shabab forces, received artillery backup from Kenyan forces, including military helicopters providing air support. Madobe would become one of the new generation of US-backed warlords drawn from the rubble of the Islamic Courts Union. He would not be the last.

IN 2010, THE WORLD CUP—the most famous sporting event in the world— was hosted by South Africa. It was the first time the final would be played in Africa, and the entire continent was transformed into one huge arena. Large screens were set up in fields and stadiums and every bar, restaurant and café broadcast the games. Uganda was no exception. On July 11, 2010, in the neighborhood of Kabalagala in the capital, Kampala, scores of people were watching the World Cup Final between the Netherlands and Spain at the Ethiopian Village restaurant. As the match reached halftime, the score was tied 0–0. Boom! An explosion rocked the restaurant, which was packed with mostly foreigners. Fifteen people were killed and scores wounded, including six Mennonite missionaries. With the match approaching its ninetieth minute, a few miles north at the Kyadondo Rugby Club in Nakawa, a second blast went off. It was followed by an explosion right at the base of the large screen where people were crowded around watching the match. In all, sixty-four people died from the Nakawa bombing, most of them Ugandans. A twenty-five-year-old US aid worker was also killed. A severed head found at the scene was reportedly that of a Somali national, believed by Ugandan authorities to be a suicide bomber. Another suicide vest was later found undetonated.

Immediately after the double bombings, speculation pointed toward al Shabab. But the group had never struck beyond its borders. Lower-ranking al Shabab members praised the attacks, with one saying he was "very happy," though they stopped short of taking responsibility. But on July 12, Sheikh Ali Mohamud Rage, al Shabab's spokesman, boldly proclaimed the group was behind the bombings. "We will carry out attacks against our enemy wherever they are," he said. "No one will deter us from performing our Islamic duty." He added: "We thank the mujahideens that carried out the attack. We are sending a message to Uganda and Burundi, if they do not take out their AMISOM troops from Somalia, blasts will continue and it will happen." While Uganda and Somalia's neighbors went on a state of high alert, back in Mogadishu al Shabab was preparing for a major campaign to take down the weak government AMISOM was protecting.

THE FIRST TWO YEARS of the Obama administration's foreign policy were largely centered on Afghanistan and Iraq—and embroiled in controversy over the prison camp at Guantánamo—but by 2010, Somalia was becoming a major area of concern. JSOC had conducted a handful of operations in the country, most notably the operation that had killed Saleh Ali Saleh Nabhan, the head of al Qaeda in East Africa. But as the United States escalated its attacks, al Shabab seemed to become more daring. Every week, the group took more territory. Al Shabab controlled the largest swath of land of any al Qaeda affiliate in the world. Somalia received the dubious honor of being named the terrorism capital of the world in Maplecroft's Global Terrorism Risk Index for 2010, with a harrowing 556 terrorist attacks between June 2009 and June 2010, which killed 1,437 people. The White House's rhetoric against al Shabab began to turn markedly more bellicose, as Obama issued Executive Order 13536, declaring a "national emergency to deal with [the Somalia] threat." Among the most serious concerns identified by the US counterterrorism community was the issue of foreign fighters, particularly those from the United States who had been used as suicide bombers.

On August 5, 2010, Attorney General Eric Holder announced the unsealing of the indictments of fourteen US-based individuals accused of giving material support to al Shabab. "These indictments and arrests—in Minnesota, Alabama, and California—shed further light on a deadly pipeline that has routed funding and fighters to al Shabab from cities across the United States," Holder said. "While our investigations are ongoing around the country, these arrests and charges should serve as an unmistakable warning to others considering joining or supporting terrorist groups like al Shabab: if you choose this route you can expect to find yourself in a U.S. jail cell or a casualty on the battlefield in Somalia." Mogadishu residents began reporting seeing surveillance planes regularly hovering over the capital.

The Obama administration was ratcheting up its operations. But so, too, was al Shabab.

On August 22, 2010, al Shabab launched what the UN Monitoring Group on Somalia and Eritrea called "its most significant military campaign since May 2009." Sheikh Rage held a press conference on August 23 to announce a "massive war" to wipe out the US-backed Somali government once and for all.

Al Shabab had been mobilizing for months, in anticipation of a much-touted AMISOM offensive that would not materialize until much later. With a force numbering between 2,500 and 5,000 militants, al Shabab mounted direct assaults on Villa Somalia and other seats of government power and attempted to beat back Somali government and AMISOM forces in key districts of Mogadishu. At least eighty people were killed and scores wounded during the week of intense violence from August 23 to August 30. Other major incidents included an attack on the Presidential Palace on August 30 and a deadly roadside bomb the next day. Two days into this "Ramadan Offensive," on August 24, three antigovernment militiamen disguised as Somali government soldiers laid siege to the Muna Hotel, which lies a few hundred yards from Villa Somalia. The attack, which involved two suicide bombers, killed at least thirty-three people, including several parliamentarians. Following the attack, Somali government forces tied the remains of one of the al Shabab attackers to the back of a vehicle and drove it through the town.

"This is a particularly outrageous act during the Islamic month of Ramadan," said John Brennan, Obama's top counterterrorism adviser, on the day of the hotel attack. "The United States will continue to partner with those who oppose terrorism, extremism and violence in all forms, and will continue to work very closely with those in Africa, particularly in the Horn of Africa in Somalia."

Two weeks later, on September 9, 2010, the airport was hit by a dual car bombing during a visit from an international delegation that included the UN special representative for the secretary general and the special representative of the African Union's chairman. These high-level officials were unscathed, though the bombings—and ensuing fighting—claimed the lives of two AMISOM troops and at least five civilians. According to the terror monitoring group Critical Threats, 23,000 Mogadishu residents had been displaced by the fighting by the end of September.

Serious battles continued throughout Mogadishu in September. Al Shabab made impressive gains in the opening salvos of the offensive, although the operation ultimately spurred AMISOM to deploy 2,000 additional troops. The offensive was eventually repelled. A significant factor in al Shabab's failure, according to the UN Monitoring Group, may have been "the overdependence of [al Shabab] on child soldiers who were unable to hold their own against AMISOM troops or, to a lesser degree," Somali government forces and pro-government militias. Al Shabab reportedly suffered major casualties, both foot soldiers and higher-ranking commanders, and in some cases lost territory to the pro-government forces. In the end, the al Shabab offensive partially succeeded in further destabilizing a Somali government that was already in critical condition. It also spurred an internal debate within the nexus of al Shabab and al Qaeda about tactics and the wisdom of trying to hold territory or overrun the capital city. In the meantime, the CIA was expanding its presence in Mogadishu.

**44** "Anwar Awlaki...
Definitely Has a Missile in His Future"

YEMEN, 2011—In January 2011, Yemeni journalist Abdulelah Haider Shaye was convicted of terrorism-related charges by a Yemeni court and sentenced to five years in prison, followed by two years of restricted movement and government surveillance. Throughout his trial, Shaye refused to recognize the legitimacy of the court and declined to present a legal defense. Human Rights Watch said the specialized court where Shaye was tried "failed to meet international standards of due process," and his lawyers argued that the little "evidence" that was presented against him relied overwhelmingly on fabricated documents. "What happened was a political not judicial decision. It has no legal basis," said Abdulrahman Barman, Shaye's lawyer, who boycotted the trial. "Having witnessed his trial I can say it was a complete farce," said Iona Craig, the *Times* of London journalist.

Several international human rights groups condemned the trial as a sham and an injustice. "There are strong indications that the charges against [Shaye] are trumped up and that he has been jailed solely for daring to speak out about US collaboration in a cluster munitions attack which took place in Yemen," said Amnesty International's Philip Luther.

There is no doubt that Shaye was reporting on stories that both the Yemeni and US governments wanted to suppress. He was also interviewing people Washington was hunting, namely, Anwar Awlaki. Although the US and Yemeni governments alleged that he was a facilitator for al Qaeda propaganda, close observers of Yemen disagreed. "It is difficult to overestimate the importance of his work," said Gregory Johnsen, the Yemen scholar at Princeton University who had been communicating with Shaye since 2008. He told me, "Without Shaye's reports and interviews we would know much less about Al Qaeda in the Arabian Peninsula than we do, and if one believes, as I do, that knowledge of the enemy is important to constructing a strategy to defeat them, then his arrest and continued detention has left a hole in our knowledge that has yet to be filled."

After Shaye was convicted and sentenced, tribal leaders pressured President Saleh to issue a pardon. "Some prominent Yemenis and tribal sheikhs visited the president to mediate in the issue and Saleh agreed to release and pardon him," recalled Barman. "We were waiting for the release of the pardon—it was printed out and prepared in a file for the president to sign and announce the next day." Word of the impending pardon leaked in the Yemeni press. That day, February 2, 2011, President Saleh received a call from President Obama. The two discussed counterterrorism cooperation and the battle against AQAP. At the end of the call, Obama "expressed concern" over the release of Shaye, whom Obama said "had been sentenced to five years in prison for his association with AQAP." In fact, Shaye had not yet been released at the time of the call, but Saleh did have the pardon for him prepared and was ready to sign it. It would not have been unusual for the White House to express concern about Yemen's allowing AQAP suspects to go free. Suspicious prison breaks of Islamist militants in Yemen had been a regular occurrence over the preceding decade, and Saleh had been known to exploit the threat of terrorism to leverage counterterrorism dollars from the United States. But this case was different: Abdulelah Haider Shaye was not an Islamist militant or an al Qaeda operative. He was a journalist. After the call from Obama, Saleh ripped up the pardon.

"Certainly Shaye's reports were an embarrassment for the US and Yemeni government, because at a time when both governments were seeking and failing to kill key leaders within AQAP, this single journalist with his camera and computer was able to locate these same leaders and interview them," Johnsen told me. "There is no publicly available evidence to suggest that Abdulelah was anything other than a journalist attempting to do his job, and it remains unclear why the US or Yemeni government refuse to present the evidence they claim to possess."

Shaye staged a brief hunger strike to protest his imprisonment, ending it after his family expressed concerns about his deteriorating health. While international media organizations, including the Committee to Protect Journalists, the International Federation of Journalists and Reporters Without Borders, called for Shaye's release, his case received scant attention in the United States. Yemeni journalists, human rights activists and lawyers charged that he remained in jail at the request of the White House. State Department spokesperson Beth Gosselin told me the United States wanted him kept behind bars. "We remain concerned about Shaye's potential release due to his association with Al Qaeda in the Arabian Peninsula. We stand by the president's comments." When asked whether the US government should present evidence to support its claims about Shaye's association with AQAP, Gosselin told me, "That is all we have to say about this case."

When *Times* of London journalist Iona Craig questioned the US ambassador to Yemen, Gerald Feierstein, about Shaye's case, she said Feierstein laughed at the question before answering. "Shaye is in jail because he was facilitating al Qaeda and its planning for attacks on Americans and therefore we have a very direct interest in his case and his imprisonment," Feierstein said. When Craig mentioned the shock waves it had sent through the journalism community in Yemen, Feierstein replied, "This isn't anything to do with journalism, it is to do with the fact that he was assisting AQAP and if they [Yemeni journalists] are not doing that they don't have anything to worry about from us."

For many journalists in Yemen, the publicly available "facts" about how Shaye was "assisting" AQAP indicated that simply interviewing al Qaeda–associated figures, or reporting on civilian deaths caused by US strikes, was a crime in the view of the US government. "I think the worst thing about the whole case is that not only is an independent journalist being held in proxy detention by the US," said Craig, "but that they've successfully [intimidated] other Yemeni journalists investigating air strikes against civilians and, most importantly, holding their own government to account. Shaye did both of those things." She added, "With the huge increase in government air strikes and US drone attacks recently, Yemen needs journalists like Shaye to report on what's really going on."

ANWAR AWLAKI'S BLOG had been shut down by the US government and the "Internet Imam" had no presence on the Web except for his essays in *Inspire* magazine. The one journalist who had dared to interview him was locked up. Now the White House wanted to finish the job. As it moved forward with its plans to assassinate Awlaki, the White House dispatched the US government's top lawyer, Attorney General Eric Holder, for a high-profile television interview on ABC's flagship morning show, *Good Morning America*. The interview was advertised as a "Blunt Warning on Terror Attacks," with a banner proclaiming that the threat of "Home Grown Terror" was causing the attorney general "Sleepless Nights." Holder said, "What I am trying to do in this interview is to make people aware of the fact that the threat is real, the threat is different, the threat is constant." He added, "The threat has changed from simply worrying about foreigners coming here, to worrying about people in the United States, American citizens—raised here, born here, and who for whatever reason, have decided that they are going to become radicalized and take up arms against the nation in which they were born." As images of Anwar Awlaki appeared, a headline flashed on screen: "New Top Terror Worry: Cleric Who Rivals Bin Laden."

The reporter brought up the "Underwear Bomber" who tried to bring down the Northwest Airlines flight on Christmas Day and the cargo plane bomb plots. Awlaki is "an extremely dangerous man. He has shown a desire to harm the United States, a desire to strike the homeland of the United States," Holder said. "He is a person who—as an American citizen—is familiar with this country and he brings a dimension, because of that American familiarity, that others do not." The danger Awlaki posed to the United States, Holder said, was an ability to incite potential terrorists to act. "The ability to go into your basement, turn on your computer, find a site that has this kind of hatred spewed...they have an ability to take somebody who is perhaps just interested, perhaps just on the edge, and take them over to the other side," he said. Awlaki "would be on the same list with bin Laden." The reporter asked Holder whether the United States preferred to capture Awlaki and put him on trial or to kill him outright. "Well, we certainly want to neutralize him. And we will do whatever we can in order to do that," Holder replied.

Awlaki had now achieved epic status as the top US outlaw across the globe. The lawyers from the ACLU and Center for Constitutional Rights who were fighting to stop the government from killing Awlaki were mystified that the government would present no evidence to back up the claims Holder and other officials were publicly making in the media and through leaks to a select group of journalists. "Even if what [Awlaki] is saying is criminal, charge him, try him. That's still not a reason to send a drone into Yemen and kill him," Pardiss Kebriaei, one of his lawyers, told me. "So whatever people may think, and whatever he may be saying, even if it has crossed the line, the point here is that the government cannot just determine, on the basis of some vague allegation of a threat, that he should be killed without due process."

The Obama administration disagreed.

The time clock in the game of cat-and-mouse with US drones and Awlaki was running out. Obama was deploying teams from JSOC and the CIA to hunt him down and kill him. Former Navy Intelligence officer Malcolm Nance told me at the time that Awlaki was "dangerous on a strategic scale" and that he "definitely has a missile in his future. You cannot allow [him] to shape the battlefield ideologically and turn that into combat capacity."

Soon after the cargo bomb plot was foiled, British media outlets reported that British SAS forces were operating in Yemen alongside JSOC and Yemen's CTU "in missions to kill or capture" AQAP leaders. In February 2011, the National Counterterrorism Center's director, Michael Leiter, briefed Congress on the top threats faced by the United States worldwide. "Al Qaeda in the Arabian Peninsula, with Al-Awlaki as a leader within that organization, is certainly the most significant risk to the U.S. homeland," he declared before the House Homeland Security Committee. "Al-Awlaki is the most well-known English-speaking ideologue who is speaking directly to folks here in the homeland."

The former DIA Yemen analyst Joshua Foust characterized Obama's response at the time like this: "He immediately sent drones and special operations guys to Yemen. It was immediately, 'Let's send JSOC.' Send in the Ninjas." Without providing details, which he said were classified, Foust asserted that he had seen targeted killing operations conducted that he believed were warranted and that he did not believe such strikes were "theoretically a bad thing." Foust, however, told me he was deeply concerned about the standards that were being used to determine who would be targeted for killing. "Frankly, most of the time when I was working on Yemen was spent arguing" with Special Operations Command-Yemen and other DIA analysts "about evidentiary standards," he said. "The evidentiary standard for actually killing people off, to me, is frighteningly low. I think it's like three separate corroborated HUMINT reports, and that's it? In a court of law, that only amounts to hearsay. I don't understand how people are that comfortable with killing people on evidence that thin." He added, "If you are going to murder someone, you need to have a very good reason to do it, and you need to have absolutely unequivocal evidence that this is necessary, and will materially advance our interests. And that just doesn't happen." Eventually, Foust said, his branch chief at the DIA "told me to back off and shut up."

# 45 The Curious Case of Raymond Davis: Act I

PAKISTAN, 2011—The burly thirty-six-year-old American would have blended in perfectly in his small hometown of Big Stone Gap, nestled in the mountainous countryside of rural southwest Virginia. With his checkered flannel shirt and blue jeans and scruffy, graying stubble, perhaps the only unusual thing about him would have been his choice of vehicle: a white Honda Civic rather than a pickup truck. But on January 27, 2011, Raymond Davis was not driving around Big Stone Gap, Virginia. He was half a world away, stuck in traffic in the chaotic streets of Pakistan's second-largest city, Lahore. There, the Honda Civic blended in perfectly. It was a local rental car and bore a Lahore plate registered as LEC-10/5545.

The full details of what happened at the Mozang Chowk intersection that day may never be known. And who exactly Raymond Davis is and what he was doing in Lahore—or in Pakistan in general—is even murkier. Within moments of Davis's vehicle coming to a stop, three people would be dead, the American would be on his way to a notorious Lahore jail, mobs of angry Pakistanis would be calling for his death and the most significant diplomatic crisis between the Pakistani and American governments since the 1979 burning and ransacking of the US Embassy in Islamabad would be in full swing.

If the official version of that day's events, as provided by Davis and senior US officials all the way up to President Obama, is to be believed, then Raymond Davis was working at the US Consulate in Lahore, a bureaucrat who stamped passports and performed administrative duties—essentially, a pencil pusher—who found himself at the wrong place at the wrong time in a very dangerous city. According to this version of the story, Davis was the victim of an attempted armed robbery by two assailants who trailed him after Davis made a withdrawal from an ATM. As Davis sat in traffic, the would-be robbers pulled in front of him on a motorbike, one of them brandishing a weapon. Davis, fearing for his life, pulled out his .9mm semiautomatic Glock pistol and shot the men through the front windshield of his car in self-defense. After a brief car chase, Davis was arrested by the Punjab police. He held in his possession a diplomatic passport, entitling him to diplomatic immunity. President Obama called Davis "our diplomat." Under the Vienna Conventions, no criminal charges could lawfully be filed against him in Pakistan, and Davis should have been handed back to US custody. Case closed.

To accept this version of the story would require believing that an administrative staffer at the consulate would, by chance, be so cool-headed and so skilled with a Glock that he would react with an assassin's precision to an attempted robbery, deftly taking down two assailants by firing his weapon from behind the steering wheel through the windshield of his car. That would be a remarkable feat for a "technical adviser" or a member of the "administrative staff," as US officials characterized Davis. Never mind that US diplomats in Pakistan are not authorized to carry weapons.

This, of course, is not the full story. In fact, the official version may actually be void of any substantial truth—save the obvious: that an American named Raymond Allen Davis shot dead two Pakistanis in broad daylight at an intersection in Lahore. The most vital pieces of this story are not Raymond Davis's diplomatic passport, what type of visa he possessed or that the United States publicly owned him as a diplomat once he was arrested. Those are details of a cover story, part of which was preconceived and part of which was cobbled together on the fly.

The Kot Lakhpat Jail on the outskirts of Lahore is home to scores of suspected militants and accused terrorists—men who would love nothing more than to have a chance in the dark of night to slit the throat of a suspected American spy. It was this jail where Raymond Davis was ultimately taken after a brief car chase through Lahore that ended in his apprehension by local police at the Old Anarkali Bazaar. Davis was not placed in the general population, but rather in an isolation cell in the jail's "high security zone." Some twenty-five suspected "jihadis" were transferred out of the jail once Davis arrived. For extra measure, the paramilitary Punjab Rangers were brought in to ring the wing of the jail. Although it was portrayed as a safety measure to protect Davis, it also served another purpose—ensuring that no one could break the American free. Pakistani intelligence knew things about Davis that inspired fears of that happening.

Soon after his arrest, Davis was brought into an interrogation room. His interrogation was captured in a grainy film shot by someone in the room. "I need to tell the embassy where I am," Davis insisted. "Just tell me the street." "You're from America?" someone shouted. "Yeah," Davis responded. Still wearing his US government ID badges around his neck, Davis lifted them one by one to show his interrogators. "You belong to American embassy?" one of them asked. "No. It's [the] Consulate General. It's not an ambassador—in here, Lahore. I just work as a consultant there," Davis responded, adding that he worked with the Regional Affairs Office, the RAO. They offered Davis a glass of water and Davis instead asked for a bottle of water. "Oh, pure water!" one of his interrogators exclaimed, sparking laughter in the room. "No money, no water," the man added, inspiring more laughs. The questioning continued. Davis eventually signed a statement affirming his story that the shooting was in self-defense and the dead men were robbers. Davis repeatedly asked for his passport, which he claimed would show he was a diplomat. "Can you search the car for my passport?" Davis asked, adding that it might be under the seat or might have fallen on the road when he was arrested.

The Pakistani authorities were indeed searching Davis's car, but his passport would be the least interesting item they'd discover. They had already recovered Davis's Glock .9mm with a stock of ammunition, including five magazines. In the vehicle, they also found two empty clips of ammo for the .9mm and another semiautomatic weapon, also with ammo. As the search continued of Davis and his car, they uncovered a cache of supplies that would seriously undermine the credibility of claims that Davis was a diplomat or a mere technical staffer at the consulate. Among the items: night-vision equipment, multiple IDs, several ATM cards, masks, a make-up kit used for disguising identity, a survival kit, a telescope, a sophisticated GPS device, a forehead-mounted flashlight, infrared equipment, a satellite phone and various wire cutters and knives. He also had an airline ticket. A check of the numbers on his multiple mobile phones revealed calls to twenty-seven militants from the terrorist group Lashkar-e-Jhangvi and Tehrik-e-Taliban, the Pakistani Taliban, according to Pakistani law enforcement sources quoted by the *Express Tribune*. On the memory card of Davis's camera, investigators found photos of religious schools and government and military institutions near the Indian border. They also found an ID showing Davis as a US Department of Defense contractor.

Meanwhile, reporters in the United States tracked down Davis's wife, Rebecca, at their home in Highlands Ranch outside Denver, Colorado. She directed them to a phone number provided to her by the US government. It was a number at CIA headquarters in Langley, Virginia.

During his interrogation, Davis told his inquisitors that he had come from the American Consulate when the attempted robbery took place. But according to the GPS device in his car, he had come from a private residence in the upscale Scotch Corner Upper Mall in eastern Lahore. "The accused has concealed the fact," a police report later noted. "He refused to reply to any question during investigations, saying the American consulate had forbidden him to answer any question." The house from which Davis departed earlier that day, if the recovered GPS data can be trusted, was well known to Pakistan's spy agency.

"BOY, WE'RE IN A WORLD OF HURT!" Lieutenant Colonel Anthony Shaffer recalled thinking the moment he heard of Davis's arrest. "The spy game between the ISI and CIA has gotten much worse." Shaffer, a veteran clandestine operator who had worked for the CIA and the Defense Intelligence Agency on highly classified operations, coordinated the Human Intelligence program in Afghanistan in the early stages of the war there and planned covert incursions into Pakistan. He knew how high the stakes were when Davis was taken into custody by the Pakistanis. "The Obama Administration, senior level, probably didn't know all of the details of what was going on," Shaffer said.

Long before the shooting at Mozang Chowk, Pakistan's Inter-Services Intelligence spy agency knew Raymond Davis was not a diplomat and that he wasn't sweating it out in the US Consulate stamping passports.

Davis had arrived in Pakistan a week before the Lahore shooting, but that was not his first time in the country. He was a seasoned Special Forces operator, an ex–Green Beret who served as a Special Operations weapons sergeant. His last assignment in the military was with the 3rd Special Forces Group based at Fort Bragg, where JSOC is headquartered. In 2003, as the Iraq occupation was swinging into full gear, Davis left the military to become a private contractor, a move that would send him straight to the heart of US covert and clandestine operations. His first known trip to Pakistan was in December 2008, when he began working for the notorious private security firm Blackwater on a secret CIA contract. His job as a contractor for the Agency's Global Response Staff (GRS) was to provide protection for CIA operatives deployed to Pakistan as part of the ever-widening presence of Agency personnel coordinating Washington's covert war there. The gig often put him in direct proximity to case officers meeting with secret sources or preparing sensitive operations. His official cover, as a regional affairs officer at the embassy, was a common cover for CIA operatives and contractors.

While Davis was working for Blackwater, the company was at the center of the CIA's most sensitive covert operations in Pakistan, helping to run its drone bombing campaign and targeted killing and capture operations. Blackwater, which had long been used by the Bush administration as an "unattributable" force that could conduct off-the-books operations cloaked in secrecy and layers of subcontracts, had its tentacles in almost every aspect of US covert ops. Not only was the company working for the CIA on its assassination program, but it also worked closely with the Joint Special Operations Command. While at Blackwater, Davis was at the nexus of the key organizations running the covert campaign.

Assigned to the company's CIA security detail, Davis moved between

Islamabad, Lahore and Peshawar. According to a former JSOC staffer who worked on its classified operations in Afghanistan and Pakistan, while Davis was working as a contractor for the CIA, he was approached by JSOC and asked to simultaneously work on its operations in Pakistan, utilizing his more palatable CIA cover. "Davis was 'vanilla' Special Forces, not a black ops guy," said the source. "There is nothing cooler for those guys than being approached by JSOC and being asked to do something for them. It was like a pro bono side gig for JSOC."

It was the beginning of Davis's foray into the muddiest realm of covert US operations in Pakistan. Davis had worked with Blackwater in Pakistan until August 2010. In September of that year, he became a free agent and signed a contract worth $200,000 for "Overseas Protective Services." As a contract vehicle, he used a company called Hyperion Protective Services, LLC, which described itself as providing "loss and risk management professionals." It was registered at an address in Las Vegas. Davis and his wife were listed, along with one other person, as its officers. The address was actually a post office box in a UPS store in a strip mall next to a Super Cuts barbershop. Davis returned to Pakistan.

The former JSOC staffer said that Davis helped to "wash" money and to establish safe houses for JSOC personnel, in addition to his work for the CIA. "All over the world we have people that, literally, are peripheral to policy and are just in-country to collect human intelligence or to facilitate special ops or espionage," he said. That is, at least in part, what Davis was doing in Pakistan. His various roles, some legit, some covers and some covers within covers—diplomat, technical adviser, Blackwater contractor, CIA bodyguard, Green Beret, JSOC asset—suggest that his story and that of the secret US war in Pakistan are far more complicated, and less benign, than official accounts have led us to believe.

That someone like Davis would end up working with JSOC is hardly a stretch. Many Blackwater operatives—quite a few of whom were former Special Ops or Special Forces—who originally went to Pakistan as security contractors eventually started working with JSOC on its targeted kill and capture operations. "The Blackwater individuals have the experience. A lot of these individuals are retired military, and they've been around twenty to thirty years and have experience that the younger Green Beret guys don't," said retired lieutenant colonel Jeffrey Addicott, a well-connected military lawyer who served as senior legal counsel for US Army Special Forces. "They're known entities. Everybody knows who they are, what their capabilities are, and they've got the experience. They're very valuable."

Special Ops veterans "make much more money being the smarts of these operations, planning hits in various countries and basing it off their experience in Chechnya, Bosnia, Somalia, Ethiopia," said a US military intelligence source. "They were there for all of these things, they know what the hell they're talking about." He added: "They hire back people that used to work for them and had already planned and executed these [types of] operations."

When exactly this began in Pakistan is unclear. Blackwater had a presence along the Afghan-Pakistan border dating back to April 2002, when it won its first "black" contract to protect CIA operations in Afghanistan in the early stages of the US war. It also held diplomatic security, logistical and CIA contracts in Pakistan. According to a former senior Blackwater executive and the military intelligence source, the relationship with JSOC intensified after President Bush authorized an expansion of Special Ops activities in Pakistan.

I asked the former senior Blackwater executive, who had extensive experience in Pakistan, for confirmation of what the military intelligence source told me—that Blackwater forces were not actively killing people in Pakistan, but rather supporting JSOC and the CIA in doing so. "That's not entirely accurate," he replied. He concurred with the military intelligence source's description of the JSOC and CIA programs, but he pointed to another role he said Blackwater played in Pakistan, not for the US government but for Islamabad. He said Blackwater worked on a subcontract for Kestral Logistics, a powerful Pakistani firm that specialized in military logistical support, private security and intelligence consulting. It was staffed with former high-ranking Pakistani army and government officials. Although Kestral's main offices were in Pakistan, it also had branches in several other countries. Kestral did a robust business in defense logistics with the Pakistani government and other nations, as well as top US defense companies. Blackwater's founder, Erik Prince, had a "pretty close relationship" with Kestral CEO Liaquat Ali Baig, according to the former Blackwater executive. "They've met many times and struck a deal, and they [offer] mutual support for one another." Working with Kestral, the former executive said, Blackwater provided convoy security for Defense Department shipments destined for Afghanistan that would arrive in the port at Karachi. Blackwater would guard the supplies as they were transported overland from Karachi to Peshawar and then west through the Torkham border crossing, the most important supply route for the US military in Afghanistan.

According to the former executive, Blackwater operatives also integrated with Kestral's forces in sensitive counterterrorism operations in the North-West Frontier Province, where they worked in conjunction with the Pakistani Interior Ministry's paramilitary force, known as the Frontier Corps (alternately referred to as "frontier scouts"). The Blackwater personnel were technically advisers, but the former executive said that the line was often blurred in the field. Blackwater was "providing the actual guidance on how to do [counterterrorism operations] and Kestral's folks are carrying a lot of them out, but they're having the guidance and the overwatch from some BW guys that will actually go out with the teams when they're executing the job," he said. "You can see how that can lead to other things in the border areas." He said that when Blackwater personnel were out with the Pakistani teams, sometimes its men engaged in operations against suspected terrorists. "You've got BW guys that are assisting…and they're all going to want to go on the jobs—so they're going to go with them," he said. "So, the things that you're seeing in the news about how this Pakistani military group came in and raided this house or did this or did that—in some of those cases, you're going to have Western folks that are right there at the house, if not *in* the house." Blackwater, he said, was paid by the Pakistani government through Kestral for consulting services. "That gives the Pakistani government the cover to say, 'Hey, no, we don't have any Westerners doing this. It's all local and our people are doing it.' But it gets them the expertise that Westerners provide for [counterterrorism]-related work." The military intelligence source confirmed Blackwater worked with the Frontier Corps, saying, "There's no real oversight. It's not really on people's radar screen."

A spokesperson for the US State Department's Directorate of Defense Trade Controls (DDTC), which is responsible for issuing licenses to US corporations to provide defense-related services to foreign governments or entities, would neither confirm nor deny that Blackwater had a license to work in Pakistan or to work with Kestral. "We cannot help you," said department spokesperson David McKeeby after checking with the relevant DDTC officials. "You'll have to contact the companies directly." Blackwater's spokesman said the company had "no operations of any kind" in Pakistan other than one employee working for the DoD. Kestral did not respond to inquiries about its relationship with Blackwater.

According to federal lobbying records, Kestral had hired former assistant secretary of state for Western Hemisphere affairs Roger Noriega, who served in that post from 2003 to 2005, to lobby the US government, including the State Department, USAID and Congress, on foreign affairs issues "regarding [Kestral's] capabilities to carry out activities of interest to the United States." Noriega was hired through his firm, Vision Americas, which he ran with Christina Rocca, a former CIA operations official who served as assistant secretary of state for South Asian affairs from 2001 to

2006 and was deeply involved in shaping US policy toward Pakistan. In October 2009, Kestral paid Vision Americas $15,000 and gave a Vision Americas–affiliated firm, Firecreek Ltd., an equal amount to lobby on defense and foreign policy issues.

IN NOVEMBER 2009, as I worked on an investigative report for the *Nation* magazine on JSOC's targeted killing operations in Pakistan, I received an unprompted call on my cell phone the day before publication from Captain John Kirby, the spokesperson for Admiral Michael Mullen, chair of the Joint Chiefs of Staff, President Obama's most senior military adviser. Kirby wouldn't explain how he got my number or how he had heard about the story. "Let's just leave it at: we heard about it," he told me bluntly. Kirby told me that my story was false but would not go on record saying that. Instead, he told me, "We do not discuss current operations one way or the other, regardless of their nature." He told me bluntly that if we published the story, which connected Blackwater to JSOC's operations in Pakistan, I would be "on thin ice."

We had confidence in our sources, so despite this clear attempt at intimidation, the *Nation* ran the story. The next day, when the article, titled "The Secret US War in Pakistan," was published, Pentagon spokesperson Geoff Morrell called it "conspiratorial" and explicitly denied that US Special Operations Forces were doing anything other than "training" in Pakistan. Morrell told reporters: "We have basically, I think, a few dozen forces on the ground in Pakistan who are involved in a train-the-trainer mission. These are Special Operations Forces. We've been very candid about this. They are—they have been for months, if not years now, training Pakistani forces so that they can in turn train other Pakistani military on how to—on certain skills and operational techniques. And that's the extent of our—our, you know, military boots on the ground in Pakistan, despite whatever conspiratorial theories that, you know, magazines…may want to cook up. There's nothing to it."

In fact, there was a lot to it.

A year after my story in the *Nation*, WikiLeaks released a series of classified cables showing that a month before Morrell denounced my report, the US Embassy was aware that US military Special Operations Forces had been conducting offensive operations inside Pakistan, helping direct US drone strikes and conducting joint operations with Pakistani forces against al Qaeda and Taliban forces in North and South Waziristan and elsewhere in the Federally Administered Tribal Areas. According to an October 9, 2009, cable classified by US ambassador to Pakistan Anne Patterson, the operations were "almost certainly [conducted] with the personal consent of [Pakistan's] Chief of Army Staff General [Ashfaq Parvez] Kayani." The operations were coordinated with the US Office of the Defense Representative in Pakistan. A US Special Operations source told me that the US forces described in the cable as "SOC(FWD)-PAK" (Special Operations Command-Forward Pakistan) were "forward operating troops" from JSOC.

In the fall of 2008, the US Special Operations Command asked top US diplomats in Pakistan and Afghanistan for detailed information on refugee camps along the Afghanistan-Pakistan border and a list of humanitarian aid organizations working in those camps. On October 6, Ambassador Patterson sent a cable marked "Confidential" to Defense Secretary Robert Gates, Secretary of State Condoleezza Rice, the CIA, US Central Command and several US embassies saying that some of the requests, which came orally and in the form of e-mails, "suggested that agencies intend to use the data for targeting purposes." Other requests, according to the cable, "indicate it would be used for 'NO STRIKE' purposes." The cable, which was issued jointly by the US Embassies in Kabul and Islamabad, declared: "We are concerned about providing information gained from humanitarian organizations to military personnel, especially for reasons that remain unclear. Particularly worrisome, this does not seem to us a very efficient way to gather accurate information." What this cable said in plain terms is that at least one person within the US Special Operations Command actually asked US diplomats in Kabul and/or Islamabad point blank for information on refugee camps, information that was to be used in a targeted killing or capture operation.

The cable also revealed that in addition to the requests from SOCOM and the US defense attaché, a SOCOM contractor had also asked US diplomats for "information on camps along the Pakistan-Afghanistan border which are housing Afghan refugees and/or Internally Displaced Persons (IDPs)." Specifically, the cable added, SOCOM and its "contractor" have "requested information on camp names and locations, camp status, number of IDS/refugees and ethnic breakdown, and NGO/humanitarian relief organizations working in the camps."

From the October 2008 cable, it is evident that US diplomats in Kabul and Islamabad were disturbed by the requests, asking various US military, intelligence and government entities for "clarification of the origin and purpose of this tasker." At the same time the cable suggested that if the CIA or Special Operations Forces wanted such information, they "should send a front channel cable to the appropriate Embassy" or a representative of the director of national intelligence rather than by e-mailing or orally requesting the information from embassy personnel. Clearly, the back-channel approach was used for a reason.

So close was Blackwater to the most highly classified, sensitive operations the CIA was conducting that its members were among the casualties in one of the deadliest known attacks against the Agency in its history, the December 2009 suicide bombing at a CIA outpost at Forward Operating Base Chapman in Afghanistan. Blackwater operatives were serving as the security team for the Agency's second-highest-ranking officer in Afghanistan. They were meeting with a source, someone traveling by car from Pakistan, whom they believed knew the whereabouts of Ayman al Zawahiri, al Qaeda's number-two man. Humam Khalil Abu-Mulal al Balawi, it turned out, was a double agent whose true allegiance was to the Pakistani Taliban. In all, seven CIA personnel and a Jordanian intelligence officer were killed when Balawi walked onto the base and blew himself up. Two of those killed were Blackwater operatives.

In addition to working on covert action planning and drone strikes, Blackwater also provided private guards to perform the sensitive task of security for secret US drone bases, JSOC camps and Defense Intelligence Agency facilities inside Pakistan, according to the military intelligence source.

THE ABILITY OF US SPECIAL OPERATIONS FORCES to operate in Pakistan was clearly viewed as a major development by the US Embassy. "Patient relationship-building with the military is the key factor that has brought us to this point," according to an October 2009 US diplomatic cable. It also noted the potential consequences of the activities leaking: "These deployments are highly politically sensitive because of widely-held concerns among the public about Pakistani sovereignty and opposition to allowing foreign military forces to operate in any fashion on Pakistani soil. Should these developments and/or related matters receive any coverage in the Pakistani or US media, the Pakistani military will likely stop making requests for such assistance."

Such statements might help explain why ambassador Richard Holbrooke, at the time the top US envoy to Afghanistan and Pakistan, misled the world when he said bluntly in July 2010: "People think that the US has troops in Pakistan; well, we don't."

In late 2010, relations between the United States and the ISI began to rapidly deteriorate. In November, a civil lawsuit filed in New York accused the ISI's chief, Ahmad Shuja Pasha, of involvement in the 2008 Mumbai bombings carried out by Lashkar-e-Taiba. In December, the CIA scrambled to whisk its Islamabad station chief out of Pakistan after local media blew his cover and reported his name, Jonathan Banks. The top spy's identity was first revealed in a lawsuit filed in Pakistan by a man from North Waziristan who alleged that two of his relatives had been killed in a drone strike. US officials accused the ISI of leaking the name in retaliation for the lawsuit that named Pasha. A US intelligence official said that Banks had to be removed because "terrorist threats against him in Pakistan were of such a serious nature that it would be imprudent not to act."

A month later, on January 20, 2011, Raymond Davis returned to Pakistan.

# 46 | The Curious Case of Raymond Davis: Act II

PAKISTAN, 2011—In Lahore, Raymond Davis lived and worked out of a US safe house in Upper Mall that he reportedly shared with five CIA security personnel. JSOC operatives also used the house. Far from being a diplomat, Davis worked on an ultrasecret, highly compartmentalized, classified team of men tasked with conducting sensitive surveillance and intelligence operations that could lead to targeted killing or capture. Among their tasks, according to US officials, was covertly gathering intel on the terror group Lashkar-e-Taiba. On January 27, Davis was conducting an "area familiarization route," putting him out in the open on the streets of Lahore for hours. He scouted several locations, including religious schools and government buildings. That's why the Pakistani authorities found, in his car, the high-tech kit of a clandestine operative: weapons with enough ammo to fight a small street war, surveillance equipment, wire cutters, knives and infrared equipment. It would also explain the collection of various identity cards bearing different job descriptions, as well as theatrical makeup. Lieutenant Colonel Shaffer told me it is common for covert operators to alter their appearance to blend in. "It's acting without a script," he said. "That is really what it comes down to. It's tradecraft."

Davis also had in his possession a "blood chit," which is distributed to all US military personnel entering a hostile environment. According to the US military's Joint Publication 3-50 on Personnel Recovery, a blood chit "is a small sheet of material on which is imprinted an American flag, a statement in English and several languages common to the populace in the operational area, and numbers in each corner and, in some cases, centered under the flag, that identify the particular chit. The blood chit identifies the bearer as an American and promises a reward by the USG [US government] to anyone providing assistance to the bearer or helping the bearer to return to friendly control." They are to be used by US military forces under siege, lost or in imminent danger of capture or harm "after all other measure(s) of independent evasion and escape have failed and the evader(s) or escapee(s) consider(s) assistance vital to survival."

At some point on January 27, as Davis traveled through Lahore, he came in contact with the men on the motorcycle, twenty-two-year-old Faizan Haider and twenty-six-year-old Faheem Shamshad, also known as Muhammad Faheem. According to the US version of events, the two men scoped out Davis as he stopped at an ATM to withdraw money and then put in place a plan to rob him. But according to four Pakistani sources who spoke to ABC News shortly after the incident, the two men were actually working for the ISI and began tracking Davis after he had crossed "a red line." Days before the incident, Davis "was asked to leave an area of Lahore restricted by the military," according to ABC's sources. "His cell phone was tracked, said one government official, and some of his calls were made to the Waziristan tribal areas, where the Pakistani Taliban and a dozen other militant groups have a safe haven. Pakistani intelligence officials saw him as a threat who was 'encroaching on their turf,'" an official said. "Yes, they belonged to the security establishment," a Pakistani security official told Karachi's *Express Tribune* newspaper. "[T]hey found the activities of the American official detrimental to our national security." Complicating all of this, other Pakistani officials emphatically denied the men were ISI.

Lieutenant Colonel Anthony Shaffer said he heard credible reports from his colleagues who work on Pakistan that the two men were in fact ISI. "They were just going to pick him up and make a point, 'We know who you are,'" Shaffer said. Because Davis had not been declared as CIA to the ISI, "they were gonna make the point to say, 'We know you're here.'"

"I know a lot more about this than I can say, unfortunately," Shaffer added. "It suffices to say that the Davis issue was prompted by the ISI, there was a provocation, there was a reason why Davis reacted the way he did and this gamesmanship had gotten to the point where CIA was basically being trailed by the very folks they're working with."

Which "red line" Davis crossed, if in fact that is what prompted the two men to track him, may never be known. Perhaps it involved getting too close to Lashkar-e-Taiba. Perhaps he was working to expose its ties to the ISI. Maybe he was scouting targets for the Agency's drone bombings. Some suggested that Davis was the CIA's new chief of station. Some Pakistani officials went so far as to offer up a wild conspiracy theory that Davis was actually working with the Taliban and other militant groups to plan attacks on civilian targets that could be blamed on terrorists. It was a common allegation hurled at Blackwater in places like Peshawar, the capital of the Federally Administered Tribal Areas, and a central front in the covert US war in Pakistan. Despite the incendiary nature of these allegations, no evidence was ever produced to back up any of these charges. "The Lahore killings were a blessing in disguise for our security agencies who suspected that Davis was masterminding terrorist activities in Lahore and other parts of Punjab," a senior Punjab police official alleged, adding that Davis had "close ties" with the Pakistani Taliban. "Davis was instrumental in recruiting young people from Punjab for the Taliban to fuel the bloody insurgency." Police officials said that the call logs from Davis's phones showed records of links with more than thirty Pakistanis, including "27 militants" from the Taliban and the militant group Lashkar-e-Jhangvi, which is designated as a terrorist group by both the United States and Pakistan.

Other Pakistani government sources alleged that Davis was in the country and known to the ISI and had been authorized to work on a CIA program conducting surveillance of al Qaeda and the Taliban. "Davis's job was to trail links of the Taliban and al Qaeda in different parts of Pakistan," a source told the *Tribune*. "But, instead, investigators found that he had developed close links" with the Taliban. "The government and security agencies were surprised to know that Davis and some of his colleagues were involved in activities that were not spelled out in the agreement." The mainstream Pakistani conspiracy theories on Davis suggested that the American operative was setting up false flag bombings to force the Pakistani government to take a more aggressive approach toward militant groups or to give the impression that the country's nuclear weapons were not secure. No evidence was ever presented to support these allegations.

The truth may never be known, but it is certainly possible that Davis was up to something with the Taliban and al Qaeda that Pakistan did not like and the US government would never want to acknowledge. "All countries conduct espionage," asserted Colonel Patrick Lang. "In the course of that task in the 'game of nations,' some things are done in 'liaison' with a country's service, in this case, the ISI, and others are not. They are done unilaterally, i.e., illegally in the country where they occur. If one does not do that, then one is vulnerable to the agenda of the 'liaison' service." The US intelligence community, Lang argued, "is often accused of not really knowing what is 'going on' in a country. The way to avoid that is to do some things 'unilaterally.' In this case are the ISI irritated? I am sure they are. Do you think we believe that Pakistan does not operate 'unilaterally' in the US? If we do, then we are fools."

In any event, given the programs Raymond Davis was known to have worked on, the US version of events and its characterization of him as a diplomat or a "technical adviser" or, as the *New York Times* characterized the US position: "a paper-shuffling diplomat who stamped visas as a day job," are impossible to believe. Perhaps he was CIA. It is also possible that his CIA status was a cover within a cover and that, as my military intelligence source suggested, he was working with JSOC. "That's common,"

Lieutenant Colonel Shaffer told me. "It all gets mish-mashed together. The sad truth is," Shaffer asserted, US officials, including ambassadors and policy makers not directly looped in to an operation, "don't really know, what's going on, anywhere. It all gets kind of blurred together." Shaffer added that Davis's cover was all about "Layering." He said, "You always have a cover within a cover and it depends on how far you are trying to throw someone off, especially if you assume you are going to be rolled up at some point in time. You always have throwaways."

It is not uncommon for CIA operatives to work under cover as diplomats. It is standard operating procedure for many nations. The RAO, where Davis said he worked, was a common cover for US spies. Everyone who needed to know was aware of such cover arrangements. When an operation goes south, it usually does not play out in public. Discreet arrangements are made, and sometimes prisoners are exchanged or payoffs authorized. It is all part of the spy game. But this particular incident occurred in broad daylight, in a crowded intersection, with scores of eyewitnesses.

If Davis had been revealed to be working for JSOC in Pakistan, that would have been the scenario most offensive to the ISI. After Obama's 2008 election, while Pakistan's government tried to curb the flow of CIA operatives into the country, the United States began increasing the number of covert personnel it allowed "cover" as diplomats. The ISI had long dealt with the CIA, but JSOC was an entirely different beast, one the ISI would find terrifying.

In addition to being the lead agency in US targeted killing operations, JSOC was also the premier US entity responsible for counterproliferation. In Pakistan, theories that the United States was plotting to snatch the country's nuclear weapons were rampant and the source of endless commentary on its news channels. The idea wasn't just paranoia. JSOC had in fact drawn up plans to secure Pakistan's nukes in the event of a coup or other destabilization. In the late 1990s, it was revealed that plans existed for JSOC to be prepared to deploy anywhere across the globe "to recover sensitive NBC [nuclear, biological, chemical] materials in the hands of terrorist groups, to slip undetected into rogue countries to gain evidence of a secret WMD development program, to sabotage such a program, and to detect, disarm, disable, or seize WMD." While such plans were hardly unique to Pakistan, they fueled the ISI's obsession with JSOC.

Former Pakistani brigadier F. B. Ali described two phases of JSOC's operations in Pakistan, the first being the "hot pursuit" arrangement with JSOC dating back to President Musharraf's time. "The second phase of the JSOC influx occurred after the US decided to undertake a large, long-term aid program for Pakistan," Ali observed. "The US applied for visas for a large number of staff and support personnel to manage the program. The ISI insisted on security vetting all visa applicants, which held up the process. The US exerted huge pressure on the government, warning that the aid program would be adversely affected." Pakistan's government, Ali alleged, acquiesced and allowed a large flow of Americans into Pakistan. That claim was backed up by an ISI official who claimed thousands of visas had been issued to US Embassy personnel over a five-month period leading up to the Davis incident, "following a government directive to the Pakistan Embassy in Washington to issue visas without the usual vetting by the interior ministry and the ISI." According to an Associated Press report in late February 2011, "Within two days of receiving that directive, the Pakistani Embassy issued 400 visas and since then thousands more have been issued." In all, according to the Pakistani Embassy in Washington, more than 3,500 visas were issued to US diplomats, military personnel and employees of "allied agencies" in 2010.

At the time of the Davis incident, Pakistan's Foreign Ministry stated that there were 851 Americans with diplomatic immunity in Pakistan, 297 of whom were not working "in a diplomatic capacity." But the Interior Ministry listed more than four hundred "special Americans," suspected by Pakistani security officials to be "operatives of US intelligence agencies who are on covert missions in Pakistan, reporting to" JSOC. "The 'official' version of what they are doing is gathering counter-terrorism intelligence," Brigadier Ali asserted. "But the ISI rank and file knew otherwise; they just couldn't get the dominant US-friendly brass to do anything about it. Until Raymond Davis gunned down a couple of ISI auxiliaries on the streets of Lahore, and the US publicly came down like a ton of bricks to get him freed."

Whatever Davis was doing and for whom he was doing it prior to pulling up at the Mozang Chowk intersection in Lahore on January 27, 2011, what happened that day was straight out of a spy movie.

At some point, Davis pegged the two guys on the motorcycle in front of him as a threat. As he told it, one of the men brandished a firearm in a menacing way. Davis grabbed his Glock 9 and fired five shots through his front windshield, with deadly precision, taking down Muhammad Faheem, who was on the back of the bike. One shot hit him in the head, just above his ear. Another pierced his stomach. The driver of the motorcycle, Faizan Haider, hopped off the bike and started to flee. Davis, Glock in hand, stepped out of his car, aimed and fired five more shots. Haider fell thirty feet from his motorcycle. At least two shots hit him in the back. He later died in the hospital.

According to eyewitnesses, after shooting the two men, Davis returned calmly to his vehicle and took out a military-grade radio. He called for backup. Before getting back into his vehicle, onlookers in the crowded intersection watched as Davis walked over to the blood-soaked bodies of the two men he had shot and photographed them. As crowds began to descend on the streets, the potential for a mob forming was strong. Traffic police called out for Davis to stop. He ignored them, got back in his car—the windshield riddled with the bullet holes made by his own Glock—and sped off. In the meantime, a Toyota Land Cruiser was speeding through the streets of Lahore. Its license plate, bearing the tag LZN-6970, was a fake. The driver of Davis's backup vehicle was not about to wait in congested traffic. He punched it, hopping onto the median of a crowded road, and then darted into incoming traffic, weaving the vehicle toward Mozang Chowk. About five hundred yards from the intersection where the shooting happened, the Land Cruiser slammed into the motorcycle of a Pakistani man, Ibadur Rehman, crushing him, and then continued on toward the scene. After discovering that Davis was already gone, the men in the Land Cruiser fled.

By the time his backup vehicle arrived, Davis had made it two miles from Mozang Chowk. But the chase ended swiftly. He was confronted by local police at a crowded market in Old Anarkali in Lahore. Davis put up no resistance and was taken into custody. He worked for the US government, Davis told them. His seven-week ordeal was just beginning. While Davis was on his way to a Punjab police station for questioning, the men on his backup team were making their getaway. Somewhere near Faletti's Hotel, several items fell from their vehicle, among them four ammunition clips, 100 bullets, a black mask, a knife with a compass and a piece of fabric emblazoned with an American flag—another blood chit. They returned to the CIA-JSOC safe house, destroyed all government documents in their possession and headed for the US Consulate. The men inside that vehicle were never heard from nor seen again in Pakistan. The United States, claiming they had diplomatic immunity, whisked them out of the country before the Pakistanis could question them. "They have flown the coop, they are already in America," a senior Pakistani official remarked.

It took less than twenty-four hours for word of the incident to spread like wildfire through Pakistan. In Lahore, angry mobs of protesters called for Davis to be hanged. Reports began emerging in the Pakistani press that Davis was CIA and a Blackwater agent. As he stood inside Lahore's Lytton Road Police Station, chaos surrounded the calm American. Police officers, investigators and others in the room spoke to one another heatedly. They stumbled to pronounce his name. Davis insisted that they find his passport. He insisted he was a consultant at the consulate in Lahore and that he had a diplomatic passport. Unlike his colleagues who had gotten themselves in trouble in Pakistan in the months before the shooting in Lahore, Davis would not be going home anytime soon. He was transferred to Kot Lakhpat Jail as Pakistani authorities intensified their investigation, including a forensic review of the crime scene. Autopsies were performed on the three dead men (the two shot by Davis and the man who was run down by his backup team) before their bodies were handed over to their families for burial.

According to the Pakistani police investigation, Davis's claim that he fired in self-defense "is not correct." The postmortem report indicated that both men who were killed by Davis were shot from behind. Witnesses told the Pakistani police that Haider was gunned down as he ran from the motorcycle "to save his life." Davis told the police that Faheem had cocked his weapon and aimed it at him. When police recovered Faheem's weapon, "the chamber of the deceased's pistol [was] empty and the bullets were in the magazine." Moreover, according to police, "no one saw them aiming at" Davis. When police asked Davis for a license for his weapons, they said he couldn't produce one. To the Punjab police, the incident quickly became a murder investigation. Davis was ordered held for six days, pending further investigation.

The particulars of the incident were not nearly as important as the high-stakes game that would play out between the United States and Pakistan. Unbeknownst to the Pakistani government, five months before Raymond Davis was taken into custody, US intelligence had made a discovery of potentially incalculable value. The CIA had located a courier linked to Osama bin Laden. They tracked his movements, which ultimately led them to a large house in Abbottabad, Pakistan. Using satellite imagery, intelligence analysts noticed the movements of a mysterious figure inside the compound. The White House believed it had found bin Laden. Just as Admiral McRaven began gaming out scenarios JSOC could use to kill or capture the al Qaeda leader, Davis had shot the men in Lahore and now sat in a Pakistani jail. The United States feared that if it raided the house in Abbottabad, Davis could be killed in retaliation for the violation of Pakistan's sovereignty. Washington had to get its man out of there.

Unaware of the US planning to go after what Washington believed was bin Laden's home inside Pakistan, the government in Islamabad viewed the Davis incident as an opportunity to win the upper hand in its intelligence wars with the United States. "For the ISI, the Davis incident is a godsend," an editorial in the *Economist* concluded. "It is furious with the way American agents work independently, tracking al-Qaeda, Taliban and other militants who have slipped into Lahore and Karachi to flee drone attacks on the mountainous border with Afghanistan."

The US government's response to Davis's arrest was clumsy. It is entirely possible that Davis's actual role in Pakistan—whether CIA, JSOC or both—was not fully known by the US Embassy. The day after Davis was arrested, a spokesman for the US Embassy in Islamabad, Alberto Rodriguez, told a Pakistani television station, "I can confirm that the person that's involved in the incident is an employee of the consulate." Soon after, on January 27, the US Embassy sent a diplomatic note to the Pakistani Foreign Ministry claiming Davis as "an employee of U.S. Consulate General Lahore and holder of a diplomatic passport." That was consistent with the statement Davis gave to police. The problem for the United States, however, was that this designation meant that the Pakistani authorities could argue that he was not entitled to full immunity but was instead covered by the 1963 Vienna Convention on Consular Relations. That treaty provided that "Consular officers shall not be liable to arrest or detention pending trial, except in the case of a grave crime and pursuant to a decision by the competent judicial authority." Surely, the Pakistanis argued, murder is a grave crime.

On February 3, the United States revised its position. This time, it labeled Davis "a member of the administrative and technical staff of the U.S. embassy." According to Pakistani officials, Davis had never been certified as a diplomat because of "unresolved queries" about him made by Pakistan to the United States.

Rage was spreading across the country. Ten days after the shooting, in a hospital bed in Faisalabad, Shumaila Kanwal, Faheem's widow, was using her last breaths to record a video statement. She had swallowed rat poison and was ending her own life to protest what she called her husband's murder at the hands of a US agent. "I want blood for blood," she said as she gasped for air and struggled to focus her eyes. "The way my husband was shot, his killer should be shot in the same fashion." Imran Haider, the brother of the other man shot by Davis, said his brother had recently learned that his wife was pregnant. He expressed anger that his brother was being "smeared" as a bandit. "He was clean," he declared. "All we want is for this American to go on trial and for a proper investigation to be done. He should face the death penalty. No deals."

Shumaila died shortly after her statement was recorded. Her death further inflamed the already outraged Pakistani public. Islamic parties staged huge demonstrations, burning effigies of Davis and declaring him a terrorist, a spy and, perhaps worst of all, an agent of Blackwater.

It soon became clear that Pakistan was not going to quietly release Davis. The United States began a feverish campaign to get him out. The CIA went so far as to cease its drone bombings in the country, reportedly at the request of the ISI. That the United States halted the drone attacks was remarkable, given their centrality to the US strategy in Pakistan. "The arrest of this guy is a very positive thing for us," declared Mullah Jihad Yar, a Pakistani Taliban commander. "Our forces used to be hit by attacks every other day. Now we can move more freely." For Agency veterans, US moves indicated how badly they wanted Davis sprung. "The Embassy/Station wants Davis back because they don't want him to start talking about whatever else they are up to unilaterally," Giraldi, the former CIA officer, suggested. As for the issue of immunity, Giraldi asserted that Davis did not have it. "To be a diplomat legally speaking you have to be accredited to the foreign ministry of the country and they have to accept your accreditation. You are then entered on the diplomatic list," he asserted. "Most US Embassy employees in most overseas posts do not have diplomatic status and therefore do not have immunity except insofar as the local government might extend some protections to them as a courtesy. There is absolutely no indication that Davis went through the accreditation procedure or anything like that even if he was traveling on a dip[lomatic] passport."

As reports flooded the Pakistani press of Davis's affiliation with the CIA, JSOC and Blackwater, major US media outlets and US government officials promoted the line that Davis was a diplomat. "We continue to make clear to the government of Pakistan that our diplomat has diplomatic immunity, in our view was acting in self-defense and should be released," declared State Department spokesman P. J. Crowley in a February 7 statement that was reported by CNN, CBS, PBS, *USA Today* and other major news outlets. "Pakistan should fulfill its international obligations under the Vienna Convention."

In response to pressure from Washington, the US-friendly government of Asif Zardari was preparing to recognize Davis as a diplomat but met resistance from its own officials. Pakistan's foreign minister, Shah Mahmood Qureshi, was asked to certify Davis as a diplomat but refused, saying the request did not match the "official record" on Davis at the Foreign Ministry. "Our expert opinion suggested that the blanket immunity the US embassy is asking for is unjustified," he later said. In response, Secretary of State Clinton snubbed Qureshi at an international security conference in Munich, Germany. Qureshi was then swiftly removed as foreign minister, he charged, because of his "principled stance" against granting Davis immunity. In taking this position, Qureshi passed the issue to the courts in Lahore, ensuring that the Davis saga would continue. Leading US lawmakers threatened to withhold US humanitarian aid to Pakistan if Davis was not released. President Zardari called such threats "counterproductive," writing in the *Washington Post*, "In an incendiary environment, hot rhetoric and dysfunctional warnings can start fires that will be difficult to extinguish."

As Raymond Davis sat in his cell in the Kot Lakhpat Jail, US officials feared for his safety. As many as three prisoners had been murdered by guards in the facility. Some Pakistani officials expressed concern that the CIA would try a spectacular prison break. Davis's food was tested for poison by dogs before being served to him. While his masters tried to free him, Davis remained cool and defiant. During an interrogation after the shooting, Davis, clean-shaven and wearing a blue pullover fleece, told his interrogator, "The US ambassador says I have [immunity], so I'm not answering any questions." Davis demanded to see his passport. "Right on the front page," he said, motioning his hands in a framing motion. "Diplomatic passport." As the interrogator attempted to question him further, Davis announced he would not answer any more questions. "I'm going back to my room," Davis told the man, then got up from the table. "You can't go like this," the interrogator declared. "You are not a diplomat." Davis simply reiterated that he would not answer any more questions as he headed for the door.

Back in Washington, the full weight of the Obama administration was being thrown behind the cause of his freedom. "In our view, he acted in self-defense, when confronted by two armed men on motorcycles," Crowley declared at the State Department. He "had every reason to believe that the armed men meant him bodily harm." He demanded Davis's release.

On February 15, with Davis still in jail and a Pakistani judge preparing to rule on whether he was entitled to immunity, Senator John Kerry, chair of the Foreign Relations Committee, arrived in Pakistan. Kerry was well known in Pakistan as the co-sponsor of a massive $7.5 billion aid package to the country. Kerry met with President Zardari and other top officials, and then with a group of Pakistani journalists in Lahore, where he made the case that Davis was a diplomat and should be released into US custody. "We have to—all of us—respect the law," Kerry said, sitting in a lounge chair surrounded by the Pakistani media. Television networks in Pakistan carried his remarks live. The law governing diplomatic immunity, Kerry said, "is not a law that Pakistan idly signed up to. Your leaders signed up for this long, long ago." Kerry spoke slowly, almost as though he were speaking to a class of children rather than journalists. "We didn't create this. We live with it and it's important for us to live with it because there are incidents that occur sometimes in one part of the world or another where diplomats are not able to do the job that they are called on to do in very dangerous circumstances sometimes unless they have that immunity."

The journalists pressed Kerry on Davis's status and asked why, in their eyes, it seemed the United States was not respecting Pakistan's laws and judicial process. "It is the strong belief of our government that this case does not belong in the court. And it does not belong in the court because this man has diplomatic immunity as an administrative, technical employee of the embassy of the United States in Islamabad," Kerry responded. "We believe the documentation makes that clear. That's our position. We're not disrespecting your court. We completely respect your courts. We want your courts to be strong and to be vibrant...but we have to respect international law." Kerry called on Pakistan to "let the facts and let the reality speak for itself here."

It is highly doubtful that John Kerry actually believed that Davis was an "administrative, technical employee of the embassy." As chair of the Foreign Relations Committee, Kerry was privy to the most sensitive US intelligence and was thoroughly briefed before departing for Pakistan.

As Kerry worked Pakistani officials, back in Washington, President Obama very publicly owned Davis. "With respect to Mr. Davis, our diplomat in Pakistan, we've got a very simple principle here that every country in the world that is party to the Vienna Convention on Diplomatic Relations has upheld in the past and should uphold in the future. And that is if—if our diplomats are in another country, then they are not subject to that country's local prosecution," Obama declared at the White House. "If it starts being fair game on our ambassadors around the world, including in dangerous places where we may have differences with those governments...and they start being vulnerable to prosecution locally, that—that's untenable. It means they can't do their job." Obama said the administration had been "very firm" in making the US demands to Pakistan clear and was working "to get this person released." Obama added, "For those who aren't familiar with the background on this, a couple of Pakistanis were killed in a incident between Mr. Davis within—in Pakistan. So, obviously, we're concerned about the loss of life. You know, we're not callous about that. But there's a broader principle at stake that I think we have to uphold."

While Obama, Kerry and other US officials publicly characterized Davis as a diplomat, several major US media outlets, most prominent among them the *New York Times*, had already learned that Davis was, in fact, working for the CIA. At the request of the Obama administration, the *Times* and other US outlets agreed to withhold that fact from their reporting on the case. The *Times* later reported that it agreed not to report Davis's CIA connection after administration officials "argued that disclosure of his specific job would put his life at risk." (The Associated Press also acknowledged that it learned that Davis was working for the CIA "immediately after the shootings," but did not report it.) *New York Times* reports referred to Davis as an "American official" and described "the mystery about what Mr. Davis was doing with this inventory of gadgets" and the speculation it had sparked in the Pakistani media, even as the *Times* knew he was working for the CIA. "It's one thing for a newspaper to withhold information because they believe its disclosure would endanger lives," constitutional lawyer and journalist Glenn Greenwald observed. "But here, the U.S. Government has spent weeks making public statements that were misleading in the extreme—Obama's calling Davis 'our diplomat in Pakistan'—while the *New York Times* deliberately concealed facts undermining those government claims because government officials told them to do so. That's called being an active enabler of government propaganda."

The first major world media outlet to report the CIA connection was London's *Guardian* newspaper. Both the CIA and Britain's MI-5 pressured the paper not to publish the information. Ultimately, the paper went ahead with the story, publishing it in its February 21 edition. "We came to the view that his CIA-ness was a critical part of the story, bound to be a factor in his trial or in attempts to have him released," Ian Katz, the *Guardian's* deputy editor in charge of news, said. "The reasons we were given for not naming him were, firstly, that it may complicate his release—that is not our job. If he was held hostage other factors would kick in but he is in the judicial process. The other reason given by the CIA was that he would come to harm in prison." Once the *Guardian* printed it, US media outlets were given permission by the CIA to publish it themselves. In its first story identifying Davis as CIA, the *Times* quoted George Little, a CIA spokesman: "Our security personnel around the world act in a support role providing security for American officials. They do not conduct foreign intelligence collection or covert operations." In reality, the line between the Agency's "security" guards and operatives was almost nonexistent after a decade of operating together in Pakistan and Afghanistan.

Senator Kerry held secret talks with Pakistan's ambassador to the United States, Husain Haqqani, where they discussed the United States paying "blood money" to the families of Davis's victims and the man run over by his backup team. While the CIA and ISI waged a war through media leaks and accusations, both the US and Pakistani governments knew that Davis would be released. The question was when and what the ISI would get from the CIA before that happened. In mid-February, after Davis had been in custody for two weeks, CIA director Panetta talked to ISI chief Pasha, who demanded that the United States identify "all the Ray Davises working in Pakistan, behind our backs." Following that discussion, the ISI agreed to help facilitate and support a plan to pay off the victims' families, paving the way for Davis's release.

In testimony before the Senate Intelligence Committee a day after Kerry's visit to Pakistan, Panetta called the CIA's relationship to the ISI "one of the most complicated relationships that I've seen in a long time." A few days later, the Associated Press obtained the draft of a statement that the ISI was preparing that indicated that the ISI "is ready to split with the CIA because of its frustration over what it calls heavy-handed pressure and its anger over what it believes is a covert U.S. operation involving hundreds of contract spies." The statement, which was never released, declared that following the Davis shooting, "Post-incident conduct of the CIA has virtually put the partnership into question.... It is hard to predict if the relationship will ever reach the level at which it was prior to the Davis episode," adding bluntly: "The onus of not stalling this relationship between the two agencies now squarely lies on the CIA."

In late February, Davis was hauled into a Lahore courtroom and asked to sign a charge sheet, acknowledging he had "murdered" the two men. Davis refused to sign and repeated his contention that he had immunity. In the meantime, the ISI was combing through the paperwork from the visa applications of hundreds of Americans issued visas over the previous six months. The ISI claimed that Davis's application contained "bogus references and phone numbers" and was looking for similar red flags in other visa files.

On February 25, police in Peshawar arrested another US security contractor, Aaron DeHaven, whose company, Catalyst Services, boasted that its team had "been involved in some of the most significant events of the last 20 years, whether it was the breakup of the former Soviet Union, the US effort in Somalia, or the Global War on Terror" and that its members had "careers in the United States Military and the United States Department of Defense." The Pakistani press immediately branded him a Davis-like spy. Reports soon appeared that dozens of "contractors" had fled the country.

The Pakistani government had to be seen as cracking down, and the United States was resigned to let it do so as long as it resulted in Davis's freedom. The CIA's George Little said that the Agency's ties to the ISI "have been strong over the years, and when there are issues to sort out, we work through them. That's the sign of a healthy partnership." Despite the CIA's public declarations, that partnership was, in reality, at an all-time low. But for the US military, the stakes were too high to let the Davis affair get any more out of hand. America's war in Afghanistan was entirely dependent on Pakistan's cooperation. Without Islamabad's support, crucial US supply routes would be shut down. The generals had had enough.

ON FEBRUARY 23, the closing act to the Davis saga was initiated far away from the jail where the American sat awaiting his fate. In fact, the deal was sealed in neither Pakistan nor the United States, but at a secluded luxury beach resort in Muscat, the capital of Oman, a nation in the Arabian Peninsula. "Where do you go to think seriously and bring sanity to a maddening situation? Far from the madding crowd to a peaceful Omani luxury resort of course. So that's what the military leadership of the US and Pakistan did," declared a Pakistani military readout of the meeting. In a private conference room, the most powerful figures in the US military met with their Pakistani counterparts. Led by Admiral Mullen, the US delegation included Admiral Eric Olson, the commander of the US Special Operations Command; General David Petraeus; and General James Mattis, the commander of CENTCOM. They met with Pakistan's top military official, General Ashfaq Parvez Kayani and Major General Javed Iqbal, its director general of military operations. "The US-Pakistan relationship is heading downhill as speculation mounts about US intentions in Pakistan," the Pakistani readout stated. "The Davis affair brought all these suspicions to the surface."

Referring to the reported rift between the CIA and ISI, the readout indicated that the US military officials "had to point out that once beyond a tipping point the situation would be taken over by political forces that could not be controlled." According to the readout, the US delegation asked the Pakistani generals "to step in and do what the governments were failing to do—especially because the US military was at a critical stage in Afghanistan and Pakistan was the key to control and resolution." It concluded, "The militaries will now brief and guide their civilian masters and hopefully bring about a qualitative change in the US-Pakistan Relationship by arresting the downhill descent and moving it in the right direction."

After the Oman meeting, sources within the ISI said that the CIA had agreed not to conduct unilateral operations in Pakistan in return for its support in freeing Davis. "They will do nothing behind our backs that will result in people getting killed or arrested," a Pakistani official told the *Guardian*. That of course was not true. It is even unclear whether the CIA said it. The *New York Times* reported that US officials "insisted...the CIA made no pledges to scale back covert operations in Pakistan or to give the Pakistani government or its intelligence agency a roster of American spies operating in the country—assertions that Pakistani officials disputed."

In any case, the United States and Pakistan began putting together a plot to use Islamic Sharia law to free Davis. From the moment Davis shot the two men in Lahore, the families of his victims and the third man killed by his backup team publicly insisted that they wanted no payments or bribes, but rather wanted Davis tried and hanged. On her deathbed, Shumaila Kanwal, Faheem's widow, said she feared that justice would not be served because of a political deal. For weeks, mobs of angry protesters demonstrated at every court hearing, demanding that Davis be charged and tried. For both the United States and Pakistan, that was not an option.

The show had gone on long enough. And its ending was carefully choreographed by both governments. Under the *diyyat* provision of Sharia law, the families of a victim could "pardon" the accused and in return accept a payment commonly referred to as "blood money." That would result in the criminal case against Davis being dismissed. But it required the consent of the victims' families.

On March 16, unidentified Pakistani agents forcibly took nineteen of the victims' family members to Kot Lakhpat Jail. It was to be the day of Raymond Davis's trial. The public was not allowed in, nor were reporters. Davis was, according to Punjab law minister Rana Sanaullah, charged with murder. But instead of witnessing the presentation of evidence, the testimony of eyewitnesses or the questioning of Davis, the family members were ordered to sign papers pardoning the American. "I and my associate were kept in forced detention for hours," claimed an attorney for the family of Faizan Haider. Each of the family members was brought before the judge and asked if he or she pardoned Davis. Under intense pressure, all of them answered yes. The judge then dismissed the case against Davis and ordered his release. "This all happened in court and everything was according to law," Sanaullah declared. "The court has acquitted Raymond Davis. Now he can go anywhere." As retired Pakistani Brigadier F. B. Ali observed, "The *diyyat* provision is much loved by the rich and powerful in Muslim societies where it is in force; it literally allows them to get away with murder."

In all, the families were paid a total of $2.3 million. On a visit to Cairo, Secretary of State Clinton praised the arrangement. "The families of the victims of the January 27th incident pardoned Mr. Davis, and we are very grateful for their decision," she said. "We appreciate the actions that they took that enabled Mr. Davis to leave Pakistan and head back home." When asked about the payments to the families, she replied, "The United States did not pay any compensation." Pakistan had in fact made the payment, which the United States would later repay out of the CIA's budget.

As Raymond Davis walked from the court after his release was ordered, tears streamed down his face as his victims' families sat in stunned silence, some of them whimpering. Davis was swiftly escorted to a convoy of diplomatic vehicles and taken immediately to an airfield where he boarded a "special" plane—the type used in the CIA's extraordinary rendition program. The plane crossed into Afghanistan's airspace, headed for Bagram, and Davis disappeared. "He's gone," Lieutenant Colonel Shaffer said, smiling.

Twenty-four hours after Davis was freed, a US drone strike killed some forty people in North Waziristan. Things, it seemed, could now go back to the way they were before l'affaire Davis. But just six weeks after Davis was whisked from Pakistan, the secret war he had been helping to fight would be thrust to front-page news the world over when JSOC helicopters penetrated Pakistani territory in the dead of night and headed for the garrison town of Abbottabad. Their mission: to kill the most wanted man in the world.

## 47 The Tsunami of Change

AUSTRIA AND YEMEN, 2011—In mid-2011, Yemen was caught up in the revolution that was sweeping the Arab world. The popular revolt against oppressive regimes in the region had begun on December 17, 2010, when Mohamed Bouazizi, a twenty-six-year-old street vendor in Tunisia, took the ultimate stand. The young fruit-and-vegetable seller struggled every day in the poor rural city of Sidi Bouzid to make ends meet, facing constant harassment from local police and municipal employees who demanded bribes from him. On this particular day, Tunisian officials stripped him of his only source of income—when they confiscated his cart and goods because he did not have the proper permit. Bouazizi, enraged, ran to the governor's offices, but the governor refused to meet him. Then, desperate and furious, he went to a nearby gas station, filled a jug with gasoline and stood in the middle of traffic. It was 11:30 in the morning. "How do you expect me to make a living?" he shouted before dousing himself in gasoline. He lit a match and his body erupted in flames.

Within months, massive protests against the US-backed regimes of the Arab world had broken out in Middle Eastern and North African capitals, an uprising that became known as the Arab Spring. Several dictators fell, one after another: Zine El Abidine Ben Ali in Tunisia was the first to go. On January 25, a rebellion began against Egyptian dictator Hosni Mubarak that would ultimately bring an end to his regime. Yemenis watched as their Arab brothers and sisters in other countries faced down the dictators that had ruled their lives for as long as they could remember.

Less than two weeks later, tens of thousands poured into a square in central Sana'a and renamed it Change Square. They announced that they would not leave until President Saleh and his family were removed from power. A new issue of *Inspire* was released just as the protests were spreading in Yemen. Its cover story on the Arab uprisings, "The Tsunami of Change," was penned by Anwar Awlaki. "The first and probably most important change that this monumental event brought is a mental one. It brought a change to the collective mind of the ummah. The revolution broke the barriers of fear in the hearts and minds that the tyrants couldn't be removed,"

Awlaki wrote. "We do not know yet what the outcome would be, and we do not have to. The outcome doesn't have to be an Islamic government for us to consider what is occurring to be a step in the right direction." Awlaki embraced the protests against the US-backed regime in Yemen, writing, "Any weakness in the central government would undoubtedly bring with it more strength for the mujahidin in this blessed land."

On March 18, 2011, more than 100,000 Yemeni protesters gathered for Friday prayers in the streets near Sana'a University. As the prayers ended and people began dispersing, government security forces and pro-Saleh militiamen opened fire on the crowd, killing more than fifty people. Some of them were shot in the head by snipers. Three days later, a severe blow was dealt to the Saleh regime when the most powerful figure in Yemen's military, General Ali Mohsin al Ahmar, commander of the 1st Armored Division, threw his support behind the protests and vowed to defend Yemen's "peaceful youth revolution." Other senior military figures soon followed suit. Senior civilian officials, including scores of ambassadors and diplomats, announced their resignations. Important tribal leaders, long the most crucial element of Saleh's grip on power, swung to the opposition.

As Yemen's revolution was heating up, the United States was beginning a bombing campaign to support armed rebels in Libya that would ultimately bring down the regime of Colonel Muammar el Qaddafi. But in Yemen, the US government was playing a very different game. The prospect of losing Ali Abdullah Saleh made Washington very nervous. After all, AQAP in Yemen had been declared the most significant external threat facing the US homeland. Those running the US military and intelligence operations agreed with Awlaki's assessment that instability in Yemen would benefit AQAP. In Egypt, longtime US-backed dictator Hosni Mubarak had been overthrown, as had leaders of other Washington client regimes. *Inspire* published an ad in its Arab Spring issue that featured a picture of Ali Abdullah Saleh holding his finger up to his mouth in a "shhhh" motion. "Hey Ali, Mubarak just fell," the ad read. "Guess who's joining the party next?"

While Secretary of State Hillary Clinton and other US officials condemned the violence in Yemen, they stopped far short of calling for an end to the regime or for international military action to confront the brutality of the Yemeni security forces. Instead, the US position was to call for a "political solution." A few days after the massacre in Sana'a, Defense Secretary Robert Gates, on a visit to Moscow, was asked if the United States still backed Saleh. "I don't think it's my place to talk about internal affairs in Yemen," Gates replied. What he said next spoke volumes about US priorities: "We are obviously concerned about the instability in Yemen. We consider Al Qaeda in the Arabian Peninsula, which is largely located in

Yemen, to be perhaps the most dangerous of all the franchises of Al Qaeda right now. And so instability and diversion of attention from dealing with AQAP is certainly my primary concern about the situation." At the time, the Obama administration was in the midst of ramping up its training and equipping of Yemen's military and security forces, including some of the very forces that were now repressing peaceful antigovernment protests.

"The feckless US response is highlighting how shortsighted our policy is there," Joshua Foust, the former DIA Yemen analyst, told me at the time. "We meekly consent to Saleh's brutality out of a misguided fear that our counterterror programs will be cut off, apparently not realizing that, in doing so, we are practically guaranteeing the next government will threaten those very programs." Gregory Johnsen told me that he shared some of Washington's concerns but said the myopic obsession with terrorism was counterproductive. Saleh's fall "could certainly have a negative impact on US CT operations in Yemen," he said, adding, "I'm particularly worried that AQAP is gaining weapons and money in some parts of the country as the military begins to break down in outlying areas." Yemen "has a number of more pressing problems that will, if left unchecked, all help AQAP gain strength in the coming years," Johnsen cautioned. "In Yemen, there is no magic missile solution to the problem of AQAP. The US simply can't bomb them out of existence."

Judging from its policies, the Obama administration apparently thought otherwise.

ANWAR AWLAKI'S YOUNGEST BROTHER, Ammar, was nothing like him. While Anwar embraced a radical interpretation of Islam and was preaching for jihad against the United States, Ammar was pursuing a career working for an oil company in Yemen. Ammar was Canadian-educated and politically well connected. He dressed in blue jeans, wore hip Armani eyeglasses and sported a goatee. His hair was slicked back and he had the latest iPhone. The last time he had seen Anwar was in 2004. In February 2011, Ammar was in Vienna, Austria, on a business trip. He had just returned to his hotel after sampling some local cuisine with an Austrian colleague when the phone rang in his room. "Hello, Ammar?" said a man with an American accent. "My wife knows your wife and I have a gift for her." Ammar went down to the lobby and saw a tall, thin white man in a crisp, blue suit. They shook hands. "Can we talk a bit?" the man asked, and the two men sat down in the lobby. "I don't actually have a gift for your wife. I came from the States and I need to talk to you about your brother."

"I'm guessing you're either FBI or CIA," Ammar said. The man smiled.

Ammar asked him for identification. "Come on, we're not FBI, we don't have badges to identify us," the man said. "The best I can do is I can show you my diplomatic passport."

"Call me Chris," the American said.

"Was that your name yesterday?" Ammar replied.

Chris made it clear he worked for the CIA and told Ammar that the United States had a task force dedicated to "killing or capturing your brother." He told Ammar that the United States wanted to bring Anwar in alive, but that time was running out. "He's going to be killed," Chris told him, "so why don't you help in saving his life by helping us capture him?" He added, "You know, there's a $5 million bounty on your brother's head. You won't be helping us for free."

When Ammar told Chris he didn't want the money, the American replied, "That $5 million would help raise [Anwar's] kids. America is very frank, and I'll just say it to you. There's a $5-million-dollar bounty, and it's up for grabs. And instead of someone else getting it, why don't you get it, and help Anwar's kids get raised decently?"

"I don't think there's any need for me to meet you [again]," Ammar told Chris, reiterating that he had no idea where Anwar was. Still, Chris told Ammar to think it over. Discuss it with his family. "We can meet when you go to Dubai in two weeks." Ammar was stunned. His tickets for that trip had not even been purchased and the details were still being worked out. Chris gave Ammar an e-mail address—a Hotmail account—and said he'd be in touch.

Ammar returned to Yemen. "I talked to my mom and my brother [not Anwar] about it. And they said, 'You stop it. Don't even reply to them, don't contact them again. Just stop.'" Ammar ignored the rest of the e-mails from Chris.

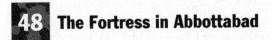

## 48 The Fortress in Abbottabad

WASHINGTON, DC, 2010–2011; PAKISTAN, 2011—As the US manhunt for Anwar Awlaki intensified, the most wanted man in the world was spending his time hiding in plain sight. For years, it was assumed that Osama bin Laden was living in a cave or hiding in the tribal areas straddling the Afghanistan-Pakistan border. Some US officials thought the United States might never catch him, while some terror analysts believed bin Laden might already be dead. But bin Laden was very much alive and was living in the middle-class Bilal Town neighborhood of Abbottabad, Pakistan, in a large compound less than a mile from the Pakistani equivalent of the West Point Military Academy.

It is unclear exactly when bin Laden had moved to Abbottabad, but construction on the residence had been completed in 2005. And it was clearly built for secrecy. The al Qaeda leader lived on the third floor of the largest house on the property with three of his wives and many of his children. Their residence was expertly designed to ensure that no one could see inside. It had almost no windows, save for some narrow openings on one of the walls. Ironically, on May 2, 2011, it was those very attributes of the home that would prevent bin Laden from seeing the well-armed US Navy SEALs who were whizzing across Pakistan on a mission to end his life.

THE LAST SERIOUS CHANCE the United States had of killing or capturing bin Laden had come a decade earlier, in the winter of 2001 in Tora Bora, Afghanistan. A collapse in coordination between the Pentagon and CIA had marred that operation, resulting in bin Laden and his deputy, Zawahiri, disappearing—some thought for good. For the next decade, a determined group of analysts from the CIA followed one lead after another to a seemingly endless string of dead ends. With no human intelligence resources inside al Qaeda, no signals intelligence coming from bin Laden himself and little hope for support from authorities in the regions he was believed to be in, the CIA was stuck. In 2005, the bin Laden unit was shuttered, though a number of analysts continued to pursue the al Qaeda leader.

Barack Obama had campaigned on a pledge to make Afghanistan and the fight against al Qaeda the centerpiece of his counterterrorism policy, and he blasted the Bush administration for dropping the ball in the hunt for bin Laden. As president, Obama had ordered CIA Director Leon Panetta to prioritize the search, labeling the killing or capture of bin Laden Panetta's "number one goal" in May 2009. Obama's orders had injected new life—and resources—into the search that had, for four years, largely been conducted by a small group of CIA analysts. While the CIA was ratcheting up its efforts to find bin Laden, not everyone in the intelligence community thought they would produce any result. In April 2010, Major General Michael Flynn told *Rolling Stone* reporter Michael Hastings, "I don't think we're going to get bin Laden," adding, "I think we'll get a call one day from the Paks: Bin Laden's dead, we captured al Zawahiri." At the time, Flynn was the highest-ranking intelligence officer in Afghanistan and Pakistan and was serving directly under General McChrystal. As Hastings pointed out, Flynn "had access to the most sensitive and detailed intelligence reports."

But in August 2010, the CIA got its biggest break in the case since Tora Bora, when a CIA asset inside Pakistan spotted Abu Ahmed al Kuwaiti in Peshawar. Kuwaiti had long been on the CIA's radar and had been identified by various al Qaeda figures captured and interrogated by US forces in the immediate aftermath of 9/11 as a top aide to bin Laden and his primary courier. The Agency's asset in Pakistan followed Kuwaiti's white Suzuki jeep on a two-hour drive from Peshawar to the garrison town of Abbottabad. As the CIA analysts examined the details of the compound, which they likened to a "fortress," they discovered it had no phone or Internet connection and that its residents burned their trash. They grew their own vegetables and raised their own chickens and cows. Every week, they would slaughter two goats. The analysts knew they had one of bin Laden's trusted aides in their scope but also knew there could be a bigger fish living in the compound—perhaps even the biggest. They decided not to try to capture Kuwaiti, hoping that he would lead them to bin Laden himself.

In late autumn, Panetta directed his bin Laden analysts to compile a list of twenty-five ways to extract intelligence from within the compound. They had already considered placing devices in the sewage system or placing a camera in a tree near the compound. Eventually, the analysts came up with thirty-eight options. According to author Peter Bergen, "One idea was to throw in foul-smelling stink bombs to flush out the occupants of the compound. Another was to play on the presumed religious fanaticism of the compound's inhabitants and broadcast from outside the compound what purported to be the 'Voice of Allah,' saying, 'You are commanded to come out into the street!'"

Eventually, the CIA enlisted a Pakistani doctor to administer a false Hepatitis B vaccination program in the neighborhood. The Agency wanted the doctor and his fake medical team to gain access to the compound and to extract DNA samples from the occupants so that they could compare them to samples the Agency already had from bin Laden's deceased sister. The doctor involved in the effort, Shakil Afridi, was from Pakistan's tribal regions. Eventually, the CIA would pay Afridi to run the fake program, which began in the poorer areas of Abbottabad in order to appear legitimate. In the end, the plan failed and Afridi and his team were unable to get any DNA samples. Afridi would later be arrested and imprisoned by Pakistani authorities for working with the CIA.

In the late summer and early fall of 2010, CIA analysts had begun circulating memos regarding the significance of the courier and his relationship to bin Laden, including one that was titled "Closing In on Usama bin Ladin's Courier" and another titled "Anatomy of a Lead."

The CIA set up a safe house in Abbottabad and expanded its "pattern of life" analysis of the compound's residents. In addition to the families of Kuwaiti and his brother, they soon discovered that there was another family living in the secluded third floor of the biggest building on the property. By analyzing shadows through aerial imagery, CIA analysts detected someone they believed to be a man who would take daily walks in the courtyard inside the compound in a small vegetable garden—but only under the cover of a tarp, which prevented the drones or satellites from getting anything more than a silhouette of his image. They could not determine the man's height. Internally, the CIA analysts called him "the Pacer."

By January 2011, the general consensus at the CIA was that the Pacer was likely bin Laden himself. President Obama asked his counterterrorism team to develop a range of options for action. Undersecretary of Defense Michael Vickers, Panetta and his deputy Mike Morell met with Admiral McRaven at CIA headquarters and read him in on the intelligence out of Abbottabad. "First of all, congratulations on getting such a good lead," McRaven told them. "Second, this is a relatively straightforward raid from JSOC's perspective. We do these ten, twelve, fourteen times a night. The thing that makes this complicated is it's one hundred and fifty miles inside Pakistan, and logistically getting there, and then the politics of explaining the raid, is the complicating factor. I want to think about it a little bit, but my instinct is to put a very seasoned member of a special unit to work directly with you who will come to the CIA every day and basically begin to plan and flesh out some options."

The *Wall Street Journal* reported that "McRaven assigned one senior special-operations officer—a Navy Captain from SEAL Team 6, one of the

top special-forces units—to work on what was known as AC1, for Abbottabad Compound 1. The captain spent every day working with the CIA team
in a remote, secure facility on the CIA's campus in Langley, Va." On paper,
any raid against the compound was to be done using CIA cover so that if
it went wrong, the United States could deny the operation. But in reality,
McRaven's men would be running the show. Within the CIA, AC1 soon
became known as "Atlantic City."

The CIA and Obama's national security team considered a number of
other options beyond the SEAL team assault. They explored doing a B-2
strike on the compound, similar to the operation that killed Zarqawi in
Iraq. But that scenario presented a number of major-league risks: it would
be nearly impossible to extract DNA to confirm bin Laden was killed, and
the bombing would certainly kill not only all of the women and children
in the compound, but potentially residents of other homes in the neighborhood. A drone strike was always an option in Pakistan, but the conditions
at the compound would have made the chance of a direct hit unpredict-
able. Looming over all of the planning was the fact that CIA contractor
Raymond Davis was sitting in a Pakistani jail cell facing murder charges
and widespread calls for his execution. Any unilateral action by the United
States would undoubtedly infuriate the Pakistani government. Some analysts feared Davis could be killed in retaliation.

Ultimately, Obama's counterterrorism team decided that a JSOC raid,
conducted by veteran Navy SEALs under the command of McRaven, would
provide the best opportunity to take out bin Laden. JSOC had conducted
raids in Pakistan before, though never this deep into the country—or with
such a sizable force. The risk of the Pakistani government spotting the US
helicopters that would have to travel 150 miles into the country—and the
possibility that the helicopters could be shot down—was serious. Admiral
McRaven began assembling a team of SEALs to start preparing for a sensitive operation, but they were not yet briefed on what that mission would
be. Once Raymond Davis was released from the Pakistani jail on March 16,
momentum picked up for the operation.

McRaven's men would prepare for the mission at a secret facility in
North Carolina and at another in the desert in Nevada.

ONE OF THE SEALS TAKING PART in the exercises was thirty-six-year-old
Matt Bissonnette, a veteran DEVGRU operator who had spent the last decade participating in a virtually nonstop run of combat deployments that
put him behind enemy lines in the expansive post-9/11 US war on terror.
Bissonnette had carried out missions in Afghanistan, Iraq, the Horn of Af-

rica and, as fate would have it, Pakistan. He had actually participated in a previous attempt to capture bin Laden in 2007 that he had dubbed a "wild-goose chase." He had risen through the Special Ops ranks to become a DEVGRU team leader.

Bissonnette and other JSOC operators were summoned to a Sensitive Compartmented Information Facility, where phones are prohibited and the walls are lined with lead to prevent the use of electronic listening devices. According to Bissonnette, "There were almost thirty people in the room, including SEALs, an EOD [Explosive Ordnance Disposal] tech, plus two support guys." The men received little information other than the fact that they were going to be headed to North Carolina for a "joint readiness exercise." They were offered no clues as to what was in store. "Overall there was a lot of experience in the room. They'd drawn us from different teams," Bissonnette recalled. "On most teams, the new guy usually carries the ladder and the sledgehammer. But looking around the room, we had all senior guys." He added, "It looked like some kind of dream team they were putting together."

According to Bissonnette, "speculation was rampant." Some of the men predicted they would be sent to Libya. Others wagered Syria or Iran. When the SEALs arrived at the North Carolina training base, they were briefed. The target of the mysterious mission was, in fact, Osama bin Laden. "No fucking way," Bissonnette declared.

Twenty-eight of DEVGRU's most senior operators were chosen for the operation, including an explosives expert. Also on the team were a combat dog named Cairo and an interpreter. There were four alternates attached to the mission in the event one of the SEALs was injured in training. In Afghanistan, the all-star troop would be joined by a SEAL Bissonnette called "Will," a self-taught Arabic speaker who would be able to conduct interrogations on the mission.

Together with the help of CIA analysts, the men committed to memory the intricately detailed mock-up of the compound that sat outside the main doors to the briefing room. The foam model stood on a five-foot by five-foot plywood base. It was locked up in a wooden box when not in use. The model showed the "house in amazing detail, right down to the small trees in the courtyard and cars in the driveway and on the road that ran along the north side of the compound," Bissonnette later wrote. "It also had the location of the compound's gates and doors, water tanks on the roof, and even concertina wire running along the top wall. Grass covered the main courtyard. Even the neighbors' houses and fields were rendered in almost exact detail."

The SEALs were introduced to the Pacer. They were given a "Road to

Abbottabad" briefing from the CIA in which they were brought up to speed on the multiyear intelligence effort to track down the al Qaeda leader. A few days after the men arrived in North Carolina, they caught their first glimpse of the Pacer via a black-and-white video feed. They watched him walk in circles under a "makeshift awning" in the compound's courtyard. On one occasion, a Pakistani military helicopter passed over the compound while the Pacer was outside. "We didn't see the Pacer sprint to a car and run. Instantly, we all thought the same thing," Bissonnette recalled. "This meant he was accustomed to hearing helicopters."

The CIA assessment informed the men that bin Laden was believed to be living on the third floor of the compound, and his son Khalid on the second. Aside from educated guesses placing the occupants of the compound on certain floors, the DEVGRU operators had no idea what the layout of the buildings would look like once they were inside. The team would use a number of "pro" words to report on the progress of the mission via radio, the idea being that short, single words would reduce radio traffic and confusion. According to Bissonnette, "On this mission, we chose pro words with a Native American theme." Bin Laden would be designated with the word "Geronimo."

As his SEALs readied for their mission, McRaven briefed the president and his national security team. "In terms of difficulty, compared to what we're doing on a nightly basis in Afghanistan, what we're doing in Iraq, this is not among the most difficult missions technically. The difficult part was the sovereignty issue with Pakistan and flying for a long stretch of time over Pakistani airspace," McRaven said. Biden's national security adviser, Tony Blinken, described the impact of McRaven's analysis. "First of all, it helps that he's from central casting," he told Bergen. "He looks and sounds the part, so he inspires confidence, but you also got the very strong impression that this was not a guy who was going to be blustering or bragging. This was a guy who was going to give his very honest assessment, and so when he did, he had a lot of credibility, and it also created a tremendous amount of reassurance. And basically what McRaven told us was after they modeled this, and gamed it, and rehearsed it, he said, 'We can do this.'"

As the SEALs war-gamed for the operation in North Carolina and the Nevada desert, a string of VIPs from the administration, the military and CIA attended some of the drills. According to Bissonnette, during one session, someone asked if the raid was a kill mission. "A lawyer from either the Department of Defense or the White House made it clear this wasn't an assassination," he recalled. "If he is naked with his hands up, you're not going to engage him," the attorney said. "I am not going to tell you how to do your job."

The SEAL team was dispatched to Jalalabad, Afghanistan, ahead of the mission. Bissonnette strung up a hammock in the plane in preparation for the lengthy trip. Some of the men popped Ambien pills for the long flight across the Atlantic. A number of analysts from the NSA and CIA joined the SEALs. As the plane took off, Bissonnette took an open seat next to one of the CIA analysts. He asked her, "What are the odds" the man in the compound was bin Laden? "One hundred percent," she told him. Bissonnette pushed back, reminding her that he had heard such proclamations from intelligence analysts before and they had fallen apart. The CIA analyst doubled down on her assessment, telling Bissonnette that she did not support the idea of the raid and would have preferred an air strike. "Sometimes JSOC can be the big gorilla in the room," she said. "I'd rather just push the easy button and bomb it." Bissonnette told her, "You guys did all the hard work to get us here," adding, "We're happy to have our thirty minutes of fun and be done."

On Friday morning, April 29, at 8:20 a.m., Obama met with National Security Adviser Thomas Donilon, his deputy Denis McDonough, John Brennan and Chief of Staff William Daley in the White House Diplomatic Reception Room. As they stood in a half circle, Obama told the men, "I've considered the decision: It's a go. And the only thing that makes it not a go is if Bill McRaven and his folks believe that either weather or conditions on the ground increase the risk to our forces."

The mission would be called Operation Neptune Spear, a tip of the hat to the trident favored by the Roman god of the sea. It is also a common insignia on Navy SEAL paraphernalia and unit crests.

On their second night in Jalalabad, Bissonnette and a number of other SEALs sat around a fire pit discussing where they should shoot bin Laden. "Try not to shoot this motherfucker in the face," said a SEAL he called "Walt." "Everybody is going to want to see this picture." The men speculated about how the raid would advance the careers of their superior officers. Bissonnette predicted McRaven would be promoted to SOCOM commander. "And we'll get Obama reelected for sure," Walt added. "I can see him now, talking about how he killed bin Laden."

The raid, planned for the evening of Saturday, April 30, coincided with the White House Correspondents' Dinner, which would have meant that the president and virtually every senior member of his national security team would be rubbing elbows with the media elite and Hollywood celebrities while the raid was taking place. Some of the president's advisers wanted the operation held back until after the dinner, concerned that if something went wrong, forcing the president and other officials to leave the event, the raid's cover could be blown. The raid was specifically planned to take place on a moonless night in order to allow the approaching helicopters to have the best cover possible. By chance, excessive cloud cover ultimately compelled McRaven to delay the raid until the next night.

Obama called McRaven for a final check-in. It was late in the evening in Jalalabad when McRaven picked up the phone. He told the president his men were ready to go. "I couldn't have any more confidence in you than the confidence I have in you and your force," the president said. "Godspeed to you and your forces. Please pass on to them my personal thanks for their service and the message that I personally will be following this mission very closely."

The president and the first lady arrived at the Washington Hilton at 7:00 p.m. on Saturday night for the Correspondents' Dinner. Panetta, Gates, Vickers and several other core members of the team planning the bin Laden raid were there as well. Obama's demeanor revealed nothing about the high-stakes preparations that were taking place on the other side of the globe. Instead, the president appeared calm and jovial, cracking a number of jokes, including one targeting billionaire Donald Trump, who was in the audience. Trump had been on a media rampage, promoting his inane theory that the president was not a US citizen. *Saturday Night Live* star Seth Meyers, who hosted the dinner, actually made a joke about bin Laden, obviously unaware that a number of people in the room were intimately involved in planning his imminent demise. "People think bin Laden is hiding in the Hindu Kush," Meyers said. "But did you know that every day from 4 to 5 p.m. he hosts a show on C-SPAN?" The camera panned to the president laughing heartily.

IN AFGHANISTAN, the final briefing before the launch of Operation Neptune Spear was "standing room only," Bissonnette wrote, with SEALs from the other squadron on the base packing in. The president had authorized the SEALs to fight off any Pakistani units that confronted them on the mission. An officer briefing the teams informed them of their cover story, should they find themselves in Pakistani custody: you were recovering a drone that had crashed. The proposal drew laughter. "The story was preposterous. We were allies with Pakistan on paper, so if we did lose a drone, the State Department would negotiate directly with the Pakistani government to get it back," an incredulous Bissonnette asserted. "The story didn't wash and would be very difficult to stick to during hours of questioning," he wrote. "The truth is, if we got to that point, no story we could come up with was going to cover up twenty-two SEALs packing sixty-pounds of high-tech gear on their backs, an EOD tech, and interpreter

for a total of twenty-four men, plus a dog, raiding a suburban neighborhood a few miles from the Pakistani military academy." The briefing was
closed by the commanding officer of DEVGRU. McRaven, he said, had
given them the green light. In twenty-four hours, the SEALs would be on
their way to Abbottabad.

Obama's national security staffers began arriving at the White House
around 8:00 a.m. on Sunday, May 1. Sandwich platters were purchased
from Costco. Multiple pizzerias were called upon to avoid making one
large conspicuous order.

At around 1:00 p.m., Obama's national security team began to assemble
in the Situation Room. Obama was finishing up a round of golf at Andrews
Air Force Base—part of the attempt to send the signal publicly that business was as usual. Over at the CIA, Panetta and his deputy, Mike Morell,
huddled with SOCOM's commander, Eric Olson, in a secure room. On
paper, Panetta was in charge of the operation. In reality, Admiral McRaven
was running Neptune Spear.

Obama returned to the White House at approximately 2:00 p.m. and,
still wearing his golf shoes and a windbreaker, went downstairs to the Situation Room, where Panetta's final overview of the operation was relayed.
But Obama and his team would not monitor the most sensitive mission in
US history from the Situation Room, which was built for such operations.
Instead, the most powerful decision makers in the United States wound up
confining themselves to a much smaller room next door.

The room had the same secure video and phone communications as the
Situation Room but could only seat seven people. Two modest-sized flat-
screen televisions were installed side by side on one wall of the room. On
the day of the bin Laden raid, the conference room was initially occupied
by Brigadier General Marshall "Brad" Webb, JSOC's assistant commanding
general. Webb and another JSOC officer were monitoring the operation in
real time through a laptop. The feed was provided by an RQ-170 stealth
drone hovering over Abbottabad. They also had secure communications
with McRaven in Jalalabad, Panetta at CIA headquarters and General Cartwright at the Pentagon's Ops Center. When the men proposed moving their
command center to the Situation Room, they were told to stay put.

Next door in the Situation Room, Obama's inner circle was arguing
about whether the president should monitor the mission live. As that debate dragged on, various senior officials, including Secretary of State Clinton and Vice President Biden, began streaming into General Webb's small
room. A short time later, the president walked into the room. "I need to
watch this," he said. The commander in chief seated himself in a folding
chair to the right of Webb. Obama later discussed the seating arrangement,
saying, "[Webb] started to get up and people were starting to go through

the protocol and figuring out how to rearrange things. I said, 'You don't worry about it. You just focus on what you're doing. I'm sure we can find a chair and I'll sit right next to him.' And that's how I ended up [on a] folding chair."

IT WAS 11:00 P.M. IN ABBOTTABAD, and the families at the bin Laden compound were already in bed. Many miles to the west, across the Pakistan-Afghanistan border, in the city of Jalalabad, twenty-three members of SEAL Team 6 were at an airbase preparing to embark on their mission. Half an hour later, the Black Hawks took off. By 2:30 p.m., the White House had received the first word that the choppers were off the ground. "It was nail-biting time and we were holding our breath," recalled Brennan.

For the mission, the SEALs would utilize two specialized MH-60 Black Hawk helicopters, flown by JSOC's "Night Stalkers." The helicopters were a stealth version of the Black Hawk that the United States had long been rumored to be developing. The unique aircraft had never been discussed publicly. The Black Hawks had been specially modified with advanced technology that would allow it to fly silently and to avoid radar detection. To further mask their presence, the pilots would fly at high speeds as close to the ground as possible, using a tactic known as "nap of the earth." General Hugh Shelton, the former commander of SOCOM, whose son is a JSOC pilot, said the Night Stalkers are the best in the US military. "They can literally—the pilots can fly a helicopter upside-down if they want to, they can land on a moving train—at night," he told me. "Any time that you've got a mission that you don't want to fail, those are the guys that you want to have doing it."

Three MH-47 Chinooks took off from the same Jalalabad airfield once the Black Hawks had entered Pakistan. One set down on the Afghan side of the border with Pakistan. The other two flew to a remote riverbank in Kala Dhaka, located in the Swat region, roughly fifty miles north of bin Laden's compound. There the Quick Reaction Force (QRF) would wait. In the event that the SEALs' raid ran into serious trouble, the QRF could get to Abbottabad in approximately twenty minutes. Meanwhile, the Black Hawks whizzed quietly toward the compound and eventually made it to the outskirts of Abbottabad.

In Afghanistan, Admiral McRaven was running the operation from a secure location in Jalalabad. In Kabul, General David Petraeus and one of his aides monitored the events in a classified control room. If the Pakistanis scrambled their fighter jets, Petraeus was poised to mobilize US warplanes to respond.

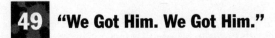 **"We Got Him. We Got Him."**

PAKISTAN, 2011—President Obama and his team huddled around a table in the small room adjacent to the Situation Room, watching grainy footage of the Black Hawks approaching Abbottabad from the northwest. It was standing room only, but everyone was silent, save for the occasional question for McRaven's deputy, General Webb. On board the choppers, some of the SEALs had tried to catnap en route to what was undoubtedly the most important mission of their careers. Navy SEAL Matt Bissonnette said he awoke fully when his helicopter was ten minutes outside of the city. He pulled his night-vision goggles down and prepared the fast-roping equipment. With his legs dangling outside the helicopter, he observed the landscape passing below his feet. "Several of the houses we passed over had lighted pools and manicured gardens behind tall stone walls. I was used to seeing mountains or villages made up of clusters of mud huts," he recalled. "From above, Abbottabad reminded me of flying over the suburbs in the United States."

Passing over the southeast wall of the compound, the Black Hawk hovered near the area where the SEALs had planned to insert. Through his night-vision goggles, Bissonnette could make out details of the ground below. "Looking down thirty feet into the compound, I could see laundry whipping on a clothesline. Rugs hung out to dry were battered by dust and dirt from the rotors. Trash swirled around the yard, and in a nearby animal pen, goats and cows thrashed around, startled by the helicopter."

That's when things began to diverge from the original plan. The Black Hawk began to drop suddenly. The high temperature was partly to blame, but it was also a consequence of the added weight of the stealth system on the aircraft. At high altitudes, a pilot can attempt to fly vertically in order to avoid the drop, but it can be deadly at low altitudes.

The pilot of the struggling Black Hawk tried to control the aircraft as it spun ninety degrees to the right. Bissonnette felt his body lifting from the floor of the chopper as he fumbled for a handhold. Packed so tightly with the other commandos, he could not scoot back. "Holy fuck, we're going in," Bissonnette thought to himself, as the wall of the compound came closer and closer. Bissonnette pulled his legs to his chest, hoping to prevent them from being smashed under the helicopter, should it roll onto its side. "The helicopter shuddered as the nose dug into the soft ground like a lawn dart. One minute, the ground was rushing up at me. The next minute, I was at a dead stop. It happened so fast, I didn't feel the impact," Bissonnette remembered.

The Chalk One pilot had managed to follow through on his contingency plan to bring the helicopter down in the compound's larger courtyard. The Black Hawk's tail was pressed against the property's twelve-foot perimeter wall at an angle that prevented the chopper's rotors from digging into the dirt and breaking into dangerous pieces of shrapnel. "If any other part of the helicopter hit the wall, or if we had tipped and the rotor hit the ground first, none of us would be walking away unscathed," Bissonnette later wrote. The pilots, he said, "pulled off the impossible."

The "hard landing" saved the lives of the SEAL team members, but the possibility of a deniable mission was gone. So, too, was any hope of surprising the compound's occupants.

The original plan had to be nixed. Instead of rappelling into the compound, the SEALs would now have to launch their raid from outside the walls. Losing the element of surprise could potentially allow their targets to arm themselves and prepare to face down against the American commandos. "My heart sank," Bissonnette recalled. "Up until I heard the go-around call, everything was going as planned. We had evaded the Pakistani radar and anti-aircraft missiles on the way in and arrived undetected. Now, the insert was already going to shit. We had rehearsed this contingency, but it was Plan B. If our target was really inside, surprise was the key and it was quickly slipping away."

There was silence in the White House as Obama and his advisers waited to hear word from the downed aircraft. "We were able to monitor the situation in real time," the president later said. "So right off the top everybody, I think, was holding their breath. That wasn't in the script."

"Those were really intense moments," Secretary of State Clinton recalled. She later told author Peter Bergen, "This was like any episode of 24 or any movie you could ever imagine." Biden, who had opposed the raid option, nervously caressed his rosary as he watched the crash unfold. "What you see there is the very first thing that was needed to happen in order for the mission to be a success as we were told, didn't happen," said Biden. "That helicopter didn't make it in the right spot and everyone went, like, 'Whoa.'"

While Obama's national security team was shaken by the crash, Admiral McRaven was not. At least he didn't give that impression. "We will now be amending the mission," McRaven calmly told Panetta. "Director, as you can see, we have a helicopter down in the courtyard. My men are prepared for this contingency and they will deal with it." McRaven's calm confidence impressed the officials in the room. "Admiral McRaven was extraordinarily unflappable and professional," Deputy National Security Adviser Ben Rhodes later said. "His demeanor did not change." Obama later called McRaven "a cool customer."

According to Obama, "We had a sense that, despite that helicopter having landed in a violent way, that the passengers inside had not been hurt and that they were still going through with the mission."

THE SEALS IN THE CRASHED CHOPPER had all survived with no serious injuries. As the second Black Hawk, which was supposed to drop its SEALs onto the roof of the building, landed instead outside the gates of the compound, Plan B kicked into gear.

Bissonnette and Will, the SEAL-translator, made their way toward the guesthouse, where they say they came under attack from AK-47 rounds and fired back. Moments later, a woman emerged from the guesthouse carrying a small child in her arms. It was Mariam al Kuwaiti, the courier's wife. "He is dead," Mariam said. "You shot him. He is dead. You killed him." Will searched her for weapons and passed her message on to Bissonnette. Crouching low, Bissonnette opened the door and looked inside. "I spotted a pair of feet lying in the doorway of the bedroom," he said. With Will at his back, he entered the guesthouse and shot Kuwaiti several more times. Although Bissonnette claimed he was fired upon, other accounts, including that of Bergen, suggested that Kuwaiti was unarmed. "The courier's AK-47 was later found by his bedside. It seems unlikely that he fired it, given its location and the fact that no casings from such a weapon were later found at the scene," Bergen wrote. Meanwhile, another group of SEALs made their way toward the main building in the compound, shooting dead two more members of Kuwaiti's family, as women and children looked on in horror.

The men had been on the ground for roughly ten minutes. The SEALs from Chalk Two had managed to enter the compound through the main gate. When the commandos stepped into bin Laden's building, they fell out of contact with Obama's team at the White House. The president later said, "There were big chunks of time in which all we were doin' was just waiting. And it was the longest forty minutes of my life with the possible exception of when Sasha got meningitis when she was three months old, and I was waiting for the doctor to tell me that she was all right. It was a very tense situation." In *Targeting Bin Laden,* a documentary for the History Channel, Obama added, "We were really in a blackout situation and it was hard for us to know what exactly was taking place. We knew that gunshots were taking place, and we knew some explosions were taking place."

Meanwhile, inside, the gate blocking the stairway was blown. The SEALs began making their way up the stairs, which "were set at ninety-degree angles, creating a sort of spiral staircase separated by small landings." There were four doors on the second floor. The SEALs cleared each room and began moving toward the third floor, where they believed the Pacer and his family resided. As they did so, they saw a head briefly pop out from behind the wall at the top of the staircase.

Intelligence analysts had indicated that bin Laden's son Khalid lived on the second floor. The intelligence reports also indicated Khalid was clean-shaven. So was the man who peered around the corner.

"Khalid," a SEAL whispered. "Khalid."

When the twenty-three-year-old worked up the nerve to peek around the corner again, he took a bullet in the face. "What was Khalid thinking at that time?" Bissonnette later asked. "Look around the corner. Curiosity killed the cat. I guess Khalid, too."

The commandos made their way up the stairs, passing over tiles wet with Khalid's blood. As the SEALs walked through the hallway of the third floor, they saw a man's head pop out from a doorway. One of the SEALs fired two suppressed rounds at the figure. The man vanished into the room. When they entered, the men encountered two women. Believing they might have had suicide vests on, one of the SEALs grabbed them and forced them into a corner, so his colleagues could continue on. Another SEAL stood face to face in the dark with a tall man. "In that second, I shot him, two times in the forehead. Bap! Bap! The second time as he's going down," he recalled. "He crumpled onto the floor in front of his bed and I hit him again, Bap! same place. That time I used my EOTech red-dot holo sight. He was dead. Not moving. His tongue was out. I watched him take his last breaths, just a reflex breath."

Bissonnette and another SEAL entered the room. "We saw the man lying on the floor at the foot of his bed," he recalled. "Blood and brains spilled out the side of his skull. In his death throes, he was still twitching and convulsing. Another assaulter and I trained our lasers on his chest and fired several rounds. The bullets tore into him, slamming his body into the floor until he was motionless."

The room was still completely dark, so Bissonnette flipped on his helmet light to better examine the man's face. It was covered in blood. "A hole in his forehead collapsed the right side of his skull," he recalled. "His chest was torn up from where the bullets had entered his body. He was lying in an ever growing pool of blood." The SEAL who originally shot the man said, "the American public doesn't want to know what that looks like."

The SEALs were not certain that the man they had shot was bin Laden. His face was now a mangled mess. They began taking DNA samples from the body and one of the SEALs sprayed the man's bloodied face with his CamelBak. Bissonnette began wiping the face. "With each swipe, the face became more familiar. He looked younger than I expected. His beard was dark, like it had been dyed. I just kept thinking about how he didn't look anything like I'd expected him to look," he wrote. One of the SEALs radioed over the command net: "We have a possible, I repeat POSSIBLE touchdown on the third deck." Bissonnette began snapping photos of the man's body. He then knelt down to focus on the man's face. He pulled his lifeless head from side to side for profile photos. He had his teammate open one of the man's eyes so he could get a tight shot of it.

On the balcony, the Arabic-speaking SEAL was questioning the women and children. An order came over the radio to prep the downed Black Hawk for demolition. Meanwhile, because the mission had gone on longer than planned, fuel for the remaining helicopters, including the rescue CH-47 hovering nearby, was running low.

Bissonnette continued to take photos while his teammate collected samples of the man's blood and saliva. The SEALs had two identical sets of the photos and DNA that would be carried back to Jalalabad in each of the Black Hawks. "This had been carefully planned so if one of the helicopters was shot down on our flight back to Jalalabad, a DNA sample and a set of pictures would survive," Bissonnette later explained.

The Arabic-speaking SEAL questioned the older woman in the room. When he asked who the dead man was, she told him, "The sheik," but declined to clarify. After being given several aliases, the SEAL turned to the children. He asked one of the little girls, and she told him the man was Osama bin Laden. When he asked if she was sure, the little girl said, "Yes." The SEAL turned back to the older woman. "Stop fucking with me now," he demanded, as he asked her again who the man in the bedroom was. She cried as she confirmed that it was Osama bin Laden. The SEAL reported the dual confirmation. Just then, two lead SEALs on the operation, including Bissonnette's squadron commander, entered the room. The commander examined bin Laden's face. "Yeah, that looks like our guy," he said. The senior SEAL stepped out of the room and radioed McRaven. "For God and country, I pass Geronimo," he said. "Geronimo E.K.I.A." Enemy Killed in Action.

In the packed White House conference room halfway around the world, Obama's national security team was overwhelmed. "We got him," Obama said quietly. "We got him." Admiral McRaven was careful to dispel any premature celebration. "Look, I've got a Geronimo call, but I need to tell you it's a first call. This is not a confirmation. Please keep your expectations managed a little here. Most operators when they are on a mission their adrenaline is sky high. Yes, they are professional, but let's not count on anything until they get back and we have some evidence." The JSOC chief added, "We've got SEALs on the ground without a ride."

The SEALs had been at the compound for a little over half an hour by the time bin Laden was killed. The possibility of an encounter with the Pakistani military was increasing with each passing second. Back on the second floor of the compound, the SEALs were attempting to gather as many of bin Laden's belongings and potential intelligence clues as possible.

Once the process of taking bin Laden's photos and DNA samples was completed, a pair of SEALs dragged his corpse out of the bedroom by the legs. Bissonnette began searching the area, grabbing papers and some cassettes. They also found two guns: an AK-47 and a holstered Makarov pistol. Neither was loaded.

Time was running short. The interpreter and the SEALs outside the compound had managed to deter curious onlookers, but Abbottabad was waking up. Pakistani authorities could arrive at any moment, and the choppers circling above were running out of fuel. The interpreter's presence was warranted, as residents of the typically tranquil neighborhood heard the sounds of helicopters and explosions and some found their electricity had been cut off. Gul Khan told *India Today*, "I saw soldiers emerging from the helicopters and advancing towards the house. Some of them instructed us in chaste Pashto to turn off the lights and stay inside." An unidentified man interviewed by CNN in the aftermath of the raid said through a translator, "We never saw their clothes but they were speaking Pashto and told us to go away. After a while, [when the] electricity blackout ended and the light came back on, they told us to turn them all off." Another man speaking to CNN through a translator added, "We tried to go there and they pointed their laser guns on us and said 'No, you can't go.' They were speaking Pashto, so we thought that they were from Afghanistan, not America."

The SEALs inside were overwhelmed with the volume of materials on hand but could only gather and carry so much. They had five minutes. "We all knew the risks of running out of gas or remaining on target too long, giving the local police or military time to react," Bissonnette later recalled. "We got what we came for: Bin Laden. It was time to get out while we still could."

Bissonnette proceeded to the landing zone. He was soon joined by the SEALs from the second floor of bin Laden's compound, who were overloaded with materials they had gathered from inside. "We looked like a gypsy camp, or like Santa Claus on Christmas Eve," he wrote. "Guys had mesh bags over their shoulders so full they seemed to waddle more than run. I saw one SEAL carrying a CPU in one hand and a leather gym bag overflowing in the other."

Bin Laden's corpse, now in a body bag, was loaded on the remaining stealth Black Hawk, which the SEALs thought had the best chance of escaping Pakistan unscathed. The big Chinook—the CH-47—would carry the remaining SEALs. Before taking off, the commandos blew up the downed Black Hawk so that its stealth technology could not be examined by the Pakistanis. Obama and his team watched the video feed of the $60-million bonfire.

News of unusual events unfolding in Abbottabad traveled fast. At 1:00 a.m., just before the SEALs took off from the compound, General Ashfaq Parvez Kayani, chief of Pakistan's army, was in his study when he received a call from his director of military operations, Major General Ishfaq Nadeem. From the initial reports he had heard, Kayani thought India might be launching some sort of a strike inside Pakistan. He called Air Chief Marshal Rao Qamar Suleman and ordered the force to confront any unidentified aircraft.

At approximately 1:08 a.m., the SEALs took off from Abbottabad. Obama told his national security team, "Inform me as soon as our helicopters are out of Pakistani airspace." The Black Hawk and the Chinook took more direct but separate routes as they exited Pakistan, with the Black Hawk stopping at a refueling point inside the country. All of the US personnel crossed the border into Afghanistan unscathed, with bin Laden's body in tow.

On the tarmac in Jalalabad, a white Toyota HiLux pickup was waiting to transport bin Laden's corpse to a nearby hangar. When the Black Hawk landed, three Army Rangers approached the helicopter to grab the al Qaeda leader's body. "Fuck no," one of the SEALs told the Rangers. "We got this."

After bin Laden's body was flown to Bagram and further DNA samples were taken, it was choppered out to the Arabian Sea, where the USS *Carl Vinson* was positioned. "Traditional procedures for Islamic burial was followed," read a May 2 e-mail sent from the *Carl Vinson* by Rear Admiral Charles Gaouette to Mullen and other military officials. "The deceased's body was washed (ablution) then placed in a white sheet. The body was placed in a weighted bag. A military officer read prepared religious remarks, which were translated into Arabic by a native speaker. After the words were complete, the body was placed on a prepared flat board, tipped up, whereupon the deceased's body slid into the sea."

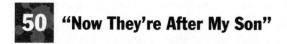

## 50 "Now They're After My Son"

SOMALIA, WASHINGTON, DC, AND YEMEN, 2011—It was 11:35 p.m., Washington time. President Obama walked down the hallway leading to the East Room of the White House. He took his place at the lectern in a dark suit with a red tie and an American flag pin on his left lapel. "Good evening," the president began. "Tonight, I can report to the American people and to the world that the United States has conducted an operation that killed Osama bin Laden, the leader of al Qaeda, and a terrorist who's responsible for the murder of thousands of innocent men, women, and children." The president did not mention the SEALs or Admiral McRaven. "At my direction, the United States launched a targeted operation against that compound in Abbottabad, Pakistan. A small team of Americans carried out the operation with extraordinary courage and capability," the president asserted. "No Americans were harmed. They took care to avoid civilian casualties. After a firefight, they killed Osama bin Laden and took custody of his body."

In the ensuing weeks, controversy would swirl as White House officials leaked details of the operation that turned out to be wildly false or exaggerated. Although the administration explicitly said that the operation was "kill or capture," and not an assassination, bin Laden was unarmed when he was killed and the weapons that were recovered in his bedroom were not loaded. Yet a senior administration official who briefed reporters soon after the raid claimed that bin Laden "did resist the assault force" and "was killed in a firefight as our operators came onto the compound." In reality, the raid was far from the dramatic firefight described initially by White House officials.

In the span of less than twenty minutes, the SEALs had shot seven of the eleven adults in the compound, killing four men and one woman. According to Pakistani officials, both women and children were injured in the raid. Peter Bergen, who gained access to the compound and many witnesses, alleged that all of those who were injured appeared to have been unarmed. The international human rights group Amnesty International described the raid as illegal in its annual report for 2011. "The US administration made clear that the operation had been conducted under the USA's theory of a global armed conflict between the USA and al-Qaeda in which the USA does not recognize the applicability of international human rights law," the report asserted. "In the absence of further clarification from the US authorities, the killing of Osama bin Laden would appear to have been unlawful."

The day after the operation, Brennan delivered an error-filled press conference that purported to give details of the raid. Brennan opened by claiming bin Laden was killed in a firefight and that there was no opportunity to take him alive. He later added that bin Laden used women in the compound as human shields. "Thinking about that from a visual perspective, here is bin Laden, who has been calling for these attacks, living in this million dollar-plus compound, living in an area that is far removed from the front, hiding behind women who were put in front of him as a shield," he said. "I think it really just speaks to just how false his narrative has been over the years. And so, again, looking at what bin Laden was doing hiding there while he's putting other people out there to carry out attacks again just speaks to I think the nature of the individual he was." Brennan also alleged that one woman who died was shot while shielding bin Laden, though she was actually killed with her own husband. The White House was later forced to retract Brennan's comments.

The leaks from the White House sparked outrage in the Special Ops community and ultimately led Bissonnette, one of the SEALs who had shot bin Laden, to write his own book on the raid, under the pen name Mark Owen, called *No Easy Day*, which he said he wrote to set the record straight. So many former SEALs and other Special Ops veterans began speaking out that McRaven issued a directive ordering all current and former Special Ops Forces to stop speaking to the media.

The night Obama had announced bin Laden's death, thousands of Americans poured into the streets in front of the White House and in New York's Times Square, chanting, "USA, USA!"

Victims' families from the 9/11 attacks spoke of bin Laden's death bringing closure. But the al Qaeda leader's demise had breathed new life into Washington's global war.

JSOC, once shrouded in secrecy, had overnight become a household name and was lionized in the media. The Disney Corporation actually tried to trademark the term "SEAL Team 6," and *Zero Dark Thirty*, a high-profile Hollywood film, was put into production; the filmmakers were even given access to sensitive material.

While the battle over the leaks—and varying and contradictory narratives over how exactly bin Laden was killed—raged in the media, behind the scenes the White House was deeply immersed in planning more lethal operations against High Value Targets. Chief among these was Anwar Awlaki.

IN APRIL 2011, Ahmed Abdulkadir Warsame, a Somali man the United States alleged had links to Somalia's al Shabab, had been captured by JSOC forces in the Gulf of Aden. Warsame was aboard a small skiff when he was snatched by an amphibious team. US counterterrorism officials alleged that he had met with Awlaki and was building ties between al Shabab and AQAP. The JSOC forces took him to a military brig aboard the USS *Boxer*, where Warsame was held incommunicado for more than two months before being transferred to New York and indicted on conspiracy charges and providing material support to al Shabab and AQAP.

Although the Obama administration won praise from some in the civil liberties community for trying him in federal court rather than sending him to Guantánamo, the International Committee of the Red Cross (ICRC) was not permitted to see him until after he had endured two months of regular interrogation on board the *Boxer*. Nor was Warsame given access to lawyers. Warsame's case ignited a legal debate over the Obama administration's policies on capturing and detaining terror suspects, particularly in light of the widening counterterrorism campaigns in Somalia and Yemen.

The executive orders that President Obama had issued two days after he was sworn into office required the US government to provide the ICRC with notification of, and timely access to, any persons in the custody of the US government. To those who had long fought the Bush administration's detainee policies, the Warsame case indicated that Obama was violating his own executive orders. "This is illegal and inexcusable. It means in effect that Mr. Warsame was disappeared for this period with all the attendant dangers such hidden detention engenders. It is reminiscent of early Guantánamo Bay and CIA 'black site' detention," alleged the Center for Constitutional Rights. The group accused the Obama administration of "stretching" the meaning of the original Authorization for Use of Military Force granted by Congress to enable pursuit of the 9/11 attackers and using it a decade later "to capture and detain, perhaps indefinitely, anyone it claims is a terrorism suspect anywhere in the world."

But the Obama administration was not simply capturing or detaining suspects: It was interrogating them as part of its intensifying campaign to hunt down terrorists. After Warsame's capture, US officials anonymously boasted to major US media outlets that he had provided them with actionable intelligence. The action sparked by that intelligence would not be in Somalia, but in Yemen, against one of Washington's most wanted targets.

"I WANT AWLAKI," President Obama told his counterterrorism team. "Don't let up on him."

Bin Laden was dead and Ayman al Zawahiri would soon take his place as the head of al Qaeda central, but it was the US citizen running around the badlands of Yemen that Obama and his team had labeled America's new Public Enemy Number One. Obama was a constitutional law professor in a different lifetime, but as president he had developed an alternative legal structure for dealing with Awlaki. President Obama's executive branch had served as prosecutor, judge and jury. As the ultimate authority, he had rendered his verdict. Now his handpicked forces would perform the execution.

Three days after Obama announced to the world that JSOC had killed Osama bin Laden, the president's counterterrorism team presented him with an urgent intelligence update on Yemen. The CIA and JSOC believed they had pinpointed Awlaki's location in the south of Yemen and said they had to seize this moment to take him out. Emboldened by the bin Laden raid, Obama's generals had been agitating for the president to authorize a blitzkrieg of sorts to deliver a "knockout blow" to al Qaeda in a variety of countries. In Yemen, JSOC was talking about "running the table" and taking the fight to the enemy.

President Obama had ordered John Brennan to update him at every Terror Tuesday meeting on all available intelligence on Awlaki. Now the president was presented with a concrete opportunity to finish him off. According to Daniel Klaidman's account, Warsame had provided crucial intelligence on Awlaki. The Navy SEALs who captured Warsame had also taken possession of his laptop, thumb drives and other data storage devices. "The hardware was filled with emails and other evidence tying him directly to Awlaki. Warsame had met with the cleric only two days before, completing a major weapons deal," according to Klaidman. "Warsame's exposure to Awlaki and other high-ranking members of AQAP gave him access to critical 'patterns of life' intelligence, which he divulged to US officials when they interrogated him. He told them how Awlaki traveled, including the kinds of vehicles he used and the configuration of his convoys. He provided information about Awlaki's modes of communications as well as the elaborate security measures he and his entourage took."

Along with signals intercepts by JSOC and the CIA and "vital details of Awlaki's whereabouts" from Yemeni intelligence, the White House now had what it believed was its best shot to date at killing Awlaki. US military aircraft were at the ready. Obama gave the green light. JSOC would run the operation. A Special Ops Dragon Spear aircraft mounted with short-range Griffin missiles blasted through Yemeni airspace, backed by Marine Harrier jets and Predator drones, and headed toward Shabwah. A Global Hawk surveillance aircraft would hover above to relay a live feed back to the mission planners.

The American cleric, well aware that the United States was trying to kill him, had taken precautions to limit the number of people with whom he communicated. He changed locations frequently and switched vehicles often. On the evening of May 5, Awlaki and some friends were driving through Jahwa, in rural southern Shabwah, when their pickup truck was rocked by a massive explosion nearby, shattering its windows. Awlaki saw a flash of light and believed a rocket had been fired at the car. "Speed up!" Awlaki yelled at the driver. He looked around the truck and took stock of the situation. No one was hurt. The back of the truck was filled with canisters of gasoline, yet the vehicle had not exploded. Alhamdulillah, Awlaki thought. "Praise God." He called for backup.

While Awlaki and his colleagues scrambled to get away from what they thought was an ambush, JSOC planners watched via satellite as his car emerged from the dust clouds the Griffin had caused. They'd missed. There had been a malfunction of the targeting pod, and the guidance system was unable to keep a lock on Awlaki's vehicle. It would now be up to the Harriers and the drone. Strike two. A massive fireball lit up the sky. Just as the celebrations were to begin, the mission's planners watched in shock as the truck emerged once again. Its back bumper had been hit, but the truck was on the run. The Harriers were running low on fuel and had to abandon the mission. The third strike had to come from the drone. Awlaki peered out the window, looking for the perpetrators of the ambush. It was then he saw it: a drone hovering in the sky. As smoke and dust engulfed the area, Awlaki told the driver not to head toward any populated areas. They pulled into a small valley with some trees.

Two brothers, Abdullah and Musa'd Mubarak al Daghari, known in the AQAP community as the al Harad brothers, had seen the strike from a distance and were speeding to Awlaki's rescue. As the drone hovered overhead, the US war planners could not see what was happening below. A former JSOC planner, who read the US after-action reports on the failed mission, told me that the mission only had satellites that provided "top down imagery." With such satellites, he said, "You can't see shit. You're looking down at ants moving. All they saw were vehicles and the people in the vehicles were smart." Dust, gravel, smoke and flames had shielded the High Value Target. The Harad brothers quickly marshaled Awlaki and his driver into their Suzuki Vitara SUV and they took Awlaki's vehicle. They gave Awlaki directions to a cliff where he could go to take shelter, if he could make it past the American missiles. Awlaki hastily said goodbye and sped off in the Suzuki. The Harad brothers then headed in the opposite direction, driving in the truck the Americans had tried to blow up moments earlier.

As two vehicles took off in opposite directions, the American war planners had to decide which one to follow. They stuck with Awlaki's truck. Awlaki looked up and saw the drones still hovering. He managed to make it to the cliff in the mountains. From there, he watched as another round of missiles shot out of the sky and blew up the truck, killing the Harad brothers.

As JSOC celebrated what it thought was a successful hit, Awlaki performed the evening prayers and reflected on the situation. Tonight has "increased my certainty that no human being will die until they complete their livelihood and [reach their] appointed time," he thought. He fell asleep in the mountains, awakened later by colleagues who took him to safety at the home of his old friend Shaykh Nadari.

Nadari was asleep when the strikes happened, but he awoke to the sound of the explosions and had felt the ground shake. "When the time of dawn approached and as the light began to spread, it brought about with it Sheikh Anwar," Nadari later recalled. "He entered upon us with a cheerful smile so we all knew that he was the one targeted." The men embraced and Awlaki debriefed him on the strikes. He estimated that ten or eleven missiles had been fired during the attacks. Nadari asked him what it was like to be bombed by the Americans. "I found it much easier than we think of it. Something of fear befalls you, but the Almighty Allah sends down tranquility," Awlaki told his friend. "This time eleven missiles missed [their] target but the next time, the first rocket may hit it." Awlaki stayed with Nadari for a few days and then moved on. It was the last time the men would see each other.

"We were hoping it was him," said a US official after the strike. As news spread of the attack, anonymous US officials confirmed that the strike had been aimed at Awlaki. And for a moment, they thought they had accomplished the mission. The US drone operators "did not know that vehicles were exchanged and resulted in the wrong people dying and [that] Awlaki [was] still alive," according to a Yemeni security official.

Awlaki may have escaped, but the United States now had a serious bead on him. "The U.S. government has been targeting al-Awlaki now for some time, [and the] pace of that operation has been increasing," said Fran Townsend, the former senior Bush administration official. "You've got to believe they had an operational plan to attack the entire leadership [of al Qaeda], that the drone attack against al-Awlaki, if they had the opportunity, was going to be timed to the operation against bin Laden so that they were going to send a very distinct message that the entire leadership of al Qaeda, wherever they could be found, would be under attack."

Nasser Awlaki could not reach his son, but he had heard from intermediaries that Anwar was alive. He knew that, having failed yet again in its mission to find and kill him, the United States would be more determined than ever to finish the job. He watched the international news reports on the bin Laden raid and listened as commentators, pundits and senior US officials compared his son to the al Qaeda leader and even suggested that Awlaki would now succeed him as its leader. "They've killed bin Laden and now they're after my son," he said.

## 51 "It Was Cold-Blooded"

PAKISTAN, 2011—Three weeks after the raid that killed Osama bin Laden, the leaders of Pakistan's ISI were still fuming. President Obama and Pakistan's President Zardari publicly presented a unified front in celebrating the death of the al Qaeda leader, and Obama thanked the Pakistani government for its assistance over the years, saying, "Our counterterrorism cooperation with Pakistan helped lead us to bin Laden and the compound where he was hiding." Zardari penned an op-ed in the *Washington Post*, praising the raid and asserting that Pakistan "did its part." Prime Minister Yousaf Raza Gillani declared, "We will not allow our soil to be used against any other country for terrorism and therefore I think it's a great victory, it's a success and I congratulate the success of this operation."

Notwithstanding the diplomatic niceties, however, the violation of Pakistan's sovereignty was a scandal in the country. "It was cold-blooded," a senior Pakistani security official said. A day after the raid, Pakistan's Foreign Office issued a statement calling the raid "an unauthorized unilateral action," asserting: "Such an event shall not serve as a future precedent for any state, including the United States."

Pakistan's former foreign minister Shah Mahmood Qureshi—who was sacked for his bold stance in the Raymond Davis case—called the raid an "unprovoked aggression" against the country, while opposition leader Chaudhry Nisar Ali Khan called for the Pakistani president and prime minister to step down. "The operation tramples on our honor and dignity, and the president and prime minister must either give an explanation or resign," he said. "The government is keeping silent and there appears to be nobody to respond to propaganda against Pakistan."

"Every Pakistani wants to know how the US troops crossed over into a sovereign and independent Pakistan without permission," said the Muttahida Qaumi Movement chief, Altaf Hussain. "How was it possible that a raid was conducted well inside Pakistani territory? How was it possible that the raiders managed to leave unhurt and undetected? How come the government and intelligence agencies remained in the dark about all this?"

The Pakistani parliament condemned the operation as a "violation of

Pakistan's sovereignty" and called on Islamabad to "revisit and review its terms of engagement with the United States." Despite the delicate state of relations between the two governments, some US officials appeared to throw gasoline on the fire. During a press conference after the raid, Brennan charged that it was "inconceivable that bin Laden did not have a support system" in Pakistan.

As a group of 1,500 Pakistanis protested the killing of bin Laden, the United States had resumed its drone strikes. Just four days after the raid, a CIA strike targeted a house in North Waziristan. Coming on the heels of the Raymond Davis saga, the bin Laden raid was seen as an ominous symbol by Pakistan's intelligence services: Washington was becoming ever bolder in its operations in Pakistan and would strike with or without the ISI's permission. Obama had made good on his threat to use unilateral force inside Pakistan.

Although the ISI could not do much to strike back at the United States directly, it began a hunt to track down any Pakistanis it believed might have assisted the Americans in the bin Laden operation. Three weeks after the raid, intelligence agents arrested Dr. Shakil Afridi, the doctor who had helped the CIA run the fake Hepatitis B vaccination program in Abbottabad. He was locked up, tried and sentenced to thirty-three years in prison. Secretary of State Clinton and leading US lawmakers pushed for Afridi's release. Senators John McCain and Carl Levin said the sentence was "shocking and outrageous" and asserted that Afridi was a hero. "Dr. Afridi set an example that we wish others in Pakistan had followed long ago," the lawmakers wrote in a joint letter. "He should be praised and rewarded for his actions, not punished and slandered." The Pakistani foreign minister later pushed back. "For us, he's no hero, believe me," she said. "He is somebody whose activity has endangered our children."

The death of Osama bin Laden certainly did not impede the pace of killing in Afghanistan. "Since the killing of the al Qaeda leader, ISAF shows no sign of slowing down or cutting back on its mission. In fact, the pace has been higher than usual the past three months," boasted an ISAF press release issued just one week after bin Laden was killed. Incursions into Pakistan continued as well. On several occasions, NATO forces based in Afghanistan conducted operations along the border, in one case killing twenty-five Pakistani soldiers. At times, teams of SEALs or members of the CIA's Special Activities Division would cross into Pakistan to conduct operations. Drone strikes continued unabated. Despite Pakistan's protests, it was clear that the Obama administration would continue to act unilaterally in Pakistan, even after bin Laden's death.

## 52 "The US Sees al Qaeda as Terrorism, and We Consider the Drones Terrorism"

YEMEN, LATE 2011—While the Obama administration was basking in the success of the bin Laden killing and JSOC and the CIA were closing in on Anwar Awlaki, the Arab uprisings were spreading. Three weeks after the raid in Abbottabad, Pakistan, President Ali Abdullah Saleh's government in Yemen was on the brink of collapse. The protests were growing and President Saleh had played almost every card he had to keep the Americans on his side. He had given the US counterterrorism machine a virtual free hand to bomb Yemen and opened the doors wide for the evolution of a not-so-covert war. But as his grip on power weakened, AQAP saw opportunity in the chaos. By the summer of 2011, the elite US-backed counterterrorism units were pulled away from the fight against AQAP to defend the regime from its own people. In southern Yemen, where AQAP had its strongest presence, the mujahedeen sought to take advantage of an imploding state whose leaders had earned a reputation for corruption as they failed to provide basic goods and services.

On May 27, 2011, several hundred militants laid siege to Zinjibar, thirty miles northeast of the strategically important southern city of Aden, killing several soldiers, driving out local officials and taking control of the city within two days. Who exactly these militants were was a matter of some dispute. According to the Yemeni government, they were AQAP operatives. But the militants who took the city did not claim to be from AQAP. Instead, they announced themselves as a new group, Ansar al Sharia, or Supporters of Sharia. Senior Yemeni officials told me that Ansar al Sharia was simply a front for al Qaeda. They pointed out that the first known public reference to the group was made a month before the attack on Zinjibar by AQAP's top cleric, Adil al Abab. "The name Ansar al Sharia is what we use to introduce ourselves in areas where we work to tell people about our work and goals, and that we are on the path of Allah," he said, adding that the new name was intended to put the focus on the message of the group so as to avoid the associations of the al Qaeda brand. Whether Ansar al Sharia had more independent origins or was merely a product of AQAP's crude rebranding campaign, as Abab claimed, the group's significance would soon extend well beyond al Qaeda's historically limited spheres of influence in Yemen, while simultaneously popularizing some of AQAP's core tenets.

Months after Zinjibar was taken, I traveled to Aden, Yemen, where I met the Yemeni general whose job it was to retake the areas seized by Ansar al Sharia. General Mohammed al Sumali sat in the passenger seat of his armored Toyota Land Cruiser as it whizzed down the deserted highway connecting Aden to Abyan Province, where the Islamist militants had overrun Zinjibar. Sumali, a heavyset man with glasses and a mustache, was the commander of the 25th Mechanized Brigade of the Yemeni armed forces and the man charged with cleansing Zinjibar of the militants. Sumali's task carried international significance: retaking Zinjibar was seen by many as a final test of the flailing Saleh regime. The only real traffic on the road consisted of refugees fleeing the fighting and heading toward Aden, and military reinforcements moving toward Zinjibar. Sumali did not want to drive out to the front lines on the day I met him. "You know there could be mortars fired at you," he told me. Twice, the militants in Zinjibar had tried to assassinate the general in that very vehicle. There was a bullet hole in the front windshield, just above his head, and another in his side window, the spider-web cracks from the bullets' impact clearly visible. When I agreed not to hold him or his men responsible for what might happen, he relented, and we piled in and took off.

As we rode along the coast of the Arabian Sea, past stacks of abandoned mortar tubes, Russian T-72 tanks dug into sand berms and the occasional wandering camel, General Sumali gave me his account of what had happened on May 27, 2011, when Ansar al Sharia took the town. Sumali attributed the takeover to an "intelligence breakdown," explaining, "We were surprised in late May with the flow of a large number of terrorist militants into Zinjibar." He added that the militants "raided and attacked some security sites. They were able to seize these institutions. We were surprised when the governor, his deputies and other local officials fled to Aden." As the Yemeni military began fighting the militants, General Sumali told me, troops from Yemen's Central Security Forces fled, abandoning heavy weaponry as they retreated. The CSF, whose counterterrorism unit was armed, trained and funded by the United States, was commanded by President Saleh's nephew Yahya. A media outlet associated with the militants reported that Ansar's forces seized "heavy artillery pieces, modern antiaircraft weapons, a number of tanks and armoured transports in addition to large quantities of different kinds of ammunition."

Sumali said that as his forces attempted to repel the attack on Zinjibar a week later, they were attacked by the militants using the artillery seized from the CSF units. "Many of my men were killed," he told me. The Islamist fighters also conducted a series of bold raids on the base of the 25th Mechanized on the southern outskirts of Zinjibar. In all, more than 230 Yemeni soldiers died in battles with the militants in under a year. "These guys are incredibly brave," the general conceded, speaking of the militants. "If I had an army full of men with that bravery, I could conquer the world."

Sumali said Zinjibar fell because of bad intelligence, but critics of the crumbling Saleh regime told me a different story. They alleged that President Saleh's forces allowed the city to fall. The fighting there began as Saleh faced mounting calls both inside and outside Yemen for his resignation. Several of his key allies had defected to the growing opposition movement. After thirty-three years of outwitting his opponents, they said, Saleh saw that the end was near. "Saleh himself actually handed over Zinjibar to these militants," charged Abdul Ghani al Iryani, a well-connected political analyst. "He ordered his police force to evacuate the city and turn it over to the militants because he wanted to send a signal to the world that, without me, Yemen will fall into the hands of the terrorists." That theory, while unproven, was not baseless. Ever since the mujahedeen war against the Soviets in Afghanistan in the 1980s and continuing after 9/11, Saleh has famously milked the threat of al Qaeda and other militants to leverage counterterrorism funding and weapons from the United States and Saudi Arabia to bolster his power within the country and neutralize opponents. A Yemeni government official, who asked to remain anonymous because he was not authorized to speak publicly about military issues, admitted that troops from the US-trained and -supported Republican Guard did not respond when the militants entered the town. Those forces were commanded by Saleh's son Ahmed Ali Saleh. Neither did those forces loyal to one of the most powerful military figures in the country, General Ali Mohsen, commander of the 1st Armored Division, move in. Two months before Zinjibar was seized, Mohsen had defected from the Saleh regime and was publicly supporting his overthrow.

General Sumali told me he could not "confirm or deny" that Ansar al Sharia was actually AQAP. "What is important for me, as a soldier, is that they have taken up arms against us. Anyone who is attacking our institutions and military camps and killing our soldiers, we will fight them regardless of if they are al Qaeda affiliates or Ansar al Sharia," he told me. "We don't care what they call themselves. And I can't confirm whether Ansar al Sharia is affiliated with al Qaeda or if they are an independent group."

Rather than fighting AQAP, the elite US-backed Yemeni units—created and funded with the explicit intent to be used only for counterterrorism operations—redeployed to Sana'a to protect the collapsing regime from its own people. The US-supported units existed "mostly for the defense of the regime," said Iryani. "In the fighting in Abyan, the counterterrorism forces have not been deployed in any effective way. They are still here in the palace [in Sana'a], protecting the palace. That's how it is." At the time, John Brennan acknowledged that the "political tumult" had caused the US-trained units "to be focused on their positioning for internal political purposes as opposed to doing all they can against AQAP." So it was left to General Sumali and his conventional forces to fight the Islamists who had taken over Zinjibar.

As we passed the first front line on the outskirts of Zinjibar, "Tiger 1," and drove a half mile to "Tiger 2," Sumali agreed to let me get out of the vehicle. "We will only stay for two minutes," he told me. "It's dangerous here." The general was soon besieged by his men. They looked thin and haggard, many with long beards and tattered uniforms or no uniforms at all. Some of them pleaded with Sumali to write them notes authorizing additional combat pay. One of the soldiers told him, "I was with you when you were ambushed. I helped fight off the attack." Sumali scribbled on a piece of paper and handed it to the soldier. The scene continued until Sumali got back into the Toyota. As we drove away, he spoke from his armored vehicle through a loudspeaker at his men. "Keep fighting. Do not give up!"

Whether it was a crass ploy on the part of a failing regime to allow the militants to overrun Zinjibar or an opportunistic power grab by AQAP, the taking of several towns across southern Yemen by Islamist forces was significant. Unlike the militant movement al Shabab in Somalia, AQAP had never taken control of significant swaths of territory in Yemen. But Ansar al Sharia was determined to do just that, declaring an Islamic emirate in Abyan. Once Ansar al Sharia and its allies solidified their grip on Zinjibar, they implemented an agenda aimed at winning popular support. "Ansar al Sharia has been much more proactive in attempting to provide services in areas in Yemen where the government has virtually disappeared," Johnsen, the Yemen scholar at Princeton University, told me at the time. "It has claimed that it is following the Taliban model in attempting to provide services and Islamic government where the central government in Yemen has left a vacuum."

Ansar al Sharia repaired roads, restored electricity, distributed food and began security patrols inside the city and its surroundings. It also established Sharia courts where disputes could be resolved. "Al Qaeda and Ansar al Sharia brought security to the people in areas that were famous for insecurity, famous for thefts, for roadblocks," said Abdul Rezzaq al Jamal, the independent Yemeni journalist who regularly interviewed al Qaeda leaders and had spent extensive time in Zinjibar. "The people I met in

Zinjibar were grateful to al Qaeda and Ansar al Sharia for maintaining security." Although the militants in Abyan brought law and order, the policies were, at times, enforced with brutal tactics such as limb amputations against accused thieves and public floggings of suspected drug users. In one incident in the Ansar al Sharia–held town of Jaar, residents said they were summoned to a gruesome event at which militants used a sword to chop off the hands of two young men accused of stealing electrical cables. The amputated hands were then paraded around the town as a warning to would-be thieves. One of the young men, a fifteen-year-old, reportedly died soon after from blood loss. In another incident, Ansar al Sharia in Jaar publicly beheaded two men it alleged had provided information to the United States to conduct drone strikes. A third man was executed in Shabwah.

AQAP took advantage of the Yemeni government's unpopularity, shrewdly recognizing that its message of a Sharia-based system of law and order would be welcomed by many in Abyan who viewed the Saleh regime as a US puppet. The US missile strikes, the civilian casualties, an almost total lack of government services and a deepening poverty all helped create the opportunity AQAP seized. "As these groups of militants took over the city, then AQAP came in and also tribes from areas that have been attacked in the past by the Yemeni government and by the US government," Iryani, the Yemeni political analyst, told me. "They came because they have a feud against the regime and against the US. There is a nucleus of AQAP, but the vast majority are people who are aggrieved by attacks on their homes that forced them to go out and fight."

As Ansar al Sharia took control of towns in the south, Washington debated how to respond. Some within the Obama administration agitated for the United States to jump into the fight. General James Mattis, who took over from Petraeus as CENTCOM commander, proposed that the president sign off on a massive air assault on the "Unity" Soccer Stadium on the outskirts of Zinjibar, where Ansar al Sharia fighters had created a makeshift base from which to attack the Yemeni military. President Obama shot down the proposal. "We're not in Yemen to get involved with some domestic conflict," the president said. "We're going to continue to stay focused on threats to the homeland—that's where the real priority is."

Instead, the United States would fly supply runs into southern Yemen via helicopter to back up General Sumali's conventional forces. The Americans also provided real-time intelligence, obtained by drones, to Yemeni forces in Abyan. "It has been an active partnership. The Americans help primarily with logistics and intelligence," Sumali told me. "Then we pound the positions with artillery or air strikes." On a few occasions, Sumali told me, the United States conducted unilateral strikes around Zinjibar that "targeted al Qaeda leaders who are on the US terrorist black list," though he added, "I did not coordinate directly in these attacks." As cities throughout southern Yemen began to fall to Ansar al Sharia and the Saleh regime crumbled, in late 2011, the Obama administration decided to pull out most of the US military personnel in Yemen, including those training Yemen's counterterrorism forces. "They have left because of the security situation," Abu Bakr al Qirbi, Yemen's foreign minister, told me at the time. "Certainly, I think if they do not return and the counterterrorism units are not provided with the necessary ammunition and equipment, it will have an impact" on counterterrorism operations.

The United States was shifting tactics. With the Saleh regime severely weakened, the Obama administration calculated that it had little to gain from that alliance at this stage. The United States would double down on its use of air power and drones, striking in Yemen at will to carry on its campaign against AQAP. The Obama administration began quick construction of a secret air base in Saudi Arabia, closer than its base in Djibouti, that could serve as a launching pad for expanded drone strikes in Yemen. Target number one remained the same: Anwar Awlaki.

THE KEY TO ACCOMPLISHING ANYTHING in Yemen is navigating its labyrinthine tribal system. For years, a tribal patronage network helped bolster Saleh's regime. Many tribes had a neutral view of AQAP or saw it as a minor nuisance; some fought against al Qaeda forces, though others gave them safe haven or shelter. The stance of many tribes toward al Qaeda depended on how they believed AQAP could forward or hurt their agendas.

But the Obama administration's Yemen policy had enraged many tribal leaders who could potentially keep AQAP in check and, over the course of three years of regular bombings, had taken away the motivation for many leaders to do so. Several southern leaders angrily told me stories of US and Yemeni attacks in their areas that killed civilians and livestock and destroyed or damaged scores of homes. If anything, the US air strikes and support for Saleh-family-run counterterrorism units had increased tribal sympathy for al Qaeda. "Why should we fight them? Why?" asked Ali Abdullah Abdulsalam, a southern tribal sheikh from Shabwah who adopted the nom de guerre Mullah Zabara, out of admiration, he told me, for Taliban leader Mullah Mohammed Omar. "If my government built schools, hospitals and roads and met basic needs, I would be loyal to my government and protect it. So far, we don't have basic services such as electricity, water pumps. Why should we fight al Qaeda?" He told me that AQAP controlled large swaths of Shabwah, conceding that the group did "provide security and prevent looting. If your car is stolen, they will get it back for you." In areas "controlled by the government, there is looting and robbery. You can see the difference." Zabara added, "If we don't pay more attention, al Qaeda could seize and control more areas."

Zabara was quick to clarify that he believed AQAP was a terrorist group bent on attacking the United States, but that was hardly his central concern. "The US sees al Qaeda as terrorism, and we consider the drones terrorism," he said. "The drones are flying day and night, frightening women and children, disturbing sleeping people. This is terrorism." Zabara told me that several US strikes in his region had killed scores of civilians and that his community was littered with unexploded cluster bombs, which at times detonated, killing children. He and other tribal leaders asked the Yemeni and US governments for assistance in removing them, he said. "We did not get any response, so we use our guns to explode them." He also said the US government should pay money to the families of civilians killed in the missile strikes of the past three years. "We demand compensation from the US for killing Yemeni citizens, just like the Lockerbie case," he declared. "The world is one village. The US received compensation from Libya for the Lockerbie bombing, but the Yemenis have not."

I met Mullah Zabara and his men at the airport in Aden, along the coast where the USS *Cole* was bombed in October 2000, killing seventeen US sailors. Zabara was dressed in black tribal clothes, complete with a *jambiya*, the traditional dagger, at his stomach. He was also packing a Beretta on his hip. Zabara was a striking figure, with leathery skin and a large scar that formed a crescent moon along his right eye. "I don't know this American," he said to my Yemeni colleague. "So if anything happens to me as a result of this meeting—if I get kidnapped—we'll just kill you later." Everyone laughed nervously. We chatted for a while on a corniche, a cliffside road along the coast, before he drove us around the city for a tour. About twenty minutes into the tour, he pulled over on the side of the road and bought a six-pack of Heineken from a shanty store, tossing one to me before cracking open a can for himself. It was 11:00 a.m.

"Once I got stopped by AQAP guys at one of their checkpoints, and they saw I had a bottle of Johnnie Walker," he recalled as he guzzled his second Heineken in ten minutes and lit a cigarette. "They asked me, 'Why do you have that?' I told them, 'To drink it.'" He laughed heartily. "I told them to bother another guy and drove off." The message of the story was clear: the al Qaeda guys don't want trouble with tribal leaders. "I am not afraid of al Qaeda. I go to their sites and meet them. We are all known tribesmen, and they have to meet us to solve their disputes." Plus, he added, "I have 30,000 fighters in my own tribe. Al Qaeda can't attack me." Zabara served as a mediator with AQAP for the Yemeni government and was instrumental in securing the release of three French aid workers held hostage by the militant group for six months. Zabara was also asked by the Yemeni minister of defense to mediate with the militants in Zinjibar on several occasions, including to retrieve bodies of soldiers killed in areas held by Ansar al Sharia. "I have nothing against al Qaeda or the government," he told me. "I started the mediation in order to stop bloodshed and to achieve peace." In Zinjibar, his efforts were unsuccessful. He told me that while mediating, he met AQAP operatives from the United States, France, Pakistan and Afghanistan.

I asked him if he ever met with top AQAP leaders. "Fahd al Quso is from my tribe," he replied with a smile, referring to one of the most wanted suspects from the *Cole* bombing. "I saw [Said] al Shihri and [Nasir] al Wuhayshi five days ago in Shabwah," he casually added, referring to the two senior AQAP leaders, both of them US-designated terrorists. "We were walking, and they said, 'Peace be upon you.' I replied, 'Peace be upon you, too.' We have nothing against them. In the past, it was unthinkable to run into them. They were hiding in the mountains and caves, but now they are walking in the streets and going to restaurants." "Why is that?" I asked. "The regime, the ministers and officials are squandering the money allocated to fight al Qaeda, while al Qaeda expands," he replied. The United States "funds the Political Security and the National Security [Forces], which spend money traveling here and there, in Sana'a or in the US, with their family. All the tribes get is air strikes against us." He added that counterterrorism "has become like an investment" for the US-backed units. "If they fight seriously, the funds will stop. They prolonged the conflict with al Qaeda to receive more funds" from the United States. In January 2013, Zabara was assassinated in Abyan. It is unknown who killed him. That same month, the Yemeni government announced that Shihri had died "after succumbing to wounds received in a counter terrorism operation."

THERE IS NO DOUBT that when President Obama took office, al Qaeda had resurrected its shop in Yemen. But how big a threat AQAP actually posed to the United States or Saleh at that historical moment was the subject of much debate. What went almost entirely undiscussed in the US discourse on AQAP and Yemen was whether US actions—the targeted killings, the Tomahawk and drone strikes—might backfire, handing AQAP an opportunity to recruit and provoking the group to escalate its own violence. "We are not generating good will in these operations," Emile Nakhleh, the former senior CIA officer, told me. "We might target radicals and potential radicals, but unfortunately...other things and other people are being destroyed or killed. So, in the long run, it is not necessarily going to help. These operations will not necessarily help to deradicalize potential recruits. To me the bigger issue is the whole issue of radicalization. How do we pull the rug from under it?" He added: "These operations might be successful in specific cases, but I don't think they necessarily contribute to a deradicalization of certain segments of those societies."

Colonel Patrick Lang, who spent his entire career in covert operations leading sensitive missions, including in Yemen, told me that the threat posed by AQAP had been "greatly exaggerated as a threat to the United States. In fact, most Americans think that anything that might kill you personally, in an airplane or walking down Park Avenue or something, is the biggest threat in the world, right? Because they're not accustomed to dealing with conditions of danger as a standard of life, you know? So to say, 'Is AQAP a threat to the United States?' Yeah. They could bring down an airliner, kill a couple hundred people. But are they an existential threat to the United States? Of course not. Of course not. None of these people are an existential threat to the United States. We've gone crazy over this. We had this kind of hysterical reaction to danger."

IN THE SAME WAY that Afghanistan and Iraq provided a laboratory for training and developing a whole new generation of highly skilled, seasoned special operators, Yemen represented a paradigm that is sure to permeate US national security policy for decades to come. It was under the Bush administration that the United States declared the world a battlefield where any country would be fair game for targeted killings, but it was President Obama who put a bipartisan stamp on this worldview that will almost certainly endure well beyond his time in office. "This is going to go on for a long time," said Lang. "The Global War on Terror has acquired a life of its own. It's a self-licking ice cream cone. And the fact that this counterterrorism/counterinsurgency industry evolved into this kind of thing, involving all these people, the foundations, and the journalists and the book writers, and the generals, and the guys doing the shooting—all of that together has a great, tremendous amount of inertia that tends to keep it going in the same direction." Lang added: "It continues to roll. It will take a conscious decision, on the part of civilian policy makers, somebody like the president, for example, to decide that 'OK, boys, the show's over.'" But Obama was far from deciding the show was over.

## 53 The Pink House

WASHINGTON, DC, AND SOMALIA, 2011—A month after the bin Laden raid, Admiral McRaven was still the toast of Washington. In June 2011, he appeared before Congress for his confirmation hearings to become head of the US Special Operations Command. The new post was a promotion from the commander in chief and would officially put McRaven in charge of the military's global targeted killing program. As he sat before the Senate Armed Services Committee, praise was heaped upon McRaven by Republicans and Democrats alike for his running of the bin Laden raid and his role in other operations. "I salute you and your colleagues in the SEALs for extraordinary operations," said Democratic senator Jack Reed. "I think your decisiveness and your feel for every level of the conflict, from the villages of Afghanistan and Pakistan all the way up here to the more complicated rooms in Washington, was amply demonstrated." Republican John McCain echoed those comments, telling McRaven, "What you had achieved in your distinguished career is already extraordinary before May 2, 2011. But on that day, by leading the mission that killed Osama bin Laden, you and your men won an enduring place in American military history."

But then the real focus of the hearings unfolded: Were McRaven and his Special Ops Forces "prepared and capable to expand" their "operations at a moment's notice worldwide?" Reed asked. McRaven told the senators that because of the dramatically increased deployment of Special Ops in the widening global battle space, more resources would be required and a new generation of operators had to be trained. Then the admiral zeroed in on the current prime targets. "From my standpoint as a former JSOC commander, I can tell you we were looking very hard at Yemen and Somalia," he declared. McRaven said that in order to expand successful "kinetic strikes" there, the United States would have to increase its use of drones, as well as on-the-ground intelligence, surveillance and reconnaissance operations. "Any expansion of manpower is going to have to come with a commensurate expansion of the enablers," McRaven declared.

When I flew into Mogadishu in the month McRaven was promoted, a rather large symbol of the not-so-quiet presence of American "enablers" was in full view from the moment I landed. Nestled in a back corner of Aden Adde International Airport was a sprawling walled compound. Set on the coast of the Indian Ocean, the facility looked like a small gated community, with more than a dozen buildings behind large protective walls and secured by guard towers at each of its four corners. I later learned from multiple Somali and US intelligence sources that it was a new counterterrorism center run by the CIA and used by JSOC operators. Somalis called it the "Pink House" because of its color. Others simply called it "Guantánamo." Adjacent to the compound were eight large metal hangars, and the CIA had its own aircraft at the airport. The site, which airport officials and Somali intelligence sources said was completed in early 2011, was guarded by Somali soldiers, but the Americans controlled access. At the facility, the CIA ran a counterterrorism training program for Somali intelligence agents and operatives aimed at building an indigenous strike force capable of snatch operations and targeted "combat" operations against al Shabab.

As part of its expanding counterterrorism program in Somalia, the CIA also utilized the secret prison buried in the basement of Somalia's National Security Agency headquarters, where prisoners suspected of being al Shabab members or of having links to the group were held. Some of the prisoners, like al Qaeda leader Saleh Ali Saleh Nabhan's alleged right-hand man, had been seized off the streets of Kenya and rendered by plane to Mogadishu. Others had been yanked off commercial flights after landing or taken from their homes in Somalia and brought to the dungeon. Although the underground prison was officially run by the Somali NSA, US intelligence personnel paid the salaries of local agents and also directly interrogated prisoners. Among the sources who provided me with information on the prison and the CIA counterterrorism center were senior Somali intelligence officials, senior members of Somalia's Transitional Federal Government, former prisoners held at the underground prison and several well-connected Somali analysts and militia leaders, some of whom worked with US personnel, including from the CIA. A US official, who confirmed the existence of both sites, told me, "It makes complete sense to have a strong counterterrorism partnership" with the Somali government.

The elevated CIA presence in Mogadishu was part of the Obama administration's counterterrorism focus on Somalia, which included targeted strikes by JSOC, drone attacks and expanded surveillance operations. The US agents "are here full time," a senior Somali intelligence official told me. At times, he said, there were as many as thirty of them in Mogadishu, but he stressed that those working with the Somali NSA did not conduct operations. Rather, they advised and trained Somali agents. "In this environment, it's very tricky. They want to help us, but the situation is not allowing them to do [it] however they want. They are not in control of the politics, they are not in control of the security," he added. "They are not controlling the environment like Afghanistan and Iraq. In Somalia, the situation is fluid, the situation is changing, personalities changing."

According to well-connected Somali sources, the CIA was reluctant to deal directly with Somali political leaders, who, despite public praise, were regarded by US officials as corrupt and untrustworthy. Instead, the United States put Somali intelligence agents directly on its payroll. Somali sources with knowledge of the program described the agents as lining up to receive $200 monthly cash payments from Americans, in a country where the average annual income was about $600. "They support us in a big way financially," said the senior Somali intelligence official. "They are the largest [funder] by far."

It was unclear how much control, if any, Somalia's president had over this counterterrorism force or if he was even fully briefed on its operations. The CIA personnel and other US intelligence agents "do not bother to be in touch with the political leadership of the country and that says a lot about the intentions," Abdirahman "Aynte" Ali, the al Shabab researcher who also had extensive sources within the Somali government, told me. "Essentially, the CIA seems to be operating, doing the foreign policy of the United States. You should have had State Department people doing foreign policy, but the CIA seems to be doing it across the country." The Somali officials I interviewed said the CIA was the lead US agency on the Mogadishu counterterrorism program, but they also indicated that US military intelligence agents are at times involved. When asked if they are from JSOC or the Defense Intelligence Agency, the senior Somali intelligence official responded, "We don't know. They don't tell us."

As the CIA built up its Somali intelligence agency, CIA Director Leon Panetta appeared before Congress and was asked about the fight against al Qaeda and its affiliates in Yemen, Somalia and North Africa. "Our approach has been to develop operations in each of these areas that will contain al Qaeda and go after them so that they have no place to escape," he said. "So we are doing that in Yemen. It's obviously a dangerous and uncertain situation, but we continue to work with elements there to try to develop counterterrorism. We're working with JSOC as well in their operations. Same thing is true for Somalia."

After I broke the story of the CIA's counterterrorism program in Somalia for the *Nation*, one Somali official told the *New York Times* that the CIA-backed spy service was becoming a "government within a government." "No one, not even the president, knows what the N.S.A. is doing," he said. "The Americans are creating a monster."

According to former detainees, the NSA's underground prison, which was staffed by Somali guards, consisted of a long corridor lined with filthy small cells infested with bedbugs and mosquitoes. One said that when he arrived in February 2011, he saw two white men wearing military boots, combat trousers, gray tucked-in shirts and black sunglasses. The former prisoners described the cells as windowless and the air as thick, moist and foul-smelling. Prisoners, they said, were not allowed outside. Many developed rashes and scratched themselves incessantly. Some had been detained for a year or more without charges or access to lawyers or family. According to one former prisoner, inmates who had been there for long periods would pace around constantly, while others leaned against walls, rocking.

A Somali journalist who was arrested in Mogadishu after filming a sensitive military operation told me that he was taken to the prison and held in a windowless underground cell. Among the prisoners he met during his time there was a man who held a Western passport (he declined to identify the man's nationality). Some of the prisoners told him they were picked up in Nairobi and rendered on small aircraft to Mogadishu, where they were handed over to Somali intelligence agents.

Once in custody, according to the senior Somali intelligence official and former prisoners, some detainees were freely interrogated by US and French agents. "Our goal is to please our partners, so we get more [out] of them, like any relationship," the Somali intelligence official told me. The Americans, he said, operated unilaterally in the country, but the French agents were embedded within AMISOM at its airport base. Indeed, in July 2011, I witnessed a French intelligence agent, with an AMISOM commander, monitoring the passengers disembarking a flight from Nairobi. Somali intelligence sources told me the French sometimes ask for passengers to be snatched from flights and questioned. According to Aynte, in some cases, "the US and other intelligence agencies have notified the Somali intelligence agency that some people, some suspects, people who have been in contact with the leadership of al Shabab, are on their way to Mogadishu on a [commercial] plane, and to essentially be at the airport for those people. Catch them, interrogate them."

The underground prison was housed in the same building once occupied by Somalia's infamous National Security Service (NSS) during the military regime of Mohamed Siad Barre, who ruled from 1969 to 1991. A former prisoner told me he actually saw an old NSS sign outside. During Barre's regime, the notorious basement prison and interrogation center, which sat behind the presidential palace in Mogadishu, was a staple of the state's apparatus of repression. It was referred to as Godka, "The Hole."

"The bunker is there, and that's where the intelligence agency does interrogate people," said Aynte, who maintained contact with Somali intelligence officials. "When CIA and other intelligence agencies—who actually are in Mogadishu—want to interrogate those people, they usually just do that." Somali officials "start the interrogation, but then foreign intelligence agencies eventually do their own interrogation as well, the Americans and the French." The US official made available to me for comment said that American operatives' "debriefing" of prisoners in the facility had "been done on only rare occasions" and always jointly with Somali agents.

In a dramatic flourish that appeared to fulfill his campaign promise to close the CIA's infamous "black sites" established under President Bush, Obama had signed Executive Order 13491 on January 22, 2009. The order required that "the CIA shall close as expeditiously as possible any detention facilities that it currently operates and shall not operate any such detention facility in the future." To human rights groups, the use of the underground prison appeared a backdoor subversion of that order. After the publication of my report on the prison in the *Nation* and a subsequent, related article by Jeffrey Gettleman in the *New York Times*, a coalition of human rights groups wrote a letter to President Obama. The articles, they said, "further call into question whether the United States is in compliance with its obligations to respect, and ensure respect for, international human rights requirements relating to *non-refoulement*, arbitrary detention, and humane treatment." Citing Obama's signing of Executive Order 13491, they told the president, "You made clear your deep commitment to ensuring that counterterrorism operations are conducted with respect for human rights and the rule of law. We urge you to reaffirm that commitment by disclosing, to the fullest extent possible, the nature of U.S. involvement in overseas detention, interrogation, and transfer operations relating to the prison in Somalia, so that there can be meaningful public dialogue regarding the extent to which such operations comply with the law."

Despite the early rhetoric from President Obama and his surrogates about the need to balance liberty and security, two years into his administration it was clear that the White House had repeatedly chosen national security over civil liberties. And though some of the excesses of the Bush era were ended and others curbed, the kill/capture program was growing, not abating. Many serious questions still loomed over the targeted killing program: Was it actually making America safer? Would these operations result in less terrorism or more? Would the actions taken by the White House in the name of defeating terrorism—drone strikes, assassinations, renditions—actually aid groups like al Shabab, AQAP and the Taliban in recruiting new members and supporters?

IN EARLY 2011, al Shabab was in firm control of a greater swath of Somalia than the Transitional Federal Government, even though the TFG was supported by thousands of US-trained, -armed and -funded African Union troops. In Mogadishu, despite increased US funding and weapons, AMISOM forces were largely confined to their bases. Instead of fighting a counterinsurgency, they opted for regular shelling of al Shabab–held neighborhoods teeming with civilians. JSOC was bumping off militant figures, but the civilian death toll of AMISOM's shelling pushed some clan leaders to lend support to al Shabab. Meanwhile, the Somali government was viewed as weak, illegitimate or worse.

"Ninety-nine percent of the government are corrupted, immoral, dishonest people, selected by the international community," Mohammed Farah Siad, a Mogadishu businessman, told me when I visited him at his home near the port of Mogadishu during the summer of 2011. Siad, who had owned his business since 1967, complained of having to regularly pay bribes and of government officials stealing from him and other importers. "I think those people must be selected by being in the category of the worst. The more you are criminal, the more you are a drug abuser, the more you will be selected as member of the Somali parliament." The government, he declared, existed "to cheat money." Siad, who adamantly condemned al Shabab and al Qaeda, said that al Shabab was far better organized than the Somali government, and he believed that if the AMISOM troops pulled out, al Shabab would take power. "Immediately, in half an hour," he exclaimed. "Less than a half an hour." Somalis, he said, were faced with a choice between the government "thieves" and the al Shabab "criminals." "We are like orphans," he concluded.

Al Shabab controlled what "amounted to be about half of Somalia, which is the size of Texas. So you could imagine the large amount of the country—including a portion of Mogadishu, the capital city," Aynte estimated. It was abundantly clear that if the Somali government was incapable of building police and military forces that could stabilize even the capital, the influence of al Shabab would continue to grow. Each suicide bombing was evidence that the government was vulnerable and every mortar that crashed into civilian areas sent a message that the government—and the US-backed African Union force—was not on the side of the people.

With most Somalis caught between a government they despised and Islamic militants they feared, the Obama administration unveiled what it referred to as a "dual-track" approach to Somalia. It would simultaneously deal with the "central government" in Mogadishu, as well as regional and clan players in Somalia. "The dual track policy only provides a new label for the old (and failed) Bush Administration's approach," observed Somalia analyst Afyare Abdi Elmi. "It inadvertently strengthens clan divisions, undermines inclusive and democratic trends and most importantly, creates a conducive environment for the return of the organized chaos or warlordism in the country."

The dual-track policy encouraged self-declared, clan-based regional administrations to seek recognition and support from the United States. "Local administrations are popping up every week," said Aynte at the time. "Most of them don't control anywhere, but people are announcing local governments in the hopes that [the] CIA will set up a little outpost in their small village."

By mid-2011, "In Washington, American officials said debates were under way about just how much the United States should rely on clandestine militia training and armed drone strikes to fight the Shabab," according to the *New York Times*. "Over the past year, the American Embassy in Nairobi, according to one American official, has become a hive of military and intelligence operatives who are 'chomping at the bit' to escalate operations in Somalia."

While the United States ratcheted up both its rhetoric and its strikes against al Shabab, its tactical successes were largely in rural areas outside of Mogadishu. In the Somali capital, the CIA-trained and -funded counterterrorism force brought few tangible gains. "So far what we have not seen is the results," the senior Somali intelligence official told me in the summer of 2011. He conceded that neither US nor Somali forces had been able to conduct a single successful targeted mission in al Shabab–controlled areas in the capital. In late 2010, according to the official, US-trained Somali agents conducted an operation in an al Shabab area that failed terribly and resulted in the death of several agents. "There was an attempt, but it was a haphazard one," he recalled. On February 3, 2011, al Shabab broadcast the execution of an alleged CIA informant on its al Kataib television channel.

While the CIA's newest project in Somalia struggled to achieve any victories, the United States waged its campaign against al Shabab primarily by continuing to support the AMISOM forces, which were not conducting their mission with anything resembling surgical precision. AMISOM regularly put out press releases boasting of gains against al Shabab and the retaking of territory, but the reality was far more complicated.

As I walked throughout the areas AMISOM had retaken in 2011, I saw a honeycomb of underground tunnels once used by al Shabab fighters to move from building to building. By some accounts, the tunnels stretched continually for miles. Leftover food, blankets and ammo cartridges lay scattered near "pop-up" positions once used by al Shabab snipers and guarded by sandbags—all that remained of guerrilla warfare positions. Not only had the al Shabab fighters been cleared from the aboveground areas, the civilians that once resided there were cleared, too. On several occasions when I was there, AMISOM forces fired artillery from their airport base at the Bakaara market, where whole neighborhoods had been totally abandoned. Houses lay in ruins and animals wandered, chewing trash. In some areas, bodies had been hastily buried in trenches with dirt barely masking the remains. On the side of the road in one former al Shabab neighborhood, a decapitated corpse lay just yards away from a new government checkpoint.

In a series of interviews in Mogadishu, several of the country's internationally recognized leaders, including President Sharif, called on the US government to quickly and dramatically increase its assistance to the Somali military in the form of training, equipment and weapons. Moreover, they argued that without viable civilian institutions, Somalia would remain vulnerable to terrorist groups that could further destabilize not only Somalia but the region. "I believe that the US should help the Somalis to establish a government that protects civilians and its people," Sharif said. But the United States had little faith in Sharif and other government officials—and with good reason. "If the [Somali government] were doing anything but pocketing all the money that has been given to it, it would have a lot more resources than al Shabab," said Ken Menkhaus, the Davidson College Somalia scholar. According to the UN Monitoring Group on Somalia, weapons and ammunition given to the Somali government "and its affiliated militias" were increasingly surfacing on the black market and ultimately ending up in the hands of al Shabab. The United Nations estimated that "the Government and pro-Government forces sell between one third and one half of their ammunition" on the black market.

In the battle against al Shabab, the United States did not cast its lot with the Somali government. The emerging US strategy on Somalia—borne out in stated policy, the expanded covert presence and funding plans—was two-pronged. On the one hand, the CIA was training, paying and at times directing Somali intelligence agents who were not firmly under the control of the Somali government, while JSOC conducted unilateral strikes without the prior knowledge of the government. On the other, the Pentagon increased its support for and arming of the counterterrorism operations of non-Somali African military forces.

By 2011, one Somali who was exercising a lot of control over his territory was Indha Adde, the former Islamic Courts Union defense minister and erstwhile al Shabab ally. When I visited him in the summer of 2011, he had rebranded himself as General Yusuf Mohammed Siad and was decked out in a military uniform bearing three stars. He had become a high-ranking officer in the Somali military. While the United States and other Western powers conducted specialized training exercises and armed and equipped the Ugandan and Burundian militaries under the auspices of AMISOM, to the tune of hundreds of millions of dollars, the Somali government could barely pay its own soldiers. The Somali military was underfunded and underarmed, its soldiers poorly paid, highly undisciplined and, at the end of the day, more loyal to their clans than to the central government. That's how the rent-a-militia program was born. And Indha Adde was a prime example of how it operated.

While Washington went to great lengths to shield its support for Somali warlords and militias, it was a barely masked public secret in Mogadishu that its proxies from Ethiopia, Kenya and AMISOM were making deals with warlords similar to those brokered with the CIA's Alliance for the Restoration of Peace and Counterterrorism in the early 2000s.

As the United States focused on its own unilateral kinetic ops, the Somali government and AMISOM turned to some unsavory characters in a dual effort: to independently build something vaguely resembling a national army and—much in the way the United States attempted with its Awakening Councils in the Sunni areas of Iraq in 2006—to purchase strategic loyalty from former allies of the current enemy. Indha Adde was given a military rank, despite never having served in an official army, while others were given government ministries in return for allocating their militia forces to the fight against al Shabab. Several were former allies of al Qaeda or al Shabab, and many had directly fought the US-sponsored Ethiopian invasion or had rallied against the US-led mission in Somalia in the early 1990s that culminated in the Black Hawk Down incident. Other militias were little more than proxies for the Ethiopian or Kenyan governments, both of which are heavily backed by Washington. In 2011, Indha Adde had become sort of a hybrid of his former selves, an Islamic warlord who believed in Sharia law, taking money and weapons from AMISOM and cultivating friendly relations with the CIA.

Large parts of Mogadishu were not accessible without Indha Adde's permission, and he controlled one of the largest militias and possessed more technicals in the city than any other warlord. His mechanic, who built specially weaponized pickups for Indha Adde's forces (and bore a striking resemblance to Mr. T), was said to be the best in Mogadishu. With a senior military rank and a flow of modern weapons, Indha Adde was more powerful—and, at least as far as he saw it, respectable—than ever. As I sat outside one of Indha Adde's homes, waiting for his entourage to prepare to head out for the front lines, a white Toyota Corolla pulled into the drive. Within moments, box after box of fresh ammunition was being unloaded.

Indha Adde took me to several front lines where his militia was fighting al Shabab. As we made our way to various positions, we were repeatedly fired on by al Shabab snipers. A few months earlier, Indha Adde's personal bodyguard was shot in the head as he stood in front of his boss in a battle with al Shabab fighters. According to witnesses, Indha Adde slung the man's body over his shoulder, carried him to a secured area, picked up an automatic weapon and then charged at his killers. "One night I fired 120 AK-47 rounds, four magazines and 250 machine gun bullets. I am the number one fighter on the front lines," he told me as we walked through the bombed-out remains of a neighborhood his men had recently retaken from al Shabab. Unlike the forces from AMISOM, Indha Adde did not wear any body armor, and he regularly stopped to take calls on his hands-free mobile. "The role of general is two-way street. In a conventional, well-funded war, the generals lead from behind with orders," he declared. "But in a guerrilla war, as we are in, the general has to be at front line to boost the morale of his men."

As we walked alongside trenches on the outskirts of Bakaara market, once occupied by fighters from al Shabab, Indha Adde's entourage stopped. In one of the trenches, the foot of a corpse poked out from a makeshift grave consisting of some sand dumped loosely over the body. One of Indha Adde's militiamen said the body was that of a foreigner who fought alongside al Shabab. "We bury their dead, and we also capture them alive," Indha Adde told me in his low, raspy voice. "We take care of them if they are Somali, but if we capture a foreigner, we execute them so that others will see we have no mercy."

I asked Indha Adde why he was now fighting on the side of the United States and against his former al Shabab allies, and he spat what sounded like memorized verses without skipping a beat: "Foreign international terrorists came into our country, started to kill our people. They killed some of our fathers, raped our women and looted our houses. It is my obligation to defend my people, my country and my religion. I have to either liberate my people or die in the course." The militants from al Qaeda and al Shabab changed, he said, not him. "The terrorists are misinterpreting the religion," he said. "If I would have known what I now know—that the guys I was protecting were terrorists—I would have handed them to the CIA without asking for any money."

ONE OF THE MORE POWERFUL FORCES that emerged in Somalia's anti–al Shabab government-militia nexus was Ahlu Sunna Wal Jama (ASWJ), a Sufi Muslim paramilitary organization. Originally founded in the 1990s as a quasi-political organization dedicated to Sufi religious scholarship and community works—and avowedly nonmilitant—ASWJ viewed itself as a buffer against what it saw as the encroachment of Wahabism in Somalia. Its proclaimed mandate was to "preach a message of peace and delegitimize the beliefs and political platform" of "fundamentalist movements." It ran madrassas and taught Koranic memorization. The sect's prayer services, which featured a lot of group chanting, more closely resembled an evangelical Sunday service than conventional Friday prayers at mosques throughout the Muslim world.

In 2008, al Shabab began targeting Ahlu Sunna leaders, carrying out assassinations and desecrating the tombs of ASWJ's elders. Al Shabab considered ASWJ to be a cult whose practices of celebrating the dead and speaking in tongues were heresy. After much debate within the ASWJ community, militias were formed to take up arms against al Shabab. At the beginning, its fighting force of undisciplined clan fighters and religious scholars left much to be desired. Then, quietly, Ethiopia started arming and financing ASWJ, as well as providing its forces with training and, eventually, boots on the ground. By early 2010, ASWJ was widely seen as an Ethiopian—and therefore US—proxy. In March 2010, after heated debate within its community, ASWJ signed a formal cooperation agreement with the Somali government.

One of the prime beneficiaries of ASWJ's new status as a paramilitary militia was Abdulkadir Moalin Noor, simply known as "the Khalifa," or the successor. His father, a widely revered holy man, died in 2009 at the age of ninety-one and had designated Noor as the new spiritual leader of the movement. Noor was educated in London and managed his family's business investments outside of Somalia. When his father died, he left his life of safety and comfort to return to Mogadishu, where he was given the title of minister of state for the presidency. Noor, however, still enjoyed the luxuries of the West. He rolled around Mogadishu in an armored SUV with animal skins over the seats. He set up a wireless Internet network in an ASWJ camp outside of the capital that didn't have indoor plumbing and his Koran was housed in a shiny new iPad. He showed me an e-mail from Ethiopia's minister of foreign affairs on his recently acquired white iPhone.

Noor, who regularly met with Western officials and intelligence agents, declined to outline who exactly was funding ASWJ from the outside, but he did single out the United States as Somalia's "number one" ally. "I'm here to thank them, because they are helping us, fighting against the terrorists," he told me. "What about on a military level?" I asked him. "I don't want to mention a lot of things," he replied. "But, they are in deep, deep. They are working with our intelligence, they are giving them training. They are working with the military personnel. They have special trained forces fighting against al Shabab here. I don't want to disclose—but I know they're doing a good job. They do have people here, fighting al Shabab. And by the help of Allah, we hope this mayhem will end soon."

By mid-2011, the ASWJ militias had emerged as some of the most effective fighters battling al Shabab forces outside of Mogadishu, winning back territory in the Mudug region and several other pockets of the country. But, like most powerful paramilitary groups in Somalia, there was far more to the group than met the eye.

The UN Monitoring Group on Somalia declared that some ASWJ militias "appear to be proxies for neighboring States rather than emergent local authorities." ASWJ also received support from Southern Ace, a private security firm. Technically registered in Hong Kong in 2007 and run by a white South African, Edgar Van Tonder, Southern Ace committed "egregious violations of the arms embargo" on Somalia, according to the United Nations, and "also began to explore prospects for arms trafficking and engaged in horticultural experiments aimed at the production of narcotic drugs, including marijuana, cocaine and opium."

Between April 2009 and early 2011, according to the United Nations, "Southern Ace and its local associates recruited and operated a well-equipped, 220-strong militia...supervised by a dozen Zimbabweans and three Westerners, at an estimated cost of $1 million in salaries and at least $150,000 in arms and ammunition. The result was one of the strongest forces...with the potential to change the balance of power in the area."

Southern Ace began acquiring arms from the weapons market in Somalia, including scores of Kalashnikovs, heavy machine guns, rocket-propelled grenade launchers and an antiaircraft ZU-23 machine gun with 2,000 rounds of ammunition. The company's arms purchases "were so substantial" that local officials "noted a significant rise in the price of ammunition and a shortage of ZU-23 rounds." Some of the weapons were mounted on four-wheel drive vehicles and pickup trucks. The company also imported to Somalia "Philippine army-style uniforms and bullet-proof jackets in support of their operations," according to the United Nations.

Backed by Ethiopia and Southern Ace, ASWJ conducted a series of major offensives against al Shabab that the United Nations alleged were supported through violations of the arms embargo. Although Ethiopia and the United States undoubtedly saw ASWJ as the best counterbalance to the rhetoric of al Shabab and al Qaeda, in just three years they transformed a previously nonviolent entity into one of the most powerful armed groups in Somalia. "To a certain extent, the resort to Somali proxy forces by foreign Governments represents a potential return to the 'warlordism' of the 1990s and early 2000s," a UN report soberly concluded. Such practices, it added, "historically proved to be counterproductive."

SOUTHERN ACE WAS HARDLY the only mercenary company to intervene in Somalia. No modern US war would be complete without the involvement of Blackwater founder Erik Prince. Even though his company's crimes and scandals were closely associated with the neoconservatives and the Bush era, Blackwater forces continued to play a significant role in the CIA's global operations under the Obama administration. With Blackwater under intense investigation and his top deputies indicted on federal conspiracy and weapons charges, Prince left the United States in 2010 and relocated to Abu Dhabi in the United Arab Emirates, a major hub for the mercenary industry and the war-contracting business as a whole. Prince had close ties to the royals, particularly the crown prince of Abu Dhabi. He said he chose Abu Dhabi because of its "great proximity to potential opportunities across the entire Middle East, and great logistics," adding that it has "a friendly business climate, low to no taxes, free trade and no out of control trial lawyers or labor unions. It's pro-business and opportunity."

From his adopted home in the UAE, Prince continued his mercenary activities. He left the United States, he said, to "make it harder for the jackals to get my money," adding that he wanted to explore new opportunities in "the energy field." A few days before Christmas 2010, Prince landed at Mogadishu's international airport, disembarked a private jet and was taken to the VIP lounge, where he met with unidentified individuals for an hour. He then got back aboard his jet and took off. "We have been hearing more and more about Blackwater's ambitions to make its mark in Somalia," a Western official told me at the time.

Prince had long been interested in building a privatized counterpiracy force that could deploy off the coast of Somalia. In late 2008, he was in talks with more than a dozen shipping companies about hiring Blackwater to protect their ships and vessels through the Horn of Africa and the Gulf of Aden. In 2006, he had purchased a 183-foot vessel, the *McArthur*, and transformed it into an antipiracy mother ship that could be equipped with Little Bird helicopters, inflatable boats, thirty-five private soldiers and a .50-caliber machine gun. "We could put vessels out there and go and stop fishing boats the pirates are using a lot cheaper than the Navy could using a billion and a half to two billion dollar war ships," Prince said. The European Union, he said, was "out there with 24 ships, trying to cover 2 million square miles of ocean in the Indian Ocean dealing with Somali pirates. That comes out to 80,000 square miles per vessel. That's just not getting it done."

Prince suggested that his force could operate like the privateers during the American Revolution. "A privateer was a private ship, with a private crew, with a private master and they would receive a hunting license. It's

called a Letter of Marque. It's actually provided for in the Constitution,"
Prince declared in a speech shortly before he left for the UAE. "They were
allowed to go hunt enemy shipping and they did very well. Even General
Washington was an investor in one of those privateer operations."

There was no doubt that piracy was expanding off Somalia's coast. Pirate
attacks continued to climb during the second half of 2010—from September 2010 to January 2011, the number of hostages held by pirates rose from
250 to 770. Pirates had begun demanding increasingly exorbitant ransoms
and were using commandeered "mother ships" to carry out more ambitious attacks.

In January 2011, US soldiers conducted a counterpiracy incursion inland, snatching three young Somali men and bringing them aboard a ship
for questioning. Soon after, the head of CENTCOM's naval forces, Vice Admiral Mark Fox, suggested that the United States should employ counterterrorism measures in the fight against Somali piracy. Citing the increasing
sophistication of the pirates' technology, as well as their links to al Shabab,
Fox spoke of countering nascent pirate attacks inland. "Al Shabab is responsible for a lot of training activity and camps and that sort of thing in
Somalia," he declared. "The pirates use these things. There cannot be a
segregation between terrorist activity, in my mind, and counter-piracy."

Although Fox may have been overstating links between al Shabab and
the pirates—many accounts indicate that al Shabab was extorting from the
pirates more than it was coordinating with them—he was correct that the
pirates were becoming bolder.

On February 16, 2011, Abduwali Muse—the lone pirate prosecuted for
the hijacking of the *Maersk Alabama,* was sentenced to thirty-three years
in prison. Two days later, an SOS was sent from a personal yacht, the *SV
Quest,* owned by California residents Jean and Scott Adam. They were captured, along with Seattle-based crewmates Phyllis Macay and Robert Rig-
gle, 275 miles from the coast of Oman. An ad hoc flotilla of naval vessels
from the US 5th Fleet began trailing the *Quest* soon after its capture was
reported, supported by helicopters and unarmed surveillance drones. The
rescue mission caught up to the *Quest* in international waters between the
northernmost tip of Puntland and the Yemeni island of Socotra.

By the next day, President Obama had authorized the use of lethal force.
But in all the ways that the takedown of the pirates who took the *Maersk
Alabama* was a success, the mission to liberate the passengers on board
the *Quest* was a disaster.

An unusually large, unwieldy band of nineteen pirates had boarded the
yacht, making the succinct "three shots, three dead pirates" conclusion of
the *Alabama* rescue impossible to replicate. So the stalemate continued

until two pirate representatives from the *Quest* willingly boarded one of the ships to negotiate with the FBI. The talks soon stalled, and FBI agents detained the pirates. The next morning, a rocket-propelled grenade was fired at one of the Navy ships, before gunfire erupted within the yacht. Two pirates were killed. US forces then sprang into action: two motorboats carried fifteen Navy SEAL commandos to the yacht, where intense hand-to-hand combat ensued. Two pirates were killed by the SEALS, one shot and the other stabbed. It was already too late for the hostages. Two had died, and the others had suffered fatal gunshot wounds. It is unclear whether the hostages had been executed or caught in the crossfire.

In a telephone press conference, Admiral Fox stated that the hostages were shot prior to the boarding and violent clearing operation. A BBC correspondent who spoke with the pirates reported that they took credit for killing the captives but had done so only after the US Navy fired the first shots, which killed the first two pirates. The fifteen remaining pirates were taken into US custody, and fourteen were later indicted on charges of piracy and kidnapping (one was a juvenile and was determined not to have been a central player in the hijacking).

Manifesting one of the qualities that defined Blackwater's ascent, Erik Prince again saw opportunity in crisis. In 2009, Blackwater had inked a deal with the government of Djibouti to operate the antipiracy ship *McArthur* from its territory (the ship was later sold to a Saracen International subsidiary). The arrangement was the result of a series of meetings between Djiboutian officials, Prince and Cofer Black, the former head of the CIA's Counterterrorism Center, who at the time was a senior executive at Blackwater. Initial estimates indicated that the company could make about $200,000 per escort job for shipping companies. The crew would consist of thirty-three US citizens, including three six-man shooter teams that would operate on a continual rotation. "Blackwater does not intend to take any pirates into custody, but will use lethal force against pirates if necessary," according to a classified US diplomatic cable on the agreement, noting that Blackwater "has briefed AFRICOM, CENTCOM, and Embassy Nairobi officials." The cable added that there was "no precedent for a paramilitary operation in a purely commercial environment."

Somalia's piracy industry was based in the semi-autonomous Puntland region, which had little interest in cooperating with the US-backed government in Mogadishu. The Puntland authorities were facing mounting pressure from the international community to crack down on the pirates, and a local Islamic militant movement was threatening its ability to sign lucrative oil and mineral exploitation contracts with large corporations. Somalia is home to significant deposits of "uranium and largely unexploited reserves of iron ore, tin, gypsum, bauxite, copper, salt, natural gas, likely oil reserves," according to the CIA. In late 2010, Puntland's government announced that it was creating its own counterpiracy/counterterrorism force, saying that it had received funding from an anonymous donor nation from the Gulf. It was later revealed that the anonymous donor country was none other than the UAE and that the company that had been contracted to train the security force was bankrolled by one of its newest residents, Erik Prince.

The company, Saracen International, was run by several veterans of the mercenary firm Executive Outcomes and had offices and shell companies in multiple countries, including South Africa, Uganda, Angola and Lebanon. Among the key figures in the company was Lafras Luitingh, a former officer in apartheid South Africa's Civil Cooperation Bureau, a notorious security force known for hunting down and killing opponents of the apartheid regime. According to a confidential intelligence report from AMISOM, Prince was "at the top of the management chain of Saracen" and "provided seed money for the Saracen contract." According to the UN Monitoring Group on Somalia, Prince and Luitingh met in Washington, DC, in October 2009, and the two then met with officials from Abu Dhabi. The UAE also hired a former US diplomat, attorney Pierre-Richard Prosper, who had served as the ambassador at large for war crimes issues under President Bush, and an ex-CIA officer, Michael Shanklin, the former CIA Mogadishu station chief. By late 2010, Saracen was training a 1,000-member counterpiracy force in northern Puntland. The force also began preparing to take on Islamic militants who were threatening big-business opportunities. The Islamic militants had complained that they had been "cut out of energy exploration deals" in their region. "You cannot have oil exploration if you have insecurity," declared Mohamed Farole, the son and adviser of Puntland's president, Abdirahman Mohamed Farole.

By May 2011, Saracen's Puntland operations were well under way: at the Bandar Siyada base near Bosaso, 470 soldiers and drivers had completed training. Plans were in place to equip the force with three transport aircraft, three reconnaissance aircraft, two transport helicopters and two light helicopters. The projected force, according to the UN Monitoring Group, would be the best-equipped indigenous military force anywhere in Somalia and the second-largest externally supported military effort after AMISOM. Photographic evidence indicated that Saracen personnel had already been deployed for VIP security and humanitarian operations.

Saracen also brokered a deal with President Sheikh Sharif's administration in Mogadishu to build a personal security detail for the president and other senior officials. Saracen's Mogadishu operations were visible by October 2010. Luitingh, Shanklin and a small group of Saracen personnel traveled to Mogadishu on October 5. Over the next three weeks they received four armored vehicles, complete with machine-gun turrets, from the UAE. It seemed that President Sharif and his prime minister had been making secret deals with Saracen and at least five other private companies that had set up shop around Mogadishu's international airport. These conspicuous activities quickly aroused the suspicions and concerns of AMISOM forces and Somali politicians. AMISOM's commander, Major General Nathan Mugisha, expressed concern about "unknown armed groups in the mission area," in reference to Saracen's operations. Meanwhile, Somali lawmakers announced at the end of 2010 that they were demanding the suspension of contracts with private security contractors, claiming that they had no idea what the contractors had actually been hired to do.

Just as Prince and Saracens' latest private war was getting under way, scandal hit. The UN Monitoring Group declared that Saracen had been operating in flagrant violation of the arms embargo on Somalia, concluding in its report that "notwithstanding Southern Ace's short-lived and unsuccessful attempts at arms dealing and drug trafficking, the most egregious violation of the arms embargo by a private security company during the course of the UN Monitoring Group's mandate was perpetrated by Saracen International, in association with an opaque web of affiliated entities." The UN Monitoring Group suggested that Saracen's continued operations could actually increase support for local Islamist militias and, possibly, al Shabab. "Saracen's presence has increased tension in north-eastern Somalia," it concluded. A year later, in response to a subsequent UN report, Saracen's lawyer accused the monitoring group of publishing "a collection of unsubstantiated and often false innuendo."

In early 2011, when Prince's involvement in Saracen became public, his spokesman, Mark Corallo, said that Prince was merely compelled by humanitarian imperative to help "Somalia overcome the scourge of piracy" and claimed he had no financial stake in Saracen's work.

"We don't want to have anything to do with Blackwater," Somalia's information minister, Abdulkareem Jama, told the *New York Times*, recalling Blackwater's killing of innocent Iraqis at Baghdad's Nisour Square in 2007. "We need help, but we don't want mercenaries." Jama didn't mention that he was among the Somali officials present during negotiations around the Saracen deal.

In the spring of 2011, Puntland announced that it was suspending Saracen's operations, pending approval by the United Nations. But a senior Somali official told me that the company was still discreetly operating in Mogadishu, working with Somali security forces. Among the other private security companies based at the Mogadishu airport were AECOM Technology Corporation, OSPREA Logistics, PAE, Agility, RA International, International Armored Group, Hart Security, DynCorp, Bancroft and Threat Management Group. Some of them trained Somali security services or supported AMISOM, while others provided logistical support for aid groups and journalists. Some companies, like Bancroft, were well known, but the roles of some others were secret and their activities shielded from effective oversight. In that way, they fit in perfectly in Somalia. They were also convenient for Washington. "We do not want an American footprint or boot on the ground," said Johnnie Carson, the Obama administration's lead official on Somalia.

Despite the increased role of the CIA and JSOC and the use of warlords-turned-generals and mercenary firms, the greatest tactical victory won in recent years in Somalia was delivered not by AMISOM, the CIA or JSOC, or by any US-backed indigenous forces, but by members of a militia fighting as part of the Somali government's chaotic local military. And it happened purely by accident.

**"Total Savagery Throughout the Country"**

SOMALIA, 2011—Fazul Abdullah Mohammed's world had grown very small. Almost all of his East African al Qaeda comrades had been assassinated by JSOC, and he lived life on the run. He had a $5 million bounty on his head, courtesy of the US government. Some intelligence reports indicated that he may have had plastic surgery, and there were periodic reports of him popping up throughout the Horn of Africa using aliases and fake passports. With many of the veteran al Qaeda leaders gone, Fazul was increasingly isolated and dealing with the complexities of Somalia's clan politics. Then, on May 2, Osama bin Laden was killed. "We shall redouble our jihad and we shall overpower our enemies," al Shabab's spokesman, Sheikh Rage, declared after bin Laden's death. "We shall never divert from the path of Sheikh Osama and we shall continue the battle till we taste the death our brother Osama faced, or achieve victory and rule the whole world."

Despite such declarations, al Shabab found itself in a weakened state. It had taken severe losses as a result of the AMISOM bombings, JSOC's targeted killings and various clan-based militias fighting to retake territory from al Shabab. If the group was to survive and continue its remarkable ascent in Somalia, it would need to adapt. By the time bin Laden died, Fazul had spent most of his adult life focused on Somalia and had grown frustrated with both al Qaeda and the al Shabab leadership. He wrote to Zawahiri complaining that al Shabab was not being sufficiently supported by al Qaeda central. "He was criticizing them for ignoring what he calls an organization that has proven its effectiveness," said a Somali source with close connections to the Somali intelligence services that read the letter. Fazul, the source said, argued "that al Qaeda central is channeling resources to other AQ outfits, who are not as effective as al Qaeda in Somalia." The source added: "He's right on that. Al Qaeda in East Africa has proven that it could actually manipulate an organization like al Shabab, connect with its leadership, be part of its highest command, and do whatever it wants with it." But Fazul was finding it increasingly difficult to deliver adequate resources from al Qaeda to al Shabab, and al Shabab sought out different means of financing and support, instead making deals with powerful clans.

So Fazul found himself at odds with al Shabab's Somali leadership. My Somali source, who was given access to some of Fazul's writings from 2011, described growing "fissures," revealing that "Fazul thought, essentially, that al Shabab is going the wrong way, that the traditional warfare that's going on between al Shabab and the government was not sustainable any-more, that al Shabab started to lose significant ground in Mogadishu, and that they had too little fighters, about 4,000 or so fighters, against about 8,000 African Union peacekeepers, and maybe 10,000 Somalis." Fazul crit-icized the al Shabab leadership for failing to recruit young Somalis—ideally between the ages of thirteen and sixteen—and train them for a long-term struggle. Fazul alleged that al Shabab was recruiting young people, but then "in a few months they're just sending them as suicide bombers. And he thought that that was such a bad idea, and that in the long run would just erode fighters out of al Shabab." The source added: "I mean this guy's looking way ahead, and he's accusing the al Shabab leadership of being shortsighted."

A month after bin Laden died, al Shabab was in serious trouble. AMISOM had increased the size of its forces and its role shifted from a peacekeeping operation to one that increasingly involved offensive operations. US-trained Ugandan and Burundian troops began pushing into al Shabab territory on the outskirts of Mogadishu, including the Bakaara market. The United States was feeding AMISOM targeting data and providing it with new tech-nology, including small Raven surveillance drones, night-vision and com-munications equipment and other surveillance gear. The pro-government militia ASWJ had routed al Shabab's forces in several key areas outside of the city, while other US-supported militias, including those of Indha Adde and Ahmed Madobe, fought them elsewhere. Al Shabab, as Fazul had warned, was relying too heavily on young, inexperienced recruits to fight on the front lines against far better trained and more experienced Somali militias and foreign-backed forces. It was a defining moment in the history of al Shabab, and also for Fazul.

LATE ON THE EVENING OF JUNE 7, 2011, a man whose South African passport identified him as Daniel Robinson was in the passenger seat of a Toyota SUV driving on the outskirts of Mogadishu when his driver, a Kenyan national, missed a turn and headed straight toward a checkpoint manned by some kids from a Somali militia. It was unheard of during this time for any vehicles to be on the streets of Mogadishu late at night, so the Somalis at the checkpoint, some of whom were high on khat, were imme-diately suspicious. After the men in the vehicle refused to comply with instructions to properly identify themselves and show their faces by turning on the lights of the car's cab, the militia guys sensed a threat and opened fire. A firefight broke out as the men in the vehicle shot back. By sunrise, the vehicle was pocked with bullet holes. When the Somali forces finally approached the vehicle, they discovered laptop computers, cell phones, documents, weapons and $40,000 in cash. The soldiers promptly looted the car and took their booty back to their villages. They left the passports and a few other items at the scene.

As soon as it was discovered that the men killed at the checkpoint were foreigners, CIA-funded Somali intelligence agents were dispatched to the scene to launch an investigation and recover the items that had been looted. "There was a lot of English and Arabic stuff, papers," recalled a Somali intelligence official who helped lead the investigation that day. The papers, he said, contained "very tactical stuff" that appeared to be linked to al Qaeda, including "two senior people communicating." The Somali agents "realized it was an important man" and informed the CIA in Mogadishu. The men's bodies were taken to the Somali NSA. The Americans took DNA samples and fingerprints, then flew them to Nairobi for processing.

Within hours, the United States confirmed that Robinson was in fact Fazul Abdullah Mohammed. At its facilities in Mogadishu, the CIA and its Somali NSA agents pored over the materials recovered from Fazul's car, which served as a mobile headquarters for the al Qaeda leader. Some deleted and encrypted files were recovered and decoded by US agents. The senior Somali intelligence official who reviewed the documents predicted the intelligence might prove more valuable on a tactical level than the cache found in Osama bin Laden's house in Pakistan, especially in light of the increasing US—and al Qaeda—focus on East Africa. The Americans, he said, were "unbelievably grateful." Secretary of State Hillary Clinton called Fazul's death "a significant blow to Al Qaeda, its extremist allies and its operations in East Africa. It is a just end for a terrorist who brought so much death and pain to so many innocents."

According to Aynte, the al Shabab expert, al Shabab's leadership at the time was primarily concerned with tactics and operations that would allow the group "to take over as much land as possible." But according to the source who reviewed Fazul's writings, Fazul advised the al Shabab leadership to instead "go back to their old ways of hit-and-run insurgency and underground operations, and to disband the areas that they control." Fazul was "arguing that Al Shabab essentially give up the vast areas that they control in Somalia, in exchange for going underground across the country, including peaceful areas, in Somaliland and Puntland, and disrupting the whole country." Fazul believed that al "Shabab simply cannot retain the status quo, cannot retain 40 percent of Somalia under its domain; that it had better give those lands up, and just wreak havoc, carry out small operations, assassinations, throughout Somalia." His vision was to allow the US puppet government to fail, while al Shabab "created a total savagery throughout the country."

On June 23, the United States carried out a strike against alleged al Shabab members near Kismayo. As with the Nabhan operation, a JSOC team swooped in on helicopters and snatched the bodies of those killed and wounded. The men were taken to an undisclosed location. On July 6, three more US strikes targeted al Shabab training camps in the same area. When I met President Sheikh Sharif in Mogadishu just after that series of strikes, he denied any knowledge of the US attacks. I asked him if such strikes strengthened or weakened his government. "Both at the same time," he replied. "For our sovereignty, it's not good to attack a sovereign country. That's the negative part. The positive part is you're targeting individuals who are criminals."

A week after the June 23 strike, President Obama's chief counterterrorism adviser, John Brennan, described an emerging US strategy that would focus not on "deploying large armies abroad but delivering targeted, surgical pressure to the groups that threaten us." Brennan singled out al Shabab, saying, "From the territory it controls in Somalia, al Shabab continues to call for strikes against the United States," adding, "We cannot and we will not let down our guard. We will continue to pummel Al Qaeda and its ilk."

SINCE 1991, Somalis had been pounded by two powerful fists: the violence of civil war, foreign intervention and terrorism; and the punishing climate of their country. In 2011, the two hit them hard in tandem. A drought, combined with misused and mismanaged international aid programs, had taken an extreme toll on Somali civilians. Rural Somalis were so desperate that thousands began flocking to the violence-rocked capital, Mogadishu, seeking food. Others fled across the border to the massively overcrowded Dadaab refugee camp in Kenya. When a famine was officially declared in July 2011, the monthly rate of refugees streaming across the border had tripled. Some 30,000 refugees had arrived that month. By that time, al Shabab had lost a crucial funding source as a result of the AMISOM offensive at the Bakaara market. When al Shabab ceded control of the market—the most important commerce point in Mogadishu—to AMISOM, it also lost its ability to collect taxes from the businesses and residents. The drought, which crippled tax-paying farmers in the south, produced a similar loss of income for al Shabab. Then the monsoon season hit, severely limiting sea-based trade and port activity. Al Shabab could literally no longer afford the war it had fought for years.

On Saturday, August 6, al Shabab fighters carried out a well-organized retreat from many of their main strongholds throughout Mogadishu. In the early morning, they left by the truckload, reportedly heading for their southern strongholds of Barawa and Merca. The retreat came after an evening of attacks on Somali government military bases and troop positions and fierce gun battles. As news of the al Shabab retreat spread, there were reports of celebrations in the street throughout the beleaguered capital. Al Shabab spokesman Sheikh Rage announced that the group had "completely vacated Mogadishu for tactical purposes" but that they "[would] be back soon. The retreat by our forces is only aiming to counter-attack the enemy. People will hear happy news in the coming hours. We shall fight the enemy wherever they are."

The Somali government and the US-backed AMISOM forces celebrated the al Shabab retreat as a great victory and the beginning of the end of al Shabab. Somalia "welcomes the success by the Somali government forces backed by [AMISOM] who defeated the enemy of al Shabab," President Sharif told reporters at Villa Somalia, and he called on Somalis to "harvest the fruits of peace." AMISOM soon announced that its forces, together with those of the Somali government, were in control of 90 percent of the city. In a sobering footnote, AMISOM noted that it would need 20,000 troops to effectively secure Mogadishu. In September, US Undersecretary of Defense for Intelligence Michael Vickers—a key player in US covert ops and the targeting of al Qaeda's leadership—said that "Al-Qaeda's elements in East Africa continue to be a primary [counterterrorism] focus of the United States in light of clear indications of their ongoing intent to conduct attacks." But Vickers added that he believed the United States had "decimated" the "leadership ranks" of al Shabab and al Qaeda in East Africa. That may have been true, but the victory declarations were premature.


IN THE FALL OF 2011, al Shabab carried out a series of major attacks in Somalia, including a massive strike in central Mogadishu, showing that despite its tactical retreat, al Shabab could still strike deep into government-controlled territory. Its operatives drove a fifteen-ton truck rigged with a bomb and positioned it outside a fortified government compound and detonated the vehicle, killing more than 100 people and injuring scores more. The scene of the attack, in the K-4 neighborhood, also housed an office of the Ministry of Education, where many students had come to check the results of a recent exam. K-4 was one of the few neighborhoods the government had claimed to fully control. "This is the biggest attack since al Shabab was defeated," an AMISOM spokesman said, apparently with no sense of the irony of his statement.

In response to al Shabab's tactical shift and recent attacks, a Burundian-led AMISOM force launched an offensive to push al Shabab from Daynile, a crucial al Shabab stronghold north of Mogadishu. The offensive, while partially successful, resulted in scores of Burundian troops being killed—as many as seventy-six, by some estimates, which would have made it the greatest loss of AMISOM lives in a single battle ever. After what al Shabab dubbed the "Battle of Daynile," its fighters piled up the bodies of Burundian soldiers onto trucks and paraded them through town. Dozens of people lined the roads cheering them on and chanting, "Allah u Akbar!" and shouting praise for al Shabab. The trucks eventually pulled into an open field, where they dumped the bodies. Some residents prostrated themselves before the fighters. Mukhtar Robow and other Somali al Shabab leaders examined the dead Burundians—still wearing their combat fatigues. In one of the uniformed corpses of an AMISOM soldier, an al Shabab fighter's machete remained driven into the chest.

"We want to tell the Muslim people to rejoice in the fact that the ones who have displaced you from your homes, caused you so much trouble and violated the honor of your women—today Allah has humiliated them too," said al Shabab's Sheikh Rage. Holding up a crucifix and a Bible he said was seized from one of the soldiers, Rage continued. "We also want to let the Muslims know that this is a war between...Islam and Christianity.... This is also a stern warning to the Kenyans who are entering our Muslim land: This will be the end that awaits your sons, by the will of Allah the Almighty. The disbelievers have sustained heavy losses, but we've only managed to carry seventy-six of their corpses. And these were the original disbelievers, particularly those from Burundi."

"Claims of al-Shabab's imminent collapse," observed Christopher Anzalone, a PhD candidate at the Institute of Islamic Studies at McGill University, whose work focused on al Shabab, "are exaggerated and belied by the movement's continued ability to launch major attacks inside Mogadishu as well as inflict significant numbers of casualties on AMISOM and [Somali government] forces." Al Shabab was fighting for its survival—and not just on the battlefield. It appeared to realize that no matter how many military victories it achieved, it would ultimately need popular support— the kind that brought the Islamic Courts to power and chased out the CIA warlords—to survive. It needed its own version of the US counterinsurgency doctrine. Forced to relinquish military control of certain areas, al Shabab redoubled its political efforts.

Al Shabab organized a series of meetings with clan elders from various regions in an effort to mend relations with them and negotiate agreements. A month after it killed the Burundian troops, al Shabab allowed reporters access to one of its own aid camps for internally displaced people, Ala-Yasir camp in southern Somalia. Although part of the point was to push back against claims that al Shabab was responsible for the humanitarian disaster and had prevented aid from reaching Somalia, a special guest was also there. Introduced as the al Qaeda envoy to the humanitarian crisis in Somalia, a white man with a keffiyeh wrapped around his face was identified as Abu Abdullah al Muhajir. Local al Shabab leaders said he was an American citizen. Journalists watched as Muhajir and his allies distributed food, Islamic books and clothes at the camp, which housed more than 4,000 people. The al Qaeda delegation also brought an ambulance. "To our beloved brothers and sisters in Somalia, we are following your situation on a daily basis," Muhajir declared in English. "And, though we are separated by thousands of kilometers, you are consistently in our thoughts and prayers." Journalists reported that the man handed out bags full of Somali shillings, equaling about $17,000.

Perhaps al Shabab was truly on the ropes, as the Somali government and AMISOM claimed. Or maybe the group had begun to implement Fazul's vision of a guerrilla terror campaign that gave up territory in favor of sowing fear throughout the country, while effectively exposing the Somali government's inability to bring stability. Al Shabab certainly faced an uphill battle in reasserting its control over territory it won as a result of the disastrous US-backed Ethiopian invasion and the overthrow of the Islamic Courts, but its future could well be determined—as so much of modern Somalia's has been—by foreign intervention.

The United States may have killed a slew of prominent al Qaeda and al Shabab figures, but in doing so it had simultaneously inspired successors to those militants—including US citizens—to rise up and continue the fight. Unlike AMISOM's forces or any other foreign troops, the members of al Shabab were largely Somali and could reintegrate into society or rebrand themselves and regroup. "Whoever thinks today that a government other than that of Islam will rule Somalia, he is indeed deluding himself and is not following the affairs of the world," Ahmed Abdi Godane, the emir of al Shabab, declared in late 2011. "A time will come in the very near future, when the Shariah of Allah rules the entire country—from one corner to the other, and Somalia becomes the foundation of the Islamic Caliphate, upon the methodology of the Prophethood. And our Jihad will continue until we reach the objective that has been defined by Allah."

AL SHABAB'S METEORIC RISE IN SOMALIA, and the legacy of terror it wrought, was a direct response to a decade of disastrous US policy, which had strengthened the very threat it was intended to crush. The multipronged US operations in Somalia, in the end, may have given the greatest boost to warlords, including those who once counted al Shabab among their allies and friends. "They are not fighting for a cause," Mohamed Ahmed Nur, the Mogadishu mayor, told me. "And the conflict will start tomorrow, when we defeat Shabab. These militias are based on clan and warlordism and all these things. They don't want a system. They want to keep that turf as a fixed post—then, whenever the government becomes weak, they want to say, 'We control here.'"

Washington seemed to have cast history aside and, with it, the hard work of supporting indigenous Somali movements that could potentially stabilize their country, opting instead to wage a war of attrition. Under President Obama, the large-scale conventional military deployments of Iraq and Afghanistan were replaced by an expansion of drone strikes and Special Ops teams conducting targeted killings. President Obama seemed intent on a strategy that presumed peace would come by killing the bad guys. But, as happened in Afghanistan, Iraq and elsewhere, this strategy appeared to fuel the movements that created those "bad guys" in the first place. "If you use the drone, and the selected killings, and do nothing else on the other side, then you get rid of individuals. But the root causes are still there," observed the former Somali foreign minister, Ismail Mahmoud "Buubaa" Hurre. "The root causes are not security. The root causes are political and economic."

The history of Somalia has been marred by extreme violence and social division. But the country has also displayed a capacity to unite in the face of foreign intervention. Although al Shabab may have been a severely weakened movement, the conditions that turned it into a Frankenstein remained. The end result of US policy from 1991 through the first term of the Obama administration was to ensure that warlordism would continue and that Somalia would remain a breeding ground for violent jihadists and an enduring interest for al Qaeda. Together, the Bush and Obama administrations managed to rewind the clock of history to the time US troops withdrew from Somalia after Black Hawk Down and abandoned the country to gangsters and warlords. From there, the hellish realities of Somalia grew even worse. Nonetheless, by late 2011, the Obama administration had established a new drone base in Ethiopia in addition to the ones in the Seychelles and Saudi Arabia.

**Abdulrahman Vanishes**

YEMEN, 2011—Abdulrahman Awlaki, the oldest son of Anwar Awlaki, was born in Denver, Colorado. Like his father, he spent the first seven years of his life in the United States, attending American schools. When he returned to Yemen, his grandparents—Anwar's mom and dad—played a huge role in his upbringing, particularly after Anwar went underground. Anwar "always thought that it is best for Abdulrahman to be with me," Nasser told me. Anwar believed that his wife and children "should not be involved at all in his problems." Nasser knew that Anwar would never return to the United States and that he was on a collision course with the US government. But still, he had hopes for his grandson. Nasser wanted Abdulrahman to excel in school and he had dreams of sending his grandson back to the United States for a college education.

Abdulrahman looked just like his father when he was a young boy, but with long wavy hair. "We were pressuring him to go to the mosque, and to perform the prayers on time, things like that," recalled Nasser, adding that Abdulrahman was not particularly religious and preferred to hang out with his friends. "His hair was very long, and his mother wanted him to have a haircut. I mean, he was as normal as anybody. He was acting like other American" teens. "Anwar used to have adventures, do things like that. Abdulrahman was not that kind," he added. "He was just from school, to the house, and then to go and play with his friends. And they go to the pizza parlors, to all kinds of places. I always tell him, 'When you grow up, I want you to study in the United States.'"

It was difficult for Abdulrahman and his siblings to grow up without their father around, but as a teenager, Abdulrahman was old enough to understand why he couldn't see his father. And it was frightening. "Definitely, he was mad about the targeting, what is happening to his father," Nasser added. "He was really concerned about his father."

Abdulrahman's aunt, Abir—Anwar's younger sister—was extremely close to him. "Abdulrahman was one of the closest people to my heart. I loved him so much and everybody did because Abdulrahman made it very easy for all of us to just adore him," she told me. "He had somehow filled his father's vacuum for me and became a brother, a really dear one." Abdul-rahman admired his father and had even chosen as his Facebook username "Ibn al Shaykh," Son of the Shaykh. But Abdulrahman was not his father.

Abdulrahman loved hip-hop music and Facebook and hanging out with his friends. They would take pictures of themselves posing as rappers, and when the Yemeni revolution began, Abdulrahman wanted to be a part of it. As massive protests shook Yemen, he would spend hours hanging out in Change Square with the young, nonviolent revolutionaries who had vowed to change their government through peaceful means. He would spend nights there with his friends, sharing his vision for the future and, at times, just goofing off. But as the revolution continued and the government was brought to the verge of collapse, Abdulrahman decided to follow his urge to see his father.

In early September, Abdulrahman woke up before the rest of the house. He tiptoed into his mother's bedroom, went into her purse, took 9,000 Yemeni rials—the equivalent of about $40—and left a note outside of her bedroom door. He then snuck out the kitchen window and into the court-yard. Shortly after 6:00 a.m., the family's guard saw the boy leave but didn't think anything of it at the time. It was Sunday, September 4, 2011, a few days after the Eid al-Fitr holiday marked the end of the holy month of Ra-madan. Nine days before, Abdulrahman had turned sixteen.

A short while later, Abdulrahman's mother woke up. She started to rouse Abdulrahman's siblings for the morning prayers and then went to find Abdulrahman. He was not in his bedroom. She called for him, and while searching the house, she found the note. "I am sorry for leaving in this kind of way. I miss my father and want to see if I can go and talk to him," the note read. "I will be back in a few days. I am sorry for taking the money. I will pay you back. Please forgive me. Love, Abdulrahman." Nasser said they were all shocked. "He would talk sometimes about his father and he wanted to see him, but nothing really which would indicate that he one day will leave us like that. He never told his mother or me or his grandmother that he would like to go and look for his father," Nasser recalled. "Because his father always thought that it is best for him to be with me. And that he should not be involved at all in his problems."

When they searched Abdulrahman's room, they determined that he had only taken a backpack. He clearly was planning a short trip. "When his mother told me about the letter, it was just like a shock for me," Abdulrah-man's grandmother, Saleha, told me. "I said, 'I think this will be just like bait for his father.'" The CIA, she feared, "might find his father through him." The family called around to Abdulrahman's friends. Someone told Nasser that a teacher at the school had recently gotten close to Abdulrahman, and Nasser believed the teacher had been encouraging Abdulrahman to find his father and to reconnect with him, that it would be good for the boy. "He had influence on him, and they used to go to a pizza parlor to eat pizza," Nasser said. When Nasser tried to find the teacher to ask him if he had any information about Abdulrahman's whereabouts, the teacher had "vanished."

Abdulrahman had already boarded a bus at Bab al Yemen, in the old city in Sana'a. His destination was Shabwah, the family's home province and the scene of repeated US air strikes aimed at killing his father.

 **Hellfire**

WASHINGTON, DC, AND YEMEN, 2011—On September 6, 2011, General David Petraeus was sworn in as the director of the CIA. A decade after 9/11, the Agency had been transformed as a result of its behind-the-scenes turf war with JSOC. And for some veteran intelligence officials, Obama's selection of Petraeus was an ominous symbol. "The CIA has become more militarized, and is working very closely with JSOC, to the extent that they're even using CIA cover, which would have been unimaginable ten years ago," former CIA case officer Phil Giraldi told me. "A considerable part of the CIA budget is now no longer spying. It's supporting paramilitaries who work closely with JSOC to kill terrorists, and to run the drone program." The CIA, he added, "is a killing machine now."

A State Department liaison who worked extensively with JSOC described Petraeus's vision for running the CIA as transforming the Agency into "a mini-Special Operations Command that purports to be an intelligence agency." For all the praise Petraeus won for his counterinsurgency strategy and the "surge" in Iraq, the liaison told me, Petraeus's most significant contribution was as a "political tool," an enabler of those within the national security apparatus who wanted to see a continuation and expansion of covert global small wars. Pointing to the "mystique that surrounds JSOC" and Admiral William McRaven, the liaison said, "Petraeus was trying to implement that kind of command climate at the CIA."

Colonel Patrick Lang told me that once Petraeus arrived at Langley, he "wanted to drag them in the covert action direction and to be a major player."

FOR TWO YEARS, the US efforts to assassinate Anwar Awlaki were based on intelligence that he was hiding in his tribal areas around Shabwah and Abyan. But the interrogation sessions with Ahmed Abdulkadir Warsame—the young Somali snatched by JSOC and held for months on board a US Navy vessel—had indicated that Awlaki had relocated to the northern Yemeni governate of Jawf, far from the scene of most of the strikes aimed at killing him. The United States had long assumed Awlaki was in Shabwah and had repeatedly conducted operations there in an effort to get him. Yemeni intelligence on the ground had corroborated the information that Warsame had given US interrogators when JSOC held him. By early September, US surveillance aircraft had pinpointed Awlaki's location at a small house in Khashef, a village in Jawf about ninety miles northeast of Sana'a. Jawf, which borders Saudi Arabia, was rife with informants on the kingdom's payroll.

Local villagers in Khashef began seeing drones hovering in the skies above. Washington's drone war had kicked into full gear in Yemen, so the presence of the aircraft was not particularly out of the ordinary, but what the villagers did not know was that the White House's counterterrorism teams were watching one specific house. Watching and waiting. Once they got a lock on Awlaki's coordinates, the CIA quickly deployed several armed Predator drones from its new base in Saudi Arabia and took operational control of some JSOC drones launched from Djibouti, as well.

The plan to assassinate Awlaki was code-named Operation Troy. The very name implied that the United States had a mole who was leading its forces to Awlaki.

As the Americans surveilled the house where Anwar Awlaki was staying in Jawf, Abdulrahman Awlaki arrived in Ataq, Shabwah. He was picked up at the bus station by his relatives, who told him that they did not know where his father was. The boy decided to wait in the hope that his father would come to meet him. His grandmother called the family he was with in Shabwah, but Abdulrahman refused to speak to her. "I called the family house and they said, 'He's OK, he's here,' but I didn't talk to him," she recalled. "He tried to avoid talking to us, because he knows we will tell him to come back. And he wanted to see his father." Abdulrahman traveled with some of his cousins to the town of Azzan, where he planned to await word from his father.

At the White House, President Obama was faced with a decision, not of morality or legality, but of timing. He had already sentenced Anwar Awlaki, a US citizen, to death without trial. A secret legal authorization had been prepared and internal administration critics sidelined or brought on board. All that remained to sort out was the day Awlaki would die. Obama, one of his advisers recalled, had "no qualms" about this kill. According to leaks from the Obama administration about the operation, US officials knew there were women and children in the house where Awlaki was staying. Although scores of US drone strikes had killed civilians in various countries around the globe, it was official policy to avoid such deaths if at all possible. When Obama was briefed on Awlaki's location in Jawf and was told that children were in the home, he was explicit that he did not want any options ruled out. Awlaki was not to escape again. "Bring it to me and let me decide in the reality of the moment rather than in the abstract," Obama told his advisers. "In this one instance," an Obama confidant recalled, "the president considered relaxing some of his collateral requirements."

Awlaki had evaded US drones and cruise missiles for at least two years. He rarely stayed in one place more than a night or two. This time was different. For some reason, he had stayed in the same house in Khashef much longer, all the while being monitored by the United States. Now the Americans had him cleanly in their sights. "They were living in this house, for at least two weeks. Small mud house," Nasser was later told by local people. "I think they wanted to make some videotape. Samir Khan was with him." On the morning of September 30, 2011, Awlaki and Khan finished their breakfast inside the house. US spy cameras and satellites broadcast images back to Washington and Virginia of the two men and a handful of their cohorts piling into vehicles and driving away from the house. They began heading toward the province of Marib. As the vehicles made their way over the dusty, unpaved roads, US drones, armed with Hellfire missiles, were dispatched to hunt them down. The drones were technically under the command of the CIA, though JSOC aircraft and ground forces were poised to jump in should the operation require their assistance. A team of commandos stood at the ready to board V-22 helicopters and take action. For extra measure, US Marine Harrier jets scrambled in a backup maneuver.

Six months earlier, Awlaki had narrowly missed death by US missiles. "This time eleven missiles missed its target but the next time, the first rocket may hit it," he had said. As the cars sped down the road, Awlaki's prophecy came true. Two of the Predator drones locked onto the car carrying Awlaki, while other aircraft hovered as backup. A Hellfire missile fired from a drone slammed into his car, transforming it into a ball of flames. A second missile hit moments later, ensuring that the men inside would never escape if they had managed to survive. "Just a few minutes after they left the house, they were going to a *wadi*, somewhere they can make this film, and they were targeted," said Nasser. "The car was completely destroyed. And [Anwar's] body was cut out of the car." The Yemeni government sent out a text message to journalists. "The terrorist Anwar Awlaki has been killed along with some of his companions," it read. It was 9:55 a.m. local time. When villagers in the area arrived at the scene of the missile strikes, they reported that the bodies inside had been burned beyond recognition. There were no survivors. Amid the rubble, they found a symbol more reliable than a fingerprint in Yemeni culture: a charred rhinoceros horn handle of a *jambiya* dagger. There was no doubt it belonged to Anwar Awlaki.

ON SEPTEMBER 30, during a visit to Fort Myer in Virginia, President Obama stepped up to a podium and addressed reporters. "Earlier this morning Anwar Awlaki, a leader of al Qaeda in the Arabian Peninsula, was killed in Yemen," Obama declared. "The death of Awlaki is a major blow to al Qaeda's most active operational affiliate." The president then bestowed upon Awlaki a label that had never been attached to him before, despite all his reported associations with al Qaeda. "Awlaki was the leader of external operations for al Qaeda in the Arabian Peninsula. In that role, he took the lead in planning and directing efforts to murder innocent Americans," Obama asserted. "The death of Awlaki marks another significant milestone in the broader effort to defeat al Qaeda and its affiliates," adding that the United States "will be resolute in our commitment to destroy terrorist networks that aim to kill Americans, and to build a world in which people everywhere can live in greater peace, prosperity and security." Obama made no mention of the fact that Awlaki was a US citizen.

Back in Yemen, the Awlaki family received word of the strike in Jawf. At first they doubted the official reports, as so many before had been false, but then they confirmed that this time they were accurate. As they mourned the death of their son Anwar, the Awlakis' attention turned to their grandson, Abdulrahman. He had gone to Shabwah to find his father, and now his father was dead.

After Abdulrahman heard the news of Anwar's death, he called home for the first time and spoke to his mother and his grandmother. "That's enough, Abdulrahman. You have to come back," his grandmother, Saleha, told him. "That's it, you didn't see your father." Abdulrahman, she recalled, sounded devastated, yet still tried to comfort her. "Be patient. Be strong," Abdulrahman told her. "Allah chose him." The conversation was brief. Abdulrahman said he would return home soon but that he wanted to wait for the roads to clear. "At the time, the roads were not very safe. The revolution was at its maybe highest point," Saleha added. There were police checkpoints and fighting on the route. Abdulrahman did not want to be detained or caught up in any violence. So the boy said he would remain with his cousins in Shabwah and return to Sana'a when things calmed down.

IN NORTH CAROLINA, Sarah Khan woke up to the news from Yemen. "In the morning when I opened the computer, I saw that they had killed Anwar Awlaki," she told me. There was no mention of her son, Samir, in the early reports. But then Sarah's husband, Zafar, called her from his office and said he had seen some reports indicating that a "Samir Khan" had also been killed in the drone strikes. "I didn't believe it," Sarah told me. "Samir is a name that is pretty common in the Middle East—it could be any Samir. Doesn't have to be my Samir. I was like, it's not true. It cannot be Samir. It has to be somebody else. I didn't want to believe in that." As more reports trickled out, they began to accept the fact that their son was dead, killed by his own government. The Khans tried to contact the State Department for information, for answers. Why was Samir killed when the FBI had told his family that he had committed no crime? The grand jury that was convened to consider charges against him a year earlier, in August 2010, had produced no indictment. Why was he condemned to death without trial? Their inquiries were met with silence.

The Khans—who had done everything they could to stay away from the media spotlight when their son became a known figure in *Inspire* magazine—decided to take their questions public. After the strike in Yemen, they wrote an open letter to the US government in a local newspaper. "It has been stated in the media that Samir was not the target of the attack; however no US official has contacted us with any news about the recovery of our son's remains, nor offered us any condolences. As a result, we feel appalled by the indifference shown to us by our government," the letter read. "Being a law abiding citizen of the United States our late son Samir Khan never broke any law and was never implicated of any crime. The Fifth Amendment states that no citizen shall be 'deprived of life, liberty or property, without due process of law,' yet our government assassinated two of its citizens. Was this style of execution the only solution? Why couldn't there have been a capture and trial? Where is the justice? As we mourn our son, we must ask these questions."

Days later, Zafar Khan received a phone call from the US State Department. The official on the line expressed the US government's "condolences" for Samir's death. "They said that they were sorry and that Samir wasn't the target," Sarah Khan told me. "They said Sammy did not do anything wrong. They said he was not the target." That only raised more questions for her. "If they knew that Samir was there, in that vehicle, then how could they do something like that?" she asked. Obama administration officials later told reporters that Khan was "collateral damage" in a strike aimed at Awlaki, but Representative Michael McCaul from Texas had another word for it. "Samir Khan was a bonus. It was a twofer," McCaul said. "It's a pretty good hit."

As word of Awlaki's death spread, politicians in the United States from both political parties hailed the assassination of one of their own citizens. "This is an extraordinary victory, a great moment for the United States," gloated Republican congressman Peter King, the chair of the House Homeland Security Committee. Awlaki, he said, had become "more dangerous than bin Laden"—indeed, he was "the No. 1 terrorist in the world." Democratic senator Dianne Feinstein, chair of the Senate Intelligence Committee, celebrated Awlaki's killing, saying in a joint statement with Republican senator Saxby Chambliss that he "posed a significant and imminent threat to the United States" and had "declared war on the United States and inspired and planned attacks against us. We commend the agencies and individuals who found him and eliminated this dangerous threat." Secretary of State Hillary Clinton said, "Like Osama bin Laden and so many other terrorist leaders who have been killed or captured in recent years, [Awlaki] can no longer threaten America, our allies, or peace-loving people anywhere in the world. Today we are all safer."

"I'm glad they did it," said Republican senator John McCain. Former vice president Dick Cheney praised Obama for killing Awlaki, saying, "I do think this was a good strike. I think the president ought to have that kind of authority to order that kind of strike, even when it involves an American citizen." CIA director Leon Panetta echoed those sentiments, declaring, "This individual was clearly a terrorist and yes, he was a citizen, but if you're a terrorist, you're a terrorist."

Although Awlaki's killing did not inspire the same spontaneous carnival-like street celebrations in the streets of Washington, DC, and New York City that marked bin Laden's death, some tabloid newspapers staged their own victory parades on their pages. "Another al Qaeda Bites the Dust; Blasted to Hell; CIA Drone Kills US-Born Terrorist al-Awlaki," declared the *New York Post*. "Remote-Control Really Hits the Splat," proclaimed another headline in the paper. "One Less Terror Big. Al Qaeda Loses Leader in Attack; Their violent hatred for US dies when a missile strike killed off an American-born monster militant," announced the New York *Daily News*.

The only voices of dissent that emanated from Washington in the immediate aftermath of Awlaki's killing came from the fringes of the Democratic and Republican parties. "If the American people accept this blindly and casually, that we now have an accepted practice of the president assassinating people who he thinks are bad guys, I think it's sad," Texas Republican Ron Paul said on the campaign trail as he waged an unsuccessful insurgent campaign for the Republican presidential nomination. "Awlaki was born here, he's an American citizen. He was never tried or charged for any crimes. To start assassinating American citizens without charges—we should think very seriously about this." Democrat Dennis Kucinich, who tried to challenge the government's assertion that it could kill US citizens without trial nearly two years before Awlaki's death, said, "The Administration has a crossed a dangerous divide and set a dangerous precedent for how the United States handles terrorism cases. This dangerous legal precedent allows the government to target U.S. citizens abroad for being suspected of involvement in terrorism, in subversion of their most basic constitutional rights and due process of law. Their right to a trial is summarily and anonymously stripped from them."

Constitutional lawyer and syndicated columnist Glenn Greenwald was among the few US commentators to look askance at the celebrations of Awlaki's killing, writing, "After several unsuccessful efforts to assassinate its own citizen, the U.S. succeeded today." He correctly predicted that few Americans would raise questions or express outrage at the killing. "What's most amazing is that its citizens will not merely refrain from objecting, but will stand and cheer the U.S. government's new power to assassinate their fellow citizens, far from any battlefield, literally without a shred of due process from the U.S. government."

In an interview the day Awlaki's death was announced, Greenwald said, "Remember that there was great controversy that George Bush asserted the power simply to detain American citizens without due process or simply to eavesdrop on their conversation without warrant. Here you have something much more severe. Not eavesdropping on American citizens, not detaining them without due process, but killing them without due process. And yet many Democrats and progressives, because it's President Obama doing it, have no problem with it and are even in favor of it." Greenwald added: "To say that the President has the right to kill citizens without due process is really to take the Constitution and to tear it into as many little pieces as you can and then burn it and step on it."

For some former senior members of the Bush administration, the killing of a US citizen by a Democratic president seemed to take the acceptable bounds of US conduct in the war on terror beyond their own lax standards. "Right now, there isn't a government on the planet that agrees with our legal rationale for these operations, except for Afghanistan and maybe Israel," said former Bush CIA director Michael Hayden. "We needed a court order to eavesdrop on" Awlaki, he noted, "but we didn't need a court order to kill him. Isn't that something?"

Even as the legal issues surrounding Awlaki's killing received little attention in the US media and barely registered a blip on the radar of the general public in the United States, a few journalists and some lawmakers on Capitol Hill began seeking information about the process of authorizing the assassination of US citizens. Only a select few in Washington knew anything specific. "There's a process that goes through the National Security Council, and then after that it goes to the president, and then the president then indicates that these individuals are on this list, and as a result of that process we followed it's legal," said Charles Albert "Dutch" Ruppersberger III, a Maryland Democrat who was the ranking member of the House Intelligence Committee at the time. "It's legitimate, and we're taking out someone who has attempted to attack us on numerous occasions, and he was on that list. It was pursuant to a process."

While the White House and some leading national security lawmakers assured journalists and the public that the process was lawful, the administration refused to make public its evidence. Some lawmakers—whose security clearances and committee assignments authorized them to review the kill process—alleged that they were not being sufficiently briefed by the White House. "It's important for the American people to know when the president can kill an American citizen, and when they can't," Senator Ron Wyden told me. Wyden, a Democrat from Oregon, had served on the Senate Intelligence Committee since 2001 and often found himself at odds with the Bush administration over secrecy and transparency issues. Now, under a Democratic president, he was waging the same battles—and new ones. He said that he repeatedly asked the administration for its legal rationale for the government killing its own citizens without trial, calling his attempts to extract this information "an enormous struggle." The American people, Wyden said, deserve "to know clearly when a president thinks an American citizen can be killed, and their life taken. These are substantial questions where I just don't think there's been a lot of detail, and the American people deserve more." In the case of Awlaki, the target had not been indicted in any US court and faced no known charges. How would he have surrendered? To whom would he even surrender? "Those questions are clearly sort of hanging in suspended animation, without answers," Wyden told me.

Giraldi, the former CIA officer, labeled Awlaki's killing an "assassination." He had reviewed the publicly available information about Awlaki and what the administration had alleged Awlaki had done. "None of those things, to me, amounted to a death sentence. And they're saying, 'Well, we have other stuff, but it's secret,'" Giraldi told me at the time. "And that's of course the thing that's always trotted out, and if there's a challenge in the courts, you come up against the State Secrets Privilege, so that the challenge goes away. So we're having a situation where people are being killed, you don't know what the evidence is, and you have no way to redress the situation."

Nasser Awlaki believed that the US and Yemeni security forces could have arrested Anwar, but that they did not want to see him stand trial and be able to present a defense. It is also possible that the United States did not want to give Awlaki a platform to spread his message more widely. "I think that they wanted to kill him, without due process, because they thought he was a legitimate military target," Nasser told me. "How is it that Umar Farouk, who tried to blow up the airplane, or Nidal Hasan, who actually killed those soldiers, how are they now having, let us say, a fair trial? My son did not get that fair trial."

## 57   Paying for the Sins of the Father

WASHINGTON, DC, AND YEMEN, 2011—Abdulrahman Awlaki was mourning his father in Shabwah. The boy's family members there tried to comfort him and encouraged him to get out with his cousins—to go for walks or go outside for meals in the fresh air. That was what Abdulrahman was doing on the evening of October 14. He and his cousins had joined a group of friends outdoors to barbecue. The boy and his cousins had laid a blanket on the ground and were about to begin their meal. There were a few other people nearby doing the same. It was about 9:00 p.m. when the drones pierced the night sky. Moments later, Abdulrahman was dead. So, too, were several other teenage members of his family, including Abdulrahman's seventeen-year-old cousin, Ahmed.

Early the next morning, Nasser Awlaki received a phone call from his family in Shabwah. "Some of our relatives went to the place where [Abdulrahman] was killed, and they saw the area where he was killed. And they told us he was buried with the others in one grave because they were blown up to pieces by the drone. So they could not put them in separate graves," Nasser told me. "They put three or four of them in one grave because they were cut into pieces. The people who were there could recognize only the back of Abdulrahman's hair. But they could not recognize his face or anything else." As the horror was setting in that their eldest grandson had been killed just two weeks after the death of their eldest child, Nasser and Saleha watched in disbelief as numerous news reports identified Abdulrahman as being twenty-one years old, with anonymous US military officials referring to him as a "military-aged" male. Some reports intimated that he was an al Qaeda supporter and that he had been killed while meeting with Ibrahim al Banna, an Egyptian citizen described as the "media coordinator" for AQAP.

"To kill a teenager is just unbelievable, really, and they claim that he is an al Qaeda militant. It's nonsense," said Nasser shortly after the strike. "They want to justify his killing, that's all." When I visited Nasser after Abdulrahman was killed, he showed me the boy's Colorado birth certificate, showing that he was born in 1995 in Denver. "When he was killed by the

US government, he was a teenager, he wasn't twenty-one. He wouldn't have been able to enlist in the military in the US. He was sixteen," he told me.

Days after the killing of Abdulrahman, the United States released a statement, as usual feigning ignorance about who was responsible for the strike, even though "unnamed officials" in the United States and Yemen had confirmed the strike to almost all media outlets that inquired. "We have seen press reports that AQAP senior official Ibrahim al Banna was killed last Friday in Yemen and that several others, including the son of Anwar al-Awlaki, were with al Banna at the time," National Security Council spokesman Thomas Vietor told the press, in a statement that strangely cast Abdulrahman as something between an al Qaeda associate and a hapless tourist. "For over the past year, the Department of State has publicly urged US citizens not to travel to Yemen and has encouraged those already in Yemen to leave because of the continuing threat of violence and the presence of terrorist organizations, including AQAP, throughout the country."

The Awlaki family members, who had declined to discuss the killing of Anwar, believed that they needed to speak out publicly about the killing of Abdulrahman. "We watched with surprise and condemnation how several prominent American newspapers and news channels twist the truth, calling Abdulrahman an Al Qaeda operative and falsely and misleadingly stating his age as 21 years old," read a statement from the family. "Abdulrahman Anwar Awlaki was born on August 26, 1995 in Denver Colorado. He was an American citizen raised in the U.S. until 2002 when his father was forced to leave the U.S. and go back to Yemen." They invited people to look up Abdulrahman's Facebook page—which revealed a teenager interested in music, video games and his friends—"to see the 'lethal terrorist', 'the 21 year old Qaeda operative' the U.S. government is claiming they killed. Look at his pictures, his friends and his hobbies. His Facebook page shows a typical kid, a teenager who paid a hefty price for something he never did and never was."

For the Awlaki family, their private pain was overwhelming. After Anwar was killed, "People flocked to our house to pay condolences and show sympathy and I was in state of complete disbelief and denial," recalled Anwar's sister, Abir. "They kept on coming for the next two weeks, when we were yet struck again by the murder of Anwar's oldest son, Abdulrahman. The skinny, smiling, curly-haired boy was murdered; and for what? What was he found guilty of?" she asked. "The shock of losing Abdulrahman only fourteen days after his father was unbearable. I can't wipe the picture of my father's reaction upon receiving the news. It is hard—hard for a father to lose his oldest son and then his first and favorite grandchild. The entire house was traumatized and hurt by every sense of the word."

Abdulrahman's grandmother, Saleha, went into a severe depression after her son and grandson were killed. She had been extremely close to Abdulrahman. After he died, when guests would come to the house to pay respects, she would serve them tea or sweets. She later told me from her home in Sana'a, "I look around the house and see if anybody will take the dishes and take them and bring them back to the kitchen." She would look for her grandson, remembering how he used to help her clean up, but he wasn't there. "I miss him a lot," Saleha said, beginning to cry. "Abdulrahman was a different boy. I have never known anybody like Abdulrahman. He was a very, very gentle boy." I asked her what her message would be to people in the United States. "Abdulrahman was not the only one killed that day. There were other children whose parents loved them very much. Just like the American people love their children," she said. "I wonder if Obama lost one of his daughters, or Mrs. Clinton, would they be happy? Are they going to be happy if they lost one of their children like that? I was wondering if this will make the American people happier?"

While they opposed Anwar's killing and believed that the United States had exaggerated its claims about his involvement with al Qaeda, Nasser told me that his family understood why he was killed. "My son believed in what he did," Nasser said, "but I am really distressed and disappointed by the killing, the brutal killing, of his son. He did nothing against the US. He was an American citizen. Maybe one day he would have gone to America to study and live there, and they killed him in cold blood."

The CIA claimed that it had not carried out the strike, asserting that the supposed target, Ibrahim Banna, was not on the Agency's hit list. That led to speculation that the strike that killed Abdulrahman and his relatives was a JSOC strike. Senior US officials told the *Washington Post* that "the two kill lists don't match, but offered conflicting explanations as to why." The officials added that Abdulrahman was an "unintended casualty." A JSOC official told me that the intended target was not killed in the strike, though he would not say who the target was. On October 20, 2011, military officials presented a closed briefing on the JSOC strike to the Senate Armed Services Committee. With the exception of the statements from anonymous US officials, the United States offered no public explanation for the strike. The mystery deepened when AQAP released a statement claiming that Banna was, in fact, still alive. "These lies and allegations announced by the government...are not unusual...the government has falsely declared the death of mujahedeens many times," the statement declared. The Awlakis began to wonder if perhaps Abdulrahman was, in fact, the target of the strike.

Senate Majority Leader Harry Reid, one of the handful of US lawmakers who would have access to all intelligence on the strike, seemed to suggest that was the case when asked about the killing of the two Awlakis and Samir Khan. "I do know this," he said on CNN, "the American citizens who have been killed overseas...are terrorists, and, frankly, if anyone in the world deserved to be killed, those three did deserve to be killed." When asked specifically about Abdulrahman's killing by my colleague, journalist Ryan Devereaux, Representative Peter King, who also sits on the Intelligence Committee, said, "I'm convinced, and I meet on a regular basis with General Petraeus and the CIA and also military leaders, that every attack that's been carried out in Yemen and Afghanistan, anywhere the US has been involved, I believe that the United States had reason to carry them out and I support them," adding, "I'm satisfied they've done the right thing." Asked whether he had specifically reviewed the Abdulrahman strike, King replied, "Yeah, that would be a logical deduction. You're trying to get me in trouble." Despite Representative King's assertion that he had reviewed the case, he later falsely portrayed Abdulrahman as having been with his father when he was killed. "If the kid was killed when he was with him, that's the breaks," King said.

Robert Gibbs, Obama's former White House press secretary and a senior official in the president's 2012 reelection campaign, was also asked about the strike that killed Abdulrahman. "It's an American citizen that is being targeted without due process of law, without trial. And, he's underage. He's a minor," reporter Sierra Adamson told Gibbs, during a press gaggle after a presidential debate where Gibbs was serving as a surrogate for Obama. Gibbs shot back: "I would suggest that you should have a far more responsible father if they are truly concerned about the well-being of their children. I don't think becoming an al Qaeda jihadist terrorist is the best way to go about doing your business."

The Awlakis were left only with questions about why their grandson had been killed. They wondered if somehow the US government had used Abdulrahman to find Anwar. Perhaps, as had happened with the killing of the Yemeni regime's political opponents in the past, the United States had been fed false intelligence about Abdulrahman's age and connections to al Qaeda. While emphasizing that they were not prone to conspiracy theories, they told me it was difficult to imagine why Abdulrahman would have been killed, especially if Banna was not there. Who, then, was the target? "It is up to the US government to be sure about the kind of information they get before they make any action against anybody. So I don't believe it was just an accident. They must have followed him," Nasser said. "But they wanted to cover up the story, and that's why they claimed that he was twenty-one years old, in order to justify his killing. Or maybe, as they mentioned, he was in the wrong place at the wrong time." He paused before adding, "I don't think we can buy this argument."

An anonymous US official later told the *Washington Post* that Abdulrahman's killing was "an outrageous mistake…They were going after the guy sitting next to him." But no one ever identified who that someone was. As far as the family knows, their grandson was sitting next to his teenage cousins, none of whom were affiliated with al Qaeda. Decisions on "targets, drones, these are made only by the highest US government authorities, the CIA and all that. Why did they specifically target these guys?" Nasser demanded. "I want answers from the United States government."

The Obama administration would fight passionately to keep those answers secret, invoking the State Secrets Privilege repeatedly—just as President Bush had done throughout his eight years in office. The killings of Anwar and Abdulrahman Awlaki represented a watershed moment in modern US history.

# EPILOGUE: PERPETUAL WAR

ON JANUARY 21, 2013, Barack Obama was inaugurated for his second term as president of the United States. Just as he had promised when he began his first campaign for president six years earlier, he pledged again to turn the page on history and take US foreign policy in a different direction. "A decade of war is now ending," Obama declared. "We, the people, still believe that enduring security and lasting peace do not require perpetual war."

Much of the media focus that day was on the new hairstyle of First Lady Michelle Obama, who appeared on the dais sporting freshly trimmed bangs, and on the celebrities in attendance, including hip-hop mogul Jay-Z and his wife, Beyoncé, who performed the national anthem. But the day Obama was sworn in, a US drone strike hit Yemen. It was the third such attack in that country in as many days. Despite the rhetoric from the president on the Capitol steps, there was abundant evidence that he would continue to preside over a country that is in a state of perpetual war.

In the year leading up to the inauguration, more people had been killed in US drone strikes across the globe than were imprisoned at Guantánamo. As Obama was sworn in for his second term, his counterterrorism team was finishing up the task of systematizing the kill list, including developing rules for when US citizens could be targeted. Admiral McRaven had been promoted to the commander of SOCOM, and his Special Ops forces were operating in more than one hundred countries across the globe.

After General David Petraeus's career was brought to a halt as a result of an extramarital affair, President Obama tapped John Brennan to replace him as director of the CIA, thus ensuring that the Agency would be headed by a seminal figure in the expansion and running of the kill program. After four years as Obama's senior counterterrorism adviser, Brennan had become known in some circles as the "assassination czar" for his role in US drone strikes and other targeted killing operations.

When Obama had tried to put Brennan at the helm of the Agency at the beginning of his first term, the nomination was scuttled by controversy over Brennan's role in the Bush-era detainee program. By the time

President Obama began his second term in office, Brennan had created a "playbook" for crossing names off the kill list. "Targeted killing is now so routine that the Obama administration has spent much of the past year codifying and streamlining the processes that sustain it," noted the *Washington Post*. Brennan played a key role in the evolution of targeted killing by "seeking to codify the administration's approach to generating capture/ kill lists, part of a broader effort to guide future administrations through the counterterrorism processes that Obama has embraced," the paper added. "The system functions like a funnel, starting with input from half a dozen agencies and narrowing through layers of review until proposed revisions are laid on Brennan's desk, and subsequently presented to the president."

Obama's counterterrorism team had developed what was referred to as the "Disposition Matrix," a database full of information on suspected terrorists and militants that would provide options for killing or capturing targets. Senior administration officials predicted that the targeted killing program would persist for "at least another decade." During his first term in office, the *Washington Post* concluded, "Obama has institutionalized the highly classified practice of targeted killing, transforming ad-hoc elements into a counterterrorism infrastructure capable of sustaining a seemingly permanent war."

In early 2013, a US Department of Justice "white paper" surfaced that laid out the "Lawfulness of a Lethal Operation Directed Against a U.S. Citizen." The government lawyers who wrote the sixteen-page document asserted that the government need not possess specific intelligence indicating that an American citizen is actively engaged in a particular or active terror plot in order to be cleared for targeted killing. Instead, the paper argued that a determination from a "well-informed high level administration official" that a target represents an "imminent threat" to the United States is a sufficient basis to order the killing of an American citizen. But, the Justice Department's lawyers sought to alter the definition of "imminent," advocating what they called a "broader concept of imminence." They wrote, "The condition that an operational leader present an 'imminent' threat of violent attack against the United States does not require the United States to have clear evidence that a specific attack on U.S. persons will take place in the immediate future." The government lawyers argued that waiting for a targeted killing of a suspect "until preparations for an attack are concluded, would not allow the United States sufficient time to defend itself." They asserted that such an operation constitutes "a lawful killing in self-defense" and is "not an assassination."

Jameel Jaffer of the ACLU called the white paper a "chilling document," saying that "it argues that the government has the right to carry out the extrajudicial killing of an American citizen." Jaffer added, "This power is going to be available to the next administration and the one after that, and it's going to be available in every future conflict, not just the conflict against al-Qaeda. And according to the [Obama] administration, the power is available all over the world, not just on geographically cabined battle-fields. So it really is a sweeping proposition."

In October 2002, as the Bush administration prepared to invade Iraq, Barack Obama gave the first major speech of his national political career. The then–state senator came out forcefully against going to war in Iraq, but he began his speech with a clarification. "Although this has been billed as an anti-war rally, I stand before you as someone who is not opposed to war in all circumstances....I don't oppose all wars." Obama declared, "What I am opposed to is a dumb war. What I am opposed to is a rash war." During his first campaign for president, Obama had blasted the Bush administration for fighting the wrong war—Iraq—and repeatedly criticized his opponent, Senator John McCain, for not articulating how he would take the fight to Osama bin Laden and al Qaeda.

As his first term in office wound down, the overwhelming majority of US military forces had been withdrawn from Iraq and plans for a similar drawdown in Afghanistan in 2014 were being openly discussed. The administration had succeeded in convincing the American public that Obama was waging a smarter war than his predecessor. As he ran for re-election, Obama was asked about charges from his Republican opponents that his foreign policy was based on appeasement. "Ask Osama bin Laden and the 22 out of 30 top al-Qaida leaders who have been taken off the field whether I engage in appeasement," Obama replied. "Or whoever is left out there, ask them about that."

As the war on terror entered a second decade, the fantasy of a clean war took hold. It was a myth fostered by the Obama administration, and it found a ready audience. All polls indicated that Americans were tired of large military deployments in Iraq and Afghanistan and the mounting US troop casualties that came with them. A 2012 poll found that 83 percent of Americans supported Obama's drone program, with 77 percent of self-identified liberal Democrats supporting such strikes. The *Washington Post*–ABC News poll determined that support for drone strikes declined "only somewhat" in cases where a US citizen was the target.

President Obama and his advisers seldom mentioned the drone program publicly. In fact, the first known confirmation of the use of armed drones by the president came several years into Obama's first term. It was not in the form of a legal brief or a press conference, but rather on a Google+ "Hangout" as the president took questions from the public. Obama was asked about his use of drones. "I want to make sure that people understand actually drones have not caused a huge number of civilian casualties," Obama said. "For the most part, they have been very precise, precision strikes against al-Qaeda and their affiliates. And we are very careful in terms of how it's been applied." He rejected what he called the "perception" that "we're just sending in a whole bunch of strikes willy-nilly" and asserted that "this is a targeted, focused effort at people who are on a list of active terrorists, who are trying to go in and harm Americans, hit American facilities, American bases and so on." Obama added: "It is important for everybody to understand that this thing is kept on a very tight leash. It's not a bunch of folks in a room somewhere just making decisions. And it is also part and parcel of our overall authority when it comes to battling al-Qaeda. It is not something that's being used beyond that."

Michael Boyle, a former adviser in the Obama campaign's counterterrorism experts group and a professor at LaSalle University, said that one of the reasons the administration was "so successful in spinning the number of civilian casualties" was the use of signature strikes and other systems for categorizing military-aged males as legitimate targets, even if their specific identities were unknown. "The result of the 'guilt by association' approach has been a gradual loosening of the standards by which the US selects targets for drone strikes," Boyle charged. "The consequences can be seen in the targeting of mosques or funeral processions that kill non-combatants and tear at the social fabric of the regions where they occur." No one, he added, "really knows the number of deaths caused by drones in these distant, sometimes ungoverned, lands."

Using drones, cruise missiles and Special Ops raids, the United States has embarked on a mission to kill its way to victory. The war on terror, launched under a Republican administration, was ultimately legitimized and expanded by a popular Democratic president. Although Barack Obama's ascent to the most powerful office on earth was the result of myriad factors, it was largely due to the desire of millions of Americans to shift course from the excesses of the Bush era. Had John McCain won the election, it is difficult to imagine such widespread support, particularly among liberal Democrats, for some of the very counterterrorism policies that Obama implemented. As individuals, we must all ask whether we would support the same policies—the expansion of drone strikes, the empowerment of JSOC, the use of the State Secrets Privilege, the use of indefinite detention, the denial of habeas corpus rights, the targeting of US citizens without charge or trial—if the commander in chief was not our candidate of choice. But beyond the partisan lens, the policies implemented by the Obama administration will have far-reaching consequences. Future US presidents—Republican or Democratic—will inherit a streamlined process for assassinating enemies of America, perceived or real. They will inherit an executive branch with sweeping powers, rationalized under the banner of national security.

In 2012, a former US constitutional law professor was asked about the US drone and targeted killing program. "It's very important for the president and the entire culture of our national security team to continually ask tough questions about 'Are we doing the right thing? Are we abiding by the rule of law? Are we abiding by due process?'" he responded, warning that it was important for the United States to "avoid any kind of slippery slope into a place where we're not being true to who we are."

That former law professor was Barack Obama.

The creation of the kill list and the expansion of drone strikes "represents a betrayal of President Obama's promise to make counterterrorism policies consistent with the US constitution," charged Boyle. Obama, he added, "has routinized and normalized extrajudicial killing from the Oval Office, taking advantage of America's temporary advantage in drone technology to wage a series of shadow wars in Afghanistan, Pakistan, Yemen, and Somalia. Without the scrutiny of the legislature and the courts, and outside the public eye, Obama is authorizing murder on a weekly basis, with a discussion of the guilt or innocence of candidates for the 'kill list' being resolved in secret." Boyle warned:

> Once Obama leaves office, there is nothing stopping the next president from launching his own drone strikes, perhaps against a different and more controversial array of targets. The infrastructure and processes of vetting the "kill list" will remain in place for the next president, who may be less mindful of moral and legal implications of this action than Obama supposedly is.

In late 2012, the ACLU and the *New York Times* sought information on the legal rationale for the kill program, specifically the strikes that had killed three US citizens—among them sixteen-year-old Abdulrahman Awlaki. In January 2013, a federal judge ruled on the request. In her decision, Judge Colleen McMahon appeared frustrated with the White House's lack of transparency, writing that the Freedom of Information Act requests raised "serious issues about the limits on the power of the Executive Branch under the Constitution and laws of the United States, and about whether we are indeed a nation of laws, not of men." She charged that the Obama administration "has engaged in public discussion of the legality of targeted killing, even of citizens, but in cryptic and imprecise ways, generally without citing to any statute or court decision that justifies its conclusions." She added, "More fulsome disclosure of the legal reasoning on which the Administration relies to justify the targeted killing of individuals, including United States citizens, far from any recognizable 'hot' field of battle, would allow for intelligent discussion and assessment of a tactic that (like torture before it) remains hotly debated. It might also help the public understand the scope of the ill-defined yet vast and seemingly ever-growing exercise."

Ultimately, Judge McMahon blocked the release of the documents. Citing her legal concerns about the state of transparency with regard to the kill program, she wrote:

> This Court is constrained by law, and under the law, I can only conclude that the Government has not violated FOIA by refusing to turn over the documents sought in the FOIA requests, and so cannot be compelled by this court of law to explain in detail the reasons why its actions do not violate the Constitution and laws of the United States. The Alice-in-Wonderland nature of this pronouncement is not lost on me; but after careful and extensive consideration, I find myself stuck in a paradoxical situation in which I cannot solve a problem because of contradictory constraints and rules—a veritable Catch-22. I can find no way around the thicket of laws and precedents that effectively allow the Executive Branch of our Government to proclaim as perfectly lawful certain actions that seem on their face incompatible with our Constitution and laws, while keeping the reasons for their conclusion a secret.

It is not just the precedents set during the Obama era that will reverberate into the future, but also the lethal operations themselves. No one can scientifically predict the future consequences of drone strikes, cruise missile attacks and night raids. But, from my experience in several undeclared war zones across the globe, it seems clear that the United States is helping to breed a new generation of enemies in Somalia, Yemen, Pakistan, Afghanistan and throughout the Muslim world. Those whose loved ones were killed in drone strikes or cruise missile attacks or night raids will have a legitimate score to settle. In an October 2003 memo, written less than a year into the US occupation of Iraq, Donald Rumsfeld framed the issue of whether the United States was "winning or losing the global war on terror" through one question: "Are we capturing, killing or deterring and dissuading more terrorists every day than the madrassas and the radical clerics are recruiting, training and deploying against us?" More than a decade after 9/11, that question should be updated. At the end of the day, US policy makers and the general public must all confront a more uncomfortable question: Are our own actions, carried out in the name of national security, making us less safe or more safe? Are they eliminating more enemies than they are inspiring? Boyle put it mildly when he observed that the US kill program's "adverse strategic effects...have not been properly weighed against the tactical gains associated with killing terrorists."

In November 2012, President Obama remarked that "there's no country on Earth that would tolerate missiles raining down on its citizens from outside its borders." He made the statement in defense of Israel's attack on Gaza, which was launched in the name of protecting itself from Hamas missile attacks. "We are fully supportive of Israel's right to defend itself from missiles landing on people's homes and workplaces and potentially killing civilians," Obama continued. "And we will continue to support Israel's right to defend itself." How would people living in areas of Yemen, Somalia or Pakistan that have been regularly targeted by US drones or missile strikes view that statement?

Toward the end of President Obama's first term in office, the Pentagon's general counsel, Jeh Johnson, gave a major lecture at the Oxford Union in England. "If I had to summarize my job in one sentence: it is to ensure that everything our military and our Defense Department do is consistent with U.S. and international law," Johnson said. "This includes the prior legal review of every military operation that the Secretary of Defense and the President must approve." As Johnson spoke, the British government was facing serious questions about its involvement in US drone strikes. A legal case brought in the United Kingdom by the British son of a tribal leader killed in Pakistan alleged that British officials had served as "secondary parties to murder" by providing intelligence to the United States that allegedly led to the 2011 strike. A UN commission was preparing to launch an investigation into the expanding US kill program, and new legal challenges were making their way through the US court system. In his speech, Johnson presented the US defense of its controversial counterterror policies:

> Some legal scholars and commentators in our country brand the detention by the military of members of al Qaeda as "indefinite detention without charges." Some refer to targeted lethal force against known, identified individual members of al Qaeda as "extrajudicial killing."
>
> Viewed within the context of law enforcement or criminal justice, where no person is sentenced to death or prison without an indictment, an arraignment and a trial before an impartial judge or jury, these characterizations might be understandable.
>
> Viewed within the context of conventional armed conflict—as they should be—capture, detention and lethal force are traditional practices as old as armies.

In the end, the Obama administration's defense of its expanding global wars boiled down to the assertion that it was, in fact, at war; that the authorities granted by the US Congress to the Bush administration after 9/11 to pursue those responsible for the attacks justified the Obama administration's ongoing strikes against "suspected militants" across the globe—some of whom were toddlers when the Twin Towers crumbled to the ground—more than a decade later. The end result of the policies initiated under President Bush and continued and expanded under his Democratic successor was to bring the world to the dawn of a new age, the era of the Dirty War on Terror. As Boyle, the former Obama campaign counterterrorism adviser, asserted in early 2013, the US drone program was "encouraging a new arms race for drones that will empower current and future rivals and lay the foundations for an international system that is increasingly violent."

Today, decisions on who should live or die in the name of protecting America's national security are made in secret, laws are interpreted by the president and his advisers behind closed doors and no target is off-limits, including US citizens. But the decisions made in Washington have implications far beyond their impact on the democratic system of checks and balances in the United States. In January 2013, Ben Emmerson, the UN special rapporteur on counterterrorism and human rights, announced his investigation into drone strikes and targeted killing by the United States. In a statement launching the probe, Emmerson characterized the US defense of its use of drones and targeted killings in other countries as "Western democracies...engaged in a global [war] against a stateless enemy, without geographical boundaries to the theatre of conflict, and without limit of time." This position, he concluded, "is heavily disputed by most States, and by the majority of international lawyers outside the United States of America."

At his inauguration in January 2013, Obama employed the rhetoric of internationalism. "We will defend our people and uphold our values through strength of arms and rule of law. We will show the courage to try and resolve our differences with other nations peacefully—not because we are naïve about the dangers we face, but because engagement can more durably lift suspicion and fear," the president declared. "America will remain the anchor of strong alliances in every corner of the globe; and we will renew those institutions that extend our capacity to manage crisis abroad, for no one has a greater stake in a peaceful world than its most powerful nation." Yet, as Obama embarked on his second term in office, the United States was once again at odds with the rest of the world on one of the central components of its foreign policy. The drone strike in Yemen the day

Obama was sworn in served as a potent symbol of a reality that had been clearly established during his first four years in office: US unilateralism and exceptionalism were not only bipartisan principles in Washington, but a permanent American institution. As large-scale military deployments wound down, the United States had simultaneously escalated its use of drones, cruise missiles and Special Ops raids in an unprecedented number of countries. The war on terror had become a self-fulfilling prophecy.

The question all Americans must ask themselves lingers painfully: How does a war like this ever end?

# ACKNOWLEDGMENTS

THIS BOOK IS THE PRODUCT of the tireless work of a team of people, spread across the globe from Brooklyn, New York, to Sana'a, Yemen; Washington, DC; Mogadishu, Somalia; Kabul, Afghanistan; and beyond. I will never forget the bravery and dedication of my fellow journalists who traveled with me and aided me in so many legs of this multiyear journey. I cannot thank by name some of the people who were most helpful in producing this book—either for their own safety or because I promised to keep their identities confidential. All of them have my deepest gratitude and respect.

Although my name is on the front of this book, many of the stories told in *Dirty Wars* would not have been possible without my dear brother Richard Rowley. Rick is an incredibly brave journalist, unbelievably calm under pressure and duress. We were shot at together on rooftops in Mogadishu, slept on dingy floors in rural Afghanistan and traveled together in the netherlands of southern Yemen. There were many times during this investigation when I really don't know if I would have had the strength or courage to carry on had it not been for Rick. He is a shining example of what journalists and friends should be.

For more than two years, my researcher Lauren Sutherland worked diligently to track down every lead we had—no matter how crazy the trail seemed. She is a ferocious investigator, and she prepared scores of meticulously documented briefings and memos on everything from Somali warlords to profiles of little-known military units to obscure legal filings. She was always cool under pressure and never once complained about the long hours she had to work. She even accompanied us on a discreet trip across the Kenya-Somalia border to meet with a Somali warlord who had been targeted by JSOC. My colleague Ryan Devereaux also provided invaluable research work for this book.

It is customary for authors to thank their agents, but Anthony Arnove is so much more than that to me. I feel truly honored to work with him. He is an incredible and loyal friend above all else, and he has my complete trust. He spent a surreal amount of time going over many versions of this book, always looking for ways to make it stronger. He has fantastic instincts and has literally devoted his entire life to supporting struggles for justice. This book could not have happened without Anthony's brilliant shepherding of the project.

My editor, Betsy Reed, is hands down the best in the business. Not only did she edit this book in about ten different iterations, but she has been my editor at the *Nation* magazine for almost a decade. She is a fierce defender of her writers and their stories, and always pushes me further than I think I can go. I have never submitted any writing to Betsy that she did not make significantly stronger in the end. I feel so lucky to work with her daily and to call her a dear friend.

I am very fortunate to have an immensely supportive family. My parents, Michael and Lisa, are my heroes. My brother, Tim, and sister, Stephanie, have always been there for me, and I am so proud to be their brother and to also call them my friends. Ksenija Scahill is an incredible, strong young woman who is wise beyond her years, has a deep curiosity about the world and always inspires me. I am so proud of her and the person she is. She means the world to me. Liliana Segura is not only a phenomenal journalist but has been selfless, loving and determined in her support of me and of this project. In ways small and big, she has always been there when it mattered. Without her or her unwavering support, this book would not have been possible. My aunts, uncles and cousins in my extended family are tremendous people whose loyalty and encouragement know no bounds. My sister-in-law, Jenny Kling-Scahill, has been such a great addition to our family, and I adore my nieces, Maya and Caitlin. Barb and Harry Hoferle, my aunt and uncle, have visited me almost everywhere I have ever lived in the world and have been tremendous in their love and support.

Carl Bromley at Nation Books is a remarkable man and a great friend. He has a brilliant, sharp wit and fantastic ideas. From the first day we met about my previous book, *Blackwater*, Carl has been one of my most trusted colleagues. He is a real treasure. Ruth Baldwin has been a fantastic ally and a tireless advocate for this project and many others over the years. The support I've received from Taya Kitman at the Nation Institute has been crucial. The staff of the Nation Institute is an outstanding group of smart and talented people. I also want to express my gratitude to Hamilton Fish for his support over the years and to Victor Navasky.

The team at Perseus Books Group and Basic Books is tremendous. Susan Weinberg has been an enthusiastic backer of this book from the day she came on board. Her positivity and passion set the tone for a great community effort on this project. Her predecessor, John Sherer, was also a pleasure to work with and laid the groundwork for this project several years ago.

Robert Kimzey did a brilliant job of moving the production of this book along, against the odds, on a very tight deadline, and did so with grace and class. Michele Wynn is an exceptional copy editor. I am also grateful to Mark Sorkin for his diligent work in proofing the book. Michele Jacob, my publicist, is a great gem and a passionate supporter of my work. She is a real pro. Alan Kaufman is a tenacious lawyer who is not afraid of the powerful and has always taken great care in protecting my journalism. Many thanks to Martin Soames, who did the British legal review of this book, for his careful work.

Many thanks to Marie Maes for the detailed index, Mike Morgenfeld and the Avalon Travel cartography department for the excellent maps and Jeff Vespa of WireImage for my author photo. Daniel LoPreto of Nation Books was invaluable in preparing the photographic insert and helping to manage the complex production of this book.

I owe a tremendous debt of gratitude to my colleagues at the *Nation* magazine. Katrina vanden Heuvel is an unshakable editor in chief who has always believed in me since we began working together in 2005. Richard Kim, Roane Carey and Emily Douglas are a joy to work with and are wonderful editors. Joliange Wright and Ellen Bollinger have always provided great encouragement, as has Jean Stein. I feel honored to be a part of the *Nation* magazine family. My friend and mentor Amy Goodman is the most loyal person I know and is one of the greatest journalists of our time. I will always consider *Democracy Now!* my university and my family.

The Puffin Foundation, the Wallace Global Fund and Lannan Foundation have been so incredible in their years of support for me and my work. Without them, nothing I have done in the past decade would have been possible. Patrick Lannan has become a dear friend and a great late-night whiskey drinking partner. Randall Wallace is a magical dude. And Perry Rosenstein has been a steadfast backer of my work. My friend Scott Roth has been so crucial to the *Dirty Wars* project, has a keen sense of justice and is one of the sharpest people I know. My gratitude also to Tony Tabatznik, Jen Robinson, Jess Search, Sandra Whipham and everyone at the Bertha Foundation and BRITDOC. The brilliant Cara Mertes from the Sundance Institute has been a solid adviser. Many thanks also to the Kindle Project for its support.

This book has also benefited tremendously from the support of my international publishers: Pete Ayrton and Hannah Westland of Serpent's Tail, Antje Kunstmann and Moritz Kirschner of Verlag Antje Kunstmann, Alexandre Sanchez and Louis-Frédéric Gaudet of Lux Éditeur, and the editorial teams of Companhia das Letras, Ediciones Paidós, Norstedts Förlag, All Prints Distributors and Publishers, and Wydawnictwo Sine Qua Non.

Thanks also to David Grossman of David Grossman Literary Agency, Isabel Monteagudo and Rosa Bertran of International Editors Co., Philip Sane of Lennart Sane Agency and the whole team at Prava I Prevodi Literary Agency.

The film *Dirty Wars* has a credit roll that includes more than two hundred people who helped make the documentary. I cannot thank every one of them here, but I would like to thank especially the remarkable team at IFC Films/Sundance Selects, Josh Braun and all of his colleagues at Submarine Entertainment, Nancy Willen of Acme Public Relations, David Harrington and Kronos Quartet, as well as the Kronos Performing Arts Association, Frank Dehn, Sue Bodine, Marc H. Simon, David Menschel of the Vital Projects Fund and Kristin Feeley of the Sundance Institute Documentary Film Program. Special thanks also to Joslyn Barnes, Bonni Cohen, Howard Gertler, Rebecca Lichtenfeld, James Schamus, Sundance Institute Creative Producing Lab, and Michael Watt.

In the course of writing this book, I was honored to work with so many incredible and brave journalists and media workers. In Afghanistan, Jerome Starkey, Jeremy Kelly and Jason Motlagh were very generous with their time and insight. My friend Raouf Hikal was a great fixer and coordinator who took serious risks to tell stories that would not otherwise have been told. Thank you also to Haji Shokat, Fatima Ayoub, Noor Islam Ahmadzia, Asif Shokat, Naqibullah Salarzai and Shafiq Ullah. Una Vera Moore offered key help. Thank you also to the Sharabuddin family in Gardez for welcoming us into your home and for sharing your utterly painful story with us. We will never forget you.

In Yemen, Saber al Haidary and Nasser Arrabyee were great coordinators and friends. Mohammed Albasha was tremendously helpful and always went the extra mile to get us into the country. Thank you also to Ashwaq Arrabyee and Adnan Arrabyee. My friend Iona Craig is a fantastic journalist and an incredibly generous soul. She helped us in too many ways to list here. Adam Baron, Gregory Johnsen and Aaron Zelin offered crucial support and insight, as did Haykal Bafana. Sheikh Saleh bin Fareed offered us great hospitality and made sure we could document the story of the bombing of al Majalah. He is a graceful and classy man. The Awlaki family welcomed us into their home and shared their stories with us. I am in awe of their ability to forgive, to be patient and to never give up their quest for justice. Dr. Nasser Awlaki was very generous with his time and his family. Saleha and Abir Awlaki cooked us amazing food and dug deep into their family photo and video collection to help us tell the story of their family. Ammar Awlaki was incredibly helpful throughout our time in Yemen. Thank you also to Omar Awlaki for the delicious honey and for welcoming us into his home.

In Somalia, we were so fortunate to work with the great Bashiir Yusuf Osman, owner of the Peace Hotel. He is a fearless man and an incredible combination of fixer, security coordinator, host and friend. I will never forget the risks Bashiir took so that we could report on Somalia. I am also grateful to Abdirahman "Aynte" Ali and Mohamed Ibrahim "Fanah" Mohamed for their assistance, as well as Sadia Ali Aden and Mohamed Olad Hassan. In Kenya, Abdirizak Haji Atosh and Daud Yussuf offered great assistance. Many thanks also to Katharine Houreld and Clara Gutteridge for all of their help.

My brother K'naan Warsame has been a true inspiration for my work. His music was the soundtrack of this book. I listened to his songs late at night in Brooklyn as I typed away and also in the streets of Mogadishu and Sana'a. His soft-spoken words and searing poetry boom throughout the world. I am so honored to call him my friend. Special thanks also to the Center for Constitutional Rights and the American Civil Liberties Union, particularly Pardiss Kebriaei, Jameel Jaffer, Hina Shamsi and Vince Warren for dealing with my constant requests for documents and interviews.

I feel blessed to have such a great community of friends, colleagues and even adversaries—all of whom challenge me and enlighten me. David Riker, who made the *Dirty Wars* film with us, is one of the most sincere and deep people I have ever met. I have learned so much from him and admire him immensely. Brenda Coughlin has been a great ally and a dear friend for many years and is always willing to do whatever needs to be done, often taking up the most thankless tasks and going the extra mile. I worked with Jacqueline Soohen before I could even grow a beard. We spent years going in and out of Iraq together. She is a great journalist and is like a sister to me. Sharif and Kareem Kouddous are my brothers and have always been there for me, through thick and thin. Thanks also to my buddies Ali Gharib, Garrett Ordower, Hani Sabra and Dan Coughlin for always reminding me to not take life so seriously. Michael Ratner and Karen Ranucci have been so generous in their support and with their love for so many years. Thank you also to the great Michael Moore for giving me one of my first "real" jobs and for always supporting my work. Oliver Stone and John Cusack have offered support, encouragement and wisdom at key moments. My dear friend Naomi Klein has always been there for me through good times and bad. She and Avi Lewis are a great force for justice.

Anamaria Segura and Phil Tisne have brightened my life. Muchas gracias also to Jorge and Clemencia Segura for all of their love and support. Wallace Segura is a scholar among scholars. Emma Kelton-Lewis and Daniel Avery have been tremendously generous in their personal support, as have Claire and Rennie Alba. Thanks to my friend Glenn Greenwald for being who he is and for keeping me sane at a few key points over the last few years. Gratitude also to Chris Hayes, my friend and colleague, for all of his encouragement and support. To my sister Ana Nogueira for being a true friend for a long time and to my pals Mike Burke and Elizabeth Press, thank you.

Among the journalists and writers I have learned from, consulted or compared notes with during the course of this project are Spencer Ackerman, Marc Ambinder, D. B. Grady, Barry Eisler, Noah Shachtman, Matthew Cole, Matthieu Aikins, Anand Gopal, Azmat Zahra Khan, Michelle Shepherd, Gareth Porter, Jeffrey Kaye, Jason Leopold, Kevin Gosztola, Adam Serwer, James Gordon Meek, Jake Tapper, Eli Lake, Ryan Grim, Michael Hastings, Josh Rogin, Charlie Savage, Jim Risen, Marcy Wheeler, Alyona Minkovski, Medea Benjamin, Jodie Evans, Kade Ellis, Nick Turse, Tom Engelhardt, Willie Geist, Justin Elliott, Rachel Maddow, Solly Granatstein, Aram Roston, Amy Davidson, Arun Gupta, Christian Parenti, Jane Mayer, Sy Hersh, Josh Gerstein, Micah Zenko, Declan Walsh, J. M. Berger, Sean Naylor, Joshua Hersh, Casey Coombs, Jonathan Larsen, Diane Shamis, Jamil Smith and Jeff Stein. Thank you all for doing what you do.

I also want to acknowledge some of the people I have had the pleasure of dialoguing with over the years (many of them on Twitter first and real life later). I have learned from all of them, sometimes through our disagreements, and they all have my respect. Among them, Brandon Webb and Jack Murphy at the Special Operations Forces Situation Report, Rob Dubois, Daveed Gartenstein-Ross, Jeff Emanuel, Rob Caruso, Dan Trombly, Joshua Foust, Clint Watts, Matthew Hoh, Andrew Exum, Nada Bakos, Will McCants, Mosharraff Zaidi, Huma and Saba Imtiaz, Omar Waraich, Andy Carvin, Caitlin Fitzgerald, Blake Hounshell, Sebastian Junger, Timothy Carney, Peter Bergen and Chris Albon. Thank you also to David Massoni, whose Thistle Hill Tavern provided me many meals while writing this book.

As of this writing, Yemeni journalist Abdulelah Haider Shaye remains locked up in a prison in Sana'a, in part due to the intervention of the White House. He should be set free.

# ACRONYMS AND ABBREVIATIONS

AC1, Abbottabad Compound 1
ACCMs, Alternative Compartmentalized
   Control Measures
AFOs, Advance Force Operations
AFRICOM, US Africa Command
AIAI, Al Itihaad al Islamiya
AMISOM, African Union Mission in Somalia
ANSF, Afghan National Security Forces
AOR, Area of Responsibility
AQAP, al Qaeda in the Arabian Peninsula
AQI, al Qaeda in Iraq
AQN ExOrd, Al Qaeda Network Execute
   Order
ASWJ, Ahlu Sunna Wal Jama
AUMF, Authorization for Use of Military
   Force

BIF, Battlefield Interrogation Facility

CAG, Combat Applications Group (also
   known as Delta Force)
CCR, Center for Constitutional Rights
CENTCOM, Central Command
CFR, Council on Foreign Relations
CID, Army Criminal Investigations Division
CINC, commander in chief
CJTF 180, Combined Joint Task Force 180
CJTF–HOA, Combined Joint Task Force–
   Horn of Africa
COIN, counterinsurgency
CONOP, Concept of Operations
CSF, Central Security Forces
CSSW, Charitable Society for Social Welfare
CT, counterterrorism
CTC, Counterterrorism Center
CTTL, Continuous Clandestine Tagging
   Tracking and Locating

DDTC, Directorate of Defense Trade Controls
DEVGRU, Naval Warfare Development
   Group (also known as Seal Team 6)

DIA, Defense Intelligence Agency
DoD, Department of Defense

E.K.I.A., Enemy Killed in Action
EC, Electronic Communications
EOD, Explosive Ordnance Disposal

FOG, Field Operations Group
FOUO, For Official Use Only

GRS, Global Response Staff
GST, Greystone
GTMO, or Gitmo, Guantánamo Bay
GWOT, Global War on Terror (or Terrorism)

HIG, Hezb-e-Islami Gulbuddin
HUMINT, human intelligence
HVT, High Value Target

IC, Intelligence Community
ICG, International Crisis Group
ICRC, International Committee of the Red
   Cross
ICU, Islamic Courts Union
IDPs, Internally Displaced Persons
INS, Immigration and Naturalization Service
IONA, Islamic Organization of North Amer-
   ica
ISAF, International Security Assistance Force
ISI, Inter-Services Intelligence
ISR, Intelligence, Surveillance Reconnais-
   sance
IWGCA, Interagency Working Group for
   Covert Action

JAG, Judge Advocate General
JIMAS, Association to Revive the Way of the
   Messenger
JPEL, Joint Prioritized Effects List
JPRA, Joint Personnel Recovery Agency
JSOC, Joint Special Operations Command

JUWTF, Joint Unconventional Warfare Task Force

KIA, killed in action

LeT, Lashkar-e-Taiba
LIMDIS, limited distribution

MLE, Military Liaison Elements

NBC, nuclear, biological, chemical
NGO, nongovernmental organization
NSA, National Security Agency
NSC, National Security Council
NSDD, National Security Decision Directive
NSPD, National Security Presidential Directive
NSS, National Security Service

OLC, Office of Legal Counsel
OSS, Office of Strategic Services

PAK, Pakistan
PET, Danish Intelligence Service
PETN, pentaerythritol tetranitrate
PNAC, Project for the New American Century
PSO, Political Security Organization

QRF, Quick Reaction Force

RAO, Regional Affairs Office
RPGs, rocket-propelled grenades

SAD, Special Activities Division of the CIA
SAP, Special Access Program
SAS, Special Air Service

SCUD, tactical ballistic missile
SEALs, Sea, Air, Land teams of the US Navy
SECDEF, or SecDef, or Secdef, secretary of defense
SELECT, an elite division of Blackwater
SERE, Survival, Evasion, Resistance and Escape
SMU, Special Mission Unit
SO/LIC, Special Operations/Low Intensity Conflict
SOC(FWD)-PAK, Special Operations Command-Forward Pakistan
SOC(FWD)-Yemen, Special Operations Command-Forward Yemen
SOCOM, Special Operations Command
SOF, Special Operations Forces
SOG, Studies and Observation Group
SOP, standard operating procedure
SSB, Strategic Support Branch

TADS, Terrorist Attack Disruption Strikes
TCCC, Tom Clancy Combat Concepts
TECS II, Treasury Enforcement Communications System
TF, Task Force
TFG, Transitional Federal Government

UAE, United Arab Emirates
USAID, US Agency for International Development
USG, US government
USSOCOM, US Special Operations Command

WFO, Washington Field Office
WMD, weapons of mass destruction

# NOTES

## Prologue

1 **they gathered for a barbecue:** Author interviews, Awlaki family members, January and August 2012. Details of the boy and the scene come from these interviews.

1 **"You are a gentle boy":** Author interview, Saleha al Awlaki, September 2012.

## 1: "There Was Concern...That We Not Create an American Hit List"

3 **10:10 a.m.:** *Joint Inquiry Briefing by Staff on US Government Counterterrorism Organizations (Before September 11, 2001) and on the Evolution of the Terrorist Threat and U.S. Response: 1986–2001, Senate Select Committee on Intelligence and House Permanent Select Committee on Intelligence, June 11, 2002.* All details of the briefing come from the transcript, unless otherwise noted.

3 **loya jirga:** Joe Havely, "The loya jirga: A Very Afghan Gathering," CNN.com, June 11, 2002.

4 **the attic, elevator, narrow staircase, counterespionage:** "Tower Report Under Wraps in the Attic," *New York Times*, February 27, 1989.

4 **most experienced:** Clarke describes his White House and counterterrorism credentials during the congressional briefing.

4 more covert action: According to the 9/11 Commission Report, in 1998 Clarke "drew up what he called 'Political-Military Plan Delenda,'" which laid out a plan to "immediately eliminate any significant threat to Americans" from the "Bin Ladin network." The plan had diplomatic and financial components but also advocated "covert action to disrupt terrorist activities, but above all to capture Bin Ladin and his deputies and bring them to trial," as well as "follow-on military action." National Commission on Terrorist Attacks upon the United States (Philip Zelikow, Executive Director; Bonnie D. Jenkins, Counsel; Ernest R. May, Senior Advisor), The 9/11 Commission Report (New York: W. W. Norton, 2004), p. 120.

5 **"splattering mud back on the Agency":** *Joint Inquiry Briefing by Staff on US Government Counterterrorism Organizations (Before September 11, 2001) and on the Evolution of the Terrorist Threat and U.S. Response: 1986–2001, Senate Select Committee on Intelligence and House Permanent Select Committee on Intelligence, June 11, 2002* (testimony of Richard Clarke). All statements made by Richard Clarke come from the briefing, unless otherwise noted.

5 **"political assassinations":** Executive Order No. 11905, Fed. Reg. 7703, 7733 (1976).

5 **"engage in, or conspire to engage in, assassination":** Executive Order No. 12036, Fed. Reg. 3674, 3688, 3689 (1978).

5 **Muammar el Qaddafi:** Seymour M. Hersh, "Target Qaddafi," *New York Times Magazine*, February 22, 1987.

5 **Saddam Hussein's palaces:** "The United States Navy in 'Desert Shield'/'Desert Storm'; V: 'Thunder and Lightning'—The War with Iraq," May 15, 1991, accessed August 5, 2012, www.history.navy.mil/wars/dstorm/ds5.htm. "TLAMs were used against chemical and nuclear weapons facilities, surface-to-air missile sites, command and control centers and Saddam's presidential palace."

5 **Desert Fox:** William M. Arkin, "The Difference Was in the Details," *Washington Post*, January 17, 1999.

6 **cruise missile attacks:** James Bennet, "U.S. Cruise Missiles Strike Sudan and Afghan Targets Tied to Terrorist Network," *New York Times*, August 21, 1998.

6 **pharmaceutical factory:** James Astill, "Strike One," *Guardian*, October 1, 2001.

6 **case-by-case basis:** Clarke says, "[The administration and the Justice Department] did not want to throw out the ban on assassination in a way that threw the baby out with the bathwater."

6 **trigger was seldom pulled:** As Clarke put it, "CIA would ask for an authority. They would rapidly get it. We would wait. Nothing would happen."

6 **"were held to the most restricted form of**

**notification":** Representative Pelosi is speaking during the joint briefing.

7 **key players:** "Statement of Principles," Project for the New American Century, June 3, 1997. Elliott Abrams, Richard Cheney, Donald Rumsfeld, Paul Wolfowitz, and I. Lewis Libby were signatories to PNAC's letter.

7 **"decade of defense neglect":** "Rebuilding America's Defenses: Strategy, Forces, and Resources for a New Century," Project for the New American Century, September 2000, p. 4.

7 **"provided a blueprint":** Ibid., Introduction, p. ii.

7 **key authors:** David Armstrong, "Dick Cheney's Song of America; Drafting a Plan for Global Dominance," *Harper's*, October 2002.

7 **"potential competitors":** Patrick E. Tyler, "U.S. Strategy Plan Calls for Insuring No Rivals Develop," *New York Times*, March 8, 1992.

8 **more powerful forces, toned down:** Jim Lobe, "Cold War 'Intellectuals' Re-enlist for War on Iraq, Arabs," Inter Press Service News Agency, November 17, 2001.

8 **"All must be easier to deploy":** Prepared address of George W. Bush, "A Period of Consequences," The Citadel, Charleston, SC, September 23, 1999.

8 **"Ardent supporters":** Lobe, "Cold War 'Intellectuals.'"

8 **"issue of the regime of Saddam Hussein":** "Rebuilding America's Defenses," p. 14.

9 **"undo the Clinton signature":** Donald Rumsfeld, fax to National Security Adviser Condoleezza Rice, "Subject: International Criminal Court," February 23, 2001, http://rumsfeld.com/library.

9 **"'the crazies are back'":** Transcript, "'The Crazies Are Back': Bush Sr.'s Briefer Discusses How Wolfowitz and Allies Falsely Led the U.S. to War," *Democracy Now!*, September 17, 2003.

9 **Rumsfeld hired Cheney:** Charlie Savage, *Takeover: The Return of the Imperial Presidency and the Subversion of American Democracy* (New York: Bay Back Books, 2008), p. 9.

9 **Congress condemned:** Ibid., pp. 25–26.

9 **overrode an attempt:** Richard L. Madden, "House and Senate Override Veto by Nixon on Curb of War Powers; Backers of Bill Win Three-Year Fight," *New York Times*, November 7, 1973.

9 **"consult with Congress":** Joint Resolution Concerning the War Powers of Congress and the President, Pub. L. No. 93-148, Sec. 3–4 (1973).

10 **"low point":** Bob Woodward, "Cheney Upholds Power of the Presidency; Vice President Praises Bush as Strong, Decisive Leader Who Has Helped Restore Office," *Washington Post*, January 20, 2005.

10 **domestic spying operations:** Select Committee to Study Governmental Operations with Respect to Intelligence Activities, Final Report; Book III: Supplementary Detailed Staff Reports on Intelligence Activities and the Rights of Americans, Senate Rep. No. 94-755 (1976).

10 **Salvador Allende:** Select Committee to Study Governmental Operations with Respect to Intelligence Activities, Staff Report, Covert Action in Chile, 1963–1973 (1975).

10 **stymied the probe:** Senate Select Committee to Study Governmental Operations with Respect to Intelligence Activities (The Church Committee), United States Senate website, accessed October 5, 2012, www.senate.gov/artandhistory/history/common/investigations/ChurchCommittee.htm.

10 **compel the FBI, rebuffed:** Adam Liptak, "Cheney's To-Do Lists, Then and Now," *New York Times*, February 11, 2007.

10 **congressional committees:** Overview of the Senate Select Committee on Intelligence, Responsibilities and Activities, SSCI website, accessed October 5, 2012, www.intelligence.senate.gov/about.html; "The CIA and Congress: The Creation of the HPSCI," CIA website, accessed October 5, 2012, www.cia.gov/news-information/featured-story-archive/2011-featured-story-archive/cia-and-congress-hpsci.html.

10 **enacted a law:** Intelligence Authorization Act for FY 1981, Pub. Law 96-450 (1980). Title V of the law—"Accountability for Intelligence Activities"—states that "the Director of the Central Intelligence and the heads of all departments, agencies, and other entities of the United States involved in intelligence activities shall…keep the Select Committee on Intelligence of the Senate and the Permanent Select Committee on Intelligence of the House of Representatives…fully and currently informed of all intelligence activities which are the responsibility of, are engaged in by, or are carried out for or on behalf of, any department, agency, or entity of the United States, including any significant anticipated intelligence activity."

10 **"seriously weakened":** Savage, *Takeover*, p. 43.

11 **"congressional resurgence," "signing statements":** Ibid.

11 **unlawful use of force:** "Case Concerning the Military and Paramilitary Activities in and Against Nicaragua (Nicaragua v. United States of America)," Summary of the Judgment, International Court of Justice, June 27, 1986.

11 **Boland Amendment:** Senate Select Committee on Secret Military Assistance to Iran and the Nicaraguan Opposition and House Select Committee to Investigate Covert Arms Transactions with Iran, Report of the Congressional Committees Investigating the Iran-Contra Affair, with Supplemental, Minority, and Additional Views, Senate Rep. No. 100-216, House Rep. No. 100-433 (1987), pp. 498–500.

11 **Fourteen members:** Paula Dwyer, "Pointing a Finger at Reagan," *Businessweek*, June 23, 1997.

11 **"minority report":** Senate Select Committee on Secret Military Assistance to Iran and the Nicaraguan Opposition and House Select Committee to Investigate Covert Arms Transactions with Iran, Report of the Congressional Committees Investigating the Iran-Contra Affair, Section II: Minority Report, Senate Rep. No. 100-216, House Rep. No. 100-433 (1987), pp. 437, 469.

12 **commissioning a study:** Tom Squitieri, "Role of Security Companies Likely to Become More Visible," *USA Today*, April 1, 2004.

12 **American Enterprise Institute:** Savage, *Takeover*, p. 67.

12 **portraits:** The second portrait was, for the time being, only a photograph, but it would later be replaced by a painting worth nearly $50,000. See Christopher Lee, "Official Portraits Draw Skeptical Gaze," *Washington Post*, October 21, 2008.

12 **"a serious threat":** Transcript, Donald Rumsfeld remarks, "DOD Acquisition and Logistics Excellence Week Kickoff—Bureaucracy to Battlefield," The Pentagon, September 10, 2001.

13 **"revolution in military affairs":** Paul C. Light, "Rumsfeld's Revolution at Defense," Brookings Policy Brief Series, Paper No. 142, Brookings Institution, July 2005.

13 **massive missile defense systems:** James M. Lindsay and Ivo H. Daalder, "The Bush Revolution: The Remaking of America's Foreign Policy," Brookings Institution, May 2003.

13 **"threat of jihadist terrorism":** Douglas Feith, *War and Decision: Inside the Pentagon at the Dawn of the War on Terrorism* (New York: Harper, 2009), p. 1.

13 **"From the start":** Ron Suskind, *The Price of Loyalty: George W. Bush, the White House, and the Education of Paul O'Neill* (New York: Simon and Schuster Paperbacks, 2004), p. 86.

13 **"laid out the case":** Bob Woodward, *State of Denial: Bush at War, Part III* (New York: Simon and Schuster Paperbacks, 2006), p. 49.

14 **"immediate priority targets":** Feith, *War and Decision*, p. 51.

14 **"The agenda was very clear":** Author interview, General Hugh Shelton (Ret.), March 2011. All information and statements attributed to General Shelton come from the author's interview, unless otherwise noted.

14 **"any shred":** Richard Clarke, *Against All Enemies: Inside America's War on Terror* (New York: Free Press, 2004), p. 32.

14 **"10 percent chance":** *9/11 Commission Report*, pp. 335–336.

14 **clashed with Wolfowitz:** "The War Behind Closed Doors," *Frontline*, PBS, February 20, 2003.

15 **"have no clear information":** Author interview, Dr. Emile Nakhleh, February 2012. Details of Dr. Nakhleh's career are from the author's interviews. Information about Dr. Nakleh's scholarship at the CIA can also be found in his biography on the American Foreign Policy Project, accessed October 5, 2012, http://americanforeignpolicy.org/iran-experts/emile-nakhleh.

15 **"humble" foreign policy:** Transcript, presidential debate between George W. Bush and Al Gore, Wake Forest University, Winston-Salem, North Carolina, October 11, 2000, www.debates.org/index.php?page=october-11-2000-debate-transcript.

15 **more than a dozen visits:** Some reports have stated that Cheney made around a dozen visits to CIA headquarters; other reports have put the number slightly lower. Dubose and Bernstein report that "Cheney made at least eight, perhaps as many as fifteen" visits, citing interviews within and connected to the CIA. Libby was reportedly a more frequent visitor. See Tom Hamburger and Peter Wallsten (*Los Angeles Times*), "Cheney's Tussles with CIA Are Subtext of Leaker Probe; Vice President's Skeptical View of Intelligence Agency Dates Back to the Late 1980's," *Baltimore Sun*, October 21, 2005; Lou Dubose and Jake Bernstein, *Vice: Dick Cheney and the Hijacking of the American Presidency* (New York: Random House, 2006, Kindle edition).

15 **mass arrests:** Martha Mendoza (AP), "One Man Still Locked Up from 9/11 Sweeps," *Washington Post*, October 14, 2006.

16 **rigorous legal and oversight system:** Joshua A. Bobich, "Note: Who Authorized This?! An Assessment of the Process for Approving U.S. Covert Action," *William Mitchell Law Review* 33 (3) (April 10, 2007): 1111–1142, 1126. The details of the Clinton administration's process for approving covert actions are from the article.

16 **closely mirrored:** Ibid., p. 1126; memorandum from George W. Bush, "Subject: Organization of the National Security Council System," February 13, 2001. The memoran-

dum is known as National Security Presidential Directive-1 (NSPD-1), and though the unclassified memorandum does not mention covert action specifically, it purports to preserve much of the structure of the national security system.

16 **"new series of authorities," covert actions:** *9/11 Commission Report*, p. 210.

16 **counterterrorism funding, retaliatory strike:** Ibid., p. 202.

17 **"taking the offensive," "breaking the back":** Ibid., p. 204.

17 **Uzbekistan, stopped short:** Ibid., p. 203.

17 **"admittedly ambitious":** Ibid., pp. 204–205.

17 **five more meetings:** Prepared testimony of Secretary Donald Rumsfeld, for delivery to the National Commission on Terrorist Attacks upon the United States, March 23, 2004.

17 **"concluded":** *9/11 Commission Report*, p. 212.

17 **began flying drones:** Ibid., p. 190.

17 **K2:** Author interview, US military intelligence source, February 2010.

17 **not yet operational:** Bill Yenne, *Attack of the Drones: A History of Unmanned Aerial Combat* (St. Paul, MN: Zenith Press, 2004), p. 86. According to Yenne, "On February 16, 2001, during tests at Nellis Air Force Base, a Predator successfully fired a Hellfire AGM-114C into a target. The notion of turning the Predator into a *predator* had been realized."

17 **Cofer Black argued:** *9/11 Commission Report*, pp. 190, 211.

17 **"in front of CNN":** Ibid., p. 211. The commission obtained and quoted from a memorandum sent by Cofer Black to Richard Clarke, January 25, 2001.

17 **shelve the use of the drones:** Ibid.

17 **"'This was new ground'":** Ibid.

18 **assistant director for collection:** "The Honorable Charles E. Allen, Principal," Chertoff Group, accessed October 5, 2012, http://chertoffgroup.com/bios/charles-allen.php.

18 **"happy to pull the trigger":** *9/11 Commission Report*, p. 211.

18 **September 4 meeting:** Ibid., p. 213.

18 **three years to implement:** Ibid.

18 **"broad covert action program'":** Ibid., p. 214.

18 **"Only a crisis":** Milton Friedman, *Capitalism and Freedom*, 40th anniv. ed. (Chicago: University of Chicago Press, 2002), Preface, 1982, p. xiv.

18 **mentored Rumsfeld:** Naomi Klein, *The Shock Doctrine: The Rise of Disaster Capitalism* (New York: Picador, 2007), p. 14.

18 **Cheney, sought his counsel:** Nina Easton, "Why Is Dick Cheney Smiling?" Money.CNN.com, November 25, 2007.

19 **"When that crisis occurs":** Friedman, *Capitalism and Freedom*, Preface, 1982, p. xiv.

19 **"a new Pearl Harbor":** "Rebuilding America's Defenses," p. 51.

19 **"duty to use his bully pulpit":** Feith, *War and Decision*, p. 51.

19 **"all necessary and appropriate force":** Joint Resolution to Authorize the Use of United States Armed Forces Against Those Responsible for the Recent Attacks Launched Against the United States, Pub. Law 107-40, Sec. 2 (2001).

19 **one opposing vote, no dissent:** Richard F. Grimmett, "Authorization for Use of Military Force in Response to the 9/11 Attacks (P.L. 107-40): Legislative History," Congressional Research Service, updated January 16, 2007.

19 **"urge the use of restraint":** "Barbara Lee's 9/14/01 Speech," YouTube video, 2:19, from footage of debate prior to passage of the "Authorization for Use of Military Force," September 14, 2001, posted by "OneVoice-PAC," September 12, 2007, www.youtube.com/watch?v=Zh_sxilhyVo.

19 **"There must be some of us":** Prepared speech of Representative Barbara Lee, in opposition to authorizing the use of force in Afghanistan, September 14, 2001.

20 **"the dark side":** Transcript, interview with Vice President Richard Cheney, *Meet the Press*, NBC, September 16, 2001.

20 **secret presidential directive:** Woodward, *Bush at War*, pp. 75, 101. Woodward outlines an earlier proposal made by CIA director George Tenet during the meetings at Camp David, titled "Going to War," which includes authorities to detain and use lethal force against members of the al Qaeda network. The September 17 finding, Woodward writes, "authorized all the steps proposed by Tenet at Camp David."

20 **Zambia, Somalia and South Africa:** Steve Coll, *Ghost Wars: The Secret History of the CIA, Afghanistan, and Bin Laden, from the Soviet Invasion to September 10, 2001* (New York: Penguin Press, 2004), p. 267.

20 **Zaire:** Ibid.

20 **CIA station chief:** Ibid., front matter.

20 **"the Ford Foundation of Sunni Islamic terrorism":** Ibid., p. 271.

20 **"operating directive":** Ibid., p. 267.

21 **not yet signed:** Ibid.

21 **"taboo in the outfit":** Bill Waugh with Tim Keown, *Hunting the Jackal: A Special Forces and CIA Ground Soldier's Fifty-Year Career Hunting America's Enemies* (New York: William Morrow, 2004), p. 143.

21 **dump his body:** Robert Young Pelton, *Licensed to Kill: Hired Guns in the War on Terror* (New York: Three Rivers Press, 2006), p. 28.

21 **"He used to come in my office":** Author interview, Colonel Lawrence Wilkerson (Ret.), May 2011.

21 **August 6, 2001, Crawford, Texas, ranch:** Michael Hirsh and Michael Isikoff, "What Went Wrong," *Newsweek*, May 27, 2002.

21 **"Bin Ladin Determined to Strike in US":** *9/11 Commission Report*, p. 261. The commission's report includes partial text of the presidential daily brief from August 6, 2001.

21 **"struck soon":** J. Cofer Black, prepared testimony for delivery to the Joint House-Senate Intelligence Committee Hearing into September 11, September 26, 2002.

21 **"I just couldn't wait":** Gordon Corera, "How Terror Attacks Changed the CIA," BBC.co.uk, March 13, 2006.

22 **"flies walking across their eyeballs":** Woodward, *Bush at War*, p. 52.

22 **"Let's go":** Ibid.

22 **"I was astonished":** Author interview, Philip Giraldi, March 2012.

22 **"your marching orders":** Gary C. Schroen, *First In: An Insider's Account of How the CIA Spearheaded the War on Terror in Afghanistan* (New York: Presidio Press, 2005), p. 38.

22 **"You'd need some DNA":** Jane Mayer, "The Search for Osama: Did the Government Let bin Laden's Trail Go Cold?" *New Yorker*, August 4, 2003, p. 27.

22 **"rock their world":** Woodward, *Bush at War*, p. 103.

23 **majority of the first Americans:** Pelton, *Licensed to Kill*, pp. 30–32.

23 **seven to two dozen:** Seymour M. Hersh, "Manhunt: The Bush Administration's New Strategy in the War Against Terrorism," *New Yorker*, December 23, 2002, p. 66; James Risen and David Johnson, "Threats and Responses: Hunt for Al Qaeda; Bush Has Widened Authority of C.I.A. to Kill Terrorists," *New York Times*, December 15, 2002.

23 **officially launched:** George W. Bush, "Presidential Address to the Nation," October 7, 2001.

23 **"partnership is sound":** Woodward, *Bush at War*, p. 175.

23 **small paramilitary capability:** *9/11 Commission Report*, p. 351.

24 **"the War Council":** Tom Lasseter, "Day Four: Easing of Laws That Led to Detainee Abuse Hatched in Secret," McClatchy, June 18, 2008.

24 **"minority report":** Chitra Ragavan, "Cheney's Guy," US News.com, May 21, 2006, www.usnews.com/usnews/news/articles/060529/29addington.htm.

24 **also included:** Lasseter, "Day Four."

24 **explicitly excluded:** Tim Golden, "After Terror, a Secret Rewriting of Military Law," *New York Times*, October 24, 2004. Golden's article refers explicitly to the exclusion of certain lawyers and officials from the internal discussions of the military tribunal policy.

24 **issue a finding, must comply:** 50 U.S.C. Sec. 413b, "Presidential Approval and Reporting of Covert Actions."

24 **Greystone:** Author interview, military intelligence source, November 2009. The existence of a program known by the abbreviation "GST" was originally reported by Dana Priest for the *Washington Post*. Priest later mentioned the name "Greystone" in an interview featured on the PBS documentary *Top Secret America*.

24 **umbrella, legitimate target:** Dana Priest, "Covert CIA Program Withstands New Furor," *Washington Post*, December 30, 2005.

24 **compartmentalized programs:** Ibid.

25 **directly order hits:** Ibid.

25 **"selected foreign counterparts," "broadened our options":** Tyler Drumheller, with Elaine Monaghan, *On the Brink: An Insider's Account of How the White House Compromised American Intelligence* (New York: Carroll and Graff, 2006), p. 32.

25 **"simply extraordinary":** Transcript, interview with John Rizzo, "John Rizzo: The Lawyer Who Approved CIA's Most Controversial Programs," PBS.org, September 6, 2011.

25 **"Status of Forces":** John Barry, Michael Isikoff, and Michael Hirsh, "The Roots of Torture," *Newsweek*, May 23, 2004.

25 **private contractors:** Ibid.

25 **"lawyered up":** Dana Priest, "Former CIA Spy Boss Made an Unhesitating Call to Destroy Interrogation Tapes," *Washington Post*, April 24, 2012.

25 **series of legal documents:** Stephen Gillers, "The Torture Memo," *Nation*, April 9, 2008.

25 **"big boy pants":** Transcript, interview with Jose A. Rodriguez Jr., *60 Minutes*, CBS, April 29, 2012.

26 **shipping containers, discrete sites, brick factory:** Jane Mayer, "The Black Sites: A Rare Look Inside the C.I.A.'s Secret Interrogation Program," *New Yorker*, August 13, 2007.

26 **"Salt Pit":** Dana Priest, "CIA Holds Terror Suspects in Secret Prisons," *Washington Post*, November 2, 2005.

26 **evolved:** Ibid. A former senior intelligence official told Priest, "We never sat down, as far as I know, and came up with a grand strategy. Everything was very reactive. That's how you get to a situation where you pick people up, send them into a netherworld and don't say, 'What are we going to do with them afterwards?'"

26 **naval vessels, Lake Kariba:** Priest, "CIA Holds Terror Suspects."

26 **funneling suspects:** Ibid.

26 **freely tortured:** Rebecca Leung, "CIA Flying Suspects to Torture?" CBSNews.com, February 11, 2009.

26 **refused to provide details:** Priest, "CIA Holds Terror Suspects."

26 **decided to reduce:** Joby Warrick and Dan Eggen, "Hill Briefed on Waterboarding in 2002," *Washington Post*, December 9, 2007.

26 **signed a presidential directive:** Jane Mayer, *The Dark Side: The Inside Story of How the War on Terror Turned into a War on American Ideals* (New York: Doubleday, 2008), p. 114.

26 **suspects to Egypt:** Stephen Grey, *Ghost Plane: The True Story of the CIA Rendition and Torture Program* (New York: St. Martin's Press, 2006), pp. 139–141.

27 **direct authorization:** Ibid., pp. 140–141. According to Grey, who interviewed Michael Scheuer for the book, the White House had signed off on the rendition policy. Lawyers signed off on each operation, and "within the CIA, authority for each operation...had to come from the director of central intelligence...or his assistant director."

27 **more than seventy renditions:** Eighth Public Hearing Before the National Commission on Terrorist Attacks upon the United States, March 24, 2004 (testimony of George Tenet, Director of the Central Intelligence Agency).

27 **Mir Aimal Kasi:** Amnesty International, "Pakistan: Imminent Execution of Mir Aimal Kasi Raises Fears for Others Taken into US Custody Without Human Rights Safeguards," 2002.

27 **Ramzi Yousef:** Richard Clarke, op-ed, "The Confusion over Renditions," *Boston Globe*, January 29, 2009.

27 **Wali Khan Amin Shah:** Christopher S. Wren, "U.S. Jury Convicts Three in a Conspiracy to Bomb Airliners," *New York Times*, September 6, 1996; rendition confirmed in "Patterns of Global Terrorism 1998," US Department of State, April 1999.

27 **Tsutomu Shirosaki:** "Patterns of Global Terrorism 1998," US Department of State, April 1999.

27 **"not to expel, extradite":** Foreign Affairs Reform and Restructuring Act, Pub. Law 105-277, Sec. 2242(a) (1998).

27 **"won in large measure":** Jim Landers, "CIA Official Says War on Terrorism Will Be Won with Great Force," Knight Ridder/Tribune News Service, October 18, 2001.

27 **"kick the (expletive) out of them":** Dana Priest and Barton Gellman, "U.S. Decries Abuse but Defends Interrogations," *Washington Post*, December 26, 2002.

27 **"probably aren't doing your job":** Ibid.

27 **"gloves come off":** *Joint Inquiry into Intelligence Community Activities Before and After the Terrorist Attacks of September 11, 2001, Hearings Before the Senate Select Committee on Intelligence and House Permanent Select Committee on Intelligence*, 107th Cong., 2nd Sess., September 26, 2002 (testimony of J. Cofer Black).

28 **Pakistani forces:** Dana Priest, "Al Qaeda-Iraq Link Recanted; Captured Libyan Reverses Previous Statement to CIA, Officials Say," *Washington Post*, August 1, 2004.

28 **"Shoe Bomber," Twentieth Hijacker, witness:** Mayer, *The Dark Side*, p. 104.

28 **"handle this":** Ibid.

28 **"genuinely friendly":** Ibid., p. 106.

28 **orders from Cofer Black:** John Barry and Daniel Klaidman, "A Tortured Debate," *Newsweek*, June 20, 2004.

28 **objected:** Garrett M. Graff, *The Threat Matrix: The FBI at War in the Age of Global Terror* (New York: Little, Brown, 2011), p. 359; Jason Vest, "Pray and Tell," *American Prospect*, June 19, 2005.

28 **"You know where you are going":** James Risen, *State of War: The Secret History of the CIA and the Bush Administration* (New York: Free Press, 2006), p. 29.

28 **USS *Bataan:*** "Top al Qaeda Leader Held Aboard U.S. Warship," CNN.com, January 8, 2002.

28 **tortured, Iraq connection:** Michael Isikoff and David Corn, *Hubris: The Inside Story of Spin, Scandal, and the Selling of the Iraq War* (New York: Three Rivers Press, 2007), pp. 122–123.

28 **Cheney's office directly intervened:** Colonel Lawrence B. Wilkerson, "The Truth About Richard Bruce Cheney," *Washington Note*, May 13, 2009.

28 **"real macho interrogation":** Transcript, interview with Ali Soufan, "The Interrogator," *Frontline*, PBS, aired September 13, 2011.

29 **"lacks specific details":** John D. Rockefeller IV and Carl Levin, letter to Vice Admiral Lowell E. Jacoby, Director, Defense Intelligence Agency, October 18, 2005. The letter contains two paragraphs of a DIA defense intelligence terrorist summary (DITSUM) from October 3, 2005, concerning claims made by Libi following his interrogation.

29 **given to Secretary of State Powell:** Isikoff and Corn, *Hubris*, p. 187.

29 **"I can trace the story":** Transcript, speech as delivered by Colin Powell before the United Nations, February 5, 2003.

29 **"what you want[ed] to hear":** Transcript, "The Interrogator," *Frontline*.

29 **directing a global manhunt:** Author interviews with former U.S. officials, August 2010, May 2011.

29 **convened a meeting, shut out:** Savage, *Takeover*, pp. 135–136, 138.

29 **had told President Bush:** Katharine Q. Seelye, "A Nation Challenged: The Prisoners; Powell Asks Bush to Review Stand on

War Captives," *New York Times*, January 27, 2002.

30 **endanger the lives:** Colin L. Powell, memorandum to Counsel to the President, Assistant to the President for National Security Affairs, "Subject: Draft Decision Memorandum for the President on the Applicability of the Geneva Convention to the Conflict in Afghanistan," January 26, 2002. Powell lists the "pros" and "cons" of applying and not applying the Geneva Conventions to the conflict in Afghanistan. Among the cons of not applying the conventions, Powell notes, is that "it will reverse over a century of U.S. policy and practice in supporting the Geneva conventions and undermine protections of the law of war for our troops, both in this specific context and in general."

30 **directive, just after:** Barry, Isikoff, and Hirsh, "Roots of Torture." Bush made his decision in early February, and by "mid-January 2002 the first plane-load of prisoners landed at Gitmo's Camp X-Ray."

30 **"We didn't tell the FBI":** Jose A. Rodriguez Jr., with Bill Harlow, *Hard Measures: How Aggressive CIA Actions After 9/11 Saved American Lives* (New York: Threshold Editions, 2012), pp. 116–117.

30 **"near total dependence on CIA":** Donald Rumsfeld, working paper sent to General Myers, "Subject: Afghanistan," October 17, 2001. Rumsfeld writes, "Given the nature of our world, isn't it conceivable that the Department ought not to be in a position of near total dependence on CIA in situations such as this?"

**2: Anwar Awlaki: An American Story**

31 **Their best hope:** Dr. James J. Zogby, "The Arab American Vote in the November 2000 Election," Arab American Institute, December 14, 2000. In an analysis commissioned by Abu Dhabi Television, Zogby writes that "a recent poll of Arab American voters shows that Arab Americans supported the candidacy of Republican George W. Bush over the candidacy of Democrat Al Gore by a margin of 45.5% to 38%." He further notes that despite the fact that Arab Americans tended to lean Democratic, "this election took place against the backdrop of escalating Israeli violence against Palestinians," which "apparently influenced the votes of a number of Arab Americans."

31 **"Freedom is one of them":** Transcript, interview with Anwar al Awlaki, "Fighting Fear," *NewsHour with Jim Lehrer*, PBS, October 30, 2001.

31 **Fulbright scholarship:** Author interview, Nasser al Awlaki, January 2012. Details of Nasser al Awlaki's family life and the early

years of Anwar al Awlaki are from the author's interview, unless otherwise noted.

31 **"My studies in the United States":** Ibid. All quotations from Nasser al Awlaki are from interview with author, unless otherwise noted.

31 **"meet people of the New World":** Personal, unpublished essay written by Nasser al Awlaki and shown to the author in January 2012.

32 **April 22, 1971:** An FBI report about Anwar lists his birthday as April 21, but Nasser says in an interview with the author that Anwar was born on the 22nd. News reports have used both dates.

32 **University of Minnesota:** "Interview: Dr. Nasser al-Awlaki on the Killing of His Son, Anwar, and His Grandson," *National Yemen*, October 6, 2012.

33 **O'Hare Airport:** Catherine Herridge, *The Next Wave: On the Hunt for Al Qaeda's American Recruits* (New York: Crown Forum, 2011), p. 78.

33 **civil engineering:** Bruce Finley, "Muslim Cleric Targeted by U.S. Made Little Impression During Colorado Years," *Denver Post*, April 11, 2010.

33 **"not [a] fully practicing Muslim":** Anwar al Awlaki, "Spilling Out the Beans; Al Awlaki Revealing His Side of the Story," *Inspire* 9 (winter 2012), released May 2012.

33 **Muslim Student Association:** Ibid.

34 **"staying in the US":** Ibid.

34 **grades were slipping:** Ibid.

34 **"termination of my scholarship":** Ibid.

34 **"I was a fundamentalist now!":** Ibid.

35 **asked him to deliver a sermon:** Author interview, Nasser al Awlaki, January 2012; Scott Shane and Souad Mekhennet, "Imam's Path from Condemning Terror to Preaching Jihad," *New York Times*, May 8, 2010.

35 **"very promising person":** Author interview, Sheikh Saleh bin Fareed, January 2012.

35 **graduated from CSU:** Finley, "Muslim Cleric Targeted by U.S."

35 **Denver Islamic Society:** Ibid.

35 **Malcolm X**: Author interview, Nasser al Awlaki, January 2012.

35 **"He had this magic":** Finley, "Muslim Cleric Targeted by U.S."

35 **"a beautiful tongue":** Shane and Mekhennet, "Imam's Path."

35 **September 13, 1995:** Author copy of Abdulrahman al Awlaki's birth certificate.

35 **Masjid al Ribat al Islami:** Shane and Mekhennet, "Imam's Path."

35 **education leadership:** Union-Tribune and Associated Press, "Anwar al-Awlaki, al-Qaida-Linked Cleric with San Diego Ties, Killed," UTSanDiego.com, September 30, 2011.

35 **"very outgoing and cheerful":** Memo-

randum for the record: telephone interview of Lincoln Higgie, prepared by Dieter Snell, FBI-San Diego Field Office, November 19, 2003. Available at the National Archive and Records Administration website, http://media.nara.gov/9-11/MFR/t-0148-911MFR-00449.pdf.

35 **"albacore fishing":** Transcript, *The Situation Room*, CNN, September 30, 2011.

36 **first run-in with the FBI**: Shane and Mekhennet, "Imam's Path."

36 **"blind sheikh":** Ibid.

36 **Holy Land Foundation:** National Commission on Terrorist Attacks upon the United States (Philip Zelikow, Executive Director; Bonnie D. Jenkins, Counsel; Ernest R. May, Senior Advisor), *The 9/11 Commission Report* (New York: W. W. Norton, 2004), p. 517.

36 **Charitable Society for Social Welfare:** Susan Schmidt, "Imam from Va. Mosque Now Thought to Have Aided al-Qaeda," *Washington Post*, February 27, 2008.

36 **"front organization":** Tom Hays (AP), "FBI Eyes NYC 'Charity' in Terror Probe," washingtonpost.com, February 26, 2004.

36 **Abdul Majeed al Zindani:** Schmidt, "Imam from Va. Mosque."

36 **US Department of Labor:** US Department of Labor, International Labor Affairs Bureau, Technical Cooperation Project Summary, for project "Alternatives to Combat Child Labor Through Education and Sustainable Services in the Middle East and North Africa (MENA) Region," www.dol.gov/ilab/projects/europe_mena/MidEast_LebanonYemen_EI_CLOSED.pdf; "Project Status—Europe, Middle East, and North Africa," Department of Labor website, accessed October 2010, www.dol.gov/ilab/projects/europe_mena/project-europe.htm.

36 **raising money for orphans:** Author interviews with Awlaki family members, January 2012.

36 **"does not meet the criterion":** J. M. Berger, *Jihad Joe: Americans Who Go to War in the Name of Islam* (Washington, DC: Potomac Books, 2011), p. 119.

37 **Two men:** Schmidt, "Imam from Va. Mosque."

37 **Nawaf al Hamzi:** *Joint Inquiry into Intelligence Community Activities Before and After the Terrorist Attacks of September 11, 2001, Hearings Before the Senate Select Committee on Intelligence and House Permanent Select Committee on Intelligence*, 107th Cong., 2nd Sess., September 26, 2002, p. 178.

37 **"spiritual adviser":** Ibid.

37 **recording CDs:** Shane and Mekhennet, "Imam's Path."

37 **extremely popular:** Author interview, Nasser al Awlaki, January 2012.

37 **more than a hundred CDs:** J. M. Berger, "Gone but Not Forgotten," *Foreign Policy*, September 30, 2011.

37 **free of obvious radicalism":** Shane and Mekhennet, "Imam's Path."

37 **"very pleased":** Alexander Meleagrou-Hitchens, "As American as Apple Pie: How Anwar al-Awlaki Became the Face of Western Jihad," The International Centre for the Study of Radicalisation and Political Violence, London, 2011.

37 **sent "moles":** Awlaki, "Spilling Out the Beans."

37 **busted twice:** "Radical Cleric Killed by Drone Was Twice Arrested with Prostitutes in San Diego," L.A. Now (blog), *Los Angeles Times*, September 30, 2011, http://latimesblogs.latimes.com/lanow/2011/09/anwar-awlaki-the-american-born-cleric-and-jihadist-killed-by-a-us-backed-drone-strike-in-yemen-spent-several-years-in-san.html.

38 **"I was surrounded by police officers":** Awlaki, "Spilling Out the Beans."

38 **"move somewhere else":** Ibid.

38 **partial scholarship:** Author interview, Nasser al Awlaki, January 2012.

38 **chaplain:** Ibid.

38 **"full force of faith":** Transcript, "Connections Between Radical Cleric, Hasan Closely Examined," *NewsHour*, PBS, November 12, 2009.

39 **backseat of a taxi:** "Former Islamic Spiritual Leader Defends Mosque," Copley News Service, September 28, 2001.

39 **screamed threats:** "Muslim Americans Suffer Terrorist Backlash," Scripps Howard News Service, September 12, 2001.

39 **closed for three days:** William Branigin, "Terror Hits Close to Home; Mix of Emotions Sweeps over Area's Residents," *Washington Post*, September 20, 2001.

39 **"How should we react?":** Susan Morse, "First Source of Comfort; When Events Overwhelm, Clergy, Not Doctors, Are on the Front Lines," *Washington Post*, September 18, 2001.

39 **security firm:** Debbi Wilgoren and Ann O'Hanlon, "Worship and Worry; Fear for Other Muslims Mixes with Support for US," *Washington Post*, September 22, 2001.

39 **Local churches:** Ibid.

39 **baseball bat:** Ibid.

39 **"heinous":** Branigin, "Terror Hits Close to Home."

39 **"Best Buy":** Brian Handwerk and Zain Habboo, "Attack on America: An Islamic Scholar's Perspective—Part 1," *National Geographic*, September 28, 2001.

40 **"knocking on my door":** Awlaki, "Spilling Out the Beans."

40 **showed him pictures:** Federal Bureau of

Investigation file on "Anwar Nasser Aulaqi," September 26, 2001. Document obtained by Intelwire, intelwire.com.

40 **attended an Awlaki sermon:** *9/11 Commission Report*, p. 229.

40 **"did not recognize":** Ibid., p. 221.

40 **Awlaki also said:** Ibid., pp. 229–230.

40 **"described Hazmi":** Ibid., p. 221.

40 **"a loner":** Federal Bureau of Investigation file on "Anwar Nasser Aulaqi."

40 **"very religious person":** Ibid.

40 **got a lawyer:** Awlaki, "Spilling Out the Beans."

40 **"Investigation continues":** Federal Bureau of Investigation file on "Anwar Nasser Aulaqi."

40 **series of phone conversations:** *9/11 Commission Report*, p. 517.

40 **"evidence is thin":** Ibid., p. 221.

41 **Nidal Malik Hasan:** Author interview, Nasser al Awlaki, January 2012. That Hasan attended Dar al Hijrah has been documented in press reports, such as David Johnston and Scott Shane, "U.S. Knew of Suspect's Tie to Radical Cleric," *New York Times*, November 9, 2009.

41 **worst massacres:** Robert D. McFadden, "Army Doctor Held in Ft. Hood Rampage," *New York Times*, November 5, 2009.

41 **"tolerance":** "Al-Awlaki Assassinated in Drone Attack," blog post on Dar al Hijrah website, September 30, 2011, www.daralhijrah.net/ns/?p=6258.

41 **"overtly political or radical":** Matthew Barakat, "Relief, Anger at Va. Mosque Where al-Qaida Figure Preached," Associated Press, September 30, 2011.

41 **"right to defend itself":** Transcript, "Fighting Fear," interview by Ray Suarez, *NewsHour with Jim Lehrer*, PBS, October 30, 2001.

41 **"go-to Muslim cleric":** Shane and Mekhennet, "Imam's Path."

42 **"merging East and West":** Laurie Goodstein, "A Nation Challenged: The American Muslims; Influential American Muslims Temper Their Tone," *New York Times*, October 19, 2001.

42 **"perverted their religion":** Handwerk and Habboo, "Attack on America."

42 **webcast:** Travis Fox, video, "Understanding Ramadan: A Day in the Life of an Imam," www.washingtonpost.com, November 18, 2001.

42 **"Our position needs to be reiterated":** Anwar al Awlaki sermon, excerpted in "Fighting Fear," *NewsHour with Jim Lehrer*, PBS, October 30, 2001.

42 **"attack on US foreign policy":** Wilgoren and O'Hanlon, "Worship and Worry."

42 **"killing of civilians in Afghanistan":**

"Muslim Students Are Wary of the War," *Washington Times*, October 11, 2001.

42 **"not going to happen":** Ellen Sorokin, "Area's Muslims Facing a Somber Ramadan; Terror Attack, War in Afghanistan Create 'Gloomy Mood,'" *Washington Times*, November 16, 2001.

42 **"rushed into this war":** Video interview from November 2001, provided to the author by Travis Fox.

43 **"freedom to the people":** Transcript, *Morning Edition*, National Public Radio (hereafter NPR), November 1, 2001.

43 **"casualties from the civilians":** Video interview from November 2001, provided to the author by Travis Fox.

43 **"radical understanding":** Ibid.

44 **vigilantes and federal agents:** See Human Rights Watch USA, "'We Are Not the Enemy': Hate Crimes Against Arabs, Muslims, and Those Perceived to Be Arab or Muslim After September 11," November 14, 2002; "NPR Special Report: Muslims in America; Part One: Profiling the Proud Americans of 'Little Mecca,'" NPR, October 21, 2001, www.npr.org/news/specials/response/home_front/features/2001/oct/muslim/011022.muslim.html.

44 **"element of feeling":** Transcript, *Talk of the Nation with Neal Conan*, NPR, November 15, 2001.

44 **"crude fashion":** Joe Cantlupe and Dana Wilkie, "Former San Diego Islamic Spiritual Defends Mosque," Copley News Service, September 28, 2001.

44 **"radical voices":** Transcript, *Morning Edition*, NPR, November 1, 2001.

44 **"American Muslims":** Jean Marbella, "Ramadan Raises Conflicting Loyalties; US Muslims Feel Pull of Nation, Solidarity; War on Terrorism," *Baltimore Sun*, October 28, 2001.

44 **"enemy of Islam":** Transcript, *Morning Edition*, NPR, November 1, 2001.

45 **"privilege":** E-mail from undisclosed sender to undisclosed recipients, subject: "RE: Luncheon Speaker—Islam and Middle Eastern politics and culture—February 5th—Response date—1/31," sent February 1, 2002, obtained by public intelligence, http://publicintelligence.net/dod-email-discussing-anwar-al-awlakis-2002-presentation-at-the-pentagon/.

45 **"secretary of the Army's":** Catherine Herridge, "Exclusive: Al Qaeda Leader Dined at the Pentagon Just Months After 9/11," FoxNews.com, October 20, 2010.

45 **"attended a luncheon":** Ibid.

45 **"East Side West Side":** E-mail from undisclosed sender, "RE: Luncheon Speaker."

45 **PBS documentary:** *Muhammad: Legacy of a Prophet*, PBS, 2002, produced by KiKim

Media and Unity Productions Foundation/A KQED Presentation, Corporation for Public Broadcasting.

45 **sweeping raids:** Jerry Markon, "Muslim Anger Burns over Lingering Probe of Charities," *Washington Post,* October 11, 2006.

46 **Operation Green Quest:** Associated Press, "Feds Launch 'Operation Green Quest,'" CBSNews.com, October 25, 2001.

46 **International Institute of Islamic Thought:** Judith Miller, "A Nation Challenged: The Money Trail; Raids Seek Evidence of Money-Laundering," *New York Times,* March 21, 2002.

46 **Graduate School of Islamic and Social Sciences:** Riad Z. Abdelkarim and Basil Z. Abdelkarim, "Islam in America: As American Muslims Face New Raids, Muslim Charities Fight Back," *Washington Report on Middle East Affairs,* May 2002, pp. 80–81.

46 **property seized:** Markon, "Muslim Anger Burns."

46 **five hundred boxes:** Ibid.

46 **"attack on every one of us":** Audio recording of Anwar al Awlaki sermon, Virginia, March 2002, transcription by Alexander Meleagrou-Hitchens, "As American as Apple Pie: How Anwar al-Awlaki Became the Face of Western Jihad," The International Centre for the Study of Radicalisation and Political Violence, London, 2011.

46 **"struggle for those rights":** Ibid.

46 **active subject:** Herridge, *The Next Wave,* p. 91.

46 **"various investigations":** Chitra Ragavan, "The Imam's Very Curious Story," *US News and World Report,* June 13, 2004, www.usnews.com/usnews/news/articles/040621/21plot.htm.

46 **flip him:** Awlaki, "Spilling Out the Beans."

46 **"across state lines":** Ragavan, "The Imam's Very Curious Story."

46 **"Why are you leaving?":** Transcript, "Connections Between Radical Cleric, Hasan Closely Examined," *NewsHour,* PBS, November 12, 2009.

47 **running for parliament:** Meleagrou-Hitchens, "As American as Apple Pie."

47 **his own TV show:** Shane and Mekhennet, "Imam's Path."

47 **"ruined him":** Meleagrou-Hitchens, "As American as Apple Pie."

47 **"war against Muslims":** Audio recording of Imam Anwar al Awlaki sermon, unconfirmed location, March 2002.

## 3: Find, Fix, Finish: The Rise of JSOC

48 **"worldwide war":** Transcript, Defense Secretary Donald Rumsfeld, "Address to the Men and Women of Fort Bragg/Pope AFB," Fort Bragg, NC, November 21, 2001.

48 **secret meeting:** Rowan Scarborough, *Rumsfeld's War: The Untold Story of America's Anti-Terrorist Commander* (Washington, DC: Regnery, 2004), pp. 8–10.

48 **"joint headquarters":** Description of Joint Special Operations Command from "Special Operations Forces Reference Manual," compiled and developed for the Joint Special Operations Forces Institute by Cubic Applications, Inc., January 1998.

49 **Operation Eagle Claw:** Mark Bowden, "The Desert One Debacle," *Atlantic,* May 2006.

49 **went down in a sandstorm:** Ibid.

49 **several crucial aircraft:** Ibid.

49 **abort mission order:** Ibid.

49 **Eight US service members:** Ibid.

49 **hostages for weapons:** Gary Sick, "The Election Story of the Decade," op-ed, *New York Times,* April 15, 1991.

49 **just minutes after:** *NBC Nightly News,* January 20, 1981, www.nbc.com/news-sports/msnbc-video/2012/01/from-the-archives-reagan-sworn-in-iran-hostages-released/.

49 **Honey Badger:** Tom Clancy, with General Carl Stiner (Ret.), *Shadow Warriors: Inside the Special Forces* (New York: Berkley Publishing Group, 2002), p. 9.

49 **Che Guevara:** Author interview, Colonel W. Patrick Lang (Ret.), September 2010. Details of Colonel Lang's background and credentials come from the author's interview. Also see "Bio of Col. W. Patrick Lang," Sic Semper Tyrannis (blog), turcopolier.typepad.com.

50 **"training and leading indigenous forces":** Ibid. All statements and information attributed to Colonel Lang come from the author's interview.

50 **force multiplier:** Lieutenant Colonel David E. Hill Jr., "The Shaft of the Spear: US Special Operations Command, Funding Authority, and the Global War on Terrorism," US Army War College Strategy Research Project, March 15, 2006.

50 **Delta Force had formed:** See Command Sergeant Major Eric L. Haney, *Inside Delta Force: The Story of America's Elite Counterterrorist Unit* (New York: Bantam Dell, 2003), pp. 1–4.

50 **founding commander:** "Seal Team Six," Special Operations Forces Situation Report (SOFREP), accessed September 5, 2012, http://sofrep.com/devgru-seal-team-6/. Other details of the origins of SEAL Team 6 come from SOFREP's brief history.

51 **Field Operations Group:** Michael Smith, *Killer Elite: The Inside Story of America's Most Secret Special Operations Team* (New York: St. Martin's Press, 2006), pp. 20–21.

51 **successful rescue operation:** Ibid., pp. 22–46.

51 **Grenada:** See Ronald H. Cole, "Operation Urgent Fury: Grenada," Joint History Office, Office of the Chairman of the Joint Chiefs of Staff, 1997.

51 **"the use of sabotage, killing":** Robert Chesney, "Military-Intelligence Convergence and the Law of the Title 10/Title 50 Debate," *Journal of National Security Law and Policy* 5 (2012): 539–629.

52 **Pablo Escobar:** See Mark Bowden, *Killing Pablo: The Hunt for the World's Greatest Outlaw* (New York: Penguin Books, 2001), pp. 147, 259.

52 **former Yugoslavia:** Paula Broadwell, with Vernon Loeb, *All In: The Education of General David Petraeus* (New York: Penguin Press, 2012), pp. 148–153; Smith, *Killer Elite,* pp. 192–193.

52 **secret presidential directive:** "Joint Special Operations Command (JSOC)," GlobalSecurity.org, accessed October 1, 2012, www.globalsecurity.org/military/agency/dod/jsoc.htm.

52 **Waco, Texas:** Philip Shenon, "Documents on Waco Point to a Close Commando Role," *New York Times,* September 5, 1999.

52 **World Cup, Summer Olympics:** "Joint Special Operations Command (JSOC)," GlobalSecurity.org.

52 **"transnational threats":** Eric Schmitt, "Commandos Get Duty on U.S. Soil," *New York Times,* January 23, 2005.

52 **80 percent:** Marc Ambinder and D. B. Grady, *The Command: Deep Inside the President's Secret Army* (Hoboken, NJ: John Wiley and Sons, 2012, Kindle edition).

52 **"ace in the hole":** Author interview, General Hugh Shelton (Ret.), March 2011. All information and statements attributed to General Shelton come from the author's interview, unless otherwise noted.

52 **most of his military career:** "General Henry Hugh Shelton Biography," website of the General H. Hugh Shelton Leadership Center at North Carolina State University, accessed October 5, 2012, www.ncsu.edu/extension/sheltonleadership/shelton-forum/documents/GENERALHENRYHUGHSHELTONBIOGRAPHYOct07.pdf.

53 **rescue of Kurt Muse:** "Delta Force Pulled Off Daring Rescue," Associated Press, January 3, 1990.

53 **war plan:** Tom Clancy, with General Carl Stiner (Ret.), *Shadow Warriors: Inside the Special Forces* (New York: Berkley Publishing Group, 2002), p. 409. Clancy writes, "'Schwarzkopf was a good example of a senior officer who did not understand special operations and was afraid of it,' said Special Forces vet Maj. General Jim Guest, who served as the J-3 at SOCOM. Schwarzkopf's mentality was, 'I have a coiled cobra in a cage and if I open

the cage, that cobra is going to get out and possibly embarrass me.'"

53 **"In 1996 alone":** U.S. Special Operations Command (SOCOM), *History of SOCOM,* 6th ed., March 31, 2008.

53 **large-scale operations:** Ibid.

53 **"reduced emphasis":** General Wayne Downing, memorandum to Rumsfeld and General Peter Pace, chairman of the Joint Chiefs, "Special Operations Forces Assessment," November 9, 2005. Retrieved from http://rumsfeld.com/library/.

53 **propose missions:** Richard H. Shultz Jr., "Showstoppers: Nine Reasons Why We Never Sent Our Special Operations Forces After al Qaeda Before 9/11," *Weekly Standard* 9 (19), January 26, 2004.

53 **included JSOC:** National Commission on Terrorist Attacks upon the United States (Philip Zelikow, Executive Director; Bonnie D. Jenkins, Counsel; Ernest R. May, Senior Advisor), *The 9/11 Commission Report* (New York: W. W. Norton, 2004), p. 136.

53 **"never used once":** Shultz, "Showstoppers."

54 **approximately twenty operations:** Ibid.

54 **"'finish' capabilities":** Downing, memorandum to Rumsfeld and Pace, "Special Operations Forces Assessment."

54 **Title 10:** See sections 153 and 163 of Title 10 of the US Code.

54 **"based on deception":** General Hugh Shelton (Ret.), *Without Hesitation: The Odyssey of an American Warrior* (New York: St. Martin's Press, 2010), pp. 401, 413.

55 **had lawyered:** Rowan Scarborough, *Rumsfeld's War: The Untold Story of America's Anti-Terrorist Commander* (Washington, DC: Regnery, 2004), p. 16. Scarborough discusses Shultz's report, for which he received top security clearances to interview senior commanders and policy makers. "Pentagon lawyers in the 1990s argued that DoD did not have the legal authority until Title 10" to authorize covert operations, Shultz wrote. "Rumsfeld overturned the Clinton policy of arguing in favor of Title 10 restrictions, and has decided that covert missions can indeed be authorized from the Pentagon," Scarborough wrote.

55 **"possibility of hunting":** Shultz, "Showstoppers."

55 **security clearance:** Scarborough, *Rumsfeld's War,* p. 14.

55 **UN peacekeeping mission:** United Nations Security Council Resolution 794, adopted December 3, 1992, accessed December 5, 2012, www.un.org/documents/sc/res/1992/scres92.htm.

55 **warlords openly defied:** Dr. Richard W. Stewart, *The United States Army in Somalia, 1992–1994,* U.S. Army Center of Military

History, accessed January 2011, www.history.army.mil/brochures/Somalia/Somalia.pdf.

55 **green light:** Mark Bowden, "How a Relief Mission Ended in a Firefight," *Philadelphia Inquirer*, December 14, 1997.

55 **descended into disaster:** Ibid.

56 **"Mogadishu disaster":** Shultz, "Showstoppers."

56 **"check off boxes":** Ibid.

57 **began briefing:** Ibid.

57 SECRET: Scarborough, *Rumsfeld's War*, p. 14.

57 **"for fifteen minutes":** Jamie McIntyre, "Rumsfeld Versus Shelton," Line of Departure (blog), Military.com, February 25, 2011, www.lineofdeparture.com/tag/rumsfeld-shelton/.

57 **"learn the right lessons":** Scarborough, *Rumsfeld's War*, p. 15.

57 **"allies and friends":** Douglas J. Feith, *War and Decision; Inside the Pentagon at the Dawn of the War on Terrorism* (New York: Harper, 2009), p. 51.

57 **"Forget about 'exit strategies'":** Donald H. Rumsfeld, "A New Kind of War," *New York Times*, September 27, 2001.

58 **"No one amongst those people":** Author interview, Malcolm W. Nance, May 2011.

58 **seven hundred covert operatives:** Jennifer Kibbe, "The Rise of the Shadow Warriors," *Foreign Affairs* 83 (2) (March–April 2004): 112.

58 **"paramilitary expertise":** Author interview, Vincent Cannistraro, August 2010. All information and statements attributed to Vincent Cannistraro come from the author's interview.

58 **"bunch of pansies":** Author interview, Colonel Lawrence Wilkerson (Ret.), May 2011.

59 **were cautioning against**: Transcript, *NewsHour*, PBS, March 26, 2004. Colin Powell: "I recommended to the president that our focus had to be on al-Qaida, the Taliban and Afghanistan. Those were the ones who attacked the United States of America on 9/11."

59 **"no choice":** Transcript, "Secretary Rumsfeld News Briefing in Brussels," December 18, 2001.

59 **draw up a list:** Seymour Hersh, "Manhunt: The Bush Administration's New Strategy in the War Against Terrorism," *New Yorker*, December 23, 2002.

60 **"exploring targets":** Memorandum to President George W. Bush, no subject, September 23, 2001, www.rumsfeld.com/library/.

**4: The Boss: Ali Abdullah Saleh**

61 **Yemen's leader:** Robert F. Worth, "For Yemen's Leader, a Balancing Act Gets Harder," *New York Times*, June 21, 2008.

61 **"The Boss":** Gregory D. Johnsen, "The Boss Falls. Then What?" *New York Times*, March 24, 2011.

61 **"We would drive around":** Author interview, Colonel W. Patrick Lang (Ret.), February 2011. All information and statements attributed to Colonel Lang come from the author's interview. Details about Colonel Lang's background are from the author's interview.

62 **coordinated and funded:** Gregory D. Johnsen, *The Last Refuge: Yemen, Al-Qaeda, and America's War in Arabia* (New York: W. W. Norton, 2013), p. 7.

62 **"sent to Afghanistan":** "An Interview with President Ali Abdullah Saleh," *New York Times*, June 28, 2008.

62 **safe haven:** Worth, "Balancing Act Gets Harder."

62 **"political pluralism":** "An Interview with President Ali Abdullah Saleh."

62 **Islamic Jihad:** Lawrence Wright, *The Looming Tower: Al-Qaeda and the Road to 9/11* (New York: Vintage Books, 2006), p. 365.

62 **southern secessionists:** Robert F. Worth, "Yemen's Deals with Jihadists Unsettle the U.S.," *New York Times*, January 28, 2008.

62 **against Shiite Houthi rebels:** Author interview, former US counterterrorism official, January 2011.

62 **"They were the thugs":** Author interview, Ali Soufan, January 2011.

62 **five hundred pounds of explosives:** William Branigin, "Two Sentenced to Die for USS Cole Attack," *Washington Post*, September 30, 2004.

63 **"charged and destroyed":** Diana Elias, "Video Offers Strong Bin Laden-USS Cole Link," ABCNews.go.com, June 19, 2001.

63 **aides had written:** Wright, *The Looming Tower*, p. 333.

63 **"50 million machine guns," "the most hostile environment":** Ibid., p. 365.

63 **had to pull out completely:** Ibid.

63 **"death threats":** Ali H. Soufan, "Closing the Case on the Cole," op-ed, *New York Times*, October 11, 2010.

63 **Saleh's government:** Soufan does note in his op-ed that the FBI team "left Yemen with most of the terrorists locked up" but says that they were soon released by the government.

63 **"No one in the Clinton White House":** Soufan, "Closing the Case on the Cole."

63 **"great victory":** Wright, *The Looming Tower*, p. 374.

63 **"denied them access":** Walter Pincus, "Yemen Hears Benefits of Joining U.S. Fight; Officials Discuss up to $400 Million in Aid," *Washington Post*, November 28, 2001.

64 **"Those who make war":** Transcript, President George W. Bush radio address, September 15, 2001, www.nytimes.com/2001/09/16/us/

after-the-attacks-the-president-s-message-a-different-battle-awaits.html.

64 **put Yemen on a list**: Eric Schmitt and Thom Shanker, *Counterstrike: The Untold Story of America's Secret Campaign Against al Qaeda* (New York: Times Books, 2011), p. 30.

64 **"graveyard for the invaders"**: Jonathan Mahler, "The Bush Administration vs. Salim Hamdan," *New York Times Magazine*, January 8, 2006.

64 **held talks:** "Issues of Interest; Yemeni-American Relations," website of the Embassy of the Republic of Yemen in Washington, DC, accessed December 1, 2012, www.yemenembassy.org/issues/ymusrelshp/index.htm.

64 **"principal partner"**: Ibid.

64 **Ritz Carlton:** Author interview, Yemeni official, January 2013.

64 **presented with an aid package:** Pincus, "Yemen Hears Benefits of Joining U.S. Fight."

65 **"counterterrorism camp"**: Philip Smucker and Howard LaFranchi, "Anti-US strike Shakes Yemen; Three US aid Workers Slain in a Hospital," *Christian Science Monitor*, December 31, 2002.

65 **permission for the CIA to fly drones:** Dana Priest, "U.S. Military Teams, Intelligence Deeply Involved in Aiding Yemen on Strikes," *Washington Post*, January 27, 2010.

65 **"knew how to survive"**: Author interview, Dr. Emile Nakhleh, January 2010.

65 **"expressed his concern"**: "Issues of Interest; Yemeni-American Relations."

65 **ordered his forces to raid a village:** Gregory D. Johnsen, "The Expansion Strategy of Al-Qa'ida in the Arabian Peninsula," *CTC Sentinel*, September 2009, pp. 8–11.

66 **nine hundred military and intelligence personnel:** Robert Schlesinger, "In Djibouti, US Special Forces Develop Base amid Secrecy," *Boston Globe*, December 12, 2002.

66 **establish operational capacity:** Priest, "U.S. Military Teams, Intelligence Deeply Involved."

## 5: The Enigma of Anwar Awlaki

67 **"Uncle Saleh, I am here"**: Author interview, Sheikh Saleh bin Fareed, January 2012. All statements and information attributed to Saleh bin Fareed come from the author's interview, unless otherwise noted.

67 **"We should be concerned"**: Audio recording of Anwar al Awlaki lecture, "Lessons from the Companions Living as a Minority," JIMAS Conference, University of Leicester, August 2002.

68 **"given permission"**: Anwar al Awlaki, "The Islamic Education of Shaikh Anwar al Awlaki," Imam Anwar's Blog, anwar-alawlaki.com, August 12, 2008.

68 **traveled to Saudi Arabia:** Author interviews, Awlaki family members, January and August 2012.

68 **"air went out of the balloon"**: Chitra Ragavan, "The Imam's Very Curious Story: A Skirt-Chasing Mullah Is Just One More Mystery for the 9/11 Panel," *US News and World Report*, June 13, 2004, www.usnews.com/usnews/news/articles/040621/21plot.htm..

68 **"support a criminal prosecution"**: National Commission on Terrorist Attacks upon the United States (Philip Zelikow, Executive Director; Bonnie D. Jenkins, Counsel; Ernest R. May, Senior Advisor), *The 9/11 Commission Report* (New York: W. W. Norton, 2004), p. 517.

68 **warrant issued:** "Justice Department Response to Fox News Regarding Colorado 2002 Awlaki Matter," FoxNews.com, May 21, 2010. For the warrant itself, see www.scribd.com/doc/29510870/Al-Awlaki-Arrest-Warrant.

68 **resolved the issue:** The letter from the Justice Department, published by FoxNews.com, says he "corrected" the mistake.

68 **"We were ecstatic"**: Joseph Rhee and Mark Schone, "How Anwar Awlaki Got Away," ABCNews.go.com, November 30, 2009.

68 **up to ten years in prison:** Ibid.

69 **TECS II:** Journalist Paul Sperry obtained information from the TECS II system concerning Awlaki; see www.sperryfiles.com/images/1-3.jpg.

69 **"Give it another shot"**: Author interview, Nasser al Awlaki, September 2012. All quotations from Nasser al Awlaki come from interviews the author conducted between January and September 2012, unless otherwise noted.

69 **intelligence memo:** *9/11 Commission Report*, p. 517.

69 **filed a motion:** Catherine Herridge, *The Next Wave: Inside the Hunt for Al Qaeda's American Recruits* (New York: Crown Forum, 2011), p. 95.

69 **"having a bad reputation"**: Joseph Rhee, "U.S. Attorney Defends Decision to Scrap Awlaki Arrest Warrant," ABCNews.go.com, December 7, 2009.

69 **arrived at JFK Airport:** TECS II "Incident Log" entry concerning arrival of Anwar at John F. Kennedy Airport, October 10, 2002, accessed March 2012, sperryfiles.com, www.sperryfiles.com/images/1-4.jpg.

69 **"ANTI-TERRORIST PASSENGER"**: Database entry following a "Secondary Inspection" of Awlaki upon his arrival at JFK Airport, October 10, 2001, accessed March 2012, sperryfiles.com, www.sperryfiles.com/images/1-1.jpg.

69 **registering as active:** Catherine Herridge, "Mueller Grilled on FBI's Release of

al-Awlaki in 2002," FoxNews.com, March 8, 2012.

70 **three hours:** TECS II "Incident Log" entry, October 10, 2002.

70 **"He is a match":** Joseph Rhee and Mark Schone, "How Anwar Awlaki Got Away," ABCNews.go.com, November 30, 2009.

70 **luggage was searched:** Database entry following a "Secondary Inspection," October 10, 2001.

70 **number was invalid:** TECS II "Incident Log" entry, October 10, 2002.

70 **track down Ammerman:** Ibid.

70 **worked the Awlaki case:** Herridge, *The Next Wave*, p. 91.

70 **"We did not find a link":** Ibid.

70 **"no explanation":** Ibid., p. 93.

70 **"WARRANT HAD BEEN REMOVED":** TECS II "Incident Log" entry, October 10, 2002.

70 **not actually removed until:** Herridge, *The Next Wave*, p. 96.

70 **"thanks for their [patience]":** TECS II "Incident Log" entry, October 10, 2002, p. 2, obtained by Paul Sperry, www.sperryfiles.com/images/1-5.jpg.

70 **"I got an apology":** Anwar al Awlaki, "Spilling out the Beans; Al Awlaki Revealing His Side of the Story," *Inspire* 9 (winter 2012), released May 2012.

70 **another charismatic preacher:** Susan Schmidt, "Imam from Va. Mosque Now Thought to Have Aided al-Qaeda," *Washington Post*, February 27, 2008.

71 **lead lecturer:** Jerry Markon, "Muslim Lecturer Sentenced to Life," *Washington Post*, July 14, 2005.

71 **cancer gene research:** Milton Viorst, "The Education of Ali al-Timimi," *Atlantic Monthly*, June 2006.

71 **"anthrax plots":** Mary Beth Sheridan, "Hardball Tactics in an Era of Threats," *Washington Post*, September 3, 2006.

71 **one of the lead investigators:** Herridge, *The Next Wave*, p. 84.

71 **"I don't think anyone wants me talking":** Ibid., p. 217.

71 **"trying to cultivate":** Ibid., p. 216.

71 **"even talked to the guy":** Author interview, Edward MacMahon, July 2012.

71 **trying to set him up:** Scott Shane and Souad Mekhennet, "Imam's Path from Condemning Terror to Preaching Jihad," *New York Times*, May 8, 2010.

71 **ultimately convicted:** Eric Lichtblau, "Scholar Is Given Life Sentence in 'Virginia Jihad' Case," *New York Times*, July 14, 2005.

72 **wearing a wire:** Herridge, *The Next Wave*, p. 85.

72 **"authority for this request":** Author copy of filing.

72 **"a national security issue":** Author

interview, Edward MacMahon, July 2012.

72 **"had Awlaki released":** Herridge, *The Next Wave*, p. 85.

72 **"pounced on the tips":** Sheridan, "Hardball Tactics in an Era of Threats."

72 **"Is there any connection":** Press release from Representative Frank Wolf, "Wolf Asks FBI Why Aulaqi Was Released from Custody in 2002," May 24, 2010, http://wolf.house.gov/press-releases/wolf-asks-fbi-why-aulaqi-was-released-from-custody-in-2002/.

73 **"pages of blankness":** Herridge, *The Next Wave*, p. 206.

73 **government witnesses:** Jerry Markon, "Views of Va. Muslim Leader Differ as Terror Trial Opens," *Washington Post*, April 5, 2005.

73 **"How did Aulaqi end up":** Wolf, "Wolf Asks FBI Why Aulaqi Was Released from Custody in 2002."

74 **"plan to attempt a recruitment":** Author interview, former senior FBI counterterrorism agent, July 2012.

74 **"how he got out":** Ragavan, "The Imam's Very Curious Story."

### 6: "We're in a New Kind of War"

75 **"godfather of terror":** Philip Smucker and Howard LaFranchi, "Anti-US Strike Shakes Yemen; Three US Aid Workers Slain in a Hospital," *Christian Science Monitor*, December 31, 2002.

75 **meeting with tribal officials:** Ibid.

75 **multiple mobile phones:** Seymour M. Hersh, "Manhunt: The Bush Administration's New Strategy in the War Against Terrorism," *New Yorker*, December 23, 2002.

75 **"compound under surveillance":** Michael DeLong, with Noah Lukeman, *Inside CentCom: The Unvarnished Truth About the Wars in Afghanistan and Iraq* (Washington, DC: Regnery, 2004), p. 70.

75 **MQ-1 Predator drone:** Hersh, "Manhunt."

75 **live video feed:** Dina Temple-Raston, *The Jihad Next Door: The Lackawanna Six and Rough Justice in the Age of Terror* (New York: PublicAffairs, 2007), p. 196.

75 **"high-speed Predator chase":** DeLong, *Inside CentCom*, p. 70.

75 **driving off in a convoy:** Temple-Raston, *The Jihad Next Door*, p. 195.

75 **"We're right over here":** Ibid., p. 196.

76 **"We didn't want publicity":** DeLong, *Inside CentCom*, pp. 70–71.

76 **twenty-five yards:** Ibid., p. 71.

76 **DNA samples:** Temple-Raston, *The Jihad Next Door*, p. 196.

76 **US citizen:** Dana Priest, "U.S. Citizen Among Those Killed In Yemen Predator Missile Strike," *Washington Post*, November 8, 2002.

76 **unindicted co-conspirator:** James Risen and Marc Santora, "Threats and Responses: The Terror Network; Slain in Yemen Tied by U.S. to Buffalo Cell," *New York Times*, November 10, 2002.

76 **"card-carrying member":** Matthew Purdy and Lowell Bergman, "Where the Trail Led: Between Evidence and Suspicion; Unclear Danger: Inside the Lackawanna Terror Case," *New York Times*, October 12, 2003. The other six men all pled guilty to terrorism-related charges and served time in federal prison. They have since been released. See Mary Friona and Claudine Ewing (WGRZ-TV), "Lackawanna Six: Ten Years Later," wgrz.com, September 14, 2012.

76 **"international killers":** Greg Miller and Josh Meyer, "U.S. Drops Bomb in Yemen, Kills Six al-Qaida Operatives," *Los Angeles Times*, November 5, 2002.

76 **"out of business":** Transcript, "DoD News Briefing—Secretary Rumsfeld and Gen. Myers," November 4, 2002.

77 **"high-tech resources":** Mark Hosenball and Evan Thomas, "The Opening Shot; in a Show of Superpower Might, the CIA Kills a Qaeda Operative in Yemen and His American Ally," *Newsweek*, November 18, 2002.

77 **"successful tactical operation":** Transcript, *CNN International*, November 5, 2002.

77 **"highly pissed":** Hosenball and Thomas, "The Opening Shot."

77 **"major problems":** DeLong, *Inside CentCom*, p. 71.

77 **"it is so difficult":** Philip Smucker, "The Intrigue Behind the Drone Strike; Yemen Official Says US Lacks Discretion as Antiterror Partner," *Christian Science Monitor*, November 12, 2002.

77 **truck bomb:** DeLong, *Inside CentCom*, pp. 70–71.

77 **"I hope so":** Hosenball and Thomas, "The Opening Shot."

77 **"deliberate killing":** Amnesty International, "Yemen/USA: Government Must Not Sanction Extra-judicial Executions," November 8, 2002.

78 **"constitutional questions":** Transcript, *Fox News Sunday*, Fox, November 10, 2002.

78 **"Assassination as a norm":** Dana Priest, "CIA Killed U.S. Citizen in Yemen Missile Strike; Action's Legality, Effectiveness Questioned," *Washington Post*, November 8, 2002.

78 **outside of Afghanistan:** Chris Woods, "'OK, fine. Shoot him.' Four Words That Heralded a Decade of Secret US Drone Killings," Bureau of Investigation Journalism, November 3, 2012.

78 **"rules of engagement":** Miller and Meyer, "U.S. Drops Bomb in Yemen."

78 **"best way":** Transcript of President Bush's prepared remarks radio address, November 16, 2002.

78 **upgrading and expanding:** Robert Schlesinger, "In Djibouti, US Special Forces Develop Base amid Secrecy," *Boston Globe*, December 12, 2002. "The base has been transformed since the first US soldiers arrived, taking over a former French installation that was in advanced disrepair. Many of the old buildings were razed, replaced with a growing number of tents and hard buildings. Hesko barriers—wire and canvas structures filled with dirt—line roads, some of which are paved, many of which are bumpy gravel. The base has two gyms and the old French pool is close to being renovated. Where midday meals were once the military's pre-packaged Meals Ready to Eat, four hot meals are now served daily."

78 **"where the action is":** Ibid.

79 **"we can speak about":** Ibid.

79 **fully operational:** Agence France-Presse, "US Anti-Terror Chief Meets President of Troubled Yemen," December 22, 2002.

79 **more than four hundred soldiers:** Transcript, "Joint Task Force Horn of Africa Briefing," January 10, 2003.

79 **"we're relentless":** Mark Fineman, "New Phase of War on Terror Moves to E. Africa; American Military Presence Is Beefed Up as Navy Vessel Becomes a Mobile Forward Base," *Los Angeles Times*, December 21, 2002.

79 **Christmas decorations:** Ibid.

79 **"If they stumble":** Ibid.

79 **met with President Saleh:** "US Anti-Terror Chief Meets President of Troubled Yemen."

79 **"coordination":** Ibid.

79 **"hunting for Qaeda members":** Patrick E. Tyler, "Yemen, an Uneasy Ally, Proves Adept at Playing Off Old Rivals," *New York Times*, December 19, 2002.

79 **"Needless to say":** Transcript, "Secretary Rumsfeld Town Hall Meeting at Camp Lemonier [*sic*], Djibouti," December 11, 2002.

## 7: Special Plans

81 **"gravest error":** Barton Gellman and Thomas E. Ricks, "US Concludes bin Laden Escaped at Tora Bora Flight; Failure to Send Troops in Pursuit Termed Major Error," *Washington Post*, April 17, 2002.

81 **"deep background":** Richard Sale, "Embarrassed Rumsfeld Fired CIA Official," United Press International, July 28, 2004.

81 **"assigned to another position":** Bob Woodward and Dan Eggen, "Aug. Memo Focused on Attacks in U.S. Lack of Fresh

Information Frustrated Bush," *Washington Post*, May 19, 2002.

81 **Rumsfeld who had Black fired:** Sale, "Embarrassed Rumsfeld Fired CIA Official."

81 **Black was replaced:** Joby Warrick and Walter Pincus, "Station Chief Made Appeal to Destroy CIA Tapes; Lawyer Says Top Official Had Implicit Approval," *Washington Post*, January 16, 2008.

81 **zealous promoter:** Jose A. Rodriguez Jr., with Bill Harlow, *Hard Measures: How Aggressive CIA Actions After 9/11 Saved American Lives* (New York: Threshold Editions, 2012), Preface, p. xiii. "I am certain, beyond any doubt, that these techniques, approved at the highest levels of the U.S. government... shielded the people of the United States from harm and led to the capture and killing of Usama bin Ladin."

81 **visiting the Agency:** Dana Priest and Walter Pincus, "Some Iraq Analysts Felt Pressure from Cheney Visits," *Washington Post*, June 5, 2003.

81 **significant push-back:** Bryan Burrough, Evgenia Peretz, David Rose, and David Wise, "The Path to War," *Vanity Fair*, November 2004, p. 228.

81 **"no credible information":** January 2003 CIA report, "Iraqi Support for Terrorism," excerpted in "Report of an Inquiry into the Alternative Analysis of the Issue of an Iraq-al Qaeda Relationship," by Senator Carl Levin, October 21, 2004.

82 **"contradict the CIA's own analyses":** Robert Dreyfuss, "The Pentagon Muzzles the CIA," *American Prospect*, November 21, 2002.

82 **"It's [Feith's] shop":** Transcript, "Department of Defense Press Briefing, Defense Secretary Donald Rumsfeld, Gen. Richard B. Myers, Chairman, JCS," October 24, 2002.

82 **"helping us sift":** Eric Schmitt and Thom Shanker, "Pentagon Sets Up Intelligence Unit," *New York Times*, October 24, 2002.

82 **justification for an invasion of Iraq:** Seymour M. Hersh, "Selective Intelligence: Donald Rumsfeld Has His Own Special Sources—Are They Really Reliable?" *New Yorker*, May 12, 2003.

82 **"do it a lot better":** Author interview, Colonel Lawrence B. Wilkerson (Ret.), May 2011.

82 **Libby, made repeated trips:** Julian Borger, "The Spies Who Pushed for War," *Guardian*, July 17, 2003.

82 **Newt Gingrich:** Ibid.

82 **William Luti:** Franklin Foer and Spencer Ackerman, "The Radical; What Dick Cheney Really Believes," *New Republic*, November 20, 2003.

83 **taken a year to produce:** Michael Isikoff and David Corn, *Hubris: The Inside Story of Spin, Scandal, and the Selling of the Iraq War* (New York: Three Rivers Press, 2007), p. 6.

83 **commandeer a conference room:** Ibid., pp. 3–4.

83 **"hell-bent":** Rodriguez, *Hard Measures*, p. 125.

83 **"unprecedented":** Ray McGovern, "Cheney Chicanery," CommonDreams.org, July 29, 2003.

83 **"'alternative' assessment":** Senator Carl Levin, "Report of an Inquiry into the Alternative Analysis of the Issue of an Iraq–al Qaeda Relationship," October 21, 2004, p. 10.

83 **Feith edited his reports:** Ibid., pp. 16–24.

83 **"conveyed a perception":** Ibid., p. 23.

83 **"deprived of the opportunity":** Ibid., p. 24.

84 **"unusual":** Ibid., p. 14.

84 **discredited intelligence:** Ibid., p. 15.

84 **CIA attempts to discredit":** Ibid.

84 **"questionable intelligence reports":** Ibid., p. 16.

84 **"operational relationship":** Stephen F. Hayes, "Case Closed: The U.S. Government's Secret Memo Detailing Cooperation Between Saddam Hussein and Osama bin Laden," *Weekly Standard* 9 (11), November 24, 2003.

### 8: Survival, Evasion, Resistance, Escape

85 **Some of the FBI personnel were disgusted:** Ali Soufan, "My Tortured Decision," *New York Times*, April 22, 2009, www.nytimes.com/2009/04/23/opinion/23soufan.html.

85 **detained more than 3,000:** James Risen and David Johnston, "Bush Has Widened Authority of C.I.A. to Kill Terrorists," *New York Times*, December 15, 2002.

85 **"It is not going right":** Memo from Donald Rumsfeld to Stephen Cambone, "Subject: Intel," May 5, 2002, rumsfeld.com.

86 **"Defense Department task":** Memo from Donald Rumsfeld to Stephen Cambone, General Myers copied, "Subject: Finding Terrorists," May 31, 2002, rumsfeld.com.

86 **rescue, resisting:** "About the Joint Personnel Recovery Agency," United States Joint Forces Command, accessed September 5, 2012, www.jpra.mil/site_public/about/about.htm.

86 **"totalitarian evil nation":** Transcript, documentary film, *Torturing Democracy*, an interview with Malcolm Nance, produced by Sherry Jones, co-produced by Carey Murphy and Washington Media Associates, in association with the National Security Archive (interview November 15, 2008).

86 **During training:** Documents provided in confidence to the author, as well as interviews with SERE participants and former in-

structors, November 2009 and January 2012; see also Jane Mayer, "The Experiment: The Military Trains People to Withstand Interrogation—Are Those Methods Being Misused at Guantanamo?" *New Yorker*, July 11, 2005.

86 **"enemy torture methods":** Author interview, Malcolm Nance, May 2011. All information and statements attributed to Malcolm Nance are from the author's interview.

86 **regimes and terror groups:** Ibid.

86 **running the interrogation, not harsh enough:** Marc Ambinder and D. B. Grady, *The Command: Deep Inside the President's Secret Army* (Hoboken, NJ: John Wiley and Sons, 2012, Kindle edition). "By October 2002, an internal JSOC assessment of interrogations at Bagram Airfield, Afghanistan, and [Gitmo] found that the resistance techniques of enemy combatants 'outmatched' the interrogation techniques of US forces. Higher [HQ] was not satisfied with the results, and JSOC picked up the rope."

86 **"From the beginning":** Colonel Steven Kleinman, prepared testimony for the Senate Armed Services Hearing, "The Treatment of Detainees in U.S. Custody," September 25, 2008. The following quotes from Kleinman are from his prepared testimony.

87 **reverse-engineered:** Senate Committee on Armed Services, Inquiry into the Treatment of Detainees in US Custody, S. Prt. 110-54, Executive Summary at xiv, November 20, 2008.

87 **"flagrantly violated the laws of war":** Donald Rumsfeld and Paul Wolfowitz, "Prepared Statement: Senate Armed Services Committee 'Military Commissions,'" December 12, 2001.

87 **"exploitation":** Senate Committee on Armed Services, Inquiry into the Treatment of Detainees, p. 6.

88 **"neither reliable nor accurate":** JPRA memorandum to Pentagon's Office of the General Counsel, "Operational Issues Pertaining to the Use of Physical/Psychological Coercion in Interrogation: An Overview," July 2002, www.washingtonpost.com/wp-srv/nation/pdf/JPRA-Memo_042409.pdf.

88 **"detainee resistance":** Senate Committee on Armed Services, Inquiry into the Treatment of Detainees, Executive Summary, at xiv.

88 **"exploitation plan":** Ibid.

88 **receiving training:** Joby Warrick and Peter Finn, "Harsh Tactics Readied Before Their Approval," *Washington Post*, April 22, 2009.

88 **"effects of waterboarding," "list of SERE techniques," Richard Shiffrin:** Senate Armed Services Committee Report, Inquiry into the Treatment of Detainees, Executive Summary, at xiv.

88 **"mind-control experiments":** Mark Mazzetti, "Ex-Pentagon Lawyers Face Inquiry on Interrogation Role," *New York Times*, June 17, 2008.

88 **same information:** Senate Committee on Armed Services, Inquiry into the Treatment of Detainees, p. 31.

88 **National Security Council:** Peter Finn and Joby Warrick, "2002 Document Referred to Extreme Duress as 'Torture,' Warned of Techniques' Unreliability," *Washington Post*, April 25, 2009.

89 **"even death":** U.S. Department of Justice Office of Legal Counsel, Office of the Assistant Attorney General, "Memo for Alberto R. Gonzales, Counsel to the President; Re: Standards for Conduct for Interrogation under 18 USC, sections 2340-2340 A," August 1, 2002.

89 **legal justification:** U.S. Department of Justice Office of Legal Counsel, Office of the Assistant Attorney General, "Memorandum for John Rizzo, Acting General Counsel of the Central Intelligence Agency," August 1, 2002.

89 **"deniability":** Transcript, "Hard Measures," interview by Lesley Stahl, *60 Minutes*, CBS, April 29, 2012.

89 **specific interrogation techniques:** Joby Warrick and Dan Egan, "Hill Briefed on Waterboarding in 2002," *Washington Post*, December 9, 2007.

89 **never briefed:** Paul Kane, "Pelosi Denies Knowing Interrogation Techniques Were Used," Capitol Briefing (blog), *Washington Post*, April 23 2009, http://voices.washingtonpost.com/capitol-briefing/2009/04/pelosi_denies_knowing_interrog.html. However, under continued public pressure, Pelosi further admitted that later, after she had left the Intelligence Committee, an aide informed her of their use; see Deirdre Walsh, "Source: Aide told Pelosi Waterboarding Had Been Used," CNN.com, May 12, 2009.

89 **claimed otherwise:** Warrick and Egan, "Hill Briefed on Waterboarding in 2002."

89 **Some were snatched:** International Committee of the Red Cross, "ICRC Report on the Treatment of Fourteen 'High Value Detainees' in CIA Custody," February 2007. The following descriptions of inhumane treatment in US custody are from the Red Cross report.

90 **"ten different sites":** Ibid., p. 6.

90 **"experimenting":** Ibid., p. 31.

91 **"designated unlawful combatants":** Ambinder and Grady, *The Command*, chap. 3, "Interrogations and Intelligence."

91 **reporting to the White House:** Greg Miller, "Cheney OK'd Harsh CIA Tactics," *Los Angeles Times*, December 16, 2008.

91 **Copper Green, Matchbox:** Ambinder

and Grady, *The Command*, chap. 3, "Interrogations and Intelligence."

91 **legal definition of covert action:** Title 50 US Code, Section 413b, "Presidential Approval and Reporting of Covert Actions."

91 **prevent scandals:** Richard A. Best Jr., "Covert Action: Legislative Background and Possible Policy Questions," Congressional Research Service, December 27, 2011.

92 **"clandestine operations":** Joint Publication 1-02, DOD Dictionary of Military and Associated Terms, November 8, 2010 (As Amended Through November 15, 2012).

92 **"Traditional Military Activities":** Joint Explanatory Statement of the Committee of Conference, H.R. 1455, July 25, 1991. "It is the intent of the conferees that 'traditional military activities' include activities by military personnel under the direction and control of a United States military commander (whether or not the U.S. sponsorship of such activities is apparent or later to be acknowledged) preceding and related to hostilities which are either anticipated (meaning approval has been given by the National Command Authorities for the activities and or operational planning for hostilities) to involve U.S. military forces, or where such hostilities involving United States military forces are ongoing, and, where the fact of the U.S. role in the overall operation is apparent or to be acknowledged publicly. In this regard, the conferees intend to draw a line between activities that are and are not under the direction and control of the military commander. Activities that are not under the direction and control of a military commander should not be considered as 'traditional military activities.'"

92 **no real-time oversight rights:** Seymour M. Hersh, "Preparing the Battlefield; The Bush Administration Steps Up Its Secret Moves Against Iran," *New Yorker*, July 7, 2008.

92 **"Preparing the Battlespace," Advance Force Operations:** Michael Respass, "Combating Terrorism with Preparation of the Battlespace," Strategy Research Project, US Army War College, July 4, 2003.

92 **work-around:** Intelligence Authorization Act for Fiscal Year 2010, H.R. Rep. No. 111-186 (2009) (accompanying H.R. 2701).

93 **delegating military assets:** 50 United States Code, Section 413b, "Presidential Approval and Reporting of Covert Actions."

93 **"organize for a manhunt," "develop a plan":** Seymour M. Hersh, "Manhunt: The Bush Administration's New Strategy in the War Against Terrorism," *New Yorker*, December 23, 2002.

93 **five-year plan:** Rowan Scarborough, "Billions Needed to Fight al Qaeda; General

Requests More Troops, Too," *Washington Times*, September 24, 2002.

93 **outpaced the military's abilities:** Eric Schmitt and Thom Shanker, "Ranks and Growing Pains in Taking Key Antiterror Role," *New York Times*, August 2, 2004.

94 **"actionable intelligence":** Hersh, "Manhunt."

94 **"intelligence wasn't good enough":** Eric Schmitt and Thom Shanker, *Counterstrike: The Untold Story of America's Secret Campaign Against Al Qaeda* (New York: Times Books, 2011).

94 **"fighting generals":** Hersh, "Manhunt."

94 **"those who support them":** "Fact Sheet on New Counter-Terrorism and Cyberspace Positions; National Director and Deputy National Security Advisor for Combating Terrorism General Wayne Downing (U.S. Army Ret.)," Office of the Press Secretary, October 9, 2001, http://georgewbush-whitehouse.archives.gov/news/releases/2001/10/20011009.html.

94 **"blacker/lower visibility force":** Memo from General Wayne Downing to Secretary of Defense and Chairman, Joint Chiefs of Staff, "Special Operations Forces Assessment," November 9, 2005, www.rumsfeld.com.

94 **"bypassed Special Operations Command":** Author interview, Colonel Lawrence Wilkerson (Ret.), May 2011.

95 **"That's dangerous":** Ibid.

95 **"Gray Fox":** Ambinder and Grady, *The Command*, chap. 8, "The Activity."

95 **mirrored the capabilities:** Barton Gellman, "Secret Unit Expands Rumsfeld's Domain; New Espionage Branch Delving into CIA Territory," *Washington Post*, January 23, 2005.

95 **handed over to the CIA:** Linda Robinson, "Moves That Matter; in the Intelligence Wars, a Pre-emptive Strike by the Pentagon Surprises Many in Congress," *US News and World Report*, August 12, 2002.

95 **Project Icon:** Barton Gellman, "Secret Unit Expands Rumsfeld's Domain; New Espionage Branch Delving into CIA Territory," *Washington Post*, January 23, 2005.

95 **"new clandestine teams":** Josh White and Barton Gellman, "Defense Espionage Unit to Work with CIA," *Washington Post*, January 25, 2005; Gellman, "Secret Unit Expands Rumsfeld's Domain."

95 **Strategic Support Branch:** Gellman, "Secret Unit Expands Rumsfeld's Domain."

95 **transferred Gray Fox:** Seymour M. Hersh, "The Coming Wars," *New Yorker*, January 24, 2005.

96 **"emerging target countries," "without detection":** Gellman, "Secret Unit Expands Rumsfeld's Domain." The following details

about "internal Pentagon documents" and the Strategic Support Branch come from the *Washington Post.*

96 **"viewed the CIA as a weak sister":** Author interview, Philip Giraldi, March 2012.

97 **lose their Geneva Convention status:** Colonel Kathryn Stone, "'All Necessary Means'—Employing CIA Operatives in a Warfighting Role Alongside Special Operations Forces," USAWC Strategy Research Project (U.S. Army War College, 2003).

97 **officially run:** Barbara Starr, "Pentagon Runs Clandestine Intelligence-Gathering Infrastructure," CNN.com, January 24, 2005.

97 **Strategic Defense Initiative:** Kerry Gildea, "Rumsfeld Adviser Brings Precise Analytical Approach to DoD Post," *Defense Daily*, January 31, 2001.

97 **special projects:** Official Department of Defense biography, "Dr. Stephen A. Cambone; Under Secretary of Defense for Intelligence," January 13, 2006.

97 **special assistant:** Ibid.

97 **"The effort has to be global":** Memo from Donald Rumsfeld to unnamed recipient(s), "Memorandum 9/23/01," www.rumsfeld.com.

97 **"Capabilities":** Memo from Donald Rumsfeld to Stephen Cambone, "Subject: Capabilities," September 23, 2001, www.rumsfeld.com.

97 **"Opportunity":** Memo from Donald Rumsfeld to Stephen Cambone, "Subject: Opportunity," September 26, 2001, www.rumsfeld.com.

97 **"They are all cast in the same mode":** Author interview, Colonel W. Patrick Lang (Ret.), September 2010. All statements and information attributed to Patrick Lang are from the author's interviews.

98 **"increase the total number":** Memo from Donald Rumsfeld to Paul Wolfowitz and Stephen Cambone, "Subject: Increase Special Forces," January 15, 2002, www.rumsfeld.com.

98 **free up as many shooters:** Memo from Stephen A. Cambone to Donald Rumsfeld, "Subject: Conventional Forces/Special Forces," September 16, 2002, www.rumsfeld.com/library/.

98 **"preliminary pre-clearance":** Rowan Scarborough, *Rumsfeld's War: The Untold Story of America's Anti-Terrorist Commander* (Washington, DC: Regnery, 2004), p. 21.

98 **"Combat Applications Group":** Marc Ambinder, "Delta Force Gets a Name Change," TheAtlantic.com, posted October 10, 2010.

98 **"number of steps":** Transcript, "DoD News Briefing—Secretary Rumsfeld and Gen. Myers," January 7, 2003.

98 **new portfolio:** Thomas E. Ricks, "Rumsfeld Stands Tall After Iraq Victory," *Washington Post*, April 20, 2003.

99 **report directly:** DoD Directive 5143.01, issued November 23, 2005, "Subject: Under Secretary of Defense for Intelligence (USD(I))," www.fas.org/irp/doddir/dod/d5143_01.pdf.

99 **"center of gravity":** Spencer Ackerman, "Rumsfeld's Intelligence Takeover," *New Republic*, June 10, 2004.

99 **"Rumsfeld wasn't an evil man":** Author interview, former aide to Special Operations commander, June 2012.

99 **original member:** Biography of Lieutenant General William G. Boykin (Ret.), www.kingdomwarriors.net/about.php. Kingdom Warriors is a ministry founded by General Boykin and Dr. Stuart K. Weber.

99 **"saw great opportunities":** Memorandum for the record prepared by Bonnie D. Jenkins, counsel on the National Commission on Terrorist Attacks upon the United States (9/11 Commission), "Interview of Major General William Boykin," November 7, 2003, www.archives.gov/research/9-11/commission-memoranda.html. The following characterizations and quotes from Boykin come from Jenkins's description of the interview.

99 **"dangerous for U.S. foreign policy":** Jennifer D. Kibbe, "The Rise of the Shadow Warriors," *Foreign Affairs* 83 (2) (March–April 2004): 102.

100 **"It kinda went wild":** Author interview, Vincent Cannistraro, August 2010.

100 **"shown a propensity":** Intelligence Authorization Act for Fiscal Year 2010, H.R. Rep. No. 111-186 (2009) (accompanying H.R. 2701).

100 **"thrown under the bus":** Author interview, Colonel Douglas Macgregor, August 2010. All information and statements attributed to Colonel Macgregor come from the author's interview, unless otherwise noted.

100 **famous tank battle:** Richard J. Newman, "Renegades Finish Last: A Colonel's Innovative Ideas Don't Sit Well with the Brass," *US News and World Report*, July 20, 1997.

101 **"By entering the friendly country":** Stone, "'All Necessary Means.'"

## 9: The Troublemaker: Stanley McChrystal

102 **son of an Army general:** Dexter Filkins, "Stanley McChrystal's Long War," *New York Times Magazine*, October 14, 2009.

102 **enrolled at West Point:** Ibid.

102 **"troublemaker":** Evan Thomas, "McChrystal's War," *Newsweek*, September 25, 2009.

102 **mock raid:** Michael Hastings, *The Operators: The Wild and Terrifying Inside Story*

*of America's War in Afghanistan* (New York: Blue Rider Press, 2012), p. 161.

102 **graduated:** "Biography of General Stanley McChrystal," Council on Foreign Relations, 2010, www.cfr.org/afghanistan/biography-general-stanley-mcchrystal/p19396. Information about McChrystal's education and military assignments comes from the biography, unless otherwise noted.

102 **"I missed Panama":** Thomas, "McChrystal's War."

102 **revolutionized:** Hastings, *The Operators*, pp. 171–172.

102 **"I've never shot anyone":** Thomas, "McChrystal's War."

103 **"My Ranger peers":** Dalton Fury, "The Pope," *Small Wars Journal*, May 14, 2009. All quotations of Dalton Fury come from this essay.

103 **"the Rangers were just as skilled":** Ibid.

103 **Military Fellowship Selection Board:** "Overview of the Studies Program, 1998–99," Council on Foreign Relations.

104 **"It is military reality":** Stanley A. McChrystal, "Memorandum to the President," in *Humanitarian Intervention: Crafting a Workable Doctrine: Three Options Presented as Memoranda to the President*, Project Director Alton Frye, Council Policy Initiative, Council on Foreign Relations (Washington, DC: Brookings Institution Press, 2000), pp. 56, 62.

104 **forward headquarters:** "Combined Joint Task Force 82," GlobalSecurity.org, accessed June 1, 2012, www.globalsecurity.org/military/agency/dod/cjtf-180.htm.

104 **ran a "hybrid organization":** Lieutenant Colonel Anthony Shaffer, *Operation Dark Heart: Spycraft and Special Ops on the Frontlines of Afghanistan—and the Path to Victory* (New York: St. Martin's Press, 2010), p.29.

104 **task force's mission:** Dr. Donald P. Wright, James R. Bird, Steven E. Clay, Peter W. Connors, Lieutenant Colonel Scott C. Farquhar, Lynne Chandler Garcia, and Dennis F. Van Wey, *A Different Kind of War: The United States Army in Operation Enduring Freedom, October 2001–September 2005* (Fort Leavenworth, KS: Combat Studies Institute Press, 2010), pp. 209–210.

104 **interrogating prisoners, night raids:** Ibid., p. 220.

104 **"blueprint for the war against terrorism":** Elizabeth Neuffer, "Fighting Terror; Afghanistan on the Front Lines: In US Strategy, Myriad Hazards; Some See Tactics Bolstering Role of Local Warlords," *Boston Globe*, July 7, 2002.

104 **prisoner abuse scandal:** Senate Committee on Armed Services, Inquiry into the Treatment of Detainees in U.S. Custody, S. Prt. 110-54, pp. 151–152 (2008).

104 **tried in connection:** Lianne Hart, "Afghan Detainee's Leg Was 'Pulpified,' Witness Says," *Los Angeles Times*, March 23, 2005.

105 **director of intelligence:** "Lieutenant General Michael T. Flynn, USA, Director, Defense Intelligence Agency," Defense Intelligence Agency, accessed August 10, 2012, www.dia.mil/about/leadership/director.html. Information about General Flynn's military career is from his official biography, unless otherwise noted.

105 **hard-partying surfer:** Hastings, *The Operators*, p. 27.

105 **"equipped with low density systems":** Second Lieutenant Ethan T. Vessels, "Pillar of Intelligence Training: The 111th MI Brigade," *Military Intelligence Professional Bulletin* 21 (4) (October 1995), at www.fas.org/irp/agency/army/mipb/1995-4/vessels.htm.

105 **"The super secret":** William Arkin, "Secret Soldiers: Will Our Military Be Dominated by Forces Shielded from Scrutiny?" op-ed, *Los Angeles Times*, June 22, 2003.

105 **one thousand personnel:** Josh White, "US Generals in Iraq Were Told of Abuse Early, Study Finds," *Washington Post*, December 1, 2004.

105 **"among the first troops":** Dana Priest and William Arkin, *Top Secret America: The Rise of the New American Security State* (New York: Little, Brown, 2011), p. 235.

106 **"There were a lot of us":** Hastings, *The Operators*, p. 90.

106 **made more difficult":** Transcript, "HBO History Makers Series with Stanley McChrystal," interview with Tom Brokaw, Council on Foreign Relations, October 6, 2011.

106 **"the daily lie," "I don't benefit," "not the best use":** Allison Stevens, "Lawmakers Split About Benefits of Private Briefings on Status of Iraq War," *Congressional Daily Monitor*, April 9, 2003.

107 **"My staff goes":** Ibid.

107 **"They simply give us the facts":** Ibid.

107 **"more extensive":** Transcript, "DoD News Briefing—[Assistant Secretary of Defense for Public Affairs Victoria] Clarke and Maj. Gen. McChrystal," April 4, 2003.

107 **"very focused targeting":** Transcript, "Special Targeting Procedures," Foreign Press Center Briefing with Major General McChrystal, April 3, 2003.

107 **"I would anticipate":** Eric Schmitt and Bernard Weinraub, "A Nation at War: Military; Pentagon Asserts the Main Fighting Is Finished in Iraq," *New York Times*, April 15, 2003.

107 **one meal, twelve miles:** Dexter Filkins,

"Stanley McChrystal's Long War," *New York Times Magazine*, October 14, 2009.

107 *Talladega Nights*, Bud Lite Lime: Michael Hastings, "The Runaway General," *Rolling Stone*, July 8, 2010.

107 **"unique warrior"**: Author interview, Andrew Exum, March 2012. All information and statements attributed to Andrew Exum are from the author's interview.

108 **Janet Reno**: Marc Ambinder, "The Night Beat: Obama Borrows the Military Back," TheAtlantic.com, June 23, 2010.

108 **"epitome of a warrior"**: Author interview, former Special Operations staffer, March 2011.

108 **"McChrystal is stubborn"**: Dalton Fury, "The Pope," *Small Wars Journal*, May 14, 2009. The following quotations of Dalton Fury come from his essay.

109 **"A third generation soldier"**: Carl Prine, "McChrystal Clear," Line of Departure (blog), Military.com, June 3, 2012.

109 **"I like Stan"**: Author interview, Colonel Douglas Macgregor, August 2010. All statements and information attributed to Colonel Macgregor come from the author's interview.

110 **"great crusade against Islam"**: Author interview with retired military officer, July 2010.

110 **Catholic convert**: James Dao, "Aftereffects: The Overseer—Man in the News; at the Helm in Shattered Iraq: Lewis Paul Bremer III," *New York Times*, May 8, 2003.

110 **"Our retribution"**: L. Paul Bremer III, "Crush Them; Let Us Wage Total War on Our Foes," op-ed, *Wall Street Journal*, September 13, 2001.

110 **"running the occupation"**: Ambassador L. Paul Bremer III, with Malcolm McConnell, *My Year in Iraq: The Struggle to Build a Future of Hope* (New York: Threshold Editions, 2006), pp. 6–7.

111 **"paramount authority figure"**: Ibid., p. 2.

111 **brainchild**: Ibid., p. 37. Bremer describes Defense Secretary Rumsfeld as giving him his "marching orders" to proceed with de-Baathification, with Feith doing the groundwork.

111 **"Order 1"**: Naomi Klein, "Baghdad Year Zero," *Harper's*, September 2004.

111 **"450,000 enemies"**: David Rieff, "Blueprint for a Mess," *New York Times Magazine*, November 2, 2003.

111 **"We are going to fight them"**: Transcript, Interview with L. Paul Bremer III, *Breakfast with Frost*, BBC, June 29, 2003, http://news.bbc.co.uk/2/hi/programmes/breakfast_with_frost/3029904.stm.

111 **"My fellow Americans"**: Transcript,

"Remarks by the President from the USS Abraham Lincoln," May 1, 2003.

111 **were killed**: Ann Scott Tyson, "Anatomy of the Raid on Hussein's Sons," *Christian Science Monitor*, July 24, 2003.

111 **"the phrase 'guerrilla war'"**: Transcript, "DoD News Briefing—Secretary Rumsfeld and Gen. Myers," June 30, 2003.

111 **"classical guerrilla-type campaign"**: Brian Knowlton, "Top US General in Iraq Sees 'Classical Guerrilla-Type' War," *New York Times*, July 16, 2003.

112 **"significant terrorist threat"**: Alissa J. Rubin, Mark Fineman, and Edmund Sanders, "Iraqis on Council to Get Guards," *Los Angeles Times*, August 13, 2003.

112 **United Nations headquarters**: Sameer N. Yacoub (AP), "Huge Explosion Rocks UN Headquarters in Iraq," *USA Today* (USAToday.com), August 20, 2003; CBS/AP, "Baghdad Bomb Crude but Deadly," CBSNews.com.

112 **alleged**: Associated Press, "CIA Feels al-Qaida Tape on Iraq Is Probably Authentic," NBCNews.com, April 7, 2004. The United States and the UN both cited the August 2003 attack in their sanctions against Zarqawi and his group. In a 2004 audiotape, a man claiming to be Zarqawi took credit for the UN attack. An unnamed agency official told journalists that the tape was "probably authentic."

112 **"determined adversaries"**: Transcript, remarks as delivered by Secretary of Defense Donald H. Rumsfeld, Veterans of Foreign Wars event, San Antonio, TX, August 25, 2003.

113 **withdraw all remaining**: Edith M. Lederer, "Annan Orders U.N. Cutbacks in Iraq Staff," Associated Press, September 25, 2003.

113 **traveled to Afghanistan**: Mary Anne Weaver, "The Short, Violent Life of Abu Musab al-Zarqawi," *Atlantic*, July–August 2006.

113 **indicted in absentia**: "Jordan Says Major al Qaeda Plot Disrupted," CNN.com, April 26, 2004.

113 **medical treatment**: Brian Ross, "CIA Questions Saddam's Ties to al Qaeda," ABCNews.go.com, October 5, 2004.

113 **"some al-Qaeda leaders"**: Transcript, "Remarks by the President on Iraq," Cincinnati Museum Center, Cincinnati, Ohio, October 7, 2002.

113 **"deadly terrorist network"**: Transcript, Colin Powell address before the United Nations Security Council, February 5, 2003, www.nytimes.com/2003/02/06/world/threats-responses-powell-s-address-presenting-deeply-troubling-evidence-iraq.html?pagewanted=all&src=pm.

113 **was a dubious one**: Senate Select

Committee on Intelligence, Postwar Findings About Iraq's WMD Programs and Links to Terrorism and How They Compare with Prewar Assessments, S. Report 109-331, p. 63 (2006).

113 **$25 million bounty:** "U.S. Raises Zarqawi Reward to $25m," CNN.com, July 1, 2004.

113 **pledge allegiance:** Weaver, "The Short, Violent Life of Abu Musab al-Zarqawi."

114 **"They killed huge numbers":** Author interview, Gareth Porter, September 2010.

114 **September 16, 2003, fifteen countries:** Priest and Arkin, *Top Secret America*, pp. 236–237.

114 **"the nexus":** Advance Questions for Lieutenant General Bryan D. Brown, USA Nominee for Commander, accessed August 10, 2012, www.globalsecurity.org/military/library/congress/2003_hr/brown.pdf.

114 **"capturing, killing, or deterring":** Donald Rumsfeld, memorandum for Gen. Richard Myers, Paul Wolfowitz, Gen. Peter Pace, and Douglas Feith, "Subject: The Global War on Terrorism," October 16, 2003, published in full by USAToday.com, May 20, 2005.

115 **consumer product:** Lisa Burgess, "Buyers Beware: The Real Iraq 'Most Wanted' Cards Are Still Awaiting Distribution," *Stars and Stripes*, April 17, 2003.

115 **"forward commander":** John Barry and Michael Hirsh, "The Hunt Heats Up," *Newsweek*, March 14, 2004.

115 **"'grow up to be 007'":** Barton Gellman, "Person of the Year 2011; Runners-Up; William McRaven: The Admiral," *Time*, December 14, 2011.

115 **constituent SEAL teams:** Ibid.

115 **debauched parties:** Ibid.

115 **"The SEALS were happy":** Ibid.

116 **"some questionable activities":** Barry and Hirsh, "The Hunt Heats Up."

116 **"end of his career":** Gellman, "Person of the Year 2011."

116 **twenty-one months:** Orr Kelly, *Brave Men—Dark Waters: The Untold Story of the Navy SEALs* (Novato, CA: Pocket Books, 1992), p. 235.

116 **"task unit":** "Admiral William H. McRaven, Commander, United States Special Operations Command, United States Navy," United States Navy, accessed August 5, 2012, www.navy.mil/navydata/bios/navybio.asp?bioID=401. Information about Admiral McRaven's subsequent assignments comes from his official biography.

116 **first graduate:** Amanda D. Stein, "USSOCOM McRaven Honors Longtime NPS Professor During SGL," Naval Postgraduate School, June 11, 2012, www.nps.edu/About/News/USSOCOM-McRaven-Honors-Longtime-NPS-Professor-During-SGL.html.

116 **"the smartest SEAL that ever lived":** Gellman, "Person of the Year 2011."

116 **fractured his pelvis:** Ibid.

117 **principal author:** Ibid.

117 **vetting and assembling:** Author interview, confidential source, June 2012.

**10: "Their Intention and Our Intention Is the Same"**

118 **secluded airstrip:** Author interview, Mohamed Afrah Qanyare, June 2011.

118 **powerful warlords:** Emily Meehan, "Notes from a Failed State: Entry 2," *Slate*, August 19, 2008.

118 **smuggling *mira*:** Author interview, Mohamed Afrah Qanyare, June 2011. See also, Ernst Jan Hogendoorn, Mohamed Abdoulaye M'Backe, and Brynjulf Mugaas, "Report of the Panel of Experts on Somalia Pursuant to Security Council Resolution 1425 (2002)," Panel of Experts on Somalia, United Nations Security Council, March 25, 2003, p. 39.

118 **Bluebird Aviation:** Ibid. Many journalists have documented the smuggling business run by Bluebird Aviation. See Donald G. McNeil Jr., "Correspondence/Touring Somalia: When All Else Fails (Like the State), Take the Drug Flight into Town," *New York Times*, February 3, 2002.

118 **"American intelligence":** Author interview, Mohamed Afrah Qanyare, June 2011. Quotations from Mohamed Afrah Qanyare come from the interview with the author, unless otherwise noted.

119 **simultaneous attacks:** Dexter Filkins, "Terror in Africa: Attacks in Mombasa; Kenyans Hunting Clues to Bombing; Toll Rises to Thirteen," *New York Times*, November 30, 2002.

119 **Arkia Israel Airlines Flight 582:** Tim Butcher, "Missiles Launched at Holiday Plane as Bombers Bring Carnage to Hotel," *Telegraph*, November 29, 2002.

119 **later indicted:** United States of America v. Usama bin Laden et al., United States District Court Southern District of New York, April 2000, cns.miis.edu/reports/pdfs/binladen/indict.pdf.

119 **assembling a team:** Johan Peleman, Edward Howard Johns, Pavanjeet Singh Sandhu, and John Tambi, "Report of the Panel of Experts on Somalia Pursuant to Security Council Resolution 1474 (2003)," UN Security Council, published November 4, 2003, pp. 29–30.

119 **weapons black market:** International Crisis Group, "Counter-Terrorism in Somalia: Losing Hearts and Minds?" Africa Report No. 95, July 11, 2005, p. 8.

119 **Tariq Abdullah:** Ibid.

119 **traced back to him:** Marc Lacey, "Threats and Responses: African Investigation; Kenya Clears Fishermen, Saying They

Had No Ties to Attackers," *New York Times*, December 14, 2002.

119 **principal intermediary:** International Crisis Group, "Counter-Terrorism in Somalia."

119 **escaped to Somalia:** J. Peleman, E. H. Johns, P. S. Sandhu, and J. Tambi, "Report of the Panel of Experts on Somalia Pursuant to Security Council resolution 1425 (2002)," UN Security Council, published March 25, 2003, pp. 29–30.

120 **Mennonite missionaries, keeping the books:** Author interview, Mohamed Afrah Qanyare, June 2011.

120 **once or twice a week:** Ibid.

120 **US team:** Sean D. Naylor, "Clandestine Somalia Missions Yield AQ Targets," *Army Times*, November 14, 2011.

120 **"The airport is inland":** Author interview, Mohamed Afrah Qanyare, June 2011.

120 **network of surveillance:** Naylor, "Clandestine Somalia Missions Yield AQ Targets."

120 **pay him $100,000–$150,000:** Author interview, Mohamed Afrah Qanyare, June 2011.

120 **"non-traditional liaison partners":** US diplomatic cable 06NAIROBI2425 from Ambassador William Bellamy, US Embassy Nairobi, "Somalia: A Strategy for Engagement," June 2, 2006, released by WikiLeaks, http://wikileaks.org/cable/2006/06/06NAI-ROBI2425.html.

120 **"Operation Black Hawk":** Naylor, "Clandestine Somalia Missions Yield AQ Targets."

121 **Radical Islam was new:** Dr. Ken Menkhaus, "Political Islam in Somalia," *Middle East Policy* 9 (1) (March 2002). Menkhaus writes, "Despite—or perhaps because of—the fact that it is the only country in the Horn of Africa which is almost entirely Muslim, Somalia has not historically been home to the same level of radical Islamic political activity as has been the case in neighboring, religiously divided states."

121 **"Either you are with us":** President Bush, "Address to a Joint Session of Congress and the American People," Washington, DC, September 20, 2001.

121 **"We are with you":** Author interview, Ismail Mahmoud Hurre, June 2011.

121 **groups and individuals, "disrupt the financial support":** Executive Order 13224, Office of the Coordinator for Counterterrorism, September 23, 2011, www.state.gov/j/ct/rls/other/des/122570.htm.

121 **largely disbanded:** International Crisis Group, "Somalia's Divided Islamists," Africa Briefing No. 74, May 18, 2010, pp. 3–4.

121 **insurrection:** David Chazan, "Who Are al-Ittihad?" BBC.co.uk, November 30, 2002.

122 **assassinations in Ethiopia:** International Crisis Group, "Somalia: Countering Terrorism in a Failed State," Africa Report No. 45, May 23, 2002, p. 10.

122 **Task Force 150:** Michael R. Gordon, "Threats and Responses: The Operations; U.S. Turns Horn of Africa into a Military Hub," *New York Times*, November 17, 2002.

122 **"not a question of 'if'":** "US Chides German Minister," BBC.co.uk, December 20, 2001.

122 **"a funny report":** Transcript, "DoD News Briefing—Secretary Rumsfeld," December 19, 2001.

122 **"ripe for misuse":** Alan Sipress and Peter Slevin, "Powell Wary of Iraq Move; U.S. Eyes Somalia in Continuing Al Qaeda Hunt," *Washington Post*, December 21, 2001.

122 **"rebuilding its infrastructure":** Ambassador William Bellamy, "Somalia: A Strategy for Engagement."

122 **"terror cells being in Somalia":** Associated Press, "U.S. Concerned About Terrorist Activity in Somalia," *Navy Times*, December 12, 2001.

122 **"Identifying Somalia as a terrorist base":** Simon Reeve, "News Analysis; U.S. Returning to a Nightmare Called Somalia," *San Francisco Chronicle*, December 16, 2001.

123 **"People mention Somalia":** Transcript, "DoD News Briefing—Deputy Secretary Wolfowitz and Rear Admiral Stufflebeem," December 10, 2001.

123 **"small potatoes":** Karl Vick, "Al Qaeda Ally in Somalia in Tatters; Only Remnants Remain of Potential U.S. Target," *Washington Post*, February 24, 2002.

123 **"There's no need":** Ibid.

123 **between ten and twelve:** Ibid.

123 **"abysmal":** Ibid.

123 **"bring the full resources":** Author interview, former task force member, March 2011.

124 **team on standby:** Naylor, "Clandestine Somalia Missions Yield AQ Targets."

124 **removed from the Somali equation":** Ambassador William Bellamy, "Somalia: A Strategy for Engagement."

124 **included in a 1998 indictment:** United States of America v. Usama bin Laden et al., United States District Court Southern District of New York, April 2000, cns.miis.edu/reports/pdfs/binladen/indict.pdf.

124 **"cut the head off":** John J. Goldman, "Testimony Shines Light on Bid [sic] Laden's Terror Strategy," *Los Angeles Times*, February 7, 2001.

124 **250 jihadists:** Lawrence Wright, *The Looming Tower: Al-Qaeda and the Road to 9/11* (New York: Vintage Books, 2006), p. 214.

124 **"The youth were surprised":** John Miller, "Greetings, America. My Name is Osama Bin Laden," *Esquire*, February 1, 1999.

124 **"never heard of bin Laden":** Reeve, "U.S. Returning to a Nightmare Called Somalia."

125 **Operation Gothic Serpent, Garrison, contingent's commander:** Michael Smith, *Killer Elite: The Inside Story of America's Most Secret Special Operations Team* (New York: St. Martin's Griffin, 2008), pp. 179–180.

125 **"This ragged place":** Lieutenant General William G. Boykin (Ret.), with Lynn Vincent, *Never Surrender: A Soldier's Journey to the Crossroads of Faith and Freedom* (New York: FaithWords, 2008), p. 276.

125 **ramping up:** Smith, *Killer Elite*, p. 189.

125 **retired:** "Pillars of Success: William F. Garrison (BBA '66)," The University of Texas-Pan American, accessed November 20, 2012, http://portal.utpa.edu/utpa_main/dua_2011/alumni_home/awards/pillars_of_success/2008/#.UOoVRxzKZcQ.

125 **exactly two days, injuries:** Haroun M. Hassan, "Gen. Mohamed Aidid, Self-Proclaimed Somali President, Is Dead," Associated Press, August 2, 1996.

125 **five members:** Wright, *The Looming Tower*, p. 305.

125 **electric shock:** Andrew Higgins and Christopher Cooper, "CIA-Backed Team Used Brutal Means to Break Up Cell in Albania," *Wall Street Journal*, November 20, 2001.

125 **"a language they will understand":** Wright, *The Looming Tower*, pp. 305–306.

125 **Ten Most Wanted List:** Dan Eggen, "Bin Laden, Most Wanted for Embassy Bombings?" *Washington Post*, August 28, 2006.

125 **payback:** Wright, *The Looming Tower*, p. 308.

125 **eighth anniversary:** Phil Hirschkorn, "Embassy Bombings Jury Asks for Even More Evidence," CNN.com, May 14, 2001.

125 **"all the means at our disposal":** Philip Shenon, "Bombings in East Africa: In Washington; Focus on Suspects in Past Attacks," *New York Times*, August 8, 1998.

126 **"not inconsistent," arresting:** *Joint Inquiry Briefing by Staff on US Government Counterterrorism Organizations (Before September 11, 2001) and on the Evolution of the Terrorist Threat and U.S. Response: 1986–2001, Senate Select Committee on Intelligence and House Permanent Select Committee on Intelligence, June 11, 2002.*

126 **"was much easier":** Richard H. Shultz Jr., "Showstoppers: Nine Reasons Why We Never Sent Our Special Operations Forces After al Qaeda Before 9/11," *Weekly Standard* 9 (19), January 26, 2004.

126 **"Don't let these SOF guys":** Ibid.

126 **scouting missions:** International Crisis Group, "Counter-Terrorism in Somalia."

126 **Operation Infinite Reach:** James Risen, "To Bomb Sudan Plant, or Not: A Year Later, Debates Rankle," *New York Times*, October 27, 1999.

126 **half of Sudan's medications:** European Sudanese Public Affairs Council, "'Confused, Inconclusive and Contradictory': An Assessment and Analysis of the American Government's 'Evidence' for the Cruise Missile Attack on Sudan," September 1998, www.espac.org/al_shifa_pages/al-shifa_1.asp.

126 **"long-term struggle":** Transcript, "Terrorism on Trial," *NewsHour with Jim Lehrer*, PBS, February 5, 2001.

127 **"small slice of Mogadishu":** Author interview, Ismail Mahmoud Hurre, June 2011.

127 **"a low-to-invisible":** General Wayne A. Downing (Ret.), Forward to report by Clint Watts, Jacob Shapiro, and Vahid Brown, "Al-Qaida's (Mis)Adventures in the Horn of Africa," The Harmony Project, Combating Terrorism Center at West Point, July 2, 2007.

127 **fly from Nairobi, ground rules:** Naylor, "Clandestine Somalia Missions Yield AQ Targets."

127 **reluctant to pull the trigger:** Author interview, Mohamed Afrah Qanyare, June 2011.

127 **captured in spring 2003:** Human Rights Watch, "Off the Record: US Responsibility for Forced Disappearances in the 'War on Terror,'" June 2007.

127 **Mohamed Dheere:** International Crisis Group, "Counter-Terrorism in Somalia."

127 **two secret prisons:** Human Rights Watch, "Off the Record: US Responsibility for Forced Disappearances."

127 **home of a Somali militant, Sudani:** International Crisis Group, "Counter-Terrorism in Somalia."

128 **According to Isse:** Paul Salopek, "'Nobody Is Watching'; America's Hidden War in Somalia," *Chicago Tribune*, November 24, 2008. Information about Isse's time in US custody comes from this article.

128 **"The scramble":** International Crisis Group, "Counter-Terrorism in Somalia."

128 **repatriate them, execute them:** Author interview, Mogadishu, Somalia, June 2011.

128 **"already heinous warlords":** Author interview, Abdirahman "Aynte" Ali, June 2011.

128 **"may seem unpalatable":** Ambassador William Bellamy, "Somalia: A Strategy for Engagement."

129 **"No mercy":** Author interview, Mohamed Afrah Qanyare, June 2011.

129 **"US government was not helping":** Author interview, Ismail Mahmoud Hurre, June 2011.

129 **"Jedi Knights":** John Barry and Michael Hirsh, "The Hidden General," *Newsweek*, June 25, 2006.

### 11: "A Defeated Enemy Is Not a Vanquished One"

130 **Shortly after 11:00 p.m.:** Owen Bowcott and David Pallister, "'The Message Is: You're Not Safe Here,'" *Guardian*, May 13, 2003.

130 **Vinnell Corporation, pro-US Saudi billionaire:** "One Bombed Compound Owned by Pro-Western Saudi," CNN.com, May 13, 2003.

130 **Al Mohaya housing compound:** "Riyadh Attack Death Toll Mounts," BBC.co.uk, November 9, 2003.

130 **campaign against al Qaeda:** Evan Osnos, "Al Qaeda Blamed for Saudi Blast; Death Toll at Seventeen; Americans Are Among Wounded," *Chicago Tribune*, November 10, 2003.

130 **Muhammad Hamdi al Ahdal:** "Yemen Arrests a Leading Member of Al Qaeda," *New York Times*, November 26, 2003.

130 **arrested more than one hundred:** Craig S. Smith, "Fire on French Tanker off Yemen Raises Terrorism Fears," *New York Times*, October 7, 2002.

130 **"There was an interlude":** *Yemen: Confronting al-Qaeda, Preventing State Failure, Hearing Before the Senate Foreign Relations Committee*, 111th Cong. 53 (2010) (prepared testimony of Gregory D. Johnsen).

131 **disillusioned:** Author interviews, former Special Operations Forces members, February 2011 and March 2011.

131 **Houthi minority launched:** Christopher Boucek, "War in Saada: From Local Insurrection to National Challenge," Carnegie Paper series Yemen: On the Brink, Carnegie Endowment for International Peace, April 2010, www.carnegieendowment.org/files/war_in_saada.pdf.

131 **special operations forces:** See US diplomatic cable 09SANAA2230 from Ambassador Stephen Seche, US Embassy Sana'a, "Subject: Yemen's Counter Terrorism Unit Stretched Thin by War Against Houthis," December 17, 2009, released by WikiLeaks, http://wikileaks.org/cable/2009/12/09SANAA2230.html.

131 **"eas[ing] the persecution":** "Yemen: Al-Qaeda Fighting Rebels 'at Government's Request,'" Adnkronos.com, January 31, 2008.

131 **backed up:** Author interviews, former US intelligence and military officials, January 2011 and February 2011.

131 **$10 million a month:** David Hughes, "Yemen's Problems Are the Region's Problems," NATO Review (blog), accessed March 2012, www.nato.int/docu/review/2010/yemen/Yemen_region_problems/EN/index.htm.

132 **$2 billion a year:** Camille Pecastaing, *Jihad in the Arabian Sea* (Stanford: Hoover Institution Press, 2011, Kindle edition).

132 **indicted in 2003:** Attorney General John Ashcroft, prepared remarks, "Indictment for the Bombing of the U.S.S. Cole," Washington, DC, May 15, 2003.

132 **"The Yemeni constitution prohibits":** "An Interview with President Ali Abdullah Saleh," *New York Times*, June 28, 2008.

132 **"dialogue council":** Barak Barfi, "Yemen on the Brink? The Resurgence of al Qaeda in Yemen," Counterterrorism Strategy Initiative Policy Paper, New America Foundation, January 2010, www.humansecuritygateway.com/documents/NAF_YemenOnTheBrink.pdf.

132 **"Yemeni state felt an urgent need":** Ane Skov Birk, "Incredible Dialogues: Religious Dialogue as a Means of Counter-Terrorism in Yemen," Series Developments in Radicalisation and Political Violence, The International Centre for the Study of Radicalisation and Political Violence, April 2009, http://icsr.info/2009/06/incredible-dialogues-religious-dialogue-as-a-means-of-counter-terrorism-in-yemen/.

132 **"gross violations":** Ibid.

132 **return to the struggle, discontinued:** Barfi, "Yemen on the Brink?"

132 **"After the *Cole*":** Author interview, former US counterterrorism official, January 2011.

132 **escaped from prison:** Associated Press, "Main Suspects in USS Cole Bombing Escape from Yemeni Prison," FoxNews.com, April 11, 2003.

133 **"Al-Qaeda intends":** Michael Sheuer, "Yemen Still Close to al-Qaeda's Heart," *Asia Times Online*, February 7, 2008.

133 **"Our operations":** James L. Pavitt, Deputy Director for Operations on Weapons Mass of Destruction (WMD) Programs, Written Statement for the Record, National Commission on Terrorist Attacks upon the United States, April 14, 2004.

### 12: "Never Trust a Nonbeliever"

134 **give Britain another shot:** Author interview, Nasser al Awlaki, September 2012.

134 **among Awlaki's sponsors:** Alexander Meleagrou-Hitchens, "As American as Apple Pie: How Anwar al-Awlaki Became the Face of Western Jihad," The International Centre for the Study of Radicalisation and Political Violence, London, 2011.

134 **"they sought to co-opt":** Ibid. All quotations of Alexander Meleagrou-Hitchens come from this paper. The author does not intend to suggest that the organizations named in this chapter in any way condoned or espoused the radical views held by Awlaki later in his life, particularly with regard to jihad. Their support for Awlaki in 2003 seems

to have been based on his ability to preach a conservative religious message with charisma and cultural savvy. As former colleagues and family members have noted, this style of preaching was quite novel at the time.

134 **"icons of Western Salafism":** Ibid.

134 **"forced down the throats":** Anwar al Awlaki, "The Life of the Prophet Muhammad: Introduction [Makkan Period]," YouTube video, 49:20, from a sixteen-CD lecture series produced by al-Bashir Audio, undated, posted by "Muslim Knight," September 12, 2012, www.youtube.com/watch?v=Ts36mQf-viE.

135 **"never, ever trust a *kuffar*":** Anwar al Awlaki, "Never, Ever Trust the (Kuffar) Non-Believer—Anwar al-Awlaki," YouTube video, 13:12, from a series of lectures delivered by Awlaki called "The Life and Times of Umar bin Khattab," at the East London Mosque in London, United Kingdom, December 2003, posted by "nevertrustther-kuffar," October 9, 2011, www.youtube.com/watch?v=4SALh9tTvZ4.

136 **"We are watching":** Anwar al Awlaki, "Imam Anwar Al-Awlaki: Stop Police Terror, Part 1 of 3," YouTube video, 10:19, from an audio recording of a lecture delivered by Awlaki as part of a London-based campaign called "Stop Police Terror" at East London Mosque on December 26, 2003, posted by "Haqq13," May 24, 2011, www.youtube.com/watch?v=3U6wGQkOLBc.

136 **"We are arresting people":** "Police Question Terror Suspects," BBC.co.uk, December 3, 2003.

136 **"there is a Guantánamo Bay":** Anwar al Awlaki, "Imam Anwar Al-Awlaki: Stop Police Terror, Part 3 of 3," from an audio recording of a lecture delivered by Awlaki as part of a London-based campaign called "Stop Police Terror" at East London Mosque on December 26, 2003, posted by "Haqq13," May 24, 2011, www.youtube.com/watch?v=T6JC4hzaTgY.

136 **"He became a social figure":** Author interview, Nasser al Awlaki, January 2012.

137 **"The Jews and the Christians":** Awlaki, "Never, Ever Trust the (Kuffar) Non-Believer."

137 **"I want to state":** Anwar al Awlaki, transcription of lecture from series, "The Story of Ibn al-Akwa: Sheikh Noor al-Din Shahaada," produced by Dar Ibn al-Mubarak, 2003, transcription by Meleagrou-Hitchens, found in "As American as Apple Pie."

137 **unable to afford:** Author interview, Nasser al Awlaki, September 2012.

137 **"I've got a feeling":** Meleagrou-Hitchens, "As American as Apple Pie."

## 13: "You Don't Have to Prove to Anyone That You Did Right"

138 **"tracking and then capturing":** Thom Shanker and Eric Schmitt, "Pentagon Says a Covert Force Hunts Hussein," *New York Times*, November 7, 2003.

138 **run by McRaven:** John Barry and Michael Hirsh, "The Hunt Heats Up," *Newsweek*, March 14, 2004.

138 **Special Activities Division, "the Activity":** "Agencies Unite to Find bin Laden," *Washington Times*, March 15, 2004.

138 **"tightening the sensor-to-shooter loop":** Ibid.

138 **given a mission:** Lieutenant Colonel Anthony Shaffer, *Operation Dark Heart: Spycraft and Special Ops on the Frontlines of Afghanistan—and the Path to Victory* (New York: St. Martin's Press, 2010), p. 192.

139 **Able Danger:** Ibid., p. 17.

139 **Shaffer, colleagues claimed:** Ibid., p. 178.

139 **told the 9/11 Commission:** Ibid., pp. 177–179.

139 **"conducted clandestine," "first DIA":** Ibid., pp. 18–19.

139 **"Bush administration lunacy":** Ibid., p. 19.

139 **"yielded nothing":** Ibid.

139 **"more than two-thirds":** Barton Gellman and Dafna Linzer, "Afghanistan, Iraq: Two Wars Collide," *Washington Post*, October 22, 2004.

139 **"nearly half":** Juan O. Tamayo, "Capture of Saddam Will Not Mean More Forces Available to Find bin Laden," Knight Ridder Newspapers, December 14, 2003.

140 **"Detainees captured by TF-121":** Josh White, "US Generals in Iraq Were Told of Abuse Early, Inquiry Finds," *Washington Post*, December 1, 2004.

140 **"Everyone knows":** Committee on Armed Services, Inquiry into the Treatment of Detainees in US Custody, S. Prt. 110-54, p. 218 (2008).

140 **"gratuitous enemies":** White, "US Generals in Iraq Were Told."

140 **former bodyguard:** Details of the operation to capture Saddam Hussein come from Michael Smith, *Killer Elite: The Inside Story of America's Most Secret Special Operations Team* (New York: St. Martin's Press, 2006), pp. 261–263.

140 **"Ladies and gentlemen":** Transcript, "Ambassador Bremer Briefing from Baghdad," December 14, 2003.

140 **$750,000 in hundred-dollar bills:** Smith, *Killer Elite*, p. 262.

140 **"I am Saddam Hussein," "regards":** "'President Bush Sends His Regards,'" CNN.com, December 15, 2003.

141 **Saddam's temporary home:** Eric Schmitt and Carolyn Marshall, "In Secret Unit's 'Black Room,' a Grim Portrait of U.S. Abuse," *New York Times*, March 19, 2006.

141 **"look to the future":** Transcript, "Ambassador Bremer Briefing from Baghdad."

141 **"coalition special operations forces":** Ibid.

141 **shared a cigar:** Barton Gellman, "Person of the Year 2011; Runners-Up; William McRaven: The Admiral," *Time*, December 14, 2011.

141 **"begin to run out of gas":** Rowan Scarborough, *Rumsfeld's War: The Untold Story of America's Anti-Terrorist Commander* (Washington, DC: Regnery, 2004), p. 62.

141 **"establishment of an insurgency":** Bob Woodward, *State of Denial: Bush at War, Part III* (New York: Simon and Schuster Paperbacks, 2006), p. 266.

142 **common cause:** Jeffrey Gettleman, "Signs That Shiites and Sunnis Are Joining to Battle Americans," *New York Times*, April 9, 2004.

142 **"exacerbating the insurgency":** Author interview, Andrew Exum, March 2012. All quotations from Andrew Exum in this chapter come from the author's interview.

142 **barely give his command the courtesy:** Author interview, General Ricardo Sanchez, June 2010.

142 **The most serious thing":** Author interview, Colonel Lawrence Wilkerson, May 2011.

143 **"tailored down":** Stanley A. McChrystal, "It Takes a Network: The New Front Line of Modern Warfare," *Foreign Policy* (March–April 2011). All quotations from General McChrystal in this chapter come from this article.

144 **four subunits:** Sean D. Naylor, "Special Ops Unit Nearly Nabs Zarqawi," *Army Times*, April 28, 2006. The article describes the task force after it has received a new code name, Task Force 145.

145 **F³EA:** McChrystal, "It Takes a Network."

145 **Copper Green, Matchbox:** Marc Ambinder and D. B. Grady, *The Command: Deep Inside the President's Secret Army* (Hoboken, NJ: John Wiley and Sons, 2012, Kindle edition).

145 **Footprint:** William M. Arkin, *Code Names: Deciphering US Military Plans, Programs, and Operations in the 9/11 World* (Hanover, NH: Steerforth Press, 2005), p. 369.

145 **"weren't getting anything substantive":** Seymour M. Hersh, "The Gray Zone: How a Secret Pentagon Program Came to Abu Ghraib," *New Yorker*, May 24, 2004.

146 **"Rumsfeld's answer":** Jane Mayer, *The Dark Side: The Inside Story of How the War on Terror Turned into a War on American Ideals* (New York: Doubleday, 2008), p. 243.

146 **"Grab whom you must'":** Hersh, "The Gray Zone."

146 **"just wasn't right":** Shaffer, *Operation Dark Heart*, pp. 257–259.

**14: "No Blood, No Foul"**

147 **in one of two structures:** Eric Schmitt and Carolyn Marshall, "Task Force 6-26: Inside Camp Nama; in Secret Unit's 'Black Room,' a Grim Portrait of U.S. Abuse," *New York Times*, March 19, 2006.

147 **"Nasty-Ass Military Area":** John H. Richardson, "Acts of Conscience," *Esquire*, September 21, 2009, www.esquire.com/features/ESQ0806TERROR_102.

147 **"don't make them bleed":** Schmitt and Marshall, "Task Force 6-26."

147 **"adopted the SOP":** Committee on Armed Services, Inquiry into the Treatment of Detainees in US Custody, S. Prt. 110-54, p. 158 (2008).

147 **"included stress positions":** Ibid., pp. 158–159.

148 **unlawful combatants:** As John Sifton and Marc Garlasco note in a report for Human Rights Watch, in the period during which the task force operated out of Camp NAMA, "U.S. and coalition forces in Iraq were bound by various provisions of the 1949 Geneva Conventions, as well as by customary international law." The administration said publicly that the Geneva Conventions applied to the treatment of Iraqis in detention but could be suspended if the detainee was a foreign fighter. However, according to an internal DoD report cited by the Senate report, the standard operating procedure used by the task force in Iraq was "influenced by the counter-resistance memorandum that the Secretary of Defense approved on December 2, 2002…and incorporated techniques designed for detainees who were identified as 'unlawful combatant.'" Military personnel who had worked with the task force told the Senate Armed Services Committee and Human Rights Watch that prisoners were denied protections under the Geneva Conventions, including Iraqi nationals. See John Sifton and Marc Garlasco, "No Blood, No Foul: Soldiers' Accounts of Detainee Abuse in Iraq," Human Rights Watch, July 23, 2006, www.hrw.org/reports/2006/07/22/no-blood-no-foul. See also Terry Frieden, "Justice Dept.: Geneva Conventions Limited in Iraq," CNN.com, October 26, 2004; and Committee on Armed Services, Inquiry into the Treatment of Detainees, p. 158.

148 **would not see lawyers:** Schmitt and Marshall, "Task Force 6-26."

148 **ninety days:** Spencer Ackerman, "How Special Ops Copied al-Qaida to Kill It," Danger Room (blog), Wired.com, September 9, 2011, www.wired.com/dangerroom/2011/09/mcchrystal-network/.

148 **often subjected to:** John Sifton and Marc Garlasco, "No Blood, No Foul: Soldiers' Accounts of Detainee Abuse in Iraq," Human Rights Watch, July 23, 2006, www.hrw.org/reports/2006/07/22/no-blood-no-foul. All information attributed to Human Rights Watch in this chapter comes from this report, unless otherwise noted.

148 **"directly from General McChrystal":** Ibid.

148 **set foot in Camp NAMA:** Ibid.

148 **"very necessary":** Ibid.

148 **rebuffed:** Ibid.

148 **up the chain of command:** Ibid.

148 **special ID:** Ibid.

148 **"running a country club":** Committee on Armed Services, Inquiry into the Treatment of Detainees, p.191.

148 **"GTMO-ize":** Ibid.

148 **"fearful of dogs":** Ibid., pp. 196–197.

148 **"can't tell our chain of command":** Sifton and Garlasco, "No Blood, No Foul."

149 **"This is the dark side":** Author interview, Lieutenant Colonel Anthony Shaffer, May 2011.

149 **"no oversight":** Author interview, Colonel Lawrence Wilkerson, May 2011.

149 **"very high levels":** Author interview, Scott Horton, September 2010. All statements attributed to Scott Horton in this chapter come from the author's interview.

150 **"two reasons":** Jonathan S. Landay, "Report: Abusive Tactics Used to Seek Iraq–al Qaida Link," McClatchy Newspapers, April 21, 2009.

150 **"tossed them back":** Rowan Scarborough, *Rumsfeld's War: The Untold Story of America's Anti-Terrorist Commander* (Washington, DC: Regnery, 2004), p. 48.

150 **"You saw the French":** Author interview, Andrew Exum, March 2012. All quotations of Andrew Exum in this chapter come from the author's interview.

151 **withdrew its interrogators:** Schmitt and Marshall, "Task Force 6-26."

151 **voicing their warnings:** Ibid.

151 **arrived at Camp NAMA:** Committee on Armed Services, Inquiry into the Treatment of Detainees, p. 191.

151 **"filtration site":** Author interview, Scott Horton, September 2010.

151 **four interrogation rooms:** Schmitt and Marshall, "Task Force 6-26."

152 **"this is the treatment":** Sifton and Garlasco, "No Blood, No Foul." All quotations of "Jeff Perry" in this chapter come from this report.

152 **interrogations there often incorporated:** Ibid.

152 **One former prisoner:** Schmitt and Marshall, "Task Force 6-26."

152 **described heinous acts:** Brigadier General Richard P. Formica, "Article 15-6 Investigations of CJSOTF-AP and 5th SF Group Detention Operations," November 8, 2004, pp. 20–21, 30; declassified June 7, 2006, released by the Department of Defense on Friday, June 16, 2006, www.dod.mil/pubs/foi/operation_and_plans/Detainee/OtherDetaineeRelatedDocuments.html.

152 **beat prisoners with rifle butts, spit in their faces:** Schmitt and Marshall, "Task Force 6-26."

152 **"beating the shit out of":** Sifton and Garlasco, "No Blood, No Foul."

153 **"pissed in a bottle":** "CID Report—Final—0016-04-CID343-69355," Army Criminal Investigative Command Report into allegations of detainee abuse at Camp NAMA, Baghdad International Airport, August 4, 2004, obtained by the American Civil Liberties Union and other human rights groups via FOIA, www.aclu.org/torturefoia/released/030705/9135_9166.pdf.

153 **interrupt non-harsh interrogations:** Sifton and Garlasco, "No Blood, No Foul."

153 **"to leverage":** Ibid.

153 **arrived at Camp NAMA:** Committee on Armed Services, Inquiry into the Treatment of Detainees, p. 173.

153 **"fundamental systemic problems":** Ibid., p. 173.

153 **They told Kleinman:** Ibid.

153 **described a chaotic situation:** Ibid.

153 **ordered to do so:** Ibid., p. 181.

153 **"I walked into the interrogation room":** Ibid., p. 176.

154 **"cleared hot to use SERE methods":** Ibid., p. 179.

154 **"unlawful order," Kleinman was told:** Ibid., p. 180.

154 **trying to break:** Ibid., pp. 181–182.

154 **"Concept of Operations":** Ibid., p. 184.

154 **"friction was developing":** Ibid.

154 **"sleep lightly":** Ibid., p. 186.

155 **special operators as interrogators:** Ibid., p. 193.

155 **"It's just that simple":** Author interview, Malcolm Nance, May 2011. All quotations of Malcolm Nance in this chapter come from the author's interview.

155 **"out of the hands of":** Human Rights Watch, "Leadership Failure: Firsthand Accounts of Torture of Iraqi Detainees by the U.S. Army's 82nd Airborne Division," Sep-

tember 23, 2005, www.hrw.org/node/11610/
section/1.

155 **complaining to Langley:** Schmitt and
Marshall, "Task Force 6-26."

156 **"more aggressive":** Committee on
Armed Services, Inquiry into the Treatment
of Detainees, p. 159.

156 **unmarked helicopters, goggles:**
Schmitt and Marshall, "Task Force 6-26."

156 **"harsh interrogation [was] approved":**
Sifton and Garlasco, "No Blood, No
Foul."

156 **nondisclosure agreements:** Ibid.

157 **"disaster waiting to happen":** Committee on Armed Services, Inquiry into the
Treatment of Detainees, p. 162.

157 **Fashad Mohammad:** Hina Shamsi,
"Command's Responsibility: Detainee
Deaths in U.S. Custody in Iraq and Afghan-
istan," Human Rights First, 2006, www.
humanrightsfirst.org/our-work/law-and-secu-
rity/we-can-end-torture-now/commands-re-
sponsibility-detainee-deaths-in-u-s-custo-
dy-in-iraq-and-afghanistan/. The Medical
Examiner's report cited was obtained by
Human Rights First: Office of the Armed
Forces Medical Examiner, Final Autopsy
Report for Autopsy No. ME-04-309 (Fashad
Mohammad), November 22, 2004.

157 **Manadel al Jamadi:** MG George R. Fay,
"AR 15-6 Investigation of the Abu Ghraib
Detention Facility and 205th Military Intelligence Brigade," completed August 23, 2004,
p. 53. The report states that "CIA representatives" brought a man to Abu Ghraib early on
November 4, 2003. He had been "captured by
Navy SEAL Team 7 during a joint-121/CIA
mission." The report goes on to describe the
circumstances of the man's death. Subsequent reporting revealed that the man's name
was Manadel al-Jamadi. See David Cloud,
"Seal Officer Hears Charges in Court-Martial
in Iraqi's Death," *New York Times*, May 25,
2005.

157 **"needs to be reined in":** Josh White,
"U.S. Generals in Iraq Were Told of Abuse
Early, Inquiry Finds," *Washington Post*,
December 1, 2004.

158 **"pored over intelligence":** Schmitt and
Marshall, "Task Force 6-26."

158 **"over a hundred 'high value detainees'":** "Report of the International Committee of the Red Cross (ICRC) on the Treatment
by the Coalition Forces of Prisoners of War
and Other Protected Persons by the Geneva
Conventions in Iraq During Arrest, Intern-
ment and Interrogation," ICRC, February
2004, http://military.piac.asn.au/sites/de-
fault/files/documents/document-03.pdf.

159 **list of complaints:** Memorandum
from Vice Admiral Lowell E. Jacoby to Under

Secretary of Defense for Intelligence Stephen
A. Cambone, "Alleged Detainee Abuse by
TF 6-26 Personnel," June 25, 2004, obtained
under the Freedom of Information Act by the
American Civil Liberties Union and other
human rights groups, available at www.aclu.
org/torturefoia/released/t2596_0297.pdf.

159 **scribbled a handwritten letter:** Schmitt
and Marshall, "Task Force 6-26."

159 **"no pattern of misconduct":** Ibid.

159 **"subject of this investigation":** Army
Criminal Investigation Command memorandum concerning allegations of abuse at Camp
Nama, May 31, 2004, obtained under the
Freedom of Information Act by the American Civil Liberties Union and other human
rights groups, www.aclu.org/torturefoia/
released/030705/9117_9134.pdf.

159 **thirty-four task force members:**
Schmitt and Marshall, "Task Force 6-26."

159 **"did not see any form of oversight":**
Author interview, former Air Force interrogator, June 2012.

160 **changed the letterhead:** Committee on
Armed Services, Inquiry into the Treatment
of Detainees, p. 167.

160 **eventually investigated:** Seymour M.
Hersh, "The General's Report: How Antonio
Taguba, Who Investigated the Abu Ghraib
Scandal, Became One of Its Casualties," *New
Yorker*, June 25, 2007.

160 **Rumsfeld's congressional testimony:** Captain Ian Fishback to Senator John
McCain, "A Matter of Honor," September
16, 2005, published by the *Washington Post*,
September 25, 2005.

161 **"For 17 months":** Ibid. All quotations
of Captain Fishback come from this letter.

161 **denied permission:** John H. Richardson, "Acts of Conscience," *Esquire*, September 21, 2009, www.esquire.com/features/
ESQ0806TERROR_102.

161 **"lapses of discipline":** General Stanley
McChrystal (US Army, Ret.), *My Share of the
Task: A Memoir* (New York: Portfolio/Pen-
guin, 2012), pp. 201–202.

161 **moved the task force:** Sifton and Garlasco, "No Blood, No Foul."

**15: The Death Star**

162 **"the Death Star":** Mark Urban, *Task
Force Black: The Explosive True Story of
the SAS and the Secret War in Iraq* (London:
Little, Brown, 2010), p. 82. Other characterizations of the JOC come from Urban's book.

162 **"experiment in intel crowdsourcing":**
Spencer Ackerman, "How Special Ops Copied al-Qaida to Kill It," Danger Room (blog),
Wired.com, September 9, 2011, www.wired.
com/dangerroom/2011/09/mcchrystal-net-
work/all/.

163 **killed in an ambush:** Jeffrey Gettleman, "Enraged Mob in Fallujah Kills Four American Contractors," *New York Times*, March 31, 2004.

163 **"Kick ass!":** Lieutenant General Ricardo S. Sanchez, with Donald T. Phillips, *Wiser in Battle: A Soldier's Story* (New York: HarperCollins, 2008), pp. 349–350.

163 **"Thugs and assassins":** Transcript, "Defense Department Operational Update Briefing," April 20, 2004.

163 **"arrogance and hubris":** Urban, *Task Force Black*, p. 40.

163 **body was discovered:** Associated Press, "Body Found on Baghdad Overpass Identified as That of American," USAToday.com, posted May 11, 2004.

163 **video appeared online:** CBS/AP, "CIA: Top Terrorist Executed Berg," CBSNews.com, posted May 13, 2004. The video was also posted with the title "Sheikh Abu Musab al-Zarqawi Slaughters an American Infidel with His Own Hands."

164 **"Jihadi Advanced University":** Author interview, Malcolm Nance, May 2011.

164 **money poured in:** Jonathan Masters and Greg Bruno, "Al-Qaeda in Iraq," Council on Foreign Relations, updated March 20, 2012, www.cfr.org/iraq/al-qaeda-iraq/p14811.

164 **"media spotlight":** Author interview, Richard Rowley, September 2011.

164 **Enron executive:** "Jim Steele, Counselor to US Ambassador for Iraqi Security Forces," Premiere Speakers Bureau, accessed August 2012, http://premierespeakers.com/jim_steele/bio.

164 **senior Iraq job:** Jon Lee Anderson, "The Uprising: Shia and Sunnis Put Aside Their Differences," *New Yorker*, May 3, 2004.

165 **key "counterinsurgency":** Peter Maass, "The Salvadorization of Iraq: The Way of the Commandos," *New York Times Magazine*, May 1, 2005.

165 **called to testify:** Christopher Drew, "Testimony on Contras Still Haunts Colonel," *Chicago Tribune*, July 7, 1991.

165 **"Salvador Option":** John Barry and Michael Hirsh, "'The Salvador Option,'" *Newsweek*, January 7, 2005.

165 **"good lesson," "cut off their hands":** Rod Nordland, "Iraq's Repairman," *Newsweek*, July 5, 2004.

165 **Special Police Commando Unit:** Maass, "The Salvadorization of Iraq."

165 **"embracing a new strategy":** Ibid.

165 **"Vital months":** Urban, *Task Force Black*, pp. 52–53.

166 **"smart and cunning":** John Barry and Michael Hirsh, "The Hunt Heats Up," *Newsweek*, March 14, 2004.

**16: "The Best Technology, the Best Weapons, the Best People—and Plenty of Money to Burn"**

167 **Joint Prioritized Effects List:** Nick Davies, "Afghanistan War Logs: Task Force 373—Special Force Hunting Top Taliban," *Guardian*, July 25, 2010.

167 **leadership targeting cell:** Lieutenant Colonel Anthony Shaffer, *Operation Dark Heart: Spycraft and Special Ops on the Frontlines of Afghanistan—and the Path to Victory* (New York: St. Martin's Press, 2010), p. 32.

167 **fake documents, Chris Stryker:** Ibid., p. 24.

167 **"started to roll into Bagram":** Ibid., p. 195.

168 **large operations center, "Death Star":** Ibid, p. 196.

168 **didn't sit well:** Ibid., p. 197.

168 **"the intel indicates," "it's not an option":** Ibid., p. 116.

169 **secret deal:** Mark Mazzetti and David Rohde, "Amid U.S. Policy Disputes, Qaeda Grows in Pakistan," *New York Times*, June 30, 2008.

169 **"violate the sovereignty of Pakistan":** Author interview, Lieutenant Colonel Anthony Shaffer, May 2011.

169 **Rules of Engagement:** Scott Lindlaw (AP), "U.S. OK'd Troop Terror Hunts in Pakistan," *Washington Post*, August 23, 2007.

169 **34 percent increase:** Jennifer D. Kibbe, "Rise of the Shadow Warriors," *Foreign Policy*, (March–April 2004).

170 **"protect U.S. citizens and interests":** Communication from the President of the United States: A Supplemental Consolidated Report, Consistent with the War Powers Resolution, To Help Ensure That the Congress Is Kept Fully Informed on U.S. Military Activities in Support of the War on Terror, Kosovo, and Bosnia Herzegovina, Pursuant to Pub. L. 93-148, H. Doc. 110-5, December 15, 2006.

170 **fifteen to twenty such countries:** Eric Schmitt and Mark Mazzetti, "Secret Order Lets US Raid al Qaeda," *New York Times*, November 8, 2008.

170 **drafted in 2003:** Documents provided to the author in confidence; author interview, Special Operations source, November 2009.

170 **"you can go after him":** Author interview, Special Operations source, November 2009.

170 **"bureaucratic drag":** Documents provided to the author in confidence.

170 **Military Liaison Elements:** Thom Shanker and Scott Shane, "Elite Troops Get Expanded Role on Intelligence," *New York Times*, March 8, 2006.

170 **"certain to increase significantly":** Ibid.

171 **"I don't interpret it that way at all":** Barton Gellman, "Secret Unit Expands

Rumsfeld's Domain; New Espionage Branch Delving into CIA Territory," *Washington Post*, January 23, 2005.

171 **"seventy-two-hour heads up," new guidelines:** Ibid.

171 **"Why aren't they telling us?":** Gellman, "Secret Unit Expands Rumsfeld's Domain."

171 **insert language:** Michael Smith, *Killer Elite: The Inside Story of America's Most Secret Special Operations Team* (New York: St. Martin's Press, 2006), p. 268; author interview, Special Operations source, January 2011.

171 **"There are a lot of things in NSPD-38":** Author interview, Special Operations source, January 2011.

172 **"pretty plainly illegal":** Author interview, Scott Horton, September 2010.

172 **"Preparation of the Battlespace":** Memorandum from Donald Rumsfeld for General Dick Myers, Doug Feith; CC: General Pete Pace, Steve Cambone, "Preparation of the Battlespace," September 2, 2004, www.rumsfeld.com/library/.

172 **nascent stage:** John Sifton, "A Brief History of Drones," *Nation*, February 27, 2012.

172 **"Unblinking Eye":** Michael T. Flynn, Rich Juergens, and Thomas L. Cantrell, "Employing ISR; SOF Best Practices," *Joint Forces Quarterly* 50 (July 2008).

173 **"Continuous Clandestine Tagging":** Doug Richardson, SOAL-T WSO, "US Special Operations Command; Continuous, Clandestine, Tagging, Tracking and Locating (CTTL)," PowerPoint presentation prepared for USSOCOM, September 5, 2007.

173 **"bioreactive taggant":** Author interviews, Hunter (pseudonym), June 2012; Richardson, "US Special Operations Command."

174 **JSOC is awesome":** "On the Record; Excerpts from Bob Woodward's Oval Office Interviews with President George W. Bush, May 20–21, 2008," *Washington Post*, www.washingtonpost.com/wp-srv/nation/specials/war-within/audio/.

174 **press commanders:** Bob Woodward, *The War Within: A Secret White House History, 2006–2008* (New York: Simon and Schuster, 2008), p. 13.

174 **"I don't even know how many":** Michael Hastings, *The Operators: The Wild and Terrifying Inside Story of America's War in Afghanistan* (New York: Blue Rider Press, 2012), p. 173.

174 **JSOC liaison offices:** Mark Urban, *Task Force Black: The Explosive True Story of the SAS and the Secret War in Iraq* (London: Little, Brown, 2010), p. 53; Shanker and Shane, "Elite Troops Get Expanded Role."

174 **"Department of Defense is very eager":** Shanker and Shane, "Elite Troops Get Expanded Role."

175 **"It's not a good idea":** Author interview, Colonel W. Patrick Lang (Ret.), September 2010.

175 **"why not go hammer?":** Author interview, Andrew Exum, March 2012.

175 **behind-the-scenes scuffle:** Mazzetti and Rohde, "Amid U.S. Policy Disputes."

175 **"would never cooperate":** Author interview, Lieutenant Colonel Anthony Shaffer, May 2011. All statements and information attributed to Lieutenant Colonel Shaffer come from the author's interview, unless otherwise noted.

175 **"biggest folly":** Mazzetti and Rohde, "Amid U.S. Policy Disputes."

176 **CIA took advantage of the disorder:** Marc Ambinder and D. B. Grady, *The Command: Deep Inside the President's Secret Army* (Hoboken, NJ: John Wiley and Sons, 2012, Kindle edition), chap. 10, "Widening the Playing Field."

176 **"SCREEN HUNTER":** Ibid.

176 **"first among equals":** Mark Mazzetti, "C.I.A. Closes Unit Focused on Capture of bin Laden," *New York Times*, July 4, 2006.

177 **"hurting because of Iraq":** Mazzetti and Rohde, "Amid U.S. Policy Disputes."

177 **"boys with toys":** Ibid.

177 **"They choppered in":** Greg Miller, "War on Terror Loses Ground," *Los Angeles Times*, July 27, 2008.

177 **"violated Pakistani airspace":** Rahimullah Yusufzai, "Forty-Six Killed in North Waziristan Fighting; Military Claims Killing Forty-one Foreign Militants," accessed April 10, 2012, www.pakdef.info/forum/printthread.php?t=6012&p-p=25&page=15.

177 **including Pakistan's Frontier Corps:** Author interview, former Blackwater executive, November 2009.

177 **Forward Operating Bases:** Erik Prince, speech given January 2010, author copy of audio.

178 **Blackwater SELECT:** James Risen and Mark Mazzetti, "C.I.A. Said to Use Outsiders to Put on Drones," *New York Times*, August 20, 2010.

178 **"Vibrant Fury":** Matthew Cole, Richard Esposito, and Brian Ross, "Mercenaries? CIA Says Expanded Role for Contractors Legitimate," ABCNews.go.com, December 11, 2009.

178 **"secondary in importance":** Letter, Ayman al Zawahiri to Musab al Zarqawi, July 9, 2005, released by the Office of the Director of National Intelligence on October 11, 2005, www.globalsecurity.org/security/library/re-

port/2005/zawahiri-zarqawi-letter_9jul2005.htm.

179 **"make you an example," Askariyya Mosque:** Seth G. Jones, *Hunting in the Shadows: The Pursuit of al Qaeda Since 9/11* (New York: W. W. Norton, 2012), p. 249.

179 **alliance with the occupation:** John Ward Anderson, "Iraqi Tribes Strike Back at Insurgents," *Washington Post,* March 7, 2006.

179 **found, fixed and finished:** Dexter Filkins, Mark Mazzetti, and Richard A. Oppell Jr., "How Surveillance and Betrayal Led to a Hunt's End," *New York Times,* June 9, 2006. Details of the Zarqawi raid can be found in this article.

**17: "A Lot of It Was of Questionable Legality"**
This chapter is based on a series of interviews in 2010 and 2011 with "Hunter," a Special Operations source. Hunter is a pseudonym created to protect the identity of the source.

180 **home of JSOC's intelligence wing:** See Marc Ambinder and D. B. Grady, *The Command: Deep Inside the President's Secret Army* (Hoboken, NJ: John Wiley and Sons, 2012, Kindle edition), chap. 8, "The Activity."

**18: The Imprisonment of Anwar Awlaki**
184 **"could not get a scholarship":** Author interview, Nasser al Awlaki, January 2012. All information and statements attributed to Nasser al Awlaki come from the author's interviews, in January, August and September 2012, unless otherwise noted. Details about Anwar from this period come from the author's interviews with Nasser and other members of the family, unless otherwise noted.

184 **study at Iman University:** Author interviews, Awlaki family members, January and August 2012; Sudarsan Raghavan, "Cleric Linked to Fort Hood Attack Grew More Radicalized in Yemen," *Washington Post,* December 10, 2009.

185 **tribal dispute:** Susan Schmidt, "Imam from Va. Mosque Now Thought to Have Aided al-Qaeda," *Washington Post,* February 27, 2008.

185 **prison in Sana'a:** Author interview, Nasser al Awlaki, January 2012.

185 **confiscated:** Schmidt, "Imam from Va. Mosque."

185 **"look after" Anwar:** Author interview, Nasser al Awlaki, January 2012.

185 **"first nine months":** Transcript, "Moazzam Begg Interviews Imam Anwar al-Awlaki," Cageprisoners, December 31, 2007, www.cageprisoners.com/our-work/interviews/item/159-moazzam-begg-interviews-imam-anwar-al-awlaki.

186 **"I was held at the request":** Transcript, "Interview with In Focus News, California," by Saaqib Rangoonwala, posted by "SoldierOfAllah" on Shaykh Anwar's Blog, October 13, 2011, http://anwar-awlaki.blogspot.com/2011/10/interview-with-in-focus-news-california.html. This is not the same domain name once used by Anwar al Awlaki.

186 **"began asking me questions":** Transcript, "Moazzam Begg Interviews Imam Anwar al-Awlaki."

186 **"at the request of the United States":** Christof Heyns, "Report of the Special Rapporteur on Extrajudicial Summary or Arbitrary Executions," submitted to the United Nations Human Rights Council, May 27, 2011, p. 395.

186 **"did not object":** Scott Shane and Souad Mekhennet, "Imam's Path from Condemning Terror to Preaching Jihad," *New York Times,* May 8, 2010.

186 **meeting between Negroponte:** Author interview, former Yemeni government minister, January 2012. Details of the meeting are from the author's interview.

186 **"Bandar Bush":** Ian Black, "Prince Bandar bin Sultan—Profile," *Guardian,* October 10, 2012.

186 **some 750,000 people:** Author interview, Sheikh Saleh bin Fareed, January 2012.

186 **"asked us to keep him in jail":** Ibid. All information and statements attributed to bin Fareed come from the author's interview.

187 **Saleh visited Washington:** Author interview, Nasser al Awlaki, January 2012; also see "Visits by Foreign Leaders of Yemen," Office of the Historian, U.S. Department of State, accessed December 15, 2012, http://history.state.gov/departmenthistory/visits/yemen. President Saleh visited the US from April 29 to May 7, 2007.

187 **stayed for two days:** Author interview, Nasser al Awlaki, January 2012.

187 **"summoned to an office":** Shaykh Harith al Nadari, "My Story with al-Awlaki," *Inspire* 9 (winter 2012), released May 2012.

187 **Yemeni intelligence insisted:** Author interview, Nasser al Awlaki, January 2012.

187 **"There was some pressure":** Transcript, "Moazzam Begg Interviews Imam Anwar al-Awlaki."

188 **"detention as a blessing":** Anwar al Awlaki, "Book Review 3: In the Shade of the Quran by Sayyid Qutb," Imam Anwar's Blog, June 22, 2008, www.anwar-alawlaki.com.

188 **"they took everything away":** Transcript, "Moazzam Begg Interviews Imam Anwar al-Awlaki."

188 **studying in Colorado:** Lawrence Wright, *The Looming Tower: Al-Qaeda and*

*the Road to 9/11* (New York: Vintage Books, 2007), p. 20.

188 **"numb to faith":** David Von Drehle, "A Lesson in Hate; How an Egyptian Student Came to Study 1950s America and Left Determined to Wage Holy War," *Smithsonian Magazine*, February 2006.

188 **arrested, put in jail:** Wright, *The Looming Tower*, p. 33.

188 **his most influential texts:** Ibid., pp. 33–34.

188 **Qutb was hanged:** Ibid., p. 37.

189 **"so immersed":** Awlaki, "Book Review 3."

189 **"particularly mean Prison Head":** Anwar al Awlaki blog post, "Book Review 9: English Novels," Imam Anwar's Blog, August 6, 2008, anwar-alawlaki.com.

189 **"staple breads":** Anwar al Awlaki, "Food Reviews from Behind Bars," Imam Anwar's Blog, August 21, 2008, anwar-alawlaki.com.

189 **"Before my imprisonment":** Transcript, "Interview with In Focus News."

190 **"alleged spiritual advisor":** US diplomatic cable 07SANAA2333, from Deputy Chief of Mission Angie Bryan, US Embassy Sana'a, "Yemeni-American Awlaqi Released from ROYG Custody," December 18, 2007, released by WikiLeaks, http://wikileaks.org/cable/2007/12/07SANAA2333.html.

190 **"kidnapping for ransom":** "Treasury Designates Anwar al-Aulaqi, Key Leader of Al-Qa'ida in the Arabian Peninsula," press release, US Department of the Treasury, July 16, 2010.

**19: "America Knows War. They Are War Masters."**

191 **first approached by the CIA:** Author interview, Yusuf Mohamed Siad, June 2011.

191 **Lower Shabelle:** Ken Menkhaus, "Governance without Government in Somalia: Spoilers, State Building, and the Politics of Coping," *International Security* 31 (3) (winter 2006–2007): 74–106, 85, www.mitpressjournals.org/doi/abs/10.1162/isec.2007.31.3.74.

191 **trafficking operations:** Bruno Schiemsky, Melvin E. Holt Jr., Harjit S. Kelley, and Joel Salek, "Report of the Monitoring Group on Somalia Pursuant to Security Council Resolution 1587 (2005)," UN Security Council, October 4, 2005, pp. 23–24.

191 **"They offered me money":** Author interview, Yusuf Mohamed Siad, June 2011. All quotations of Indha Adde come from the author's interview, unless otherwise noted.

192 **five specific terrorists:** US diplomatic cable 06NAIROBI2425, from Ambassador William Bellamy, US Embassy Nairobi, "Somalia: A Strategy for Engagement," June 2, 2006, released by WikiLeaks, http://

wikileaks.org/cable/2006/06/06NAIROBI2425.html. "Fazul [Abdullah Mohammed], [Saleh Ali Saleh] Nabhan, [Abu Talha] el-Sudani, [Ahmed] Abdi [Godane] and [Aden Hashi] Ayrow must be removed from the Somali equation."

192 **"start an open war in Mogadishu":** US diplomatic cable 06NAIROBI1484, from Ambassador William M. Bellamy, US Embassy Nairobi, "Ambassador to Yusuf: Alliance Against Terror Not Directed at TFG," April 4, 2006, released by WikiLeaks, http://wikileaks.org/cable/2006/04/06NAIROBI1484.html.

193 **small, regional Islamic courts:** Cedric Barnes and Harun Hassan, "The Rise and Fall of Mogadishu's Islamic Courts," *Journal of Eastern African Studies* 1 (2) (July 2007).

193 **twelve courts united:** Author interview, Abdirahman "Aynte" Ali, June 2011.

193 **receiving shipments:** Schiemsky et al., "Report of the Monitoring Group on Somalia," p. 15. The Monitoring Group reported that "another State in the region provided support to the opposition and the Oromo National Liberation Front [a Somali nationalist guerrilla group operating along the border] in the form of arms. That State provided arm[s] to opposition allies including Sheik Yusuf Indohaadde…Sheik Hassan Dahir Aweys…and other[s] for the purpose of countering support provided to the TFG by Ethiopia." The country being reported was confirmed to be Eritrea by subsequent UN and other reports.

193 **supporting the CIA's warlords:** Schiemsky et al., "Report of the Monitoring Group on Somalia," pp. 20–21.

193 **"whole mess started from that point":** Author interview, Ali Mohamed Gedi, June 2011.

193 **officially announcing:** "Somali Warlords Battle Islamists," BBC News, February 21, 2006, http://news.bbc.co.uk/2/hi/africa/4735614.stm.

193 **endorsed the US campaign:** Mark Mazzetti, "Efforts by C.I.A. Fail in Somalia, Officials Charge," *New York Times*, June 8, 2006.

193 **"work with responsible individuals":** Emily Wax and Karen DeYoung, "U.S. Secretly Backing Warlords in Somalia," *Washington Post*, May 17, 2006.

194 **"suitcases filled with dollars":** Salim Lone, "Destabilizing the Horn," *Nation*, January 22, 2007.

194 **"This war is easy":** Author interview, Mohamed Afrah Qanyare, June 2011. All quotations from Mohamed Afrah Qanyare are from the author's interview, unless otherwise noted.

194 **"some of the most violent":** Wax and

DeYoung, "U.S. Secretly Backing Warlords in Somalia."

194 **"clandestine third-country"**: Schiemsky et al., "Report of the Monitoring Group on Somalia," p. 15.

194 **"rallying to the cause"**: US diplomatic cable 06NAIROBI1261, from Leslie Rowe, Deputy Chief of Mission US Embassy Nairobi, "Worst Combat in Five Years Put at USG Doorstep," March 20, 2006, released by WikiLeaks, http://wikileaks.org/cable/2006/03/06NAIROBI1261.html.

194 **"thwarted counterterrorism efforts"**: Mazzetti, "Efforts by C.I.A. Fail in Somalia, Officials Charge."

194 **"join the jihad"**: Mohamed Olad Hassan (AP), "Ethiopian Troops off to Somalia," News24.com, November 11, 2006.

194 **"killing [of] prayer leaders"**: Author interview, Abdirahman "Aynte" Ali, June 2011. Quotations of Aynte come from the author's interview, unless otherwise noted.

195 **"end to the warlords' ruthlessness"**: Author interview, Sheikh Ahmed "Madobe" Mohammed Islam, June 2011.

195 **"promise of order and security"**: International Crisis Group, "Somalia's Islamists," Africa Report No. 100, December 12, 2005.

196 **"We share no objectives"**: Simon Robinson, "Somalia's Islamic Leaders Deny a Link to Terror," *Time*, June 6, 2006.

196 **sometime in 2003**: Abdirahman "Aynte" Ali, "The Anatomy of al Shabaab," unpublished paper, June 2010, www.radiodaljir.com/audio/docs/TheAnatomyOfAlShabaab.pdf.

196 **explosives expert, financing**: Clint Watts, Jacob Shapiro, and Vahid Brown, "Al-Qaida's (Mis)Adventures in the Horn of Africa," Combating Terrorism Center at West Point, July 2, 2007, Appendix B: Cast of Characters from the Horn of Africa, pp. 131–132, www.ctc.usma.edu/posts/al-qaidas-misadventures-in-the-horn-of-africa.

197 **1972 or 1974**: Profile of Fazul Abdullah Mohammed, United Nations Security Council al-Qaida Sanctions List, accessed August 14, 2012, www.un.org/News/Press/docs/2012/sc10755.doc.htm. Fazul reportedly possessed other documents stating that his date of birth was in 1976 and 1971. Fazul removed from the sanctions list on August 12, 2012.

197 **Fazul grew up**: Watts, Shapiro, and Brown, "Al-Qaida's (Mis)Adventures in the Horn of Africa," pp. 89–90.

197 **"got confirmed"**: Ibid., p. 93. The authors cite a letter sent from Fazul to his brother Omar in 1991.

197 **first mission**: United States of America v. Usama bin Laden et al., S(9) 98 Cr. 1023, Indictment, p. 16.

197 **Fazul claimed**: Watts, Shapiro, and Brown, "Al-Qaida's (Mis)Adventures in the Horn of Africa," p. 94.

198 **renting the house**: Ibid., p. 96.

198 **relocated his family**: Ibid., pp. 94–95.

198 **learned it from CNN**: Ibid., p. 95.

198 **resulted in raids**: Ibid.

198 **operate out of Liberia**: Ibid., p. 97.

198 **regularly travel to Somalia**: Ibid., p. 98.

199 **contracted Mohamed Dheere**: Ibid., p. 99; Desmond Butler, "Threats and Responses: Terrorism; Three-Year Hunt Fails to Net Qaeda Suspect in Africa," *New York Times*, June 14, 2003.

199 **Internet café, "Fazul was too smart"**: Sean D. Naylor, "Years of Detective Work Led to al-Qaida Target," *Army Times*, November 21, 2011.

199 **intercepted communications**: Watts, Shapiro, and Brown, "Al-Qaida's (Mis)Adventures in the Horn of Africa," p. 99.

199 **"most wanted fugitives"**: International Crisis Group, "Counterterrorism in Somalia: Losing Hearts and Minds?" Africa Report No. 95, July 11, 2005, p. 9.

200 **"the special group"**: International Crisis Group, "Somalia's Islamists," Africa Report No. 100, December 12, 2005, p. 11.

200 **Italian cemetery**: Ali, "The Anatomy of al Shabaab," p. 28.

200 **"headline-grabbing assassinations"**: Ibid.

201 **video teleconferences**: Naylor, "Years of Detective Work Led to al-Qaida Target."

201 **took control of Mogadishu**: "Islamic Militia Claims Mogadishu," CNN.com, June 5, 2006.

201 **"wonderful piece of news"**: Transcript, "Islamic Militia Takes Control of Somali Capital," *NewsHour*, PBS, June 6, 2006.

202 **"establish a friendly relationship"**: Sheikh Sharif Sheikh Ahmed, letter to governments and international organizations, "The Union of Islamic Courts in Mogadishu Break the Silence," June 6, 2006, www.hiiraan.com/news/2006/jun/somali_news6_7.aspx.

202 **"invite an investigative team"**: US diplomatic cable 06NAIROBI2640, from Ambassador William Bellamy, US Embassy Nairobi, "Islamist Advances, Prospects for Dialogue, but Still No Admission of the Al Qaida Presence," June 15, 2006, released by WikiLeaks, http://wikileaks.org/cable/2006/06/06NAIROBI2640.html. The cable includes the text of a letter sent from Sheikh Sharif on June 14.

202 **"litmus test"**: Ibid.

202 **"moderate"**: See US diplomatic cable 07NAIROBI5403, from Ambassador Michael Ranneberger, US Embassy Nairobi, "Somalia—Sheikh Sharif and the Future Role of Islamic Courts Moderates," January 1, 2007,

released by WikiLeaks, http://wikileaks.org/cable/2007/01/07NAIROBI5403.html.

202 **"contemplate killing Sharif":** Jon Lee Anderson, "The Most Failed State," *New Yorker*, December 14, 2009.

202 **"onto everybody's radar screen":** Author interview, Daveed Gartenstein-Ross, March 2011. All quotations of Gartenstein-Ross are from the author's interview.

202 **"There is instability in Somalia":** Transcript, "President's Remarks to the Travel Pool at Laredo Border Patrol Sector Headquarters," June 6, 2006.

203 **insane maze of roadblocks:** Mohammed Olad Hassan, "Life Under Somalia's Islamists," BBC.news.co.uk, July 11, 2006.

203 **ports and the airport:** "Mogadishu's Port Reopened," AlJazeera.com, August 23, 2006.

203 **felt safer:** Xan Rice, "Mogadishu's Miracle: Peace in the World's Most Lawless City," *Guardian*, June 25, 2006.

203 **US officials acknowledged:** US diplomatic cable 06NAIROBI3441, from Economic Counselor John F. Hoover, US Embassy Nairobi, "Horn of Africa, State-US-AID Humanitarian Cable Update Number 8," August 8, 2006, released by WikiLeaks, http://wikileaks.org/cable/2006/08/06NAIROBI3441.html.

203 **"some semblance of order":** Author interview, Ismail Mahmoud Hurre, June 2011.

203 **"rally with Ethiopia":** Memorandum from "Ennifar" (likely Azouz Ennifar, Deputy Special Representative for UN mission in Ethiopia and Eritrea), "Meeting with US Assistant Secretary of State for African Affairs," June 26, 2006, released by WikiLeaks, http://wikileaks.org/wiki/US_encouraged_Ethiopian_invasion_of_Somalia:_UN_meeting_memo_with_Jenday_Frazer,_Secretary_of_State_for_African_Affairs,_2006.

204 **training its notorious Agazi:** Michael R. Gordon and Mark Mazzetti, "U.S. Ethiopian Campaign Routed Islamic Militants in Somalia," *International Herald Tribune*, February 23, 2007.

204 **began setting up shop:** Thomas P. M. Barnett, "The Americans Have Landed," *Esquire*, June 27, 2007, www.esquire.com/features/africacommando707.

204 **Task Force 88:** Michael R. Gordon and Mark Mazzetti, "U.S. Used Base in Ethiopia to Hunt al Qaeda," *New York Times*, February 23, 2007.

204 **ratchet up its rhetoric:** See Stephanie McCrummen, "Interview with Meles Zenawi," WashingtonPost.com, December 14, 2006.

204 **went on national radio:** Author interview, Mohamed Afrah Qanyare, June 2011.

204 **"reconnaissance missions":** US Diplomatic cable 06ADDISABABA1904 from Vicki Huddleston, Chargé d'Affaires, US Embassy Addis Ababa, "Corrected Copy—Ethiopia: GOE Says No Incursion in Somalia," July 12, 2006, released by WikiLeaks, http://wikileaks.org/cable/2006/07/06ADDISABABA1904.html.

205 **"Shabab was a sideline organization":** Author interview, Malcolm Nance, May 2011. Quotations of Malcolm Nance come from the author's interview.

205 **"We warn all the nations":** Osama bin Laden, transcript of audio recording, July 2, 2006, translation from The Middle East Media Research Institute (MEMRI), accessed December 2010, www.memri.org/report/en/print1872.htm.

206 **privately warned their superiors:** US diplomatic cable 06NAIROBI2618, from Ambassador William Bellamy, US Embassy Nairobi, "Jowhar Falls," June 14, 2006, released by WikiLeaks, http://wikileaks.org/cable/2006/06/06NAIROBI2618.html. "The UN has reports that an Ethiopian brigade positioned along the Somali border has been reinforced with armor and helicopters, sparking fears about an Ethiopian incursion to Somalia. Such a move could lead to greatly expanded conflict and could ultimately cause the TFIs to fail. In this light, we advise a high-level call to Ethiopia to dissuade movement of troops into Somalia...squadron of armor and MI-24 Hind B helicopters."

206 **"Jihad in Allah's way":** Sheikh Sharif Sheikh Ahmed, "Islamists Declare Jihad (Holy War) on Neighboring Ethiopia Following the Fall of Key Town to Ethiopian-back[ed] Somali Government Forces," October 10, 2006, video and transcription from Reuters.

206 **"executive order" written in Arabic:** US diplomatic cable 06ADDISABABA3212, from Ambassador Donald Yamamoto, US Embassy Addis Ababa, "Somali Prime Minister Gedi Highlights Foreign Extremist Support for ICU," December 6, 2006, released by WikiLeaks, http://wikileaks.org/cable/2006/12/06ADDISABABA3212.html.

207 **John Abizaid:** US diplomatic cable 06ADDISABABA3240, from Ambassador Donald Yamamoto, US Embassy Addis Ababa, "Ethiopia: Meles Alters Stance on Military Action," December 8, 2006, released by WikiLeaks, http://wikileaks.org/cable/2006/12/06ADDISABABA3240.html; Xan Rice and Suzanne Goldenberg, "How US Forged an Alliance with Ethiopia over Invasion," *Guardian*, January 12, 2007.

207 **"chance of a lifetime":** Alex Perry, "Somalia on the Edge," *Time*, November 29, 2007.

207 **"They are terrorists"**: David Gollust, "US Says al-Qaida Elements Running Somali Islamic Movement," Voice of America, December 14, 2006.

207 **"Growing Al-Qaeda Menace"**: Julie Hollar, "Rediscovering Somalia; Press Downplays U.S. Role in Renewed Crisis," Fairness and Accuracy in Reporting, March 1, 2008, http://fair.org/extra-online-articles/rediscovering-somalia/.

207 **"a safe haven"**: Ibid.

207 **"here in East Africa"**: Transcript, *Newsroom*, CNN, January 6, 2007.

207 **"hard and fast views"**: Karen DeYoung, "U.S. Sees Growing Threats in Somalia," *Washington Post*, December 18, 2006.

207 **"idiotic"**: Ibid.

207 **"making a bad bet"**: Ibid.

208 **across the Somali border:** Jeffrey Gettleman, "Ethiopian Warplanes Attack Somalia," *New York Times*, December 24, 2006.

208 **40,000–50,000 troops:** David Axe, "Wikileaked Cable Confirms U.S.' Secret Somalia Op," Danger Room (blog), Wired.com, December 2, 2010, www.wired.com/dangerroom/2010/12/wikileaked-cable-confirms-u-s-secret-somalia-op/; Scott Baldauf, "In Somalia, Foreign Intervention Won't Resolve Al Shabab Threat," *Christian Science Monitor*, September 2, 2010. Axe reports that "some 50,000 Ethiopian troops" participated in the invasion; the *Christian Science Monitor* reports 40,000.

208 **"attack Addis Ababa"**: Xan Rice, "Somali Hardliner Calls for Foreign Jihadists," *Guardian*, December 23, 2006.

208 **"The warlord era"**: Stephanie McCrummen, "Somali Islamic Fighters Flee Toward Kenya," *Washington Post*, January 2, 2007.

208 **demonstrations broke out:** Reuters, "Anti-Ethiopian Protests Rock Mogadishu," *Toronto Star*, January 6, 2007.

**20: Prison Break**

210 **escaped, maximum security prison:** Mark Trevelyan (Reuters), "Jailbreak in Yemen Stirs Concern Abroad; Inside Job Seen in Qaeda Escape," *Boston Globe*, February 10, 2006.

210 **later boasted:** Wuhayshi later recounted the escape in an article for an Arabic-language publication, which was later translated by Gregory D. Johnsen. See Nasir al-Wuhayshi, "The New Leader of al-Qaeda in Yemen Relates the Details of the Escape of al-Qaeda Members from an Intelligence Prison," *al-Ghad*, June 25, 2007.

210 **"serious problem"**: Barbara Starr, "Yemen Prison Break Raises Alarms at Sea," CNN.com, February 7, 2006.

210 **"Saleh knows how to play the game"**: Author interview, former US counterterrorism official, January 2011. All statements and quotations attributed to the former US counterterrorism official are from the author's interview.

210 **"They play it for survival"**: Author interview, Dr. Emile Nakhleh, January 2010.

211 **"an inside job"**: Sam Kimball, "Whose Side Is Yemen On?" *Foreign Policy*, August 29, 2012.

211 **"would seem impossible"**: Ibid.

212 **major expansion of Camp Lemonnier:** Joseph Giordono, "U.S. Military Plans to Expand Camp Lemonier in Djibouti; Lease to Provide for More Housing and Security," *Stars and Stripes*, July 9, 2006.

212 **"Some teams use the base"**: Ibid.

212 **President Bush's top aide:** US diplomatic cable 07SANAA1989, from Ambassador Stephen Seche, US Embassy Sana'a, "Townsend-Saleh Meeting Provides Opening for Additional CT Cooperation," October 30, 2007, released by WikiLeaks, http://wikileaks.org/cable/2007/10/07SANAA1989.html. Details of Saleh's meeting with Townsend come from this cable.

212 **"Despite the Somalia UN arms embargo"**: "Security Council Committee on Somalia and Eritrea Issues List of Individuals Identified Pursuant to Paragraph 8 of Resolution 1844 (2008)," Department of Public Information, UN Security Council, April 12, 2010, www.un.org/News/Press/docs/2010/sc9904.doc.htm.

213 **"way over their heads"**: Author interview, former US military official, February 2012.

213 **"put a great deal of pressure"**: *Yemen: Confronting al-Qaeda, Preventing State Failure, Hearing Before the Senate Foreign Relations Committee*, 111th Cong. 53 (2010) (prepared testimony of Gregory D. Johnsen).

213 **hardened jihadist:** Gregory D. Johnsen, *The Last Refuge: Yemen, Al-Qaeda, and America's War in Arabia* (New York: W. W. Norton, 2012), p. 163.

214 **"become more strident"**: Gregory D. Johnsen, "Al-Qaeda in Yemen Reorganizes Under Nasir al-Wahayshi," *Terrorism Focus* 5 (11) (March 18, 2008), www.jamestown.org/single/?no_cache=1&tx_ttnews%5Btt_news%5D=4796.

**21: Hot Pursuit**

215 **first basement-level recruit:** "Robert M. Gates; Secretary of Defense," accessed September 10, 2012, http://georgewbush-whitehouse.archives.gov/government/gates-bio.html.

215 **"was close to many figures"**: Lawrence

E. Walsh, "Final Report of the Independent Counsel for Iran/Contra Matters; Volume I: Investigations and Prosecutions," August 4, 1993, p. 223.

215 **US-fueled war in Afghanistan:** Yaroslav Trofimov, "Soviets' Afghan Ordeal Vexed Gates on Troop-Surge," *Wall Street Journal*, November 30, 2009.

216 **"direct action authorities":** Committee on Armed Services, Afghanistan, S. Hrg. 110-269 (2007) (testimony of Lieutenant General Douglas E. Lute).

216 **"pushing hard":** Sean D. Naylor, "Spec Ops Raids into Pakistan Halted," *Army Times*, September 26, 2008.

216 **"Pakistanis looked the other way":** Author interview, Lieutenant Colonel Anthony Shaffer, May 2011.

216 **grown by 60 percent:** Ann Scott Tyson, "New Plans Foresee Fighting Terrorism Beyond War Zones," *Washington Post*, April 23, 2006.

217 **"bitter disagreements":** Mark Mazzetti and David Rohde, "Amid U.S. Policy Disputes, Qaeda Grows in Pakistan," *New York Times*, June 30, 2008.

217 **"unprovoked and cowardly":** Kamran Haider, "Pakistan Condemns 'Cowardly' US Attack; Eleven Dead," Reuters, June 11, 2008.

217 **approved a secret order:** Eric Schmitt and Mark Mazzetti, "Bush Said to Give Orders Allowing Raids in Pakistan," *New York Times*, September 10, 2008.

217 **"Bill rapidly expanded operations":** Author interview, Special Operations source, August 2010.

218 **Angoor Adda:** Christina Lamb, "Playing with Firepower," *Sunday Times* (London), September 14, 2008.

218 **"two dozen suspected Qaeda fighters":** Schmitt and Mazzetti, "Bush Said to Give Orders Allowing Raids in Pakistan."

218 **according to local villagers:** Lamb, "Playing with Firepower."

218 **"gross violation of Pakistan's territory":** US diplomatic cable 08ISLAMABAD2907, from Ambassador Anne Patterson, US Embassy Islamabad, "GOP Condemns Alleged ISAF September 3 Incident in South Waziristan," September 3, 2008, released by WikiLeaks, http://wikileaks.org/cable/2008/09/08ISLAMABAD2907.html.

## 22: "Every Step Taken by the US Benefited al Shabab"

219 **near Dire Dawa:** Eric Schmitt and Mark Mazzetti, "Secret Order Lets U.S. Raid Al Qaeda," *New York Times*, November 9, 2008.

219 **"It's kinetic":** Author interview, Malcolm Nance, May 2011.

219 **unarmed US Predator drone:** David Axe, "Hidden History: America's Secret Drone War in Africa," Danger Room (blog), Wired.com, August 13, 2012, www.wired.com/dangerroom/2012/08/somalia-drones/all/.

219 **strafed the convoy:** Jeffrey Gettleman, "More Than Fifty Die in U.S. Strikes in Somalia," *New York Times*, January 9, 2007.

219 **Reports suggested:** Michael R. Gordon and Mark Mazzetti, "U.S. Used Base in Ethiopia to Hunt Al Qaeda," *New York Times*, February 23, 2007.

219 **"al Qaeda leader":** Gettleman, "More Than Fifty Die in U.S. Strikes in Somalia."

219 **bloodied passport:** Gordon and Mazzetti, "U.S. Used Base in Ethiopia to Hunt Al Qaeda."

220 **"near the Kenyan border":** US diplomatic cable 07ADDISABABA90, from Ambassador Donald Yamamoto, US Embassy Addis Ababa, "Scenesetter for Deputy USTR Allgeier's Visit to Ethiopia," January 12, 2007, released by WikiLeaks, http://wikileaks.org/cable/2007/01/07ADDISABABA90.html.

220 **took credit:** "US Somali Air Strikes 'Kill Many,'" BBC.co.uk, January 9, 2007.

220 **"Qaeda Clobbered":** Andy Soltis, "Qaeda Clobbered; U.S. Somalia Raid Kills Embassy Fiend," *New York Post*, January 11, 2007.

220 **randomly killed:** Alex Perry, "Somalia on the Edge," *Time*, November 29, 2007.

220 **"no combatants amongst them":** Aaron Glantz, "U.S. Air Strikes in Somalia Condemned for Killing Innocent Civilians," *OneWorld US*, January 20, 2007.

220 **"paying the price":** Anne Penketh and Steve Bloomfield, "US Strikes on al-Qa'ida Chiefs Kill Nomads," *Independent* (London), January 13, 2007.

221 **US-designated terrorist:** "Individuals and Entities Designated by the State Department Under E.O. 13224," Bureau of Counterterrorism, US Department of State, December 17, 2012, www.state.gov/j/ct/rls/other/des/143210.htm.

221 **"helped the Americans easily trace us":** Author interview, Sheikh Ahmed "Madobe" Mohammed Islam, June 2011. All quotations of Madobe are from the author's interview.

222 **"The Ambassador told Sharif":** US diplomatic cable 07NAIROBI5403, from Ambassador Michael Ranneberger, US Embassy Nairobi, "Sheikh Sharif and the Future Role of the Islamic Courts Moderates," January 2, 2007, released by WikiLeaks, http://wikileaks.org/cable/2007/01/07NAIROBI5403.html.

222 **"preferable to co-opt":** US diplomatic

cable 07ADDISABABA311, from Ambassador Donald Yamamoto, US Embassy Addis Ababa, "PM Meles Highlights Land Reform as Key to Clan Reconciliation and Political Stability in Somalia," February 1, 2007, released by WikiLeaks, http://wikileaks.org/cable/2007/02/07ADDISABABA311.html.

222 **escaped from Somalia to Kenya:** Jeffrey Gettleman, "Somali Islamists' No. Two Leader Surrenders in Kenyan Capital," *New York Times*, January 23, 2007.

222 **"working with the CIA":** Author interview, Ali Mohamed Gedi, June 2011.

222 **In Yemen:** "Somali Islamist Travels to Yemen," BBC.co.uk, February 8, 2007.

222 **"at least 150":** Human Rights Watch, "Why Am I Still Here? The 2007 Horn of Africa Renditions and the Fate of Those Still Missing" (2008). All information about renditions attributed to Human Rights Watch comes from this report.

223 **sent to Guantánamo:** Human Rights Watch, "Why Am I Still Here?" p. 4. Kenyan national Mohammed Abulmalik was arrested in Mombasa in February 2007 and ultimately ended up in the prison in Guantánamo Bay.

223 **left his family:** Clint Watts, Jacob Shapiro, and Vahid Brown, "Al-Qaida's (Mis) Adventures in the Horn of Africa," Combating Terrorism Center at West Point, July 2, 2007, Appendix B: Cast of Characters from the Horn of Africa, p. 99.

223 **"as the lions eat their prey":** Lydia Khalil, "Foreign Fighters Face Obstacles Joining the Somali Jihad," *Terrorism Focus* 4 (24) (July 25, 2007), www.jamestown.org/single/?-no_cache=1&tx_ttnews[tt_news]=4326.

224 **"help of all these foreign fighters":** Author interview, Yusuf Mohamed Siad, June 2011. Quotations of Indha Adde come from the author's interview unless otherwise noted.

224 **went underground:** Garowe Online, "Islamists Do Not Recognize 'Colonial Government,' Says War Chief," Biyokulule.com, December 10, 2007; "US Warns Eritrea over 'Terrorism'; Asmara Told to Stop Supporting Somalia Fighters to Avoid 'Terrorism Sponsor' Label," AlJazeera.com, September 9, 2007.

224 **receiving support:** Matt Bryden, Gilbert Charles Barthe, Charles Lengalenga, and Ignatius Yaw Kwantwi-Mensah, "Report of the Monitoring Group on Somalia Pursuant to Security Council Resolution 1811 (2008)," UN Security Council, December 10, 2008, p. 25.

224 **snipers, disproportionate fire:** Human Rights Watch, "Shell-Shocked: Civilians Under Siege in Mogadishu," August 13, 2007, www.hrw.org/reports/2007/08/12/shell-shocked.

224 **"like goats":** Amnesty International, "Routinely Targeted: Attacks on Civilians in Somalia," May 6, 2008, www.amnesty.org/en/library/info/AFR52/006/2008.

224 **large proportion of those:** Ibid.

224 **Some 6,000 civilians:** Ibid. The report cites estimates from Somalia-based Elman Human Rights Organization, and the UN, respectively.

224 **335,000 Somali refugees:** "Somalia—Complex Emergency, Situation Report No. 1, Fiscal Year 2008," USAID, December 20, 2007, http://transition.usaid.gov/our_work/humanitarian_assistance/disaster_assistance/countries/somalia/template/fs_sr/somalia_ce_sr01_12-20-2007.pdf.

224 **"major problem":** Author interview, Daveed Gartenstein-Ross, March 2011. All quotations from Gartenstein-Ross come from the author's interview, unless otherwise noted.

225 **"break that they were looking for":** Author interview, Abdirahman, "Aynte" Ali, June 2011. All quotations from Aynte come from the author's interview, unless otherwise noted.

225 **four-day battle:** Salad Duhul (AP), "Somali Fighting Kills 381; Government Warns of New Offensive," *Deseret News*, April 2, 2007.

225 **dragged Ethiopian soldiers:** "Crowd Drags Ethiopian Corpse, Echoing 1993 Brutality," CNN.com, November 8, 2007.

225 **Toyota Land Cruiser:** "Somali Prime Minister Survives Bomb Attack," CNN.com, June 3, 2007.

225 **"tremendous success":** "Interview: Ethiopian Prime Minister Meles Zenawi," by Alex Perry, *Time*, September 6, 2007, www.time.com/time/magazine/article/0,9171,1659420,00.html.

226 **officially designated:** "Designation of al-Shabaab as a Foreign Terrorist Organization," Office of the Coordinator for Counterterrorism, US Department of State, February 26, 2008, www.state.gov/j/ct/rls/other/des/102446.htm.

226 **missile strikes:** Agence France-Presse, "US Missile Strike Targets 'Al-Qaeda Leader' in Somalia," March 3, 2008; Jeffrey Gettleman and Eric Schmitt, "U.S. Forces Fire Missiles into Somalia at a Kenyan," *New York Times*, March 4, 2008.

226 **five Tomahawk cruise missiles:** Stephanie McCrummen and Karen DeYoung, "U.S. Airstrike Kills Somali Accused of Links to Al-Qaeda," *Washington Post*, May 2, 2008.

226 **weeks of surveillance:** Eric Schmitt and Jeffrey Gettleman, "Qaeda Leader Reported Killed in Somalia," *New York Times*, May 2, 2008.

226 **bodies of sixteen people:** McCrummen and DeYoung, "U.S. Airstrike Kills Somali Accused of Links to Al-Qaeda."

226 **bio of their slain leader:** Daveed Gartenstein-Ross, "The Strategic Challenge of Somalia's Al-Shabaab," *Middle East Quarterly* (fall 2009), www.meforum.org/2486/somalia-al-shabaab-strategic-challenge#_ftn22.

226 **"short-term disruption":** US diplomatic cable 08NAIROBI1363, from Ambassador Michael Ranneberger, US Embassy Nairobi, "Somalia—Ayrow's Demise," June 3, 2008, released by WikiLeaks, http://wikileaks.org/cable/2008/06/08NAIROBI1363.html.

226 **agreement signed in Djibouti:** United Nations Security Council Department of Public Information, "Security Council, in Presidential Statement, Welcomes Signing of Djibouti Agreement on Reconciliation by Parties to Somalia Conflict," UN Security Council press release, September 4, 2008.

227 **refused to discuss:** Author interview, President Sheikh Sharif Sheikh Ahmed, June 2011.

227 **"favorite puppet":** Abdirahman "Aynte" Ali, "The Anatomy of al Shabaab," unpublished paper, June 2010, www.radiodaljir.com/audio/docs/TheAnatomyOfAlShabaab.pdf.

227 **indigenous diversity:** Ibid., p. 28.

227 **sense of empowerment:** Ibid., p. 20.

228 **diplomatic "visits":** International Crisis Group, "Somalia: To Move Beyond the Failed State," Africa Report No. 147, December 23, 2008, p. 12.

228 **lengthy negotiations:** Ibid., pp. 12–13.

228 **dismantling of roadblocks:** Mark Bradbury, "State-Building, Counterterrorism, and Licensing Humanitarianism in Somalia," briefing paper, Feinstein International Center, October 2010.

228 **"a caricature":** International Crisis Group, "Somalia: To Move Beyond the Failed State," p. 14.

228 **reminiscent of the Taliban:** Ibid.

228 **"the only organization":** Committee on Foreign Relations, *Al Qaeda in Yemen and Somalia: A Ticking Time Bomb*, S. Prt. 111-40, p. 16 (2010).

228 **"far more popular":** Ali, "The Anatomy of al Shabaab," p. 37.

229 **"Fight on, Champions":** Khaled Wassef (CNET), "Bin Laden Urges Somalis to 'Fight On,'" CBS.com, March 19, 2009.

## 23: "If Your Son Does Not Come to Us, He Will Be Killed by the Americans"

230 **discovered a US spy drone:** US diplomatic cable 07SANAA473, from Chargé d'Affaires Nabeel Khoury, US Embassy Sana'a, "Unmanned USG Aircraft Washes Ashore, Official Media Reports Downed Iranian 'Spy Plane,'" April 2, 2007, released by WikiLeaks, http://wikileaks.org/cable/2007/04/07SANAA473.html. Descriptions of the drone incident are based on this cable.

230 **floating prison:** David Campbell and Richard Norton-Taylor, "US Accused of Holding Terror Suspects on Prison Ships," *Guardian*, June 1, 2008.

230 **against oil and gas facilities:** Hassan M. Fattah, "Suicide Attacks Foiled at Two Oil Sites, Yemen Says," *New York Times*, September 16, 2006.

230 **chief criminal investigator:** Gregory D. Johnsen, "Is Al-Qaeda in Yemen Regrouping?" *Terrorism Focus* 4 (15) (May 30, 2007), www.jamestown.org/single/?no_cache=1&tx_ttnews%5Btt_news%5D=4174.

230 **audiotaped message:** *Yemen: Confronting al-Qaeda, Preventing State Failure, Hearing Before the Senate Foreign Relations Committee*, 111th Cong. 53 (2010) (prepared testimony of Gregory D. Johnsen).

231 **convoy of Spanish tourists:** Ahmed al-Hajj (AP), "Suicide Attacker Kills Nine at Yemen Temple," *Washington Post*, July 2, 2007. According to Johnsen in his Senate testimony, the death toll was ultimately higher than originally reported.

231 **went home to his family:** Author interviews, family members, January 2012.

231 **"I would like to travel":** "Moazzam Begg Interviews Imam Anwar al-Awlaki," Cageprisoners, December 31, 2007, www.cageprisoners.com/our-work/interviews/item/159-moazzam-begg-interviews-imam-anwar-al-awlaki.

231 **"truth of the matter":** Anwar al Awlaki, "The Lies of the Telegraph," Imam Anwar's Blog, anwar-alawlaki.com, December 27, 2008.

231 **"a few opportunities":** "Moazzam Begg Interviews Imam Anwar al-Awlaki," Cageprisoners, December 31, 2007.

231 **"In the old times":** Anwar al Awlaki, "Assalamu alaykum all," Imam Anwar's Blog, anwar-alawlaki.com, May 31, 2008.

232 **"Do You Like Cheese?":** Anwar al Awlaki, "Do You Like Cheese?" Imam Anwar's Blog, anwar-alawlaki.com, November 25, 2008.

232 **"If you are a person":** Anwar al Awlaki, "Is the Franklin Morphing into the Washington?!" Imam Anwar's Blog, anwar-alawlaki.com, October 6, 2008.

232 **"do not try to infiltrate":** Anwar al Awlaki, "A Question About the Method of Establishing Khilafa," Imam Anwar's Blog, anwar-alawlaki.com, August 29, 2008.

233 **"an interesting assortment of sins":**

Awlaki, "Is the Franklin Morphing into the Washington?!"

233 **"There is good reason to believe":** Susan Schmidt, "Imam from Va. Mosque Now Thought to Have Aided al-Qaeda," *Washington Post*, February 27, 2008.

233 **believed to have been recorded:** Alexander Meleagrou-Hitchens, "As American as Apple Pie: How Anwar al-Awlaki Became the Face of Western Jihad," The International Centre for the Study of Radicalisation and Political Violence, 2011, p. 55.

233 **first operational leader:** International Crisis Group, "Saudi Arabia Backgrounder: Who Are the Islamists?" Middle East Report No. 31, September 21, 2004, p. 13.

234 **"Whenever you see the word terrorist":** Anwar al Awlaki, "Constants on the Path of Jihad," 2005.

234 **"al Awlaki crosses this bridge":** Author interview, Dr. Emile Nakhleh, January 2010. All quotations of Nakhleh come from the author's interview.

234 **"The Americans were very, very angry":** Author interview, Sheikh Saleh bin Fareed, January 2012. All quotations of bin Fareed come from the author's interview.

234 **"He was harassed":** Author interview, Nasser al Awlaki, January 2012. All information and statements attributed to Awlaki come from this interview, unless otherwise noted.

235 **"surveillance and harassment":** Shaykh Harith al Nadari, "My Story with al-Awlaki," *Inspire* 9 (winter 2012), released May 2012.

235 **go to Ataq:** Author interviews with family members, January 2012.

235 **"you put me in jail":** Author interview, Sheikh Saleh bin Fareed, January 2012.

235 **the family's small village:** Author interviews, Awlaki family members, August 2012.

235 **telling friends and family:** Ibid.

235 **kamikaze attack:** Shane Bauer, "U.S. Embassy Hit in Yemen, Raising Militancy Concerns," *Christian Science Monitor*, September 18, 2008.

236 **"This attack is a reminder":** Agence France-Presse, "Bush Says Yemen Attack Shows Need to Fight Extremists," September 17, 2008.

236 **met in Qatar:** *Nominations Before the Senate Armed Services Committee: Hearings on the Nominations of Gen. David D. McKeirnan; LTG. Raymond T. Odierno; LTG Walter L. Sharp; Gen. David H. Petraeus; Hon. Nelson M. Ford; Joseph A. Benkert; Sean J. Stackley; Frederick S. Celec; Michael B. Doley; Gen. Norton A. Schwartz; and Gen. Duncan J. McNabb, Day 3, Before the Armed Services Committee*, 110th Congress, 145 (2008) (testimony of Gen. David H. Petraeus).

236 **"It just reminds us":** Athena Jones, "Obama Discusses Yemen Attack," National-Journal.com, September 17, 2008.

236 **"seems to have stabilized":** Michael Sheuer, "Yemen's Role in al-Qaeda's Strategy," *Terrorism Focus* 5 (5) (February 7, 2008), www.jamestown.org/programs/gta/single/?tx_ttnews%5Btt_news%5D=4708&tx_ttnews%5BbackPid%5D=246&no_cache=1.

236 **"US money starts flowing":** Author interview, former senior counterterrorism official, January 2011.

237 **"targeting and then killing people":** Author interview, former JSOC aide, 2010.

237 **"There was no such thing":** Associated Press, "McCain, Obama Spar over Al Qaeda in Iraq," CBSNews.com, June 18, 2009.

237 **"the least of the two evils":** Anwar al Awlaki. "Voting for the American President," Imam Anwar's Blog, anwar-alawlaki.com, October 31, 2008.

238 **"very little difference":** Anwar al Awlaki, "Part 2: Voting for the American President," Imam Anwar's Blog, anwar-awlaki.com, November 3, 2008.

238 **"an al-Qaeda supporter":** Gordon Rayner, "Muslim Groups 'Linked to September 11 Hijackers Spark Fury over Conference,'" *Telegraph*, December 27, 2008.

238 **"This is a baseless claim":** Anwar al Awlaki, "The Lies of the Telegraph," Imam Anwar's Blog, anwar-alawlaki.com, December 27, 2008.

238 **plot to attack Fort Dix:** Evan Kohlmann, "Investigating Ft. Hood: Anwar al-Awlaki's 'Constants on the Path of Jihad,'" Counterterrorism Blog, November 9, 2009, http://counterterrorismblog.org/2009/11/investigating_ft_hood_anwar_al.php.

238 **traveled to Somalia:** Andrea Elliott, "A Call to Jihad, Answered in America," *New York Times*, July 11, 2009.

239 **"fills our hearts":** Anwar al Awlaki, "Salutations to the al-Shabab of Somalia," Imam Anwar's Blog, anwar-alawlaki.com, December 21, 2008.

239 **"beloved Sheikh Anwar":** "Al-Shabaab: Reply to the Greeting and Advice of Sheikh Anwar," Imam Anwar's Blog, anwar-alawlaki.com, December 27, 2008.

239 **"The illegal state of Israel":** Anwar al Awlaki, "The Meaning of Gaza," Imam Anwar's Blog, anwar-alawlaki.com, December 28, 2008.

240 **"There are many soldiers":** Nidal Hasan, e-mail to Anwar Awlaki, December 17, 2008, published by Intelwire on July 19, 2012, http://news.intelwire.com/2012/07/the-following-e-mails-between-maj.html.

240 **"condenses the Al Qaeda philosophy":** Scott Shane, "Born in U.S., a Radical Cleric Inspires Terror," *New York Times*, November 18, 2009.

240 **did not speak Arabic:** Wesley Yang, "The Terrorist Search Engine," *New York*, December 5, 2010.

241 **"little surprise":** Kohlmann, "Investigating Ft. Hood."

241 **"he preaches in English":** Author interview, Joshua Foust, January 2011.

241 **"call from the pulpits":** Anwar al Awlaki, "Yemeni-American Jihadi Cleric Anwar Al-Awlaki in First Interview with al-Qaeda Media calls on Muslim US Servicemen to Kill Fellow Soldiers," transcription of interview with Al-Malahem Media, May 23, 2010, by the Middle East Media Research Institute (MEMRI), www.memritv.org/clip_transcript/en/2480.htm.

242 **"The US has come to the conclusion":** Anwar al Awlaki, "A New Year: Reality and Aspirations," Imam Anwar's Blog, anwar-alawlaki.com, December 31, 2008.

242 **"Jihad will carry on":** Ibid.

## 24: "Obama Is Set to Continue the Course Set by Bush"

244 **"I am opposed to":** Barack Obama, "Transcript: Obama's Speech Against the Iraq War," October 2, 2002, transcript available via NPR.org, www.npr.org/templates/story/story.php?storyId=99591469.

244 **"Let's be the generation":** Barack Obama, "Illinois Sen. Barack Obama's Announcement Speech," February 10, 2007, transcript available via Associated Press, www.washingtonpost.com/wp-dyn/content/article/2007/02/10/AR2007021000879.html.

244 **"harshest interrogation techniques":** Scott Shane, David Johnston, and James Risen, "Secret U.S. Endorsement of Severe Interrogations," *New York Times*, October 4, 2007.

245 **"This is an example":** Transcript, "Barack Obama on MSNBC," October 4, 2007, transcript available via NYTimes.com, www.nytimes.com/2007/10/04/us/politics/04obama-text.html?pagewanted=all.

245 **"governed by fear":** "Oct. 30 Democratic Debate Transcript," October 30, 2007, transcript available via MSNBC.com, www.msnbc.msn.com/id/21528787/ns/politics-the_debates/t/oct-democratic-debate-transcript/#.UPeUQhzKZcR.

245 **"a terrible mistake":** Associated Press, "Obama Says He Might Send Troops to Pakistan," NBCNews.com, August 1, 2007.

245 **"You don't broadcast":** Andy Merten, "Presidential Candidates Debate Pakistan; McCain, Clinton Criticize Obama for Threatening to Order Attacks," NBCNews.com, February 28, 2008.

245 **"the right strategy":** "Feb. 26 Democratic Debate Transcript," February 26, 2007, transcript available via MSNBC.com, www.msnbc.msn.com/id/23354734/ns/

politics-the_debates/t/feb-democratic-debate-transcript/#.UPeVjBzKZcR.

245 **"John McCain likes to say":** Obama Blasts McCain, Lays Out His Own Agenda," CNN.com, August 28, 2008.

246 **"reassuring":** Karl Rove, "Thanksgiving Cheer from Obama; He's Assembled a First-Rate Economic Team," *Wall Street Journal*, November 28, 2008.

246 **"I am gobsmacked":** Max Boot, "Obama's Picks," *Commentary*, posted November 11, 2008, www.commentarymagazine.com/2008/11/25/obamas-picks/.

246 **"continue the course":** Michael Goldfarb, "Obama the Realist," Weekly Standard (blog), November 26, 2008, www.weeklystandard.com/weblogs/TWSFP/2008/11/obama_the_realist_1.asp.

247 **"we need to look forward":** Transcript, *This Week with George Stephanopoulos*, ABC, January 11, 2009.

247 **"take down a lot of those policies":** Transcript, *Face the Nation*, CBS, May 10, 2009.

## 25: Obama's Signature Strikes

248 **"message we are sending":** Jake Tapper, Jan Crawford-Greenburg, and Huma Khan, "Obama Order to Shut Gitmo, CIA Detention Centers," ABCNews.go.com, January 22, 2009.

248 **Hayden briefed him:** Daniel Klaidman, *Kill or Capture: The War on Terror and the Soul of the Obama Presidency* (New York: Houghton Mifflin Harcourt, 2012), p. 39.

248 **The first strike:** Reprieve, "Complaint Against the United States of America for the Killing of Innocent Citizens of the Islamic Republic of Pakistan to the UN Human Rights Council," February 23, 2012, http://reprieve.org.uk/media/downloads/2012_02_22_PUB_drones_UN_HRC_complaint.pdf?utm_source=Press+mailing+list&utm_campaign=89f3db0a75-2012_02_23_drones_UN_complaint&utm_medium=email. The complaint was filed on behalf of the victims of different strikes, including Ejaz Ahmad, whose relatives were among those killed and injured by the strike in question.

248 **The second struck:** Klaidman, *Kill or Capture*, p. 39.

248 **"five al Qaeda militants," "Good":** Bob Woodward, *Obama's Wars* (New York: Simon and Schuster, 2010), p. 93.

248 **straight to the president:** Klaidman, *Kill or Capture*, p. 40.

248 **between seven and fifteen:** "Obama 2009 Pakistan Strikes," *Bureau of Investigative Journalism*, August 10, 2011, www.thebureauinvestigates.com/2011/08/10/obama-2009-strikes/.

249 **One boy, loss of an eye:** Reprieve,

"Complaint Against the United States of America."

249 **"wrong house":** "Obama 2009 Pakistan Strikes."

249 **"pro-government peace committee":** Klaidman, *Kill or Capture*, p. 40.

249 **first the new president had heard:** Ibid., pp. 40–41.

249 **added a constraint:** Ibid., p. 42.

249 **But he didn't:** Obama has reportedly made other small changes to the signature strike protocol, such as bringing the State Department, namely, the ambassador in Islamabad, into the process. Adam Entous, Siobhan Gorman, and Julian E. Barnes, "U.S. Tightens Drone Rules," *Wall Street Journal*, November 4, 2011.

249 **"crash course":** Klaidman, *Kill or Capture*, p. 120.

249 **"tutorial":** Eric Schmitt and Thom Shanker, *Counterstrike: The Untold Story of America's Secret Campaign Against al Qaeda* (New York: Times Books, 2011), p. 232.

250 **most of the ExOrds:** Ibid., p. 245.

250 **"reached a tacit agreement":** R. Jeffrey Smith, Candace Rondeaux, and Joby Warrick, "Two U.S. Airstrikes Offer a Concrete Sign of Obama's Pakistan Policy," *Washington Post*, January 24, 2009.

250 **"fully endorsed":** Woodward, *Obama's Wars*, p. 93.

250 **"all the key personnel":** Jane Mayer, "The Predator War: What Are the Risks of the C.I.A.'s Covert Drone Program?" *New Yorker*, October 26, 2009.

250 **"the real [secret]":** Woodward, *Obama's Wars*, p. 6.

250 **"number one goal":** Peter Bergen, *Manhunt: The Ten-Year Search for Bin Laden—from 9/11 to Abbottabad* (New York: Crown, 2012), p. 116.

250 **"detailed operation plan":** Jake Tapper, "Chapter Six: The President Takes Aim," in Terry Moran, Martha Raddatz, Nick Schifrin, Brian Ross, and Jake Tapper, *Target: Bin Laden—the Death and Life of Public Enemy Number One*, ABCNews.go.com, June 9, 2011.

250 **Scores of civilians:** "Obama 2009 Pakistan Strikes."

250 **"After the prayers":** Agence France-Presse, "US Drone Fires on Taliban Territory," *National* (UAE), June 24, 2009.

251 **"among the mourners":** Mayer, "The Predator War."

251 **father-in-law's house:** Ibid.

251 **"target boxes":** Klaidman, *Kill or Capture*, p. 121.

251 **as many drone strikes:** "2009: The Year of the Drone," Counterterrorism Strategy Initiative, New America Foundation, accessed

December 17, 2012, http://counterterrorism. newamerica.net/drones/2009.

251 **"hidden bases":** James Risen and Mark Mazzetti, "C.I.A. Said to Use Outsiders to Put Bombs on Drones," *New York Times*, August 20, 2009.

251 **"With an ACCM":** Author interview, US military intelligence source, October 2009. All information from and quotations of the "military intelligence source" come from the author's interview.

253 **introduced legislation:** Transparency and Accountability in Military and Security Contracting Act of 2007, S. 674, 110th Cong. (2007).

## 26: Special Ops Want to "Own This Shit Like They Did in Central America in the '80s"

254 **prisoner number 372:** Associated Press, "Report: Ex-Gitmo Detainee Now al-Qaeda's No. 2 in Yemen," USAToday.com, January 23, 2009.

254 **"al Qaeda travel facilitator":** Memorandum from DoD Office for the Administrative Review of the Detention of Enemy Combatants at US Naval Base Guantanamo Bay, Cuba, to Said Ali Jabir al Khathim al Shihri, "Unclassified Summary of Evidence for Administrative Review Board in the Case of Said Ali Jabir al Khathim al Shihri," June 16, 2005, accessed December 18, 2012, http://projects.nytimes.com/guantanamo/detainees/372-said-ali-al-shihri/documents/1/pages/411#3.

254 **went missing:** Robert F. Worth, "Freed by the U.S., Saudi Becomes a Qaeda Chief," *New York Times*, January 22, 2009.

254 **"By Allah":** Agence France-Presse, "Former Guantanamo Detainee Elevated to Senior Qaeda Rank," January 23, 2009.

255 **"transformed al Qaeda in Yemen":** Barak Barfi, "Yemen on the Brink? The Resurgence of al Qaeda in Yemen," Counterterrorism Strategy Initiative Policy Paper, New America Foundation, January 2010, p. 5.

255 **"85 Most Wanted":** Ibid., p. 8.

255 **"deteriorated significantly":** Associated Press, "U.S. Report Says Pakistan Terror Attacks Up," USAtoday.com, April 30, 2009.

255 **"I don't think there's any doubt":** *Hearing to Receive Testimony of Afghanistan, Before the Senate Committee on Armed Services*, 111th Cong. p. 63 (December 2, 2009) (testimony of Hillary Rodham Clinton, Secretary of State).

255 **"toothpaste in a tube":** *Annual Threat Assessment Hearing, Before the Permanent Select Committee on Intelligence*, 111th Cong. (February 25, 2009) (testimony of Admiral Dennis Blair, Director of National Intelligence).

256 **"a very persistent enemy"**: Transcript, "Media Roundtable with CIA Director Leon E. Panetta," February 25, 2009, transcript from Federal News Service.

256 **"immediate threat"**: Bob Woodward, *Obama's Wars* (New York: Simon and Schuster, 2010), p. 8.

256 **"adequate plans"**: Ibid., p. 35.

256 **"establishing new safe-havens"**: Dan Pfeiffer, "The Same Old Washington Blame Game," The White House Blog, December 30, 2009, www.whitehouse.gov/blog/2009/12/30/same-old-washington-blame-game.

256 **Almost half**: Worth, "Freed by the U.S., Saudi Becomes a Qaeda Chief."

256 **Khobar Towers**: Pam Benson, "Obama to Name John Brennan to Lead CIA," Security Clearance (blog), CNN.com, January 7, 2013, http://security.blogs.cnn.com/2013/01/07/obama-to-name-john-brennan-to-lead-cia/.

257 **"direct and immediate"**: "Profile: John O. Brennan," Who Runs Gov, WashingtonPost.com, accessed December 15, 2012.

257 **released 176 of the men**: "Yemen Frees 176 al-Qaeda Suspects," AlArabiya.net, February 9, 2009.

257 **South Korean tourists**: "Tourists Die in Yemen Explosion," BBC.co.uk, March 15, 2009.

257 **"repeatedly rebuffed"**: US diplomatic cable 09SANAA495, from Chargé d'Affaires Angie Bryan, "Saleh Shows No Flexibility on GTMO Detainees," March 23, 2009, released by WikiLeaks, http://wikileaks.org/cable/2009/03/09SANAA495.html. The author relies on this cable for details of the meeting.

257 **"praised Yemen's efforts"**: Saba (Yemen), "Yemeni Leader Receives Letter from US President," BBC Monitoring International Reports, March 16, 2009.

257 **addressed the Guantánamo situation**: Bryan, "Saleh Shows No Flexibility on GTMO Detainees."

258 **"We are not obedient soldiers"**: Kevin Peraino, "Our Main Enemy Is Al Qaeda," *Newsweek*, April 17, 2009.

258 **"know how to deal with us"**: Author interview, Colonel W. Patrick Lang, February 2011. All quotations of Lang come from the author's interview.

258 **pushed hard**: Gareth Porter, "True Believer: Petraeus and the Mythology of Afghanistan," *Truthout*, December 20, 2012.

258 **"Success against the extremist networks"**: General David H. Petraeus, Commander US Central Command, "The Afghanistan-Pakistan Strategic Review and the Posture of U.S. Central Command," prepared statement for Senate Armed Services Committee, April 1, 2009.

258 **approved a plan**: "Yemen," excerpt from General David H. Petraeus, Commander US Central Command, statement before the Senate Armed Services Committee on the Afghanistan-Pakistan Strategic Review and the Posture of US Central Command, March 16, 2010, www.centcom.mil/yemen/.

258 **"inability of the Yemeni government"**: Petraeus, "The Afghanistan-Pakistan Strategic Review and the Posture of U.S. Central Command," April 1, 2009.

259 **advised President Obama, under Petraeus's command**: Marc Ambinder, "Obama Gives Commanders Wide Berth for Secret Warfare," *Atlantic*, May 25, 2010, www.theatlantic.com/politics/archive/2010/05/obama-gives-commanders-wide-berth-for-secret-warfare/57202/.

259 **boarded a Yemeni Air Force helicopter**: US diplomatic cable 09SANAA1015 from Ambassador Stephen Seche, US Embassy Sana'a, "Saleh Sees Foreign Hand Behind Yemen's Internal Woes," May 31, 2009, released by WikiLeaks, http://wikileaks.org/cable/2009/05/09SANAA1015.html. The author relies on this cable for details of the meeting.

260 **US military recruiting center**: CNN Wire Staff, "Man Pleads Guilty to Recruiting Center Killing, Gets Life," CNN.com, July 25, 2011.

260 **literature by Anwar Awlaki**: Kristina Goetz (Commercial Appeal, Memphis), "Muslim Who Shot Soldier in Arkansas Says He Wanted to Cause More Death," Knoxnews.com, November 13, 2010.

260 **"If you ever get out"**: James Dao, "Suspect's Lawyer Outlines Defense in Killing of Soldier," *New York Times*, June 4, 2009.

260 **he was investigated**: Pierre Thomas, Richard Esposito, and Jack Date, "Recruiter Shooting Suspect Had Ties to Extremist Locations," ABCNews.go.com, June 3, 2009.

260 **told police officials**: Steve Barnes and James Dao, "Gunman Kills Soldier Outside Recruiting Station," *New York Times*, June 1, 2009.

260 **"a jihadi attack"**: "Arkansas Recruiting Center Killing Suspect: 'This Was a Jihadi Attack,'" CNN.com, January 22, 2010.

260 **"might be trying to link himself"**: James Dao, "Man Claims Terror Ties in Little Rock Shooting," *New York Times*, January 21, 2010.

261 **"recklessness cloaked in righteousness"**: Remarks by Richard B. Cheney, American Enterprise Institute, May 21, 2009, www.aei.org/article/foreign-and-defense-policy/regional/india-pakistan-afghanistan/remarks-by-richard-b-cheney/.

261 **"doubled down on Bush policy"**: Au-

thor interview, Joshua Foust, January 2011.

261 **"These guys are scalpels"**: Author interview, former aide to Special Operations commander, February 2011.

262 **fly drones and US helicopters:** US diplomatic cable 09STATE72112, from Secretary of State Hillary Clinton to US Embassy in Sana'a, "Eliciting Yemeni Cooperation for Arms Smuggling Interdiction Efforts," July 9, 2009, released by WikiLeaks, http://wikileaks. org/cable/2009/07/09STATE72112.html. The author relies on this cable for details of Ambassador Seche's talking points.

262 **laying the groundwork:** US diplomatic cable 08SANAA1947, from Ambassador Stephen Seche, US Embassy Sana'a, "Saleh Tells Petraeus: 'No Restrictions' on CT Cooperation," August 9, 2009, released by WikiLeaks, http://wikileaks.org/cable/2009/08/09SA-NAA1430.html. The author relies on this cable for details of the meeting.

262 **deployed his nephew:** Gregory D. Johnsen, "The Expansion Strategy of Al-Qa'ida in the Arabian Peninsula," *CTC Sentinel*, January 3, 2010, www.ctc.usma. edu/posts/the-expansion-strategy-of-al-qa-ida-in-the-arabian-peninsula-2.

262 **posting a video online:** Ibid.

263 **"I worry about safe havens"**: Transcript, "Defense Language Institute All Hands Call," Defense Language Institute, Monterey, CA, August 10, 2009, www.jcs.mil/speech. aspx?id=1230.

263 **"got free training"**: Author interview, former aide to Special Operations commander, December 2010.

**27: Suicide or Martyrdom?**

264 **"Today the world turns upside down"**: Anwar al Awlaki, "Suicide or Martyrdom?" Imam Anwar's Blog, anwar-alawlaki.com, January 22, 2009.

264 **"the greatest terrorists of all"**: Anwar al Awlaki, "An Offer to Retract and Unite," Imam Anwar's Blog, anwar-alawlaki.com, February 14, 2009.

264 **"speaking to you from Yemen"**: Anwar al Awlaki, "State of the Ummah—Imam Anwar Al-Awlaki," YouTube video (audio), 48:51, from a lecture delivered by Anwar al Awlaki via teleconference on March 1, 2009, posted by "Moahroah," July 3, 2012, www. youtube.com/watch?v=PIpxw2tupdQ.

265 **"when the president was calling me"**: Author interview, Nasser al Awlaki, January 2012.

265 **positioning their vehicles:** Author interview, Nasser al Awlaki, August 2012.

265 **"what the president wants"**: Ibid.

266 **"I will not allow the Americans"**: Author interview, Nasser al Awlaki, January 2012.

266 **"It was a heated discussion"**: Author interview, Nasser al Awlaki, September 2012.

266 **"You and the Americans"**: Author interview, Sheikh Saleh bin Fareed, January 2012.

266 **"What am I accused of?"**: Anwar al Awlaki, "Anwar al-Awlaki May 2010 Interview Video," transcript of interview with Al-Malahem Media, released May 23, 2010, translation from Public Intelligence, May 26, 2010, http://publicintelligence.net/an-war-al-awlaki-may-2010-interview-video/.

266 **"Unguided Rockets into Israel?"**: Nidal Hasan, e-mail to Anwar al Awlaki, January 16, 2009, released by Intelwire, July 19, 2012, http://news.intelwire.com/2012/07/the-following-e-mails-between-maj.html.

266 **"This can assure privacy"**: Nidal Hasan, e-mail to Anwar al Awlaki, February 16, 2009, released by Intelwire, July 19, 2012, http://news.intelwire.com/2012/07/the-following-e-mails-between-maj.html. This was from the first of four e-mails Hasan sent on February 16.

267 **"$5,000.00 scholarship"**: Ibid., from the third of four e-mails Hasan sent on February 16.

267 **"I pray this message reaches you"**: Anwar al Awlaki, e-mail to Nidal Hasan, February 16, 2009, released by Intelwire, July 19, 2012, http://news.intelwire.com/2012/07/the-following-e-mails-between-maj.html.

267 **"looking for a wife"**: Nidal Hasan, e-mail to Anwar al Awlaki, February 16, 2009, released by Intelwire, July 19, 2012, http://news.intelwire.com/2012/07/the-following-e-mails-between-maj.html. This was from the fourth of four e-mails Hasan sent on February 16.

267 **"Thanks for the offer"**: Anwar al Awlaki, e-mail to Nidal Hasan, February 22, 2009, released by Intelwire, July 19, 2012, http://news.intelwire.com/2012/07/the-following-e-mails-between-maj.html.

267 **"I know your busy"**: Nidal Hasan, e-mail to Anwar al Awlaki, March 7, 2009, released by Intelwire, July 19, 2012, http://news.intelwire.com/2012/07/the-following-e-mails-between-maj.html.

267 **"the issue of 'collateral damage'"**: Nidal Hasan, e-mail to Anwar al Awlaki, May 31, 2009, released by Intelwire, July 19, 2012, http://news.intelwire.com/2012/07/the-fol-lowing-e-mails-between-maj.html.

268 **"The first face to face fight"**: Anwar al Awlaki, "The Army of Yemen Confronts the Mujahideen," Imam Anwar's Blog, anwar-alawlaki.com, August 1, 2009.

268 **"Surprise of the Season?"**: Anwar al

Awlaki, "Could Yemen Be the Next Surprise of the Season?" Imam Anwar's Blog, an-war-alawlai.com, October 7, 2009.

269 **"If we go back to 2001 or 2002"**: Author interview, Abdul Rezzaq al Jamal, January 2012.

269 **"I lived in the US"**: Anwar al Awlaki, "Anwar Al Awlaki's Posthumous Call to Jihad (Part 1)," YouTube video, 12:48, from an address delivered by Anwar al Awlaki in March 2010 and produced by Al-Malahem Media, posted by "ClarionProductions," December 21, 2011, www.youtube.com/watch?v=EOcFKofJ5PA.

**28: Obama Embraces JSOC**

270 **fewer than one hundred**: Joshua Partlow, "In Afghanistan, Taliban Leaving al-Qaeda Behind," *Washington Post*, November 11, 2009.

270 **"a coup attempt"**: Agence France-Presse, "UN Somalia Envoy Accuses Islamist of Coup Attempt," May 13, 2009.

270 **highly produced videos:** Agence France-Presse, "Somali Terror Group Raps in English for Recruits," March 31, 2009.

270 **Syrian immigrant:** Abu Mansuur al-Amriiki, "The Story of an American Jihaadi, Part One," accessed May 17, 2012, http://azelin.files.wordpress.com/2012/05/omar-hammami-abc5ab-mane1b9a3c5a-br-al-amrc4abkc4ab-22the-story-of-an-amer-ican-jihc481dc4ab-part-122.pdf. For details of Omar Hammami's life, the author relied on his autobiography, published online under the nom de guerre Abu Mansuur al-Amriiki, unless otherwise noted.

271 **"I made it my goal"**: Andrea Elliott, "The Jihadist Next Door," *New York Times Magazine*, January 27, 2010.

271 **"a multinational counterterrorism team"**: Ibid.

271 **federal, terror-related charges:** Associated Press, "American Is Charged in U.S. for Activities in Somalia," *Washington Post*, February 14, 2007.

271 **a potential asset:** Elliott, "The Jihadist Next Door."

271 **"Oh, Muslims of America"**: Ibid.

271 **450 foreign fighters:** Agence France-Presse, "Lawless Somalia Draws Influx of Foreign Fighters," March 27, 2009.

271 **"The only reason"**: Omar Hammami, "A Converted American Who Joined Al Qaeda," YouTube video, 3:12, from a CNN broadcast featuring an excerpt of the Shabab-produced recruitment video "Ambush at Bardal," posted by "shahzad-khan007," July 22, 2009, www.youtube.com/watch?v=dvEdB9riTI0.

271 **"If you can encourage"**: Omar Hamma-mi, "Two Americans in Shabaab," YouTube video, 3:38, from the Shabab-produced video "Ambush at Bardal" released March 31, 2009, posted by "RabieAbuBakr," April 15, 2009, www.youtube.com/watch?v=HMU9Vgix6E0.

271 **"We're calling all the brothers"**: "Somali Terrorist Group Releases Recruitment Video Featuring 'the American,'" Anti-Defamation League, September 8, 2009, www.adl.org/main_Terrorism/al_shabaab_video_the_american.htm.

271 **key al Shabab leaders:** In 2012, Hammami and al Shabab had an apparent falling out, with Hammami charging in two online videos that "friction" with other leaders had put his life in danger. Al Shabab denied the allegations, calling Hammami "narcissistic," and accused him of "sowing disunity" among the mujahedeen. See Omar Hammami, "urgentmessage," YouTube video, 1:09, posted by "somalimuhajirwarrior," March 16, 2012, www.youtube.com/watch?v=GAr2srINqks; The Middle East Media Research Institute, "In Second Urgent Message, American Al-Shabab Commander Hammami Confirms Major Schism Between Somali and Foreign Al-Shabab Fighters, Urges Al-Qaeda Leadership to Intervene," translation of online video message from Omar Hammami, October 19, 2012, www.memri.org/report/en/print6766.htm; HSM Press Office, "Abu Mansur Al-Amriki: A Candid Clarification," statement from Harakat Al-Shabab Al-Mujahideen posted on their Twitter feed, December 17, 2012, www.twitlonger.com/show/kcjrkc.

271 **Shirwa Ahmed**: Pierre Thomas and Jason Ryan, "Feds Probing Possible Minn. Terror Group," ABCNews.go.com, November 25, 2008.

272 **"fight terrorism with lethal force"**: Daniel Volman, "Obama, AFRICOM, and U.S. Military Policy Toward Africa," Working Paper No. 14, Program of African Studies, Northwestern University, 2009. Volman cites Senator Obama's written responses to a questionnaire given to the 2008 presidential candidates by the Leon H. Sullivan Foundation. The questionnaire—but not the responses—can be found at, www.afjn.org/focus-campaigns/other/other-continental-issues/82-general/399-presidential-town-hall-meeting-africa-questionnaire.html.

272 **"just a failed state"**: Hillary Clinton during confirmation hearing, Senate Committee on Foreign Relations, January 13, 2009, transcript by CQ Transcriptions, released via NYTimes.com, www.nytimes.com/2009/01/13/us/politics/13text-clinton.html?pagewanted=1&_r=0.

272 **arms shipments:** Marina Litvinsky

and Jim Lobe, "Somalia: U.S. Confirms Arms Shipments to Bolster Besieged Gov't," Inter Press Service News Agency, June 25, 2009.

272 **better paid:** Roland Marchal, "The Rise of a Jihadi Movement in a Country at War; Harakat Al-Shabaab al Mujaheddin in Somalia," National Centre for Scientific Research, March 2011, p. 8. Al Shabab reportedly paid its recruits' salaries far more regularly than other Somali actors, including the government, although the stated salaries themselves could be comparably modest.

272 **double-suicide attacks:** Edmund Sanders, "Eleven African Soldiers Killed in Somalia," *Los Angeles Times*, February 23, 2009.

272 **"unprecedented level":** "Somali Militants Kill Eleven Burundian Soldiers in Mogadishu," *Pana Press*, February 23, 2009.

273 **"heaviest of its kind":** Mohamed Ibrahim, "Fighting in Somalia Kills at Least Fifteen," *New York Times*, February 24, 2009.

273 **"walking slowly":** Greg Jaffe and Karen DeYoung, "Obama Team Mulls Aims of Somali Extremists," *Washington Post*, April 11, 2009.

273 **at least twenty cases:** Andrea Elliott, "A Call to Jihad, Answered in America," *New York Times*, July 11, 2009.

273 **cracked down substantially:** Maalik Eng, "Somalia Piracy Falls to Six-Year Low as Guards Defend Ships," Shabelle Media Network, October 22, 2012.

273 **for-profit fishery:** Johan Peleman, Edward Howard Johns, Pavanjeet Singh Sandhu, and John Tambi, "Report of the Panel of Experts on Somalia Pursuant to Security Council Resolution 1474 (2003)," UN Security Council, November 4, 2003, p. 32.

273 **illegal waste dumping:** "Report of the Secretary-General on the Protection of Somali Natural Resources and Waters," United Nations Security Council, October 25, 2011, pp. 12–13.

273 **Somali coastguard:** Najad Abdullahi, "'Toxic Waste' Behind Somali Piracy," AlJazeera.com, October 11, 2008.

274 **counter-piracy training:** "American Crew Regains Control of Hijacked Ship, One Pirate in Custody," FoxNews.com, April 8, 2009.

274 **a secured safe room:** Chip Cummins and Sarah Childress, "On the Maersk: 'I Hope if I Die, I Die a Brave Person,'" *Wall Street Journal*, April 16, 2009.

274 **maneuvered the *Alabama*'s rudders:** "Crewman's E-mail Gives Harrowing Details of Hijacking," CNN.com, April 20, 2009.

274 **FV *Win Far 161*:** Jay Bahadur, *The Pirates of Somalia: Inside Their Hidden World* (New York: Pantheon Books, 2011, Kindle edition).

274 **US Defense Department contractor:**

Mark Mazzetti and Sharon Otterman, "U.S. Captain Is Hostage of Pirates; Navy Ship Arrives," *New York Times*, April 8, 2009.

274 **since the early 1800s:** James Bone, "Maersk Alabama Crew Return to US to Tell of Somali Pirate Ordeal," *Times Online* (London), April 18, 2009.

274 **deployment of a destroyer:** Mazzetti and Otterman, "U.S. Captain Is Hostage of Pirates."

274 **taken hostage:** Ibid.

274 **Two other ships:** "More Pirates Searching for Lifeboat, Official Says," CNN.com, April 10, 2009.

274 **"virtually immediately":** Scott Wilson, Ann Scott Tyson, and Stephanie McCrummen, "'Three Rounds, Three Dead Bodies'; Precision Volley by Navy SEALs Ended a Five-Day Ordeal for an American Seaman, but Piracy Off Somalia Continues," *Washington Post*, April 14, 2009.

274 **first authorization:** Transcript, *Larry King Live*, CNN, April 12, 2009.

274 **tried to escape:** Wilson, Tyson, and McCrummen, "'Three Rounds, Three Dead Bodies.'"

274 **threw into the ocean:** Mark Owen, with Kevin Maurer, *No Easy Day: The Firsthand Account of the Mission That Killed Osama Bin Laden* (New York: Dutton, 2012), p. 94.

275 **second authorization:** Transcript, *Larry King Live*, CNN, April 12, 2009.

275 **"the first time I know of":** Author interview, Marc Ambinder, December 2010. All quotations of Marc Ambinder come from the author's interview.

275 **deploy to the Horn of Africa:** Owen, *No Easy Day*, p. 89.

275 **based at Manda Bay:** Marc Ambinder, "Obama Gives Commanders Wide Berth for Secret Warfare," TheAtlantic.com, May 25, 2010.

275 **"They're deadly accurate":** Author interview, General Hugh Shelton, March 2011.

275 **Three shots:** Wilson, Tyson, and McCrummen, "'Three Rounds, Three Dead Bodies,'"

276 **publicly used the name:** Marc Ambinder, "SEAL Team Six v. the Pirates," theAtlantic.com, April 12, 2009. The White House provided a backgrounder to journalists, which stated that President Obama called military officials after the operation, including "Vice Admiral William McRaven, Commander Joint Special Operations Command."

276 **"The President personally invited":** Author interview, Special Operations source, August 2010.

277 **bold attack:** Alex Perry, "Behind the Suicide Bombing in Somalia," *Time*, June 19, 2009.

277 **Mogadishu's police chief:** Associated Press, "Somali Police Chief Among Seventeen Dead in Clashes," MSNBC.com, June 17, 2009.

277 **few hundred yards:** Jeffrey Gettleman, "In Somalia, a Leader Is Raising Hopes for Stability," *New York Times*, September 16, 2009.

277 **"weakened by the rebel forces":** Al Arabiya/Agencies, "Somalia Seeks Foreign Military Aid amid Crisis," AlArabiya.net, June 20, 2009.

277 **shipment of forty tons:** Mary Beth Sheridan, "U.S. Has Sent Forty Tons of Munitions to Aid Somali Government," *Washington Post*, June 27, 2009.

277 **"best hope we've had":** Transcript, "Remarks with Somali Transitional Federal Government President Sheikh Sharif Sheikh Ahmed," August 6, 2009.

277 **"a number of actions and initiatives":** John O. Brennan, "A New Approach to Safeguarding Americans," prepared remarks, Center for Strategic and International Studies, August 6, 2009, www.whitehouse.gov/the-press-office/remarks-john-brennan-center-strategic-and-international-studies.

### 29: "Let JSOC Off the Leash"

278 **received a phone call:** "Saudi Prince Spoke to Bomber on Phone Before Attack," Reuters, September 2, 2009.

278 **fled the kingdom:** Al Arabiya/Reuters, "Qaeda Names Man Who Tried to Kill Saudi Prince," AlArabiya.net, August 30, 2009.

278 **recruited:** Abdullah Al-Oreifij (Saudi Gazette), "Saudi Interior Ministry Names Suicide Bomber in Attack on Prince," BBC Monitoring International Reports, August 31, 2009.

278 **"I need to meet":** "Saudi Prince Spoke to Bomber on Phone Before Attack."

278 **pick him up:** Al Arabiya/Reuters, "Qaeda Names Man."

278 **"Asiri said":** Richard Barrett, "Al-Qaida and Taliban Status Check: A Resurgent Threat?" Washington Institute for Near East Policy, September 29, 2009, transcript by Federal News Service, www.teachingterror.net/resources/AQ%20Status%20check.pdf. All quotations and information attributed to Barrett come from these remarks.

278 **one-pound bomb:** CBS/AP, "Saudi Bombmaker Key Suspect in Yemen Plot," CBSNews.com, November 1, 2010.

279 **Asiri's brother:** "Profile: Al-Qaeda 'Bomb Maker' Ibrahim al-Asiri," BBC.co.uk, May 9, 2012.

279 **delivering a personal letter:** US diplomatic cable 09JEDDAH343, from Consul General Martin R. Quinn, US Consulate in Jeddah, "Presidential Assistant Brennan's

Sept. 5 Discussion with Saudi Interior Minister Prince Naif," September 11, 2009, released by WikiLeaks, http://wikileaks.org/cable/2009/09/09JEDDAH343.html.

279 **"I met with Prince Mohammed bin Nayef":** Transcript, interview with Gloria Borger, *State of the Union with John King*, CNN, January 4, 2010.

279 **"We're very concerned":** Transcript, *Meet the Press*, NBC, January 3, 2010.

279 **"There was no indication":** Ibid.

279 **sat face to face:** US diplomatic cable 09SANAA1669, from Ambassador Stephen Seche, US Embassy Sana'a, "Brennan-Saleh Meeting September 6, 2009," September 15, 2009. Released by WikiLeaks, http://wikileaks.org/cable/2009/09/09SANAA1669.html. Details of this meeting between Brennan and President Saleh come from this cable.

280 **subsequent classified cable:** Ibid.

280 **"doesn't mean a damn thing":** Author interview, Colonel W. Patrick Lang, February 2011.

281 **"initiative to help Yemen":** Reuters, "US Offers Yemen Help in 'Fight Against Terrorism,'" AlArabiya.net, September 7, 2009.

281 **authorizing plans:** Author interviews, Special Operations sources, May–July 2010.

281 **"Not enough people":** "Al Qaeda Extends to Somalia, Yemen," *Washington Times*, September 10, 2009.

281 **"under more pressure":** *Eight Years After 9/11: Confronting the Terrorist Threat to the Homeland, Hearing Before the Senate Committee on Homeland Security and Government Affairs*, 111th Cong. (September 30, 2009) (testimony of Michael Leiter, Director, National Counterterrorism Center), video available at www.senate.gov/fplayers/I2009/urlPlayer.cfm?fn=govtaff093009&st=840&dur=8355.

281 **"witnessed the reemergence":** Ibid.

282 **convened a meeting:** Sunlen Miller, "A Look at the President's Meetings on Afghanistan and Pakistan," ABCNews.go.com, November 10, 2009.

282 **seven-page secret order:** Marc Ambinder, "Obama Gives Commanders Wide Berth for Secret Warfare," TheAtlantic.com, May 25, 2010.

282 **permission slip:** Mark Mazzetti, "U.S. Is Said to Expand Secret Actions in Mideast," *New York Times*, May 24, 2010.

282 **"more systematic and long term":** Ibid.

282 **"reluctant to allow such an expansion":** Ambinder, "Obama Gives Commanders Wide Berth."

283 **intelligence gathering:** Mazzetti, "U.S. Is Said to Expand Secret Actions."

283 **"cannot or will not be accomplished":** Ibid.

283 **"The temptation for the leadership":**

Author interview, Colonel W. Patrick Lang, February 2011.

283 **"Pentagon is already empowered":** Author interview, Special Operations source, May 2010.

284 **"insulate the president":** Author interview, former aide to Special Operations commander, May 2010.

284 **discreet trip to Yemen:** "Yemen, U.S. Talks on Cooperation in Military, Combating Terror Fields," President Saleh website, October 4, 2009, www.presidentsaleh.gov.ye/ shownews.php?lng=en&_nsid=7743.

284 **"cooperation between the U.S. and Yemen":** "Senior Military Official Visits Yemen," press release from the US embassy in Sana'a, Yemen, October 4, 2009, http:// yemen.usembassy.gov/smov.html.

284 **"implementation of some special operations":** Muhammad al Ahmadi, "Al Qaeda to Respond to Obama's Strategy in Yemen," *al-Ghad*, December 6, 2009.

284 **"We're developing geostrategic principles":** Bob Woodward, *Obama's Wars* (New York: Simon and Schuster, 2010), pp. 227–228.

### 30: Samir Khan: An Unlikely Foot Soldier

285 **Soldier Readiness Processing Center:** Ana Campoy, Peter Sanders, and Russell Gold, "Hash Browns, Then Four Minutes of Chaos," *Wall Street Journal*, November 9, 2009.

285 **prosecuted for war crimes:** Brooks Egerton, "Fort Hood Captain: Hasan Wanted Patients to Face War Crimes Charges," *Dallas Morning News*, November 17, 2009.

285 **complained to friends:** James McKinley Jr. and James Dao, "Fort Hood Gunman Gave Signals Before His Rampage," *New York Times*, November 8, 2009.

285 **"It's getting harder":** Dana Priest, "Fort Hood Suspect Warned of Threats Within the Ranks," *Washington Post*, November 10, 2009.

285 **imminent deployment:** Staff and wire reports, "Suspect Was to Deploy to Afghanistan," *Army Times*, November 5, 2009.

286 **"did not alert":** Scott Shane and James Dao, "Investigators Study Tangle of Clues on Fort Hood Suspect," *New York Times*, November 14, 2009.

286 **"ordered nor pressured":** Sudarsan Raghavan, "Cleric Says He Was Confidant to Hasan," *Washington Post*, November 16, 2009.

286 **"is a hero":** Anwar al Awlaki, "Nidal Hassan Did the Right Thing," Imam Anwar's blog, anwar-alawlaki.com, November 9, 2009.

286 **"not recruited by Al-Qaida":** "MEMRI TV Clip No. 3240: AQAP Video Features American-Yemeni Cleric Anwar al-Awlaki Calling On American Muslims to Either

Leave or Follow the Example of Nidal Hassan," transcript of AQAP-produced video featuring Anwar al Awlaki, November 2011, transcript from Middle East Research Institute (MEMRI), December 20, 2011, www. memritv.org/clip/en/3240.htm.

286 **"undertake a full review":** Transcript, "Weekly Address: President Obama Calls for Comprehensive Review of Events Leading to Tragedy at Fort Hood," November 14, 2009.

286 **"most destructive terrorist attack":** Agence France-Presse, "Army Base Shooting Was 'Terrorist Attack': US Lawmaker," November 18, 2009.

286 **call for preemptive strikes:** Jordan Fabian, "Lieberman: Yemen Will Be 'Tomorrow's War' If Pre-emptive Action Not Taken," Briefing Room (blog), *The Hill*, December 27, 2009, http://thehill.com/blogs/blog-briefing-room/ news/73651-lieberman-yemen-will-be-tomorrows-war-if-preemptive-action-not-taken.

287 **Wild West Domains:** Author search, August 2011, http://who.is/whois/an-war-alawlaki.com/.

287 **"They shut down my website":** Anwar al Awlaki, interview with Al-Malahem Media, aired May 23, 2010, transcript provided by MEMRI, www.memrijttm.org/clip_tran-script/en/2480.htm.

287 **landed in Sana'a:** Transcript, "Grand Jury Focuses on NC Man Tied to Jihad Magazine," *Morning Edition with Steve Inskeep*, NPR, August 18, 2010.

287 **"He's a Christmas child":** Author interview, Sarah Khan, April 2012. All information and quotations attributed to Sarah Khan come from the author's interview.

287 **Samir's grandparents' house:** Ibid.

287 **classmates recall:** Matthew Chayes, Anthony M. Destefano, Robert E. Kessler, Greg Lacour, and Victor Manuel Ramos, "Samir Khan, al-Qaida Figure, Grew Up on Long Island," *Newsday*, October 7, 2011; Timothy Bolger, "Slain al Qaeda Mouthpiece Samir Khan's Westbury Roots," LongIsland-Press.com, October 6, 2011.

288 **"a practicing Muslim":** Michael Moss and Souad Mekhennet, "An Internet Jihad Aims at US Viewers," *New York Times*, October 15, 2007.

288 **Islamic Thinkers Society:** Ibid.

288 **"Does he think like them?":** Chayes et al., "Samir Khan, al-Qaida Figure, Grew Up on Long Island."

288 **first of several interventions:** Robbie Brown and Kim Severson, "Second American in Strike Waged Qaeda Media War," *New York Times*, September 30, 2011.

288 **"If you give Satan an inch":** Chayes et al., "Samir Khan, al-Qaida Figure, Grew Up on Long Island."

288 **community college:** Moss and

Mekhennet, "An Internet Jihad Aims at US Viewers."

288 **debates with fellow attendees:** "American Editor Brings US Savvy to Jihad Outreach," *Morning Edition*, NPR, October 12, 2010.

289 **retiring blogs:** Alice Fordham, "A 'Proud Traitor': Samir Khan Reported Dead Alongside Aulaqi," Checkpoint Washington (blog), *Washington Post*, September 30, 2011.

289 **Muslimpad:** Moss and Mekhennet, "An Internet Jihad Aims at US Viewers."

289 **top 1 percent:** Ibid.

289 **"scholars of Islam":** "About," The Ignored Puzzle Pieces of Knowledge, revolution.muslimpad.com.

289 **Zachary Chesser:** "Alleged American Jihadists—Connecting the Dots," CNN.com, October 10, 2012.

289 **"unlikely foot soldier":** Moss and Mekhennet, "An Internet Jihad Aims at US Viewers."

289 **"brought great happiness to me":** Ibid.

289 **told a local news station:** Ibid.

290 **hired a lawyer:** "American Editor Brings US Savvy to Jihad Outreach."

290 **following him closely:** Michael Moss, "What to Do About Pixels of Hate," *New York Times*, October 21, 2007.

290 **"shut [Khan] down":** Fordham, "A 'Proud Traitor.'"

290 **"FBI dispatched a spy":** Samir Khan, "I Am Proud to Be a Traitor to America," *Inspire* 2 (fall 2010), published October 2010. All excerpts of Khan's writing come from this article, unless otherwise noted.

290 **invited an Imam:** Moss and Mekhennet, "An Internet Jihad Aims at US Viewers."

290 **"a moderate Muslim":** Steven Stalinsky and R. Sosnow, "The Life and Legacy of American al-Qaeda Online Jihad Pioneer Samir Khan—Editor of al-Qaeda Magazine 'Inspire' and a Driving Force Behind al-Qaeda's Push for 'Lone-Wolf' Terrorist Attacks in the West," Middle East Research Institute (MEMRI), September 28, 2012, www.memri.org/report/en/print6713.htm#_edn39.

290 **became very much convinced":** Chayes et al., "Samir Khan, al-Qaida Figure, Grew Up on Long Island."

290 **"I tried to bring arguments":** Moss and Mekhennet, "An Internet Jihad Aims at US Viewers."

290 **already received an invitation:** Steve Inskeep, "Grand Jury Focuses on NC Man Tied to Jihad Magazine," *Morning Edition*, NPR, August 18, 2010.

291 **"How could anyone claim sanity":** Abu Yazeed, "Samir Khan: The Face of Joy," *Inspire* 9 (winter 2012), released May 2012. The author claims to be publishing a "last will" left by Samir Khan on his hard drive.

291 **first met Anwar Awlaki:** Paul Cruickshank and Tim Lister, "The Danish Biker and the Trail That Led to al Qaeda's Most Wanted," CNN.com, October 24, 2012.

291 **Murad Storm:** Ibid.

291 **first armed robbery:** Ray Weaver, "Former Biker Infiltrated al-Qaeda," *Copenhagen Post*, October 8, 2012.

292 **Bandidos:** Ibid.

292 **converted to Islam, moved to Yemen:** Ibid.

292 **named him Osama:** Ibid.

292 **video from 2005:** Cruickshank and Lister, "The Danish Biker and the Trail That Led to al Qaeda's Most Wanted."

292 **student at Iman University:** Ibid.

292 **"talked freely":** Ibid.

292 **"not what I thought":** Weaver, "Former Biker Infiltrated al-Qaeda."

292 **claimed he approached:** Cruickshank and Lister, "The Danish Biker and the Trail That Led to al Qaeda's Most Wanted."

292 **saw me as his friend":** Ibid.

292 **"materials and electronic equipment":** Ibid.

292 **"discussed the terrorist attacks":** Ibid.

292 **"part of a conspiracy to get Anwar":** E-mail sent to author from Awlaki family, December 2012.

293 **married a second Yemeni wife:** Author interviews, Awlaki family members, August 2012.

293 **"companion in hiding":** Cruickshank and Lister, "The Danish Biker and the Trail That Led to al Qaeda's Most Wanted."

293 **"There are two things":** Duncan Gardham, "Morten Storm: A Radical Life," *Telegraph*, December 3, 2012.

293 **launched an assault:** Cruickshank and Lister, "The Danish Biker and the Trail That Led to al Qaeda's Most Wanted."

293 **"overjoyed":** "The Terrorist's Bride," *Jyllands-Posten* documentary, 12:11, December 16, 2012.

293 **"The idea was to find someone":** Ibid.

293 **"That was the plan":** Weaver, "Former Biker Infiltrated al-Qaeda."

### 31: Blowback in Somalia

294 **plastic surgery:** Profile of Fazul Abdullah Mohammed, United Nations Security Council al-Qaida Sanctions List, accessed August 14, 2012, https://www.un.org/News/Press/docs//2012/sc10755.doc.htm.

294 **"senior trainer":** US diplomatic cable 09NAIROBI1395, from Ambassador Michael Ranneberger, US Embassy Nairobi, "Somalia—the TFG, Al-Shabaab, and Al Qaeda," July 6, 2009, released by WikiLeaks, http://wikileaks.org/cable/2009/07/09NAIROBI1395.html.

294 **burst through the door, Wilson Airport:**

Author interview, Clara Gutteridge, July 2011.

294 **"They put a bag on my head":** Author copy of written testimony of Ahmed Abdullahi Hassan.

294 **taken to a secret prison:** Author interview, Clara Gutteridge, July 2011.

295 **"former personal assistant":** Author copy, Kenyan intelligence report, October 2010.

295 **"CIA no longer operates":** Leon E. Panetta, "Message from the Director: Interrogation Policy and Contracts," Central Intelligence Agency, April 9, 2009, https://www.cia.gov/news-information/press-releases-statements/directors-statement-interrogation-policy-contracts.html.

295 **"United States provided information":** Author interview, US official, July 2011.

295 **"right-hand man":** Author interview, Somali intelligence official, June 2011.

295 **took off in helicopters:** Sean D. Naylor, "JSOC Closes Chapter on al-Qaida Leader: Somalia Raid Nets Body of Man Wanted in Bombing," *Army Times*, September 18, 2009.

295 **regular trips:** Bill Roggio, "Commando Raid in Somalia Is Latest in Covert Operations Across the Globe," *Long War Journal*, September 15, 2009.

295 **According to witnesses:** Ewen MacAskill, "Somali Insurgents Vow Revenge for US Killing of Leader," *Guardian*, September 15, 2009.

295 **collected at least two:** Jeffrey Gettleman and Eric Schmitt, "U.S. Kills Top Qaeda Militant in Southern Somalia," *New York Times*, September 14, 2009.

295 **"any alleged operation":** MacAskill, "Somali Insurgents Vow Revenge."

295 **al Shabab confirmed:** Gettleman and Schmitt, "U.S. Kills Top Qaeda Militant in Southern Somalia."

296 **"I am a firm believer":** Author interview, Malcolm Nance, May 2011. All quotations of Malcolm Nance come from the author's interview.

296 **"like summary executions":** Naylor, "JSOC Closes Chapter on al-Qaida Leader."

296 **"The truth is closer to the opposite":** Ibid.

296 **free to interrogate the prisoners:** Author interview, Somali intelligence official, June 2011.

296 **"Hassan's case suggests":** Statement, legal team of Ahmed Abdullahi Hassan, July 2011.

297 **at least seven US citizens:** Bobby Ghosh, "Domestic-Terrorism Incidents Hit a Peak in 2009," *Time*, December 23, 2009.

297 **issued his update:** Mark Mazzetti, "U.S. Is Said to Expand Secret Actions in Mideast," *New York Times*, May 24, 2010.

298 **"purely military solution":** Peter Spiegel, "Gates Says Somalia Government Is Key to Problem," *Wall Street Journal*, April 14, 2009.

298 **"National Security Council":** Johnnie Carson, prepared testimony, "Developing a Coordinated and Sustainable Strategy for Somalia," Hearing of Senate Foreign Relations Subcommittee on African Affairs, May 20, 2009, www.state.gov/p/af/rls/rm/2009/123729.htm.

298 **"following the course":** Daniel Volman, "Obama Administration Budget Request for AFRICOM Operations and for Security Assistance Programs in Africa in FY 2010," African Security Research Project, May 2009, http://concernedafricascholars.org/african-security-research-project/?p=18. The figures of US budget requests for FY 2010 come from Volman's report.

298 **government of the Seychelles:** Craig Whitlock and Greg Miller, "U.S. Assembling Secret Drone Bases in Africa, Arabian Peninsula, Officials Say," *Washington Post*, September 20, 2011.

298 **"It would be a mistake":** Volman, "Obama Administration Budget Request for AFRICOM Operations."

298 **expanded to 5,200:** "Report of the Secretary-General on Somalia Pursuant to Security Council Resolution 1872 (2009)," United Nations Security Council, October 2, 2009.

299 **post-Ramadan offensive:** Mohammed Ibrahim and Jeffrey Gettleman, "African Union Base in Somalia Is Hit," *New York Times*, September 17, 2009.

299 **two UN Land Cruisers:** Details of the attack are from ibid.

299 **single deadliest attack:** Malkhadir M. Muhumed (AP), "Death Toll Rises to Twenty-one in Somalia Suicide Attack," *Seattle Times*, September 17, 2009.

299 **"We have got our revenge":** Ibrahim Mohamed, "Suicide Car Bombers Hit Main AU Base in Somalia," Reuters, September 17, 2009.

299 **speaking English:** Ibid.

299 **was a US citizen:** Jeffrey Gettleman, "American Helped Bomb Somalia Base, Web Site Says," *New York Times*, September 25, 2009.

299 **established in 2002:** "Overviews," Benadir University website, www.benadiruniversity.net/Overviews.aspx.

299 **video of the ceremony:** Author copy, video of graduation ceremony at Benadir University, December 2009. Many details of the attack are from the video.

300 **five Somali government ministers:** "Somalia Ministers Killed by Hotel Suicide Bomb," BBC.co.uk, December 3, 2009.

300 **higher education minister:** Stepha-

nie McCrummen, "Attack at Graduation Ceremony Kills Nineteen in Somali Capital," *Washington Post*, December 4, 2009.

300 **health minister:** Allie Shah, "Minneapolis Surgeon Feels Calling Back to Somalia," *Star Tribune*, December 19, 2009.

300 **"Suddenly, the hall shook":** Abdinasir Mohamed, "'I Looked to My Right and Saw a Colleague Dead and Bleeding,'" *Wall Street Journal*, December 4, 2009.

300 **"national disaster":** Associated Press, "Bomber Dressed as Woman Kills Twenty-two Somalis," FoxNews.com, December 3, 2009.

300 **"We beg the world":** McCrummen, "Attack at Graduation Ceremony."

300 **Danish citizen:** "Somalia Suicide Bomber 'Was from Denmark,'" BBC.co.uk, December 10, 2009.

301 **"did not mastermind that explosion":** Ibrahim Mohamed, "Somali Rebels Deny They Carried Out Suicide Bombing," *Reuters*, December 4, 2009.

301 **"The struggle against violent extremism":** Transcript, "Remarks by the President in Address to the Nation on the Way Forward in Afghanistan and Pakistan," West Point Military Academy, December 1, 2009.

301 **"Perhaps the most profound issue":** Transcript, "Remarks by the President at the Acceptance of the Nobel Peace Prize," Oslo, Norway, December 10, 2009.

302 **"superb," "tough":** Tweet from CBS White House Correspondent Mark Knoller (@markknoller), December 11, 2009, http://twitter.com/markknoller/status/6567810262.

302 **"liberal president":** Margaret Talev, "Unlikely Support: GOP Loved Obama's Nobel Speech," McClatchy Newspapers, December 11, 2009.

302 **"most explicitly pro-war speech":** Glenn Greenwald, "The Strange Consensus on Obama's Nobel Address: Why Did So Many Liberals and Conservatives Both Find So Much to Cheer in the President's Foreign Policy Speech?" Salon.com, December 11, 2009.

**32: "If They Kill Innocent Children and Call Them al Qaeda, Then We Are All al Qaeda"**

303 **three alleged AQAP members:** Daniel Klaidman, *Kill or Capture: The War on Terror and the Soul of the Obama Presidency* (New York: Houghton Mifflin Harcourt, 2012), p. 199.

303 **just forty-five minutes:** Ibid.

303 **some seventy-five officials:** Ibid., p. 200.

303 **"near the village of al-Majalah":** Ibid., p. 199.

303 **"heavy pressure exerted":** Ibid., p. 210.

304 **BlackBerry started ringing:** Author interview, Sheikh Saleh bin Fareed, January 2012. All information and quotations attributed to bin Fareed are from the author's interview, unless otherwise noted.

304 **read a press release:** "'Dozens Killed' in Yemen Raids," AlJazeera.com, December 18, 2009.

304 **arrived in southern Yemen:** Paula Dear, "Britain's Long Relationship with Yemen," BBC News Magazine, January 12, 2010, http://news.bbc.co.uk/2/hi/uk_news/magazine/8441263.stm.

304 **Crown colony:** Ibid.

304 **British withdrew:** Ibid.

305 **but he had overslept:** Phil Hirschkorn, "Who Was Fahd al-Quso?" CBSNews.com, May 7, 2012.

305 **"People saw the smoke":** Author interview, Muqbal, January 2012. All quotations of Muqbal come from the author's interview.

306 **"I was making bread":** Author interview, female survivor, January 2012.

306 **fourteen women and twenty-one children:** Amnesty International, "Yemen: Cracking Down Under Pressure," August 25, 2010.

306 **three more people were killed:** Chris Woods, "The Civilian Massacre the US Neither Confirms Nor Denies," *Bureau of Investigative Journalism*, March 29, 2012.

306 **"We were only exposed to Western media":** Author interview, Kamal Sharaf, January 2012. All quotations of Kamal Sharaf come from the author's interview.

306 **his relationship, through marriage:** Ibid.

306 **US Treasury Department–designated:** Specially Designated Nationals List, Office of Foreign Assets Control, US Department of the Treasury, January 17, 2013, www.treasury.gov/ofac/downloads/t11sdn.pdf.

307 **tried on a suicide vest:** See, for example, Gregory D. Johnsen, *The Last Refuge: Yemen, Al-Qaeda, and America's War in Arabia* (New York: W. W. Norton, 2013), pp. 235–238.

307 **"Special Access Program":** Scott Shane, Mark Mazzetti, and Robert F. Worth, "Secret Assault on Terrorism Widens on Two Continents," *New York Times*, August 14, 2010.

307 **US-Yemen joint operations center:** Dana Priest, "US Military Teams, Intelligence Deeply Involved in Aiding Yemen on Strikes," *Washington Post*, January 27, 2010.

307 **surveillance aircraft:** Woods, "The Civilian Massacre the US Neither Confirms Nor Denies." According to Woods, local residents had noticed a "spotter plane" overhead well before the strike.

307 **another strike:** Kimberly Dozier, "U.S.

Leading Assaults on al Qaeda in Yemen," CBSNews.com, January 3, 2010.

308 **preparing for strikes:** Robert F. Worth, "Yemen Says Strikes Against Qaeda Bases Killed Thirty-Four," *New York Times*, December 17, 2009.

308 **a big fish:** US diplomatic cable 09SA-NAA2250, from Ambassador Stephen Seche, US Embassy Sana'a, "Yemen Abuzz with Talk of CT Operations; Attention Slowly Turns to U.S. Role," December 21, 2009, released by WikiLeaks, http://wikileaks.org/cable/2009/12/09SANAA2250.html.

308 **"an imminent attack":** Brian Ross, Richard Esposito, Matthew Cole, Luis Martinez, and Kirit Radia, "Obama Ordered U.S. Military Strike on Yemen Terrorists," ABCNews.go.com, December 18, 2009.

308 **"JSOC operation with borrowed Navy subs":** Author interview, military source, November 2010.

308 **"successful pre-emptive operations":** Ian Black, "Yemen 'Kills Thirty-four al-Qaida Members in Raids,'" *Guardian*, December 17, 2009.

308 **"carried out simultaneous raids":** Embassy of the Republic of Yemen; Office of Media and Public Affairs, Washington, DC, "Press Statement," December 24, 2009.

308 **"thank him for his cooperation":** "Obama Hails Yemen's Efforts in Fighting Terror in Phone Call to President Salih," Yemen News Agency (SABA), December 17, 2009.

308 **Hosni Mubarak also phoned:** "Saleh Receives Phone Call from Egyptian President," Yemen News Agency (SABA), December 17, 2009.

308 **questioned whether Yemen:** Amnesty International, "Yemen: Cracking Down Under Pressure."

308 **BLU 97 A/B cluster bomblets:** Ibid. Details of the bomblets and munitions are also from the Amnesty International report.

308 **Yemen's arsenal:** Kim Sengupta, "US Cruise Missile Parts Found in Yemeni Village Where Fifty-two Died," *Independent* (UK), June 7, 2010.

309 **"We've actually done quite a bit":** Gordon Lubold, "Yemen's Air Strike on Al Qaeda May Signal New US Focus," *Christian Science Monitor*, December 24, 2009.

309 **"largely nomadic, Bedouin families":** US diplomatic cable 09SANAA2251, from Ambassador Stephen Seche, US Embassy Sana'a, "ROYG Looks Ahead Following CT Operations, but Perhaps Not Far Enough," December 21, 2009, released by WikiLeaks, http://wikileaks.org/cable/2009/12/09SA-NAA2251.html.

309 **gathering of tribal leaders:** Author

interview, Sheikh Saleh bin Fareed, January 2012. The author relies on bin Fareed's account for his description of the tribal gathering.

311 **"Al Qaeda's war in Yemen":** Johnsen, *The Last Refuge*, pp. 255–256.

311 **another cruise missile attack:** Robert Worth, "Is Yemen the Next Afghanistan?" *New York Times Magazine*, July 6, 2010.

311 **on-the-ground investigation:** Author copy, Yemen Parliamentary Investigation. Details of the delegation's findings are from this report.

312 **were puzzled:** Author interviews, Yemeni journalists and security analysts, January 2012.

312 **"the involvement of the United States":** Eric Schmitt and Robert F. Worth, "US Widens Terror War to Yemen, a Qaeda Bastion," *New York Times*, December 27, 2009.

312 **sent a cable from Sana'a:** Ambassador Stephen Seche, "ROYG Looks Ahead Following CT Operations, but Perhaps Not Far Enough."

312 **Pentagon would not respond:** Amnesty International, "Yemen: Cracking Down Under Pressure."

312 **"military strike of this kind":** Ibid.

312 **"cited strained resources":** Shane, Mazzetti, and Worth, "Secret Assault on Terrorism Widens on Two Continents."

312 **$100,000 to pay off the victims:** Ambassador Stephen Seche, "ROYG Looks Ahead Following CT Operations, but Perhaps Not Far Enough."

312 **"conducted very methodically":** Shane, Mazzetti, and Worth, "Secret Assault on Terrorism Widens on Two Continents."

313 **"If I were Catholic":** Klaidman, *Kill or Capture*, p. 210.

313 **"non-stop until we eradicate this disease":** Ambassador Stephen Seche, "ROYG Looks Ahead Following CT Operations, but Perhaps Not Far Enough."

313 **"stay quiet":** US diplomatic cable 09SANAA2274, from Chargé d'Affaires Angie Bryan, US Embassy Sana'a, "ROYG Acknowledges US Intel Assistance in AQAP Strikes, Makes Case Before Parliament," December 27, 2009, released by WikiLeaks, http://wikileaks.org/cable/2009/12/09SANAA2274.html.

313 **"intelligence aid from Saudi Arabia":** Ahmed al-Haj (AP), "Yemen Claims Thirty Killed in Raid on Qaida Hide-Outs," Guardian.co.uk, December 24, 2009.

313 **"It was cruise missile strikes":** Dozier, "U.S. Leading Assaults on al Qaeda in Yemen."

313 **taken into custody and interrogated:**

David E. Sanger and Eric Schmitt, "Threats Led to Embassy Closings in Yemen, Officials Say," *New York Times*, January 3, 2010.


**33: "The Americans Really Wanted to Kill Anwar"**

314 **"He called me at three o'clock":** Author interview, Nasser al Awlaki, January 2012. All information and quotations attributed to Nasser al Awlaki come from the author's interview, unless otherwise noted.

314 **US forces carried out an air strike:** Scott Shane, Mark Mazzetti, and Robert F. Worth, "Secret Assault on Terrorism Widens on Two Continents," *New York Times*, August 14, 2010.

314 **According to official accounts:** Sudarsan Raghavan and Michael D. Shear, "US-aided Attack in Yemen Thought to Have Killed Aulaqi, Two al-Qaida Leaders," *Washington Post*, December 25, 2009.

314 **"Yemeni and foreign oil targets":** Reuters, "Army Kills Dozens of Suspected Al-Qaeda Members," France24.com, December 24, 2009.

314 **"a huge victory":** Christopher Boucek, "Airstrike in Yemen Targets Terror Operatives," interview with Jeffrey Brown, *NewsHour*, PBS, December 24, 2009.

314 **"doesn't really change anything":** Dana Priest, "U.S. Military Teams, Intelligence Deeply Involved in Aiding Yemen on Strikes," *Washington Post*, January 27, 2010.

315 **"escaped the brunt of criticism":** US diplomatic cable 09SANAA2250, from Ambassador Stephen Seche, US Embassy Sana'a, "Yemen Abuzz with Talk of CT Operations; Attention Slowly Turns to U.S. Role," December 21, 2009, released by WikiLeaks, http://wikileaks.org/cable/2009/12/09SANAA2250.html.

315 **"far from his house":** CBS/AP, "Ft. Hood Suspect's Cleric Killed in Yemen?" CBSNews.com, December 24, 2009.

315 **Shaye's interview was tough:** "Transcript of interview with al-Awlaki," from Al Jazeera interview with Anwar al Awlaki, December 23, 2009, released via NBC News, December 23, 2009, www.msnbc.msn.com/id/34579438/ns/us_news-tragedy_at_fort_hood/t/transcript-interview-al-awlaki/.

317 **singing Christmas carols:** Peter Baker, "Obama's War over Terror," *New York Times Magazine*, January 4, 2010.

317 **Northwest Airlines Flight 253:** "Investigators Cross Globe Looking for Details of Plane Bombing Suspect," FoxNews.com, December 27, 2009.

317 **Abdulmutallab's father:** Seth G. Jones, *Hunting in the Shadows: The Pursuit of al*

*Qaeda Since 9/11* (New York: W. W. Norton, 2012), p. 345.

317 **"every teacher's dream":** "Profile: Umar Farouk Abdulmutallab, BBC.co.uk, October 12, 2011.

317 **studying Arabic:** Peter Kenyon, "Going Radical: Yemen a Turning Point for Christmas Bomb Suspect," *Morning Edition*, NPR, February 19, 2010.

317 **enrolled in college:** Mark Hosenball, "The Radicalization of Umar Farouk Abdulmutallab," *Newsweek*, January 1, 2010.

317 **traveled to the United States:** Dan Eggen, Karen DeYoung, and Spencer S. Hsu, "Plane Suspect Was Listed in Terror Database After Father Alerted US Officials," *Washington Post*, December 27, 2008.

317 **Islamic institute in Texas:** Tom Abrahams, "Terror Suspect Attended Classes in Houston," KTRK-TV Houston, http://abclocal.go.com/ktrk/story?section=news/local&id=7193124.

317 **"the real Islam":** Andrew Gregory, "Syringe Bomber Umar Abdulmutallab Chilling Text Messages to Dad," *Mirror* (UK), January 1, 2010, www.mirror.co.uk/news/uk-news/syringe-bomber-umar-abdulmutallab-chilling-191630.

317 **US Embassy in Nigeria:** Jill Dougherty, "Official: Dad Warned U.S. of Son but 'No Suggestion' of Terrorist Act," CNN.com, December 28, 2009.

317 **"extreme religious views":** "Father of Terror Suspect Reportedly Warned U.S. About Son," FoxNews.com, December 2, 2009.

318 **"Explosive device":** Ron French, "Inside Story of Terror on Flight 253," *Detroit News*, March 18, 2010.

318 **cited as evidence:** Peter Bergen, "Analysis: Similar Explosive on Plane Used in Saudi Attack," CNN.com, December 27, 2009.

318 **sent on a suicide mission:** Victor Morton, "Awlaki Personally Blessed Detroit Attack," *Washington Times*, December 29, 2009.

318 **"voice-to-voice communication":** Sudarsan Raghavan, "Investigators Scrutinize Yemeni American Cleric's Ties to Plane Suspect," *Washington Post*, January 1, 2010.

318 **"He was watering trees":** Author interview, Mullah Zabara, January 2012. All quotations and information attributed to Mullah Zabara come from the author's interview.

318 **one of his "students":** Transcript, "Interview: Anwar al-Awlaki," AlJazeera.com, February 7, 2010.

318 **sources in Shabwah:** Author interviews, tribal members, January 2012.

318 **"Yes, there was some contact":** Transcript, "Interview: Anwar al-Awlaki," AlJazeera.com.

319 **"technical error"**: Peter Baker and Scott Shane, "Obama Seeks to Reassure US After Bombing Attempt," *New York Times*, December 28, 2009.

319 **AQAP released a video:** Matthew Cole, Brian Ross, and Nasser Atta, "Underwear Bomber: New Video of Training, Martyrdom Statements," ABCNews.go.com, April 26, 2010.

320 **"season for second-guessing"**: Mark Hosenball, "The Radicalization of Umar Farouk Abdulmutallab," *Newsweek*, January 1, 2010.

320 **"The Obama administration came in"**: Transcript, *Fox News Sunday*, Fox News, December 27, 2009.

320 **"trying to pretend we are not at war"**: Mike Allen, "Dick Cheney: Barack Obama 'Trying to Pretend,'" *Politico*, December 30, 2009.

320 **"in the hands of the law enforcement people"**: Sam Stein, "Bush Waited Six Days to Discuss Shoe Bomber with No GOP Complaints," *Huffington Post*, March 18, 2010.

320 **"it makes us less safe"**: Allen, "Dick Cheney: Barack Obama 'Trying to Pretend.'"

320 **"A lot of the knuckleheads"**: Baker, "Obama's War over Terror."

321 **"Our nation is at war"**: Transcript, "Inaugural Address," January 20, 2009, The American Presidency Project, www.nytimes.com/2009/01/20/us/politics/20text-obama.html?pagewanted=all.

321 **"We have a growing presence there"**: Transcript, *Fox News Sunday*.

321 **"Are we sending troops into Yemen?"**: Transcript, Admiral Mike Mullen at the Naval War College, January 8, 2010, www.jcs.mil/speech.aspx?id=1312.

321 **"We've known throughout this year"**: Olivia Hampton, "Obama: No U.S. Troops to Somalia, Yemen," Agence France-Presse, January 11, 2010.

321 **"steadily growing military elements"**: "Report of Inspection; Embassy Sanaa, Yemen," US Department of State and the Broadcasting Board of Governors Office of the Inspector General, June 2010, http://oig.state.gov/documents/organization/145254.pdf.

321 **authority to approve all personnel:** "NSDD-38: Staffing at Diplomatic Missions and Their Overseas Constituent Posts," text of NSDD-38, June 2, 1982, released by the Office of Management Policy, Rightsizing, and Innovation, April 26, 2005, www.state.gov/m/pri/nsdd/.

322 **more than two dozen:** Priest, "U.S. Military Teams, Intelligence Deeply Involved in Aiding Yemen on Strikes."

322 **operating its own drones:** David S. Cloud (Tribune), "White House Considers Yemen Drone Strikes, Officials Say," *Los Angeles Times*, November 7, 2010.

322 **"After the December thing"**: Author interview, Dr. Emile Nakhleh, January 2010. All quotations and information attributed to Dr. Nakhleh come from the author's interview.

322 **another round of meetings:** US diplomatic cable 10SANAA4, from Ambassador Stephen Seche, US Embassy Sana'a, "General Petraeus' Meeting with Saleh on Security Assistance, AQAP strikes," January 4, 2010, released by WikiLeaks, http://wikileaks.org/cable/2010/01/10SANAA4.html. Details of the meetings between Saleh and Petraeus come from this cable.

323 **"100 percent Yemeni forces"**: Haley Sweetland Edwards, "US Lends Firepower to Yemen Fight," *Global Post*, January 24, 2010.

323 **"it is believed by most Yemenis"**: Ibid.

323 **take matters into their own hands:** Author interviews, Special Operations sources, 2010 and 2011.

323 **"Given the unsettled situation"**: Peter Finn, "Return of Yemeni Detainees at Guantanamo Bay Is Suspended," *Washington Post*, January 5, 2010.

323 **"unconscionable"**: Ibid.

323 **"The instability in Yemen"**: Transcript, "Remarks with Qatar Prime Minister Sheikh Hamad bin Jassim bin Jabr al-Thani After Their Meeting," Washington, DC, January 4, 2010.

324 **more air strikes:** Robert F. Worth, "Senior Qaeda Figures Killed in Attack, Yemen Says," *New York Times*, January 15, 2010.

324 **formally designated:** Transcript, press statement from Philip J. Crowley, Assistant Secretary of State, Bureau of Public Affairs, "Designations of Al-Qa'ida in the Arabian Peninsula (AQAP) and Senior Leaders," January 19, 2010.

324 **took similar action:** "U.N. Security Council Sanctions al Qaeda's Yemen Wing," Reuters.com, January 19, 2010.

324 **"support the U.S. effort"**: Transcript, Philip J. Crowley, "Designations of Al-Qa'ida in the Arabian Peninsula (AQAP) and Senior Leaders."

324 **killed senior AQAP figures:** Hammoud Mounasser, "Yemen Air Strikes Pound Qaeda Leader's Home: Military," Agence France-Presse, January 20, 2010.

324 **local leader Ayad al Shabwani:** The first strike was not in Marib but reportedly killed al Shabwani; the second reportedly hit near his home.

324 **"seventeen raids inside Marib"**: "Airstrikes Target al-Qaida in Yemen," Voice of America, January 19, 2010.

### 34: "Mr. Barack Obama...I Hope That You Reconsider Your Order to Kill...My Son"

325 **"Both the CIA and the JSOC":** Dana Priest, "U.S. Military Teams, Intelligence Deeply Involved in Aiding Yemen on Strikes," *Washington Post*, January 27, 2010.

325 **"a very dubious legality":** Author interview, Colonel W. Patrick Lang, September 2010.

325 **"Obviously, if U.S. forces are fighting":** Glenn Greenwald, "Presidential Assassinations of U.S. Citizens," Salon.com, January 27, 2010.

326 **"terrorist No. 1":** Adam Entous, "U.S. Targets American-Born Cleric in Yemen: Officials," Reuters, April 6, 2010.

326 **"a decision to use lethal force":** To Prohibit the Extrajudicial Killing of United States Citizens, and for Other Purposes, H.R. 6010, 111th Cong. (July 30, 2010). Representative Kucinich cites the statement in his bill. It was not included in the public record of Blair's testimony before the Permanent Select Committee on Intelligence, on February 3, 2010.

326 **"There is some unease about this approach":** Author interview, Dr. Emile Nakhleh, January 2010.

326 **"We are very pleased":** Priest, "U.S. Military Teams, Intelligence Deeply Involved."

326 **write directly to Obama:** Author copy of letter from Nasser al Awlaki to President Barack Obama.

### 35: One Night in Gardez

328 **nomination had been held up:** Yochi J. Dreazen, "Lawmakers Hold Up a Top General's Nomination," *Wall Street Journal*, May 1, 2008.

328 **McChrystal was instrumental:** Marc Ambinder, "Obama Gives Commanders Wide Berth for Secret Warfare," *Atlantic*, May 25, 2010, www.theatlantic.com/politics/archive/2010/05/obama-gives-commanders-wide-berth-for-secret-warfare/57202/.

328 **heated debate:** "Sharp Division Inside White House on Afghanistan, Analyst Says," CNN.com, October 5, 2009.

328 **advocated for a shift:** Peter Baker, "How Obama Came to Plan for 'Surge' in Afghanistan," *New York Times*, December 5, 2009.

328 **"I don't foresee the return":** Transcript, interview with General James Jones on *State of the Union with John King*, CNN, October 4, 2009.

329 **"a fairly good relationship":** Author interview, confidential source, December 2010.

329 **surge in Afghanistan:** Karen DeYoung and Scott Wilson, "Obama to Send 34,000 Troops to Afghanistan," *Washington Post*, December 1, 2009.

329 **"Disrupt, dismantle and defeat":** Transcript of President Barack Obama remarks, "Address to the Nation on the Way Forward in Afghanistan and Pakistan," West Point Military Academy, West Point, New York, December 1, 2009.

329 **"I was somewhat stunned":** Author interview, Colonel Lawrence Wilkerson, May 2011.

329 **"The Kabul Command":** Author interview, Scott Horton, September 2010.

330 **McChrystal made it clear:** Spencer Ackerman, "Special Operations Chiefs Quietly Sway Afghanistan Policy," *Washington Independent*, November 9, 2009.

330 **"heavy COIN presence":** Ibid.

330 **"They're focusing on the main population":** Ibid.

330 **embracing its core tenets:** General Stanley McChrystal, Commander ISAF (COMISAF) Initial Assessment (Declassified), released September 21, 2009, accessed December 1, 2012, www.washingtonpost.com/wp-dyn/content/article/2009/09/21/AR2009092100110.html.

330 **"essential to [the] credibility":** *Hearing to Consider the Nominations of Admiral James G. Stavridis, USN for Reappointment to the Grade of Admiral and to be Commander, U.S. European Command and Supreme Allied Commander, Europe; Lieutenant General Douglas M. Fraser, USAF to be General and Commander, U.S. Southern Command; And Lieutenant General Stanley A. McChrystal, USA, to be General and Commander, International Security Assistance Force and Commander, U.S. Forces, Afghanistan, Day 5, Before the Senate Armed Services Committee*, 111th Cong. (June 2, 2009) (testimony of General Stanley McChrystal).

330 **significantly reduced air strikes:** Dexter Filkins, "U.S. Tightens Airstrike Policy in Afghanistan," *New York Times*, June 21, 2009.

330 **ninety-seven Afghan civilians:** Dan De Luce, "We Failed to Follow Bombing Rules: Pentagon," Agence France-Presse, June 8, 2009.

330 **"any entry into an Afghan house":** Memorandum, from International Security Assistance Force Headquarters, Kabul, Afghanistan, July 6, 2009, www.nato.int/isaf/docu/official_texts/Tactical_Directive_090706.pdf. The memo contains unclassified excerpts of a tactical directive sent out by McChrystal on July 2, 2009.

330 **1,000 Special Operations Forces:** Rowan Scarborough, "Pentagon Quietly Sending 1,000

Special Operators to Afghanistan in Strategy Revamp," FoxNews.com, June 5, 2009.

331 **SOF teams set to mowing down:** Associated Press, "Analysis: Gen. Petraeus Promotes Special-Ops Success to Show Part of Afghan War US Is Winning," FoxNews.com, September 3, 2010.

331 **"By any objective reckoning":** Author interview with Gareth Porter, September 2010.

331 **more than 2,000 people:** Nick Davies, "Afghanistan War Logs: Task Force 373—Special Forces Hunting Top Taliban," *Guardian,* July 25, 2010.

331 **increased fourfold:** Julian E. Barnes, "U.S. Steps Up Special Operations Mission in Afghanistan," *Los Angeles Times,* December 16, 2009.

331 **"This is Gen. McChrystal's play":** Ibid.

331 **own detainee operations:** Kimberly Dozier (AP), "Afghanistan Secret Prisons Confirmed by U.S.," *Huffington Post,* April 8, 2011.

331 **Field Detention Sites:** Anand Gopal, "America's Secret Afghan Prisons," *Nation,* January 28, 2010.

331 **ninety-six hours:** Ibid.

331 **nine weeks:** Dozier, "Afghanistan Secret Prisons Confirmed by U.S."

331 **Black Jail:** Alissa J. Rubin, "Afghans Detail Detention in 'Black Jail' at U.S. Base," *New York Times,* November 28, 2009.

331 **forced nudity, environmental manipulation, solitary confinement:** Dozier, "Afghanistan Secret Prisons Confirmed by U.S."

331 **being beaten:** Rubin, "Afghans Detail Detention in 'Black Jail' at U.S. Base."

331 **record number:** Joshua Partlow, "July Becomes Deadliest Month for U.S. Troops in Nearly Nine-Year Afghan War," *Washington Post,* July 31, 2010.

332 **enter their areas of responsibility:** Author interviews, Afghan police commanders, October 2010.

332 **"U.S. and NATO presence":** Matthew Hoh, letter of resignation to Ambassador Nancy J. Powell, Director General of the Foreign Service and Director of Human Resources, U.S. Department of State, September 10, 2009, www.washingtonpost.com/wp-srv/hp/ssi/wpc/ResignationLetter.pdf.

332 **"sent ripples":** Karen DeYoung, "U.S. Official Resigns over Afghan War," *Washington Post,* October 27, 2009.

332 **"If he really wanted to affect policy":** Ibid.

332 **"need to be killed":** Author interview, Matthew Hoh, September 2010. All quotations attributed to Matthew Hoh are from the author's interview, unless otherwise noted.

333 **McChrystal knew how to promote:** Michael Hastings, "The Runaway General," *Rolling Stone,* July 8, 2010.

333 **"facilitators," "suspected militants":** Open Society Foundations and The Liaison Office, "The Cost of Kill/Capture: Impact of the Night Raid Surge on Afghan Civilians," September 19, 2011.

334 **important promotion:** Jerome Starkey, "Nato 'Covered Up' Botched Night Raid in Afghanistan That Killed Five," *Times* (UK), March 13, 2010.

334 **newborn son:** "Man Loses Five Family Members in Disputed NATO Raid," CNN Afghanistan Crossroads (blog), CNN.com, April 6, 2010.

334 **sixth day of a child's life:** Author interview, Jerome Starkey, October 2010.

334 **two dozen people, three musicians:** Jerome Starkey, "US Special Forces 'Tried to Cover Up' Botched Khataba Raid in Afghanistan," *Times Online* (UK), April 5, 2010.

334 **"We invited many guests":** Author interview, Mohammed Tahir, October 2010. All quotations attributed to Mohammed Tahir are from the author's interviews, unless otherwise noted.

334 **not ethnic Pashtun:** Author interviews, Sharabuddin family members, October 2010. Details about the family and the night of the raid are from the author's interviews, unless otherwise noted.

334 **main light:** "Man Loses Five Family Members in Disputed NATO Raid."

334 **lasers scoping the grounds:** Author interviews, Sharabuddin family members, October 2010.

335 **both hit by sniper rounds:** Starkey, "Nato 'Covered Up' Botched Night Raid."

335 **"When my father went down":** Author interview, Abdul Ghafar, October 2010. All quotations attributed to Abdul Ghafar are from the author's interviews, unless otherwise noted.

335 **"When I ran outside":** Author interview, Mohammed Sabir, October 2010.

335 **pregnant:** Author interviews, Sharabuddin family members, October 2010. Early press reports, namely, the reporting of Jerome Starkey, also stated that two of the women were pregnant.

335 **sixteen children among them:** Richard A. Oppel Jr., "U.S. Admits Role in February Killing of Afghan Women," *New York Times,* April 4, 2010.

336 **prepared burial shrouds:** Jerome Starkey, "Nato Accused of Cover Up over Killing of Pregnant Women," *Scotsman,* March 13, 2010.

336 **handcuffing them:** Author copy of "briefing note" by United Nations Assistance Mission in Afghanistan (UNAMA) Human Rights unit, dated February 14, 2010.

336 **barefoot, on a brutal winter morning, their hands tied:** Ibid.

336 **assaulted by the US and Afghan team:** Ibid. According to the UNAMA briefing note, "The same witness reported having seen at least 10 people, including the 65 year old house owner, being seriously assaulted by US and Afghan Forces."

336 **"They told us that they were informed":** Author interview, Hajji Sharabuddin, October 2010.

337 **"suffered from cruel, inhuman, degrading treatment":** UNAMA briefing note. All information attributed to the UN is from this report, unless otherwise noted.

338 **"hidden in an adjacent room":** "Joint Force Operating in Gardez Makes Gruesome Discovery," ISAF Joint Command, February 12, 2010, accessed December 1, 2012, www.dvidshub.net/news/45240/joint-force-operating-gardez-makes-gruesome-discovery#. UOLyVBzKZcQ .

338 **"criminals and terrorists":** "Afghan, International Force Kills Enemy Fighters," American Forces Press Service, February 12, 2010.

338 **men, women and children, medical support:** "Joint Force Operating in Gardez Makes Gruesome Discovery."

338 **"It has the earmarks":** "Bodies Found Gagged, Bound After Afghan 'Honor Killing,'" CNN.com, February 12, 2010.

338 **Paktia Province police chief:** Rod Nordland, "Afghanistan: Different Accounts Offered About Civilian Deaths," *New York Times,* February 13, 2010.

338 **deep cuts and puncture wounds:** Richard A. Oppel Jr. and Abdul Waheed Wafa, "Afghan Investigators Say U.S. Troops Tried to Cover Up Evidence in Botched Raid," *New York Times,* April 5, 2010.

338 **inaccurate, falsified tip-off:** Lemar Niazai, "Intelligence Official Among Five Killed by NATO Troops," *Pajhwok Afghan News,* February 12, 2010.

339 **"We strongly condemn this":** Amir Shah, "NATO: Raid Killed Militants; Family Says Civilians," Associated Press, February 12, 2010.

339 **barred from entering:** Starkey, "US Special Forces 'Tried to Cover Up' Botched Khataba Raid."

339 **"wouldn't let us come near":** Laura King, "Probe Targets Elite Unit; an Inquiry into a Raid That Killed Five Afghan Civilians May Shed Light on the Role of U.S. Special Forces," *Los Angeles Times,* April 9, 2010.

339 **top criminal investigator:** Starkey, "US Special Forces 'Tried to Cover Up' Botched Khataba Raid."

339 **"extraordinary and intriguing story":** Author interview, Jerome Starkey, October

2010. All quotations attributed to Jerome Starkey come from the author's interview, unless otherwise noted.

340 **denied having been a part of:** Starkey, "Nato 'Covered Up' Botched Night Raid."

340 **"This operation was a mistake":** Starkey, "Nato Accused of Cover Up over Killing of Pregnant Women."

340 **should have left information:** Ibid.

341 **"You don't have to be fired upon":** Starkey, "Nato 'Covered Up' Botched Night Raid."

341 **"categorically false":** "ISAF Rejects Cover Up Allegation," International Security Assistance Force (ISAF), March 13, 2010, accessed December 12, 2012, www.dvidshub.net/news/46637/isaf-rejects-cover-up-allegation#.UOL9RhzKZcQ.

341 **"Called up rival outlets":** Michael Hastings, *The Operators: The Wild and Terrifying Inside Story of America's War in Afghanistan* (New York: Blue Rider Press, 2012), p. 294.

341 **"The tapes, do not exist":** Jerome Starkey, "U.S.-led Forces in Afghanistan Are Committing Atrocities, Lying and Getting Away with It," Nieman Watchdog (blog), March 22, 2010, www.niemanwatchdog.org/index.cfm?fuseaction=background.view&backgroundid=00440.

341 **"I don't want money":** Jerome Starkey, "Survivors of Family Killed in Afghanistan Raid Threaten Suicide Attacks," *Times* (London), March 15, 2010.

342 **"naming of a newborn child":** Ibid.

342 **"I want the killers brought to justice":** Ibid.

342 **General McChrystal had decided:** Richard A. Oppel Jr. and Rod Nordland, "U.S. Is Reining in Special Operations Forces in Afghanistan," *New York Times,* March 15, 2010.

342 **"ever know how they died":** Ibid.

342 **"burn ourselves to death":** Ibid.

343 **"joint force firing at the men":** "Gardez Investigation Concludes," International Security Assistance Force—Afghanistan (ISAF), April 4, 2010, accessed December 12, 2012, www.isaf.nato.int/article/isaf-releases/gardez-investigation-concludes.html.

344 **"soldiers dug bullets out":** Starkey, "US Special Forces 'Tried to Cover Up' Botched Khataba Raid."

344 **"There was a mess":** Oppel Jr. and Wafa, "Afghan Investigators Say U.S. Troops Tried to Cover Up Evidence in Botched Raid."

344 **"simply is no evidence":** Ibid.

344 **"operational control":** Gareth Porter and Ahmad Walid Fazly, "U.S.: McChrystal's Special Ops Probe Excluded Key Eyewitnesses," Inter Press Service News Agency, July 6, 2010.

344 **"no evidence of a cover-up":** Ibid.

344 **personally travel:** Author interviews, Sharabuddin family members, October 2010.

345 **"When people come to your gate":** Jerome Starkey, "US Army Chief Begs Afghans to Forgive," *Times* (London), April 12, 2010.

345 **"an ancient Afghan ritual":** Author interview, Jerome Starkey, October 2010.

345 **"Sir, you and I are very different, this awful tragedy":** Jerome Starkey, "US Army Chief Begs Afghans to Forgive."

345 **Almost $30,000:** Julius Kavendish, "US Special Forces Apologise for Botched Night Raid," *Independent* (UK), April 9, 2010.

346 **accepted McRaven's apology:** Nick Shifrin and Aleem Agha, "U.S. Vice Admiral Apologizes for Afghan Deaths," ABCNews.go.com, April 8, 2010.

347 **"those damn acts of war":** Author interview, General Hugh Shelton (Ret.), March 2011.

347 **"scold you in the morning":** Hastings, *The Operators*, p. 175.

347 **75 percent increase:** Phil Stewart, "Civilian Casualties Rising in Afghanistan," Reuters, May 12, 2010.

347 **"In the nine-plus months":** Justin Elliott, "Gen. McChrystal: We've Shot 'An Amazing Number of People' Who Were *Not* Threats," TPMMuckraker, April 2, 2010.

348 **1,000 night raids a month:** Gareth Porter, "New Light Shed on US's Night Raids," *Asia Times Online*, September 27, 2010.

348 **"automatically categorized, as insurgents":** Gareth Porter, "True Believer: Petraeus and the Mythology of Afghanistan," *Truthout*, December 20, 2012.

348 **"encouraging the people, hatred against Americans":** Author interview, Mullah Abdul Salam Zaeef, October 2010. All quotations attributed to Mullah Zaeef come from the author's interview, unless otherwise noted.

348 **since 2005:** "Mullah Zaeef Freed from Guantanamo," Dawn.com, September 12, 2005.

348 **longest-running war:** Thomas Nagorski, "Editor's Notebook: Afghan War Now Country's Longest," ABCNews.go.com, June 7, 2010.

348 **passed the 1,000 mark:** James Dao and Andrew W. Lehren, "Grim Milestone: 1,000 Americans Dead," *New York Times*, May 18, 2010.

348 **more than 900:** Gareth Porter, "Petraeus Spin on IED War Belied by Soaring Casualties," Inter Press Service News Agency, September 9, 2010.

349 **"remarkable career in uniform":** Transcript, "Statement by the President in the Rose Garden," June 23, 2010.

349 **pace of night raids increased:** Gareth Porter, "True Believer: Petraeus and the Mythology of Afghanistan," *Truthout*, December 20, 2012.

349 **air strikes resumed:** Julian E. Barnes, "Petraeus Resets Afghan Airstrike Rules," *Wall Street Journal*, August 1, 2010.

349 **civilian death toll mounted:** David S. Cloud, "Afghan Civilian Deaths Caused by Allied Forces Rise," *Los Angeles Times*, November 2, 2010.

**36: The Year of the Drone**

350 **"There's no daylight":** Author interview, Hunter (pseudonym), August 2010. All quotations and information attributed to Hunter come from the author's interview.

351 **at least three entities:** Dana Priest and William M. Arkin, *Top Secret America: The Rise of the New American Security State* (New York: Little, Brown, 2012), p. 204.

351 **"parallel, more cloistered process":** Jo Becker and Scott Shane, "Secret 'Kill List' Proves a Test of Obama's Principles and Will," *New York Times*, May 29, 2012.

351 **little oversight:** Priest and Arkin, *Top Secret America*, p. 205.

351 **"more complex and risky strikes":** Becker and Shane, "Secret 'Kill List' Proves a Test of Obama's Principles and Will."

351 **At least twice a month:** Priest and Arkin, *Top Secret America*, p. 209.

351 **"was really more than one":** Ibid., p. 207.

351 **personally signing off:** President Obama would not necessarily sign off on every operation right before it happened, but he would sometimes approve the concepts of operations in advance. See Eric Schmitt and Thom Shanker, *Counterstrike: The Untold Story of America's Secret Campaign Against al Qaeda* (New York: Times Books, 2011), p. 235: "Cognizant that some high-profile terrorist might pop up only briefly and then vanish, [Secretary of Defense Robert] Gates created a system where options for potential types of missions were discussed with the president in advance so that the commander in chief could delegate authority beforehand to strike fleeting targets."

351 **"secret 'nominations' process":** Becker and Shane, "Secret 'Kill List' Proves a Test of Obama's Principles and Will."

352 **"groomed":** Author interview, JSOC sources, June 2012.

352 **Terrorist Attack Disruption Strikes:** Becker and Shane, "Secret 'Kill List' Proves a Test of Obama's Principles and Will."

352 **"conducting the most aggressive":** Daniel Klaidman, *Kill or Capture: The War on Terror and the Soul of the Obama Presiden-*

*cy* (New York: Houghton Mifflin Harcourt, 2012), p. 121.

353 **"If John Brennan is the last guy"**: Becker and Shane, "Secret 'Kill List' Proves a Test of Obama's Principles and Will."

353 **"Their policy is to take out"**: Ibid.

353 **"the politically advantageous thing"**: Ibid.

354 **"perhaps the most remarkable surprise"**: Jack Goldsmith, *Power and Constraint: The Accountable Presidency After 9/11* (New York: W. W. Norton, 2012), Introduction, p. x.

354 **refused to release its findings:** Catherine Herridge, "Obama Administration Pressed for Accountability After Americans Killed in Anti-Terror Airstrikes," FoxNews.com, October 25, 2011.

354 **"This is an easy one"**: Becker and Shane, "Secret 'Kill List' Proves a Test of Obama's Principles and Will."

354 **This program rests on the personal legitimacy"**: Ibid.

354 **"where people are being killed"**: Author interview, Philip Giraldi, March 2012.

354 **sixty countries to seventy-five countries:** Karen DeYoung and Greg Jaffe, "U.S. 'Secret War' Expands Globally as Special Operations Forces Take Larger Role," *Washington Post*, June 4, 2010.

354 **4,000 people:** Ibid.

354 **"Special Operations capabilities"**: Ibid.

354 **"will not merely respond"**: Transcript, "Remarks by Assistant to the President for Homeland Security and Counterterrorism John Brennan at CSIS," May 26, 2010.

355 **"ongoing unilateral actions"**: Author interview, Special Operations source, June 2010.

355 **"things that the previous administration"**: DeYoung and Jaffe, "U.S. 'Secret War' Expands Globally as Special Operations Forces Take Larger Role."

### 37: Driving Anwar Awlaki to Hell

356 **"We advise you"**: Reuters, "Yemen's al-Qaeda Calls for Jihad Against Jews, Christians," *Times of Oman*, February 8, 2010.

356 **United States struck again:** Scott Shane, Mark Mazzetti, and Robert F. Worth, "Secret Assault on Terrorism Widens on Two Continents," *New York Times*, August 14, 2010.

356 **"A US strike targeted our brother"**: "Al-Jazeera Airs Audio Confirming Al-Qai'dah Deaths in Yemen," BBC Worldwide Monitoring, May 17, 2010.

356 **"Brigade of the martyr"**: Shane, Mazzetti, and Worth, "Secret Assault on Terrorism Widens on Two Continents."

356 **"ongoing counterterrorism cooperation"**: Press release, "Undersecretary of Defense Visits Yemen," Embassy of the United States, Sana'a, Yemen, March 22, 2010, http://yemen.usembassy.gov/udv3.html.

356 **closed-door briefing:** Congressional Record—Daily Digest, April 29, 2010, US Government Printing Office, www.gpo.gov/fdsys/pkg/CREC-2010-04-29/pdf/CREC-2010-04-29-pt1-PgD460.pdf#page=2.

356 **internal e-mail:** Author copy of e-mail.

357 **president green-lit a strike:** Daniel Klaidman, *Kill or Capture: The War on Terror and the Soul of the Obama Presidency* (New York: Houghton Mifflin Harcourt, 2012), p. 255.

357 **struck a convoy of vehicles:** Mohammed Ghobari and Mohamed Sudam, "Air Strike Kills Yemen Mediator," Reuters, May 25, 2010.

357 **his cousin Ayad:** Adam Entous, Julian E. Barnes, and Margaret Coker, "U.S. Doubts Intelligence That Led to Yemen Strike," *Wall Street Journal*, December 29, 2011.

357 **"on a mediation mission"**: "Yemen Strike Kills Mediator, Tribesmen Hit Pipeline," Reuters, May 25, 2010.

357 **Supreme Security Council apologized:** "Air Raid Kills Yemeni Mediator," AlJazeera.com, May 25, 2010.

357 **attacked the main oil pipeline:** Ibid.

357 **"We think we got played"**: Entous, Barnes, and Coker, "U.S. Doubts Intelligence That Led to Yemen Strike."

357 **"How could this have happened?"**: Klaidman, *Kill or Capture*, p. 255.

358 **shift from JSOC's Tomahawk strikes:** Entous, Barnes, and Coker, "U.S. Doubts Intelligence That Led to Yemen Strike."

358 **"The drones are flying over Marib"**: Jeb Boone, Abdul-Aziz Oudah, and Shuaib M. al-Mosawa, "Marib Sheikh: US Drones Fly over Wadi Abida Every Day," *Yemen Observer*, October 28, 2010, www.yobserver.com/front-page/10020035.html.

358 **"At the end of the day"**: Shane, Mazzetti, and Worth, "Secret Assault on Terrorism Widens on Two Continents."

358 **series of US strikes:** Hush Tomlinson, Michael Evans, and Iona Craig, "'Secret' US War on al-Qaeda in Yemen Killing Civilians," *Times* (UK), December 9, 2010.

358 **"It is incredibly dangerous"**: Laura Kasinof, "US Cluster Bombs in Yemen: The Right Weapon in Al Qaeda Fight?" *Christian Science Monitor*, June 7, 2010.

359 **bold raid:** BBC News, "Yemen Gunmen in Deadly Raid on Aden Security Service HQ," BBC.co.uk, June 19, 2010.

359 **launched a dozen attacks:** Christopher Boucek, "The Evolving Terrorist Threat

in Yemen," *CTC Sentinel* 3 (9) (September 2010).

359 **use of "motorbikes in terrorist operations":** "Yemen Bans Motorcycles in Qaida-Infested Abyan," *Xinhua*, September 16, 2010.

359 **"in retaliation to American cruise missiles":** Anwar al Awlaki, "Message from Sheikh Anwar al-Awlaki to the American people," YouTube video, 14:59, from a videotape released by Al-Malahem Media in March 2010, posted by "0109vip," March 3, 2012, www.youtube.com/watch?v=GrdK6m9TKf8.

360 **"the agency lacked specific evidence":** David Ignatius, "For Lack of Hard Evidence, a Terrorist Evaded Capture," *Washington Post*, March 26, 2010.

360 **"the Americans want to kill you":** Transcript, "Interview: Anwar al-Awlaki," AlJazeera.com, February 7, 2010.

361 **"circling our valley twenty-four hours":** Author interview, Saleh bin Fareed, January 2012. All quotations and information attributed to bin Fareed are from the author's interview.

362 **"The First and Exclusive Meeting":** "Anwar Al Awlaki Al Malahem Interview [FULL] ENGLISH Translation," YouTube video, 45:27, from interview with Anwar al Awlaki by Al-Malahem Media, May 23, 2010, posted by "EastLdnMuslima," March 19, 2012, www.youtube.com/watch?v=q70_PQkqnt-g&playnext=1&list=PLcFlly8jyVao4CYWvx-S9dYvik4J9NiBsy&feature=results_main.

362 **"he's literally middle management":** Author interview, Joshua Foust, January 2011. All quotations and information attributed to Foust come from the author's interview, unless otherwise noted.

363 **"I think it's an exaggeration":** Author interview, Dr. Emile Nakhleh, January 2010. All quotations and information attributed to Nakhleh come from the author's interview, unless otherwise noted.

363 **"Anwar al Awlaki was not a leader":** Author interview, Abdul Razzaq al Jamal, January 2012.

363 **"He never said":** Author interview, Nasser al Awlaki, January 2012. All quotations and information attributed to Nasser come from the author's interview, unless otherwise noted.

363 **"always been looked at as a preacher":** Charles Fromm, "Yemen Refuses to Hunt al-Awlaki for US," Inter Press Service, April 13, 2010. http://ipsnorthamerica.net/news.php?idnews=2991.

**38: The CIA's Dating Service**

364 **messages on websites:** Paul Cruickshank, Tim Lister, and Nic Robertson, "The Danish Agent, the Croatian Blonde and the Plot to Get al-Awlaki," CNN.com, October 24, 2012.

364 **track star in high school:** Darko Marinkovi /VLM, Darko Pavi i , Renata Rašovi / VLM, "Al-Qa'idina teroristica Amina bila je vrsna trka ica na sto metara" [Al Qaeda terrorist Amina was a great 100-meter track star], *Vecernji List* (vecernji.hr), October 25, 2012.

364 **"I was wondering will he search for second wife":** "The Terrorist's Bride," *Jyllands-Posten* documentary, 12:11, December 16, 2012.

364 **"overjoyed":** Ibid.

364 **suitcase outfitted with a tracking device:** Ibid.

364 **"If you visit her":** Cruickshank, Lister, and Robertson, "The Danish Agent, the Croatian Blonde and the Plot to Get al-Awlaki."

365 **international bus station:** Ibid.

365 **multiple receipts:** "The Terrorist's Bride," *Jyllands-Posten* documentary.

365 **"done specifically for Sister Aminah":** Ibid.

365 **"nervous":** Ibid.

365 **"it's me without the scarf":** Cruickshank, Lister, and Robertson, "The Danish Agent, the Croatian Blonde and the Plot to Get al-Awlaki."

365 **"Warm weather clothing":** "The Terrorist's Bride," *Jyllands-Posten* documentary.

365 **"the Hook," "the sister":** Ibid.

365 **"We sat there, had a barbecue":** Ibid.

365 **"Congratulations brother":** Cruickshank, Lister, and Robertson, "The Danish Agent, the Croatian Blonde and the Plot to Get al-Awlaki."

366 **handcuffed to the briefcase:** "The Terrorist's Bride," *Jyllands-Posten* documentary.

366 **"Try 007":** Cruickshank, Lister, and Robertson, "The Danish Agent, the Croatian Blonde and the Plot to Get al-Awlaki."

366 **Multiple sources confirmed:** "The Terrorist's Bride," *Jyllands-Posten* documentary.

366 **could not bring her suitcase:** Ibid.

366 **sent Storm a message:** Cruickshank, Lister, and Robertson, "The Danish Agent, the Croatian Blonde and the Plot to Get al-Awlaki."

**39: "The Auction of the Assassin"**

367 **"I don't support it—period":** Author interview, Representative Dennis Kucinich, February 2010. All quotations and information attributed to Representative Kucinich come from the author's interview.

368 **introduced a bill:** To Prohibit the Extrajudicial Killing of United States Citizens, and for Other Purposes, H.R. 6010, 111th Cong. (July 30, 2010).

368 **"almost a dozen":** Dina Temple-Raston, "U.S. Turns Up Heat on Internet Imam

Awlaki," *Morning Edition*, NPR, July 29, 2010.

368 **"a very important opportunity"**: Author interview, Pardiss Kebriaei, March 2012. All quotations and information attributed to Kebriaei come from the author's interview.

369 **legal partners in Yemen:** "Obama Administration Claims Unchecked Authority to Kill Americans Outside Combat Zones; Federal Court Hears Arguments Today in ACLU and CCR Case Challenging Administration's Claimed Authority to Assassinate Americans It Designates Threats," Center for Constitutional Rights and American Civil Liberties Union, November 8, 2010.

369 **"I will do my best":** Paula Newton, "CNN Exclusive: Al-Awlaki's Father Says Son Is 'Not Osama bin Laden,'" CNN.com, January 11, 2010.

369 **"involved himself in every aspect":** "Treasury Designates Anwar al-Awlaki Key Leader of AQAP," U.S. Treasury Department, July 16, 2010.

369 **sued the Treasury Department**: ACLU and CCR v. Geithner, 1:10-cv-013 (DDC August 3, 2010).

369 **allowing the lawyers:** "CCR and ACLU Receive License from OFAC to Pursue Challenge to Targeted Killing," American Civil Liberties Union, August 4, 2010.

369 **"The summary use of force":** Nasser Al-Aulaqi v. Barack Obama, Robert Gates, Leon Panetta ("Al-Aulaqi v. Obama et al."), 1:10-cv-01469-JDB (DDC August 30, 2010).

370 **"puts directly at issue":** Al-Aulaqi v. Obama et al., 1:10-cv-01469-JDB (DDC September 25, 2010).

370 **"to protect intelligence sources":** Al-Aulaqi v. Obama, 1:10-cv-01469-JDB, "Declaration and Formal Claim of State Secrets Privilege and Statutory Privileges by Leon E. Panetta, Director, Central Intelligence Agency" (DDC September 25, 2010).

370 **"exceptionally grave harm":** Al-Aulaqi v. Obama, Case 1:10-cv-01469-JDB, "Public Declaration and Assertion of Military and State Secrets Privilege by Robert M. Gates, Secretary of Defense" (DDC September 25, 2010).

370 **"The government's sweeping invocation":** Al-Aulaqi Versus Obama, Case 1:10-cv-01469-JDB, "Reply Memorandum in Support of Plaintiff's Motion for a Preliminary Injunction and in Opposition to Defendant's Motion to Dismiss by Jameel Jaffer, Ben Wizner, Jonathan M. Manes, Pardiss Kebriaei, Maria C. LaHood, William Quigley, and Arthur B. Spitzer (DDC October 9, 2010).

371 **its own legal framework:** Charlie Savage, "Secret U.S. Memo Made Legal Case to Kill a Citizen," *New York Times*, October 8, 2011.

371 **"loved the idea":** Daniel Klaidman, *Kill or Capture: The War on Terror and the Soul of the Obama Presidency* (New York: Houghton Mifflin Harcourt, 2012), pp. 214–215.

372 **"set his own legal standard":** Ibid., p. 216.

372 **"US targeting practices"**: Speech, Harold Hongju Koh, Annual Meeting of the American Society of International Law, Washington, DC, March 25, 2010, www.state.gov/s/l/releases/remarks/139119.htm.

373 **"To the Muslims in America":** Anwar al Awlaki, "Message from Sheikh Anwar al-Awlaki to the American People," YouTube video, 14:59, from a videotape released by Al-Malahem Media in March 2010, posted by "0109vip," March 3, 2012.

374 **"To go from that individual":** Ahmed al-Haj and Brian Murphy (AP), "Al-Awlaki: From Voice for Jihad to al Qaeda Figure," *Washington Times*, September 30, 2011.

**40: "Martyrdom Is Why We Came Here, My Brother"**

375 **"He was heartbroken":** Abu Yazeed, "Samir Khan: The Face of Joy," *Inspire* 9 (winter 2012), released May 2012. All quotations and information attributed to Abu Yazeed are from this essay.

375 **"for what seemed like years":** Samir Khan, "I Am Proud to Be a Traitor to America," *Inspire* 2 (fall 2010), released October 2010. All quotations and information attributed to Samir Khan are from this essay.

376 **"They came to know":** Author interview, Sarah Khan, April 2012. All quotations and information attributed to Sarah Khan are from the author's interview.

377 **studied Internet technology:** Author interview, Sarah Khan, April 2012.

377 **"connecting and facilitating disparate groups":** Author interview, Aaron Zelin, August 2012.

378 **MI-6:** Richard Norton-Taylor, "British Intelligence Used Cupcake Recipes to Ruin al-Qaida Website," *Guardian*, June 2, 2011.

378 **"'And inspire the believers to fight'":** "Letter from the Editor," *Inspire* 1 (summer 2010), released July 2010.

379 **commissioned a dozen cartoons:** Stephen Castle, "Mohamed Cartoons Provoke Bomb Threats Against Danish Newspaper," *Independent* (UK), February 1, 2006.

379 **"Everybody Draw Mohammed Day":** "'Draw Muhammad' Cartoonist Goes into Hiding at FBI's Insistence After Assassination Threat," FoxNews.com, September 16, 2010.

379 **"I would like to express my thanks":** Anwar al Awlaki, "May Our Souls Be Sacrificed for You!" *Inspire* 1 (summer 2010), released July 2010.

380 **changed her name and moved:** Mark D. Fefer, "On the Advice of the FBI, Cartoonist

Molly Norris Disappears from View," *Seattle Weekly*, September 15, 2010.

380 **"The more the US talked about *Inspire*"**: Author interview, Gregory Johnsen, August 2012.

381 **ordered his deputy**: Osama bin Laden, letter to Shaykh Mahmud (Attiya Abd al-Rahman), SOCOM-2012-0000003-HT 27, August 27, 2010, released by the Combating Terrorism Center at West Point, May 3, 2012.

### 41: The Persecution of Abdulelah Haider Shaye

382 **"He was focusing"**: Author interview, Kamal Sharaf, January 2012. All quotations and information attributed to Kamal Sharaf come from the author's interview.

382 **"Abdulelah was threatened many times"**: Author interview, Abdulrahman Barman, January 2012. All quotations and information attributed to Abdulrahman Barman come from the author's interview.

383 **"a very smart journalist"**: Interview with Mohamed Abdel Dayem, "Jeremy Scahill: Why Is President Obama Keeping Yemeni Journalist Abdulelah Haider Shaye in Prison?" *Democracy Now!*, March 15, 2012. All quotations and information attributed to Mohamed Abdel Dayem come from his appearance on the show.

383 **using his paychecks**: Author interview, US media source, March 2012.

383 **"I was persuaded"**: Dexter Filkins, "After the Uprising: Can Protesters Find a Path Between Dictatorship and Anarchy?" *New Yorker*, April 11, 2011.

384 **put in a cell together**: Author interview, Kamal Sharaf, January 2012.

384 **thirty-four days**: Iona Craig, "Yemen: Press Freedom a Distant Hope," *Index on Censorship*, October 27, 2010.

384 **asked for more time**: Nasser Arrabyee, "Yemeni Journalist Sentenced to Five Years for Terror Links," Nasser Arrabyee (blog), January 18, 2011, narrabyee-e.blogspot.ca.

385 **"paced slowly around the white cell"**: Craig, "Yemen: Press Freedom a Distant Hope."

385 **"When they hid murderers"**: "Yemeni Journalist Accused of Being 'Media Man' for Al-Qaeda," YouTube video, 0:30, from second court appearance, October 26, 2010, posted by "ioniocraig," October 26, 2010, www.youtube.com/watch?v=6J6RgbEx6Zc.

### 42: The President Can Write His Own Rules

386 **"Progress against violent extremists"**: Transcript, "Remarks with British Foreign Secretary David Miliband and Yemeni Foreign Minister Abu Bakr Abdullah al-Qirbi," London, UK, January 27, 2010.

386 **"greatly expanded"**: Aaron W. Jost,

"A Comprehensive Approach to Yemen," The White House Blog, September 24, 2010, www.whitehouse.gov/blog/2010/09/24. All statements and information attributed to Jost come from the post.

386 **"adverse impact on the poor"**: "Joint Statement from the Ministerial Meeting of the Friends of Yemen," New York, September 24, 2010, www.fco.gov.uk/en/news/latest-news/?view=PressS&id=22916622.

387 **"Saleh doesn't really want us"**: Author interview, Colonel W. Patrick Lang, February 2011.

387 **"Security forces have taught the terrorists"**: Fawaz al Haidari, "Yemen Army 'Regains Control' of Southern Town," Agence France-Presse, August 25, 2010.

387 **"dearth of solid intelligence"**: Scott Shane, Mark Mazzetti, and Robert F. Worth, "Secret Assault on Terrorism Widens on Two Continents," *New York Times*, August 14, 2010.

387 **"All Land Rovers"**: Greg Miller, Greg Jaffe, and Karen DeYoung, "U.S. Drones on Hunt in Yemen," *Washington Post*, November 7, 2010.

388 **"For the first time"**: Greg Miller, "CIA Sees Increased Threat in Yemen," *Washington Post*, August 25, 2010.

388 **"mount a more intense"**: Adam Entous and Siobhan Gorman, "U.S. Weighs Expanded Strikes in Yemen," *Wall Street Journal*, August 25, 2010.

388 **"on the upswing"**: Miller, "CIA Sees Increased Threat in Yemen."

388 **"The Agency has taken advantage"**: Gareth Porter, "Behind Drone Issue, a Struggle to Control Covert Ops," Inter Press Service, November 10, 2010.

388 **"elite U.S. hunter-killer teams"**: Julian E. Barnes and Adam Entous, "Yemen Covert Role Pushed; Foiled Bomb Plot Heightens Talk of Putting Elite U.S. Squads in CIA Hands," *Wall Street Journal*, November 1, 2010.

388 **another offensive against AQAP**: Laura Kasinof, "Yemen Goes on Offensive Against al Qaeda," *Christian Science Monitor*, September 22, 2010.

389 **"discussed cooperation"**: "Statement by National Security Council Spokesman Mike Hammer on the Visit of Assistant to the President for Counterterrorism and Homeland Security John Brennan to Yemen," The White House, September 20, 2010, www.whitehouse.gov/the-press-office/2010/09/20/statement-national-security-council-spokesman-mike-hammer-visit-assistan.

389 **late-night phone call**: Mark Mazzetti and Robert F. Worth, "U.S. Sees Complexity of Bombs as Link to al Qaeda," *New York Times*, October 30, 2010.

389 **"potential terrorist threat":** David Jackson, "Obama Monitoring Possible Terrorist Plot, Spokesman Says," *USA Today*, October 29, 2010.

389 **tracking numbers:** Eric Schmitt and Scott Shane, "Saudis Warned U.S. of Attack Before Parcel Bomb Plot," *New York Times*, November 5, 2010.

389 **before arriving at 2:13 a.m.:** Vikram Dodd, Richard Norton-Taylor, and Paul Harris, "Cargo Plane Bomb Found in Britain Was Primed to Blow Up over US," *Guardian*, November 20, 2010.

389 **kept for further tests:** Matt Apuzzo, Eileen Sullivan, and David Rising (AP), "Race to Find Mail Bombs Zigzagged as Cargo Dodged Screens," *Denver Post*, November 7, 2010.

389 **Defense Science and Technology Laboratory:** Duncan Gardham, "Al-Qaeda Plane Bomb Seventeen Minutes from Going Off," *Telegraph*, November 4, 2010.

390 **"activation could have occurred":** Dodd, Norton-Taylor, and Harris, "Cargo Plane Bomb Found in Britain Was Primed to Blow Up over US."

390 **"one of the most sophisticated":** Ibid.

390 **discovered in Dubai:** Scott Shane and Robert F. Worth, "Earlier Flight May Have Been Dry Run for Plotters," *New York Times*, November 1, 2010.

390 **long-dead historical figures:** Ron Grossman and Christi Parsons, "Bomb Plot Becomes Historic Jigsaw Puzzle," *Chicago Tribune*, November 4, 2010.

390 **emergency landing:** Michael Scotto, "JFK-Bound Jet Escorted as Part of Increased Security Following 'Credible' Terror Threat," NY1.com, October 29, 2010.

390 **planes being swept:** "Terror Probe Leads to Searches in NY, NJ," NewYork. CBSlocal.com, October 29, 2010.

390 **"credible terrorist threat":** Jesse Lee, "President Obama: 'A Credible Terrorist Threat Against Our Country, and the Actions That We're Taking," The White House Blog, October 29, 2010.

390 **"We have succeeded":** "Operation Hemorrhage," *Inspire* (November 2010), Special Issue, released November 2010.

391 **dismissed suggestions:** "Dubai Officials Dismiss Claim of Blast on Plane," CNN. com, November 6, 2010.

391 **"maximum losses to the American economy":** Head of Foreign Operations, "The Objectives of Operation Hemorrhage," *Inspire* (November 2010), Special Issue, released November 2010.

391 **indicted Awlaki in absentia:** "Yemen Orders Arrest of al-Awlaki," AlJazeera.com, November 6, 2010.

391 **"How is it that judicial approval is re-**quired":** Al-Aulaqi v. Obama, 1:10-cv-01469-JDB, "Memorandum Opinion by Judge John D. Bates" (DDC December 7, 2010).

392 **If the court's ruling is correct":** Charlie Savage, "Suit over Targeted Killings Is Thrown Out," *New York Times*, December 7, 2010.

### 43: Al Qaeda's "Foothold in Somalia Has Probably Been Facilitated"

393 **"agreement for unification":** Text of agreement, "Somali Website Publishes Islamists' Agreement to Unite with al-Qaidah," *Biyokulule Online*, February 2, 2010, www. biyokulule.com/view_content.php?articleid=2511.

393 **"United States has launched air strikes":** Committee on Foreign Relations, "Al Qaeda in Yemen and Somalia: A Ticking Time Bomb," S. Prt. 111-40, p. 16 (2010).

394 **reaching an agreement:** "Somalia: Islamist MP Resigns After 'Cheating' Ethiopia Jail," *Garowe Online*, April 4, 2009.

394 **As he tells it:** Author interview, Sheikh Ahmed "Madobe" Mohammed Islam, June 2011. All statements and information attributed to Madobe come from the author's interview, unless otherwise noted.

394 **Madobe announced:** Radio Shabelle, "Hizbul Islam Declare War on Al-Shabab in Southern Somalia," *Mareeg*, February 28, 2010, www.mareeg.com/fidsan. php?sid=15312&tirsan=3. Fighting between Madobe's forces and al Shabab had been going on for weeks at this point.

394 **"most important source of income":** Matt Bryden, Jörg Roofthooft, Ghassan Schbley, Babatunde Taiwo, "Report of the Monitoring Group on Somalia and Eritrea Pursuant to Security Council Resolution 1916 (2010)," UN Security Council, July 18, 2011, p. 28.

394 **"training and support":** Paul Cruickshank, "Kenya's High Stakes Shabaab Offensive," Security Clearance (blog), CNN. com, October 24, 2011, http://security.blogs. cnn.com/2011/10/24/kenya's-high-stakes-shabaab-offensive/.

395 **Ethiopian Village restaurant:** Josh Kron, "Bombers Kill More Than Fifty in Attacks in Uganda Capital," *New York Times*, July 11, 2010.

395 **halftime:** Xan Rice, "Uganda Bomb Blasts Kill at Least Seventy-Four," *Guardian*, July 12, 2010.

395 **ninetieth minute:** "Somali Militants Claim Responsibility for Uganda Bombings," CNN.com, July 12, 2010.

395 **Kyadondo Rugby Club:** Vision reporter, "Over Forty Die in Kampala Bomb Blasts," *New Vision* (Kampala), July 12, 2010.

395 **severed head:** Haggae Matsiko, "Ugan-

da: An Unexploded Suicide Vest Found in Makindye, Kampala," *Independent* (Kampala), July 13, 2010.

395 **"very happy"**: "'Somali Link' as Seventy-four World Cup Fans Die in Uganda Blasts," BBC.co.uk, July 12, 2010.

395 **"We will carry out attacks"**: Xan Rice, "Somali Militants Say They Carried Out Deadly Uganda World Cup Blasts," *Guardian*, July 12, 2010.

395 **"We thank the mujahideens"**: "Al-Shabab Claims Uganda Bombings; Twin Attacks Targeting World Cup Fans in Kampala Kill at Least Seventy-four People," AlJazeera.com, July 13, 2010.

396 **terrorism capital**: "Somalia Tops Terror Attack List," UPI, November 18, 2010.

396 **"national emergency"**: Executive Order 13536 (April 12, 2010).

396 **"These indictments and arrests"**: Attorney General Eric Holder, remarks as prepared for delivery at press conference, Washington, DC, August 5, 2010.

396 **"most significant military campaign"**: Bryden et al., "Report of the Monitoring Group on Somalia and Eritrea Pursuant to Security Council Resolution 1916 (2010)," p. 17.

396 **"massive war"**: Associated Press, "Militants Slaughter Lawmakers at Somali Hotel," MSNBC.com, August 24, 2010.

397 **laid siege to the Muna Hotel:** Bryden et al., "Report of the Monitoring Group on Somalia and Eritrea Pursuant to Security Council Resolution 1916 (2010)," p. 17.

397 **tied the remains:** Mohamed Olad Hassan and Malkhadir M. Muhumed (AP), "Somalia Suicide Bomber, Gunmen Attack Muna Hotel, Thirty-two Killed," *Huffington Post,* August 24, 2010.

397 **"This is a particularly outrageous act"**: Transcript, Press briefing by Deputy Press Secretary Bill Burton and Assistant to the President for Counterterrorism and Homeland Security John Brennan," Vineyard Haven, MA, August 24, 2010.

397 **dual car bombing:** Bryden et al., "Report of the Monitoring Group on Somalia and Eritrea Pursuant to Security Council Resolution 1916 (2010)," p. 18.

397 **week of intense violence:** Abdi Sheikh, "Somalia's al Shabaab Rebels Push Towards Palace," Reuters, August 25, 2010.

397 **deadly roadside bomb:** Mohamed Ibrahim, "Somalia: Roadside Bomb Kills Eight Civilians," *New York Times,* August 31, 2010.

397 **displaced by the fighting:** The Editors, "Quick Take: Map of al Shabaab's Mogadishu Offensive," *Critical Threats,* September 23, 2010, www.criticalthreats.org/somalia/quick-take-map-al-shabaabs-mogadishu-offensive.

397 **"overdependence of [al Shabab] on child soldiers"**: Bryden et al., "Report of the Monitoring Group on Somalia and Eritrea Pursuant to Security Council Resolution 1916 (2010)," p. 18.

### 44: "Anwar Awlaki…Definitely Has a Missile in His Future"

398 **convicted of terrorism-related charges:** Iona Craig, "Obama Intervention Puts Yemen Reporter in Jail," *Index on Censorship,* February 7, 2011.

398 **"failed to meet international standards"**: Human Rights Watch, World Report 2011, "Yemen," www.hrw.org/world-report-2012/world-report-2012-yemen.

398 **"It has no legal basis"**: Author interview, Abdulrahman Barman, January 2012. All statements and information attributed to Abdulrahman Barman come from the author's interview, unless otherwise noted.

398 **"Having witnessed his trial"**: Author interview, Iona Craig, March 2012. All statements and information attributed to Iona Craig come from the author's interview, unless otherwise noted.

398 **"There are strong indications"**: "Yemeni Journalist Jailed After Alleging US Involvement in Missile Attack," Amnesty International, January 19, 2011, www.amnesty.org/en/news-and-updates/yemeni-journalist-jailed-after-alleging-us-involvement-missile-attack-2011-01-19.

398 **"It is difficult to overestimate"**: Author interview, Gregory Johnsen, March 2012. All statements and information attributed to Gregory Johnsen come from the author's interview, unless otherwise noted.

399 **call from President Obama:** "Readout of the President's Call with President Saleh of Yemen," The White House, February 3, 2011.

399 **brief hunger strike:** Iona Craig, "Yemen: Shaye Commences Hunger Strike," *Index on Censorship,* February 14, 2012.

399 **"We remain concerned"**: Author interview, Beth Gosselin, March 2012.

400 **"Shaye is in jail"**: Iona Craig, "US Has 'Direct Interest' in Shaye's Case," Iona Craig's Blog, February 21, 2012, http://ionacraig.tumblr.com/post/17969745744/us-ambassador-response-to-shaye-imprisonment.

400 **"the threat is constant"**: Eric Holder, interview with Pierre Thomas, *Good Morning America,* ABC, December 21, 2010.

401 **"Even if what [Awlaki] is saying"**: Author interview, Pardiss Kebriaei, March 2012.

401 **"definitely has a missile in his future"**: Author interview, Malcolm Nance, May 2011.

401 **in missions to kill or capture"**: Duncan Gardham and Richard Spencer, "Cargo

Bomb Plot: SAS Hunting al-Qaeda in Yemen," *Telegraph*, November 2, 2010.

401 **"Al Qaeda in the Arabian Peninsula":** *Understanding the Homeland Threat Landscape—Considerations for the 112th Congress, Hearing Before the House Homeland Security Committee,* 111th Cong. (February 9, 2011) (testimony of Michael Leiter).

402 **"He immediately sent drones":** Author interview, Joshua Foust, January 2011.

**45: The Curious Case of Raymond Davis: Act I**

403 **Big Stone Gap:** Mark Mazzetti, Ashley Parker, Jane Perlez, and Eric Schmitt, "American Held in Pakistan Worked with C.I.A.," *New York Times*, February 21, 2011.

403 **Lahore plate:** Raja Riaz, "'Raymond Davis Tried to Trick Investigators,'" *Daily Times*, February 15, 2011, www.dailytimes.com.pk/default.asp?page=2011\02\15\story_15-2-2011_pg7_17.

403 **withdrawal from an ATM:** "US Official Raymond Davis on Lahore Murder Charges," BBC.co.uk, January 28, 2011.

403 **pulled in front of him:** Declan Walsh, "A CIA Spy, a Hail of Bullets, Three Killed and a US-Pakistan Diplomatic Row," *Guardian*, February 20, 2011.

403 **Davis was arrested:** Riaz, "'Raymond Davis Tried to Trick Investigators.'"

404 **"our diplomat":** Transcript of White House press briefing by Jake Tapper, "Spending Cuts and an American Imprisoned in Pakistan: Todays Qs for O's WH—2/15/11," Political Punch (blog), ABCNews.go.com, February 15, 2011.

404 **Vienna Conventions:** Charlie Savage, "Pakistan Case Tests Laws on Diplomatic Immunity," *New York Times*, February 22, 2011.

404 **"technical adviser":** Matthew Cole, Kirit Radia, and Lee Ferran, "American Official Involved in Pakistan Shooting Identified," ABCNews.go.com, January 28, 2011.

404 **not authorized:** Asif Chaudhry, "US Official Guns Down Two Motorcyclists in Lahore," Dawn.com, January 28, 2011.

404 **Old Anarkali Bazaar:** Walsh, "A CIA Spy, a Hail of Bullets."

404 **"high security zone":** Declan Walsh and Ewen MacAskill, "American Who Sparked Diplomatic Crisis over Lahore Shooting Was CIA Spy," *Guardian*, February 20, 2011.

404 **transferred out of the jail:** Ewen MacAskill and Declan Walsh, "US Gives Fresh Details of CIA Agent Who Killed Two Men in Pakistan Shootout," *Guardian*, February 21, 2011.

404 **Punjab Rangers:** "Rangers Deployed at Kot Lakhpat," *Dawn*, February 14, 2011.

404 **served another purpose:** Ansar Abbasi, "Multiple Security Layers Erected for Raymond Davis," *News International* (PAK), February 11, 2011.

404 **grainy film:** "Raymond Davis Investigation by Punjab Police," YouTube video, 3:06, from a video shot of Davis's initial interrogation, broadcast on the Geo News network, posted by "shoaib748," February 11, 2011, www.youtube.com/watch?v=AkqBF-Dk4Zuo.

405 **least interesting item:** Riaz, "'Raymond Davis Tried to Trick Investigators.'" Unless otherwise noted, this inventory is based on the Riaz article, which claims to have reprinted excerpts of the Punjab police report following Davis's arrest.

405 **multiple IDs:** Greg Miller and Karen DeYoung, "U.S., Pakistan Officials at Diplomatic Odds in Fatal Shooting," *Washington Post*, February 10, 2011.

405 **masks:** Mazzetti et al., "American Held in Pakistan Worked with C.I.A."

405 **calls to twenty-seven militants:** Qaiser Butt, "'CIA Agent Davis Had Ties with Local Militants,'" *Express Tribune*, February 22, 2011.

405 **religious schools:** Brigadier (Ret.) F. B. Ali, "#Update: The Raymond Davis Affair," Sic Semper Tyrannis (blog), February 19, 2011, http://turcopolier.typepad.com/sic_semper_tyrannis/2011/02/update-the-raymond-davis-affair-fb-ali.html.

405 **military institutions:** Walsh, "A CIA Spy, a Hail of Bullets."

405 **Department of Defense contractor:** Jane Perlez, "Mystery over Detained American Angers Pakistan," *New York Times*, February 8, 2011.

405 **number at CIA headquarters:** Walsh and MacAskill, "American Who Sparked Diplomatic Crisis."

405 **"The accused has concealed":** Riaz, "'Raymond Davis Tried to Trick Investigators.'"

405 **well known to Pakistan's spy agency:** Asad Kharal, "Retracing the Path: Trailing Raymond Davis," *Express Tribune*, February 22, 2011.

406 **"Boy, we're in a world of hurt!":** Author interview, Lieutenant Colonel Anthony Shaffer, May 2011.

406 **arrived in Pakistan:** Kharal, "Retracing the Path."

406 **Special Operations weapons sergeant:** Miller and DeYoung, "U.S., Pakistani Officials at Diplomatic Odds in Fatal Shooting."

406 **left the military:** Walsh and MacAskill, "American Who Sparked Diplomatic Crisis."

406 **private security firm Blackwater:** Matthew Cole, "Raymond Davis Is CIA

Contractor, U.S. Officials Say," ABCNews. go.com, February 21, 2011. Details of Davis's reported work with the Global Response Staff are from Cole's reporting.

406 **common cover:** Mazzetti et al., "American Held in Pakistan Worked with C.I.A."

406 **run its drone bombing campaign:** James Risen and Mark Mazzetti, "C.I.A. Said to Use Outsiders to Put Bombs on Drones," *New York Times,* August 20, 2009.

406 **moved between:** Cole, "Raymond Davis Is CIA Contractor."

407 **"Davis was 'vanilla' Special Forces":** Author interview, former JSOC staffer, March 2011. All statements and information attributed to the former JSOC staffer are from the author's interview.

407 **signed a contract worth $200,000:** Munir Ahmed (AP), "Disagreements in Pakistan over Held American; ex-Foreign Minister Disputes Immunity Claim," *Star Tribune,* February 16, 2011.

407 **"loss and risk management professionals":** Cole, Radia, and Ferran, "American Official Involved in Pakistan Shooting Identified."

407 **address in Las Vegas:** Summary of registration, Hyperion Protective Services LLC, business registry database from the website of the Colorado Secretary of State. Screenshot of Colorado registration summary available via Jim White, "Does Raymond Davis Recruit Intelligence Agents in US?" My FDL (blog), My Firedoglake, February 17, 2011, http://my.firedoglake.com/jimwhite/2011/02/17/does-raymond-davis-recruit-intelligence-agents-in-us/.

407 **post office box:** "The UPS Store--#3627, Las Vegas, NV," www.theupsstorelocal.com/3627/.

407 **"The Blackwater individuals":** Author interview, Lieutenant Colonel Jeffrey Addicott, November 2009. All statements and information attributed to Addicott come from the author's interview.

407 **"make much more money":** Author interview, US military intelligence source, November 2009. All statements and information attributed to the military intelligence source come from the author's interview.

408 **first "black" contract:** Robert Young Pelton, *Licensed to Kill: Hired Guns in the War on Terror* (New York: Three Rivers Press, 2006), pp. 36–41; author interviews, former Blackwater and intelligence officials, February–September 2006.

408 **"That's not entirely accurate":** Author interview, former Blackwater executive, November 2009. Details of Blackwater's relationship with Kestral Logistics come from the author's interview.

408 **powerful Pakistani firm:** "Kestral Group of Companies," Kestral Logistics, www.kestral-logistics.com/.

409 **"We cannot help you":** Author interview, David McKeeby, November 2009.

409 **"no operations of any kind":** Mark Corallo, e-mail to author, November 20, 2009.

409 **federal lobbying records:** Lobbying records filed on behalf of Kestral-USA, from the Lobbying Disclosure Act Database, accessed December 2012, http://soprweb.senate.gov/index.cfm?event=submit-SearchRequest.

409 **Kestral had hired:** Lobbying Report, required under the Lobbying Disclosure Act of 1995, Quarter 4 of 2009, Roger F. Noriega, with the DC-based consulting firm Vision Americas, on behalf of Kestral-USA.

409 **Vision Americas:** "Ambassador Roger F. Noriega," Vision Americas website, accessed December 2012, www.visionamericas.com/noriega.php.

409 **Christina Rocca:** "Ambassador Christina Rocca," Vision Americas website, accessed December 2012, www.visionamericas.com/rocca.php.

410 **paid Vision Americas $15,000:** Lobbying report, filed by Roger F. Noriega, Vision Americas, Quarter 3, 2009.

410 **Firecreek Ltd.:** See records of Firecreek Ltd.'s lobbying on behalf of Kestral-USA, Lobbying Disclosure Act Database, accessed December 2012, http://soprweb.senate.gov/index.cfm?event=submitSearchRequest.

410 **called it "conspiratorial":** Transcript, "DoD News Briefing with Geoff Morrell from the Pentagon," November 24, 2009.

411 **"personal consent, Chief of Army Staff General Kayani":** US diplomatic cable 09IS-LAMABAD2449, from Ambassador Anne W. Patterson, US Embassy Islamabad, "Pakistan Army GHQ Again Approves Embedding," October 9, 2009, released by WikiLeaks, http://wikileaks.org/cable/2009/10/09IS-LAMABAD2449.html.

411 **"forward operating troops":** Author interview, Special Operations source, December 2010.

411 **detailed information on refugee camps:** US diplomatic cable 08ISLAM-ABAD3183, from Ambassador Anne W. Patterson, US. Embassy Islamabad, "Taskings for IDP/Refugee Information," October 6, 2008, released by WikiLeaks, http://cablegatesearch.net/cable.php?id=08ISLAM-ABAD3183&q=for%20idp-refugee%20information%20taskings.

412 **Forward Operating Base Chapman:** See Joby Warrick, *The Triple Agent: The al-Qaeda Mole Who Infiltrated the CIA* (New York: Doubleday, 2011).

412 **"Patient relationship-building"**: Ambassador Anne W. Patterson, "Pakistan Army GHQ Again Approves Embedding."

412 **"well, we don't"**: Times Wire, "Bomb Exposes U.S. in Pakistan," *Tampa Bay Times*, February 10, 2010.

412 **civil lawsuit**: Aliza I. Kassim, "Pakistan Defies U.S. Court in Lawsuit over Mumbai Attacks," CNN.com, December 30, 2010.

412 **blew his cover**: Greg Miller and Karin Brulliard, "CIA's Pakistan Chief Removed," *Washington Post*, December 18, 2010.

413 **"terrorist threats against him"**: Ibid.

413 **Davis returned to Pakistan**: Kharal, "Retracing the Path."

**46: The Curious Case of Raymond Davis: Act II**

414 **five CIA security personnel**: Asad Kharal, "Retracing the Path: Trailing Raymond Davis," *Express Tribune* (PAK), February 22, 2011; Matthew Cole, "Raymond Davis Is CIA Contractor, U.S. Officials Say," ABCNews.go.com, February 21, 2011.

414 **also used the house**: Author interview, former Blackwater executive, March 2011.

414 **gathering intel on the terror group Lashkar-e-Taiba**: Mark Mazzetti, "A Shooting in Pakistan Reveals Fraying Alliance," *New York Times*, March 12, 2011.

414 **"area familiarization route"**: Cole, "Raymond Davis Is CIA Contractor."

414 **"It's acting without a script"**: Author interview, Lieutenant Colonel Anthony Shaffer, May 2011. All statements and information attributed to Lieutenant Colonel Shaffer are from the author's interview, unless otherwise noted.

414 **"blood chit"**: Raja Riaz, "'Raymond Davis Tried to Trick Investigators,'" *Daily Times* (PAK), February 15, 2011. The police report describes it as a "chit of the embassy."

414 **"small sheet of material"**: Joint Publication 3-50, Personnel Recovery, January 5, 2008, IV-8, www.dtic.mil/dpmo/laws_directives/documents/joint_pu_3_50.pdf.

414 **"after all other measure(s)"**: Department of Defense memorandum, "Department of Defense Policy on Blood Chits," July 20, 2006, www.dtic.mil/dpmo/personnel_accounting/documents/dod_policy_on_blood_chits.pdf.

415 **crossed "a red line"**: Nick Schifrin, "Did Ray Davis Shoot Two Pakistani Agents?" ABCNews.go.com, February 9, 2011.

415 **"belonged to the security establishment"**: Kamran Yousaf, "Raymond Davis Case: Men Killed in Lahore Were Intelligence Operatives, Says Official," *Express Tribune*, February 5, 2011.

415 **emphatically denied**: "Agencies Rule Out Any Link with Lahore Killing Incident," *News International*, February 8, 2011.

415 **new chief of station**: Rob Crilly, "Raymond Davis 'Was Acting Head of CIA in Pakistan,'" *Telegraph*, February 22, 2011.

415 **"a blessing in disguise"**: Qaiser Butt, "'CIA Agent Davis Had Ties with Local Militants,'" *Express Tribune*, February 22, 2011.

416 **"Davis's job"**: Ibid.

416 **false flag bombings**: Ibid.

416 **"All countries conduct espionage"**: Colonel W. Patrick Lang, comment thread for post by Brigadier (Ret.) F. B. Ali, "#Update: The Raymond Davis Affair," Sic Semper Tyrannis (blog), http://turcopolier.typepad.com/sic_semper_tyrannis/2011/02/update-the-raymond-davis-affair-fb-ali.html.

416 **"a paper-shuffling diplomat"**: Mazzetti, "A Shooting in Pakistan Reveals Fraying Alliance."

417 **drawn up plans**: Marc Ambinder and D. B. Grady, *The Command: Deep Inside the President's Secret Army* (Hoboken, NJ: John Wiley and Sons, 2012, Kindle edition).

417 **"detect, disarm, disable, or seize WMD"**: Glenn W. Goodman Jr., "Deep Underground Tunnels: Counterproliferation Mission Takes SOF Commandos into Tough New Environments," *Armed Forces Journal*, accessed November 2012, www.specialoperations.com/Literature/AFJI/CP.htm.

417 **"second phase of the JSOC influx"**: Brigadier (Ret.) F. B. Ali, "The Fallout from the Davis Affair," Sic Semper Tyrannis (blog), March 1, 2011, http://turcopolier.typepad.com/sic_semper_tyrannis/2011/03/the-fallout-from-the-davis-affair-fb-ali.html.

418 **"following a government directive"**: Kathy Gannon and Adam Goldman, "Pakistan's Intelligence Ready to Split with CIA," Associated Press, February 23, 2011.

418 **more than 3,500 visas**: Karin Brulliard, "In Aftermath of Shooting, Rising Skepticism About American Presence in Pakistan," *Washington Post*, February 22, 2011.

418 **"in a diplomatic capacity"**: Asad Kharal, "After Davis' Arrest, US Operatives Leaving Pakistan," *Express Tribune*, February 28, 2011.

418 **"special Americans"**: Ibid.

418 **"The 'official' version"**: Ali, "The Fallout from the Davis Affair."

418 **pierced his stomach**: Riaz, "'Raymond Davis Tried to Trick Investigators.'"

418 **At least two shots**: Declan Walsh, "A CIA Spy, a Hail of Bullets, Three Killed and a US-Pakistan Diplomatic Row," *Guardian*, February 20, 2011.

419 **photographed them**: Ibid.

419 **license plate**: Asif Chaudhry, "US

Official Guns Down Two Motorcyclists in Lahore," Dawn.com, January 28, 2011.

419 **slammed into the motorcycle:** Walsh, "A CIA Spy, a Hail of Bullets."

419 **made it two miles:** Ibid.

419 **Faletti's Hotel:** Riaz, "'Raymond Davis Tried to Trick Investigators.'"

419 **destroyed all government documents:** Cole, "Raymond Davis Is CIA Contractor."

419 **"They have flown the coop":** Declan Walsh and Ewen MacAskill, "American Who Sparked Diplomatic Crisis over Lahore Shooting Was CIA Spy," *Guardian*, February 20, 2011.

419 **called for Davis to be hanged:** "Rallies Demand Public Execution of Davis," Dawn.com, February 12, 2011.

420 **"is not correct":** Riaz, "'Raymond Davis Tried to Trick Investigators.'"

420 **ordered held for six days:** Karin Brulliard and Aoun Sahi, "U.S. Embassy Demands Release of 'Unlawfully Detained' Diplomat Who Shot Two Pakistanis," *Washington Post*, January 29, 2011.

420 **The United States feared:** Peter Bergen, *Manhunt: The Ten-Year Search for Bin Laden—from 9/11 to Abbottabad* (New York: Crown Publishers, 2012), p. 171.

420 **"Davis incident is a godsend":** "Stuck With You; a Clash Between Spy Agencies Is Boosting the ISI—but Is Doing Pakistan No Favours," *Economist*, March 3, 2011.

421 **"I can confirm":** "American Kills Two Pakistanis in Lahore: US Embassy Spokesman Says Investigations Underway," YouTube video, 3:53, footage from broadcast of Pakistan's Express 24/7 news network, posted by "theexpresstribune," January 27, 2011, https://www.youtube.com/watch?v=mXHjR12GGXo.

421 **"employee of U.S. Consulate":** Glenn Kessler, "Who Is Raymond Davis?" *Washington Post*, February 22, 2011.

421 **"except in the case of a grave crime":** Vienna Convention on Consular Relations, 1963; created April 24, 1963 (entered into force on March 19, 1967), United Nations.

421 **"administrative and technical staff":** Kessler, "Who Is Raymond Davis?"

421 **"unresolved queries":** Baqir Sajjad Syed, "FO Did Not Grant Diplomatic Status to Davis: US," Dawn.com, February 4, 2011.

421 **"I want blood for blood":** Babar Dogar (AP), "Shumaila Kanwal, Pakistani Woman, Commits Suicide After U.S. Shooting," *Huffington Post*, February 6, 2011.

421 **"He was clean":** Rob Crilly, "Widow of Man Shot Dead by US Consul Official Commits Suicide," *Telegraph*, February 7, 2011.

422 **"The arrest of this guy":** Ron Moreau and Sami Yousafzai, "Killings Spark CIA Fears in Pakistan," *Newsweek*, February 17, 2011.

422 **"whatever else they are up to unilaterally":** Philip Giraldi, on comment thread for post by Brigadier (Ret.) F. B. Ali, "#Update: The Raymond Davis Affair," Sic Semper Tyrannis (blog), http://turcopolier.typepad.com/sic_semper_tyrannis/2011/02/update-the-raymond-davis-affair-fb-ali.html.

422 **"We continue to make clear":** Associated Press, "US Ups Pressure on Pakistan over Detained American," FoxNews.com, February 8, 2011.

422 **preparing to recognize:** Ahmad Norrani, "Is Presidency Pushing for Backdated Immunity to Raymond?" *News International*, February 12, 2011.

422 **"Our expert opinion":** Shah Mahmood Qureshi, "Raymond Davis Does Not Enjoy Immunity," YouTube video, 7:40, from coverage of a press conference held by Mr. Qureshi, broadcast on the Express 24/7 network, posted by "MrPoliticians," February 17, 2011, www.youtube.com/watch?v=VsF3HpHZdzc.

422 **snubbed Qureshi:** Karen DeYoung and Karin Brulliard, "U.S.-Pakistan Relations Strained Further with Case of Jailed Diplomat," *Washington Post*, February 8, 2011.

422 **"principled stance":** Qureshi, "Raymond Davis Does Not Enjoy Immunity."

422 **threatened to withhold:** Shaun Tandon, "US Threatens to Cut Pakistan Aid over Shooting," Agence France-Presse, February 8, 2011.

422 **"In an incendiary environment":** Asif Ali Zardari, "As Pakistan Battles Extremism, It Needs Allies' Patience and Help," op-ed *Washington Post*, March 6, 2011.

423 **three prisoners:** Matthew Cole, "U.S. Fears for Life of Outed CIA Contractor in Pakistan Prison," ABCNews.go.com, February 22, 2011.

423 **tested for poison:** Ibid.

423 **"I'm not answering any questions":** "New Video of Raymond Davis Interrogation by Punjab Police, Lahore, Pakistan—WatchGeoNews.com," YouTube video, 1:03, filmed interrogation of Raymond Davis by Punjab police, broadcast on February 15, 2011, posted by "feelpkcom," February 15, 2011, www.youtube.com/watch?v=3hye2lLBZfI.

423 **"In our view, he acted in self-defense":** Agence France-Presse, "US Defends 'Diplomat' Accused of Killing Two in Pakistan," *Dawn*, February 1, 2011.

423 **met with President Zardari:** Jane Perlez, "Pakistan Delays Ruling on Jailed American," *New York Times*, February 17, 2011.

423 **"We have to, respect the law":** Senator John Kerry, "Kerry Regrets Raymond Davis Killing," YouTube video, 33:03, Express 24/7 network coverage of John Kerry's media appearance in Lahore, Pakistan, February 15,

2011, posted by "theexpresstribune," February 15, 2011, https://www.youtube.com/watch?v=dIIXQcOG3tY. Details of the media appearance come from Express 24/7 coverage of the event.

424 **"With respect to Mr. Davis"**: Transcript, "Press Conference by the President," February 15, 2011.

424 **"argued that disclosure of his specific job"**: Mark Mazzetti, Ashley Parker, Jane Perlez, and Eric Schmitt, "American Held in Pakistan Worked with C.I.A.," *New York Times*, February 21, 2011.

424 **"immediately after the shootings"**: Adam Goldman and Kimberly Dozier (AP), "Arrested US Official Raymond Allen Davis Is Actually a CIA Contractor," *Christian Science Monitor*, February 21, 2011.

425 **"American official"**: Waqar Gillani and Jane Perlez, "Pakistan Extends Jailing of American Held in Two Deaths," *New York Times*, February 11, 2011.

425 **"inventory of gadgets"**: Jane Perlez, "Mystery over Detained American Angers Pakistan," *New York Times*, February 8, 2011.

425 **"It's one thing"**: Glenn Greenwald, "The NYT's Journalistic Obedience," Salon.com, February 21, 2011.

425 **"the view that his CIA-ness"**: Chris Elliott, "Open Door: Dangerous Decisions," *Guardian*, February 27, 2011.

425 **"Our security personnel"**: Mazzetti et al., "American Held in Pakistan Worked with C.I.A."

425 **secret talks**: Declan Walsh and Ewen MacAskill, "CIA Spy Escapes Murder Case in Pakistan After US Pays 'Blood Money,'" *Guardian*, March 16, 2011.

425 **"all the Ray Davises"**: Babar Dogar and Chris Brummitt (AP), "Contractor Accused of Murder Released in Pakistan," *Huffington Post*, March 16, 2011.

426 **"one of the most complicated relationships"**: *Current and Projected National Security Threats to the United States, Hearing Before the Select Committee on Intelligence,* 111th Cong. 59 (February 16, 2011) (testimony of Leon Panetta, Director of Central Intelligence).

426 **"ready to split with the CIA"**: Kathy Gannon and Adam Goldman (AP), "Case of Jailed American Causes Deep Rift in Pakistani Spy Agency's Relationship with CIA," *Star Tribune*, February 24, 2011.

426 **refused to sign**: Associated Press, "American: I'm Immune from Pakistan Murder Charge," CBSNews.com, February 25, 2011.

426 **"bogus references"**: Gannon and Goldman, "Case of Jailed American Causes Deep Rift."

426 **another US security contractor**: Declan Walsh, "Pakistan Arrests US Security Contractor as Rift with CIA Deepens," *Guardian*, February 25, 2011.

426 **"most significant events of the last 20 years"**: "Another Mysterious American in Pakistan," Outpost Washington (blog), Radio Free Europe Radio Liberty, February 25, 2011, www.rferl.org/content/pakistan_raymond_davis_america_cia_isi/2321321.html.

426 **fled the country**: Asad Kharal, "After Davis' Arrest, US Operatives Leaving Pakistan," *Express Tribune*, February 28, 2011.

426 **"have been strong"**: Walsh, "Pakistan Arrests US Security Contractor as Rift with CIA Deepens." Some officials claimed to be reviewing "thousands" of visas.

427 **"Where do you go to think seriously"**: General Jehangir Karamat, "The Oman Retreat," *Pakistan Today*, February 26, 2011. *Pakistan Today* published the "readout" of the meeting in Oman between top US and Pakistani officials.

427 **US delegation included**: Kevin Baron, "U.S., Pakistan Military Chiefs Hold Secret Talks in Oman," *Stars and Stripes*, February 23, 2011.

427 **"They will do nothing behind our backs"**: Walsh and MacAskill, "CIA Spy Escapes Murder Case in Pakistan After US Pays 'Blood Money.'"

427 **"CIA made no pledges"**: Carlotta Gall and Mark Mazzetti, "Hushed Deal Frees C.I.A. Contractor in Pakistan," *New York Times*, March 16, 2011.

428 **wanted Davis tried and hanged**: "CIA Contractor Ray Davis Freed over Pakistan Killings," BBC.co.uk, March 16, 2011.

428 **forcibly took**: Huma Imtiaz, "Behind the Scenes of Raymond Davis's Release," *Foreign Policy*, March 16, 2011.

428 **charged with murder**: Walsh and MacAskill, "CIA Spy Escapes Murder Case in Pakistan After US Pays 'Blood Money.'"

428 **"I and my associate"**: "CIA Contractor Ray Davis Freed over Pakistan Killings."

428 **"Now he can go anywhere"**: Babar Dogar (AP), "'Blood Money' Frees CIA Contractor in Pakistan," *Washington Times*, March 16, 2011.

428 **"The *diyyat* provision"**: Brigadier (Ret.) F. B. Ali, "The Davis Saga ends," Sic Semper Tyrannis (blog), March 16, 2011, http://turcopolier.typepad.com/sic_semper_tyrannis/2011/03/the-davis-saga-ends-fb-ali.html.

428 **"did not pay any compensation"**: Transcript, "Remarks to the Traveling Press," Cairo, Egypt, March 16, 2011.

428 **made the payment**: Gall and Mazzetti, "Hushed Deal Frees C.I.A. Contractor in Pakistan."

428 **"special" plane:** "Did Davis Board Viper with His Victims' Heirs?" *News International*, March 17, 2011.

429 **headed for Bagram:** Ron Moreau and Sami Yousafzai, "Blood Money Buys CIA Contractor's Freedom," *Newsweek*, March 16, 2011.

429 **US drone strike:** "US Drone Strike 'Kills Forty' in Pakistani Tribal Region," BBC.co.uk, March 17, 2011.

### 47: The Tsunami of Change

430 **confiscated his cart:** John Thorne, "Bouazizi Has Become a Tunisian Protest 'Symbol,'" *National* (UAE), January 13, 2011.

430 **refused to meet him:** Kareem Fahim, "Slap to a Man's Pride Set Off Tumult in Tunisia," *New York Times*, January 21, 2011.

430 **nearby gas station:** "Tunisia and the Spark That Launched Uprisings," *60 Minutes*, CBS, February 20, 2011.

430 **"The first and probably most important change":** Anwar al Awlaki, "The Tsunami of Change," *Inspire* 5 (spring 2011), released March 2011.

431 **opened fire on the crowd:** Adrian Blomfield, "Yemen Protests: Evidence Snipers Shot to Kill," *Telegraph*, March 19, 2011.

431 **"peaceful youth revolution":** Laura Kasinof, "Yemen General Says Opposition Will Be Ally Against Terrorism," *New York Times*, June 22, 2011.

431 **"political solution":** Indira A. R. Lakshmanan, "U.S. Facing Loss of Key Ally Against al-Qaeda Group in Yemen," Bloomberg, March 22, 2011.

431 **"I don't think it's my place":** Transcript, "Media Availability with Secretary Robert Gates from Moscow, Russia," March 22, 2011.

432 **"The feckless US response":** Author interview, Joshua Foust, March 24, 2011.

432 **"could certainly have a negative impact":** Author interview, Gregory Johnsen, March 2011.

432 **"Hello, Ammar?":** Author interview, Ammar al Awlaki, August 2012. The author relies on Ammar's account of the meeting in Vienna.

### 48: The Fortress in Abbottabad

434 **construction on the residence:** Peter Bergen, *Manhunt: The Ten-Year Search for bin Laden—from 9/11 to Abbottabad* (New York: Crown Publishers, 2012), p. 3. For readers wishing to study the events leading up to the bin Laden raid and the raid itself, the most comprehensive books thus far on these events are Bergen's *Manhunt* and Mark Owen, with Kevin Maurer, *No Easy Day: The Firsthand Account of the Mission That Killed Osama Bin Laden* (New York: Dutton, 2012).

434 **narrow openings:** Ibid., p. 4.

434 **bin Laden unit was shuttered:** Transcript, "Hunt for Osama Bin Laden Shifts Gears," *Morning Edition*, NPR, July 3, 2006.

435 **"number one goal":** Bergen, *Manhunt*, p. 116.

435 **"I think we'll get a call":** Michael Hastings, *The Operators: The Wild and Terrifying Inside Story of America's War in Afghanistan* (New York: Blue Rider Press, 2012), p. 92.

435 **identified by various al Qaeda figures:** Michael Isikoff, "How Profile of bin Laden Courier Led CIA to Its Target," NBCNews.com, May 4, 2011.

435 **followed Kuwaiti's white Suzuki:** Bergen, *Manhunt*, p. 123.

435 **"fortress":** Ibid., p. 124.

435 **burned their trash:** Mark Mazzetti, Helene Cooper, and Peter Baker, "Behind the Hunt for Bin Laden," *New York Times*, May 2, 2011.

435 **grew their own vegetables:** Bergen, *Manhunt*, pp. 12–13.

435 **twenty-five ways:** Ibid., pp. 125–126.

435 **"throw in foul-smelling stink bombs":** Ibid., p. 126.

436 **false Hepatitis B vaccination program:** Saeed Shah, "CIA Organised Fake Vaccination Drive to Get Osama bin Laden's Family DNA," *Guardian*, July 11, 2011.

436 **unable to get any DNA samples:** Bergen, *Manhunt*, p. 127.

436 **"Anatomy of a Lead":** Adam Goldman and Matt Apuzzo, "The Man Who Hunted Osama bin Laden," Associated Press, July 5, 2011. Peter Bergen supplies more details of the memos—the title "Closing In on Usama bin Ladin's Courier" is also from Bergen, *Manhunt*, p. 127.

436 **"pattern of life" analysis:** Bergen, *Manhunt*, p. 131.

436 **"the Pacer":** Bob Woodward, "Death of Osama bin Laden: Phone Call Pointed U.S. to Compound—and to 'the Pacer,'" *Washington Post*, May 6, 2011.

436 **"First of all, congratulations":** Ibid., pp. 166–167.

436 **"McRaven assigned":** Siobhan Gorman and Julian E. Barnes, "Spy, Military Ties Aided bin Laden Raid," *Wall Street Journal*, May 23, 2011.

437 **"Atlantic City":** Ibid.

437 **number of other options:** Ibid. Also see Bergen, *Manhunt*, p. 167.

437 **feared Davis could be killed:** Gorman and Barnes, "Spy, Military Ties Aided bin Laden Raid."

437 **desert in Nevada:** Bergen, *Manhunt*, p. 184.

438 **"wild-goose chase"**: Owen, *No Easy Day*, p. 5.

438 **"almost thirty people in the room"**: Ibid., p. 147.

438 **"some kind of dream team"**: Ibid., pp. 147–148.

438 **"speculation was rampant"**: Ibid., p. 149.

438 **"No fucking way"**: Ibid., p. 154.

438 **chosen for the operation**: Details of the team makeup come from ibid., p. 158.

438 **"house in amazing detail"**: Ibid., p. 160.

438 **"Road to Abbottabad"**: Ibid., p. 163.

439 **"accustomed to hearing helicopters"**: Ibid., p. 173.

439 **"On this mission"**: Ibid., p. 168.

439 **"In terms of difficulty"**: Bergen, *Manhunt*, pp. 185–186.

439 **"it helps that he's from central casting"**: Ibid., p. 185.

439 **"A lawyer from either"**: Owen, *No Easy Day*, p. 177.

440 **"What are the odds"**: Conversation between Bissonnette and "Jen," ibid., pp. 182–184.

440 **8:20 a.m.**: Mark Mazzetti and Helene Cooper, "Detective Work on Courier Led to Breakthrough on Bin Laden," *New York Times*, May 2, 2011.

440 **"It's a go"**: Tom Donilon, interview for History Channel special, *Targeting Bin Laden*, broadcast September 6, 2011.

440 **"Try not to shoot"**: Owen, *No Easy Day*, p. 192.

440 **promoted to SOCOM commander**: Ibid., p. 275.

440 **"And we'll get Obama reelected"**: Ibid., p. 193.

441 **moonless night**: Bergen, *Manhunt*, p. 192.

441 **delay the raid**: Ibid., p. 208.

441 **"I couldn't have any more confidence"**: Jake Tapper, "President Obama to National Security Team: 'It's a Go,'" Political Punch (blog), ABCNews.go.com, May 2, 2011.

441 **Correspondents' Dinner**: "2011 White House Correspondents' Dinner," C-Span video, 1:28:17, coverage of the White House Correspondents' Dinner on April 30, 2011, www.c-spanvideo.org/program/299256-1.

441 **"standing room only"**: Owen, *No Easy Day*, p. 194.

441 **"The story was preposterous"**: Ibid., p. 195.

442 **given them the green light**: Ibid., p. 196.

442 **around 8:00 a.m.**: Bergen, *Manhunt*, p. 212.

442 **Costco**: Nicholas Schmidle, "Getting Bin Laden: What Happened That Night in Abbottabad," *New Yorker*, August 8, 2011.

442 **Multiple pizzerias**: Interview with President Barack Obama, "Inside the Situation Room," *Rock Center*, NBC, May 2, 2012.

442 **At around 1:00 p.m.**: Bergen, *Manhunt*, p. 213.

442 **round of golf**: Darlene Superville (AP), "Obama's Golf Shoes a Clue to bin Laden Raid?" NBCnews.com, May 3, 2011.

442 **could only seat seven people**: Bergen, *Manhunt*, p. 217.

442 **RQ-170 stealth drone, secure communications**: Schmidle, "Getting Bin Laden."

442 **told to stay put**: Bergen, *Manhunt*, p. 217.

442 **inner circle was arguing**: Ibid.

442 **"I need to watch this"**: Schmidle, "Getting Bin Laden."

443 **"ended up [on a] folding chair"**: Interview with President Barack Obama, "Inside the Situation Room."

443 **11:00 p.m. in Abbottabad**: Bergen, *Manhunt*, p. 214.

443 **Black Hawks took off**: Schmidle, "Getting Bin Laden."

443 **"It was nail-biting time"**: Interview with John Brennan, *Targeting Bin Laden*, History Channel special, broadcast September 6, 2011.

443 **rumored to be developing**: Christopher Drew, "Attack on Bin Laden Used Stealthy Helicopter That Had Been a Secret," *New York Times*, May 5, 2011.

443 **"nap of the earth"**: Bergen, *Manhunt*, p. 215.

443 **"Any time that you've got a mission"**: Author interview, General Hugh Shelton, March 2011.

443 **Three MH-47 Chinooks**: Bergen, *Manhunt*, p. 216.

443 **Kala Dhaka**: Schmidle, "Getting Bin Laden."

443 **twenty minutes**: Bergen, *Manhunt*, p. 220.

443 **monitored the events**: Ibid., p. 216.

**49: "We Got Him. We Got Him."**

444 **occasional question**: Peter Bergen, *Manhunt: The Ten-Year Search for bin Laden—from 9/11 to Abbottabad* (New York: Crown Publishers, 2012), p. 218.

444 **ten minutes**: Mark Owen, with Kevin Maurer, *No Easy Day: The Firsthand Account of the Mission That Killed Osama Bin Laden* (New York: Dutton, 2012), p. 210.

444 **"Several of the houses we passed"**: Ibid., pp. 210–211.

444 **"Looking down thirty feet into the compound"**: Ibid., p. 6.

444 **high temperature, weight of the stealth system**: Bergen, *Manhunt*, p. 218.

444 **"we're going in"**: Owen, *No Easy Day*, p. 8.

445 **"The helicopter shuddered"**: Ibid., p. 214.

445 **"If any other part of the helicopter"**: Ibid., p. 215.

445 **"My heart sank"**: Ibid., p. 7.

445 **"That wasn't in the script"**: Interview with Barack Obama, History Channel special, *Targeting Bin Laden*, broadcast September 6, 2011.

445 **"Those were really intense moments"**: Bergen, *Manhunt*, p. 219.

445 **"everyone went, like, 'Whoa'"**: Interview with Joe Biden, "Inside the Situation Room," *Rock Center*, NBC, May 2, 2012.

445 **"We will now be amending"**: Bergen, *Manhunt*, p. 220.

446 **"His demeanor did not change"**: Interview with Ben Rhodes, History Channel special, *Targeting Bin Laden*, broadcast September 6, 2011.

446 **"a cool customer"**: Interview with Barack Obama, "Inside the Situation Room," *Rock Center*, NBC, May 2, 2012.

446 **"We had a sense that"**: Interview with Barack Obama, History Channel special, *Targeting Bin Laden*.

446 **"He is dead"**: Owen, *No Easy Day*, p. 222.

446 **"I spotted a pair of feet"**: Ibid., p. 223.

446 **"The courier's AK-47"**: Bergen, *Manhunt*, p. 221.

446 **another group of SEALs**: Owen, *No Easy Day*, p. 226.

446 **they fell out of contact**: Nicholas Schmidle, "Getting Bin Laden: What Happened That Night in Abbottabad," *New Yorker*, August 8, 2011.

446 **"big chunks of time"**: Transcript, "Obama on bin Laden: The Full '60 Minutes' Interview," by Steve Kroft, *60 Minutes*, CBS, May 4, 2011.

447 **"We were really in a blackout situation"**: Interview with Barack Obama, *Targeting Bin Laden*.

447 **"were set at ninety-degree angles"**: Owen, *No Easy Day*, p. 230.

447 **"Khalid"**: Ibid., p. 231.

447 **"What was Khalid thinking"**: Transcript, "Killing bin Laden," *60 Minutes*, CBS, September 9, 2012.

447 **fired two suppressed rounds**: Owen, *No Easy Day*, p. 235.

447 **"In that second"**: Phil Bronstein, "The Man Who Killed Osama bin Laden...Is Screwed," *Esquire*, February 11, 2013, http://www.esquire.com/features/man-who-shot-osama-bin-laden-0313. The account of the SEAL who shot bin Laden differs from Bissonnette's in a few key places. "The Shooter," as he is called in the *Esquire* piece, says that the women were tackled in the hallway, and that bin Laden was alive and standing in the room when the SEAL shot him in the face. He also claims to have been certain of bin Laden's identity on sight. In his book, Bissonnette appears to assume that bin Laden was fatally shot as the SEALs were coming up the stairs. The differences are likely attributable to the men's different positions in the house on the night of bin Laden's death, and readers are encouraged to review both sources.

447 **"We saw the man lying on the floor"**: Owen, *No Easy Day*, p. 236.

447 **"A hole in his forehead"**: Ibid., p. 239.

448 **"the American public doesn't want to know"**: Bronstein, "The Man Who Killed Osama bin Laden."

448 **"With each swipe"**: Owen, *No Easy Day*, p. 241.

448 **"This had been carefully planned"**: Ibid., p. 245.

448 **questioned the older woman**: Ibid., pp. 245–246.

448 **"Geronimo E.K.I.A."**: Ibid., p. 247.

448 **"We got him"**: Interview with Ben Rhodes, *Targeting Bin Laden*.

449 **"I've got a Geronimo call"**: Bergen, *Manhunt*, p. 225.

449 **gather as many of bin Laden's belongings**: Owen, *No Easy Day*, p. 252.

449 **found two guns**: Ibid., pp. 248–249.

449 **"I saw soldiers emerging"**: Qaswar Abbas and Sandeep Unnithan, "How Pak Is Trapped in Web of Deceit," *India Today*, May 16, 2011.

449 **"We never saw their clothes"**: Transcript, *Anderson Cooper 360 Degrees*, CNN, May 12, 2011.

449 **"We all knew the risks of running out of gas"**: Owen, *No Easy Day*, p. 251.

449 **"We looked like a gypsy camp"**: Ibid., p. 252.

450 **the remaining stealth Black Hawk**: Ibid., p. 253.

450 **$60-million bonfire**: Bob Woodward, "Death of Osama bin Laden: Phone Call Pointed U.S. to Compound—and to 'the Pacer,'" *Washington Post*, May 6, 2011. The price tag of the helicopter was revealed when Woodward reported President Obama's retort to the news of a SEAL lying down next to bin Laden's corpse to measure his height: "We donated a $60 million helicopter to this operation. Could we not afford a tape measure?"

450 **1:00 a.m., just before the SEALs took off**: Zahid Hussain, Matthew Rosenberg, and Jeremy Paige, "Slow Dawn After Midnight Raid," *Wall Street Journal*, May 9, 2011.

450 **"Inform me as soon as our helicopters are out"**: Bergen, *Manhunt*, p. 228.

450 **separate routes:** Ibid.

450 **On the tarmac in Jalalabad:** Owen, *No Easy Day*, p. 262.

450 **choppered out to the Arabian Sea:** Schmidle, "Getting Bin Laden."

450 **"Traditional procedures for Islamic burial":** Associated Press, "Military Emails Reveal Details of bin Laden Burial," CBSNews.com, November 22, 2012.

## 50: "Now They're After My Son"

451 **"Good evening":** Transcript, "Remarks by the President on Osama bin Laden," May 2, 2011.

451 **"did resist the assault force":** Transcript, "Press Briefing by Senior Administration Officials on the Killing of Osama bin Laden," May 2, 2011.

451 **seven of the eleven adults:** Peter Bergen, "A Visit to Osama bin Laden's Lair," CNN.com, May 3, 2012.

451 **According to Pakistani officials:** Robert Booth, Saeed Shah, and Jason Burke, "Osama bin Laden Death: How Family Scene in Compound Turned to Carnage," *Guardian*, May 5, 2011.

451 **"The US administration made clear":** Amnesty International, Annual Report 2012, "United States of America," 2012, https://www.amnesty.org/en/region/usa/report-2012.

452 **"nature of the individual he was":** Transcript, "Press Briefing by Press Secretary Jay Carney and Assistant to the President for Homeland Security and Counterterrorism John Brennan," May 2, 2011.

452 **forced to retract:** Reuters, "Woman Killed in Bin Laden Raid Not His Wife: White House," National Post, May 2, 2011.

452 **issued a directive:** Kimberly Dozier, "McRaven Tells Troops to Pipe Down," Associated Press, The Big Story (bigstory.ap.org), August 12, 2012.

452 **tried to trademark:** Ethan Smith and Julian E. Barnes, "Walt Disney Surrenders to Navy's SEAL Team 6," *Wall Street Journal*, May 26, 2011.

452 **access to sensitive material:** Mark Hosenball, "Senate Panel to Examine CIA Contacts with 'Zero Dark Thirty' Filmmakers," Reuters, January 2, 2013.

453 **snatched by an amphibious team:** Daniel Klaidman, *Kill or Capture: The War on Terror and the Soul of the Obama Presidency* (New York: Houghton Mifflin Harcourt, 2012), p. 238.

453 **transferred to New York and indicted:** United States of America v. Ahmed Abdulkadir Warsame, indictment 11 CRIM 559 (DC Southern district of New York July 5, 2011), graphics8.nytimes.com/packages/pdf/world/Warsame_Indictment.pdf.

453 **endured two months:** Charlie Savage, "U.S. Tests New Approach to Terrorism Cases on Somali Suspect," *New York Times*, July 6, 2011.

453 **provide the ICRC:** Executive Order No. 13491, 74 Fed. Reg. 4893, 4893-94 (January 27, 2009).

453 **"This is illegal and inexcusable":** "U.S. May Have Violated Domestic and International Law in Capturing and Holding Somali for Months at Sea," Center for Constitutional Rights, July 7, 2011, http://ccrjustice.org/newsroom/press-releases/u.s.-may-have-violated-domestic-and-international-law-capturing-and-holding-somali-months-sea.

453 **anonymously boasted:** Pete Williams and Jonathan Dienst, "Member of Terrorist Group Brought to US to Stand Trial," NBCNews.com, July 5, 2011.

453 **"I want Awlaki":** Klaidman, *Kill or Capture*, p. 261.

454 **"knockout blow," "running the table":** Ibid., p. 252.

454 **ordered John Brennan:** Ibid., p. 261.

454 **"The hardware was filled":** Ibid., pp. 262-263.

454 **"vital details of Awlaki's whereabouts":** Margaret Coker, Adam Entous, and Julian E. Barnes, "Drone Targets Yemeni Cleric," *Wall Street Journal*, May 7, 2011.

454 **Dragon Spear aircraft:** Martha Raddatz, "US Missiles Missed Awlaki by Inches in Yemen," ABCNews.go.com, July 19, 2011. Unless otherwise noted, details of the military strikes on May 5, 2011, are from this article.

455 **"Speed up!":** Unless otherwise noted, on-the-ground details of this strike are based on the essay by Shaykh Harith al Nadari, "My Story with al-Awlaki," *Inspire* 9 (winter 2012), released May 2012.

455 **al Harad brothers:** Gregory D. Johnsen, *The Last Refuge: Yemen, Al-Qaeda, and America's War in Arabia* (New York: W. W. Norton, 2013), p. 275.

455 **"You can't see shit":** Author interview, former JSOC planner, October 2012.

455 **Suzuki Vitara SUV:** Mohammed Jamjoom and Hakim Almasmari, "Yemeni Source: Drone Strike Misses al-Awlaki, Hits Two Supporters," CNN.com, May 7, 2011.

456 **stuck with Awlaki's truck:** Ibid.

456 **"We were hoping it was him":** Transcript, *CBS Evening News*, May 6, 2011.

456 **"vehicles were exchanged":** Jamjoom and Almasmari, "Yemeni Source."

456 **"U.S. government has been targeting al-Awlaki":** Transcript, "Deciphering bin Laden's Messages; Drone Strikes; Targeting Awlaki," *John King, USA*, CNN, May 6, 2011.

457 **"now they're after my son":** Tom Finn,

"I Fear for My Son, Says Father of Anwar al-Awlaki, Tipped as new Bin Laden," *Observer*, May 7, 2011.

### 51: "It Was Cold-Blooded"

458 **"counterterrorism cooperation with Pakistan":** Transcript, "Remarks by the President on Osama bin Laden," May 2, 2011.

458 **"did its part":** Asif Ali Zardari, "Pakistan Did Its Part," op-ed *Washington Post*, May 2, 2011.

458 **"We will not allow":** Sajjad Tarakzai, "Bin Laden Dead as Joyful US Says Justice Is Done," Agence France-Presse, May 2, 2011.

458 **"It was cold-blooded":** Kamran Haider and Augustine Anthony, "No Resistance in 'Cold-Blooded' U.S. Raid: Pakistan Officials," Reuters, May 5, 2011.

458 **"an unauthorized unilateral action":** Jane Perlez and David Rohde, "Pakistan Pushes Back Against U.S. Criticism on Bin Laden," *New York Times*, May 3, 2011.

458 **"unprovoked aggression":** Express/AFP, "Zardari and Gilani Should Resign: Qureshi," *Express Tribune*, May 7, 2011.

458 **"Every Pakistani wants to know":** "Altaf Asks Military, Govt to Apologise over US Raid," Dawn.com, May 5, 2011.

458 **"violation of Pakistan's sovereignty":** "Terms of Engagement with US Be Reviewed: Resolution," Dawn.com, May 15, 2011.

459 **"inconceivable":** Transcript, "Press Briefing by Press Secretary Jay Carney and Assistant to the President for Homeland Security and Counterterrorism John Brennan," May 2, 2011.

459 **1,500 Pakistanis protested:** "U.S. Drone Strike in Pakistan; Protests over bin Laden," Reuters, May 6, 2011.

459 **sentenced to thirty-three years:** Jon Boone, "Doctor Who Helped US in Search for Osama Bin Laden Jailed for Thirty-three Years," *Guardian*, May 23, 2012.

459 **"shocking and outrageous":** Senator John McCain and Senator Carl Levin, "Statement by Senators McCain and Levin on Sentencing of Pakistani Doctor Who Assisted in bin Laden Search," press release, May 23, 2012, www.mccain.senate.gov/public/index.cfm?ContentRecord_id=7a9e4f17-9a3f-f98a-ad20-f9fb18505c1d&-FuseAction=PressOffice.PressReleases.

459 **"For us, he's no hero":** Kimberly Dozier and Bradley Klapper, "Pakistan to Talk Counterterrorism with US, Afghans," Associated Press, September 20, 2012.

459 **"Since the killing of the al Qaeda leader":** Master Sergeant Michael O'Connor, "ISAF Mission at Full Speed Following Death of Al Qaeda Leader," ISAF Headquarters, May 12, 2011.

459 **Pakistani soldiers:** Salman Masood and Eric Schmitt, "Tensions Flare Between U.S. and Pakistan After Strike," *New York Times*, November 26, 2011.

### 52: "The US Sees al Qaeda as Terrorism, and We Consider the Drones Terrorism"

460 **counterterrorism units were pulled away:** Margaret Coker, "Rebel General Fights Yemen Regime," *Wall Street Journal*, June 2, 2011.

460 **laid siege to Zinjibar:** Laura Kasinof, "Islamists Seize a Yemeni City, Stoking Fears," *New York Times*, May 29, 2011.

460 **announced themselves as a new group:** Hakim Almasmari and Margaret Coker, "Yemen Unrest Spreads South," *Wall Street Journal*, May 30, 2011.

460 **front for Al Qaeda:** Author interviews, senior Yemeni officials, January 2012.

460 **"The name Ansar al Sharia":** "Online Question and Answer Session with Abu Zubayr Adel al-Abab, Shariah Official for Member of Al-Qaeda in the Arabian Peninsula [AQAP]," April 18, 2011, translation by Amany Soliman, The International Centre for the Study of Radicalization and Political Violence, http://islamopediaonline.org/sites/default/files/abdu_zubayr_english.pdf.

461 **"there could be mortars":** Author interview, General Mohammed al Sumali, January 2012. All statements and information attributed to General al Sumali come from the author's interview.

461 **"heavy artillery pieces":** Madad News Agency, "After Great Attrition of Ali Saleh's Forces on the Doofos Front; Ansar Al-Shari'ah Announces a New Strategy and Different Tactics for Urban Warfare," News Report Issue No. 1, September 2011, translation of online news magazine by Ansar Al-Mujahideen English Forum, released via Jihadology, December 26, 2011, http://azelin.files.wordpress.com/2011/10/ane1b9a3c481r-al-sharc4abah-in-yemen-22news-report-issue-122-en.pdf.

462 **more than 230 Yemeni soldiers:** Fawaz al Haidari, "Yemen Says Hundreds Killed in Qaeda Fight," Agence France-Presse, September 11, 2011.

462 **"handed over Zinjibar to these militants":** Author interview, Abdul Ghani al Iryani, January 2012. All statements and information attributed to Iryani come from the author's interview.

462 **did not respond:** Author interview, Yemeni government official, January 2012.

463 **"political tumult":** Kimberly Dozier (AP), "Al Qaeda Reeling, US Terror Chief Says," Boston.com, September 2, 2011.

463 **declaring an Islamic emirate:** Al Bawaba News, "Yemen: Al Qaeda Declares South Province as 'Islamic Emirate,'" *Eurasia Review*, March 31, 2011.

463 **"Ansar al Sharia has been much more proactive":** Author interview, Gregory Johnsen, January 2012. All information and statements attributed to Johnsen come from the author's interview.

463 **repaired roads, restored electricity:** Sasha Gordon, "Abyani Tribes and al Qaeda in the Arabian Peninsula in Yemen," *Critical Threats*, July 25, 2012, www.criticalthreats.org/yemen/gordon-abyani-tribes-and-al-qaeda-arabian-peninsula-july-25-2012#_edn21.

463 **"brought security to the people":** Author interview, Abdul Rezzaq al Jamal, January 2012. All information and statements attributed to Jamal come from the author's interview.

464 **a gruesome event:** "Al Qaeda Severs Boy's Hand," *Yemen Post*, September 25, 2011, http://yemenpost.net/Detail123456789.aspx?ID=3&SubID=4117.

464 **beheaded two men:** "Islamist Militants Execute Three Men in South Yemen," Reuters, February 12, 2012.

464 **third man executed:** Ibid.

464 **massive air assault:** Daniel Klaidman, *Kill or Capture: The War on Terror and the Soul of the Obama Presidency* (New York: Houghton Mifflin Harcourt, 2012), pp. 253–254.

464 **"where the real priority is":** Ibid., p. 256.

464 **fly supply runs:** Author interview, General Mohammed al Sumali, January 2012.

465 **decided to pull out:** Robert Burns (AP), "U.S. Military Trainers Have Returned to Yemen," *Army Times*, May 8, 2012.

465 **"They have left":** Author interview, Abu Bakr al Qirbi, January 2012.

465 **secret air base:** Greg Miller and Julie Tate, "CIA Shifts Focus to Killing Targets," *Washington Post*, September 1, 2011. The *Washington Post* first reported the construction of the base, revealing only that it was somewhere on the Arabian Peninsula. More than a year later, the *New York Times* confirmed that the base was in Saudi Arabia. See Robert F. Worth, Mark Mazzetti, and Scott Shane, "Drone Strikes' Risks to Get Rare Moment in the Public Eye," *New York Times*, February 5, 2013.

465 **Several southern leaders:** Author interviews, tribal leaders, January 2012.

465 **"Why should we fight them?":** Author interview, Sheikh Ali Abdullah Abdulsalam (Mullah Zabara), January 2012. All information and statements attributed to Mullah Zabara come from the author's interview.

466 **Zabara was assassinated:** Nasser Arrabyee, "Al Qaeda Suspects Killed Tribal Leader, Mediator, Political Asylum Seeker," Nasser Arrabyee (blog), January 10, 2013, http://narrabyee-e.blogspot.com/2013/01/qaeda-suspects-killed-tribal-leader.html.

466 **Shihri had died:** Press statement from the Supreme National Security Committee in the Republic of Yemen, January 24, 2013.

467 **three French aid workers:** Agence France-Presse, "Three French hostages Freed in Yemen Head for Home," November 14, 2011.

468 **"We are not generating good will":** Author interview, Dr. Emile Nakhleh, January 2010.

468 **"greatly exaggerated as a threat":** Author interview, Colonel W. Patrick Lang, February 2011.

## 53: The Pink House

469 **"I salute you and your colleagues":** *Hearing to Consider the Nominations of Lt. Gen. John Allen, Vice Adm. William McRaven, and Gen. James Thurman, Before the Senate Committee on Armed Services,* 111th Cong. (June 28, 2011) (testimony of Admiral William McRaven), video available at www.c-spanvideo.org/program/300255-1.

470 **new counterterrorism center:** Author interviews, Somali and US intelligence sources, June and July 2011.

470 **counterterrorism training program:** Author interviews, Mogadishu, Somalia, June 2011.

470 **"It makes complete sense":** Author interview, US official, July 2011. All statements attributed to the US official come from the author's interview.

470 **"are here full time":** Author interview, Somali intelligence official, June 2011. All information and statements attributed to the senior intelligence official come from the author's interview.

471 **corrupt and untrustworthy:** The corruption of the TFG administration at this time was well documented. See International Crisis Group, "Somalia: The Transitional Government on Life Support," Africa Report No. 170, February 21, 2011: Despite hopes early on that President Sharif would clean up the government, by early 2011 the ICG [International Crisis Group] reported that "corruption has continued unchecked and is now, by most accounts, more pernicious and serious than ever, presided over by powerful establishment figures and permeating every tier of government," p. 12.

471 **$200 monthly cash payments:** Author interviews, Mogadishu, Somalia, June 2011.

471 **"do not bother to be in touch":** Author interview, Abdirahman "Aynte" Ali, June 2011. Unless otherwise noted, all information and statements attributed to Aynte come from the author's interview.

471 **"Same thing is true for Somalia":** *Hearing to Consider the Nomination of Hon. Leon*

*E. Panetta to be Secretary of Defense, Before the Senate Committee on Armed Services*, 111th Cong. (June 9, 2011) (testimony of Leon E. Panetta).

471 **"creating a monster":** Jeffrey Gettleman, Mark Mazzetti, and Eric Schmitt, "U.S. Relies on Contractors in Somalia Conflict," *New York Times*, August 10, 2011.

472 **two white men:** Author interview, former prisoner, June 2011.

472 **pace around constantly:** Author copy of written testimony of Ahmed Abdulahi Hassan.

472 **A Somali journalist:** Author interview, Somali journalist, June 2011.

472 **snatched from flights:** Author interviews, Mogadishu, Somalia, June 2011.

472 **same building:** Author interviews, Somali sources with direct knowledge of NSA operations, June 2011.

472 **"The Hole":** See United States Bureau of Citizenship and Immigration Services, "Somalia: National Security Service Prison (Godka), Mogadishu, Somalia," January 8, 1998, accessed November 15, 2012, www.unhcr.org/refworld/docid/3dfobc514.html.

473 **"shall close as expeditiously as possible":** Executive Order 13491, 74 Fed. Reg. 4893 (January 27, 2009).

473 **"further call into question":** Letter sent by eight organizations to President Obama, "Clarify Alleged CIA Role in Detention and Interrogation in Somalia," September 6, 2011. Sent by the American Civil Liberties Union, Amnesty International USA, Center for Victims of Torture, Physicians for Human Rights, National Religious Campaign Against Torture, The Open Society Foundations, Human Rights First, Human Rights Watch. Accessed November 10, 2012, www.hrw.org/news/2011/09/20/letter-president-obama-clarify-alleged-cia-role-detention-and-interrogation-somalia.

474 **regular shelling:** "Somalia: MPs Condemn Amisom for Shelling Mogadishu's Populated Areas," *Shabelle Media Network*, June 6, 2011.

474 **"We are like orphans":** Author interview, Mohammed Farah Siad, June 2011.

474 **"dual-track":** Johnnie Carson, Assistant Secretary of State for African Affairs, "State Department: A Dual-Track Approach to Somalia," speech at the Center for Strategic and International Studies, October 20, 2010, video available at http://csis.org/event/state-department-dual-track-approach-somalia.

474 **"new label":** Afyare Abdi Elmi, "Dual Track Policy in Somalia Misses the Point," AlJazeera.com, June 9, 2011.

475 **"escalate operations in Somalia":** Gettleman, Mazzetti, and Schmitt, "U.S. Relies on Contractors in Somalia Conflict."

475 **broadcast the execution:** "Shabaab al-Mujahideen Announces Execution of 'CIA' 'Cooperator,'" translation of communiqué released by al Shabab on February 3, 2011, coinciding with the broadcast of the execution, Flashpoint Partners, https://flashpoint-intel.com/inteldocument/flashpoint_shabaab-kataibo211.pdf.

476 **"I believe that the US should help":** Author interview, President Sheikh Sharif Sheikh Ahmed, June 2011.

476 **"more resources than al Shabab":** Lauren Sutherland, "Inside Kenya's Overflowing Refugee Camps," *Nation*, August 15, 2011, www.thenation.com/article/162792/inside-kenyas-overflowing-refugee-camps#.

476 **"between one third and one half":** Matt Bryden, Jörg Roofthooft, Ghassan Schbley, and Babatunde Taiwo, "Report of the Monitoring Group on Somalia and Eritrea Pursuant to Security Council Resolution 1916 (2010)," UN Security Council, July 18, 2011, pp. 43–44.

477 **barely pay its own soldiers:** Katharine Houreld (AP), "Unpaid Somali Soldiers Desert to Insurgency," *Hiiraan Online*, April 28, 2010.

478 **few months earlier:** Author interviews, Mogadishu, Somalia, June 2011.

478 **"One night I fired 120 AK-47 rounds":** Author interview, Yusuf Mohamed Siad, June 2011. All information and statements attributed to Indha Adde come from the author's interviews, unless otherwise noted.

478 **Originally founded:** International Crisis Group, "Somalia's Islamists," Africa Report No. 100, December 12, 2005.

479 **"preach a message":** Ibid.

479 **assassinations, desecrating the tombs:** Author interview, Abdulkadir Moallin Noor, June 2011; International Crisis Group, "Somalia's Divided Islamists," Africa Briefing No. 74, May 18, 2010.

479 **much debate:** Author interview, Abdulkadir Moallin Noor, June 2011.

479 **arming and financing:** Matt Bryden, Arnaud Laloum, and Jörg Roofthooft, "Report of the Monitoring Group on Somalia Pursuant to Security Council Resolution 1853 (2008)," March 10, 2010, p. 12.

479 **boots on the ground:** Matt Bryden, Jörg Roofthooft, Ghassan Schbley, and Babatunde Taiwo, "Report of the Monitoring Group on Somalia and Eritrea Pursuant to Security Council Resolution 1926 (2010)," July 18, 2011, p. 51.

479 **formal cooperation agreement:** International Crisis Group, "Somalia's Divided Islamists."

479 **holy man:** Author interview, Ab-

dulkadir Moallin Noor, June 2011. The following details about Noor's background and return to Mogadishu come from the interview with the author.

479 **"number one":** Ibid. All information and statements attributed to Noor come from the author's interview.

480 **Mudug:** Author interview, Abdulkadir Moallin Noor, June 2011.

480 **"appear to be proxies":** Bryden et al., "Report of the Monitoring Group on Somalia and Eritrea," p. 11.

480 **received support:** Ibid., p. 269.

480 **"most egregious violations":** Ibid., p. 255.

480 **"production of narcotic drugs":** Ibid., p. 53.

480 **"change the balance of power":** Ibid.

480 **"so substantial," four-wheel drive vehicles, "Philippine army-style":** Ibid., p. 268.

480 **"return to the 'warlordism'":** Ibid., p. 11.

481 **close ties to the royals:** Mark Mazzetti and Eric Schmitt, "Private Army Formed to Fight Somali Pirates Leaves Troubled Legacy," *New York Times*, October 4, 2012.

481 **"pro-business and opportunity":** Kareem Shaheen, "Blackwater Founder Questioned in Abu Dhabi," *National* (UAE), August 25, 2010.

481 **"harder for the jackals":** Robert Young Pelton, "Erik Prince, an American Commando in Exile," *Men's Journal*, November 2010.

481 **"make its mark in Somalia":** Author interview, Western official, December 2010.

481 **more than a dozen shipping companies:** Philip Ewing, "Blackwater: Thirteen Firms Want Pirate Protection," *Navy Times*, October 26, 2008.

481 **183-foot vessel:** US diplomatic cable 09DJIBOUTI113, from Ambassador James Swan, US Embassy, Djibouti City, "Djibouti Approves Blackwater for Commercial Counter-Piracy Operations," February 12, 2009, released by WikiLeaks, http://wikileaks.org/cable/2009/02/09DJIBOUTI113.html. Other details about the vessel and its equipment come from the cable.

481 **"We could put vessels out there":** Author copy of recording, Erik Prince speech, January 2010.

482 **250 to 770:** Cheryl Pellerin, "Piracy Challenges Maritime Security off Somalia," America Forces Press Service, January 26, 2011.

482 **snatching three young Somali men:** "'US Marines' Land in Central Somalia, Arrest Suspected Pirate," Shabelle Media Network, January 21, 2011.

482 **"Al Shabab is responsible":** Lolita C. Baldor (AP), "Admiral Calls for Counterterror

Approach to Piracy," Boston.com, January 26, 2011.

482 **extorting from the pirates:** Bryden et al., "Report of the Monitoring Group on Somalia and Eritrea," p. 283. "It is the Monitoring Group's assessment that this arrangement [between the pirates and al Shabab] is local and, to a large extent, clan-based, and no evidence has been found to suggest any broader or more systematic involvement of Al-Shabaab in piracy."

482 **thirty-three years:** Press release from the United States Attorney, Southern District of New York, "Somalian Pirate Sentenced in Manhattan Federal Court to 405 Months in Prison for Hijacking Three Ships and for Hostage Taking," February 16, 2011.

482 **SOS:** Jeffrey Gettleman, "Somali Pirates Hijack Yacht with Americans Aboard," *New York Times*, February 19, 2011.

482 **275 miles:** "Somali Pirates Seize American Yacht Crew off Oman," bbc.co.uk, February 18, 2011.

482 **supported by helicopters:** Kevin Dolak, Luis Martinez, and Jeremy Hubbard, "Warship Tracking Yacht Hijacked by Somali Pirates," ABCNews.go.com, February 20, 2011.

482 **unarmed surveillance drones:** Transcript, "DOD News Briefing with Vice Adm. Fox via Telephone from Bahrain on Somali Piracy Aboard the S/V Quest," February 22, 2011.

482 **lethal force:** David Jackson, "Obama Notified of Pirate Killings at 4:42 a.m.," *USA Today*, February 22, 2011.

483 **willingly boarded:** Eric Schmitt, "Seizing of Pirate Commanders Is Questioned," *New York Times*, February 23, 2011.

483 **hand-to-hand combat:** Transcript, "DOD News Briefing with Vice Adm. Fox."

483 **too late:** Adam Nagourney and Jeffrey Gettleman, "Pirates Brutally End Yachting Dream," *New York Times*, February 22, 2011.

483 **took credit:** "Pirates Could Face Trial in US over American Deaths," BBC.co.uk, February 23, 2011.

483 **fifteen remaining pirates:** Hanna Siegel, "Pirates Charged in Death of American Yachters," ABCNews.go.com, March 10, 2011.

483 **inked a deal:** Ambassador James Swan, "Djibouti Approves Blackwater for Commercial Counter-Piracy Operations." Details of the arrangement and the ship come from the cable.

484 **"likely oil reserves":** "Somalia," CIA World Factbook, https://www.cia.gov/library/publications/the-world-factbook/geos/so.html.

484 **counterpiracy/counterterrorism force:** Associated Press, "One-Thousand-Man Mi-

litia Being Trained in North Somalia," *USA Today*, December 1, 2010.

484 **later be revealed:** Mark Mazzetti and Eric Schmitt, "Blackwater Founder Said to Back Mercenaries," *New York Times*, January 20, 2011.

484 **Executive Outcomes:** Ibid.

484 **offices and shell companies:** Bryden et al., "Report of the Monitoring Group on Somalia and Eritrea," p. 274.

484 **Civil Cooperation Bureau:** Desmond Tutu, Alex Boraine, Mary Burton, Bongani Finca, Sisi Khampepe, Richard Lister, Wynand Malan, Khoza Mgojo, Hlengiwe Mkhize, Dumisa Ntsebeza, Wendy Orr, Fazel Randera, Yasmin Sooka, and Glenda Wildschut, Truth and Reconciliation Commission of South Africa Report, vol. 2, October 29, 1998, pp. 138–139. Lafras Luitingh is described by the commission as a "core member" of the CCB who held the position of "administrative or production manager" on its management board.

484 **"seed money":** Ibid.

484 **officials from Abu Dhabi:** Bryden et al., "Report of the Monitoring Group on Somalia and Eritrea," p. 274.

484 **also hired:** Associated Press, "One-Thousand-Man Militia Being Trained in North Somalia."

484 **1,000-member counterpiracy force:** Ibid.

484 **"You cannot have oil exploration":** Ibid.

484 **well under way:** Bryden et al., "Report of the Monitoring Group on Somalia and Eritrea." The following details of Saracen's work in Somalia are found pp. 53, 276–279, and 281–282.

485 **traveled to Mogadishu:** Ibid., p. 275.

485 **at least five other private companies:** Mohamed Ibrahim and Jeffrey Gettleman, "Parliament Takes on Contractors in Somalia," *New York Times*, December 30, 2010.

485 **"unknown armed groups":** Bryden et al., "Report of the Monitoring Group on Somalia and Eritrea," p. 275.

485 **demanding the suspension:** Ibrahim and Gettleman, "Parliament Takes on Contractors in Somalia."

485 **"opaque web of affiliated entities":** Matt Bryden et al., "Report of the Monitoring Group on Somalia and Eritrea pursuant to Security Council resolution 1926 (2010)," p. 53.

485 **"increased tension":** Ibid., p. 282.

485 **overcome the scourge of piracy:** Katherine Houreld (AP), "Blackwater Founder Secretly Backing Somali Militia," Salon.com, January 20, 2011.

485 **"anything to do with Blackwater":** Jeffrey Gettleman, "Somalia Is Likely to Cut Ties to Mercenaries, Official Says," *New York Times*, January 23, 2011.

485 **negotiations around the Saracen deal:** Bryden et al., "Report of the Monitoring Group on Somalia and Eritrea," p. 275.

485 **suspending Saracen's operations:** Ibid., p. 273.

485 **discreetly operating:** Author interview, senior Somali official, June 2011.

485 **other private security companies:** Bryden et al., "Report of the Monitoring Group on Somalia and Eritrea," p. 256.

486 **"American footprint":** Gettleman, Mazzetti, and Schmitt, "U.S. Relies on Contractors in Somalia Conflict."

**54: "Total Savagery Throughout the Country"**

487 **$5 million bounty:** Malkhadir M. Muhumed and Jason Straziuso (AP), "Fazul Abdullah Mohammed, Alleged U.S. Embassy Bomber, Dead: Somali Government," *Huffington Post*, June 11, 2011.

487 **"We shall redouble our struggle":** Abdi Sheikh, "Somalia's al Shabaab Vows to Avenge bin Laden," Reuters, May 7, 2011.

487 **"He was criticizing them":** Author interview, Mogadishu, Somalia, June 2011. All information and statements attributed to the "Somali source" come from the author's interview.

487 **finding it increasingly difficult:** Author interview, Mogadishu, Somalia, June 2011.

488 **increased the size of its forces:** Abdi Sheikh, "Burundi Sends 1,000 Extra AU Troops to Somalia," Reuters, March 12, 2011.

488 **pushing into al Shabab territory:** Agence France-Presse, "Amisom Pinning Back Rebels in Mogadishu," News24.com, April 7, 2011.

488 **new technology:** Associated Press, "Pentagon Sends Drones, Anti-Terror Equipment to Counterterror Forces Dealing with Somalia," FoxNews.com, June 26, 2011.

488 **South African passport:** Malkhadir M. Muhumed (AP), "Young Somali Soldier: I Killed Top al-Qaida Operative," NBCnews.com, June 14, 2011.

488 **high on khat:** Mohamed Odowa, "Fazul's Last Moments; Soldiers Tell of Shootout That Killed Al-Qaeda Commander," SomaliaReport.com, June 16, 2011.

489 **refused to comply with instructions:** Author interviews, Somali militia members at the scene, June 2011, and a senior Somali intelligence official, June 2011.

489 **they discovered:** Jeffrey Gettleman, "Somalis Kill Mastermind of Two U.S. Embassy Bombings," *New York Times*, June 11, 2011.

489 **promptly looted the car:** Author interview, Somali intelligence official, June 2011.

489 **"There was a lot of English and Arabic stuff"**: Ibid. All information and statements attributed the Somali intelligence official come from the author's interview.

489 **The men's bodies were taken**: Details of what happened after the raid are from the author's interview with the Somali intelligence official.

489 **"significant blow to Al Qaeda"**: Secretary Clinton's statement to the press, "Death of Harun Fazul," June 11, 2011, www.state.gov/secretary/rm/2011/06/165942.htm.

489 **"to take over as much land as possible"**: Author interview, Abdirahman "Aynte" Ali, June 2011. All information and statements attributed to Aynte come from the author's interview.

490 **United States carried out a strike**: Malkhadir M. Muhumed (AP), "Somalia Says US Forces Snatch Militants Hit in Drone Strike," Boston.com, July 2, 2011.

490 **three more US strikes**: Aweys Cadde, "Airstrikes Hit Lower Juba...Again," SomaliaReport.com, July 6, 2011.

490 **"Both at the same time"**: Author interview, President Sheikh Sharif Sheikh Ahmed, June 2011.

490 **"We will continue to pummel"**: John Brennan, "Ensuring al-Qa'ida's Demise," prepared remarks for delivery at the Paul H. Nitze School of Advanced International Studies, Washington, DC, June 29, 2011.

490 **extreme toll on Somali civilians**: Daniel Maxwell and Merry Fitzpatrick, "The 2011 Somalia Famine: Context, Causes, and Complications," *Global Food Security* 1 (1) (December 2012), http://dx.doi.org/10.1016/j.gfs.2012.07.002.

490 **flocking to the violence-rocked capital**: Jane Ferguson and Moni Basu, "Amid Famine, Somalis Flock Back to the War-Torn City They Fled," CNN.com, July 22, 2011.

490 **30,000 refugees had arrived**: Lauren Sutherland, "Inside Kenya's Overflowing Refugee Camps," *Nation*, August 15, 2011.

490 **lost its ability to collect taxes**: Dr. Afyare Abdu Elmi and Abdi Aynte, "Somalia: The Case for Negotiating with al-Shabaab," Al Jazeera Center for Studies, January 16, 2012, http://studies.aljazeera.net/ResourceGallery/media/Documents/2012/2/16/20122161343 14443734Somalia_The%20Case%20for%20 Negotiating%20with%20al-Shabab.pdf.

490 **monsoon season hit**: Associated Press, "Taxes Hastened Somalia's Famine, Militant Retreat," FoxNews.com, October 1, 2011.

491 **well-organized retreat**: Jeffrey Gettleman and Mohammed Ibrahim, "Shabab Concede Control of Capital to Somalia Government," *New York Times*, August 6, 2011.

491 **evening of attacks**: Mohamed Ahmed

and Ibrahim Mohamed, "Somali Government Declares Islamist Rebellion Defeated," Reuters, August 6, 2011.

491 **"completely vacated Mogadishu"**: Gettleman and Ibrahim, "Shabab Concede Control of Capital to Somalia Government."

491 **"We shall fight the enemy wherever they are"**: "Somalia's al-Shabab Rebels Leave Mogadishu," BBC.co.uk, August 6, 2011.

491 **"harvest the fruits of peace"**: Jeffrey Fleishman and Lutfi Sheriff Mohammed, "Somali Shabab Militants Retreat from Mogadishu," *Los Angeles Times*, August 6, 2011.

491 **90 percent of the city**: Abdi Sheikh Mohamed Ahmed, "Fighting Erupts in Somali Capital After Rebels Say Leaving," Reuters, August 7, 2011.

491 **20,000 troops**: "World Must Aid Somalia at Historic Juncture on Its Road to Stability—UN Envoy," UN News Centre, August 10, 2011.

491 **"Al-Qaeda's elements in East Africa"**: Michael G. Vickers, Under Secretary of Defense for Intelligence, "The Evolution of Al-Qaeda and Associated Movements," prepared remarks for delivery at a National Defense University symposium, September 13–14, 2011, www.ndu.edu/inss/docupload-ed/VICKERS.pdf.

491 **fifteen-ton truck**: Mohamed Ibrahim and Jeffrey Gettleman, "Truck Bomb Kills Dozens in Somalia's Capital," *New York Times*, October 4, 2011.

491 **"This is the biggest attack"**: Clar Ni Chonghaile, "Mogadishu Truck Bomb: al-Shabaab Insurgents Claim Responsibility," *Guardian*, October 4, 2011.

492 **launched an offensive**: Jeffrey Gettleman, "African Union Force Makes Strides Inside Somalia," *New York Times*, November 24, 2011.

492 **"Battle of Daynile"**: "The Burundian Bloodbath: Battle of Dayniile," video, 32:28, propaganda video from al Shabab's Al-Kata'ib Media Foundation, released November 12, 2011, posted on Vimeo by "Saadaal Wacan," November 12, 2011, http://vimeo.com/32059413. The author relies on the video for details of Shabab's treatment of the slain soldiers, and for the statement from Sheik Rage.

492 **"Claims of al-Shabab's imminent collapse"**: Christopher Anzalone, "Al-Shabab's Setbacks in Somalia," *CTC Sentinel* 4 (10) (October 2011).

493 **series of meetings**: Ibid.

493 **"To our beloved brothers and sisters"**: Jamal Osman, "Al-Qaida Targets Somalia Drought Victims with Cash Handouts," *Guardian*, November 1, 2011.

493 **"Whoever thinks today"**: "Speech of

Mujahid Sheikh Mukhtar Abu Al-Zubeyr About the Death of Qaddafi and the Historical Battle of Dayniile," translation and transcription of speech delivered by Mukhtar Abu al-Zubeyr (aka Ahmed Abdi Godane), posted on the Ansar al-Mujahideen forum on November 17, 2011, www.ansar1.info/show-thread.php?t=36981.

494 **"They are not fighting for a cause":** Author interview, Mohamed Ahmed Nur, June 2011.

494 **"If you use the drone":** Author interview, Ismail Mahmoud Hurre, June 2011.

494 **new drone base in Ethiopia**: Craig Whitlock, "U.S. Drone Base in Ethiopia Is Operational," *Washington Post*, October 27, 2011.

## 55: Abdulrahman Vanishes

495 **"always thought that it is best":** Author interview, Nasser al Awlaki, January 2012. All statements and information attributed to Nasser al Awlaki come from the author's interview, unless otherwise noted.

495 **one of the closest people to my heart:** Author interview, Abir al Awlaki, September 2012.

496 **"Ibn al Shaykh":** Facebook page of Abdulrahman al Awlaki, screenshot downloaded by author.

496 **loved hip-hop music:** Author interviews, Awlaki family members, August 2012. The following details about Abdulrahman come from the author's interviews with family members.

496 **Abdulrahman woke up:** Author interview, Nasser al Awlaki, January 2012. Details about Abdulrahman's departure come from the author's interview with Awlaki, unless otherwise noted.

496 **had turned sixteen:** Author copy of Abdulrahman al Awlaki's birth certificate.

496 **"I am sorry for leaving":** This description of Abdulrahman's note is based on the recollections of family members.

496 **"find his father through him":** Author interview, Saleha al Awlaki, September 2012.

## 56: Hellfire

498 **"The CIA has become more militarized":** Author interview, Philip Giraldi, March 2012. All information and statements attributed to Philip Giraldi are from the author's interview.

498 **"a mini-Special Operations Command":** Author interview, State Department liaison, November 2012.

498 **"be a major player":** Author interview, Colonel W. Patrick Lang, November 2012.

498 **interrogation sessions with Ahmed Abdulkadir Warsame**: Daniel Klaidman, *Kill or Capture: The War on Terror and the Soul of*

the Obama Presidency (New York: Houghton Mifflin Harcourt, 2012), p. 263.

499 **small house in Khashef:** David S. Cloud, Jeffrey Fleishman, and Brian Bennett, "U.S. Drone Strike in Yemen Kills U.S.-Born Al Qaeda Figure Awlaki," *Los Angeles Times*, October 1, 2011.

499 **kingdom's payroll:** Mark Mazzetti, Eric Schmitt, and Robert F. Worth, "C.I.A. Strike Kills U.S.-Born Militant in a Car in Yemen," *New York Times*, October 1, 2011.

499 **seeing drones hovering:** Sudarsan Raghavan, "Anwar al-Aulaqi, US-Born Cleric Linked to al-Qaeda, Killed in Yemen," *Washington Post*, October 1, 2011.

499 **took operational control:** Greg Miller, "Strike on Aulaqi Demonstrates Collaboration Between CIA and Military," *Washington Post*, September 30, 2011.

499 **Operation Troy:** "U.S. Officials Warn of Possible Retaliation After al Qaeda Cleric Is Killed," CNN.com, September 30, 2011.

499 **arrived in Ataq:** Interview, Nasser al Awlaki, August 2012. All information and statements attributed to Nasser al Awlaki come from the author's interview, unless otherwise noted. The details of Abdulrahman's movements in Shabwah are based on the author's interview.

499 **"I called the family house":** Interview, Saleha al Awlaki, August 2012. All information and statements attributed to Abdulrahman's grandmother, Saleha, are from the author's interview.

499 **"no qualms":** Klaidman, *Kill or Capture*, p. 264.

500 **"Bring it to me and let me decide":** Ibid.

500 **"collateral requirements":** Ibid.

500 **stayed in the same house:** Ibid.

500 **finished their breakfast:** Sudarsan Raghavan, "Awlaqi Hit Misses Al-Qaeda Bombmaker, Yemen Says," *Washington Post*, September 30, 2011.

500 **JSOC aircraft and ground forces:** David Martin, "Al-Awlaki Strike Plan Included Jets, Special Ops," CBSNews.com, September 30, 2011.

500 **"eleven missiles missed":** Shaykh Harith al Nadari, "My Story with al-Awlaki," *Inspire* 9 (winter 2012), released May 2012.

500 **"Anwar Awlaki has been killed":** "Anwar al-Awlaki Killed in Yemen," AlJazeera.com, September 30, 2011.

500 **9:55 a.m. local time:** "U.S. Officials Warn of Possible Retaliation After al Qaeda Cleric Is Killed."

500 *jambiya* **dagger:** Author interview, Nasser al Awlaki, January 2012.

501 **"Earlier this morning":** Transcript, "Remarks by the President at the 'Change of Office' Chairman of the Joint Chiefs of Staff

Ceremony," Fort Myer, VA, September 30, 2011.

501 **doubted the official reports:** Author interviews, Awlaki family members, April 2012.

502 **"when I opened the computer":** Author interview, Sarah Khan, April 2012. All information and statements attributed to Sarah Khan are from the author's interview.

502 **FBI had told his family:** Author interview, Sarah Khan, April 2012.

502 **"It has been stated in the media":** Tim Funk, "Family of al Qaida Blogger Samir Khan 'Appalled' by U.S. Actions," *Charlotte Observer*, October 6, 2011.

502 **"collateral damage":** Klaidman, *Kill or Capture*, p. 264.

502 **"It was a twofer":** David S. Cloud, Jeffrey Fleishman, and Brian Bennett (Tribune), "U.S. Drones Kill Influential Al-Qaida Operative in Yemen," *Spokesman Review*, October 1, 2011.

503 **"This is an extraordinary victory":** Tim Mak, "Peter King Praises Obama for al-Awlaki Killing," *Politico*, September 30, 2011.

503 **"significant and imminent threat":** Senator Dianne Feinstein and Senator Saxby Chambliss, "Feinstein, Chambliss Release Statement on Death of al-Awlaki," press release from Senator Feinstein's website, September 30, 2011, www.feinstein. senate.gov/public/index.cfm/press-releases?ID=08023496-6f2d-4600-af42-ec-642488cea9.

503 **"like Osama bin Laden":** Transcript, "Remarks at the Kumpris Distinguished Lecture Series," Clinton Presidential Center, Little Rock, AR, September 30, 2011.

503 **"I'm glad they did it":** Craig Whitlock, "U.S. Airstrike That Killed American Teen in Yemen Raises Legal, Ethical Questions," *Washington Post*, October 22, 2011.

503 **"I do think this was a good strike":** Transcript, *State of the Union with Candy Crowley*, CNN, October 2, 2011.

503 **"This individual was clearly a terrorist":** Michael Martinez, "U.S. Drone Killing of American al-Awlaki Prompts Legal, Moral Debate," CNN.com, September 30, 2011.

503 **"Another al Qaeda Bites the Dust":** Front page of the *New York Post*, October 1, 2011, retrieved from Nexis.

503 **"Remote-Control Really Hits the Splat":** Chuck Bennett, "Remote-Control Really Hits the Splat," *New York Post*, October 1, 2003.

503 **"One Less Terror Big":** Joseph Straw, Aliyah Shahid, and Larry McShane, "One Less Terror Big: Al Qaeda Loses Leader in Attack," *Daily News* (New York), October 1, 2011.

503 **"Awlaki was born here":** Martinez, "U.S. Drone Killing of American al-Awlaki Prompts Legal, Moral Debate."

504 **"crossed a dangerous divide":** Representative Dennis Kucinich, "Kucinich on the Extrajudicial Killing of Anwar al-Awlaki: Wrong Legally, Constitutionally and Morally," press release from Representative Kucinich's website, September 30, 2011, http://kucinich.house.gov/news/documentsingle.aspx?DocumentID=262506.

504 **"After several unsuccessful efforts":** Glenn Greenwald, "The Due-Process-Free Assassination of U.S. Citizens Is Now Reality," Salon.com, September 30, 2011.

504 **"Remember that there was great controversy":** Transcript, "With Death of Anwar al-Awlaki, Has U.S. Launched New Era of Killing U.S. Citizens Without Charge?" *Democracy Now!* September 30, 2011.

504 **"there isn't a government on the planet":** Doyle McManus, "Who Reviews the U.S. 'Kill List'?" *Los Angeles Times*, February 5, 2012.

505 **"There's a process":** Brian Witte (AP), "Rep. Ruppersberger Discusses al-Awlaki Death," FederalNewsRadio.com, September 30, 2011.

505 **"It's important for the American people to know":** Author interview, Senator Ron Wyden, March 2012.

## 57: Paying for the Sins of the Father

507 **encouraged him to get out with his cousins:** Author interviews, Awlaki family members, January and August 2012. Details of Abdulrahman's activities on the night of October 14 are from the author's interviews, unless otherwise noted.

507 **seventeen-year-old cousin, Ahmed:** Author interview, Nasser al Awlaki, January 2012.

507 **"Some of our relatives went":** Ibid.

507 **"military-aged":** Hamza Hendawi (AP), "Yemen: Abdul-Rahman Al-Awlaki, Anwar Al-Awlaki's Son, Among Al Qaeda Militants Killed in U.S. Drone Strike," *Huffington Post*, October 15, 2011.

507 **while meeting with Ibrahim al Banna:** Ibid.

507 **"To kill a teenager is just unbelievable":** Peter Finn and Greg Miller, "Anwar al-Awlaki's Family Speaks Out Against His Son's Death in Airstrike," *Washington Post*, October 17, 2011.

507 **"When he was killed by the US government":** Author interview with Nasser al Awlaki, January 2012. All information and statements attributed to Nasser al Awlaki are from the author's interview, unless otherwise noted.

508 **"We have seen press reports":** Finn and Miller, "Anwar al-Awlaki's Family Speaks Out."

508 **"We watched with surprise and condemnation":** Statement released by the Awlaki family, October 2011, available at http://upstatedroneaction.org/wordpress/2011/11/23/a-family-mourns/.

508 **"People flocked to our house":** Author interview, Abir al Awlaki, August 2012.

509 **"I look around the house":** Author interview, Saleha al Awlaki, September 2012.

509 **JSOC strike:** Greg Miller, "Under Obama, an Emerging Global Apparatus for Drone Killing," *Washington Post*, December 27, 2011.

509 **"the two kill lists don't match":** Ibid.

509 **was, in fact, still alive:** Author interview with a JSOC official, January 2013.

509 **closed briefing:** Craig Whitlock, "U.S. Airstrike That Killed American Teen in Yemen Raises Legal, Ethical Questions," *Washington Post*, October 22, 2011.

509 **"These lies and allegations":** Agence France-Presse, "Yemen's Al-Qaeda Denies Death of Its Media Chief," October 30, 2011.

510 **"I do know this":** Transcript, *State of the Union with Candy Crowley*, CNN, March 11, 2012.

510 **"I'm convinced":** Representative Peter King, interview by Ryan Devereaux, March 2012.

510 **"that's the breaks":** "Romney Rep. Peter King: Presidential Kill List Totally Constitutional," video, 1:53, Luke Rudkowski of We Are Change interviewing Representative King at an event for the October 22, 2012, presidential debate, WeAreChange.org, October 23, 2012.

510 **"you should have a far more responsible father":** "Obama Top Adviser Robert Gibbs Justifies Murder of Sixteen Year Old American Citizen," YouTube video, 3:26, Sierra Adamson of We Are Change interviewing Robert Gibbs at an event for the October 22, 2012, presidential debate, posted by "wearechange," October 23, 2012, www.youtube.com/watch?feature=player_embedded&v=7MwB2znBZ1g.

510 **"It is up to the US government to be sure":** Author interview, Nasser al Awlaki, January 2012.

511 **"an outrageous mistake":** Karen DeYoung, "A CIA Veteran Transforms U.S. Counterterrorism Policy," *Washington Post*, October 24, 2012.

**Epilogue**

513 **"A decade of war":** Transcript, "Inaugural Address by President Barack Obama," January 21, 2013.

513 **US drone strike:** Reuters, "U.S. Drone Strike Kills Four in Yemen: Sources," January 21, 2013.

513 **more people had been killed:** According to available estimates, in 2012 drone strikes killed at least 246 people in Pakistan, and at least 185 people in Yemen. In Somalia, there were only two confirmed strikes—although operations in Somalia are especially likely to go underreported—killing at least a dozen people. See Chris Woods, Jack Serle, and Alice K. Ross, "Emerging from the Shadows: US Covert Drone Strikes in 2012," *Bureau of Investigative Journalism*, January 3, 2013. As of November 2012, there were 166 people in detention at Guantánamo Bay; see Associated Press, "Report Shows U.S. Jails Could House Guantanamo Detainees," CBSNews.com, November 2012.

513 **systematizing the kill list:** Greg Miller, Ellen Nakashima, and Karen DeYoung, "CIA Drone Strikes Will Get Pass in Counterterrorism 'Playbook,' Officials Say," *Washington Post*, January 19, 2013.

513 **one hundred countries:** Admiral William McRaven, Commander, US Special Operations Command, "Posture Statement," prepared for the Senate Armed Services Committee, March 6, 2012.

513 **nomination was scuttled:** Pamela Hess (AP), "Potential CIA Chief Cites Critics in Ending Bid," *Seattle Times*, November 26, 2008.

514 **"playbook":** Miller, Nakashima, and DeYoung, "CIA Drone Strikes Will Get Pass."

514 **"now so routine":** Greg Miller, "Plan for Hunting Terrorists Signals U.S. Intends to Keep Adding Names to Kill Lists," *Washington Post*, October 23, 2012. The following details of Brennan's role and the "Disposition Matrix" are from the *Washington Post* article.

514 **"white paper":** Department of Justice white paper, "Lawfulness of a Lethal Operation Directed Against a U.S. Citizen Who Is a Senior Operational Leader of Al-Qa'ida or An Associated Force," obtained by NBC News, released February 4, 2013, http://msnbcmedia.msn.com/i/msnbc/sections/news/020413_DOJ_White_Paper.pdf.

514 **"chilling document":** Michael Isikoff, "Exclusive: Justice Department Memo Reveals Legal Case for Drone Strikes on Americans," NBCNews.com, February 4, 2013.

515 **"This power is going to be available":** Transcript, "Kill List Exposed: Leaked Obama Memo Shows Assassination of U.S. Citizens 'Has No Geographic Limit,'" *Democracy Now!*, February 5, 2013.

515 **"I don't oppose all wars":** Barack Obama, "Transcript: Obama's Speech Against the Iraq War," October 2, 2002, transcript

available via NPR.org, www.npr.org/templates/story/story.php?storyId=99591469.

515 **"Ask Osama bin Laden"**: Jim Kuhnhenn (AP), "Obama Answers Appeasement Charge: 'Ask Bin Laden,'" *AP Online*, December 8, 2011.

515 **2012 poll**: Scott Wilson and Jon Cohen, "Poll Finds Broad Support for Obama's Counterterrorism Policies," WashingtonPost.com, February 8, 2012.

516 **"I want to make sure that people understand"**: "Obama Addresses Drone Strikes During 'Hangout,'" YouTube video, 4:04, Obama response to question during Google+ video forum on January 30, 2012, posted by "TheDailyConversation," January 30, 2012, www.youtube.com/watch?v=2rPMPMqO-jKY.

516 **"spinning the number of civilian casualties"**: Michael J. Boyle, "The Costs and Consequences of Drone Warfare," *International Affairs* 89 (1) (2013).

517 **"It's very important for the president"**: Transcript, "Debate Night in America," CNN, October 22, 2012.

517 **"represents a betrayal"**: Michael Boyle, "Obama's Drone Wars and the Normalisation of Extrajudicial Murder," op-ed, Guardian.co.uk, June 11, 2012.

517 **ruled on the request**: New York Times v. Department of Justice, and ACLU v. Department of Justice, 1:11-cv-09336-CM, "Corrected Opinion Granting the Government's Motion for Summary Judgment and Denying Plaintiffs' Cross Motion for Summary Judgment by Judge Colleen McMahon" (DCSNY January 3, 2013). The *New York Times* and the ACLU filed two distinct but similar suits in 2012 that were ultimately combined.

518 **"winning or losing"**: Donald Rumsfeld, memorandum for Gen. Richard Myers, Paul Wolfowitz, Gen. Peter Pace, and Douglas Feith, "Subject: The Global War on Terrorism," October 16, 2003, published in full by USAToday.com, May 20, 2005.

519 **"adverse strategic effects"**: Boyle, "The Costs and Consequences of Drone Warfare."

519 **"there's no country on Earth"**: Transcript, "Remarks by President Obama and Prime Minister Shinawatra in a Joint Press Conference," Government House, Bangkok, Thailand, November 18, 2012.

519 **"If I had to summarize"**: Jeh Charles Johnson, "The Conflict Against Al Qaeda and Its Affiliates: How Will It End?" speech at Oxford University, November 30, 2012, full text of remarks available via Lawfare (blog), www.lawfareblog.com/2012/11/jeh-johnson-speech-at-the-oxford-union/#_ftn1. All statements attributed to Jeh Johnson come from the speech.

519 **"secondary parties to murder"**: Ravi Somaiya, "Drone Strike Prompts Suit, Raising Fears for U.S. Allies," *New York Times*, January 30, 2013.

519 **UN commission**: Owen Bowcott, "UN to Investigate Civilian Deaths from US Drone Strikes," Guardian.co.uk, October 25, 2012.

520 **"encouraging a new arms race"**: Boyle, "The Costs and Consequences of Drone Warfare."

520 **"Western democracies"**: Ben Emmerson, "Statement by UN Special Rapporteur on Counter-Terrorism and Human Rights Concerning the Launch of an Inquiry into the Civilian Impact, and Human Rights Implications of the Use [of] Drones and Other Forms of Targeted Killing for the Purpose of Counter-Terrorism and Counter-Insurgency," news release from the Office of the UN High Commissioner for Human Rights, January 1, 2012.

520 **"We will defend our people"**: Barack Obama, transcript, "Inaugural Address," January 2013.

# INDEX

US military
and Gardez raid/massacre, version of, 338
kill list, 351
reorganization of, 12–13
US military aid
to Somalia, 476
to Yemen, 64–65, 236, 322
US Naval War College, 102
US Navy SEAL Team 3, 116
US Navy SEAL Team 4, 116
US Navy SEAL Team 5, 157
US Navy SEAL Team 6, 50–51, 98, 103,
108–109, 115, 116
and bin Laden raid and killing, at Abbottabad compound, 437–441, 441–450,
451–452
and *Maersk Alabama*, hijacking of,
275–276
US Navy SEALs
in Pakistan, 217–218
and piracy industry in Somalia, 483
and prisoner deaths, 157
Special Naval Warfare Group I, 116
US-Yemen joint operations, 307
USAID. *See* US Agency for International
Development
USS *Ashland*, 230
USS *Bainbridge*, 274–275
USS *Boxer*, 274, 453
USS *Cole* bombing in Yemen, 16, 61, 62–63,
65–66, 130–131, 466, 467
and Quso, Fahd al-, 305, 318
and Yemen and al Qaeda suspects, 132–133,
210, 213
USS *Halyburton*, 274
USS *Mount Whitney*, 79
USSOCOM, 114
Uzbekistan, 17, 252

Van Tonder, Edgar, 480
"Vanilla" Special Forces, 50
Vibrant Fury, 179
Vickers, Michael, 282, 356–357, 436, 441, 491
Vietnam, 114
Vietor, Thomas, 508
Vinnell Corporation, 130
Volman, Daniel, 298

War
and presidential power, 3–4
right to declare, 19–20
War against Islam, 110
War Council, 24, 29
War on terror, 27, 30, 47, 54, 113, 193–194,
320, 384
War Powers Act, 9–10
Wardak, Aziz Ahmad, 338
Warlords, Somali
and bin Laden, 198
brutality of, 193
and CIA alliance, 191–195
hatred for, 195

US campaign to fund, 193–194
*See also* Dheere, Mohamed; Qanyare, Mohamed Afrah; Siad, Yusuf Mohammed
Warsame, Ahmed Abdulkadir, 454
and Awlaki, Anwar, 498–499
capture of, 453
Waterboarding, 89. *See also* Interrogation and
torture/techniques
Waugh, Billy, 21
Wazir, Payo Jan, 218
Weaponized drones, 172. *See also* Drone
strikes
Weapons of mass destruction. *See* WMDs
Webb, Marshall B. "Brad," 442
West, Tony, 370
West Point, 109
Whitman, Bryan, 295
Wild West Domains, 287
Wilkerson, Lawrence, 21, 58
and Camp NAMA, 148
and Cheney, and presidential power, assumption of, 59
and Iraqi WMDs, 82
and JSOC, and abuse of power, 142–143
and JSOC, secrecy of, 329
and SOFs, 93, 94, 95, 99–100
WMDs (weapons of mass destruction), 417
and Iraq, 15, 28–29, 82, 139, 150
Wolf, Frank, 72
Wolf Brigade. *See* Special Police Commando
Unit
Wolfowitz, Paul
and Bremer, 110
and Cheney, defense plan of, 7–8
and drone strikes, in Yemen, 77
and Iraq and 9/11–Saddam and al Qaeda
connection, 14–15, 82, 84
and JSOC, and global manhunt, 170
and 9/11 attacks, exploitation of, 19
and Somalia, 123
and Steele, 164
Woodward, Bob, 13–14
World Bank, 64
World Cup fan bombings, in Uganda, 395
Wright, Lawrence, 63
Wuhayshi, Nasir al- (aka Abu Basir), 210,
230–231, 306, 314, 315, 379, 467
and AQAP, 255
and Awlaki, Anwar, 381
as detainee at Guantánamo, 254
and Saleh, Ali Abdullah, 213
Wyden, Ron, 505

Yarmad, Merza Mohammed, 344
Yazeed, Abu, 377
Yemen, 32–33
and al Qaeda, recruitment in, 358
and al Qaeda, resurgence of, 130–133
al Qaeda in, 62, 64, 65, 66, 122, 210–214,
235–237, 255–256, 257, 268, 269, 304–305
AQAP in, 258–260, 262–263, 269, 281, 284,
298, 323–324, 386–389

**NATION BOOKS**

# The Nation Institute

Founded in 2000, **Nation Books** has become a leading voice in American independent publishing. The inspiration for the imprint came from the *Nation* magazine, the oldest independent and continuously published weekly magazine of politics and culture in the United States.

The imprint's mission is to produce authoritative books that break new ground and shed light on current social and political issues. We publish established authors who are leaders in their area of expertise, and endeavor to cultivate a new generation of emerging and talented writers. With each of our books we aim to positively affect cultural and political discourse.

Nation Books is a project of The Nation Institute, a nonprofit media center dedicated to strengthening the independent press and advancing social justice and civil rights. The Nation Institute is home to a dynamic range of programs: the award-winning Investigative Fund, which supports ground-breaking investigative journalism; the widely read and syndicated website TomDispatch; the Victor S. Navasky Internship Program in conjunction with the *Nation* magazine; and Journalism Fellowships that support up to 25 high-profile reporters every year.

For more information on Nation Books, The Nation Institute, and the *Nation* magazine, please visit:

www.nationbooks.org

www.nationinstitute.org

www.thenation.com

www.facebook.com/nationbooks.ny

Twitter: @nationbooks